Jasper Johns
Mind/Mirror

Jasper Johns

Carlos Basualdo and Scott Rothkopf

With contributions by Emmanuel Alloa, Andrianna Campbell-LaFleur, Carroll Dunham, Flavio Fergonzi, Ruth Fine, Michio Hayashi, Terrance Hayes, Michael Ann Holly, Ralph Lemon, Alexander Nemerov, R. H. Quaytman, Jennifer L. Roberts, Drew Sawyer, Sandra Skurvida, Colm Tóibín, and Hannah Yohalem

Mind/Mirror

Philadelphia Museum of Art
Whitney Museum of American Art, New York
Distributed by Yale University Press, New Haven and London

Introductory texts by Scott Rothkopf, with Carlos Basualdo, Sarah B. Vogelman, and Lauren Young

Sponsor Statement

At Bank of America, we believe in the power of the arts to help economies thrive, educate and enrich societies, and create greater cultural understanding. That is why we are helping the arts flourish across the globe by supporting more than two thousand nonprofit cultural institutions each year. The Bank of America Art Program is part of our commitment to grow responsibly, advancing economic and social progress and sharing success with the communities we serve.

We are pleased to support *Jasper Johns: Mind/Mirror* at the Philadelphia Museum of Art and the Whitney Museum of American Art. Both of these institutions have been longtime partners of Bank of America, and we value the integral role they play in the local economy as well as the global cultural community.

Brian Moynihan

Chief Executive Officer
Bank of America

Foreword

The Philadelphia Museum of Art and the Whitney Museum of American Art are honored to be partners in the landmark retrospective *Jasper Johns: Mind/Mirror*. Our shared, long-standing commitments to modern and contemporary American art stretch back to early championing of the Ashcan School and American Realism, but our museums have never before collaborated on an exhibition because of our close proximity and potentially intersecting audiences in Philadelphia and New York. *Jasper Johns: Mind/Mirror*, however, offers an unprecedented occasion to take advantage of our locations to present a single exhibition in two places, providing the space that an ambitious retrospective of the artist's singular, prolific, and nearly seventy-year career demands.

Like many museums, the Philadelphia Museum of Art and the Whitney Museum of American Art have formed close relationships with particular artists through our collections and exhibitions. It is somewhat unusual, however, for multiple institutions to engage so deeply with the same artist, but as Scott Rothkopf notes in the archival section of this volume, "Few, if any, artists in recent history have had careers as intimately entwined with museums as Jasper Johns." The Philadelphia Museum of Art and the Whitney are privileged to be two such institutions—both of which have had the good fortune to work closely with the artist at significant moments since early in his career. Johns's work not only has been an important part of our legacies and collections but has forever transformed the history of art in the United States and internationally.

It would be fair to say that the Philadelphia Museum of Art has been a destination point and a source of reference for Johns throughout his career. The connecting thread is Marcel Duchamp, whose work first brought Johns to Philadelphia in 1957, three years after the great collection of modern art that Walter and Louise Arensberg bequeathed to the museum was installed. As friends and patrons of Duchamp, the Arensbergs had assembled the single largest collection of his work, and its inaugural presentation, along with the installation of Duchamp's *Large Glass* (1915–23), a bequest from another of the artist's American friends, Katherine S. Dreier, drew many young artists to Philadelphia to learn more about this great yet enigmatic artist. In November 1968, following Duchamp's death the month before, Johns wrote in *Artforum*: "The art community feels Duchamp's presence and his absence. He has changed the condition of being here."

Perhaps because many of the Philadelphia Museum of Art's earliest acquisitions of Johns's work were graphics, the first solo exhibition it devoted to him, in 1970, was *Jasper Johns: Prints, 1960–1970*, a survey that heralded the well-deserved recognition he has continued to receive as one of the most accomplished and innovative printmakers of his generation. Among the most significant exhibitions of Johns's work undertaken by the museum was *Jasper Johns: Work Since 1974*, presented at the American Pavilion at the 43rd Venice Biennale in 1988. Organized by Mark Rosenthal, then the museum's curator of twentieth-century art, the exhibition charted the artist's development over the course of a decade, beginning with his crosshatch paintings of the mid-1970s and ending with the complex and enigmatic series of four paintings known as the Seasons (1985–86), widely considered to be one of Johns's greatest achievements. The exhibition was lauded as a critical success and awarded the International Prize—Golden Lion by the biennale jury.

Since 1970, the Philadelphia Museum of Art has continued to exhibit Johns's work on a regular basis, drawing upon both its own holdings and, increasingly, generous long-term loans from the artist himself. In 2001, following its tradition of devoting individual galleries to artists of great stature in the history of modern and contemporary art such as Constantin Brancusi, Duchamp, and Cy Twombly, the museum dedicated a gallery to Johns, a decision supported by the collectors and museum trustees Keith L. and Katherine Sachs. This decision also reflected a growing commitment to the acquisition of Johns's work, as evident in the purchase of *Catenary (I Call to the Grave)* (1998) and, more recently, the promised gift from the Sachses of important paintings such as *5 Postcards* (2011) and *Nines* (2006), as well as drawings such as the superb *Voice 2* (1982).

Johns's relationship with the Whitney began in 1959 when he was the first of his generation to be included in that year's Annual Exhibition of Contemporary American Painting with *Two Flags* (1959). Since its founding in 1930, the Whitney has focused on notions of Americanness, and it is hard to imagine a more appropriate object of attention than the American flag for Johns's debut in an annual. However, the painting of two flags must have stood out amid works by first- and second-generation Abstract Expressionist artists Willem de Kooning, Adolph Gottlieb, Franz Kline, Alfred Leslie, and Joan Mitchell; hard-edge painters Ellsworth Kelly and Ad Reinhardt; as well as established figures Edward Hopper, Georgia O'Keeffe, and Ben Shahn. Johns went on to appear in thirteen Whitney Annuals and Biennials, eventually joined by his contemporaries, including Robert Rauschenberg in 1961; James Rosenquist in 1963; Thomas Wesselmann, Jim Dine, and Roy Lichtenstein in 1965; and Andy Warhol in 1967. Clearly, the curators of these exhibitions were fascinated not just by the flag as subject and object but by Johns's work as a whole, presenting a wide range of drawings and assemblages as well as remarkable paintings of everyday objects in the works *Target* (1960), *Painting with Two Balls* (1961), and *Map* (1963). It is easy to imagine that the curators were drawn not just to the unique subjects but to the inscrutable choice and treatment of those subjects and to the deft, subtle, glorious handling of materials—hallmarks of Johns's work throughout his career.

In addition to its inclusion in Whitney Annuals and Biennials, Johns's art has been shown in sixty-four Whitney exhibitions, ranging from thematic exhibitions and collection displays to traveling exhibitions and five monographic shows, including a retrospective in 1977–78. Today the Whitney possesses more than two hundred works by the artist, among them significant prints and masterpieces such as *White Target* (1957), *Three Flags* (1958), *0 through 9* (1961), *Studio* (1964), and *Racing Thoughts* (1983). Recent major acquisitions include the painting *Untitled* (2018) and the sculpture *Painted Bronze* (1960), gifts by Whitney Chairman Emeritus and Johns aficionado Leonard A. Lauder, who has donated or contributed to the acquisition of forty-eight works by Johns over four decades.

Three Flags has been closely identified with the Whitney since it entered the collection in 1980. Although the painting might be remembered by some as the first work by a living American artist to break the million-dollar sales mark, it is a painting, or a relief of sorts, that embodies and questions the intrinsic nature of painting and sculpture, the symbolic and the real, perception and experience. And in the context of the Whitney, it embodies the viewer's relationship to the United States and our enduring fascination with all things denoting and symbolizing America. (The Whitney possesses hundreds of works that include or refer to the American flag.) When looking at this truly unforgettable, intimate painting, its emphatic and imperative nature is clear. Exquisitely painted, with its bright colors and repetitively advancing subject, the painting, although relatively small, could easily be considered an insistent, declarative proclamation of presence and essence. It is not only an assertion but an interrogation of our identity—something that is particularly relevant for the Whitney and its focus on American art—and asks us to consider questions of who we are, what is a nation, what is America, and what is belonging.

The Philadelphia Museum of Art and the Whitney Museum of American Art are fortunate not only to have had deep connections to this remarkable artist throughout our respective histories but to be able to extend that legacy to the present with the two exceptional curators of *Jasper Johns: Mind/Mirror*: Carlos Basualdo, Philadelphia's Keith L. and Katherine Sachs Senior Curator of Contemporary Art, and Scott Rothkopf, the Whitney's Senior Deputy Director and Nancy and Steve Crown Family Chief Curator. Their relationships with the artist, depth of understanding of his work, vision for the two-part exhibition, and close collaboration during one of the most challenging times in recent history have resulted in an exhibition unlike any other—one that is truly fitting for Johns.

Without the generosity of many individuals and institutions, ambitious exhibitions such as *Jasper Johns: Mind/Mirror* could not be realized. We are extraordinarily grateful to Bank of America for its sponsorship of the retrospective in both New York and Philadelphia, and to Leonard and Judy Lauder, Matthew Marks, the Ellsworth Kelly Foundation and Jack Shear, Agnes Gund, Helen and Charles Schwab, Constance R. Caplan, Marsha and Jeffrey Perelman, Aaron and Leslee Cowen, Kathy and Richard Fuld, Mrs. Ronnie F. Heyman, and Richard and Nancy Lubin for their support of the presentations in both cities. This publication accompanying the exhibition has been made possible with the additional support of the Wyeth Foundation for American Art, The Davenport Family Foundation, Barbara Bertozzi Castelli, Jean-Christophe Castelli and Lisa Silver, and Craig F. Starr.

In Philadelphia, we would like to express our deep thanks to Constance Hess Williams and Sankey Williams, who have provided generous leadership support for the exhibition. We are also grateful for the support provided through the museum's endowment, the Daniel W. Dietrich II Fund for Excellence in Contemporary Art, the Annenberg Foundation Fund for Major Exhibitions, the Jill and Sheldon Bonovitz Fund for Exhibitions, the Robert Montgomery Scott Endowment for Exhibitions, and the Kathleen C. and John J. F. Sherrerd Fund for Exhibitions. Major support was provided by the museum's Contemporary Art Committee, The Davenport Family Foundation, Ms. Jennifer S. Rice and Mr. Michael C. Forman, The Sachs Charitable Foundation, and the Women's Committee of the Philadelphia Museum of Art—including special gifts from the estates of Patricia Sweet Clutz and Phyllys "Fifi" Fleming. Our thanks also go to the Robert Lehman Foundation, Irma and Norman Braman, Clarissa Alcock Bronfman and Edgar Bronfman Jr., Isabel and Agustín Coppel, Roberta and Carl Dranoff, Jaimie and David Field, Linda and George Kelly, Sueyun and Gene Locks, Susan and James Meyer, Leslie Miller and Richard Worley, the Mitchell and Hilarie Morgan Family Foundation, The Pew Center for Arts & Heritage, Lyn M. Ross, Howard Sacks and Vesna Todorović Sacks, Katie and Tony Schaeffer, Karen Goodman Tarte, Robbi and Bruce Toll, and three anonymous donors.

In New York, we are deeply indebted to Leonard and Judy Lauder for recognizing the importance of organizing a Jasper Johns retrospective at this moment and for their unparalleled support of the artist's work and the curators' ambitions. Kenneth C. Griffin and Susan and John Hess provided extremely generous funding that was essential to realizing the exhibition. We extend great thanks to Delta and Ralph Lauren for sponsoring the Whitney's presentation. Our sincere appreciation goes to Judy Hart Angelo; Neil G. Bluhm; and Kevin and Rosemary McNeely, Manitou Fund, all of whom have been steadfast partners in this endeavor. The exhibition also greatly benefited from the kindness of the Barbara Haskell American Fellows Legacy Fund; the Brown Foundation, Inc., of Houston; Nancy and Steve Crown; Anne and Joel Ehrenkranz; Kristen and Alexander Klabin; the Whitney's National Committee; and an anonymous donor. We are fortunate to have the important support of Constance R. Caplan, Marguerite Steed Hoffman and Tom Lentz, the Jon and Mary Shirley Foundation, Sueyun and Gene Locks, Susan and Larry Marx, Donna Perret Rosen and Benjamin M. Rosen, and Stefan T. Edlis and H. Gael Neeson Foundation. Our gratitude also goes to Aaron and Leslee Cowen, Johanna and Leslie Garfield, Ashley Leeds and Christopher Harland, Sheila and Bill Lambert, Barbara and Richard Lane, Margo Leavin, Janie C. Lee, Richard and Nancy Lubin, Martin Z. Margulies, Monique and Gregg Seibert, Norman Selby and Melissa Vail Selby, and Gloria Spivak.

Both the Philadelphia Museum of Art and the Whitney received a vital grant from the National Endowment for the Arts and an indemnity from the Federal Council on the Arts and the Humanities. Opening events at both museums were graciously funded by Christie's.

We are incredibly appreciative of all the lenders, individuals and institutions alike, that selflessly agreed to part with important works from their collections for an extended period of time so that visitors can see the full sweep of Johns's career at our institutions.

Above all, our thanks go to Jasper Johns, who not only embraced the ambitious project of this exhibition but loaned a number of extraordinary works from his own collection, some exhibited publicly for the first time. He has been extremely generous with his time despite being actively engaged in the production of many important new works. His friendship and unflagging support throughout the long and complex preparations for the exhibition and this book have been invaluable to the curators and to our institutions as a whole. We are deeply grateful for his generosity, his art, and his unstinting belief in this momentous project.

Timothy Rub
George D. Widener Director and Chief Executive Officer
Philadelphia Museum of Art

Adam D. Weinberg
Alice Pratt Brown Director
Whitney Museum of American Art

Acknowledgments

Planning a retrospective to honor nearly seven decades of Jasper Johns's art is both a daunting task and an extraordinary privilege. We have been aware of the magnitude of our endeavor since our very first conversation about the possibility of tackling this exhibition together. Many distinguished scholars who came before us brilliantly and comprehensively charted the unbelievably rich territory of Johns's work, and their accomplishments have allowed us to present his art in a way that is both innovative and accessible to a new generation of viewers. That is what we set out to do with *Jasper Johns: Mind/Mirror*, and it would not have been possible without the selfless support of many.

At Johns's studio, we are deeply indebted to Maureen Pskowski for guiding us through various challenges and decisions with grace and aplomb. Our gratitude also goes to John Delk in the archive, John Lund in the print studio, and Ryan Smith in the studio, who all kindly enabled us to view important works and shared their extensive knowledge and experience. For their generosity in facilitating loans and fielding numerous other requests and inquiries, we extend great thanks to Matthew Marks, Jacqueline Tran, Alex Fang, and Cynthia Garvey at Matthew Marks Gallery.

The planning for this project started more than five years ago, in early 2016. Initially, the exhibition was scheduled to open in the fall of 2020, but as the COVID-19 pandemic took hold in the United States in the spring of 2020, we were forced to confront a new reality, including the temporary closure of our museums and the delay of the exhibition. Our buildings have fortunately reopened to visitors, but as we write this, the future is still uncertain; the pandemic has deeply affected the global economy and society in ways that are not yet fully understood. As the preparations for the show continued under duress, the efforts of our colleagues became even more valuable, and we appreciate their remarkable perseverance and professionalism in such challenging circumstances.

From the very start, we benefited from the unwavering support of Timothy Rub, George D. Widener Director and Chief Executive Officer of the Philadelphia Museum of Art, and Adam D. Weinberg, Alice Pratt Brown Director of the Whitney Museum of American Art. We thank them for their devotion to the artist, steadfast commitment to this ambitious project, and insights and mentorship along the way.

For their dedication, organizational prowess, and key research, we owe an enormous debt of gratitude to the project's curatorial team: in New York, Lauren Young and Jessica Man, current and former curatorial assistants; Kyle Croft, Madeleine Seidel, and Anes Sung, research assistants; and Laura Busby, Adelaide Dunn, Chloe Powers, and Alice Zheng, interns; and in Philadelphia, Sarah B. Vogelman, exhibition assistant; and Jordan Garlic, Jino Rahimi, Laurel Rand-Lewis, and Elisabeth Rubin, interns. Lauren DiLoreto, senior exhibitions manager at the Whitney, and Yana Balson, director of exhibition planning at the Philadelphia Museum of Art, brilliantly orchestrated all aspects of the exhibition planning between the two institutions.

At the Philadelphia Museum of Art, we appreciate the contributions of Gail Harrity, president and chief operating officer; Deborah Johnston, chief financial officer; Alice Beamesderfer, Pappas-Sarbanes Deputy Director for Collections and Programs; Jeffrey Blair, secretary and general counsel; Regine Metellus, associate director of administration; and Mary-Jean Huntley, senior executive assistant to the director, in the executive offices. We are grateful to all our curatorial colleagues and recognize, in particular, the following individuals: Erica Battle, John Alchin and Hal Marryatt Associate Curator of Contemporary Art; Amanda Sroka, assistant curator of contemporary art; and Charlotte Lowrey, coordinator of curatorial initiatives in contemporary art. In the Prints, Drawings, and Photographs department, we extend our gratitude to Louis Marchesano, Audrey and William H. Helfand Senior Curator of Prints, Drawings, and Photographs; Sharon Hildebrand, head preparator; Clare Kobasa, former Suzanne Andrée Curatorial Fellow; Theresa Cunningham and Jillian Kruse, current and former Margaret R. Mainwaring Curatorial Fellows; and Lisa Morra and Jane Landis, current and former coordinators of collections. We also thank Nicole Stribling and Cassandra DiCarlo, current and former exhibition project managers; Kristen Regina, Arcadia Director of the Library and Archives; Margaret Huang, Martha Hamilton Morris Archivist; Rose Chiango, former associate archivist and records manager; Jonathan Hoppe, digital asset librarian; Richard Sieber, former librarian for reader services; Jack Schlechter, Park Family Director of Exhibition Design; Jamie Montgomery, exhibition designer; Andrew Slavinskas, lighting designer; Natalia Quinteros, former junior exhibition designer; Wynne Kettell, interim head of registration for exhibitions; Kara Furman, associate registrar for exhibitions; Morgan Webb, interim head of registration for collections; Mark Tucker, Neubauer Family Director of Conservation; Cindy Albertson, Theodor Siegl Conservator of Modern and Contemporary Paintings; Sally Malenka, John and Chara Haas Senior Conservator of Decorative Arts and Sculpture; Katherine Cuffari, associate conservator of decorative arts and sculpture; Thomas Primeau, conservator of works of art on paper; Dave Gallagher, manager of installations and packing; and Eric Griffin, installation coordinator. Crucial fundraising leadership was provided by Jonathan Peterson, director of development; Nico Hartzell, deputy director of development, institutional support; Danielle Smereczynski, deputy director of development, individual giving; Jane M. Allsopp, former principal gifts officer; Kate Virdone, director of corporate relations; Jackie Killian, grants manager; Caroline New, director of donor engagement and communications; and Lindsey Nevin, senior manager of donor engagement. In the education department, we offer our gratitude to Damon Reaves, interim senior curator of education; Barbara Bassett, Constance Williams Curator of Education, School and Teacher Programs; Justina Barrett, interim head of public programs; Linnea West, manager of adult public programs; Greg Stuart, coordinator of adult public programs and museum educator; Jenni Drozdek, former assistant director of interpretation; Rosalie Hooper, interim head of interpretation; and Adam Rizzo, coordinator of college and pre-professional programs and museum educator. We are appreciative of the marketing and communications, editorial and graphic design, and information and interpretive technologies teams, under the leadership of, respectively, Marcia L. Birbilis, senior marketing manager, and Norman Keyes, director of communications; Luis Bravo, creative and brand engagement director; and William Weinstein, John H. McFadden and Lisa D. Kabnick Director of Information and Interpretive Technologies. We also thank Nisa Qazi, director of content; Caitlin Mahony, manager of digital marketing; Jessica Sharpe, director of visitor operations and membership; Al Shaikoli, director of engineering, facilities and operations; Richard Reinert, manager of operations; Jeanine Kline, facilities project manager; Andrew M. Wurst, director of protection services; and Warren Peter Duane, deputy director of protection services, and all our colleagues upon whom the safety and security of our visitors, art, staff, and the museum itself depend.

At the Whitney, we thank I.D. Aruede, co-chief operating officer and chief financial officer; Amy Roth, co-chief operating officer; Nicholas S. Holmes, general counsel; Jen Leventhal, chief of staff; and Justin Romeo, executive coordinator. The curatorial department has supported this endeavor in countless ways, and we offer particular gratitude to Emily Russell, director of curatorial affairs; Jane Panetta, curator and director of the collection; Kim Conaty, Steven and Ann Ames Curator of Drawings and Prints; David Breslin, DeMartini Family Curator and Director of Curatorial Initiatives; Jennie Goldstein, assistant curator; and Joanna Epstein, assistant to the chief curator. As always, Christy Putnam, associate director for exhibitions and collections management, provided expert leadership of the Whitney's remarkable exhibitions team: Emilie Sullivan, registrar, exhibitions; Melissa Cohen, consulting registrar; Barbi Spieler, head registrar, permanent collection; Melanie Taylor, director of exhibition design; Jared Huggins, associate exhibition designer; and Joshua Rosenblatt, director of exhibition and collection preparation, and the team of art handlers in exhibitions and collection preparation. Conservation efforts were led by Carol Mancusi-Ungaro, Melva Bucksbaum Associate Director for Conservation and Research, and executed by Clara Rojas-Sebesta, Ellsworth Kelly Conservator of Works on Paper; Matt Skopek, associate conservator; Margo Delidow, assistant conservator; and Heather Cox, executive coordinator, conservation. Crucial fundraising leadership was provided by Pamela Besnard, chief advancement officer; Marilou Aquino, director of philanthropy; Stephanie Adams, director of individual and planned giving; Eunice Lee, director of strategic partnerships and events; and Morgan Arenson, director of foundation and government relations. Gina Im, manager of special events, orchestrated opening events. Farris Wahbeh, Benjamin and Irma Weiss Director of Research Resources; Anita Duquette, former senior visual resources manager; Tara Hart, managing archivist; and Michael Beiser, research resources assistant, provided research assistance. Interpretive and program initiatives were led by Anne Byrd, director of interpretation and research; Megan Heuer, director of public programs and public engagement; Heather Maxson, director of school, youth, and family programs; and Dyeemah Simmons, director of access and community programs. Marketing and communications efforts were overseen by Brianna O'Brien Lowndes, chief marketing officer, and Lindsay Pollock, chief communications and content officer, along with their colleagues Danielle Bias, director of communications; Hilary Greenbaum, director of graphic design; Jackie Foster, senior digital content manager; Benjamin Lipnick, tourism sales and marketing manager; and June Yoon, graphic designer. Wendy Barbee-Lowell, assistant director of visitor and member experience, ensured seamless visits for numerous people. Peter Scott, chief facilities officer, led the museum's indefatigable facilities and securities teams, with Larry DeBlasio, director of security, and all the guards providing essential support to keep visitors and art secure.

This catalogue, conceived as a key to the retrospective's unique bipartite structure, was possible thanks to the close collaboration between our institutions. We are sincerely grateful to Beth Huseman, director of publications; Jacob Horn, editorial coordinator; and Youngweon Lee, Babi Oloko, and Rebecca Yuste-Golob, interns, at the Whitney; and to Katie Reilly, deputy director for digital resources and content management (and former William T. Ranney Director of Publishing); Richard Bonk, interim head of publishing, production; Kathleen Krattenmaker, interim head of publishing, editorial; David Updike, editor at the book's inception; and Katie Brennan and Mary Cason, editors, at the Philadelphia Museum of Art; as well as to freelance editor Sarah Noreika, who expertly saw the book through to completion. Designer Scott Williams of A2/SW/HK was a sensitive and thoughtful partner in its making. Sue Medlicott and Nerissa Dominguez Vales offered valuable insight at key moments. We also thank Joseph Newland at the Menil Collection in Houston and Caitlin Sweeney at the Wildenstein Plattner Institute in New York for generously sharing resources.

We are indebted to the curators, academics, artists, and writers for their insights and invaluable contributions to this volume and to the broader scholarship on Johns. Our sincere thanks go to Emmanuel Alloa, Andrianna Campbell-LaFleur, Carroll Dunham, Flavio Fergonzi, Ruth Fine (who also shared her tremendous expertise in the development of our checklist), Michio Hayashi, Terrance Hayes, Michael Ann Holly, Ralph Lemon, Alexander Nemerov, R. H. Quaytman, Jennifer L. Roberts, Drew Sawyer, Sandra Skurvida, Colm Tóibín, and Hannah Yohalem.

An exhibition such as this can exist only through the enormous goodwill and generosity of its lenders. Over the past years, the following institutions and individuals fielded numerous requests and site visits, and, ultimately, temporarily parted with much-treasured parts of their collections for this unprecedented endeavor. For this, we are grateful to: Allen Family Collection; Judy Hart Angelo; Archives of American Art, Smithsonian Institution, Washington, DC; the Art Institute of Chicago; the Baltimore Museum of Art; David R. Baum and Tilly Macalister-Smith; Bayerische Staatsgemäldesammlungen, Pinakothek der Moderne, Munich; Jason Blum; Irma and Norman Braman; the Broad Art Foundation; the Eli and Edythe L. Broad Collection; Barbara Bertozzi Castelli; the Cleveland Museum of Art; Nancy and Steve Crown; Dallas Museum of Art; Des Moines Art Center, Iowa; Beth Rudin DeWoody; Glenn Dubin and Dr. Eva Dubin; Mr. and Mrs. Michael D. Eisner; Abigail R. Esman; Aaron I. Fleischman Collection; Forman Family Collection; Kathy and Richard S. Fuld, Jr.; Larry Gagosian; Gail and Tony Ganz; Kate Ganz; Glenstone, Potomac, Maryland; Greenville County Museum of Art, South Carolina; Esther Grether Family Collection; Anne Dias Griffin; Maxine Groffsky and Winthrop Knowlton; Agnes Gund; Marlene Hess and James D. Zirin; Samuel and Ronnie Heyman; Rocio and Boris Hirmas Collection; Hirshhorn Museum and Sculpture Garden, Smithsonian Institution, Washington, DC; Marguerite and Robert Hoffman; the Jewish Museum, New York; Jasper Johns; Kristen and Alex Klabin; Kolodny Family Collection; Kravis Collection; Laura Kuhn; Kunstmuseum Basel, Switzerland; Kunstsammlung Nordrhein-Westfalen; Emily Fisher Landau; Barbara and Richard S. Lane; Janie C. Lee; Thomas H. Lee and Ann Tenenbaum; Susan Lorence; Los Angeles County Museum of Art; Ludwig Museum Koblenz, Germany; Matthew Marks;

Katy Martin; Susan and Larry Marx; the Menil Collection, Houston; the Metropolitan Museum of Art, New York; the Robert and Jane Meyerhoff Collection; Minneapolis Institute of Art; MMK Museum für Moderne Kunst, Frankfurt am Main; Andrew Monk; Ugo Mulas Archive, Milan; Museum Ludwig, Cologne; Museum of Contemporary Art, Chicago; the Museum of Contemporary Art, Los Angeles; the Museum of Fine Arts, Houston; the Museum of Modern Art, New York; National Gallery of Art, Washington, DC; Nerman Family Collection; the Newhouse Collection; Marsha and Jeffrey Perelman; Meredith and Conley Rollins; the Rose Art Museum, Brandeis University, Waltham, Massachusetts; Donna Perret Rosen and Benjamin M. Rosen; Ryobi Foundation; the Keith L. and Katherine Sachs Collection; San Francisco Museum of Modern Art; Louisa Stude Sarofim; Andrew and Denise Saul; Virginia Cowles Schroth; Seattle Art Museum; Monique H. and Gregg G. Seibert; Jeffrey Seller and Josh Lehrer; Sezon Museum of Modern Art, Nagano, Japan; David and Lindsay Shapiro; Jack Shear; Jon and Mary Shirley; Ayea and Mikey Sohn; the Sonnabend Collection; Irving Stenn, Jr., Family Collection; Margaret Leng Tan; Lisa and Steven Tananbaum; Toyama Prefectural Museum of Art and Design, Japan; Walker Art Center, Minneapolis; Mildred L. and Morris L. Weisberg; Zygi and Audrey Wilf; Yale University Art Gallery, New Haven; and private collections.

We are equally thankful to the many individuals and institutions who so generously granted us access to artworks, shared their expertise, made connections, and aided our research: Acquavella Galleries, New York; Terri Anderson; Virginia M. G. Anderson; Stéphane Aquin; Greg Bell; Roberta Bernstein; Flora Miller Biddle; Daniel Birnbaum; Broc Blegen; Caitlin Brague; Irma and Norman Braman; Emily Braun; Anna Katherine Brodbeck; Clarissa and Edgar Bronfman; Barbara Bertozzi Castelli; Christophe Cherix; Tyler Chryssicas; Harry Cooper; Mary Lee Corlett; Andrew Culver; Barbara Cura; Emily Cushman; Nina del Rio; Lisa Dennison; Edith Devaney; Jason Dibley; Leah Dickerman; Stephan Diederich; Sandra Divari; Tricia Dixon; Fiona Donovan; James Elliot; Catherine Foster Ellison; Amze Emmons; Teresa Encalada; Melissa English; Elleree Erdos; Sara Friedlander; Larry Gagosian; Nicole Gallo; Vicki Gambill; Kate Ganz; Gary Garrels; Susan and David Gersh; Lily Goldberg; Ann Goldstein; Danica Gomes; Jillian Griffith; Charlotte Gutzwiller; Wade Guyton; Kayla Hagen; Jenny Harris; Harvard Art Museums/Fogg Museum, Cambridge, Massachusetts; Heller Group LLC, particularly Adrian Pohric and Chloé K. Geary; Joanne Heyler; Katherine Hinds; Susan Hirschfeld; Antonio Homem; Motoaki Hori; Cynthia Iavarone; Hiroko Ikegami; Laura Kadi; Laurence Kanter; Bill Katz; Alex Kirillov; Shelly Langdale; Julie Lazar; Patricia Lent; Dominique Lévy; Jen Levy; Amanda Lo Iacono; Amy MacKinnon; Catharina Manchanda; Jayne Manuel; Fergus McCaffrey; James Meyer; Tobias Meyer; Gretchen Shie Miller; Yuko Mizuta; Bob Monk; Kelly Montana; Montclair Art Museum, New Jersey; Hannah Murray; Jenna Nugent; Suzie Oppenheimer; Sam Orlofsky; Mike Ovitz and Nu Nguyen; Gary Owen; Carlotta Owens; Theresa Papanikolas; Kelly Parody; Mark Pascale; Suzanne Penn; Giselle Pique; Mary-Ellen Powell; Alessandra Pozzati; Jeanette Preston; Anne Randall; Katie Rashid; Charlie Ritchie; Nancy Rosen; Jennifer Russell; Ed Schad; Rachel Schumann; Cynthia Schwarz; Piers Secunda; Mizuka Seya; Jenna Shaw; Miwako Shinkai; Anna Simonovic; Leah Singsank; Deborah Solomon; Sogetsu Art Center Archive at Keio University, Tokyo; Craig Starr; Hideki Sugino; Margaret Sundell; Elizabeth Szancer; Chikako Takaoka; Kelly Taxter; Michael Taylor; Ann Temkin; Craig Tessler; Anna Testar; Maya Urich; Ryan VanGrack; Carrie Van Horn; Yvonne Force Villareal; Sheena Wagstaff; Kiriko Watanabe; Oliver Wicks; Queenie Wong; Dena Woodall; and Mary Zlot.

We would not have been able to persevere through countless meetings, numerous trips, and sometimes passionate arguments, as well as the difficult times of the pandemic without the understanding and loving support of our families: Jonathan Burnham, Monica Amor, and Maya and Lucas Basualdo.

Johns's work has been the subject of fascination, study, puzzlement, awe, and delight for countless museum visitors, artists, scholars, critics, curators, and writers dating back to the late 1950s. With *Jasper Johns: Mind/Mirror*, we aimed to engage new audiences with his extraordinary oeuvre by opening it to fresh frameworks and conversations. We have been uniquely fortunate to have the best possible accomplice in this task, the artist himself. We owe our deepest gratitude to Jasper, who greeted our unorthodox approach to his work with patience, openness, generosity, and a keen sense of adventure.

Carlos Basualdo
Keith L. and Katherine Sachs Senior Curator of Contemporary Art
Philadelphia Museum of Art

Scott Rothkopf
Senior Deputy Director and Nancy and Steve Crown Family Chief Curator
Whitney Museum of American Art, New York

Jasper Johns: Mind/Mirror

Scott Rothkopf

Jasper Johns (b. 1930) has been making and showing his art for so long and so widely that it has come to seem like an immovable feature in a landscape against which contemporary life continues to unfold. At the time of this writing, Johns is nearly ninety-one years old and has been considered an important—if not the most important—living American artist for more than sixty years. This longevity is both easy to take for granted and hard to truly fathom, like the presence of subatomic particles or galaxies beyond our view. Few, if any, artists in history have existed in the shadow of such precocious achievement and influence for such a long time. Before turning thirty, Johns had made an indelible mark on the international art scene, and his ascent coincided with a growing and unprecedented international interest in contemporary art on the part of the press, museums, and an enthralled though sometimes skeptical public. By the time he reached fifty, he had been the subject of three New York museum retrospectives and landed on the front page of the *New York Times* for his record-setting prices, a dubious distinction in the annals of art if not the popular imagination. His work helped create the very conditions into which it was so smoothly assimilated—the conditions in which contemporary art and artists still largely exist today.

Johns gained immediate attention in the late 1950s for his paintings of flags, targets, and numbers, which remain the enduring emblems of his art. Yet nothing about these early paintings would predict the multifarious experiments of the decades that followed. Indeed, if one lined up the first five years of his work alongside random samples from the next sixty, an untrained eye might be hard-pressed to recognize them as the products of the same artist. Whatever the general conception of his work may be, Johns was surely not on autopilot. This was a point that curator Kirk Varnedoe argued in the catalogue of Johns's fourth and, until now, most recent New York retrospective, at the Museum of Modern Art (MoMA) in 1996–97.[1] He endeavored to pry loose Johns's art from the restrictive and reductive amber that had calcified around it even then. Comparing Johns to the mythical figure of Prometheus, who stole fire from the gods, Varnedoe credited the artist with sparking countless new ideas. Just the first ten years of Johns's mature work paved the way for Pop art, linguistically oriented Conceptualism, literalist painting and Minimalist sculpture, quasi-referential abstraction, process- and materials-based tendencies, and many more isms and trends that followed in his wake. Varnedoe's account makes it difficult to imagine a modern artist who lit more fires faster, while continuing to blaze new trails of his own.

Despite Johns's preternatural and protean impact, today his work can sometimes feel more rooted in the past than the present. Like an injection in art's coursing vein, his hyperstimulating inventions were almost immediately absorbed and then outstripped by those of wilder progeny that now perhaps seem more of our time. Consider, the truculent, high-finish sculptures of Donald Judd or the omnivorous oeuvre of Andy Warhol, two artists who were born just before Johns and emerged just after him. Or take slightly younger figures such as Eva Hesse and David Hammons, whose work challenges traditional formats more obviously than Johns's. As much as he shifted the course of art history, Johns has remained true to earlier modes of thinking and making—careful humanist inquiry, the easel picture, the graphite drawing, the canvas and the brush. Whether we see him as the last of a line, the first of one, or both is to a certain degree a matter of perspective, but he undeniably opened a door to our age. To trade one overreaching analogy for another, Johns might be less Prometheus than Moses, someone who led his people to the Promised Land but didn't go inside.

This is one reason why Johns's art presents such a pertinent and powerful model for reexamination: it helps us to understand an inflection point in history, to sense how we got from where we were to where we are. To appreciate this we cannot merely presume the disruptive impulse of his pictures, but rather we must envision them as the charged products of a moment and a mind. It can be hard to regain this spirit of discovery and éclat in objects that have assumed the patina and reverence of icons, yet to grasp fully Johns's achievement we must try. This is one aim of *Jasper Johns: Mind/Mirror*. My cocurator, Carlos Basualdo, and I have not approached this retrospective as a straightforward reconstruction of an oeuvre or a rote reaffirmation of its putative greatness. Rather, we have attempted to segment it into pointed, discontinuous chapters that rekindle a sense of brisk curiosity in both the works and their beholders. Our goal has been to make one of the best-known artists of the past century seem somewhat strange and unfamiliar, to make his older art feel as alive as when it was new and the new work equally crucial to his story. Johns still goes to the studio almost every day. In fickle times, his assiduousness and quiet evolution are scarce qualities from which we can learn a great deal.

We began work on this project in early 2016 at a time of concentrated interest in Johns's work. The groundbreaking catalogues raisonnés of his paintings and sculptures and of his drawings, respectively, were nearing completion.[2] The Broad in Los Angeles and the Royal Academy of Arts in London were preparing a traveling survey of his work that would reintroduce it to their audiences for the first time in many years.[3] And Johns's art, entering its seventh decade, was itself on the cusp of transition from the forlorn Regrets series to an even more mournful body of work centered on an image of James Farley, a grieving marine in Vietnam. All this auspicious energy galvanized Carlos and me to embark on the most comprehensive exhibition ever of Johns's art, jointly organized by the Philadelphia Museum of Art and the Whitney Museum of American Art. Although Johns had been the subject of the 1996–97 retrospective at MoMA, the arc of his sedulous career had grown considerably since then, and we fixed on 2020 as an opportunity to celebrate the year he would turn ninety.

Each of us and our respective museums have had intimate relationships with Johns and his art, offering rich histories, expertise, and collections that would inform and support so ambitious a project. Our conjecture was that the unique contexts of the two institutions would shape a visitor's experience in different ways. The Philadelphia Museum of Art is encyclopedic and historically inclined, positioning Johns in the near company of some of his most beloved European influences, including Paul Cézanne, Marcel Duchamp, and Pablo Picasso. The Whitney is more oriented toward younger artists, so that Johns's work would be part of a lively dialogue with a new generation. But there remained a pressing obstacle: how the exhibition would unfold in time and space. Our two cities were too close—and the anticipated loans too dear—to imagine a show that traveled from one venue to the next over an extended duration. As a thought experiment, we wondered how a retrospective might play out simultaneously in two cities proximate enough that dedicated viewers could visit them both. Doubling the show in scale would allow for a much deeper investigation of a sprawling, labyrinthine oeuvre. We could look beyond greatest hits and paintings to surprising finds and in-depth treatments of Johns's indispensable works on paper. More important, this doubling could foster our curatorial intent to revivify Johns's art for both those familiar with it and for those encountering it with fresh eyes.

As soon as we decided to stage a single exhibition synchronously in two parts, the problem arose of how to make sense of the division. We recognized that the great majority of visitors would see only one of the presentations, so we needed to provide them with a coherent, self-sufficient narrative. But for those traveling between the two museums, the installations could not seem redundant. Why, after all, bother to mount two similar exhibitions at the same time? The sum of the experiences had to be greater than that of each part, and the novel structure had to convey conceptual integrity rather than caprice. One solution would have been to apportion Johns's career chronologically or by medium between the museums, but that would give most visitors too partial an account. So instead we scoured Johns's oeuvre for clues to an organizational framework that grew out of his art rather than one superimposed atop it. This bipartite structure would have to exploit the gap—in time and space—between the encounter in each city, creating the sense of a whole composed of two interrelated, echoing fragments. After nearly a year of research and debate, a compelling rubric emerged from Johns's lifelong preoccupation with mirroring and doubling—crucial twin concepts that have served as both image and operation since the inception of his mature work.

Once identified, this principle proved omnipresent. Mirroring pervades numerous compositions based on bilateral symmetry, where the left and right halves of a work reflect each other. Some, such as *Device* (1961–62; p. 193, pl. 20) and *Corpse and Mirror II* (1974–75; pp. 178–79, pl. 2), play abstractly with the logic of similitude and difference, while the more recent Regrets and Farley series are impelled by a curiosity about how images metamorphose through a mirroring of their parts. In other works, key passages reflect one another across a horizontal seam, or Johns toys with mirror writing by reversing the letters in a title or his name, as in *Mirror's Edge* (1992; p. 188, pl. 4). Pairs and doubles are even more ubiquitous. A single work often contains adjacent duplicate elements, such as flags or maps, or the uncanny pair of cast ale cans in the two editions of *Painted Bronze* (1960; p. 177, pl. 1; and p. 185, pl. 1). Later on, motifs often recur in less rigid arrangements within the same scene. Countless more works exist as cognates of one another, marked by shifts in scale, medium, or palette, as with the dozens of examples of an image executed in both color and black and white. Johns often pursues these experiments with matrices that aid in the reproduction (and, at times, reversal) of an image, such as stamps, silkscreens, and stencils, as well as the myriad tools of the printshop that have fueled his vast graphic corpus. Evident in all these instances and so many more, the mirror and the double thus suggested themselves as the devices—to borrow a typically Johnsian term—that would give the retrospective structure. They are not the exhibition's theme but its organizational metaphor, a logic by which to articulate a single exhibition across two sites. But what then is reflected?

Early in our process, we decided that the chapters of the exhibition would not hew to given series or periods but would articulate Johns's protean turns of mind. The aim would be to take viewers inside his work—if not quite his head—and give them various glimpses of the ideas, processes, moments, and themes that inform and animate his work. We ultimately selected ten discrete methodological lenses through which to consider his art. Some depend on long-standing readings of his work, such as a semiotic analysis of his use of common two-dimensional motifs, including flags and numbers. Others are less canonical and more expressive or essayistic—for example, a biographical reading of Johns's art in relation to places in which he has lived and worked. Still others focus on key working methods, such as his abiding preoccupation with making suites of unique prints or his intermittent execution of large-scale paintings that anthologize previous works and inspire future ones. The title *Jasper Johns: Mind/Mirror* speaks to the exhibition's mirror structure and to its various reflections on the artist's mind.

Each of these views on Johns's art is articulated through two case studies presented, respectively, in Philadelphia and New York. Visitors to either venue encounter the same ten overarching ideas, but the supporting evidence through which these concepts are expressed differs completely at each site. So, for instance, at the Philadelphia Museum of Art, the gallery exploring the importance of place probes deeply Johns's relationship with Japan, while the one at the Whitney delves into South Carolina, where he grew up and later spent time as an adult. In New York, the gallery devoted to early motifs focuses on flags and maps; in Philadelphia, it envelops visitors in a profusion of numbers. In some cases, the cognate galleries each contain closely related works from the same series or vintage that are distinguished from one another through their contrasting emotional timbres. In Philadelphia, for example, Johns's expressive turn to a surfeit of new imagery during the 1980s and 1990s takes on a nightmarish cast, while in New York many of the same subjects conjure a lighter, dreamy air. This yin-yang dynamic reverses in the subsequent galleries in each city, which concern Johns's recent meditations on mortality. Pallid tones and an ethereal atmosphere predominate in the Philadelphia ensemble, while in New York agitated dusky surfaces evoke death and despair. In every case, we took pains not to privilege Johns's "masterpieces" or rely solely on his most recognizable imagery but to mix them with less-known subjects and works on paper, some rarely or never before exhibited in public.

The galleries at both museums proceed largely in chronological order, although not without some curatorial sleight of hand. Several cognate rooms marshal works from the same period to support their twin takes on a common interpretive idea. For example, the galleries treating early motifs—numbers in Philadelphia, flags and maps at the Whitney—come second in the narrative sequence of each show, while the light and dark views on the most recent works conclude the coeval stories. In other cases, the cognate galleries explore the same concept at two distinct moments in Johns's career, as in the rooms that re-create his solo exhibitions at the Leo Castelli Gallery in New York in 1960 and 1968. To maintain the chronological flow at each venue, the restaging of the 1960 room comes earlier in the Philadelphia enfilade than the 1968 room does at the Whitney. And this, conversely, implies the flip-flopping of another pair, so that the gallery unpacking *According to What* (1964; pp. 150–51, pl. 2) in New York precedes the one devoted to *Untitled* (1972; pp. 158–59, pl. 2) in Philadelphia. Such structural inversions are wholly invisible to a visitor at either venue, but those interested in unpuzzling the exhibition's parallel plots will discover that their mirroring is purposefully imperfect. Indeed, the two halves of the exhibition are at once complete and commensurate while also partial and asymmetrical.

The two strands of the exhibition come together in a third site: the catalogue. A kind of Rosetta stone or decoder ring for the project as a whole, this volume is the only place where one encounters side by side the ten sets of dual case studies. A curatorial text introduces each methodological lens—or turn of mind—and its pair of supporting examples, followed by related images for each venue. On every spread, the reproductions are arranged as intricate visual essays. Sometimes, they expound on and amplify specific interrelationships explored in the galleries, while in other instances they present new connections not necessarily evident in the physical spaces of the exhibition. Each of these sections concludes with texts by a wide range of authors, from long-standing art-historical authorities on Johns's work to artists, poets, and philosophers, most of whom are writing about his art for the first time. Their essays more or less obliquely expound on the curatorial theses and works in the paired galleries, often refracting them further through new contextual and interpretive prisms. The final, eleventh bipartite section points back to the exhibition's actual sites at the Whitney and the Philadelphia Museum of Art. Here, archival materials tell parallel histories of Johns's deep and intimate relationship with each institution. Glimpses behind the backstage curtain, they thread the two venues directly into the site of the book. A coda on Johns's sketchbooks provides another window into his mind and art.

Originally scheduled to appear in 2020, the exhibition arrives in 2021, having been postponed due to the COVID-19 pandemic. It no longer celebrates Johns's ninetieth birthday, and much has happened since then. Yet despite the upheavals of the intervening year, Johns's example feels no less timely, nor does its study demand so pat an occasion. His constancy and patient dedication bracingly remind us of the importance of longer timelines, a life in the world and in art that carries on through many seasons. I remember an early conversation about the exhibition with Johns, in which I pointed out that when the show opened he would be ninety. I stumbled over whether to use the simple future or conditional tense. He paused before answering with his usual precision, "The possibility of my future existence has nothing to do with this show." He was right, of course. It's the art that lives on.

1 Kirk Varnedoe, "Fire: Johns's Work as Seen and Used by American Artists," in *Jasper Johns: A Retrospective*, ed. Kirk Varnedoe, exh. cat. (New York: Museum of Modern Art, 1996), 93–115.

2 Roberta Bernstein, *Jasper Johns: Catalogue Raisonné of Painting and Sculpture*, 5 vols. (New York: Wildenstein Plattner Institute, 2017); and Menil Collection, ed., *Jasper Johns: Catalogue Raisonné of Drawing*, 6 vols. (Houston: Menil Collection, 2018).

3 Roberta Bernstein, ed., *Jasper Johns*, exh. cat. (London and Los Angeles: Royal Academy of Arts in collaboration with the Broad, 2017).

On "Jasper Johns"
Carlos Basualdo

What Is an Exhibition?

For what seems like a long time already, I have been surprised by the tacit and widespread assumption that the form of an exhibition is somewhat standard, a priori, and independent of what is on display. The bibliography on both the history of exhibitions and the experimental forms of display that were so frequent in the first half of the twentieth century has grown exponentially in the last couple of decades and continues to do so, but the visible effects of that research in the practice of exhibition making seems to be, to put it mildly, quite restricted. For the most part, display has become synonymous with neutrality,[1] as if the ideation of an exhibition consists in determining only its contents, not its form—or worse, as if content and form, in the case of an exhibition, could be considered as independent terms. Interestingly enough, recent radical challenges to the accepted form of an exhibition have come from artists rather than curators. In this regard, the French artist Philippe Parreno is exemplary. For him, exhibition and form are one, so that far from an assemblage of discrete objects or installations, his shows become projects in themselves. In general, though, the operative consensus is normative: shows are manifestations of an established language that adapts to the temporal and spatial requirements and context of the institution. As such, all that remains for curators to do is to fill these spaces with content, be it objects, projections, or performances.

The exhibition, considered as a medium, is supposed to be elastic and transparent, a perfectly inexpressive tool. Any manifest disconnection between form and content, however, always masks the work of ideology in its purest and most pernicious state. In the case of exhibitions, that divide implies that shows are contained and objectifiable experiences intended to passively display objects or objectified actions for more-or-less passive consumption. The form of the show is the apparatus through which these assumptions are realized.

As a matter of fact, exhibitions are time-based events and not codified texts, and exhibition making should not be considered the articulation of an established language. On the contrary, exhibition making is a true praxis, and shows are an experiential choreography that needs to be reimagined according to the subject on display. In this context, efforts to relate form and content might actually be perceived as disruptive. The question is whether that disruptive potential can be made to correspond to the experience of the work. This is perhaps the fundamental question to be posed at the beginning of any curatorial project. Given a particular content, what form of display does it seem to call for? Or, put another way, what exhibition structure could best express the content and its potentialities, so that they are experienced as one and the same?

It seems to me that the form of an exhibition should resonate with the work on display. By "resonate," I mean rhyme with it, correspond to the work in a way that is both material and experiential, that can be perceived and reflected upon, so that the show becomes not just an assemblage of discrete objects but an active interpreter of the artistic strategies on display. In general terms, the temporal dimension usually allocated to a show in a museum context is the first and most powerful constraint. An exhibition has to take (its) place and occupy the space during a limited time, often about three months. Most museum spaces for temporary exhibitions have a similar size—around ten thousand square feet—so that shows can easily travel from venue to venue. No doubt these spatiotemporal parameters are further examples of the conventional template exhibitions are made to inhabit. Last, it is important to note that it is rare for an institution to agree to a show whose contents could increase or decrease. Space and time are defined beforehand and regulated internally according to a number of noncuratorial, institutional needs that include public circulation, conservation requirements of the works on display, and marketing opportunities. More often than not, these institutional limitations stifle attempts at experimentation. In the case of a vast and complex body of work such as that of Jasper Johns, they become severe restrictions.

The Imitation of Nature

Jasper Johns is one of the most influential artists of the postwar period. His impact on contemporary art has been so pervasive and profound that at times it might be taken for granted. In the United States, his work is assumed to have opened doors for many of the most important developments of art in the 1960s and beyond. A recent text by Flavio Fergonzi on Johns's reception in Italy provides an excellent overview of the groundbreaking effect the exhibition of his work has had abroad.[2] For almost seventy years, Johns has developed a polyphonic practice through a variety of media, including painting, sculpture, drawing, and prints. He has managed to reinforce the various media in which he works while questioning and ultimately undermining their conventions. He has done this through a persistent and precise method that consists of exploring the boundaries of each medium with tools borrowed from another one, in order ultimately to erase those boundaries, as well as any hierarchies with which they are traditionally associated.

Throughout his work, Johns emphasizes process to a degree that borders on obsession and the use of an ever-growing constellation of signs that recur in a variety of mutating contexts that contribute to the instability of their presumed meanings. Johns's subversive use of the conventions of each medium is echoed and amplified by the circularity of the logic by which he deploys the motifs in his oeuvre. Far from a linear progression, the work seems to be constructed around constant bifurcations, unexpected recurrences, and blatant fragmentation. Any examination of the work through a progressive, chronological narrative or from the perspective of one privileged medium—painting, for example—risks giving the viewer only a partial impression of the complexity of the artist's project. Only when considered simultaneously across media does the logic of the work become apparent. By logic of the work, I mean the set of methodologies, procedures, and motifs that recur as observable patterns in the artist's production. It is the conceptual fabric of a certain artistic practice that ultimately bears the responsibility for its singularity. Given the historical perspective that is afforded to any consideration of Johns, including the fact that most of his work across media has been rigorously catalogued, the challenge of presenting his oeuvre today coincides with the possibility of presenting its logic, and not just in the display of a discrete series of thematically or chronologically related objects. Thus, two questions immediately arise: Is it possible to grasp, effectively, the logic of Johns's work—or that of any artist? And, assuming that it is, at least partially, how is it possible—if at all—to put this logic on display?

From the artist's own sanctioned beginning of his work in 1954, Johns has posed a number of unsolvable questions to his public and critics. Around those questions, in an almost compensatory fashion, the public discourse on the work has grown and developed. Through the years, Johns—"Sybille des cibles" (Sybil of targets), as Marcel Duchamp once described him[3]—has been read according to the changing times and in response to changes in culture and the art world, which he often found himself at the center of. Layer upon layer of discourse has sedimented around the work, both enabling and obscuring the perception of access to its core. For an artist who has chosen to persistently reflect on the question of meaning, starting with the meaning of his own practice, a prodigious number of preconceptions and assumptions have accumulated around his works, his words, and his silences. Language generates more language. It is, as it used to be said, an ever-spreading virus. Any attempt to display the logic of the work necessitates, first and foremost, the ability to not listen—or to listen selectively—to the exegetical cacophony around it. Or, as Jacques Lacan once put it, to be able to listen to the floating signifier rather than the conventional meaning of the word. But is this feasible? Or, to express the same question in a language closer to that of the artist, is it possible to see before language determines what we see? Are language/meaning and seeing one and the same act?

The question, then, seems to concern not the language of the work but its structure. Not its meaning, but the form taken by its practice. Not its interpretation, but its experience. The tools to use in search of these attributes are, first, Johns's own statements about his work—offered more generously during the first decades of his career through interviews and more rarely in his writings—and second, the extraordinary perspective offered by the extensive catalogues raisonnés of his work in all the media he has so eloquently used and productively misused so far.

Of the many working strategies that Johns has declared to use, it seems to me that mirroring and duplication are the most pervasive. His insistence on the paradoxes associated with the equivocal relation between fragment and whole, plagued by duplications and reversals, seems equally important. Johns's work enacts a constant tension to both hide and display physical elements and their possible meanings, to make present what is not there while erasing what is. In the exhibition at the Philadelphia Museum of Art and the Whitney Museum of American Art, we have tried to incorporate the recurring strategies that constitute the logic of Johns's work. How do we do that? It seems obvious that such a show could not exist in a single space. Dealing with mirrors and repetition requires that the experience be divided in a way that forces the viewer to acknowledge the incompleteness of a unified narrative. It became evident in conceptualizing the show that it had to be distributed between two sites, with each site mirroring or duplicating the other through the somewhat distorting lenses of the corresponding institutional histories, civic contexts, and actual spaces. Taking place concurrently in two different cities along the US East Coast, the exhibition is an experience dispersed in time and space. The viewer is thus invited to travel from one locale to the other and, more important, to remember in the presence of one of its parts what was seen in the other. Internally, each exhibition space is structured according to the relation between fragment and totality. Each half is composed of a collection of rooms, organized mostly chronologically, so that each room represents a singular and autonomous point of view on the work. Accordingly, the curatorial process responded to the diversity of semiotic materials deployed by Johns by incorporating multiple perspectives in the organization of the show. The two-part exhibition is not the enunciation of a singular curatorial voice, or the fictive presumption of art history's objectivity, but rather a chorus of coordinated perspectives that hopefully will allow viewers to access the work from multiple points of view. It is one exhibition in two semiautonomous spaces, each half made of a sequence of rooms composing a number of diverse approaches, so that the show is eventually completed by the necessarily incomplete and fragmentary experience of a multiplicity of viewing experiences. To put it succinctly, our objective was that the pliant form of the exhibition become expressive in relation to its content, so that it ultimately informs and inflects viewers' perceptions of the work.

Once the structure of the show was established, it became impossible for Scott Rothkopf, my cocurator, and me not to replicate it in the internal conception of the rooms, as if the mechanism of mirroring and fragmentation, once begun, could not help but reproduce itself. At that point the curatorial work became, as John Cage once put it in describing Johns's artistic practice, "the imitation of nature in her manner of operation"[4]—in this case, an unintended but inevitable imitation of Johns's work in its compositional logic.

Desiring Machines

An exhibition that intends to become an orchestrated constellation of perspectives on Johns's work by definition cannot be the responsibility of a single author. The work with Scott necessitated that each of us assume the perspective of the other, or others. When working with Scott, I was constantly reminded of the first sentences of Gilles Deleuze and Félix Guattari's *A Thousand Plateaus*, a book that, as a young adult in Argentina in the 1980s, I read and reread to exhaustion: "The Two of us wrote *Anti-Oedipus* together. Since each of us was several, there was already quite a crowd. Here we have made use of everything that came within range, what was closest as well as farthest away. We have assigned clever pseudonyms to prevent recognition. Why have we kept our own names? Out of habit, purely out of habit."[5]

1 Here I am referring mainly to exhibitions taking place in major museums in the United States and abroad. I am well aware that exhibitions are still treated as experimental forms in many contexts throughout the world. Many large-scale international exhibitions provide excellent examples.

2 Flavio Fergonzi, "Jasper Johns e gli artisti italiani: Manzoni, Schifano, Paolini" (unpublished manuscript, August 30, 2019), Microsoft Word file.

3 When Johns acquired a copy of Duchamp's *Green Box* in 1960, Duchamp inscribed it "for Jasper Johns / Sybille des cibles." See Carlos Basualdo and Erica F. Battle, eds., *Dancing around the Bride: Cage, Cunningham, Johns, Rauschenberg, and Duchamp*, exh. cat. (Philadelphia: Philadelphia Museum of Art, 2012), 326.

4 John Cage, "Jasper Johns: Stories and Ideas," in *Jasper Johns*, by Alan R. Solomon, exh. cat. (New York: Jewish Museum, 1964), 22.

5 Gilles Deleuze and Félix Guattari, *A Thousand Plateaus: Capitalism and Schizophrenia*, trans. Brian Massumi (Minneapolis: University of Minnesota Press, 1987), 3.

Jasper Johns in 1954: The Time Machine

Alexander Nemerov

There is something ceremonial about Jasper Johns's *Untitled* of 1954 (p. 49, pl. 24). With its expressionless face and pasted newspapers, the box's air of renunciation matches Johns's actions and statements from that year—his ritual destruction of all his previous work, his realization that it was time to stop intending to be an artist and actually become one.[1] The impassive features of his friend Rachel Rosenthal, like the thought-balloon of newsprint extending vertically above her face, suggest a mystical abatement of everything beyond the box. Headlines muddle in the art's zone of calm. German words and Chinese characters suggest how foreign the outside world has become.

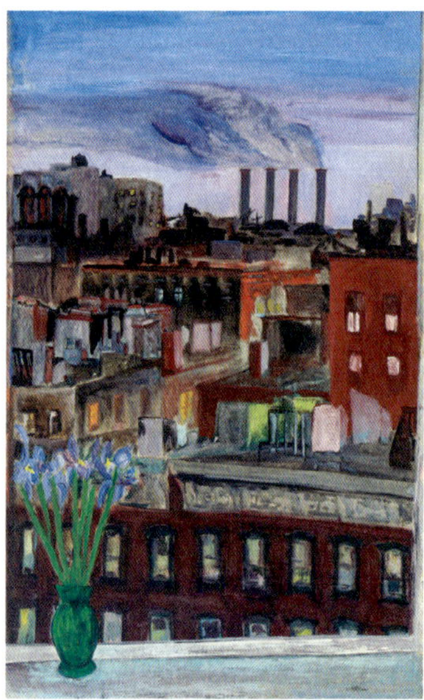

Fig. 1 **Jane Freilicher (American, 1924–2014). *Early New York Evening*, 1954**
Oil on linen, 51 ¾ × 31 ⅞ in. (131.5 × 81 cm). Whitney Museum of American Art, New York; gift of Elizabeth Hazan and Stephen Hicks in memory of John Ashbery, 2018.231

That world in 1954 was the New York in which Johns lived. Paintings of the city from that year give a sense of all that he let go. Jane Freilicher's *Early New York Evening* shows the view outside her Manhattan apartment (fig. 1). A painterly invention, the picture is also an objective view, showing "not her own note but that of things," in the words of Freilicher's friend the poet John Ashbery. Her aim was to reveal "each element's poignant desire to make its own point, to put itself across, to be accepted on its own terms."[2] The flowers on the windowsill make such a claim; so do the smokestacks. Rhymes between them build up—sky and sill make designs upon each other. But the pictorial connections, far from being fanciful, only assert "what there is there," in the words of the poet Kenneth Koch.[3] This *there*—the smoking, flowering New York of 1954—is what Johns forsook.

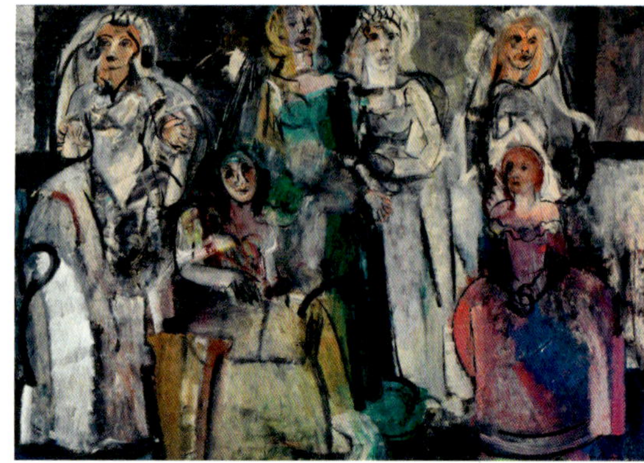

Fig. 2 **Grace Hartigan (American, 1922–2008). *Grand Street Brides*, 1954**
Oil on canvas, 72 ⅝ × 102 ⅜ in. (184.5 × 260 cm). Whitney Museum of American Art, New York; purchase with funds from an anonymous donor, 55.27

He let go of Manhattan at street level, too. Grace Hartigan's *Grand Street Brides*, another painting of 1954, portrays the bridal shop windows in Hartigan's downtown neighborhood (fig. 2). Combining Diego Velázquez and Pablo Picasso with her friend Walter Silver's photographs of mannequins, Hartigan addressed the "empty ritual" of weddings, the isolation of women in postwar culture. Dazed, regal, blank, the gathered brides seem to wonder, in the artist's words, "What are we doing? What do we mean to each other?"[4] The "we" is to some extent the already twice-married Hartigan—she is all of them, multiplied, tall at the altar, ruggedly autobiographical, ever-willing to read from the diary of her life, as her then dear friend Frank O'Hara's roommate Joe LeSueur noted.[5] The power of *Grand Street Brides* is just this social and personal topicality; it is also the painting's weakness. Helen Frankenthaler privately disparaged her friend Hartigan as a "subject matter avant-gardist," an artist who sought shortcut relevance in the present by prematurely giving up on the timeless and more challenging power of abstraction.[6] Johns, for his part, rejected the timely and the timeless alike. The plaster face of Rachel Rosenthal dreams of a privacy no topic of the day can puncture. Yet it is a privacy made up of the daily life the plaster face abjures, a baffled palimpsest of headlines grown cloudy and amber-like in the box.

Johns also avoided the embodied world of New York in 1954. Larry Rivers's *Still Life with Grapefruit and Seltzer Bottle*, another painting from that year, shows what was within arm's reach of the artist back then: the fruit on the table, the bottle and its special pump, a can or jar with the word "Mars" printed on it. The canvas, likewise within reach of the artist, is a drawing board of bright colors and instant possibilities, a warm reassurance in tandem with the things it shows. Painting is itself a refreshment, a respite from the stale and the stained, the mordant and over-philosophical. Focusing on the vibrancy of nearby things, it defies the expiration of laughter and song. Rivers's carefully preserved momentariness—what Fairfield Porter called in 1954 his "conscious spontaneity and constant awareness"[7]—says that conviviality never grows old, that it will remain as fresh as the bowls of fruit and bottles of beer in Édouard Manet's *Bar at the Folies-Bergère*. Yet the big-handled seltzer bottle is the artifact of a bygone world, as distant as a demolished Parisian café-concert, and the social rituals the bottle once centered with its reassuring spritz have likewise become echoes and aftertastes. A decorative wall-like surface, *Still Life with Grapefruit and Seltzer Bottle* would be like a Pompeian dining-room fresco, if the New York of 1954 were Pompeii, which in a way it is, thanks to the never-ending eruption of time that Johns aimed to suspend.

In *Untitled* time sleeps, and in sleeping is preserved, set to wake on another day. The Manhattan of 1954 lies only in abeyance, not in disappearance. The dormancy of the work is not sphinxlike. It does not require us to decipher the headlines for the figure to open its eyes. Instead we must recognize, first, the box's dreamy material of time—its way of conjuring a long-ago world (long ago even when the headlines were new, when Johns pasted the papers down), its way of cradling and archiving that world, turning it slow and thick as temporal honey. Second, we must recognize that this sleeping world is not dead. The plaster face evokes a death mask but is not one. The whole work portrays a time that might be dead but is not. The box is like an hourglass without sand, with time in a steady state, held in balance and poise, as by a time machine whose purpose is to suspend the flow of years in a magic structure of quiescence. That suspension of time would, in turn, extend to the world outside it, as if Johns's purpose, in suspending time within his box, were to lull the whole world around him to sleep. A charm would fall over the city of 1954 like drowsy snow, like dusk, bringing the blaring horns and shining lights to a stalled blur.

Our third recognition consists in this: *Untitled* suggests that the world it holds in suspension can swing back into motion. In 1955, Johns made *Tango*, a construction of encaustic and collage with a music box the viewer could wind up. Something of this "winding up" informs *Untitled*, even if it does not feature a device like *Tango*. Here it is not the box that would be wound up but the world outside it. That world—all of it ceremonially paused long ago when *Untitled* came into being—would be restored to life, we feel, if we could manipulate the box correctly. But maybe this restoration does not require us, and never did. Maybe it is simply that the box will reach its appointed time—the old age of the artist, for example—and then will activate the world it once had suspended, so that back then the artist could become himself. Now, many years later, he has reached the point when his own career, magically set running by the stillness of the rest of the world, can finally loosen the charm that, long ago, required that he make it seem as though nothing else except his own work existed.

Once he does that, then the pedestrians who one day in 1954 had been lifted from the sidewalks will be set down again, in the places where they were, their strides uninterrupted, with no consciousness that it is not still 1954. The artist, we see, was never hostile to his time. He just needed it to be quiet. He needed to imagine it did not exist. And when, decades in the future, he was finished with all his work, he could set that long-ago world back into motion, right where he left it. Summa cum laude, only he could turn the key to bring it all right in the end.

1 For Johns's break with who he was, see Lilian Tone, "Chronology and Plates," in *Jasper Johns: A Retrospective*, ed. Kirk Varnedoe, exh. cat. (New York: Museum of Modern Art, 1996), 124.
2 John Ashbery, "Jane Freilicher at Fischbach," *Art in America* (May–June 1975): https://www.artinamericamagazine.com/news-features/news/from-the-aia-archive-john-ashbery-on-jane-freilicher/ (accessed December 12, 2019).
3 Kenneth Koch, quoted in Ashbery, "Jane Freilicher."
4 Grace Hartigan, quoted in Cathy Curtis, *Restless Ambition: Grace Hartigan, Painter* (New York: Oxford University Press, 2015), 126.
5 Joe LeSueur, *Digressions on Some Poems by Frank O'Hara* (New York: Farrar, Straus and Giroux, 2003), 103.
6 Helen Frankenthaler, letter to Sonya Rudikoff, March 2, 1953, Sonya Rudikoff Papers, Princeton University Library, Princeton, NJ.
7 Fairfield Porter, "Rivers Paints a Picture," *ARTnews* (January 1954), quoted in Larry Rivers with Arnold Weinstein, *What Did I Do? The Unauthorized Autobiography* (New York: Harper Collins, 1992), 289.

Some Notes on Jasper Johns's European Reception, 1958–1964

Flavio Fergonzi

A particular trajectory of Jasper Johns's critical reception in Europe can be traced from 1958, with the initial arrival of his work in Italy, to 1964, when Johns attained international renown following his major retrospective at the Jewish Museum in New York, a version of which traveled to London, and the presentation of his work in that year's Venice Biennale. In this essay, I will consider reactions to Johns's work in Paris, London, and Italy during this period, with a close look at the impact of his practice on three emerging Italian artists—Piero Manzoni, Mario Schifano, and Giulio Paolini—at turning points in their careers.

In November 1962, Ileana Sonnabend opened her Paris gallery with an exhibition of paintings by Johns, a carefully calculated decision. After the polemical reactions in Paris to the exhibition of Robert Rauschenberg's Combine paintings in April 1961 at Galerie Daniel Cordier,[1] Sonnabend turned her focus on Johns, who was already in her stable and practicing extremely elegant and intellectually sophisticated painting. The result was considerable media attention and positive reactions from the demanding and somewhat biased Parisian public. Sonnabend wrote to Leo Castelli, "Jap's opening was a great success. A lot of people came, drank champagne, admired what they could see of the show. Some said it was the first time they saw Jap this way."[2] The success, however, was not commercial. In France, marked by the just-concluded Algerian crisis and the uncertainty following the elections of October 1962, it was difficult to sell paintings costing more than $1,500, particularly as many collectors had begun putting their work on the market, as Sonnabend complained in the same letter to Castelli. Nonetheless, Johns's exhibition represented a well-calibrated introduction to the sequence of shows of American artists that the gallery would present in Paris over the next two years: Rauschenberg (shown in two parts), Jim Dine, and Roy Lichtenstein, in 1963; and Claes Oldenburg, James Rosenquist, and Andy Warhol, in 1964. Indeed, Johns's painting brought together skillful pictorial craft and an acute investigation into the process of seeing: two themes then commonplace in European artistic research that could offer a still-unprepared public an introduction to the violent eruption of Pop subjects in subsequent exhibitions.

Johns had already had two solo exhibitions in Paris prior to 1962. The first, at Jean Larcade's Galerie Rive Droite in February 1959, was received with disinterest and perplexity.[3] Critical reactions to the second show, at the same gallery in June–July 1961, however, reflected a decisive change of heart, particularly in response to the pictorial and graphic series 0 through 9 (p. 82, pls. 18–20) and to the two *Painted Bronze* sculptures (p. 177, pl. 1; and p. 185, pl. 1). After the success of this exhibition, the art critic Pierre Restany, under the aegis of Nouveau Réalisme, attempted to link French and American artists through a joint presentation. According to Restany, each of the featured artists—including the French Arman (Armand Fernandez), François Dufrêne, Raymond Hains, Yves Klein, and Jacques Villeglé; the Swiss sculptor Jean Tinguely; and the Americans Johns and Rauschenberg—shared the "impassioned adventure of reality understood in and of itself and not through the prism of conceptual or imaginative transcription."[4] In a September 1961 article in the journal *Cimaise*, Restany celebrated Johns's international role within the new tendency that marked the return of the object, proclaiming that a veritable "Johns miracle" had occurred. The American artist was "a demystifier of the preconception, a metaphysician of the commonplace" because the banal images in his paintings invite "a sense of reality conceived as a full availability of vision." By starting from this "ground zero" of vision, pictorial expressiveness could be brought back into play, since "through the commonplace thus freed from its straitjacket of logical indifference, it is a work of art that appears and that is imposed on us by its objective qualities."[5]

Restany's text is particularly important because in it he reconsiders his deeply rooted belief in the superiority of French artists over American artists. He had confirmed this position only a few months earlier, in his introduction to the catalogue for the exhibition *Le Nouveau réalisme à Paris et à New York* (in which Johns was represented with the painting *Entr'acte* [1961] and the sculpture *Painted Bronze* [1960; p. 206, pl. 2]), presented at the Galerie Rive Droite from July to September 1961. The American Neo-Dadaists, according to Restany, were still too mindful of the pictorial modes of Abstract Expressionism and, at the same time, too prone to the literalism of the object; their practice was "more ambiguous, more exhibitionistic, more aestheticizing," while the French were returning "to the sociological reality, due to a need for pure air, and not to breathe the incense of a new form of worship"—that of the object understood in and of itself.[6]

Thus, between 1961 and 1962, the European perception of Johns had begun to change. In the spring of 1962 at the XVIII Salon de Mai in Paris, the exhibition of Johns's recent work *Slow Field*, with its powerful visual impact, helped confirm the consistent evolution of an artist who, working on the object-painting, allegorically staged the condition of painting and did not renounce the expressive values of pictorial touch. Over the course of that year, the international success of the exhibition *4 Amerikanare: Jasper Johns, Alfred Leslie, Robert Rauschenberg, Richard Stankiewicz*, which opened at the Moderna Museet in Stockholm before traveling to the Stedelijk Museum in Amsterdam and the Kunsthalle Bern, had resolutely positioned Johns within the hierarchy of international art, and two emerging curators and newly appointed museum directors, Pontus Hultén in Stockholm and Harald Szeemann in Bern, had recognized the artist's propulsive role.[7] Leo Steinberg, in an article published in the Italian journal *Metro* in May 1962, suggested that Johns was the most radical and coherent artist of his time, because, as Steinberg wrote, Johns "has built himself a composite language in which paint and words, object and emblems converge in a single image-meaning."[8]

In late 1962, the reviews that accompanied Johns's solo exhibition at the Galerie Sonnabend thus succeeded in overcoming the French annoyance with rhetoric regarding the banal subject, still understood as a polemical American trademark. The plastic qualities and conceptual complexity of the artist's work were beginning to seduce French critics.[9]

The French case is an example of how an organized group of young artists such as the Nouveaux Réalistes could mediate and guide critical reaction to Johns: an artist whose premises, both ideological and formal, were profoundly different. The same was true in England.

The intelligent critical reaction to the Johns retrospective at the Whitechapel Gallery in London in December 1964 can also be explained in relationship to critical themes raised by young painters returning to figuration, such as Peter Blake, David Hockney, and R. B. Kitaj.[10]

The case in Italy is perhaps the most interesting of all, since, around 1960, no recognizable pictorial movement there had yet placed the representation of the object at the center of its poetics. But at this time, Johns's works constituted an inescapable point of comparison for Italian artists who were abandoning abstract painting and beginning to face a new problem: the incorporation of an image, however simple, into the pictorial field. Thus, they were obliged to radically reconsider the significance they had given to the pictorial surface of their paintings.

From the late 1950s to the early 1960s, three moments in the relationship between Italian artists and Johns are of particular interest for this study. The first coincides with the initial arrival of Johns's works in Italy: at the 1958 Venice Biennale, which included the paintings *Flag* (1954–55; p. 66, pl. 7), *Green Target* (1955), and *Gray Alphabets* (1956); and then, in March 1959, the artist's solo exhibition at the Galleria del Naviglio in Milan. The second, from approximately 1960 to 1963, encompasses the first visual dissemination and critical discussions of Johns's work in art periodicals and international catalogues accessible to Italian artists. The third was the presentation at the 1964 Venice Biennale of twenty-one works by Johns in relationship to works by Rauschenberg and the American Pop artists Jim Dine and Claes Oldenburg, an installation that became a subject of great interest in Italian art criticism: some interpreted Johns's lesson as a call to end painting; others understood that, rather than calling for an abandonment of the medium, Johns was questioning the significance of what was being objectified, separate from the ego of the artist who had created it.[11]

For each of these three moments, a different Italian artist—Piero Manzoni, Mario Schifano, and Giulio Paolini, respectively—represents an example of a particular way of confronting Johns's work. At the 1958 Venice Biennale, *Flag*, *Green Target*, and *Gray Alphabets* were greeted with general indifference.[12] But the twenty-five-year-old Milanese artist Piero Manzoni was the first to understand the reasons behind the inconsistent relationship between the banality of the represented image and the technical complexity with which it was rendered. Above all, he intuited that the new function of the subject was chosen by Johns for its possibilities of interrogating the laws of vision. The work he must have dwelled on at greatest length at the biennale was *Gray Alphabets*, a painting disturbingly concrete in its combined techniques of collage and encaustic painting and without any internal hierarchy in its composition. This approach represented to Manzoni a frontal attack on the rigorous neoplasticism of Piet Mondrian, which had received increased attention with the recent monographic exhibition at the Galleria Nazionale d'Arte Moderna in Rome in 1956. In fact, in Johns's painting, all resources of invention and execution aimed to increase the ambiguity of perception. Was the viewer meant to interpret *Gray Alphabets* as a stenciled alphabet or a sumptuous pictorial surface? Did Johns privilege the tautological coldness of the contents or the materiality of the painting?

Manzoni may have deduced a decisive lesson from his observation of *Gray Alphabets*. His aspiration to the infinite could be achieved through a paradoxical operation: not through overcoming the physicality of the work but rather through emphasizing this physicality. The constriction of the format, in fact, made it possible to transform the painting into an object rather than a vision and to interrogate, within the physical limits of the object, the significance of the pictorial surface. During the second half of 1958, in some of his *Achromes* (fig. 1), Manzoni purposely contended with Johns's *Gray Alphabets*.[13] Within the grid-like framework of these works, an infinite variety of superficial motifs comes into play. As in *Gray Alphabets*, a finite and strongly constrictive order seems contrasted by infinity and the unpredictability of the painting's surface. The viewer's attention is forced to oscillate between the dominant graphic theme (the grid) and its constituent parts (the individual squares). The indifference of the composition inevitably brings focus to the function of the background surface and, above all, to the mysterious, contradictory relationship that ties the grid to its background.

Fig. 1 **Piero Manzoni (Italian, 1933–1963). *Achrome*, 1958–59**
Kaolin on canvas, 39 3/8 × 27 1/2 in. (100 × 70 cm). Private collection

Following the 1958 biennale, Johns's subsequent solo exhibition at the Galleria del Naviglio confirmed his intentions for Manzoni. Johns's series of white numbers, including *Large White Numbers* (1958) and *0 through 9* (1958), convinced Manzoni that a breakthrough could be made in a conceptual direction. Manzoni's belief in Johns's guiding role for modern painting was further supported that year by the Italian artist's inclusion of an illustration of Johns's *Target with Plaster Casts* (1955; p. 168, fig. 1) in the inaugural issue of *Azimuth*, which Manzoni coedited, in September 1959.

Approximately two years later, between 1961 and 1962, in a statement to critic Maurizio Calvesi, Mario Schifano, a young, emerging Roman painter, maintained that "the academic idea" that interested him most was that of Jasper Johns, because the American artist "focused his preference on the subject."[14] In 1960, Schifano had begun painting heavily material, monochrome canvases. Then, starting in

1961 and continuing throughout 1962, everyday images, including details of street signs and advertising posters, began to enter his paintings. It is at this point that his dialogue with Johns can first be identified. By importing and recomposing simple graphic themes into his work, Schifano was focusing more on the paradoxical richness of the chromatic surfaces than on the synthesis of the drawing. In the sequence of vertical white and red stripes in his 1962 painting *Cartello Piccolo* (*Small Billboard*) (fig. 2), Schifano concentrates on a detail of Johns's 1958 *Flag* (p. 72, pl. 31). He understood, even from a reproduction (most likely a color slide he had seen thanks to Ileana Sonnabend),[15] the reasoning and expressive power of a painting that turned a well-known image (the American flag) into an exercise for testing the mental mechanism of seeing. The heart of Schifano's pictorial interest was above all the application of paint in relation to the repetitiveness of the abstract scheme; in other words, he emphasized the tension between drawing and the pictorial surface.

Fig. 3 **Mario Schifano. *Qualcos'altro* (*Something Else*), 1962**
Enamel on paper applied on canvas, 78 ¾ × 90 ½ in. (200 × 230 cm).
Fondazione Marconi, Milan

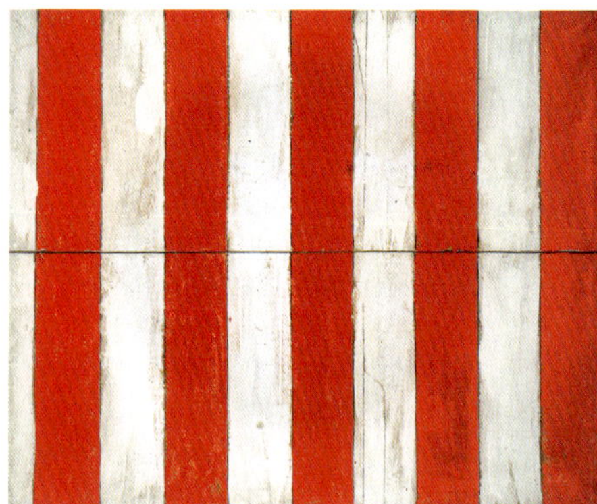

Fig. 2 **Mario Schifano (Italian, 1934–1998). *Cartello Piccolo* (*Small Billboard*), 1962**
Enamel on paper applied on canvas, 39 ⅜ × 47 ¼ in. (100 × 120 cm).
Private collection

This particular way of looking at Johns—that is, the isolation of the purely pictorial fact—became one of the fundamental aspects of Schifano's subsequent research. In his last completely aniconic paintings, his application of paint becomes thinner and his brushstrokes freer and more expressive:[16] the large *Qualcos'altro* (*Something Else*) (1962; fig. 3) is an eloquent example. Upon seeing one of these works, two distinct moments can be identified: when the viewer focuses on the canvas as a self-contained object, without any subject in it; and when, on the contrary, the surface, painted in such a lyrical, personal manner, pushes the viewer to dwell on the disturbing vitality of the painting. In the winter of 1963, Schifano became the first of his generation to directly confront the work of Johns and the cultural and environmental milieu in which it was produced, by spending six months in New York, from December 1963 to June 1964. The effect of seeing original works by the American painter was decisive. In a letter to Cesare Vivaldi, a Roman poet and art critic who had been the first to mention Johns's name in Italy, Schifano recounted his astonishment upon seeing the actual works, with their rich materiality and unexpected dimensions.[17]

Schifano's principal challenge, upon his return to Rome from New York, was to reintroduce the human figure, previously absent, into his painting. In *Corpo in moto e in equilibrio* (*Body in Motion and in Balance*) (1964), he made a first attempt at composition (seen in the two distinct groups) and at allusion to a second plane (the shapes in shadow). Above all, Schifano convincingly experimented with the interference between parts, between those that allude to a pure pictorial plane (the horizontal stripes of the color scale) and those that indicate the action of figures (the bodies). The source for the figures' poses seems to be a photograph of dancers performing in Merce Cunningham's 1958 ballet *Summerspace*, for which Rauschenberg had designed the sets with Johns's help.[18] Perhaps the experience of seeing a painting such as Johns's *Diver* (1962)—in which the outstretched arms of a diver, frozen in the moment, are visible within an abstract background—led Schifano to understand that the pictorial surface is capable of accommodating both the figure and its action.[19]

Beginning in 1961, the young Turinese artist Giulio Paolini, inspired by reproductions of Johns's work published in various periodicals, had staged, through canvas-objects, a sort of allegory for the American painter's work using the materials and tools he utilized: the exposed stretcher frame, the canvas, the brushes, and the colors applied to the canvas's surface.[20] Paolini first saw original works by Johns at the 1964 Venice Biennale, where he was confronted by the artist's pictorial application, the richness and variety of which constituted a true surprise for those who, until then, had known his work only in reproduction. Paolini was particularly struck by Johns's perceptually subtler canvases such as *Gray Rectangles* (1957; p. 47, pl. 17), whose concrete-like surface, nearly entirely covered in paint and interrupted by only the geometric contours of three rectangles, appealed to the Italian artist's investigation of the surface of the canvas as an objective field. In his 1965 painting *Made in B.* (fig. 4),[21] Paolini shows he has intuited the profound significance of *Gray Rectangles*. Using as a model a photograph of one of his aniconic paintings resting against a wall, he covered the entire canvas with gray oil paint in a tangled pattern with an almost illusionistic virtuosity, denoting the central picture with only a rectangular outline. Thus, Johns, with his indeterminate pictorial covering, suggested to Paolini a way to separate the significance of the painting (the object) from the significance of painting (the process), and he pushed him to reflect on the impossibility of recomposing this separation.

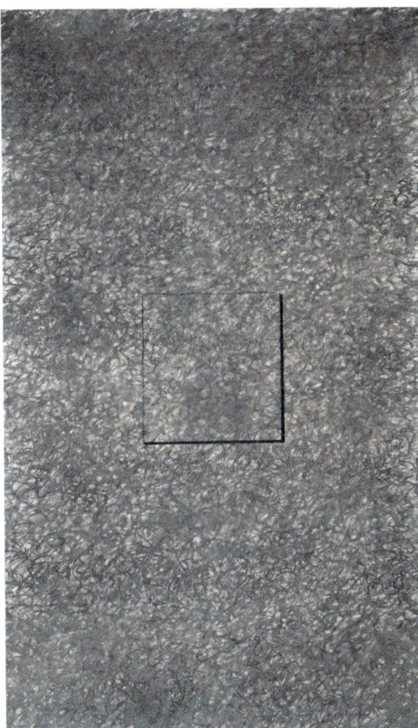

Fig. 4 **Giulio Paolini (Italian, b. 1940). *Made in B.*, 1965**
Oil and photographic emulsion on canvas, 61 × 37 ⅜ in. (155 × 95 cm). Private collection

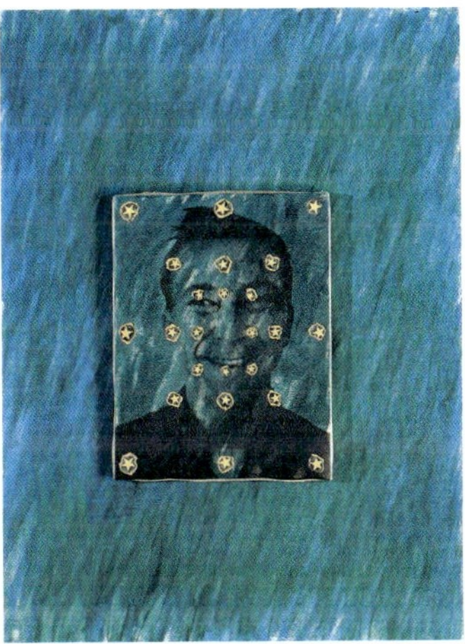

Fig. 5 **Giulio Paolini. *Jasper Johns*, 1967**
Oil on photographic canvas and primed canvas, collage on photo canvas, and nylon thread, 37 × 27 ½ in. (94 × 70 cm). Private collection

Two years later, in 1967, Paolini would make visible his relationship with Johns, covering a photograph of the American painter's face with blue paint that imitated, in application and rhythm, Johns's painting, and embellishing the face with the stars of the American flag, Johns's most celebrated symbol (fig. 5). He arranged the stars, cut out from a reproduction of Johns's *Three Flags* (1958; p. 62, pl. 2), in a pattern resembling crosshairs.[22] The beginning of Paolini's new period of research, including his renunciation of painting and his calling into question the drawing of outline and the literal object, was in homage to an artist who had inspired him to reflect on the fact that painting was a "veil" that had to be eradicated in order to arrive at the heart of the image.

Translated from the Italian by Marguerite Shore

1 On this exhibition and its reception, see Hiroko Ikegami, *The Great Migrator: Robert Rauschenberg and the Global Rise of American Art* (Cambridge, MA: MIT Press, 2010), 27-34.

2 Ileana Sonnabend to Leo Castelli, November 18, 1962, quoted in Lilian Tone, "Chronology and Plates," in *Jasper Johns: A Retrospective*, ed. Kirk Varnedoe, exh. cat. (New York: Museum of Modern Art, 1996), 198.

3 Luce Hoctin complained of a lamentable "ironical challenge to painting," and Georges Boudaille ridiculed Johns as "an ardent nationalist, passionate about shooting, who is learning to count." See Luce Hoctin, "Jasper Johns," *Arts*, no. 707 (January 28, 1958): 12; and Georges Boudaille, "Jasper Johns," *Lettres françaises*, no. 759 (February 11, 1959): 11. See also Pierre Schneider, "Art News from Paris," *ARTnews* 58, no. 1 (March 1959): 47-48.

4 Pierre Restany, "Les Nouveaux réalistes: Premier manifeste du Nouveau réalisme," in *Les Nouveaux réalistes*, exh. cat. (Milan: Galleria Apollinaire, 1960), n.p.

5 Pierre Restany, "Jasper Johns et la métaphysique du lieu commun," *Cimaise* 8, no. 55 (September 1961): 90.

6 Pierre Restany, "La réalité dépasse la fiction," in *Le Nouveau réalisme à Paris et à New York* (Paris: Galerie Rive Droite, 1961), n.p.

7 See K. G. [Pontus] Hultén, introduction to *4 Amerikanare: Jasper Johns, Alfred Leslie, Robert Rauschenberg, Richard Stankiewicz*, ed. K. G. [Pontus] Hultén, exh. cat. (Stockholm: Moderna Museet, 1962); and Harald Szeemann, introduction to *4 Amerikaner: Jasper Johns, Alfred Leslie, Robert Rauschenberg, Richard Stankiewicz*, exh. cat. (Bern: Kunsthalle Bern, 1962).

8 Leo Steinberg, "Jasper Johns: The First Seven Years of His Art," *Metro* 3, nos. 4-5 (May 1962): 90.

9 See Michel Ragon, "L'Amérique à Paris," *Arts*, no. 891 (November 15, 1962): 13; and, especially, Jean-Jacques Lévêque, "Jasper Johns," *Aujourd'hui: Art et architecture* 7, no. 40 (January 1963): 46.

10 See Andrew Forge, "The Emperor's Flag," *New Statesman*, December 11, 1964, 938-39; Edward Lucie-Smith, "Everything That Is in the Case," *The Listener*, December 17, 1964, 982; and Neville Wallis, "Images and Irony," *The Spectator*, December 18, 1964, 843-44.

11 See Marisa Volpi, "Che cos'è la 'pop-art'?," *Avanti!*, August 15, 1964; Carla Lonzi, "Una categoria operativa," *Marcatrè*, July-September 1964, 193; Renato Barilli, "L'offensiva americana alla Biennale," *Il Verri*, no. 14 (1964): 93; Alberto Boatto, "Manhattan Dada e Pop," *Marcatrè*, nos. 11-13 (February 1965): 304-6; and Maurizio Calvesi, "Un pensiero concreto II," *Marcatrè*, nos. 16-18 (July-September 1966): 241-51. The artist Luciano Fabro declared that Johns, by isolating the "pictorial fact," had demonstrated that painting was a weakened double for the "experience of things" and for this reason was being abandoned. See Luciano Fabro, "Discorsi: Carla Lonzi Intervista Luciano Fabro," *Marcatrè*, nos. 19-22 (April 1966): 376.

12 See Angelo Dragone, "Aperta a Venezia la XXIX Biennale," *Il Popolo Nuovo*, June 14, 1958; Palma Bucarelli, "La ventinovesima Biennale espressione viva dell'arte moderna," *La Sera*, June 16, 1958; and Mario Lepore, "Vecchi avanguardisti," *Visto*, July 5, 1958.

13 A juxtaposition between Manzoni's *Achromes* and Johns's work is proposed in Kirk Varnedoe, "Fire: Johns's Work as Seen and Used by American Artists," in Varnedoe, *Johns: A Retrospective*, 95-96 and fig. 7.

14 Mario Schifano, untitled statement (n.d.), quoted in Maurizio Calvesi, "Cronache e coordinate di un'avventura," in *Roma Anni '60: Al di là della Pittura*, ed. Maurizio Calvesi and Rosella Siligato, exh. cat. (Rome: Carte Segrete, 1990), 16.

15 *Flag* had been included in Johns's 1962 solo exhibition at Sonnabend's Paris gallery. That same year, Sonnabend signed a contract with Schifano. See Giorgia Gastaldon, "Ileana Sonnabend e Mario Schifano: Un epistolario (1962-1963)," *Storia dell'Arte*, no. 140 (January-April 2015): 148-76.

16 This latter characteristic is also seen in Johns's canvases from the period of 1955 to 1962, which Schifano studied and Leo Steinberg documented in his 1962 article in *Metro* (see p. 38, pl. 6; p. 45, pl. 5; p. 47, pls. 14, 16; p. 48, pl. 19; p. 100, pl. 5; and p. 149, pl. 1). See Steinberg, "Johns: The First Seven Years," 82-109.

17 Mario Schifano to Cesare Vivaldi, n.d. [January-February 1964], Biblioteca Fondazione Mario Novaro, Fondo Cesare Vivaldi, Genoa.

18 For an illustration of the photograph, see "Collazione: Spazio e movimento," *Collage* 2, nos. 3-4 (December 1964): 63.

19 *Diver* was included in the Johns retrospective at the Jewish Museum in New York from February to April 1964, which Schifano is recorded as having attended. See Furio Colombo, "La lunga strada di Manhattan," in *Words & Drawings*, by Frank O'Hara and Mario Schifano (Rome: Archivio Mario Schifano, 2017), 265-71.

20 For examples of Paolini's canvas-objects, see Maddalena Disch, *Giulio Paolini: Catalogo Ragionato*, vol. 1, *1960-1982* (Milan: Skira, 2008), nos. 8-12, 16-17, 28-49.

21 The title *Made in B.* refers to "made in Belgium," where the oil paint was produced.

22 Both the photograph of Johns, which was taken by the artist Ed Meneeley, and the illustration of *Three Flags* were illustrated in Steinberg, "Jasper Johns," 86, 93.

Note to the Reader

Works reproduced in the plates are listed under the location where they were exhibited. Occasionally exceptions occur and are noted as follows: * indicates a work that is illustrated but not exhibited, † indicates a work shown in Philadelphia but illustrated in a New York section, and ‡ indicates a work shown in New York but illustrated in a Philadelphia section. Works in the exhibition but not illustrated are listed on pages 331–33.

Whenever possible, dimension and medium lines follow Roberta Bernstein, *Jasper Johns: Catalogue Raisonné of Painting and Sculpture*, 5 vols. (New York: Wildenstein Plattner Institute, 2017); Menil Collection, ed., *Jasper Johns: Catalogue Raisonné of Drawing*, 6 vols. (Houston: Menil Collection, 2018); and Richard S. Field, *The Prints of Jasper Johns, 1960–1993: A Catalogue Raisonné* (West Islip, NY: Universal Limited Art Editions, 1994). Dimensions are given in inches followed by centimeters, with height preceding width preceding depth as applicable. For prints, dimensions refer to the sheet size. Frames are included in the dimensions when the artist conceived of the frame as part of the work.

Print captions include the credited printer and publisher, following *The Prints of Jasper Johns, 1960–1993* whenever possible. Abbreviations used for printers and publishers are as follows: Gemini for Gemini Graphic Editions Limited, JJ for Jasper Johns, SPA for Simca Print Artists, and ULAE for Universal Limited Art Editions. Abbreviations used for proofs include AP for artist's proof, PP for printer's proof, TP for trial proof, and WP for working proof.

Captions and, except as noted, dates for sketchbook pages are based on the reproductions and transcriptions in Kirk Varnedoe, ed., *Jasper Johns: Writings, Sketchbook Notes, Interviews* (New York: Museum of Modern Art, 1996).

Years noted in credit lines for long-term loans reflect the beginning of the loan.

Early Work

In the fall of 1954, Jasper Johns destroyed all of his work in his possession. Then twenty-four, he had moved to New York in the summer of 1953, after his discharge from the army in South Carolina. Several months later, he met Robert Rauschenberg, "the first person I knew," Johns recalled, "who was a real artist."[1] The two began an intense creative and romantic relationship and worked intermittently together, and Rauschenberg's art had a profound impact on Johns's. They spent time with the avant-garde composer John Cage and his boyfriend, the dancer and choreographer Merce Cunningham, whose interests in chance and an aesthetic of openness to everyday life also affected Johns deeply. Reflecting on this formative moment, he remarked, "There was a change in my spirit, in my thought and my work, as well as some doubt and terror."[2] Then, as his friend Rachel Rosenthal remembered, "One day he destroyed everything, all the old work. It seemed as if his whole new conception was created in his mind."[3] For Johns, this metamorphosis and rupture involved distancing himself not only from his earlier work but also from the prevalent modes of painting in New York, where Abstract Expressionism by the likes of Willem de Kooning and Norman Lewis was the leading style of the day, while a figurative tradition also carried on in the hands of artists such as Grace Hartigan, Fairfield Porter, and Larry Rivers. "I decided to do only what I meant to do, and not what other people did," Johns said. "When I could observe what others did, I tried to remove that from my work. My work became a constant negation of impulses."[4]

One new path Johns forged was to approach his paintings in relation to the common signs and objects all around him. In some cases, he transposed them directly in paint from the world onto the canvas, as in his series of Flags, Maps, and Targets, so that the painting itself acted as the very thing it depicted. As early as 1957, critics associated these works with Dada and the readymades of Marcel Duchamp, with whose work Johns was not yet familiar.[5] Prompted by this commentary, that same year he and Rauschenberg ventured to see the extensive Duchamp holdings at the Philadelphia Museum of Art, and they would meet the artist himself in late 1958 or early 1959, cementing Johns's lifelong fascination.

Johns not only made paintings that acted as surrogates for found objects, but he also experimented with turning objects themselves into paintings. In *Book* and *Newspaper* (both 1957; pp. 36–37, pl. 4; and p. 39, pl. 13), he covered the titular items with encaustic, a mixture of wax and colored pigment, while leaving their physical thingness evident. The scumbled surfaces impart the reading materials an air of unknowable mystery, so they vacillate ambiguously between quotidian detritus and rarefied artwork. Johns also attached actual objects to canvases that he brushed over with flickering fields of encaustic, as in the stretched canvas sandwiched face-first to *Canvas* (1956; p. 34, pl. 2) and the cast plaster replica of a writing instrument in *Fountain Pen* (1961; p. 38, pl. 5). In slightly later examples such as *Fool's House* (1961–62; p. 33, pl. 1) and *Device* (1962; p. 38, pl. 9), the broom and rulers attached, respectively, to their surfaces played a role in the production of the work by serving as the tools that pushed or scraped the paint. All these paintings convey a sense of sculptural tinkering that brought them into a charged new relation to the world. They act neither like fictive windows onto other realms nor like the resolute abstractions prevalent in their day—nor, for that matter, like the common stuff they incorporate or evoke. Rather, they test the relationships between image and object, artwork and thing, process and product, in a manner both plainspoken and deeply philosophical. In so doing, they pointed the way to the literalism of Pop, Minimalism, and the process-based sculpture alongside which Johns's work would continue to evolve throughout the 1960s.

While the readymade was one means by which Johns's work would become "a constant negation of impulses" (both in distinguishing his art from that of others and in narrowing its focus), it is possible to see negation itself as both a powerful operation and affect in his art of this time. The cast plaster faces cropped at the eyeline above *Target with Four Faces* (1955; p. 42, pl. 2) eerily allude to the violence of a shooting gallery and to blindness, a state amplified by the hinged lid that might completely hide these impassive visages from us—or us from them. This sense of disorientation and lost vision recurs in the sooty field of *Night Driver* (1960; p. 48, pl. 21), which was inspired by Johns's first memory of driving through the dark. *Tennyson* (1958; p. 47, pl. 14) and *Disappearance II* (1961; p. 48, pl. 19) both feature a folded canvas drawn across their surfaces. In *Alley Oop* (1958; p. 46, pl. 11) and *Numbers* (1960–65; p. 46, pl. 10), Johns obliterated a printed page by tracing over its forms with his brush. The "doubt and terror" he sensed in charting his own artistic course became topoi to explore.

In 1961, Johns and Rauschenberg broke off their romantic relationship, resulting in some of the most doleful and riley works of Johns's career. *No* (p. 47, pl. 12), *Liar* (p. 45, pl. 5), *Painting Bitten by a Man* (p. 44, pl. 4), and *Water Freezes* (p. 47, pl. 15), all 1961, roil with accusation, lament, and the chill of loneliness, while the tipped empty cup of *Good Time Charley* (p. 47, pl. 16) has been interpreted as a reference and riposte to Rauschenberg's ebullient charm. Although Johns has long been said to have rejected the heroic passion and putative soul baring of Abstract Expressionism, his very resistance to that stance struck an equally powerful emotional chord. In place of bravura open gestures, one finds aimless, tightly clustered strokes congealed in wax. Gutsy confidence yields to silence, absence, refusal, and loss.

—Scott Rothkopf, with Carlos Basualdo, Sarah B. Vogelman, and Lauren Young

1 Jasper Johns, quoted in Mark Stevens with Cathleen McGuigan, "Super Artist: Jasper Johns, Today's Master," *Newsweek*, October 24, 1977; reprinted in Kirk Varnedoe, ed., *Jasper Johns: Writings, Sketchbook Notes, Interviews* (New York: Museum of Modern Art, 1996), 165.

2 Jasper Johns, quoted in Vivien Raynor, "Jasper Johns: 'I Have Attempted to Develop My Thinking in Such a Way That the Work I've Done Is Not Me,'" *ARTnews* 72, no. 3 (March 1973): 22; quoted in Lilian Tone, "Chronology and Plates," in *Jasper Johns: A Retrospective*, ed. Kirk Varnedoe, exh. cat. (New York: Museum of Modern Art, 1996), 124.

3 Rachel Rosenthal, quoted in an unpublished interview with Calvin Tomkins, June 2, 1978; quoted in Tone, "Chronology," 124.

4 Jasper Johns, quoted in Michael Crichton, *Jasper Johns* (New York: Harry N. Abrams and Whitney Museum of American Art, 1977), 27.

5 See, for example, Robert Rosenblum, "Castelli Group," *Arts* 31, no. 8 (May 1957): 53.

Early Work

Real Things as Paintings

PHILADELPHIA MUSEUM OF ART

1 ***Fool's House*, 1961–62**
Oil, Sculp-metal, and charcoal on canvas with objects
72 × 36 in. (182.9 × 91.4 cm)
Private collection

2 ***Canvas*, 1956**
Encaustic and collage on canvas
30 × 25 in. (76.2 × 63.5 cm)
Collection of the artist; on long-term loan to the San Francisco Museum of Modern Art, 2000

3 ***Target*, 1958**
Oil and collage on canvas
36 × 36 in. (91.4 × 91.4 cm)
Collection of the artist; on long-term loan to the National Gallery of Art, Washington, DC, 1986

4 ***Book*, 1957***
Encaustic on book and wood
9 ½ × 12 ⅞ in. (24.1 × 32.7 cm)
Collection Martin Z. Margulies

5 ***Fountain Pen*, 1961**
Encaustic on wood with object
7 ¼ × 5 ½ in. (18.4 × 14 cm)
Private collection

6 ***Drawer*, 1957**
Encaustic on canvas with objects
30 ½ × 30 ½ in. (77.5 × 77.5 cm)
The Rose Art Museum, Brandeis University, Waltham, Massachusetts; Gevirtz-Mnuchin Purchase Fund, 1962.133

7 ***Untitled (Gray Painting with Spoon)*, 1962**
Encaustic on canvas with objects
26 × 20 ⅛ in. (66 × 51.1 cm)
Private collection

8 ***Painting with Two Balls*, 1960**
Encaustic and collage on canvas with objects (three panels)
65 × 54 ⅛ in. (165.1 × 137.5 cm) overall
Collection of the artist; on long-term loan to the Philadelphia Museum of Art, 1979

9 ***Device*, 1962**
Oil on canvas with objects
40 × 30 in. (101.6 × 76.2 cm)
The Baltimore Museum of Art; purchased with funds provided by the Dexter M. Ferry, Jr., Trustee Corporation Fund and by Edith Ferry Hooper, 1976.1

10 ***Painting with Ruler and "Gray,"* 1960***
Oil and collage on canvas with objects
32 × 32 in. (81.3 × 81.3 cm)
Frederick R. Weisman Art Foundation, Los Angeles

11 ***Target*, 1957**‡
Encaustic and collage on canvas mounted on cardboard
7 ⅜ × 7 ¼ in. (18.7 × 18.4 cm)
Private collection

12 ***Flag*, 1960–66**
Encaustic and collage over lithograph mounted on canvas
17 ½ × 26 ¾ in. (44.5 × 68 cm)
The Middleton Family Collection

13 ***Newspaper*, 1957***
Encaustic and collage on canvas
27 × 34 ¾ in. (68.6 × 88.3 cm)
Private collection

14 ***Star*, 1954**
Encaustic and collage on canvas with glass and painted wood
22 ½ × 19 ½ in. (57.2 × 49.5 cm)
The Menil Collection, Houston

Disappearance and Negation

WHITNEY MUSEUM OF AMERICAN ART

1 ***Diver*, 1962–63**
Charcoal, pastel, and paint on two sheets of paper mounted on two adjoined canvas supports
86 ⅛ × 71 ¼ in. (218.8 × 181 cm)
The Museum of Modern Art, New York; partial gift of Kate Ganz and Tony Ganz in memory of their parents, Victor and Sally Ganz, and in memory of Kirk Varnedoe; Mrs. John Hay Whitney Bequest Fund; gift of Edgar Kaufmann, Jr., gift of Philip L. Goodwin, bequest of Richard S. Zeisler, and anonymous gift (all by exchange); acquired by the Trustees of the Museum of Modern Art in memory of Kirk Varnedoe, 377.2003.a–b

2 ***Target with Four Faces*, 1955**
Encaustic and collage on canvas with objects
29 ¾ × 26 in. (75.6 × 66 cm)
The Museum of Modern Art, New York; gift of Mr. and Mrs. Robert C. Scull, 8.1958

3 ***Target with Four Faces*, 1968**
Graphite pencil, charcoal, and pastel over screenprint on paper
34 ½ × 29 ¾ in. (87.6 × 75.6 cm)
Private collection

4 ***Painting Bitten by a Man*, 1961**
Encaustic on canvas
9 ½ × 6 ⅞ in. (24.1 × 17.5 cm)
The Museum of Modern Art, New York; gift of Jasper Johns in memory of Kirk Varnedoe, Chief Curator of the Department of Painting and Sculpture, 1989–2001, 211.2007

5 ***Liar*, 1961**
Encaustic, Sculp-metal, and graphite on paper
21 ¼ × 17 in. (54 × 43.2 cm)
Collection of Gail and Tony Ganz

6 ***White Target*, 1957**
Encaustic on canvas
30 × 30 in. (76.2 × 76.2 cm)
Whitney Museum of American Art, New York; purchase, 71.211

7 ***Targets*, 1966**
Encaustic and collage on canvas
72 × 48 in. (182.9 × 121.9 cm)
MMK Museum für Moderne Kunst, Frankfurt am Main; former collection of Karl Ströher, Darmstadt, 1981/12

8 ***Green Target*, 1958***
Graphite pencil, encaustic, and collage on paper
7 ½ × 6 ¾ in. (19.1 × 17.2 cm)
Collection of the artist

9 ***Alphabets*, 1957***
Collage, graphite wash, and graphite pencil on printed card mounted on paper
19 ⅞ × 15 ⅞ in. (50.5 × 40.3 cm)
Private collection

10 ***Numbers*, 1960–65**
Encaustic over lithograph mounted on canvas
17 × 13 ¼ in. (43.2 × 33.7 cm)
Irving Stenn, Jr., Family Collection

11 ***Alley Oop*, 1958**
Oil and collage on cardboard mounted on fiberboard
23 ¼ × 18 in. (59.1 × 45.7 cm)
The Newhouse Collection

12 ***No*, 1961**
Encaustic, Sculp-metal, and collage on canvas with objects
68 × 40 ½ in. (172.7 × 102.9 cm)
Kravis Collection

13 ***Voice*, 1964–67**
Oil on canvas with objects (two panels)
96 ⅜ × 69 ⅜ in. (244.8 × 176.2 cm) overall
The Menil Collection, Houston

14 ***Tennyson*, 1958**
Encaustic and collage on canvas (two panels)
73 ½ × 48 ¼ in. (186.7 × 122.6 cm) overall
Des Moines Art Center, Iowa; purchased with funds from the Coffin Fine Arts Trust; Nathan Emory Coffin Collection of the Des Moines Art Center, 1971.4

15 ***Water Freezes*, 1961**
Encaustic and collage on canvas and wood with objects (two panels)
31 × 25 ½ in. (78.7 × 64.8 cm) overall
Collection of Marguerite and Robert Hoffman

16 ***Good Time Charley*, 1961**
Encaustic on canvas with objects
38 × 24 in. (96.5 × 61 cm)
Private collection

17 ***Gray Rectangles*, 1957***
Encaustic on canvas with objects
60 × 60 in. (152.4 × 152.4 cm)
The George Economou Collection

18 ***Disappearance I*, 1960***
Encaustic and collage on canvas
40 × 40 in. (101.6 × 101.6 cm)
Private collection

19 ***Disappearance II*, 1961**
Encaustic and collage on canvas
40 × 40 in. (101.6 × 101.6 cm)
Toyama Prefectural Museum of Art and Design, Japan

20 ***Disappearance II*, 1962***
Ink on plastic
18 × 18 in. (45.7 × 45.7 cm)
Collection of Kate Ganz

21 ***Night Driver*, 1960**
Charcoal, pastel, and collage on paper
51 × 42 ⅛ in. (129.5 × 107 cm)
The Robert and Jane Meyerhoff Collection

22 ***Star*, c. 1957***
Ink and graphite pencil on paper
10 ⅜ × 8 ¼ in. (26.4 × 21 cm)
Collection of the artist

23 ***Untitled*, 1954***
Graphite pencil on paper
14 × 11 in. (35.6 × 27.9 cm)
The Menil Collection, Houston; promised gift from the collection of Louisa Stude Sarofim

24 ***Untitled*, 1954***
Oil and collage on canvas with glass, painted wood, and object
26 ¼ × 8 ¾ in. (66.7 × 22.2 cm)
Hirshhorn Museum and Sculpture Garden, Smithsonian Institution, Washington, DC; Regents Collections Acquisition Program with Matching Funds from the Thomas M. Evans,

Jerome L. Greene, Joseph H. Hirshhorn, and Sydney and Frances Lewis Purchase Fund, 1987, 87.20

25 ***Dish*, 1969***
Graphite powder on paper
16 ¼ × 20 ¼ in. (41.3 × 51.4 cm)
Collection of the artist

26 ***Untitled*, 1960–61**
Plaster and wire
3 ⅜ × 12 ⅛ × 6 ⅜ in.
(8.6 × 30.8 × 16.2 cm)
Collection of the artist; on long-term loan to the Philadelphia Museum of Art, 2007

27 ***Target with Four Faces*, 1955**
Graphite pencil and pastel on paper
9 ¼ × 7 ⅞ in. (23.5 × 20 cm)
Collection of the artist

Real Things as Paintings

PHILADELPHIA MUSEUM OF ART

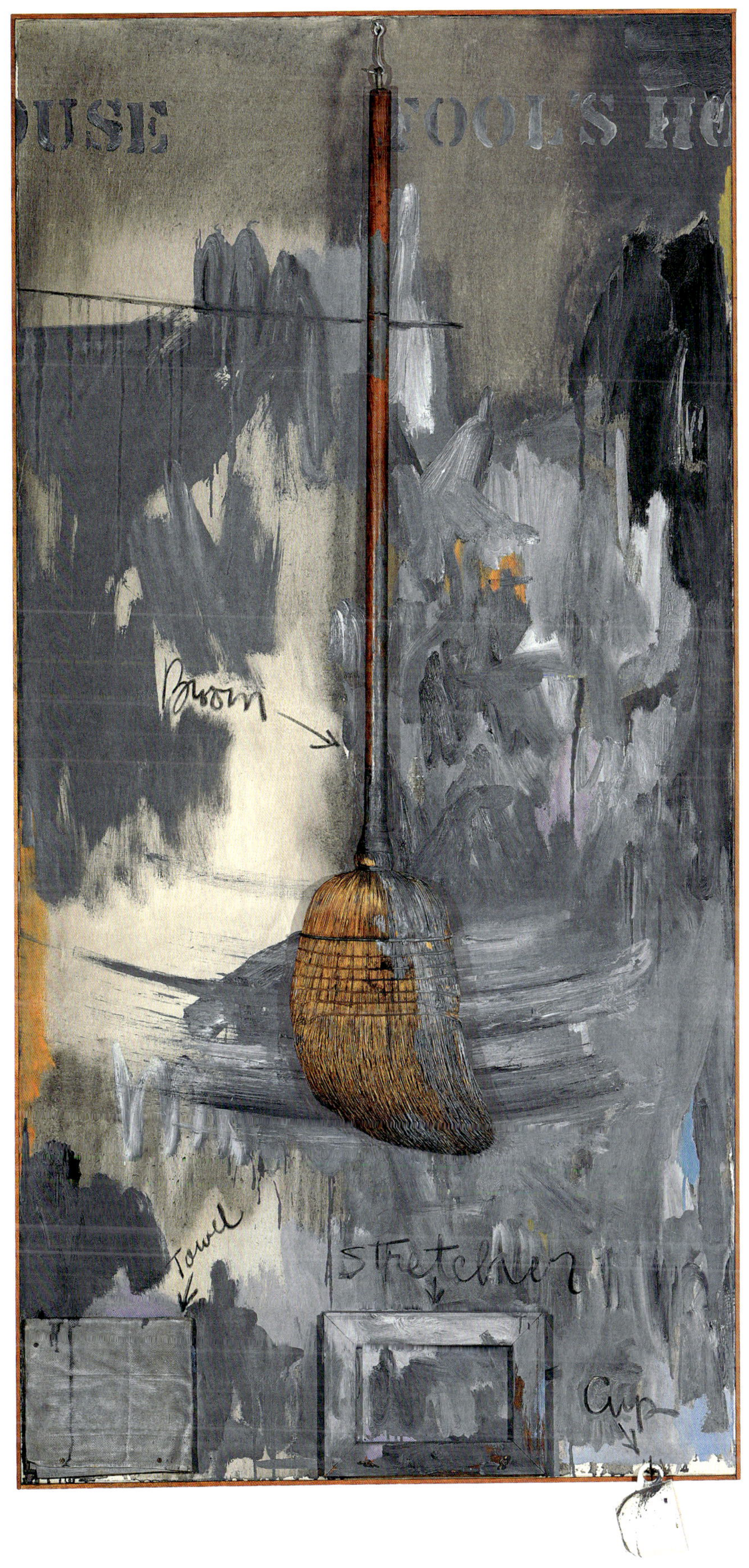

1 *Fool's House*, 1961–62

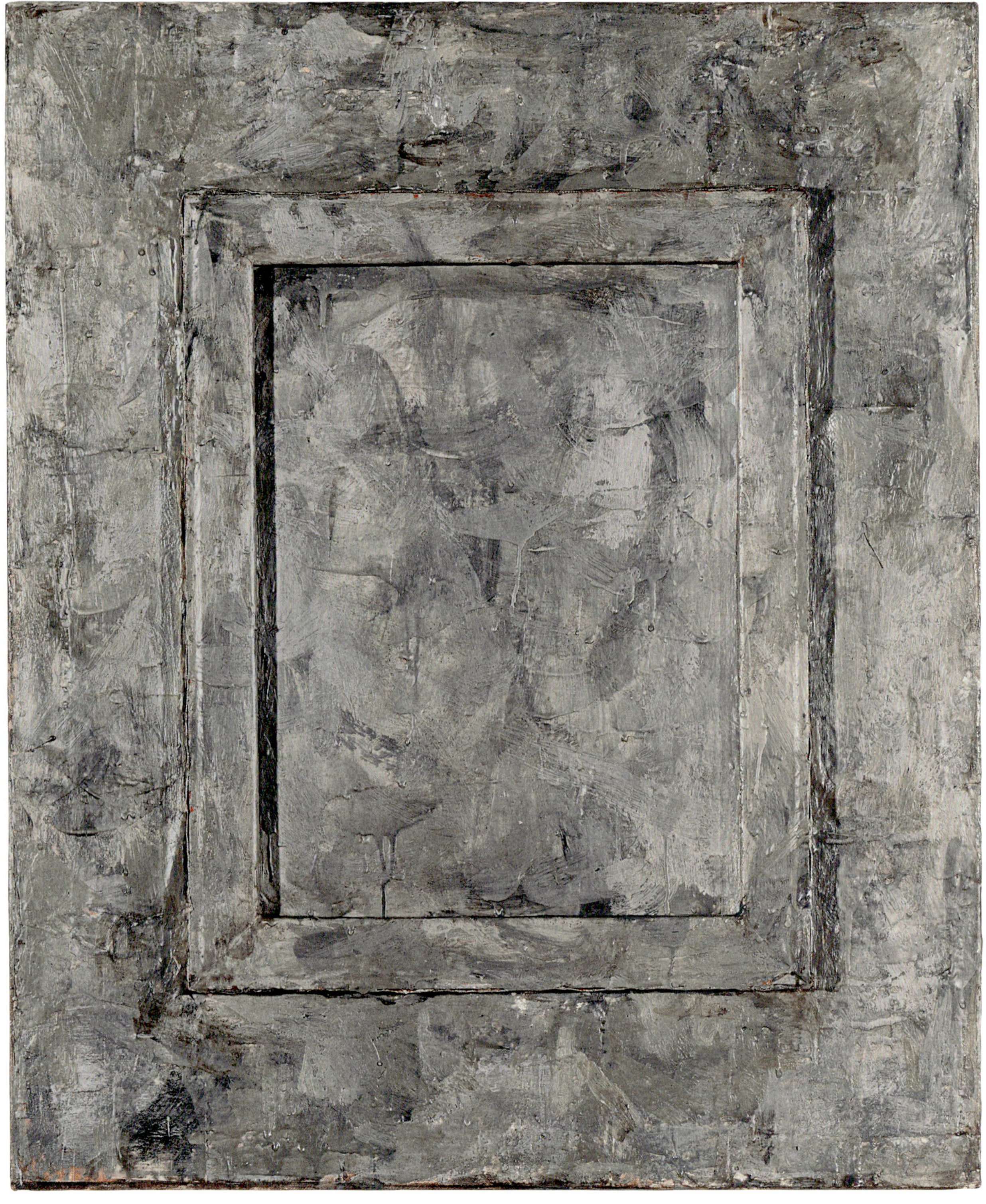

2 *Canvas*, 1956

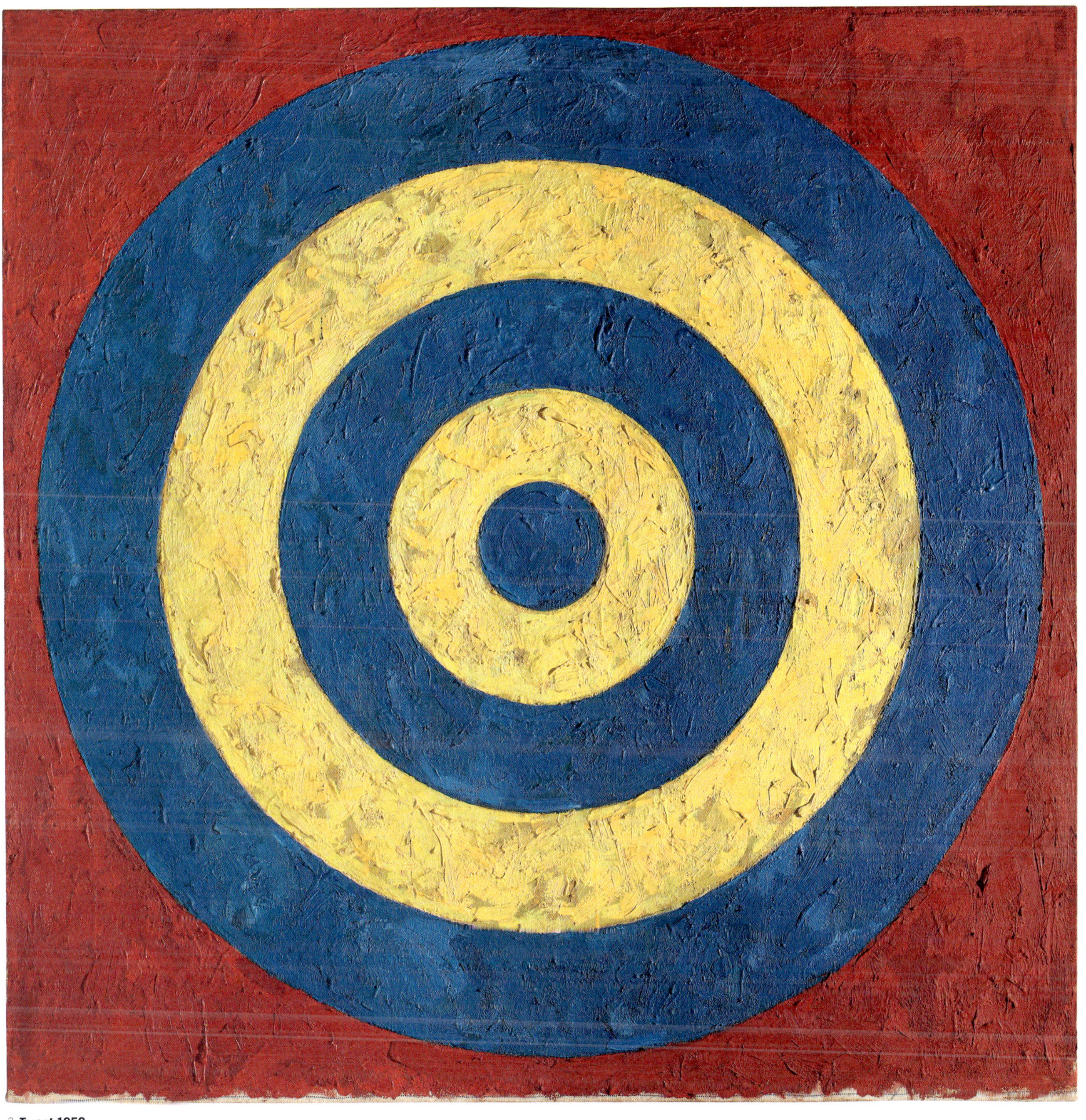

3 ***Target*, 1958**

4 ***Book*, 1957**

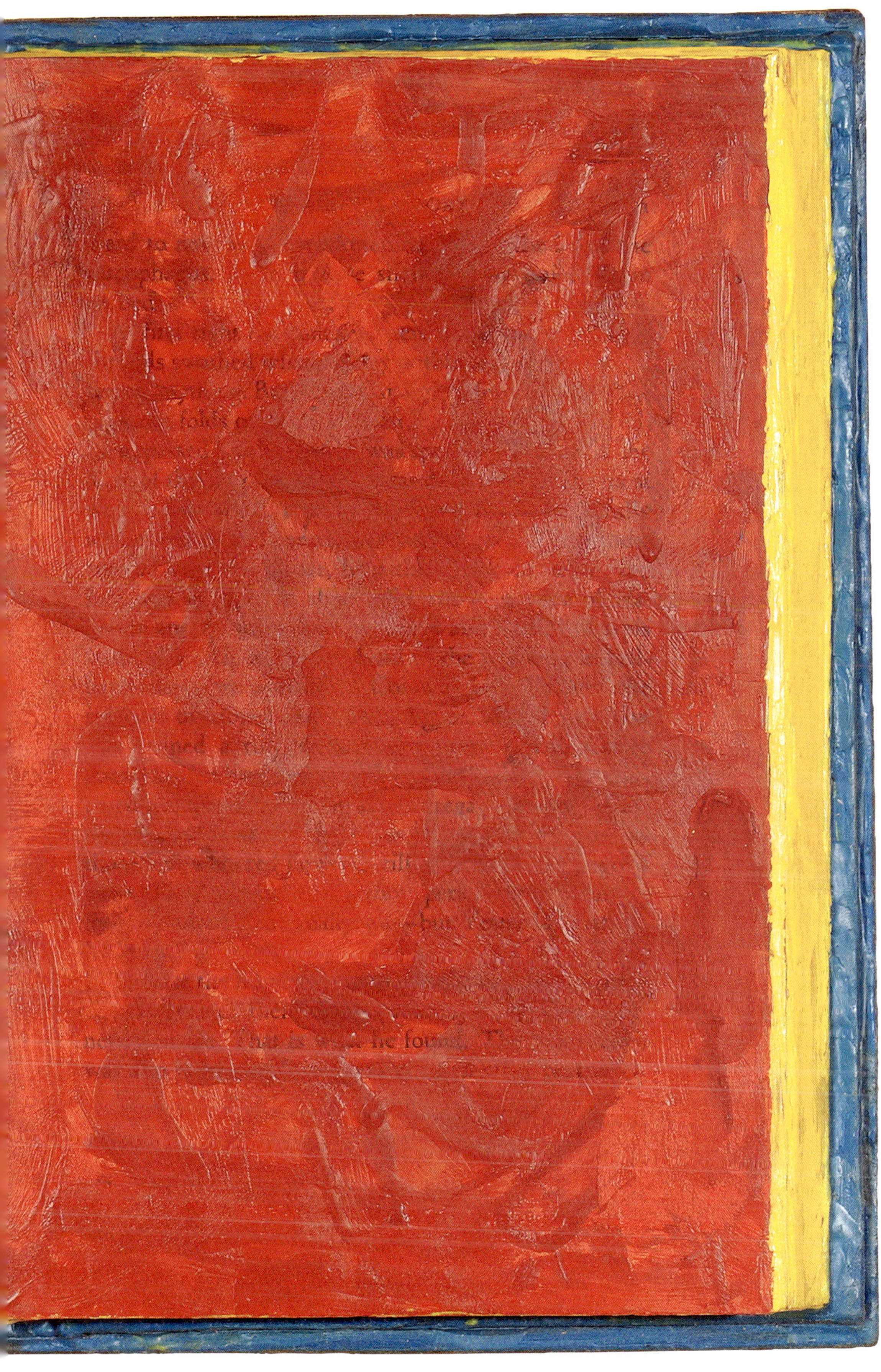

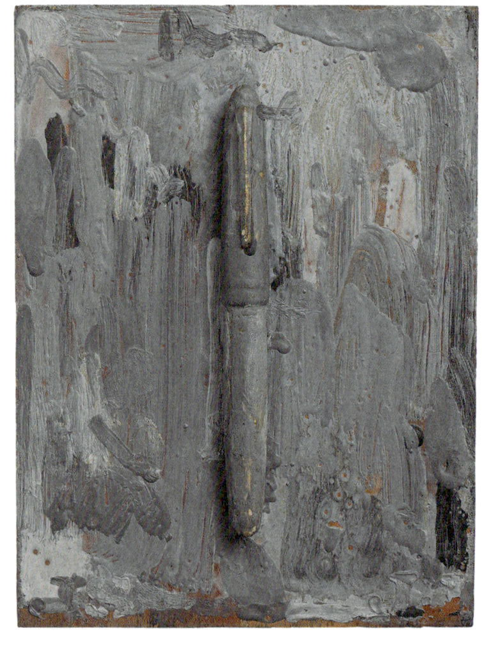

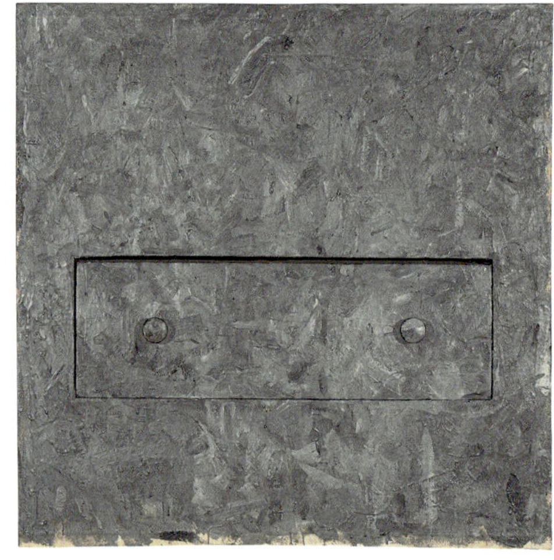

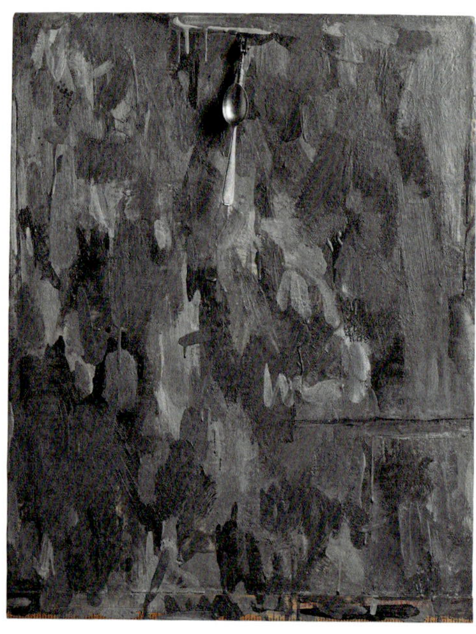

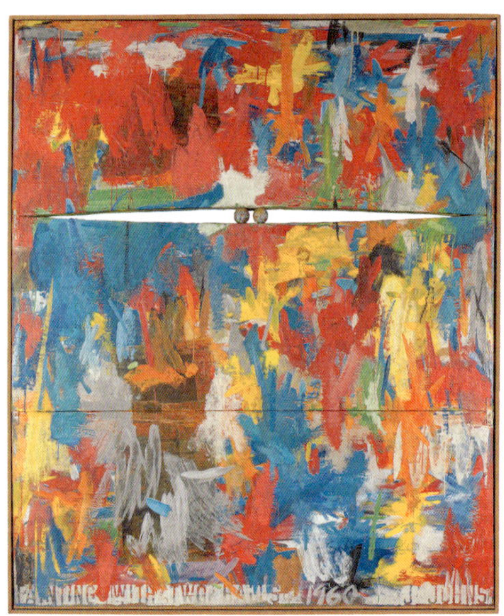

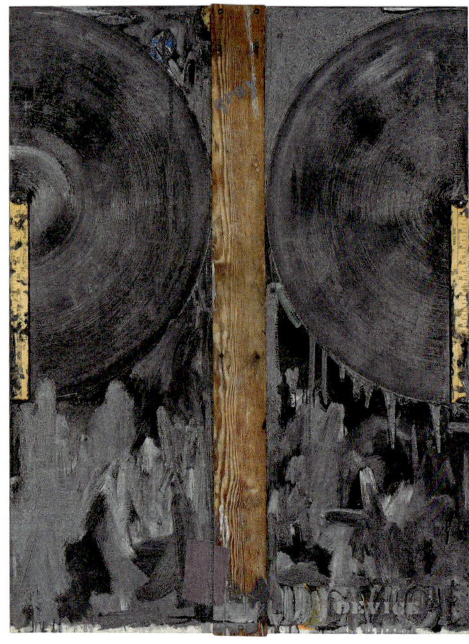

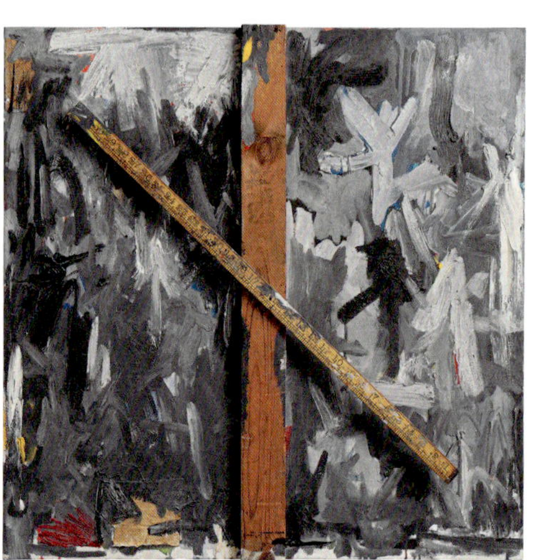

5 ***Fountain Pen***, 1961
8 ***Painting with Two Balls***, 1960

6 ***Drawer***, 1957
9 ***Device***, 1962

7 ***Untitled (Gray Painting with Spoon)***, 1962
10 ***Painting with Ruler and "Gray,"*** 1960

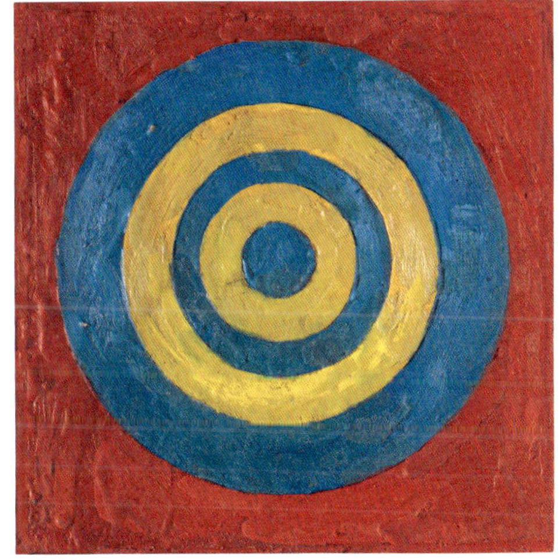

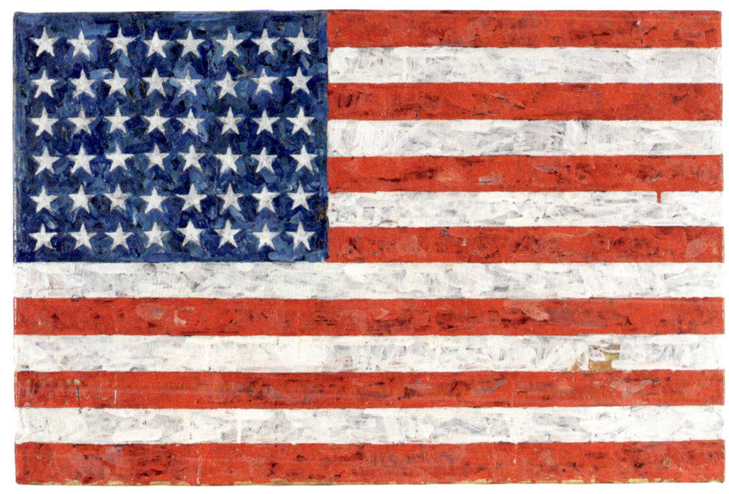

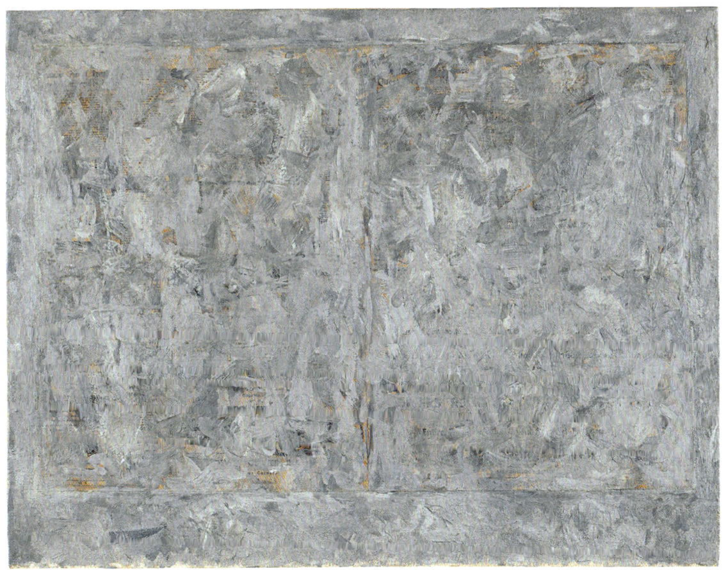

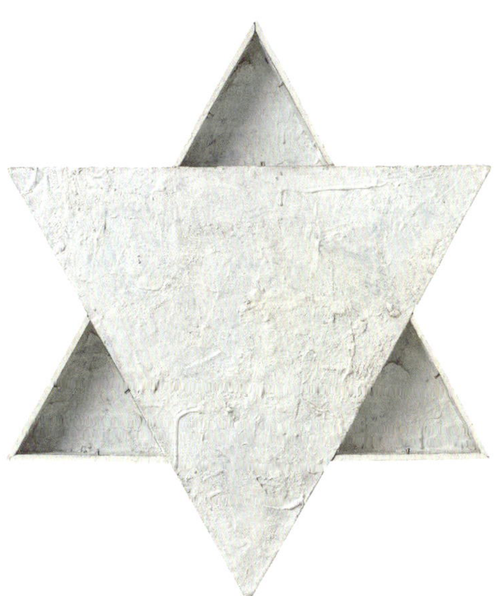

11 ***Target*, 1957**
13 ***Newspaper*, 1957**

12 ***Flag*, 1960–66**
14 ***Star*, 1954**

Disappearance and Negation

WHITNEY MUSEUM OF AMERICAN ART

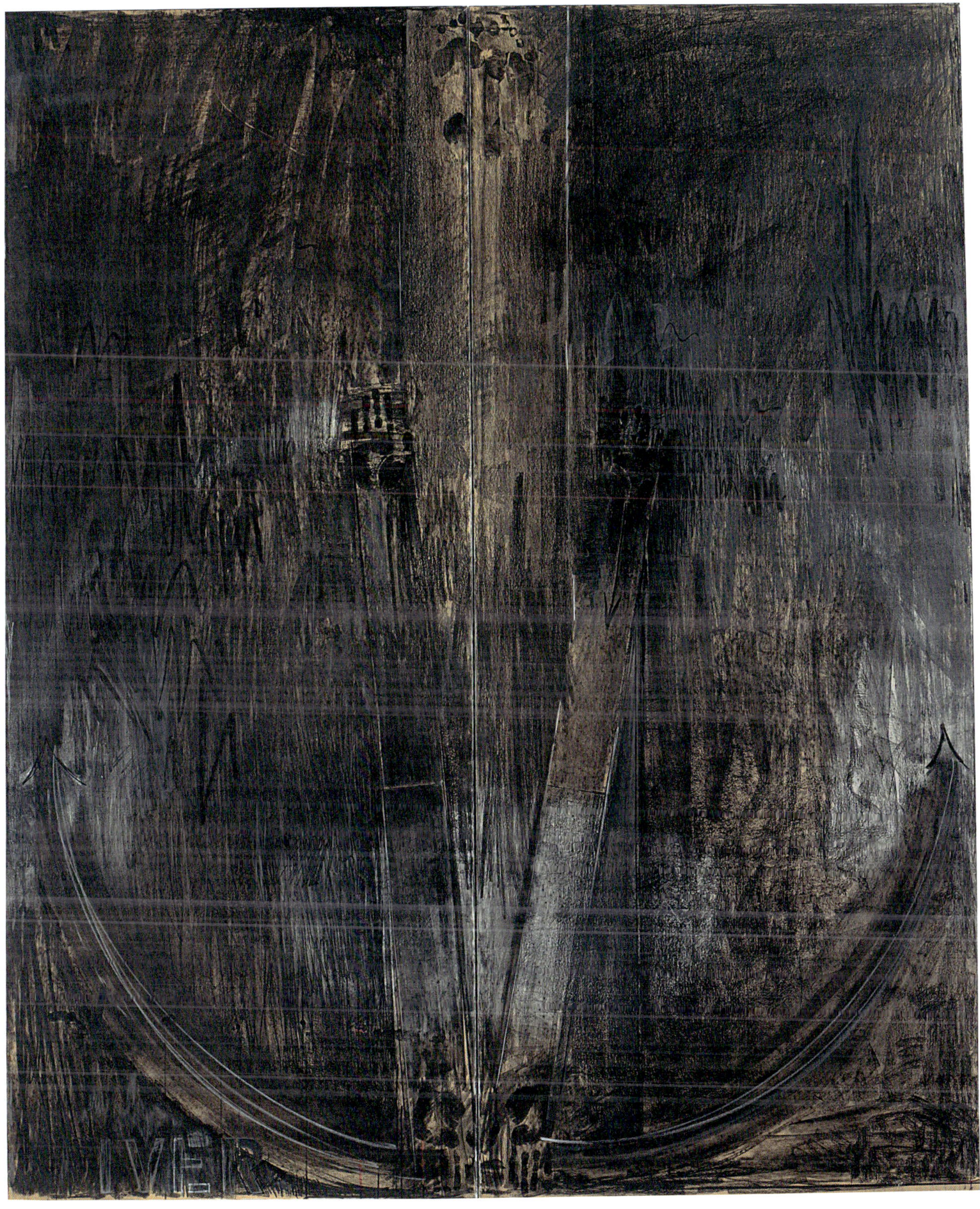

1 *Diver*, 1962–63

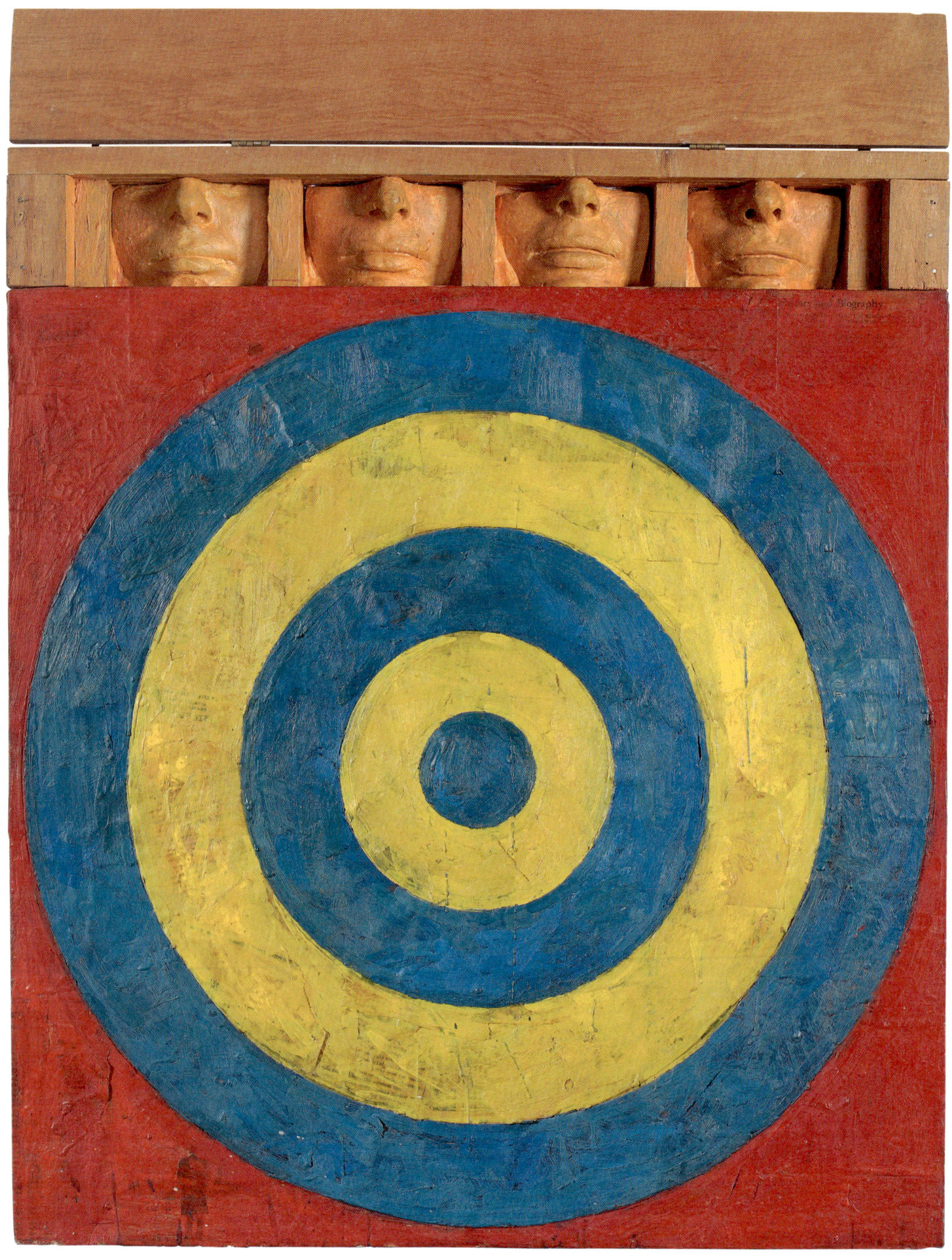

2 ***Target with Four Faces*, 1955**

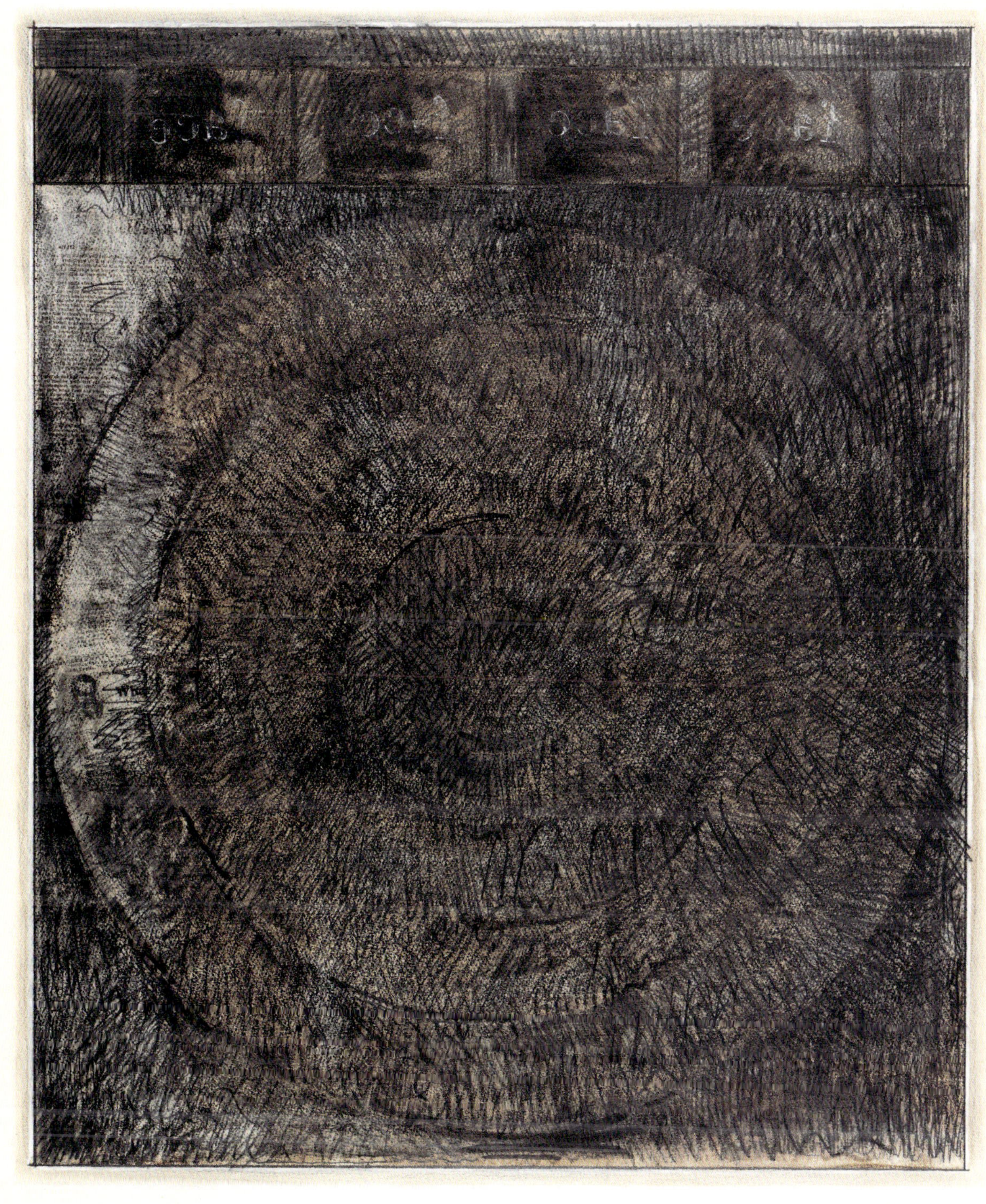

3 ***Target with Four Faces*, 1968**

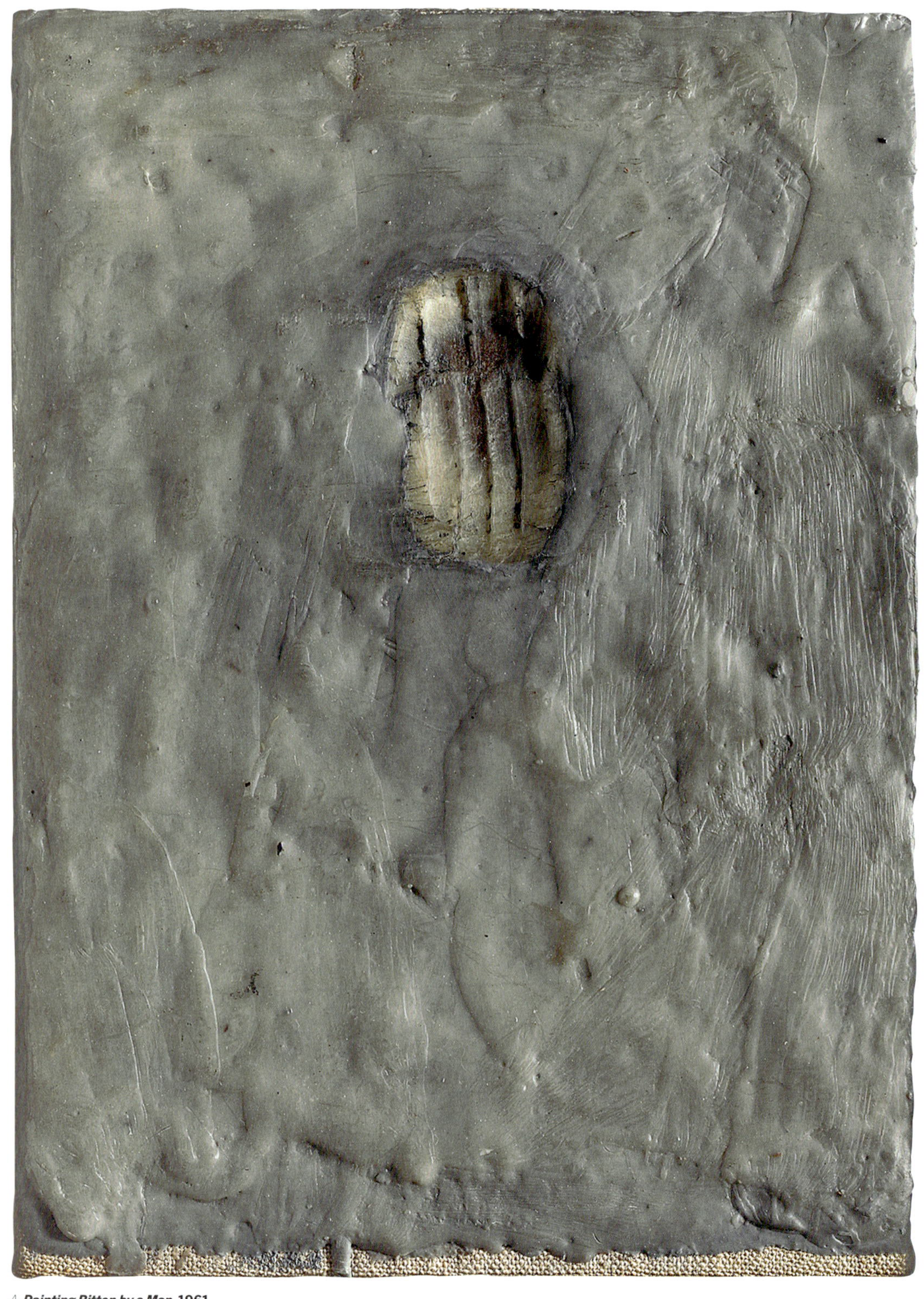

4 ***Painting Bitten by a Man*, 1961**

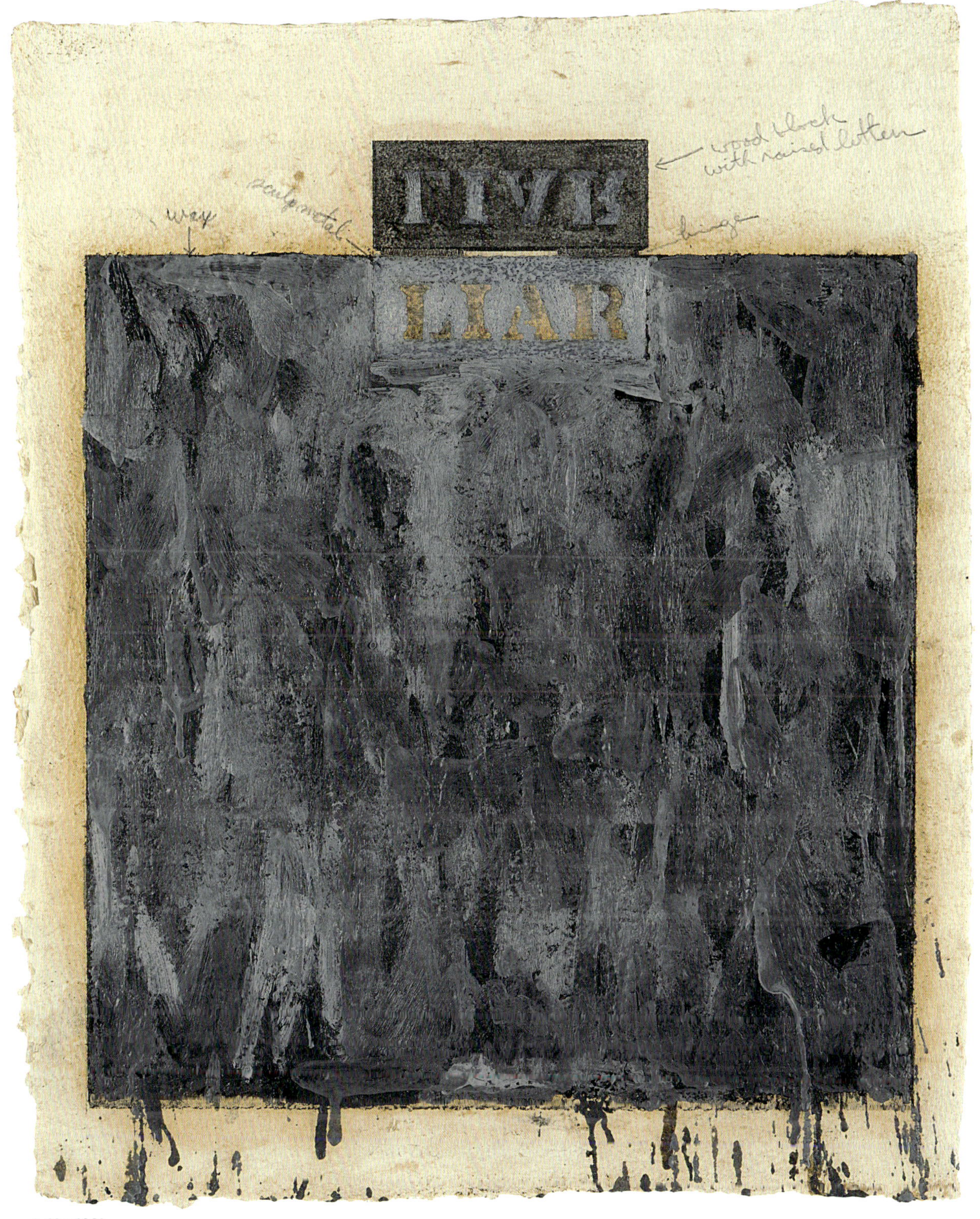

5 ***Liar***, **1961**

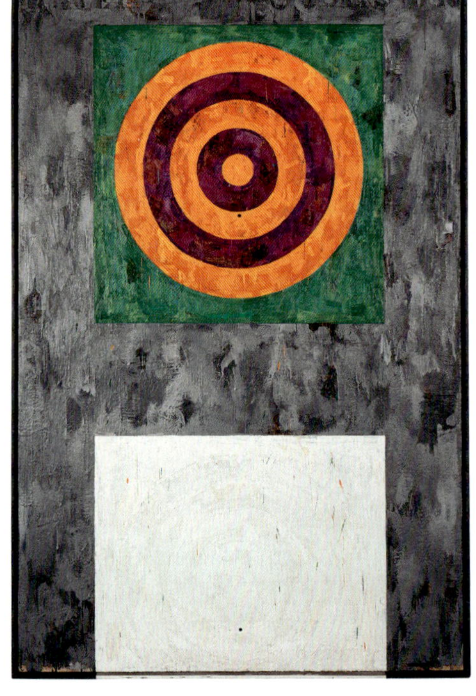

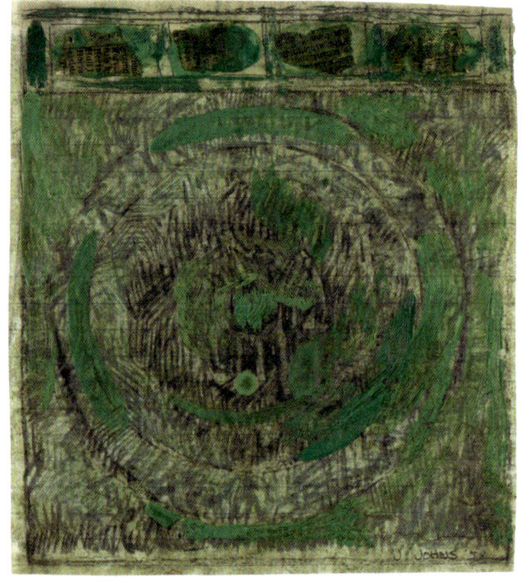

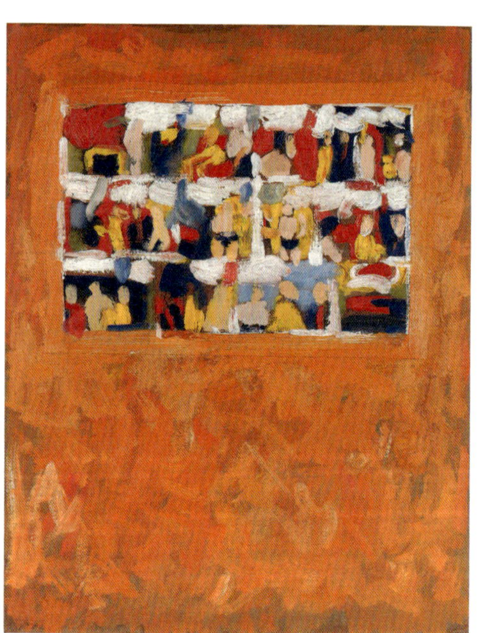

6 ***White Target***, **1957**
9 ***Alphabets***, **1957**

7 ***Targets***, **1966**
10 ***Numbers***, **1960–65**

8 ***Green Target***, **1958**
11 ***Alley Oop***, **1958**

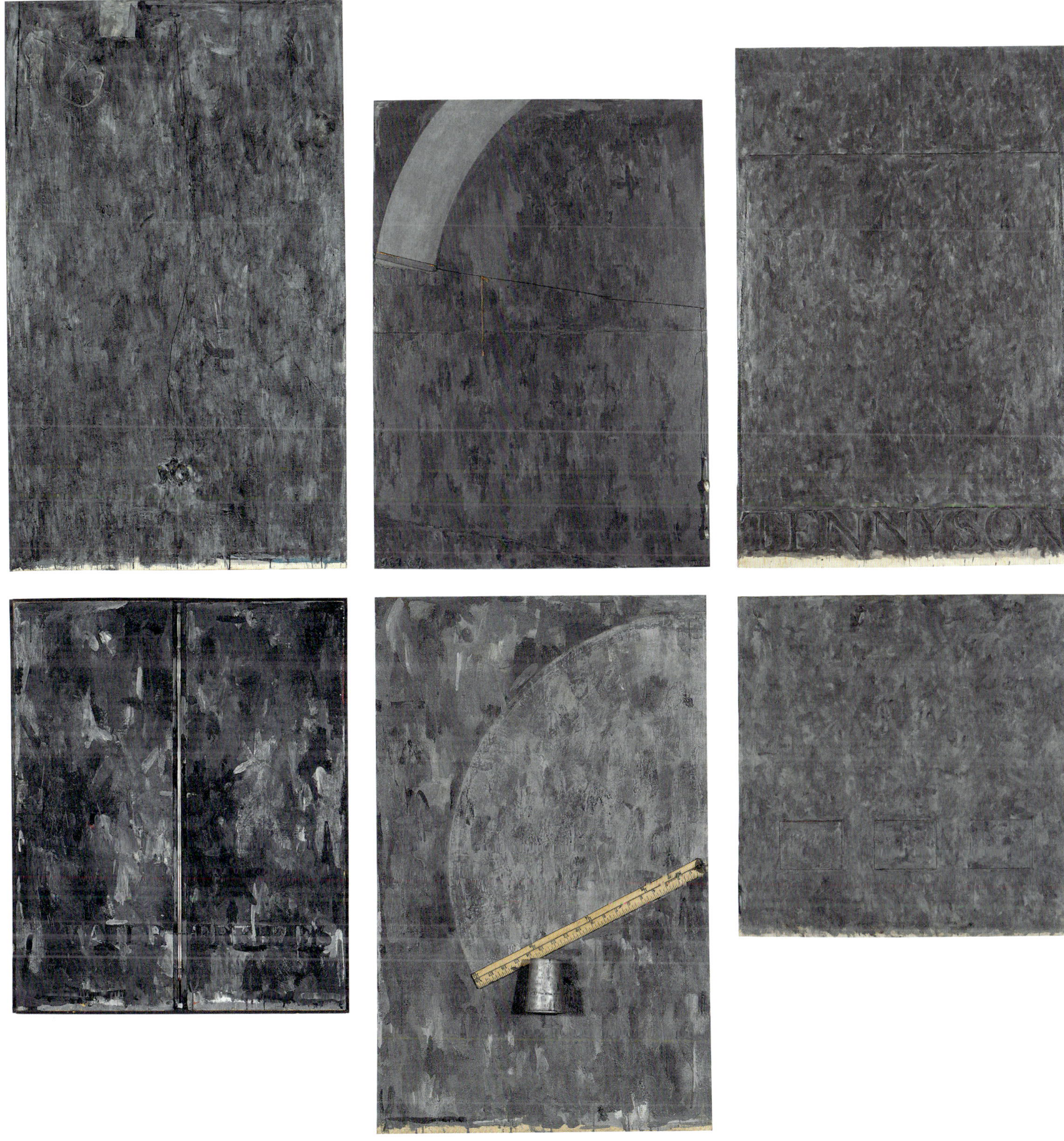

12 ***No***, **1961**
15 ***Water Freezes***, **1961**

13 ***Voice***, **1964–67**
16 ***Good Time Charley***, **1961**

14 ***Tennyson***, **1958**
17 ***Gray Rectangles***, **1957**

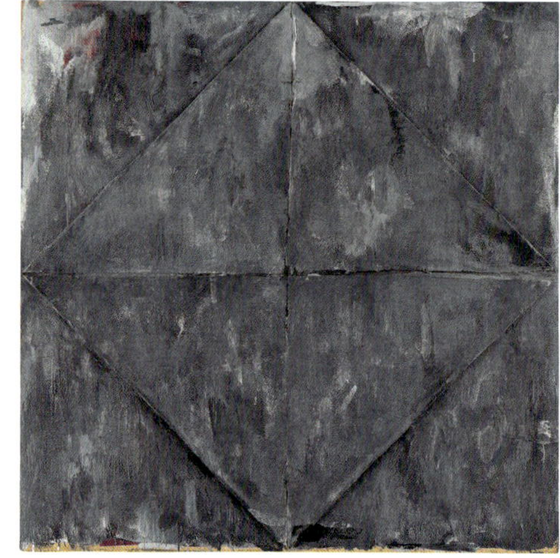

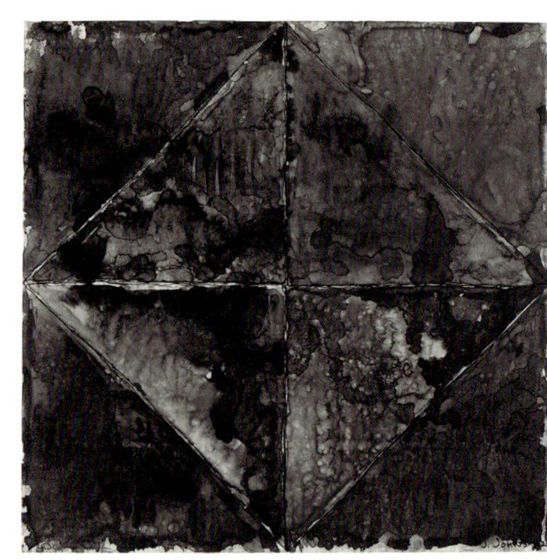

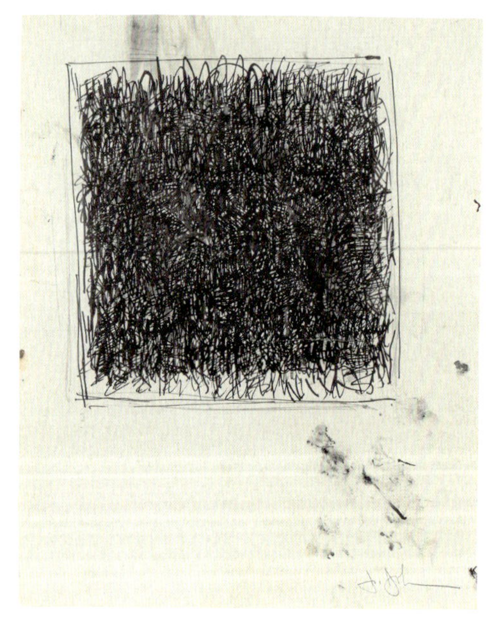

18 ***Disappearance I*, 1960**
21 ***Night Driver*, 1960**

19 ***Disappearance II*, 1961**
22 ***Star*, c. 1957**

20 ***Disappearance II*, 1962**
23 ***Untitled*, 1954**

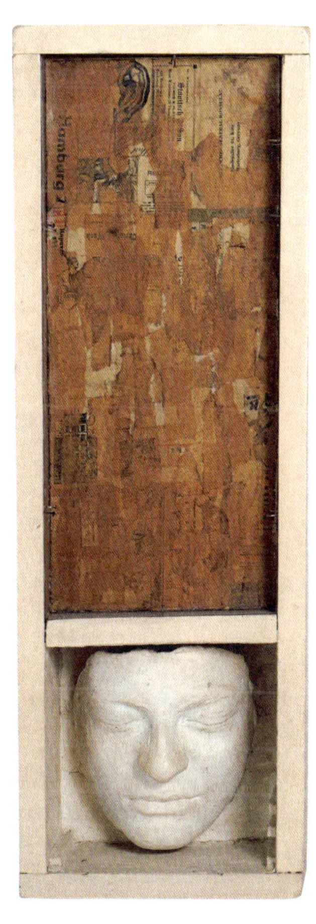

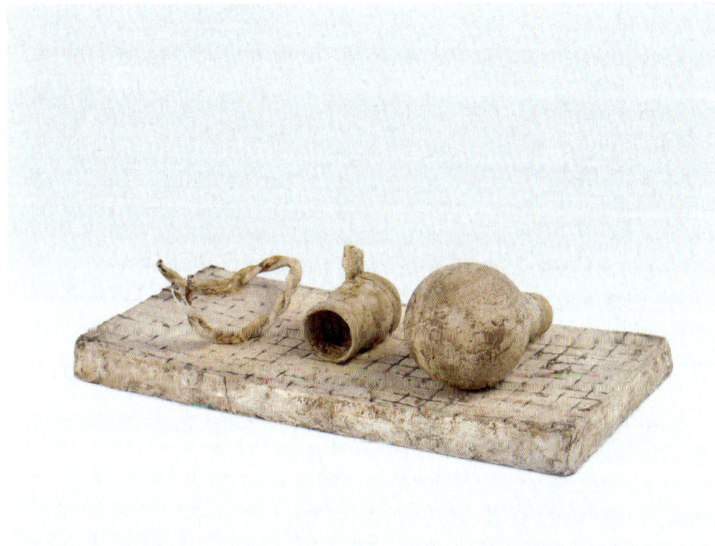

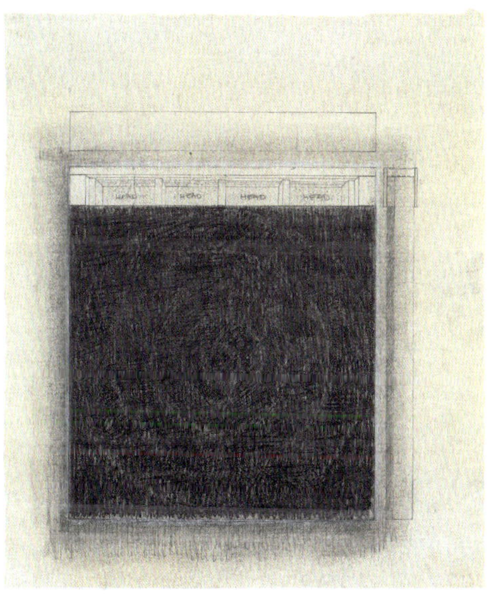

24 ***Untitled*, 1954**
26 ***Untitled*, 1960–61**

25 ***Dish*, 1969**
27 ***Target with Four Faces*, 1955**

Devices in Jasper Johns's Paintings
Andrianna Campbell-LaFleur

> Make something
> Find a use for it
> and / or
> Invent a function
> Find an object[1]

The real is that which is genuine in its material existence.[2] To speak of the real in a work by Jasper Johns is to acknowledge the addition of objects in his paintings. As a twenty-nine-year-old artist, Johns articulated and reticulated his conceptual desires.[3] As early as 1958, we see in his work an interplay of the real and the simulated, when Johns began collecting, casting, and hand-forming commonplace objects. Within a year, he added these alongside paint to build accretionary pictorial surfaces into and on his paintings.[4] I propose that Johns made these paintings with two types of "devices": first, contrivances that are sutured, glued, and hinged into their canvas and panel surfaces; and second, devices that are visually repetitive patterns that network across their surfaces.[5] These dual meanings of device (visual and semantic) led Johns to a mode of division and then devising in the late 1950s, to which he would return in the Catenary paintings of the 1990s and 2000s (see, for example, p. 267, pl. 1; and p. 272, pl. 5).[6]

If we trace the word *device* to its Latinate roots, it can be understood as a means of devising and composing, rather than its later usage in art academicism to refer to the trompe l'oeil, witty and illusionistic effects of "fooling the eye," or the ironic, self-revelatory, and anti-illusionistic aspects of modernism's "truth to materials." Thus, the thingness of the objects in Johns's paintings sits alongside the painterly illusion of the painting painted: both are part of an expressive sincerity of genuine materiality combined with a fictive alternate to the earnestly material. Morgan Meis was one of the first to summarize that Johns "opened up new areas in which paintings could be both things-in-the-world and paintings of those things."[7]

In *Device Circle* (1959; p. 100, pl. 7), Johns inscribed literalness into the painted surface.[8] The compass circle embedded in the surface refers to *device* both as a commonplace object, the material for the making of a painting—a measuring stick glued to the surface—and as a conceit for measurement, the arc seen here in the swoop that forms the gray diameter of the circle.[9] In this work, critic Leo Steinberg noted "a device for circle-making" wherein "subject, title, and form suddenly coincided."[10] Johns used standard stencils to inscribe the painting's descriptive title on its surface.[11] When asked by Steinberg about his choice of lettering, Johns replied, "That's how the stencils come."[12] Through his application of stencils, he acknowledged the literal function of lettering to label and name the painting.[13]

Quotidian and recognizable are the flags, targets, beer cans, plaster faces, and maps—objects both familiar and pulchritudinous in their simple design. Steinberg thought there was little difference between an actual flag and Johns's painted flag.[14] Yet I maintain that these everyday objects are supported in their thingness by natural materials of cotton, cork, aluminum, plaster, and thin vellum. These are materials that Johns sought, avoiding particular displays of ostentation or gaudy beauty.[15] Thus, Johns's materialized object—at times a Duchampian appropriation of the actual object and other times a recreation of the object as a device—is not engaged in Steinberg's position on the flags, targets, and so on. Those become signs, imagistic and motile.

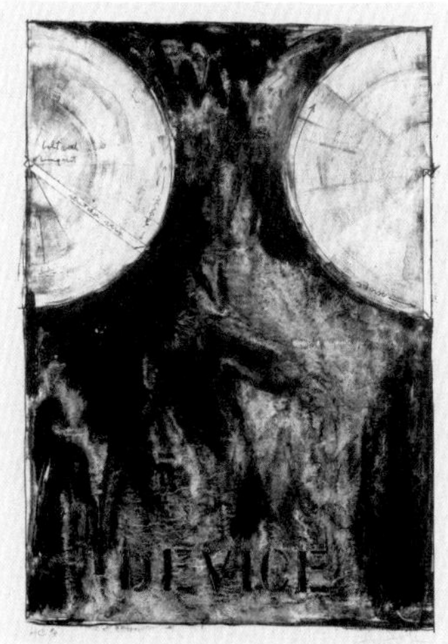

Fig. 1 ***Device*, 1962**
Lithograph: one stone, 31 ½ × 22 ¾ in. (80 × 57.8 cm). Robert Blackburn/ULAE. Edition of 6. Private collection

Between 1961 and 1962, Johns produced four works titled *Device*: a painting with two spinning wheels and a blue-and-orange camouflage (p. 193, pl. 20); a black-and-gray painting (p. 38, pl. 9); and an ink-on-plastic drawing and a related print (fig. 1).[16] We know that for Johns these devices were not meant as allegorical, nor as abstract meaning taking a physical form; rather, they are anti-illusionistic in their assertion of material form.[17] This enhances the enjoyment of the real. The spinning wheels of *Device*, for example, remind us that Johns composed by gravitational lilt, devising space in balletic brushstrokes. Johns wrote of two kinds of "space," where "linguistically, perhaps, the verb is important."[18] To see measurement and its associated verb in a painting is, as he said, "visual, intellectual activity, perhaps; 'recreation.'"[19] I disagree with Max Kozloff, who wrote that in these works "art, or rather artifice, may well transcend natural fact."[20] Here, perceiving the swoops and sweeps is to see ease: an interlacing of more fact than fiction and (together) visions of creation and recreation.

1 Jasper Johns, "Book A, p. 42, c. 1963–64," in *Jasper Johns: Writings, Sketchbook Notes, Interviews*, ed. Kirk Varnedoe (New York: Museum of Modern Art, 1996), 54 (hereafter abbreviated Varnedoe, *WSI*). See also Barbara Rose, "Jasper Johns: 'Take an object. Do something to it. Do something else to it,'" *RA Magazine*, September 7, 2017, https://www.royalacademy.org.uk/article/magazine-jasper-johns (accessed March 2, 2020).

2 Barbara Ann Kipfer, *Roget's 21st-Century Thesaurus* (New York: Bantam Dell, 2005), 684.

3 See Morgan Meis, "Is the Painting Counting?," in *Jasper Johns*, ed. Roberta Bernstein, exh. cat. (London: Royal Academy of Arts in collaboration with the Broad, 2017), 40. See also Roberta Bernstein, *Jasper Johns's Paintings and Sculpture, 1954–1974: "The Changing Focus of the Eye"* (Ann Arbor, MI: UMI Research Press, 1975), 46–47, 91–97.

4 At this time, Johns was also casting bronze objects with Japanese collaborators. He credits this accretionary mode of working to Robert Rauschenberg and other artists he met in this period.

5 The commonplace and the device are favored themes in Johns discourse. Early on, Roberta Bernstein noticed his use of device. Most recently, Jennifer Roberts has written of the printing press as Johnsian, a device space of transformation. See Jennifer L. Roberts, "The Metamorphic Press: Jasper Johns and the

Monotype," in *Jasper Johns: Catalogue Raisonné of Monotypes*, by Susan M. Dackerman and Jennifer L. Roberts (New York: Matthew Marks Gallery; New Haven: Yale University Press, 2017), 12.

6 "Catenary" refers to a free-form line created by gravity and the weight of a string as it hangs between two points affixed to nonparallel positions. This device as painting strategy is particularly penetrating in the Catenary paintings, which Johns began in 1997. Johns, who had long been working in abstraction, took the step toward reintroducing what Scott Rothkopf has termed a "literal ballast." Rothkopf defines "catenary" as capable of including the Romantic notions of painting; however, Johns played with the anti-materialist shadow as form. Alongside the rational definition of an "attendant mathematical equation," these two qualities of emotionality and reason constitute innovation in Johns's methodology of attaching things into the paintings. See Scott Rothkopf, "Suspended Animation," in *Jasper Johns: Catenary*, exh. cat. (New York: Matthew Marks Gallery, 2005), 5.

7 Meis, "Is the Painting Counting?," 40.

8 Leo Steinberg, "Jasper Johns: The First Seven Years of His Art" (1962), in *Other Criteria: Confrontations with Twentieth-Century Art* (New York: Oxford University Press, 1972), 28.

9 Scott Rothkopf calls these objects of measurement Johns's "various visual devices." See Rothkopf, "Suspended Animation," 16.

10 Steinberg, "Johns: The First Seven Years," 38. For another example of such a painting, see *Painting with Ruler and "Gray"* (1960; p. 38, pl. 10).

11 Between 1954 and 1959, Johns created the paintings most associated with his style, which followed his having destroyed his previous work. He spent this time in the company of Rauschenberg, Merce Cunningham, and many others developing what critics would call Neo-Dada. Kirk Varnedoe understood *Device Circle* as the "first" of these paintings. See Kirk Varnedoe, ed., *Jasper Johns: A Retrospective*, exh. cat. (New York: Museum of Modern Art, 1996), 163. Richard Fields wrote about Johns's use of stencils in the lithograph *Fragment—According to What: Bent Stencil* (1971; p. 154, pl. 8) as diagrammatic and illusionary: "The topmost is clearly a drawn image, subtle and diagrammatic. The middle contains two darker, flat, gray areas that seem to share the flatness of the paper. The lower figure is an illusion of the stencil itself—the apparatus that purportedly (and in the painting, literally) was the template." Richard S. Fields, *Jasper Johns: Matrix 20*, exh. brochure (Hartford, CT: Wadsworth Atheneum, 1976), n.p.

12 Jasper Johns, quoted in Steinberg, "Johns: The First Seven Years," 32.

13 Michael Crichton, *Jasper Johns* (New York: Harry N. Abrams in association with the Whitney Museum of American Art, 1977), 14. In interviews, Johns uses the word *literalness* to refer to the objects, to mixing media such as encaustic and the color gray, which has a literal quality. See Joseph E. Young, "Jasper Johns: An Appraisal," *Art International* 13, no. 7 (September 1969); reprinted in Varnedoe, *WSI*, 129–34.

14 Steinberg, "Johns: The First Seven Years," 28: "The position of modern anti-illusionism finds here its logical resting place. The street and the sky—they can only be simulated on canvas; but a flag, a target, a 5—these can be made, and the completed painting will represent no more than what it actually is."

15 Max Kozloff, *Jasper Johns* (New York: Harry N. Abrams, 1967), 34–35.

16 Johns revisited the theme in 1972 in the prints *Device* and *Device Black State*. See Richard S. Field, *The Prints of Jasper Johns, 1960–1993: A Catalogue Raisonne* (West Islip, NY: Universal Limited Art Editions, 1994), nos. 107–8.

17 See Selden Rodman, "The Artist as Antihumanist," in *The Insiders: Rejection and Rediscovery of Man in the Arts of Our Time* (Baton Rouge: Louisiana State University Press, 1960), 36; excerpted and reprinted in Varnedoe, *WSI*, 82.

18 Jasper Johns, "S-29. Book B, c. 1967," in Varnedoe, *WSI*, 61.

19 Jasper Johns, interview by David Sylvester for the BBC, June 1965, in Varnedoe, *WSI*, 117.

20 Kozloff, *Jasper Johns*, 34–35.

Once More, with Feeling: Jasper Johns and Queer Art Histories
Drew Sawyer

Since the 1950s, perhaps no American artist has confounded critics more than Jasper Johns. He is notorious for avoiding questions that pertain to meaning, and he concedes that the explication of his works depends on the viewer.[1] This resistance to authorial intent has often been seen as a reaction to the introspection of Abstract Expressionism and the beginnings of the "postmodern turn" in postwar American art. In the mid-1980s through the mid-1990s, however, a younger generation of critics and scholars found new meanings through the lens of Johns's relationship with Robert Rauschenberg between 1954 and 1961. At stake in these interpretations was the place not only of biographical and iconographical readings in contemporary art history and criticism, but also of queer identities in the canonical history of twentieth-century art. These readings were crucial to expanding the discourse around sexuality in art history, but how should they be understood today, when neither artist has discussed the nature of their relationship or sexual orientation, and when queer theory has shifted toward destabilizing identity categories and considering how sexuality intersects with race, gender, and class?

In a 1977 essay for *Artforum*, Moira Roth was among the first to acknowledge "the homosexuality and bisexuality permissible and even common among the new aesthetic group" that included Johns and Rauschenberg as well as John Cage and Merce Cunningham. Her main thesis—that these artists created an "aesthetic of indifference" within the conservative and secretive political climate of the McCarthy era—would be central to later arguments that expanded upon her comment.[2] In the mid-1980s, scholars such as Jonathan David Katz and Kenneth Silver began analyzing how Johns and Rauschenberg's relationship and a newly emerging gay subjectivity may have been expressed in their works.[3] Silver eventually published the essay "Modes of Disclosure: The Construction of Gay Identity and the Rise of Pop Art" in a 1992 exhibition catalogue for the Museum of Contemporary Art in Los Angeles.[4] A year later, Katz's "The Art of Code: Jasper Johns and Robert Rauschenberg" appeared in an edited volume.[5] More studies followed, including an essay by Caroline Jones, who characterized the work of Cage, Johns, and Rauschenberg in terms of a "homosexual aesthetic"; a monograph by Fred Orton that discussed Johns's relationship with Rauschenberg; and an unauthorized biography by Jill Johnston, for which Johns denied image permissions.[6]

Rather than an "aesthetic of indifference," the studies that followed Roth's found a politics of difference by introducing to art history nearly two decades of scholarship drawn from the fields of history and literature that explored the construction of homosexuality as a modern identity and the beginnings of the gay liberation movement in the United States.[7] For instance, John D'Emilio's *Sexual Politics, Sexual Communities* (1983), which Jones and Katz cite in their essays, assesses how Alfred Kinsey's reports on sexuality, particularly his *Sexual Behavior in the Human Male* (1948), "implicitly encouraged those still struggling in isolation against their sexual preference to accept their homosexual inclinations and search for sexual comrades" but also magnified "the proportions of the danger they [homosexuals] allegedly posed" (fig. 1).[8] The most publicized homophobic event in the wake of Kinsey's report was a 1950–53 series of Senate hearings on "Employment of Homosexuals and Other Sex Perverts in the U.S. Government." Within this historical framework, art historians began to interrogate how artists helped construct gay subcultures in cities like New York, where systemic oppression still required queer people to code their expressions in plain sight.

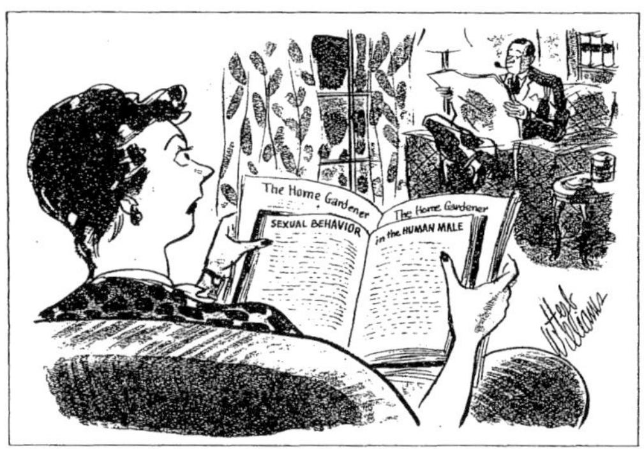

Fig. 1 **Cartoon by Herb Williams, *New York Times Book Review*, February 29, 1948, p. 2**

Literary critic Eve Kosofsky Sedgwick's *Epistemology of the Closet* (1990) provided additional theoretical tools for interpreting queer experiences in repressive cultures.[9] Using Sedgwick's notion of "the closet-in-view," Jones argues that Johns and Rauschenberg "allude only tangentially to their lives as gay artists in New York. Secrets become the engine of their art, but that engine's autobiographical chuffing can be heard, however faint."[10] Silver uses a similar language of secrets and codes: "Johns's early work is situated in a discourse, for those who could decipher it, of gay identity."[11] He interprets *Painting with Two Balls* (1960; p. 38, pl. 8) as camp; *In Memory of My Feelings—Frank O'Hara* (1961; p. 134, pl. 11) as a memorial to Johns's deteriorating relationship with Rauschenberg; and *Target with Plaster Casts* (1955; p. 168, fig. 1), which features molds of male genitalia and other body parts, as a "portrait of the homosexual man of the post-war period [in which] … the besieged gay body—and gay psyche—is fragmented and sorted into compartments, each one capable of being alternately closeted or exposed."[12] For Katz, Johns's appropriation of cultural symbols, as in his iconic *Flag* (1954–55; p. 66, pl. 7), are instances where the artist's "gayness" has led him "away from a celebration of the individual and toward the bedrock of culture where all meaning is made."[13] Following Sedgwick and other historians, these interpretations demonstrated a new understanding of sexuality as socially constructed rather than innate.[14]

While these scholars contextualized Johns's work within 1950s discourses on male sexuality, they were writing in a post-Stonewall era of visibility and solidarity heightened by fierce public debates over the AIDS epidemic and images of homosexuality by artists such as Robert Mapplethorpe. Historians and critics doubled down in their attempts to expose queer histories and destabilize normative narratives around sexuality and gender, and many found models for artists using abstraction to code homosexual experiences.[15] Several made connections between Johns's art of the 1950s and 1960s and the work of early twentieth-century American literary and artistic figures.[16] Johnston, Jones, and Katz all discuss Johns's paintings in relation to the American poet Hart Crane (1899–1932), who committed suicide by jumping off a steamship after allegedly coming on to a male crew member, and whose poems were read by scholars in the 1990s as "closeted" texts of thwarted homosexual desire. Orton postulates that Johns could have read Crane's poem "Passage" as a "complexly displaced homosexual autobiography, as a poem determined by and effecting a knowledge of a homosexual self or identity or want-of-being in a moment of transition."[17] All four authors note that Johns made several works after his relationship with Rauschenberg ended, in 1961, that allude to the poet's life and work, including *Passage* (1962), *Diver* (1962–63; p. 41, pl. 1), and *Periscope (Hart Crane)* (1963; p. 182, pl. 6).

Johns's other "gay antecedents," as Silver called them, were found among artists in the Stieglitz Circle.[18] Around the same time that Katz initiated his research on Johns and Rauschenberg's relationship, Jonathan Weinberg began writing a dissertation on the modernist painters Charles Demuth and Marsden Hartley, which he published as a groundbreaking book in 1993.[19] While both artists made numerous paintings with overtly homoerotic content, they also created what Weinberg and others saw as highly coded or symbolic portraits of lovers and friends.[20] For example, Weinberg interprets Hartley's *Portrait of a German Officer* (1914; fig. 2), with its patterning of flags, medals, and other military regalia, as a coded memorial to a lost lover. Several scholars saw this work and others as precedents for Johns's homages to Crane and O'Hara.[21] Comparing Johns's paintings to the work of Demuth and Hartley, Silver concludes, "In the work of his gay predecessors Johns found a language—shaped, as it were, by the closet—which could vouchsafe his passage as a modernist, American, gay painter."[22]

These scholars' attempts to attest to queer experiences in earlier periods were echoed by contemporary artists whose work made visible queer life, love, and loss as a mode of resistance, from AIDS activist groups such as Gran Fury to photographers such as Nan Goldin. Conversely, the interpretation of Johns's art as coded was validated by contemporary artists who referenced queer culture through the language of abstraction or in readymades, rather than through explicit homoerotic imagery. These artists withheld or deconstructed images of the body or sex acts that were often instrumentalized by the radical right as well as by progressive institutions and commercial forces. Prominent artists working in this vein during the late 1980s and early 1990s include Robert Gober and Donald Moffett, long-term partners who frequently deployed "encoded symbolism" indebted to the strategies of earlier "same-sex attracted" artists, as Gober has acknowledged.[23] Moffett's *Target* (1993), displayed in the 1993 Whitney Biennial along with works by Gober (fig. 3), is made of synthetic flowers in the shape and pattern of a target. It recalls not only Moffett's earlier lithograph *He Kills Me* (1987), a commentary on AIDS inaction that features an orange-and-black target beside a photo of Ronald Reagan with the title printed underneath, but also Johns's Target paintings, including a target-shaped work made of flowers that he created for the performance *Hommage à David Tudor* in Paris in 1961.[24]

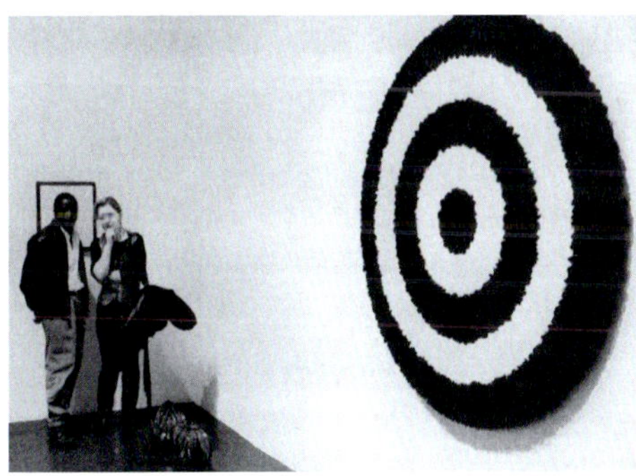

Fig. 3 **Donald Moffett (American, b. 1955). *Target*, 1993**
Acrylic and synthetic flowers laid on panel. Installation view, Whitney Biennial 1993, Whitney Museum of American Art, New York, March 4–June 20, 1993

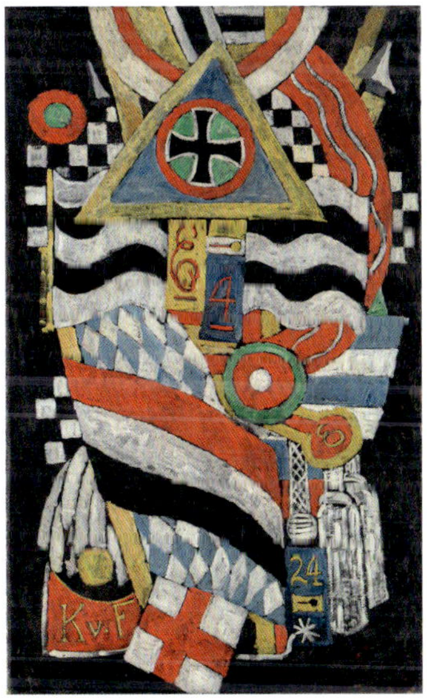

Fig. 2 **Marsden Hartley (American, 1877–1943). *Portrait of a German Officer*, 1914**
Oil on canvas, 68 ¼ × 41 ⅜ in. (173.4 × 105.1 cm). The Metropolitan Museum of Art, New York; Alfred Stieglitz Collection, 49.70.42

These studies exploring the work of central figures of postwar American art were critical to developing the discourse around sexuality in art history and contemporary practices, and prompted larger critical debates in the field. Yet most have still been relegated to the footnotes of monographs on Johns. The catalogue for the last major survey of Johns's work, organized by Kirk Varnedoe at the Museum of Modern Art (MoMA) in New York in 1996, makes only a passing reference to the artist's "close personal relationship" with Rauschenberg and mentions Silver's essay in just a single note.[25] More recent exhibitions on Rauschenberg, Johns, and their circle, such as the Philadelphia Museum of Art's *Dancing around the Bride: Cage, Cunningham, Johns, Rauschenberg, and Duchamp* (2012–13) and MoMA's *Robert Rauschenberg: Among Friends* (2017), did not explicitly explore the nature of their relationships and how they may have affected their work. This is in part due to Johns's continued reticence to discuss his relationship with Rauschenberg or his sexuality. Unlike Demuth, who produced homoerotic imagery and died decades before this scholarship emerged, Johns is a living artist with the ability to respond, which has made him a difficult or ambivalent figure to claim within the pantheon of queer art history.

These elisions also reflect a general resistance to biographical and iconographical interpretations from scholars of contemporary art, as well as to "identity politics" from both sides of the political spectrum.[26] Michael Kimmelman's *New York Times* review of the volume in which Katz's essay appeared exemplifies the more conservative line of criticism as well as the politics of "outing" at the time: "Mr. Katz's essay epitomizes the pitfalls of art writing that sees everything through the lens of sexual politics. Forget, for the moment, the propriety of such an essay when Mr. Rauschenberg and Mr. Johns have never explicitly said they were lovers during the 1950's. Mr. Katz is not the first to write about their relationship, but to him it is not only grist for public discussion; it is also the determining factor in much of their art of the period. The idea that one might be gay without making it the subject of one's art does not seem to have crossed his mind."[27] Typical of such rebukes, Kimmelman's construes a reading that involves issues around sexuality as discounting all others rather than offering an additional and more complex account of an artist's life and work in relation to larger social structures and historical subjectivities.

Even sympathetic scholars have criticized these interpretations as the methodologies and the stakes of scholarship on histories of sexual and gender identities have shifted in recent decades.[28] Since the 1990s, historians, critics, and artists have increasingly embraced queer theory methodologies that reflect a loss of faith in the coherence of stable "gay" identities or binary thinking around sexualities, and have considered a range of identities and practices beyond the relatively privileged position of gay white men.[29] To this end, many in the field have attempted to expand the canon to include queer cultural producers systematically excluded from mainstream histories due not only to sexuality but also to other social factors such as gender, race, and class. It is important to note that, in their original analyses, Jones, Katz, and Silver intentionally adopted what literary critic Gayatri Chakravorty Spivak has called "strategic essentialism," which advocates provisionally accepting essentialist notions of identity as a tactic for collective representation in order to pursue chosen political ends.[30]

Over the past thirty years, Katz has continued to write on Johns, Rauschenberg, Cage, and others. His more recent essays have argued persuasively for the performative value of silence or "ironic negation" in their art as a queering of binary identities and a way to deflect attention from personal meanings or authorial intent during the McCarthy era. This approach reflects queer theory methodologies and perhaps more closely aligns with these artists' fluidity around sexuality, as well as Johns's continued silence about the meaning of his works.[31] Similarly, Gavin Butt's 2005 study on the production and circulation of gossip around male homosexuality in the American art world during the 1950s and 1960s provided a new framework for understanding the reception of *Target with Plaster Casts*, which Alfred H. Barr supposedly refused to acquire for MoMA due to the fact that one of the casts was of a penis. Arguing that the Kinsey Report unsettled rather than reassured the American public, Butt explores how postwar anxiety over male sexuality suffused works such as *Target*. He examines in particular the obscenity debates provoked by the legal fight over Allen Ginsberg's poem "Howl" (1956), which centered on whether references to particular body parts were inherently obscene. For Butt, the "Howl" ruling, which found that the poem was not obscene because the work's primary aim was not erotic, had the effect of "overturning the idea that the representation of homosexuality was necessarily obscene in and of itself."[32] In other words, Johns exhibited *Target* in the middle of a profound transformation regarding the representation of sex.

From this perspective, it seems fitting that Johns's work has undergone reconsideration during other sea changes around the representation and categorization of sexuality, first in the late 1980s and now in the late 2010s and early 2020s. The discussion of Johns's sexuality in this volume indicates another moment in the institutionalization of queer identities within art history—and demonstrates how art museums have always been particularly slow to recognize such shifts.[33] In 2019, fifty years after the Stonewall riots, museums and galleries around the United States mounted exhibitions to commemorate the contributions of LGBTQ+-identifying artists, catching up with scholarship and cultural production from the past five decades. Many of these shows were the first museum surveys of important yet under-recognized figures, such as the photographer Alvin Baltrop and the artist Harmony Hammond, among many others. There is a desire and need to challenge institutions even further. While Johns is no longer at the center of these debates, his centrality to the postmodern turn in American art means that his sexuality is still relevant to its historicization, as well as to many viewers of his work. Simultaneously, his continued opposition to categorization makes him a model for other artists in the twenty-first century.

1 In 1963, when asked about the relationship of the spectator to the meaning of his art, Johns responded, "I think he brings everything more. He brings himself, which is something else again. And then it is a question of how he can use it.... I mean, the use of it need not involve the intentions of the maker." Johns, interview by Billy Klüver, March 1963, in *Jasper Johns: Writings, Sketchbook Notes, Interviews*, ed. Kirk Varnedoe (New York: Museum of Modern Art, 1996), 88.

2 Moira Roth, "The Aesthetic of Indifference," *Artforum* 16, no. 3 (1977): 46–53. Calvin Tomkins also mentions the circle of gay and bisexual artists and makes a discreet reference to Rauschenberg and Johns in his book *Off the Wall: Robert Rauschenberg and the Art World of Our Time* (Garden City, NY: Doubleday, 1980).

3 Early discussions of the relationship between Johns and Rauschenberg also include Charles Harrison and Fred Orton, "Jasper Johns: Meaning What You See," *Art History* 7, no. 1 (March 1984): 76–101; and Roni Feinstein, "Random Order: The First Fifteen Years of Robert Rauschenberg's Art, 1949–1964" (PhD diss., Institute of Fine Arts, New York University, 1990), 170–79, 234–69.

4 Kenneth E. Silver, "Modes of Disclosure: The Construction of Gay Identity and the Rise of Pop Art," in *Hand-Painted Pop: American Art in Transition, 1955–62*, ed. Russell Ferguson, exh. cat. (Los Angeles: Museum of Contemporary Art, 1992), 178–203. Silver first presented the paper "Belated 'Notes on Camp': Homosexuality, Representation, and the Decline of Abstract Expressionism" at the 1986 College Art Association Conference in New York, on one of the first panels to address the issue of homosexuality in art history. Silver later presented additional papers on Johns, including "The Body Electric: Jasper Johns' Song of Himself," at the Lesbian and Gay Studies Conference at Yale University in 1988. This conference, organized by Yale's Lesbian and Gay Studies Center in 1987, 1988, and 1989, played a crucial role in constituting the field of LGBT studies at a critical early moment in its development and fostered important scholars in the field, including Judith Butler and George Chauncey.

5 Jonathan D. Katz, "The Art of Code: Jasper Johns and Robert Rauschenberg," in *Significant Others: Creativity and Intimate Partnership*, ed. Whitney Chadwick and Isabelle de Courtivron (New York: Thames and Hudson, 1993). Katz had presented some of this research in a talk, "Subculture Representations in the Art of Jasper Johns and Robert Rauschenberg: Identity and Community among Postwar New York Artists," at the 1991 College Art Association Conference in Washington, DC, and would go on to publish a series of essays on Johns and Rauschenberg and their circle of friends over the next two decades.

6 Caroline A. Jones, "Finishing School: John Cage and the Abstract Expressionist Ego," *Critical Inquiry* 19, no. 4 (Summer 1993): 639; Fred Orton, *Figuring Jasper Johns* (London: Reaktion, 1994); Jill Johnston, *Jasper Johns: Privileged Information* (London: Thames and Hudson, 1996).

7 Among the texts that these authors cite are John D'Emilio's *Sexual Politics, Sexual Communities: The Making of a Homosexual Minority in the United States, 1940–1970* (Chicago: University of Chicago Press, 1983) and Eric Marcus's *Making History: The Struggle for Gay and Lesbian Equal Rights, 1945–1990* (New York: HarperCollins, 1992).

8 D'Emilio, *Sexual Politics, Sexual Communities*, 37.

9 Eve Kosofsky Sedgwick, *Epistemology of the Closet* (Berkeley: University of California Press, 1990).

10 Jones, "Finishing School," 651–52.

11 Silver, "Modes of Disclosure," 185.

12 Silver, 190.

13 Katz, "Art of Code," 200.

14 This idea was developed by the French historian and philosopher Michel Foucault in his book *The History of Sexuality, Volume I: An Introduction*, trans. Robert Hurley (New York: Pantheon, 1978).

15 For recent discussions of "queer abstraction," see David Getsy, "Ten Queer Theses on Abstraction," in *Queer Abstraction*, ed. Jared Ledesma, exh. cat. (Des Moines, IA: Des Moines Art Center, 2019), 65–75; and Travis Jeppesen, "Queer Abstraction (Or How to Be a Pervert with No Body): Some Notes toward a Probability," *Mousse Magazine*, no. 66 (Winter 2019): 182–91.

16 For examples, see several monographs that were published around this time and cited by Jones, Katz, and Silver: Thomas E. Yingling, *Hart Crane and the Homosexual Text: New Thresholds, New Anatomies* (Chicago: University of Chicago Press, 1990); M. Jimmie Killingsworth, *Whitman's Poetry of the Body: Sexuality, Politics, and the Text* (Chapel Hill: University of North Carolina Press, 1989); and Byrne R. S. Fone, *Masculine Landscapes: Walt Whitman and the Homoerotic Text* (Carbondale: Southern Illinois University Press, 1992).

17 Orton, *Figuring Jasper Johns*, 76.

18 Silver, "Modes of Disclosure," 186.

19 Jonathan Weinberg, *Speaking for Vice: Homosexuality in the Art of Charles Demuth, Marsden Hartley, and the First American Avant-Garde* (New Haven: Yale University Press, 1993).

20 Weinberg built on a 1974 essay by Kermit Champa that discussed Demuth's strategy of expressing his homosexuality through visual codes, similar to how Katz and Silver interpreted Johns's work. See Kermit Champa, "'Charlie Was Like That,'" *Artforum* 12, no. 6 (March 1974): 54–59.

21 Silver notes that Johns claimed to have been unaware of Hartley's homage to Crane. Silver, "Modes of Disclosure," 203.

22 Silver, 186, 188.

23 In a 2014 interview, Gober said, "I grew up studying artists, great seminal American artists, who were same-sex attracted but who expressed that through an encoded symbolism within their work—I grew up learning from this in a very useful and creative way." "In Conversation: Robert Gober with Jarrett Earnest," *Brooklyn Rail*, December–January 2014–15, brooklynrail.org/2014/12/art/robert-gober-with-jarrett-earnest (accessed November 1, 2019).

24 For a discussion of the work and performance, see Hiroko Ikegami, *The Great Migrator: Robert Rauschenberg and the Global Rise of American Art* (Cambridge, MA: MIT Press, 2010), 35–36.

25 Kirk Varnedoe, ed., *Jasper Johns: A Retrospective*, exh. cat. (New York: Museum of Modern Art, 1996), 35n35, 95.

26 See, for example, Branden Joseph's discussion of interpretations of Robert Rauschenberg's work in *Random Order: Robert Rauschenberg and the Neo-Avant-Garde* (Cambridge, MA: MIT Press, 2003), 67.

27 Michael Kimmelman, "The Peephole Approach to Artist Couples," *New York Times*, August 15, 1993.

28 See, for example, Gavin Butt's *Between You and Me: Queer Disclosures in the New York Art World, 1948–1963* (Durham, NC: Duke University Press, 2005).

29 Caroline Jones acknowledged the problem of essentialism, writing it "should be seen as unavoidable linguistic essentializations of what are instead shifting fabrics of historically determined, socially constructed, and discursively maintained sexual differences." Jones, "Finishing School," 652.

30 Gayatri Chakravorty Spivak, "Subaltern Studies: Deconstructing Historiography," in *Selected Subaltern Studies*, ed. Ranajit Guha and Gayatri Chakravorty Spivak (New York: Oxford University Press, 1988), 3–32.

31 Jonathan D. Katz, "Performative Silence and the Politics of Passivity," in *Making a Scene*, ed. Henry Rogers (Birmingham, UK: Birmingham University Press, 1999), 97–103. Other essays by Katz include "Dismembership: Jasper Johns and the Body Politic," in *Performing the Body / Performing the Text*, ed. Amelia Jones and Andrew Stephenson (New York: Routledge, 1999), 170–85; and "The Silent Camp: Queer Resistance and the Rise of Pop Art," in *Visions of a Future: Art and Art History in Changing Contexts*, ed. Kornelia Imesch and Hans-Jörg Heusser (Zurich: Swiss Institute for Art Research, 2004), 147–58.

32 Butt, *Between You and Me*, 143.

33 It is worth noting that Katz included Johns's work in the groundbreaking and controversial 2010–11 exhibition *Hide/Seek: Difference and Desire in American Portraiture* at the National Portrait Gallery in Washington, DC.

First Motifs

"One night I dreamed that I painted a large American flag, and the next morning I got up and I went out and bought the materials to begin it. And I did."[1] This was late in 1954, and despite his initial celerity, it took Johns nearly six months to finish the painting (p. 66, pl. 7) that would soon define the public image of his work and shift the course of art history. He crafted the stars and stripes on a bedsheet with collaged bits of newspaper and, at first, enamel paint, which he subsequently abandoned for encaustic, a mixture of wax and pigment that he favored because it sets quickly and can leave each brushstroke distinct. But even more important than his adoption of what would become his signature medium was the relationship of image to support. Johns had dreamed, tellingly, that he painted a flag, not that he made a painting *of* one. This flag does not exist within space—against a sky or on a table—but flatly fills the rectangular frame of the support edge to edge.

Johns's intuitive act inaugurated a way of working that has continued to varying degrees throughout his career: the direct transposition of two-dimensional images and signs from the world onto the surface of his art. In his early years, these images included flags, maps, targets, alphabets, and numbers, subjects he described as "things the mind already knows."[2] By relying on these common, preexisting motifs, Johns implicitly turned away from the expressive intentionality of Abstract Expressionism, dominant at the time, and from the illusionism of figurative painting, which was anathema to critical orthodoxy. By contrast, Johns's paintings function both as the things they describe *and* as depictions of them—a flag itself and its picture—leading us to question the distinction between the two, as well as that between an artwork and a common object or sign. And because his chosen motifs suggested the possibility of repeated rather than individual examples (*any* American flag or target, not a specific face or flower), they lent themselves to endless, often serial, unspooling and formal variety. These "things which suggest the world," as Johns later put it, not only connected his art to lived experience, but also freed him to focus on mark making, scale, color, medium, and the way these characteristics of his art intermingle in our perception and thought.[3]

Although Johns has repeatedly professed no particular interest in the nationalistic associations of the American flag, critics and scholars have long explored myriad possible meanings of this symbol in his work. Biographical accounts have linked the subject to Johns's military service or to his namesake, a Revolutionary War hero who rescued the flag in battle, while more sociological studies have analyzed it in relation to US geopolitical circumstances during the Cold War when he first painted it.[4] When the flags are seen in conjunction with Johns's recurrent, simultaneous depictions of maps of the United States, they inevitably serve as wellsprings for meditations on the nation and its history, present, and even future. From 1955 to the 1980s, Johns subjected these motifs to prodigious variations across media, often in black and white or in red, white, and blue, at scales ranging from diminutive to monumental, and with a touch that varies from sensual to aggressive. These formal qualities conjure a sweep of emotional and intellectual attitudes toward a divided country—jubilance and despair, hope and pessimism. Yet even these readings refuse fixity, since one could equally associate the optical zing of *Three Flags* (1958; p. 62, pl. 2) with either optimistic or hectoring patriotism. Likewise, the creamy *Two Maps* (1965; p. 61, pl. 1) might evoke futility and disappearance or a nascent state of possibility, while the maps' darker variants suggest an ominous take on the nation. Several works offer an even more pointed critique. In a painting and two prints from 1965 and 1969, respectively, Johns rendered the flag in its complementary colors, turning the red stripes green, the blue canton orange, and the white stripes and stars their inverse, black (see p. 66, pl. 8; and p. 72, pl. 32). The resultant images are jarring, acrid even, at a time when the nation was riven with conflicts over civil rights and the Vietnam War. Johns made the printed works in support of the Committee Against the War in Vietnam, and inscribed one "MORATORIUM" in solidarity with the antiwar marches occurring that year.

Of all Johns's recurrent motifs, none has appeared more insistently in his oeuvre than numbers. From the 1950s until today, he has created more than 170 paintings, drawings, prints, and sculptures that feature numerals in one of four principal structures: as individual figures; as superimpositions; and in sequences of zero to nine, either in two stacked rows or arranged in larger grids. Like flags, maps, and targets, numbers are preexisting signs open to a variety of aesthetic and interpretative operations. Yet unlike his other motifs, numbers inherently suggest a recursive stream of endless proliferation. They are part of a combinatory system with a given order that can repeat and unspool over and over again. They lack any essential scale or innate color and so offer a perfect matrix for formal experimentation and play. In Johns's work, numerals zoom in and out of scale and focus; flicker from one color to the next; and disappear into busy grounds or emerge declaratively from them. This potentially excessive, even manic, accretion offers an artistic analogy for a digital age in which numerals function as the basic building blocks of data sets and code, summoning the ceaseless protocols of production, automation, and transmission that undergird our daily lives.

—Scott Rothkopf, with Carlos Basualdo, Sarah B. Vogelman, and Lauren Young

1 Jasper Johns, quoted in Emile de Antonio and Mitch Tuchman, *Painters Painting: A Candid History of the Modern Art Scene, 1940-1970* (New York: Abbeville, 1984), 97; quoted in Lilian Tone, "Chronology and Plates," in *Jasper Johns: A Retrospective*, ed. Kirk Varnedoe, exh. cat. (New York: Museum of Modern Art, 1996), 124.

2 Jasper Johns, quoted in "His Heart Belongs to Dada," *Time*, May 4, 1959; reprinted in Kirk Varnedoe, ed., *Jasper Johns: Writings, Sketchbook Notes, Interviews* (New York: Museum of Modern Art, 1996), 82 (hereafter abbreviated Varnedoe, *WSI*).

3 Jasper Johns, interview by David Sylvester for the BBC, June 1965, in Varnedoe, *WSI*, 113.

4 For excellent treatment of these readings, see Roberta Bernstein, "'A Picture of an American Flag': Flags, 1954-2014," chap. 1 in *Jasper Johns: Redo an Eye* (New York: Wildenstein Plattner Institute, 2017).

First Motifs

Flags and Maps

WHITNEY MUSEUM OF AMERICAN ART

1 ***Two Maps*, 1965**
Encaustic and collage on canvas (two panels)
90 1/8 × 70 1/4 in. (228.9 × 178.4 cm) overall
Whitney Museum of American Art, New York; gift of the American Contemporary Art Foundation, Inc., Leonard A. Lauder, President, 2002.275

2 ***Three Flags*, 1958**
Encaustic on canvas (three panels)
30 7/8 × 45 3/4 in. (78.4 × 116.2 cm) overall
Whitney Museum of American Art, New York; purchase with funds from the Gilman Foundation, Inc., The Lauder Foundation, A. Alfred Taubman, Laura-Lee Whittier Woods, Howard Lipman, and Ed Downe in honor of the Museum's 50th Anniversary, 80.32

3 ***Map*, 1961**
Oil on canvas
78 × 123 1/4 in. (198.1 × 313.1 cm)
The Museum of Modern Art, New York; gift of Mr. and Mrs. Robert C. Scull, 277.1963

4 ***White Flag*, 1955**
Encaustic, oil, and collage on fabric (three panels)
78 1/4 × 120 3/4 in. (198.8 × 306.7 cm) overall
The Metropolitan Museum of Art, New York; purchase, Lila Acheson Wallace, Reba and Dave Williams, Stephen and Nan Swid, Roy R. and Marie S. Neuberger Foundation, Inc., Louis and Bessie Adler Foundation, Inc., Paula Cussi, Maria-Gaetana Matisse, The Barnett Newman Foundation, Jane and Robert Carroll, Eliot and Wilson Nolen, Mr. and Mrs. Derald H. Ruttenberg, Ruth and Seymour Klein Foundation, Inc., Andrew N. Schiff, The Cowles Charitable Trust, The Merrill G. and Emita E. Hastings Foundation, John J. Roche, Molly and Walter Bareiss, Linda and Morton Janklow, Aaron I. Fleischman, and Linford L. Lougheed Gifts, and gifts from friends of the Museum; Kathryn E. Hurd, Denise and Andrew Saul, George A. Hearn, Arthur Hoppock Hearn, Joseph H. Hazen Foundation Purchase, and Cynthia Hazen Polsky and Leon B. Polsky Funds; Mayer Fund; Florene M. Schoenborn Bequest; gifts of Professor and Mrs. Zevi Scharfstein and Himan Brown; and other gifts, bequests, and funds from various donors, by exchange, 1998.329

5 ***Map*, 1962-63**
Encaustic and collage on canvas
60 × 93 in. (152.4 × 236.2 cm)
The Museum of Contemporary Art, Los Angeles; gift of Marcia Simon Weisman, 90.17

6 ***Flag on Orange Field*, 1957**
Encaustic on canvas
66 × 48 3/4 in. (167.6 × 123.8 cm)
Museum Ludwig, Cologne; Ludwig Donation, 1976 ML 01050

7 ***Flag*, 1954-55**†
Encaustic, oil, and collage on fabric mounted on wood (three panels)
41 1/4 × 60 3/4 in. (104.8 × 154.3 cm) overall
The Museum of Modern Art, New York; gift of Philip Johnson in honor of Alfred H. Barr, Jr., 106.1973

8 ***Flags*, 1965**
Oil on canvas with object
72 × 48 in. (182.9 × 121.9 cm)
Collection of the artist; on long-term loan to the Walker Art Center, Minneapolis, 1988

9 ***Flag*, 1960-87***
Silver
12 3/4 × 19 1/8 in. (32.4 × 48.6 cm)
Collection of the artist

10 ***Flag*, 1957**
Pastel, graphite, and collage on gesso board
14 × 18 in. (35.6 × 45.7 cm)
Collection of Kate Ganz

11 ***Flag on Orange Field*, 1957**
Fluorescent paint, watercolor, pastel, and graphite pencil on paper
10 1/2 × 7 3/4 in. (26.7 × 19.7 cm)
The Menil Collection, Houston; promised gift of Janie C. Lee in honor of her grandfather, Alfred C. Glassell, Sr.

12 ***Three Flags*, 1960***
Charcoal and graphite pencil on three sheets of paper mounted on three boards
12 1/8 × 17 1/8 in. (30.8 × 43.5 cm)
Solomon R. Guggenheim Foundation, New York and Venice; Hannelore B. and Rudolph B. Schulhof Collection, bequest of Hannelore B. Schulhof, 2012.65

13 ***Flags*, 1968***
Lithograph with stamps: five stones, one aluminum plate, one rubber stamp
34 3/8 × 25 1/2 in. (87.3 × 64.8 cm)
Zigmunds Priede, Fred Genis/ULAE
Ed. no. 9/43
Whitney Museum of American Art, New York; gift of the artist, 69.121

14 ***Two Maps II*, 1966**
Lithograph: one stone
33 × 26 1/2 in. (83.8 × 67.3 cm)
Ben Berns/ULAE
Ed. no. 28/30
Whitney Museum of American Art, New York; purchase with funds from Leonard A. Lauder, 2020.12

15 ***Two Maps I*, 1966**
Lithograph: one stone, one aluminum plate
33 × 26 in. (83.8 × 66 cm)
Ben Berns/ULAE
Ed. no. 30/30
Whitney Museum of American Art, New York; purchase with funds from Leonard A. Lauder, 2020.11

16 ***Green Map above White*, 1966-67**
Acrylic and metallic powder on paper and encaustic on synthetic vellum mounted on canvas
12 1/8 × 10 1/8 in. (30.8 × 25.7 cm)
Private collection

17 ***Two Flags*, 1969***
Graphite pencil and collage on paper
22 1/4 × 31 in. (56.5 × 78.7 cm)
The Menil Collection, Houston

18 ***Flag*, 1959***
Graphite wash and graphite pencil on paper
12 × 16 in. (30.5 × 40.6 cm)
Kravis Collection

19 ***Map*, 2012**
Graphite pencil on paper
9 1/2 × 6 7/8 in. (24.1 × 17.5 cm)
Collection of Ayea and Mikey Sohn

20 ***Map*, 1960**
Encaustic on paper mounted on fiberboard
8 1/2 × 11 in. (21.6 × 27.9 cm)
Allen Family Collection

21 ***Green Flag*, 1956**
Graphite pencil, colored pencil, and crayon on three adjoined pieces of paper
7 7/8 × 9 3/4 in. (20 × 24.8 cm)
Private collection

22 ***Flag above White*, 1957**
Graphite pencil and collage on paper
8 1/8 × 6 1/2 in. (20.6 × 16.5 cm)
Collection of the artist

23 ***Map*, 1965**
Graphite wash, metallic powder, graphite pencil, and pastel on paper
19 × 24 3/4 in. (48.3 × 62.9 cm)
Collection of the artist

24 ***Map*, 1963**
Encaustic and collage on canvas
60 × 93 1/4 in. (152.4 × 236.9 cm)
Collection of Agnes Gund

25 ***Map*, 1961-62**
Oil on paper mounted on fiberboard
6 1/4 × 10 1/4 in. (15.9 × 26 cm)
Private collection

26 ***Map*, 1965**
Charcoal and oil on canvas
43 3/4 × 70 1/2 in. (111.1 × 179.1 cm)
Ryobi Foundation

27 ***Flag*, 1965**
Encaustic and collage on canvas
7 3/4 × 11 1/4 in. (19.7 × 28.6 cm)
Collection of Marsha and Jeffrey Perelman

28 ***Flag*, 1958**
Printed silk covered with paraffin with wood frame
2 3/4 × 3 3/4 in. (7 × 9.5 cm) overall
Collection of Laura Kuhn

29 ***Flag*, 1957**
Oil and graphite pencil on paper
3 1/8 × 3 7/8 in. (7.9 × 9.8 cm)
Collection of Virginia Cowles Schroth

30 ***Flag*, 1960***
Plaster
12 3/8 × 19 1/8 in. (31.4 × 48.6 cm)
Collection of the artist

31 ***Flag*, 1958***
Encaustic on canvas
41 3/8 × 61 in. (105.1 × 154.9 cm)
Private collection

32 ***Moratorium*, 1969**
Offset lithograph
22 1/2 × 28 3/4 in. (57.2 × 73 cm)
Printer unknown/Committee Against the War in Vietnam
Unnumbered proof
Whitney Museum of American Art, New York; purchase with funds from Scott Rothkopf in honor of Leonard A. Lauder, 2020.98

33 ***Flag*, 1958***
Graphite pencil and graphite wash on tracing paper mounted on paper
9 7/8 × 12 in. (25.1 × 30.5 cm)
Collection of Barbara Bertozzi Castelli

34 ***Flag*, 1957***
Oil on paper mounted on cardboard
11 7/8 × 16 3/4 in. (30.2 × 42.6 cm)
The Metropolitan Museum of Art, New York; gift of William S. Lieberman, in honor of the artist, 1999.425

35 ***Flags I*, 1973**
Silkscreen: thirty-one screens
27 1/2 × 35 in. (69.9 × 88.9 cm)
Kenjiro Nonaka, Hiroshi Kawanishi, Takeshi Shimada/JJ and SPA
Ed. no. 64/65

Whitney Museum of American Art, New York; gift from the Emily Fisher Landau Collection, 2015.274

36 ***Two Flags*, 1960**
Graphite wash and graphite pencil on paper mounted on board
29 ½ × 21 ¾ in. (74.9 × 55.3 cm)
Collection of the artist

37 ***Flags II*, 1970***
Lithograph with stamp: five stones, five aluminum plates, one rubber stamp
34 × 25 in. (86.4 × 63.5 cm)
Bill Goldston/ULAE
Ed. no. 5/9
The Metropolitan Museum of Art, New York; gift of Dr. Joseph I. Singer, 1974.666.1

38 ***Untitled (Envelope)*, 1959**
Watercolor and graphite pencil on paper envelope
4 ⅛ × 9 ½ in. (10.5 × 24.1 cm)
Whitney Museum of American Art, New York; purchase with funds from the American Contemporary Art Foundation, Inc., Leonard A. Lauder, President, 2016.163a–b

Numbers

PHILADELPHIA MUSEUM OF ART

1 ***0 through 9*, 1960**
Oil on canvas
72 ½ × 54 in. (184.2 × 137.2 cm)
Private collection

2 ***Figure 2*, 1963**
Graphite wash, charcoal, and pastel on paper mounted on canvas
28 ¼ × 23 ¼ in. (71.8 × 59.1 cm)
Minneapolis Institute of Art; the William Hood Dunwoody Fund, 70.71

3 ***Figure 2*, 1955**
Encaustic and collage on canvas
17 ¼ × 14 in. (43.8 × 35.6 cm)
The Newhouse Collection

4 ***White Numbers*, 1958***
Encaustic on fabric
28 ⅛ × 22 ⅛ in. (71.4 × 56.2 cm)
Simonyi Collection, Seattle

5 ***Numbers*, 2007 (cast 2008)‡**
Aluminum
107 ¾ × 83 in. (273.7 × 210.8 cm)
Glenstone, Potomac, Maryland

6 ***Figure 7*, 1959**
Oil on canvas
10 × 8 in. (25.4 × 20.3 cm)
Private collection

7 ***Figure 0*, 1959***
Oil and collage on canvas
10 × 8 in. (25.4 × 20.3 cm)
Private collection

8 ***Figure 1*, 1956***
Graphite pencil and colored pencil on paper mounted on board with foil edges
10 ⅝ × 8 ⅞ in. (27 × 22.5 cm)
Private collection

9 ***Figure 4*, 1967***
Encaustic and collage on canvas
53 ⅝ × 41 ½ in. (136.2 × 105.4 cm)
Private collection

10 ***Figure 3*, 1960**
Oil on canvas and wood (two-sided)
11 × 8 in. (27.9 × 20.3 cm)
Yale University Art Gallery, New Haven; gift of Richard Brown Baker, BA 1935, 1995.32.7

11 ***Figure 2*, 1959‡**
Encaustic and collage on canvas
3 ⅛ × 2 ¾ in. (7.9 × 7 cm)
Private collection

12 ***Figure 6*, 1964–72**
Sculp-metal and collage on canvas
9 ¾ × 7 ⅝ in. (24.8 × 19.4 cm)
Private collection

13 ***Figure 4*, 1959**
Encaustic and collage on canvas
20 × 15 ⅛ in. (50.8 × 38.4 cm)
The Art Institute of Chicago; gift of Edlis Neeson Collection, 2015.120

14 ***Figure 7*, 1955**
Encaustic and collage on canvas
17 ¼ × 14 in. (43.8 × 35.6 cm)
Los Angeles County Museum of Art; gift of Robert H. Halff through the Modern and Contemporary Art Council, M.2005.38.1

15 ***Figure 8*, 1959**
Encaustic and collage on canvas
20 × 15 in. (50.8 × 38.1 cm)
The Sonnabend Collection

16 ***4 Leo*, 1970**
Encaustic and collage on canvas and wood
50 ¾ × 35 ¾ in. (128.9 × 90.8 cm)
Collection of Barbara Bertozzi Castelli; on long-term loan to the Philadelphia Museum of Art, 1999

17 ***Figure 5*, 1959***
Graphite pencil and pastel on paper
11 ⅝ × 9 ⅞ in. (29.5 × 25.1 cm)
Collection of Audrey Irmas

18 ***0 through 9*, 1961**
Oil on canvas
54 × 41 ¼ in. (137.2 × 104.8 cm)
Whitney Museum of American Art, New York; gift of the American Contemporary Art Foundation, Inc., Leonard A. Lauder, President, 2002.222

19 ***0 through 9*, 1961**
Oil on canvas
54 × 41 ¼ in. (137.2 × 104.8 cm)
Hirshhorn Museum and Sculpture Garden, Smithsonian Institution, Washington, DC; gift of Joseph H. Hirshhorn, 1966, 66.2598

20 ***0 through 9*, 1961***
Oil on canvas
54 × 41 ¼ in. (137.2 × 104.8 cm)
Tate, London; presented by the Friends of the Tate Gallery, 1961, T00454

21 ***0 through 9*, 1961**
Charcoal, pastel, and graphite pencil on paper
54 ¼ × 41 ⅝ in. (137.8 × 105.7 cm)
Private collection

22 ***0 through 9*, 1980**
Ink on plastic
12 ⅝ × 10 ⅛ in. (32.1 × 25.7 cm)
Nerman Family Collection

23 ***0 through 9*, 1960**
Oil and collage over lithograph mounted on fiberboard
29 ¾ × 22 ⅛ in. (75.6 × 56.2 cm)
Collection of Samuel and Ronnie Heyman, Palm Beach

24 ***0 through 9*, 1960**
Charcoal on paper
28 ⅞ × 23 in. (73.3 × 58.4 cm)
Collection of the artist

25 **Study for *0 through 9*, 1960***
Graphite wash and graphite pencil on paper
12 ¾ × 11 in. (32.4 × 27.9 cm)
Private collection

26 ***0 through 9*, 1961 (cast 1964)**
Aluminum
26 ⅜ × 19 ⅞ in. (67 × 50.5 cm)
Ed. no. 1/4
Collection of the artist

27 ***0 through 9*, 1965**
Charcoal and graphite pencil on paper
30 × 22 ½ in. (76.2 × 57.2 cm)
Kristen and Alex Klabin

28 ***0 through 9*, 1970‡**
Graphite pencil, graphite powder, acrylic, and colored pencil on paper mounted on board
3 ½ × 3 ⅞ in. (8.9 × 9.8 cm) sight
Collection of Abigail R. Esman

29 ***0 through 9*, 1961**
Plaster
26 ¾ × 20 in. (68 × 50.8 cm)
Collection of the artist

30 ***0–9*, 2008 (cast 2009)‡**
Silver (two-sided)
20 ⅛ × 37 ⅞ in. (51.1 × 96.2 cm)
Private collection

31 ***0–9*, 2009–12***
Copper (two-sided)
19 ¼ × 37 ¼ in. (48.9 × 94.6 cm)
Private collection

32 ***0–9*, 2009‡**
Bronze (two-sided)
20 × 37 ¾ in. (50.8 × 95.9 cm)
Collection of Nancy and Steve Crown

33 ***0–9*, 2008‡**
Bronze (two-sided)
19 ⅞ × 37 ¾ in. (50.5 × 95.9 cm)
Philadelphia Museum of Art; promised gift of Keith L. and Katherine Sachs

34 ***Gray Numbers*, 1959–61‡**
Encaustic on canvas
5 ⅝ × 4 ¼ in. (14.3 × 10.8 cm)
Private collection

35 ***Numbers*, 2006**
Ink and crayon on paper mounted on paper
38 ⅜ × 32 ⅜ in. (97.5 × 82.2 cm)
Private collection; courtesy Acquavella Galleries, New York

36 ***0–9*, 1958**
Charcoal and graphite pencil on paper
16 × 12 in. (40.6 × 30.5 cm)
Kolodny Family Collection

37 ***0–9*, 1962**
Encaustic, graphite pencil, and oil over lithograph on paper
20 ½ × 15 ¾ in. (52.1 × 40 cm)
Collection of Marsha and Jeffrey Perelman

38 ***Numbers*, 1963 (cast 1968)‡**
Aluminum
57 ¼ × 43 ½ in. (145.4 × 110.5 cm)
Allen Family Collection

39 ***Numbers*, 1963**
Sculp-metal and collage on canvas
57 ⅞ × 43 ⅞ in. (147 × 111.4 cm)
Philadelphia Museum of Art; centennial gift of the Woodward Foundation, 1975-81-6

40–49 ***Figures 0–9*, from Color Numeral Series, 1969**
Lithographs: one stone, two aluminum plates
38 × 31 in. (96.5 × 78.7 cm) each
Kenneth Tyler, Dan Freeman (*Figure 1*); Kenneth Tyler, James Webb (*Figures 2, 6, 8*); Kenneth Tyler, Charles Ritt (*Figures 3–5, 7, 9*)/Gemini
Editions of 40
Private collection

Flags and Maps

WHITNEY MUSEUM OF AMERICAN ART

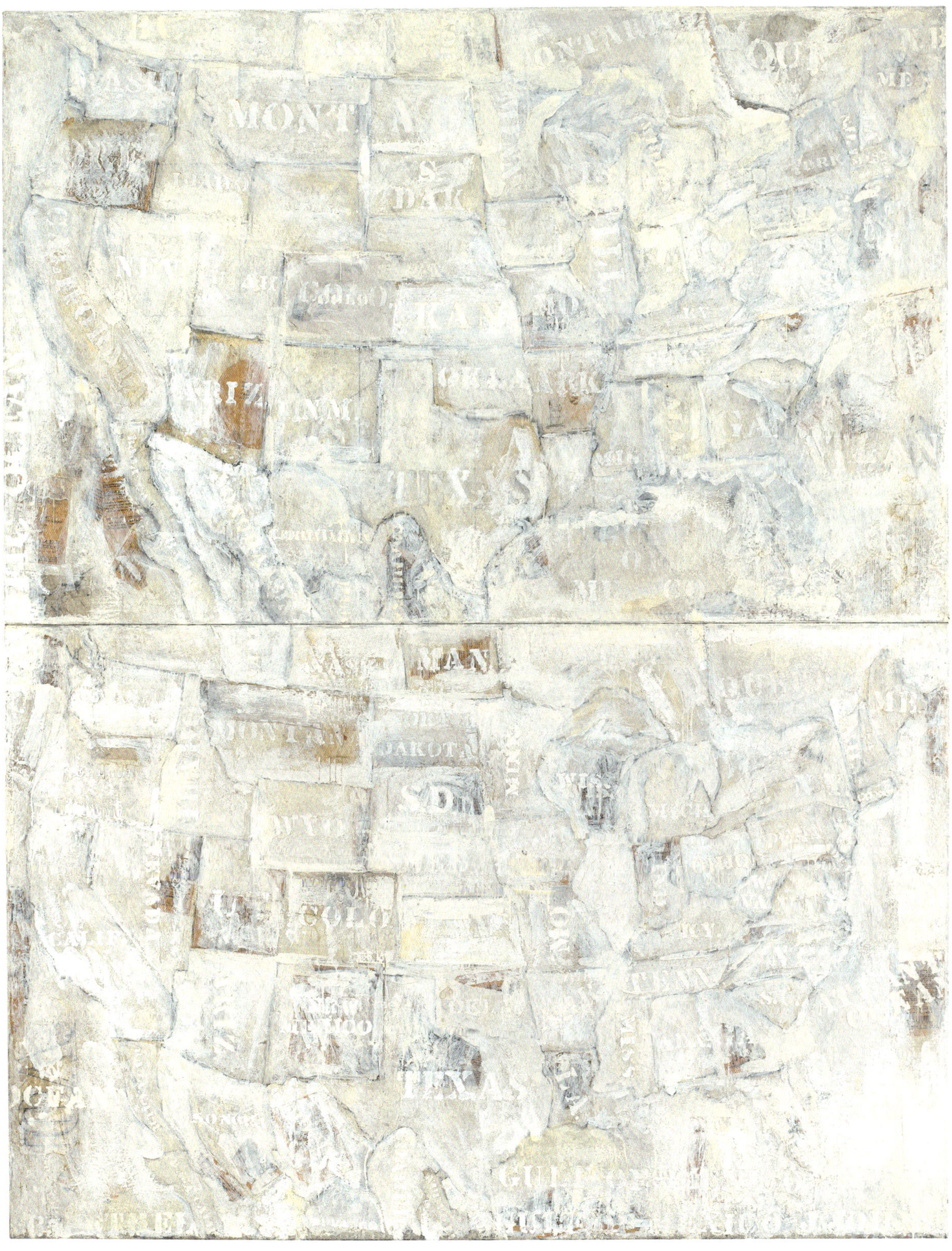

1 ***Two Maps*, 1965**

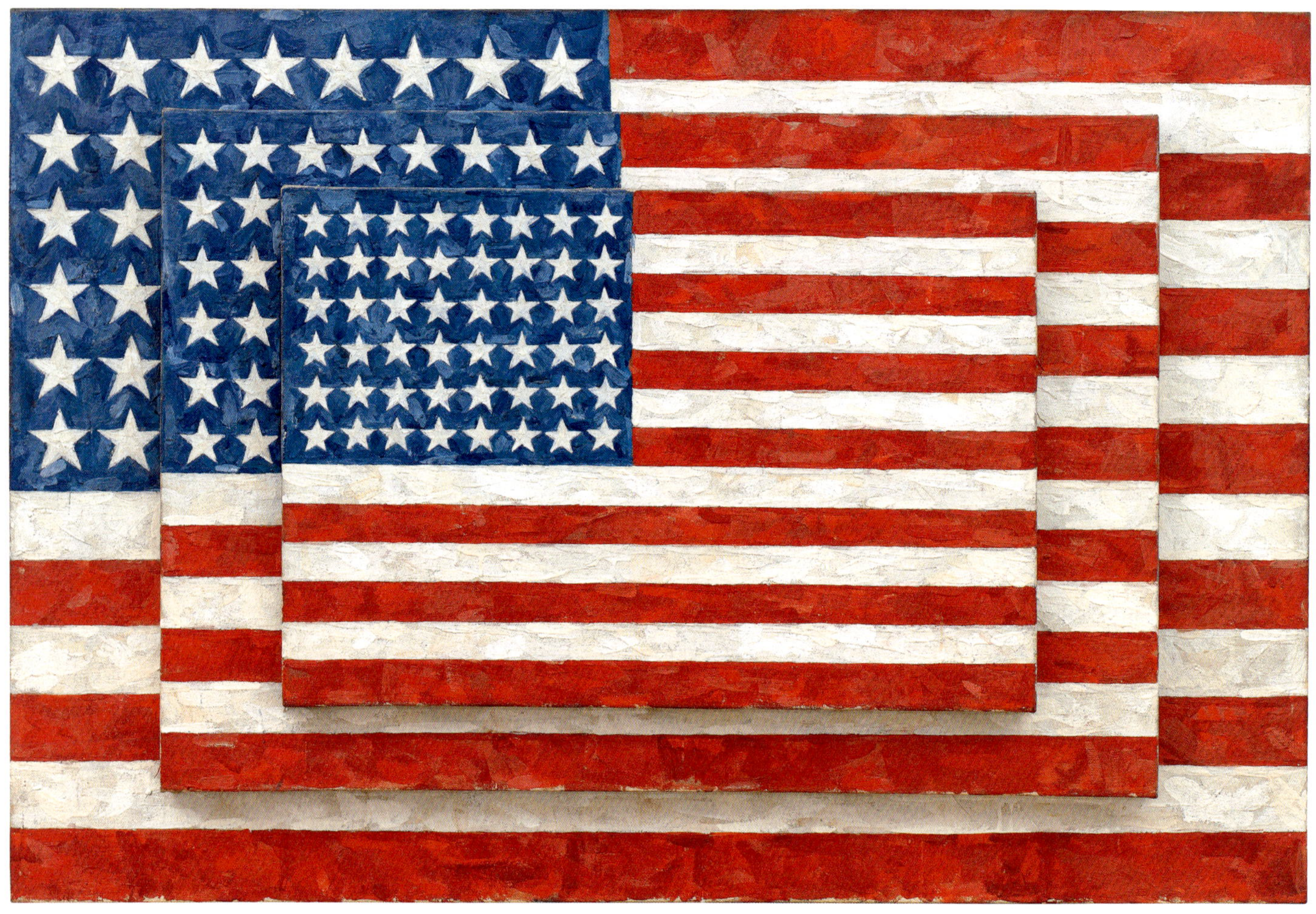

2 *Three Flags*, 1958

MONTANA
NORTH DAKOTA
SOUTH DAKOTA
OREGON
NEVADA
ONTARIO
ARIZONA
MICH
PENN
NEW YORK
GEORGIA
MISS
KENTUCKY
MISSOURI

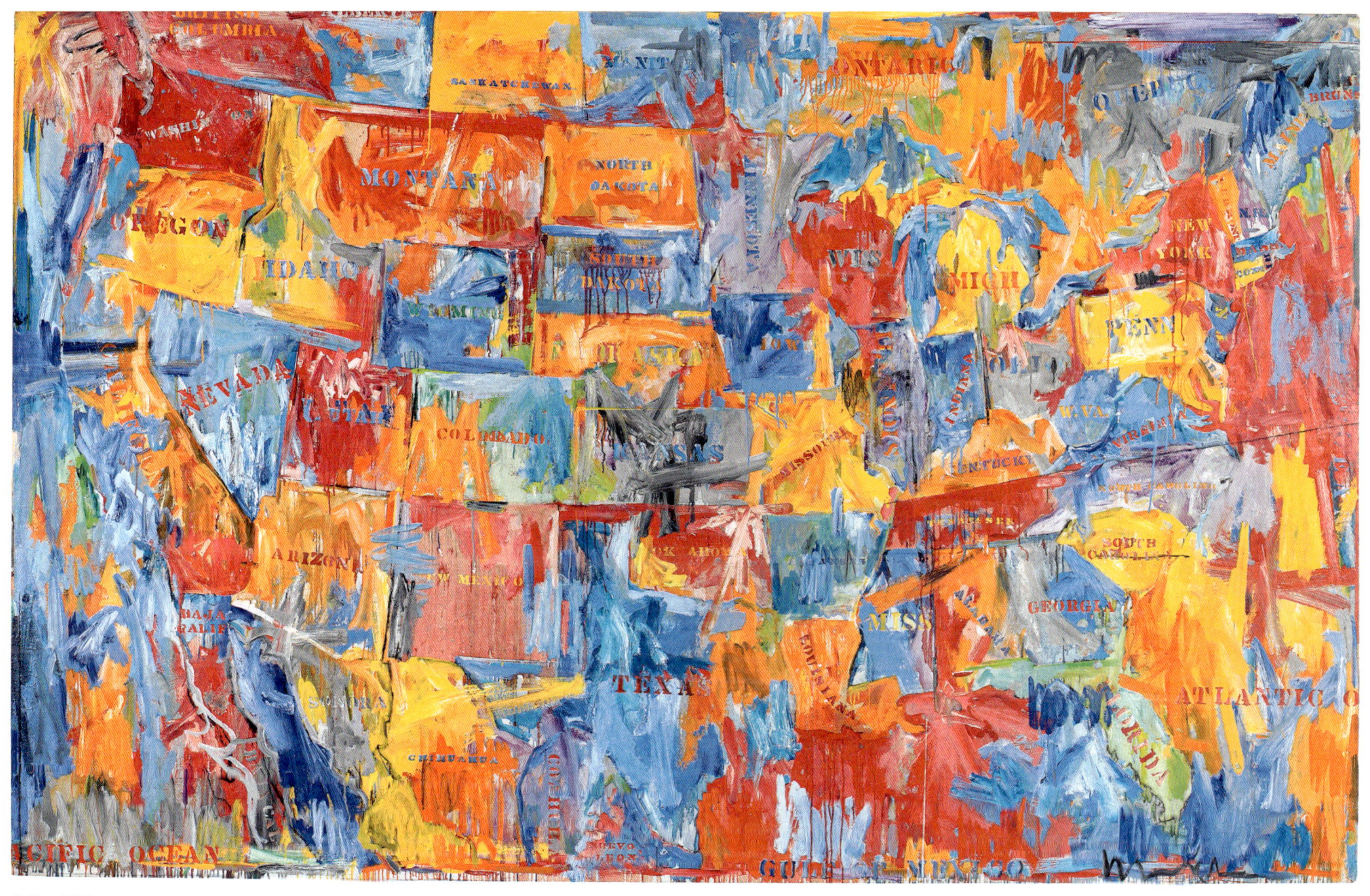

3 ***Map*, 1961**

4 ***White Flag*, 1955**

COLUMBIA
SASKATCHEWAN
NEB
IOWA
SD
MO
KY
W VA
ALA
FLA
BAJA
CALIF
SONORA
CHIHUAHUA

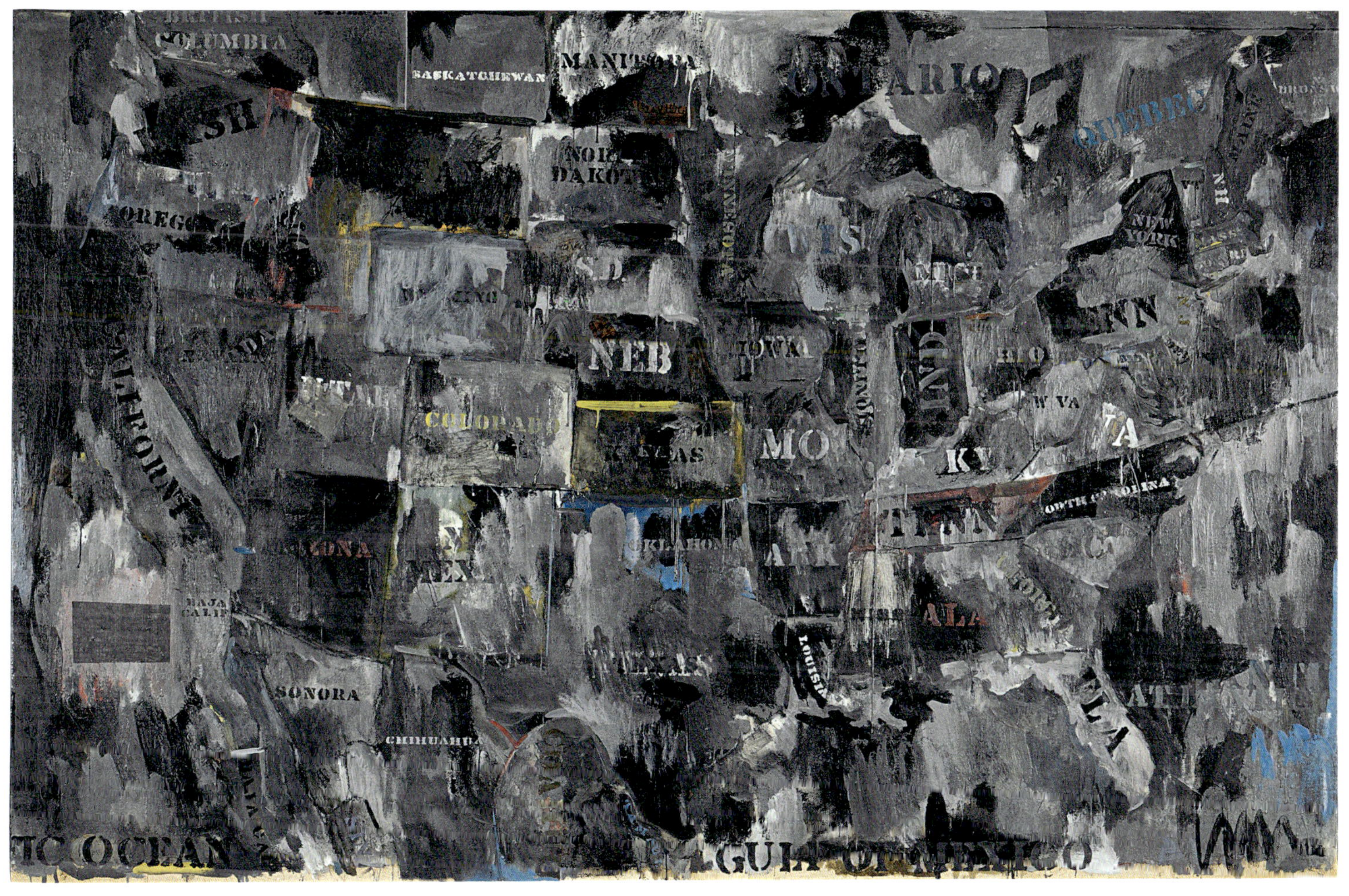

5 ***Map*, 1962–63**

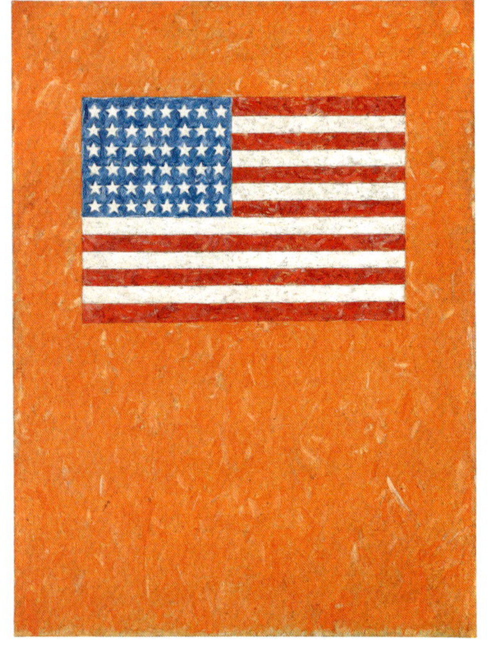

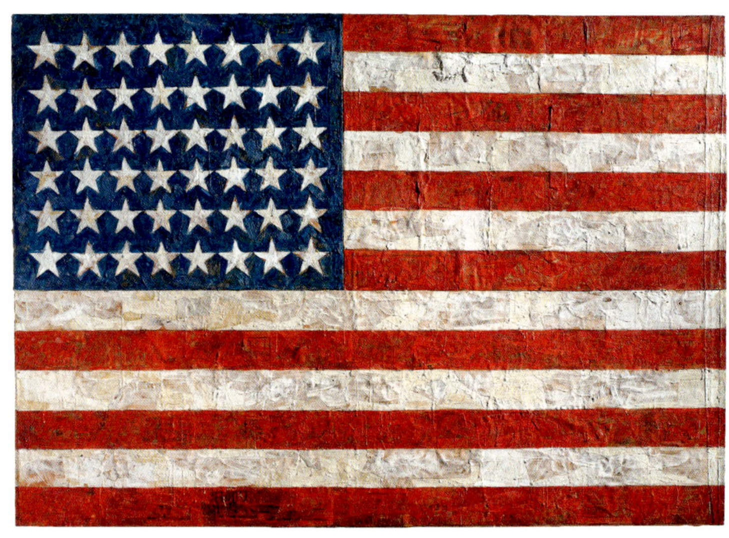

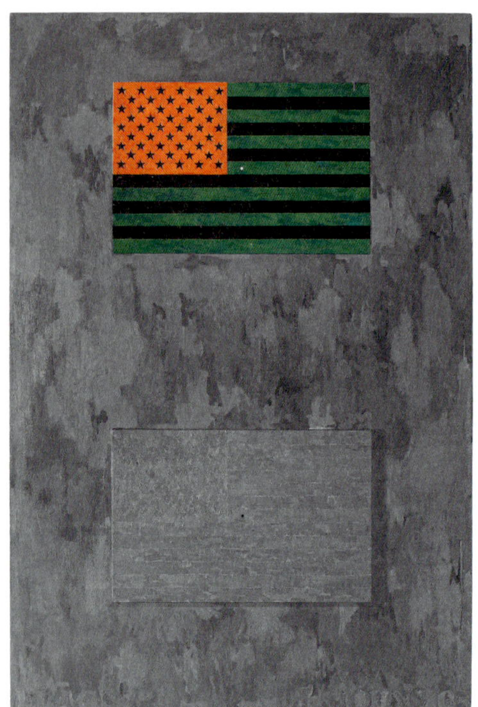

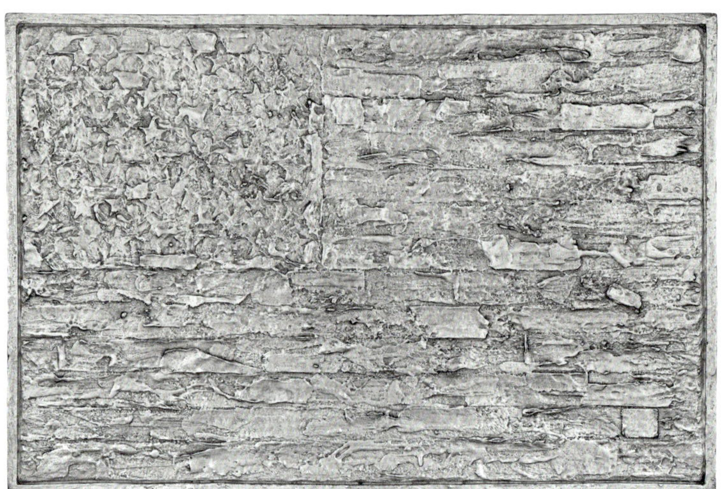

6 ***Flag on Orange Field*, 1957**
8 ***Flags*, 1965**

7 ***Flag*, 1954–55**
9 ***Flag*, 1960–87**

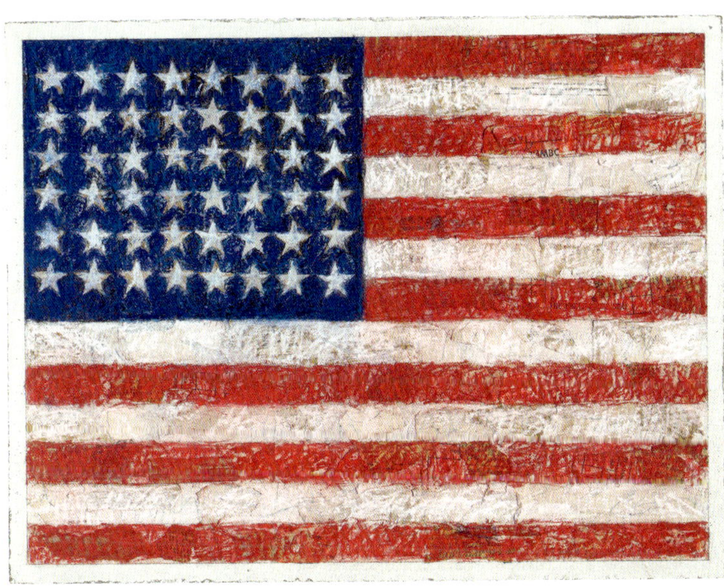

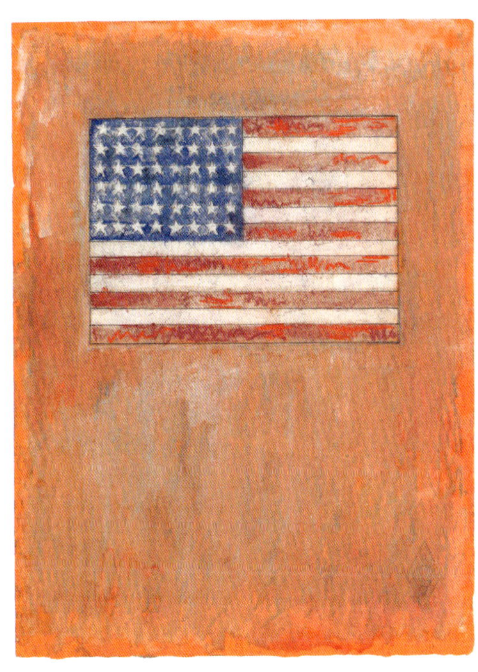

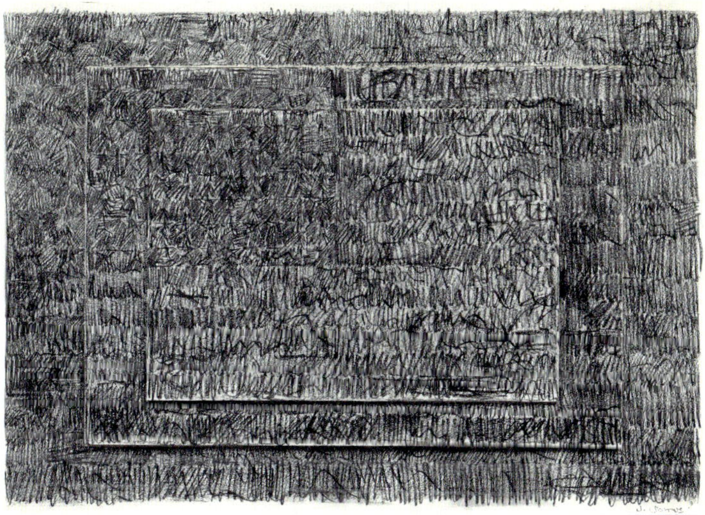

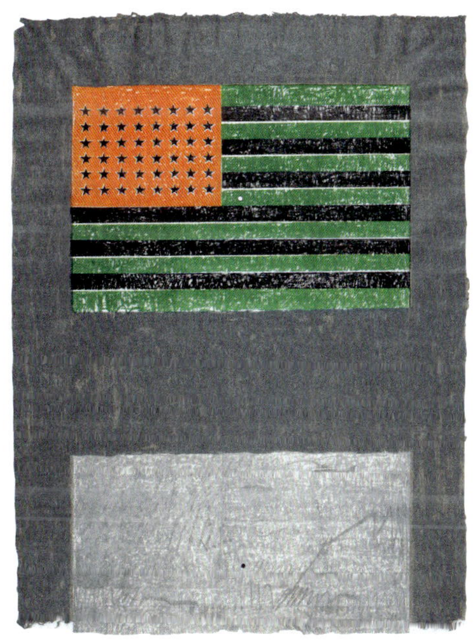

10 ***Flag*, 1957**
12 ***Three Flags*, 1960**

11 ***Flag on Orange Field*, 1957**
13 ***Flags*, 1968**

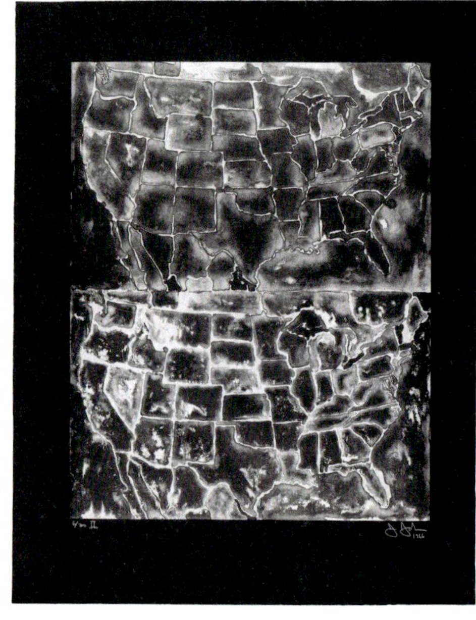

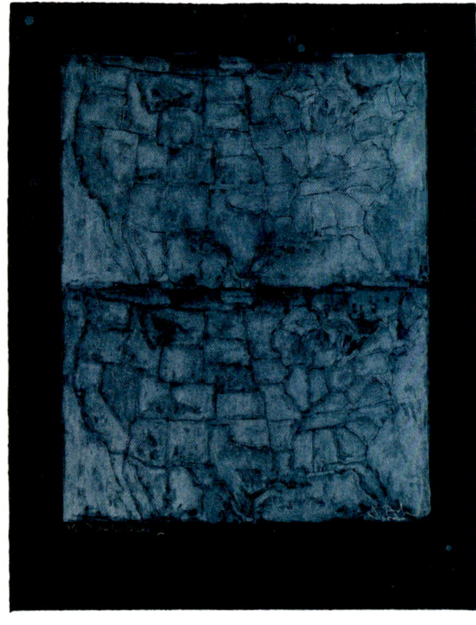

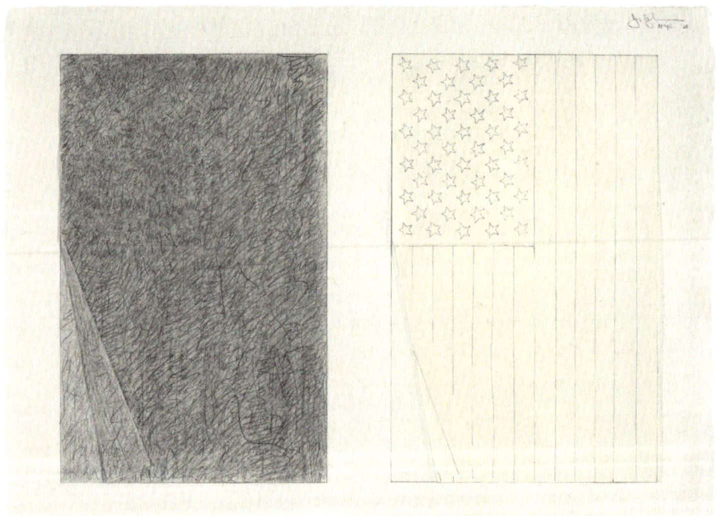

14 ***Two Maps II*, 1966**
17 ***Two Flags*, 1969**

15 ***Two Maps I*, 1966**
18 ***Flag*, 1959**

16 ***Green Map above White*, 1966–67**

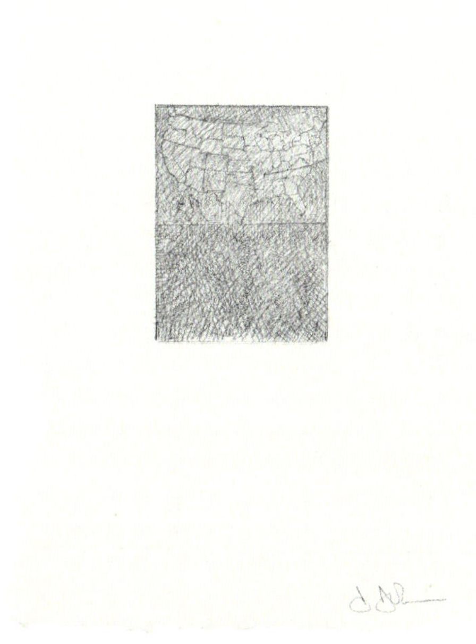

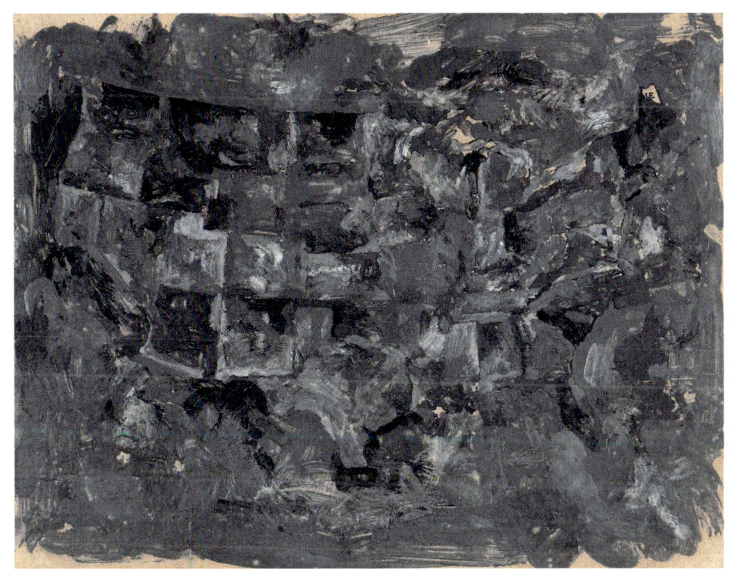

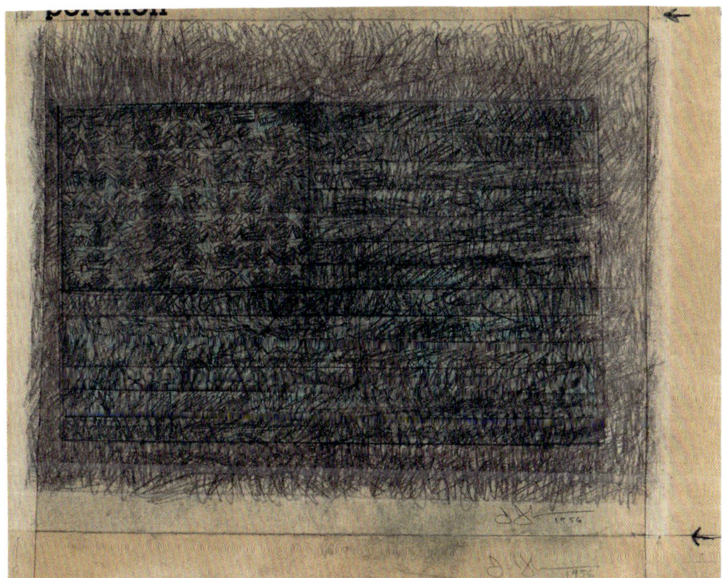

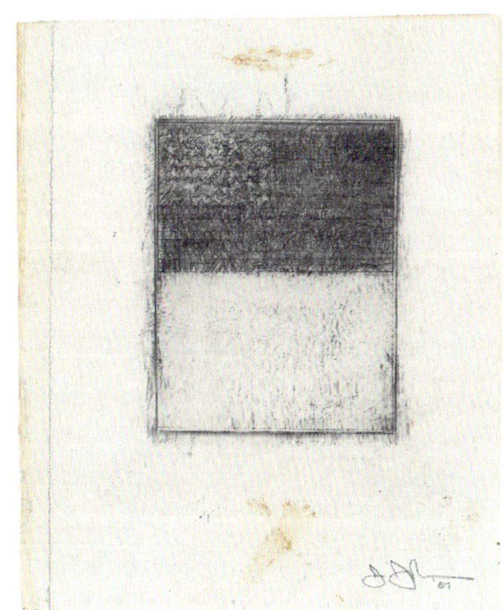

19 ***Map*, 2012**
21 ***Green Flag*, 1956**

20 ***Map*, 1960**
22 ***Flag above White*, 1957**

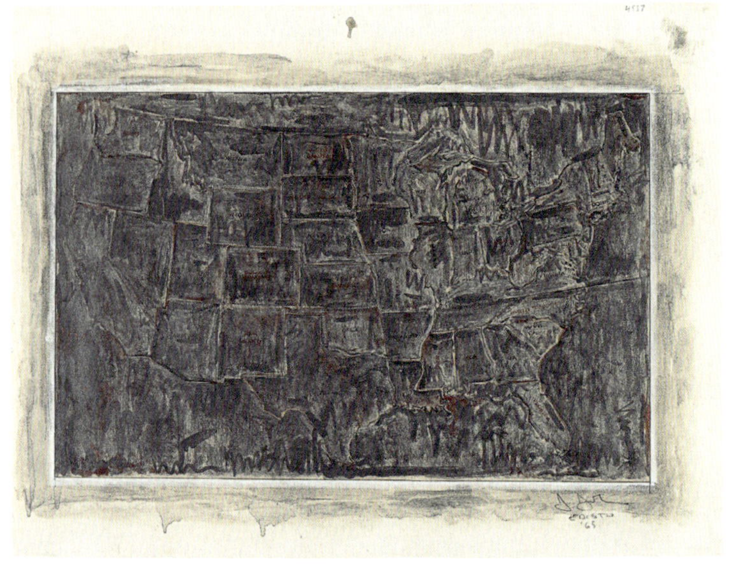

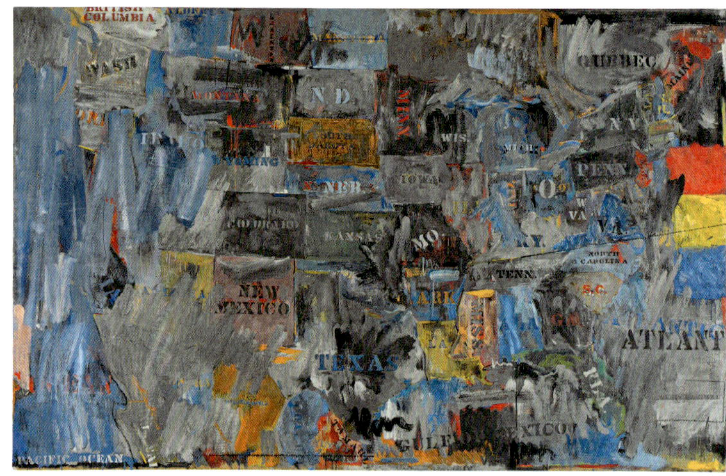

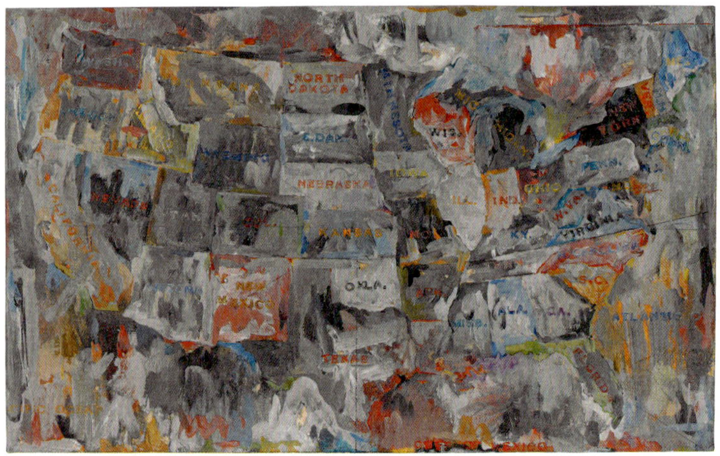

23 ***Map*, 1965**
25 ***Map*, 1961–62**

24 ***Map*, 1963**
26 ***Map*, 1965**

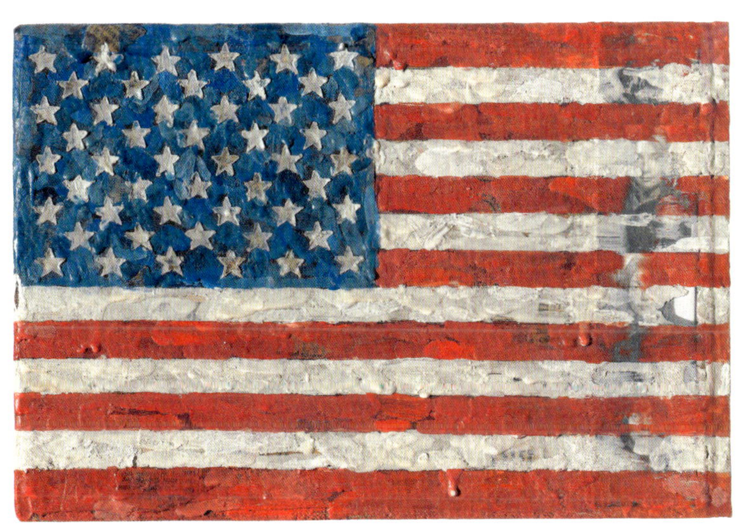

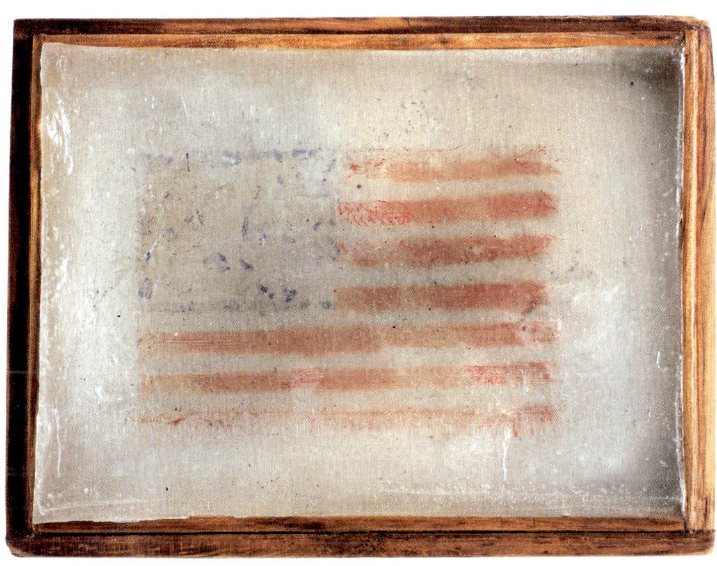

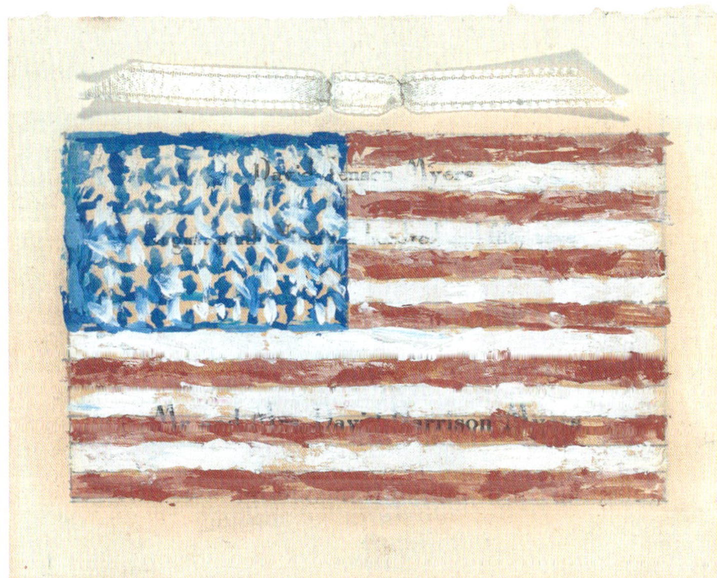

27 ***Flag*, 1965**
29 ***Flag*, 1957**

28 ***Flag*, 1958**
30 ***Flag*, 1960**

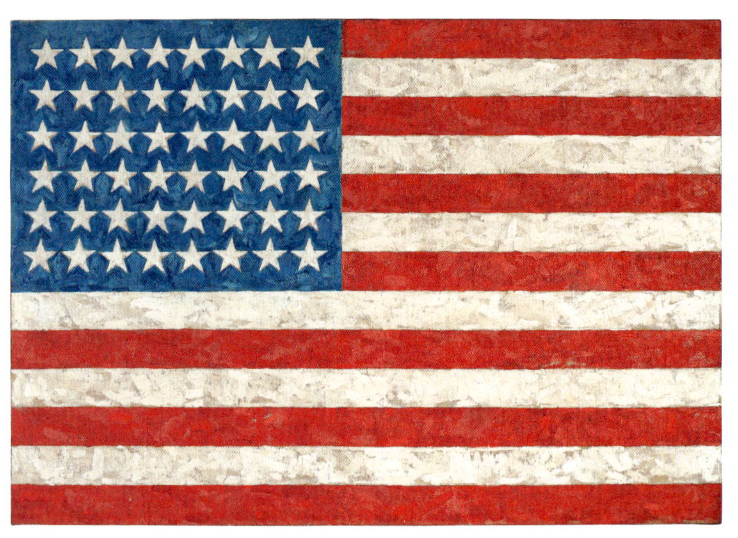

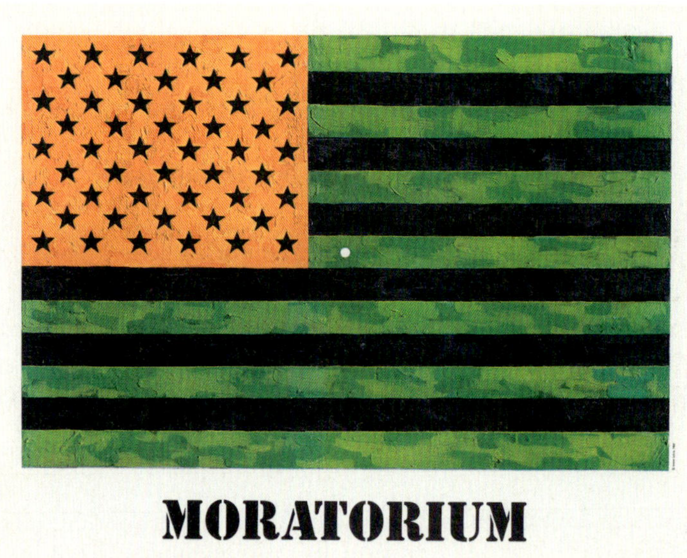

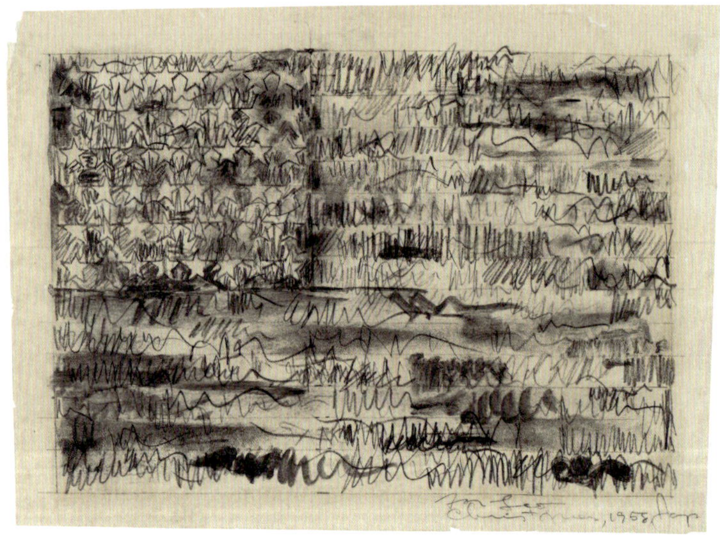

31 ***Flag*, 1958**
33 ***Flag*, 1958**

32 ***Moratorium*, 1969**
34 ***Flag*, 1957**

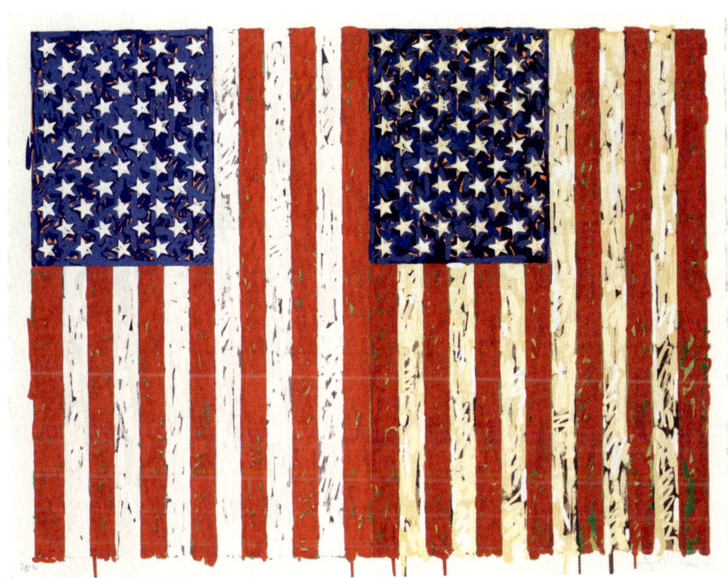

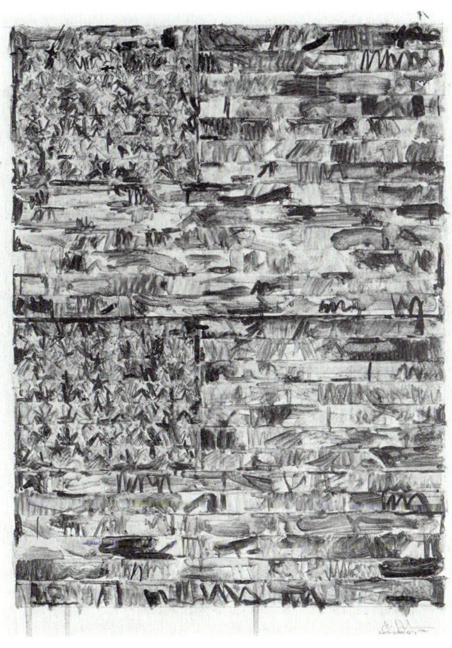

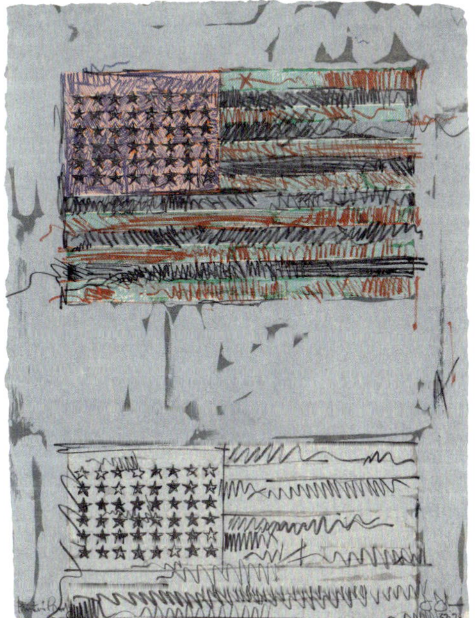

35 ***Flags I***, 1973
36 ***Two Flags***, 1960
37 ***Flags II***, 1970
38 ***Untitled (Envelope)***, 1959

Numbers

PHILADELPHIA MUSEUM OF ART

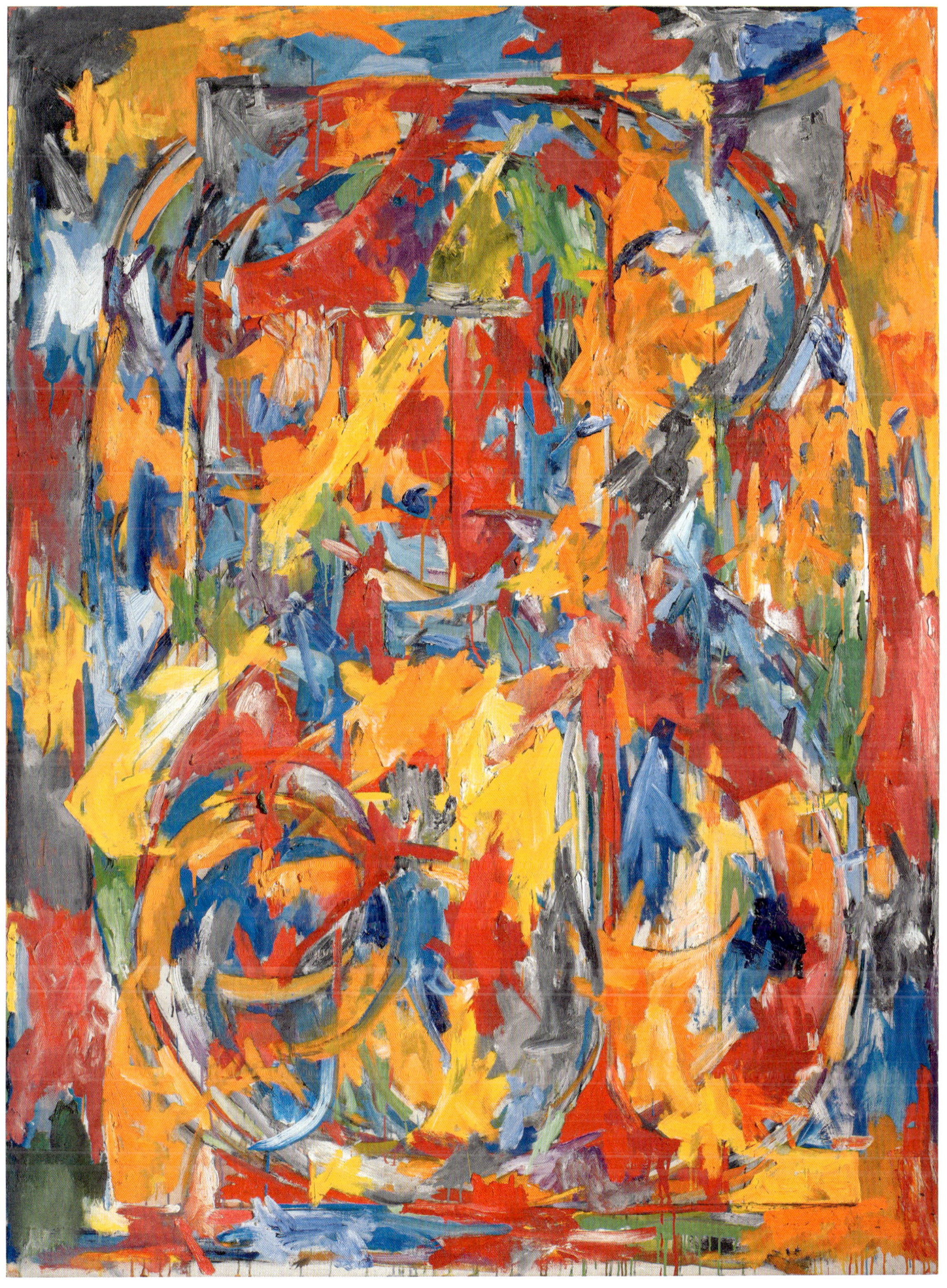

1 ***0 through 9*, 1960**

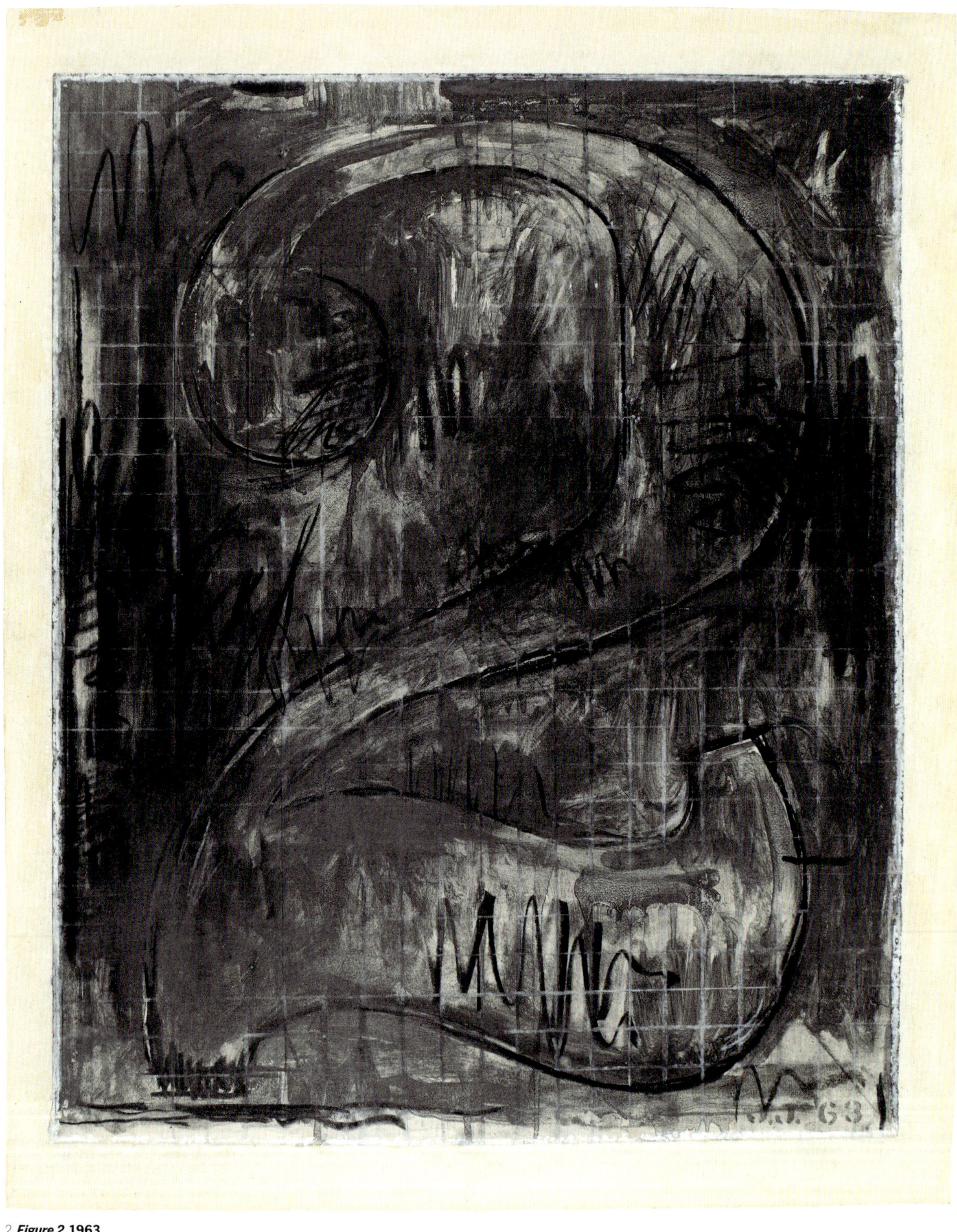

2 ***Figure 2*, 1963**

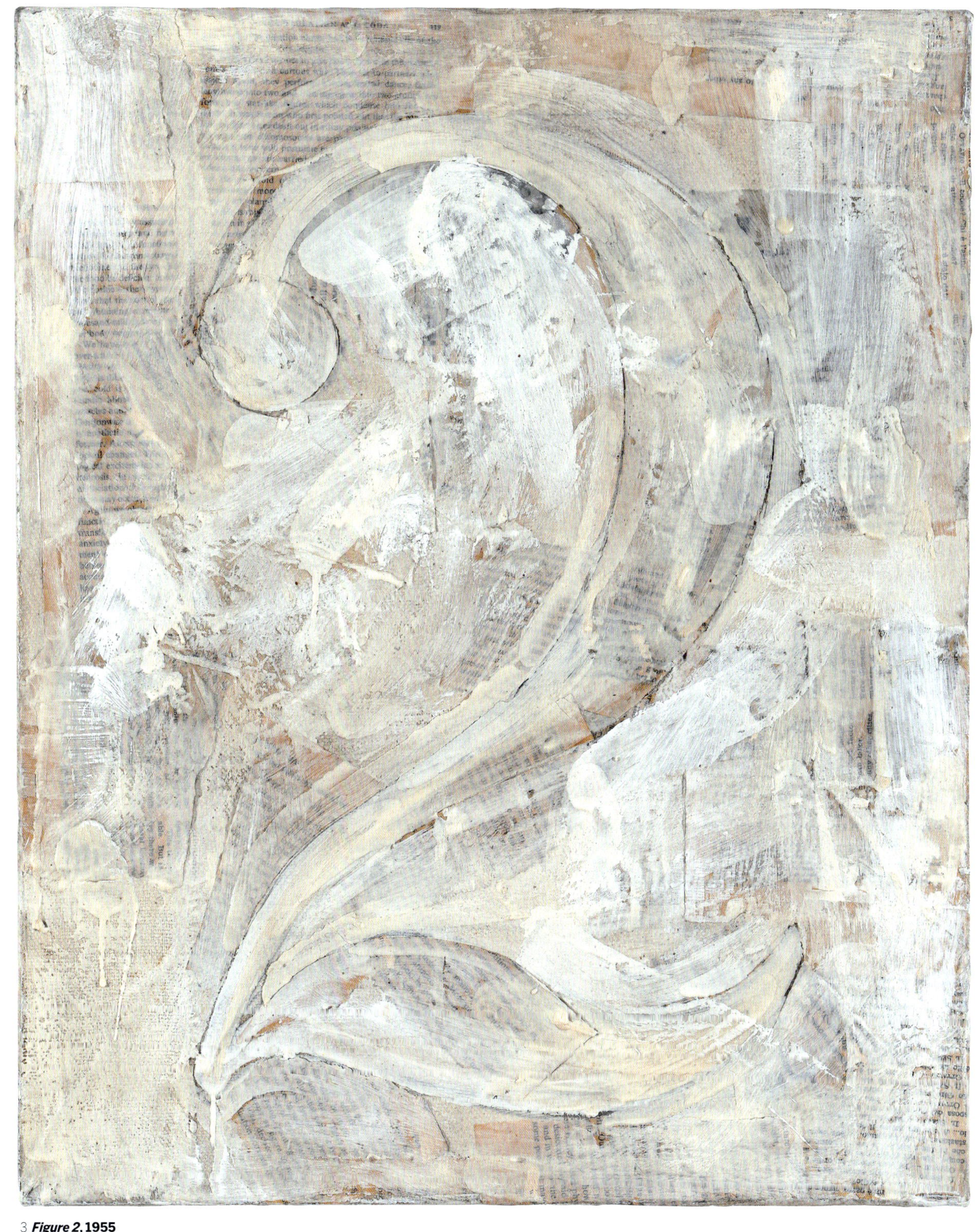

3 ***Figure 2***, **1955**

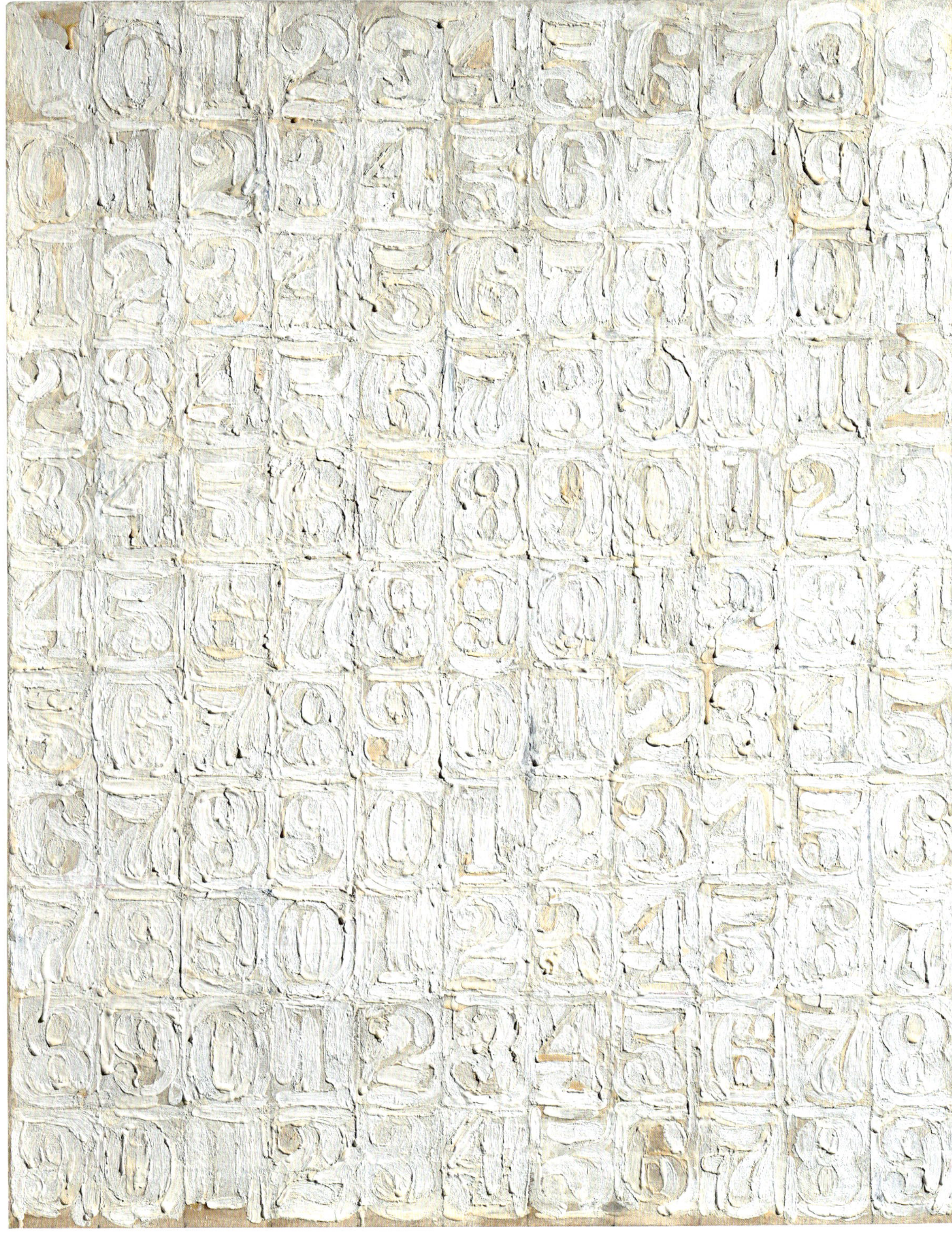

4 ***White Numbers*, 1958**

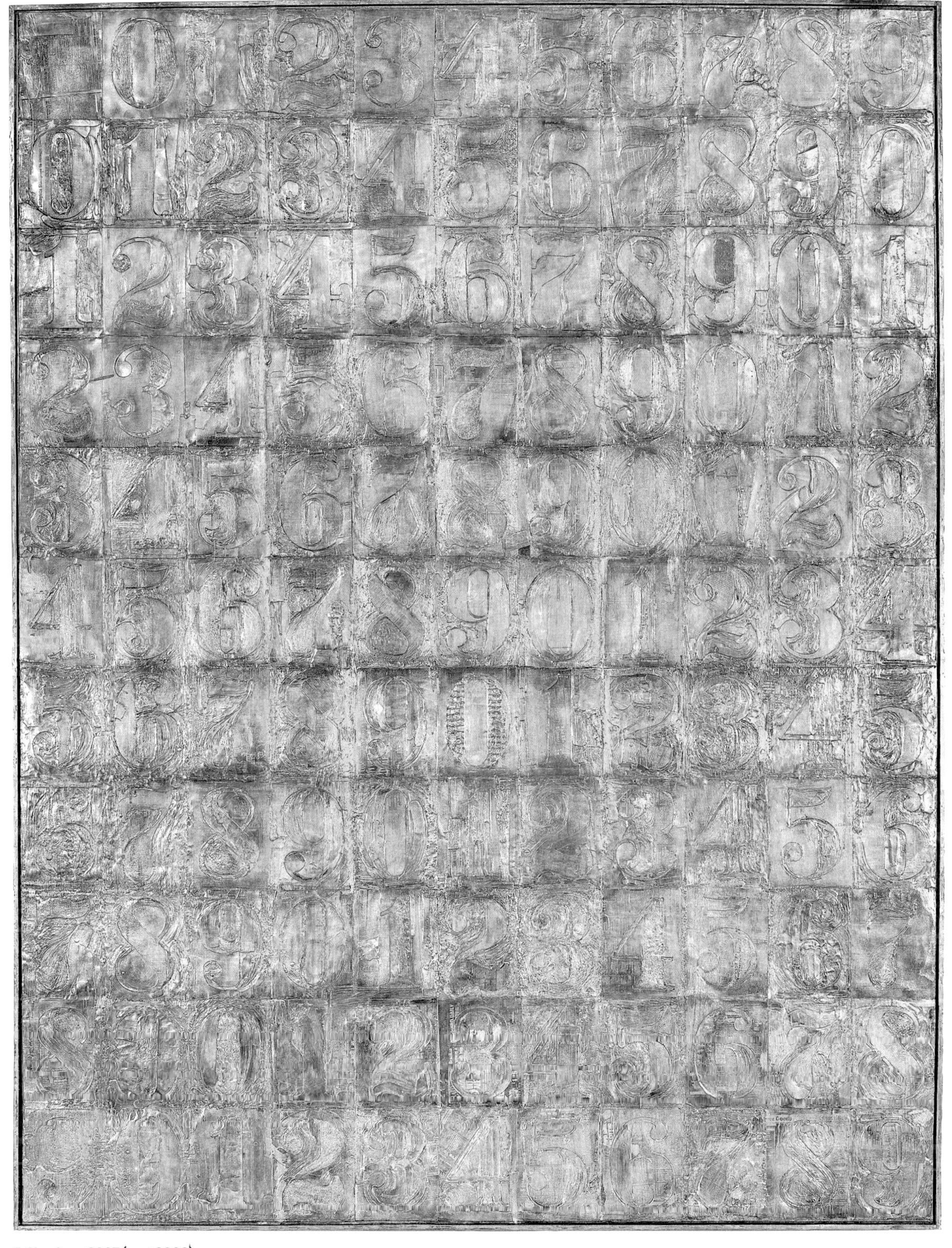

5 *Numbers*, 2007 (cast 2008)

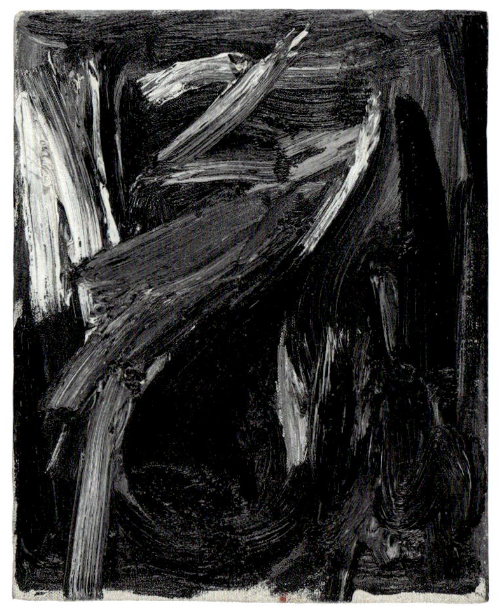

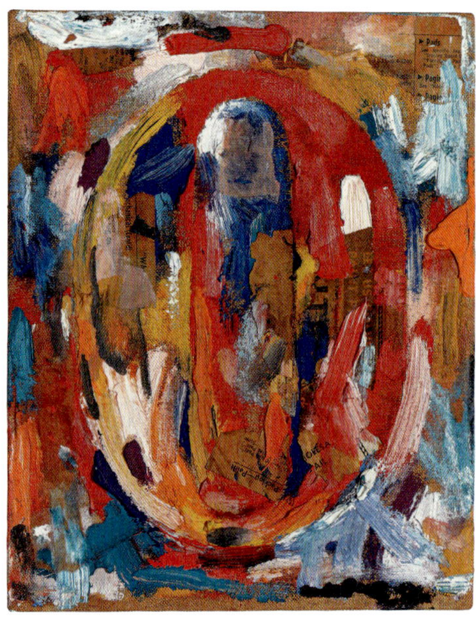

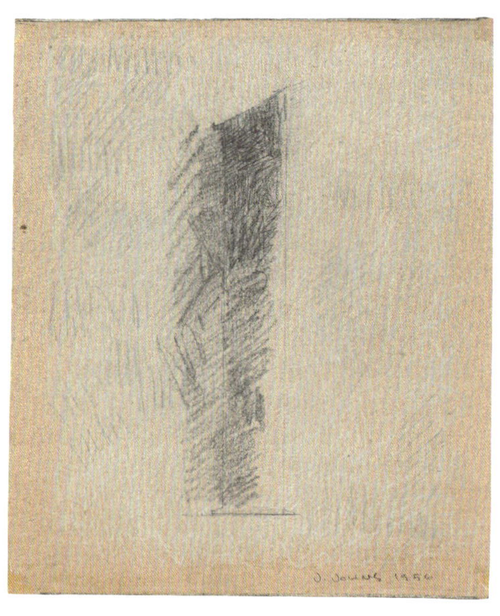

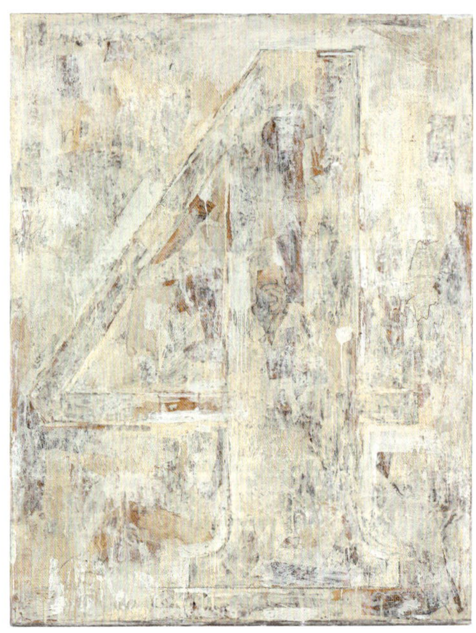

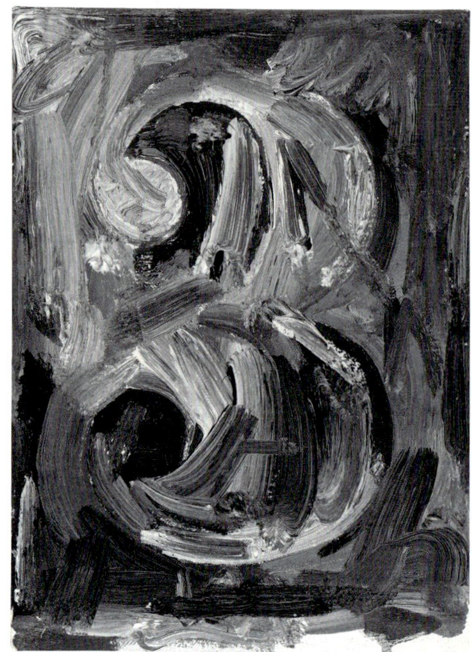

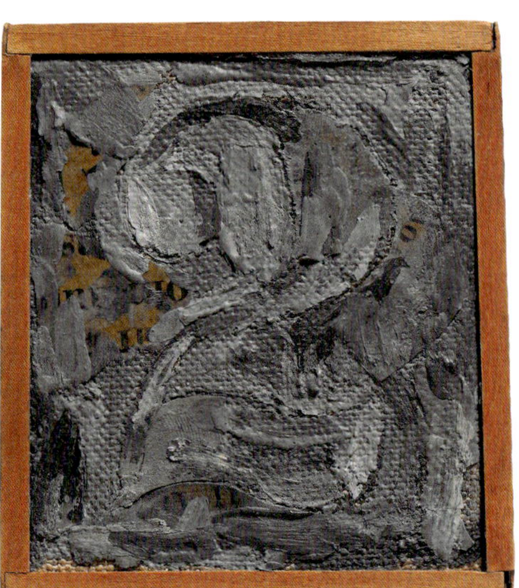

6 ***Figure 7***, 1959
9 ***Figure 4***, 1967

7 ***Figure 0***, 1959
10 ***Figure 3***, 1960

8 ***Figure 1***, 1956
11 ***Figure 2***, 1959

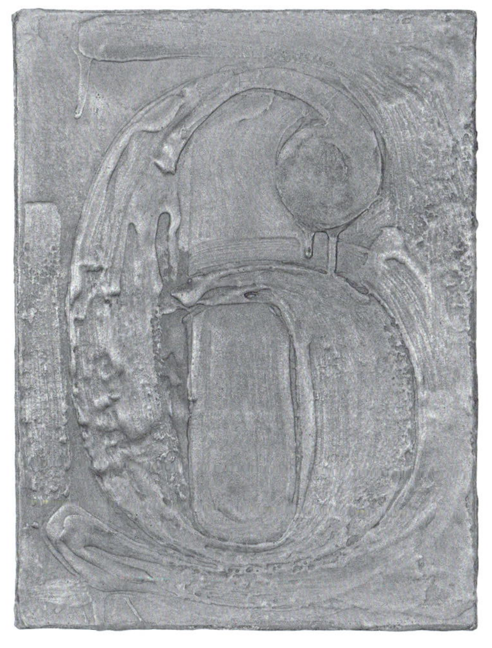

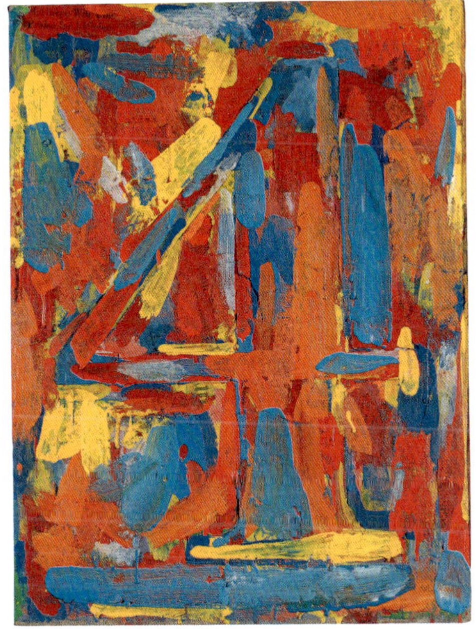

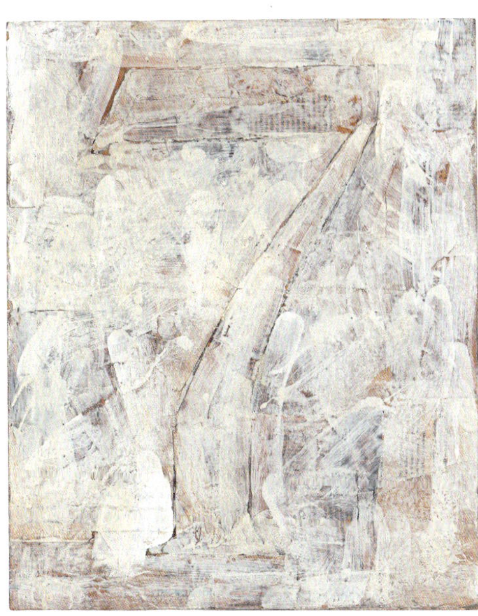

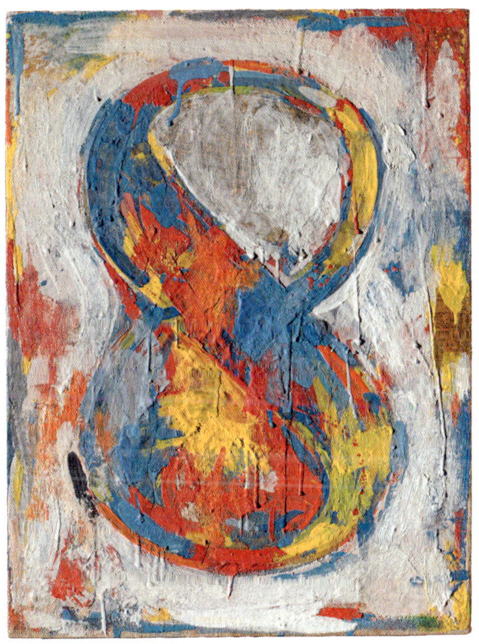

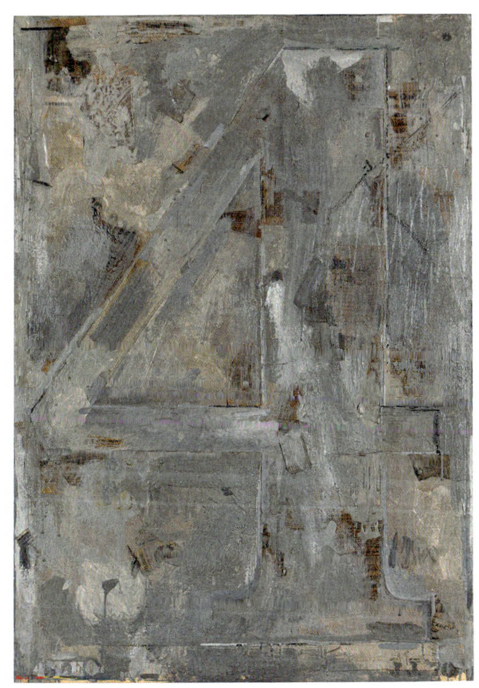

12 ***Figure 6***, **1964–72**
15 ***Figure 8***, **1959**

13 ***Figure 4***, **1959**
16 ***4 Leo***, **1970**

14 ***Figure 7***, **1955**
17 ***Figure 5***, **1959**

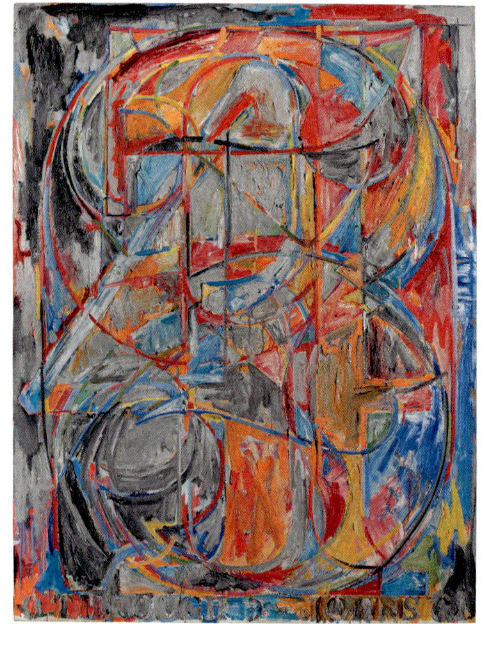
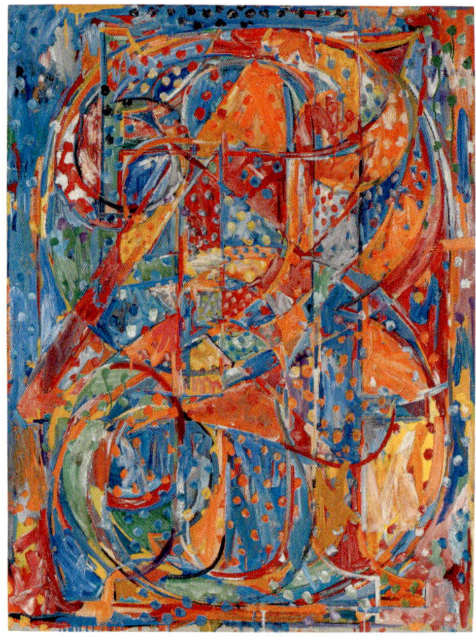
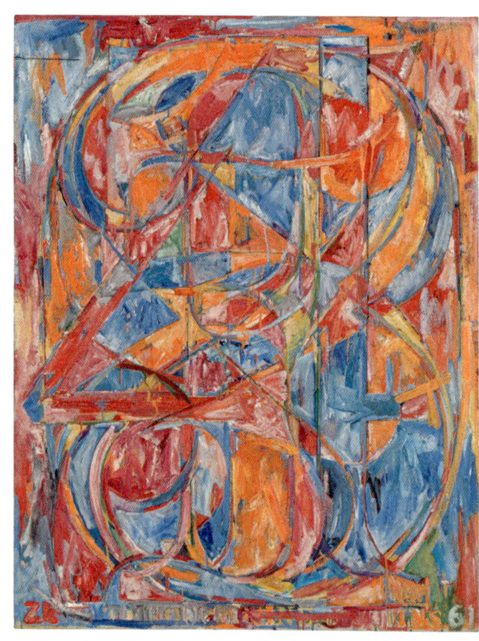
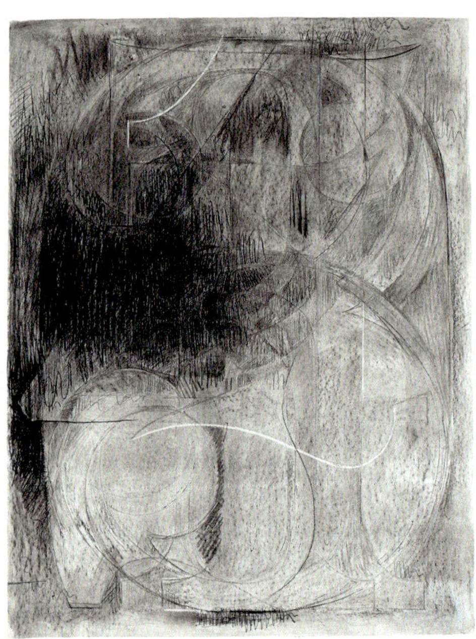
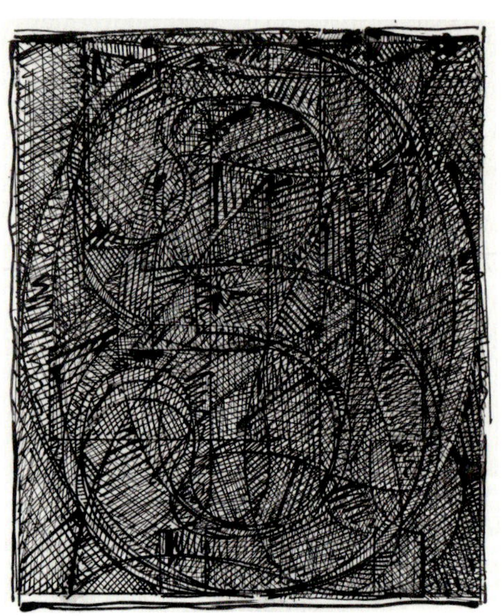
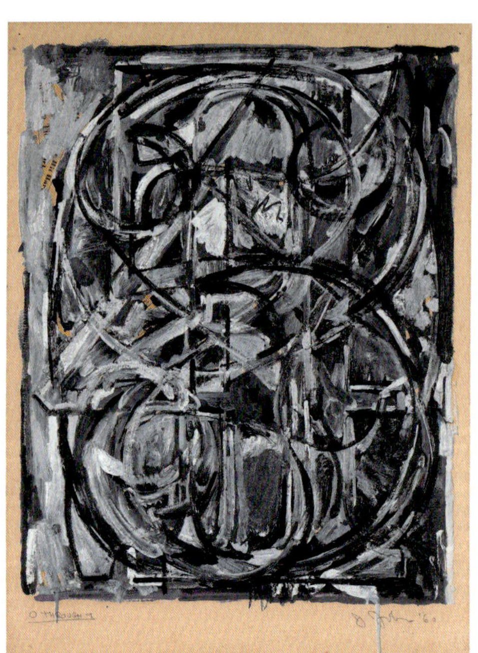

18 ***0 through 9*, 1961**
21 ***0 through 9*, 1961**

19 ***0 through 9*, 1961**
22 ***0 through 9*, 1980**

20 ***0 through 9*, 1961**
23 ***0 through 9*, 1960**

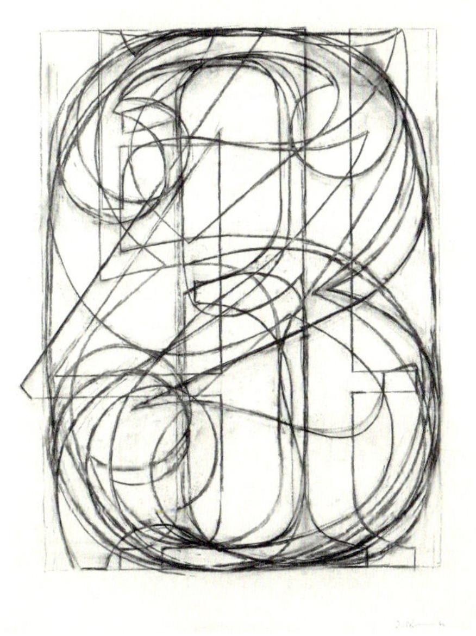

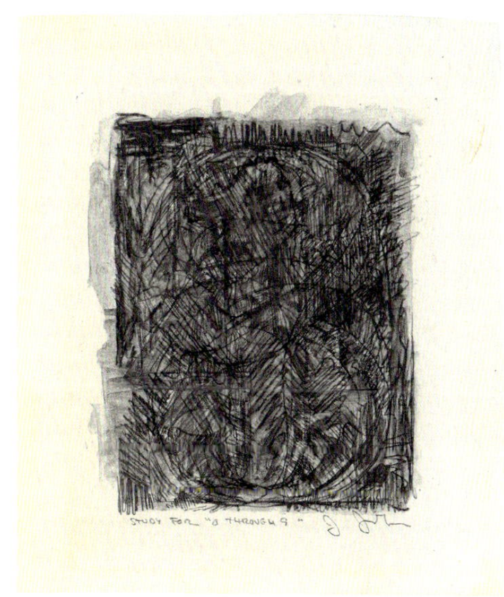

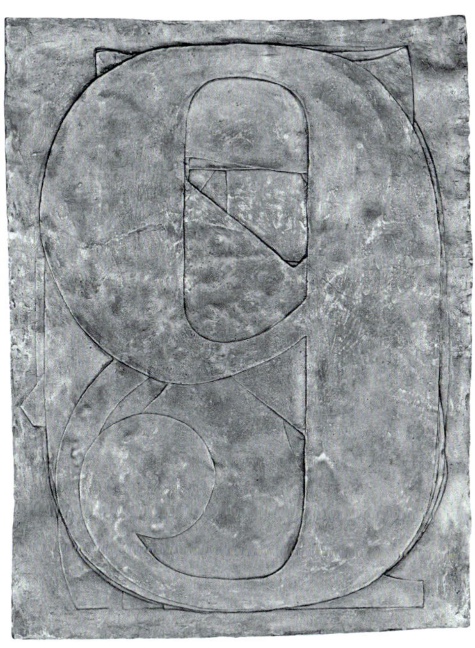

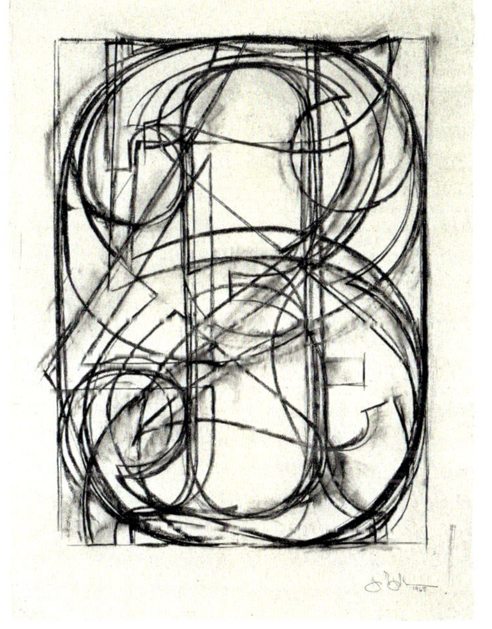

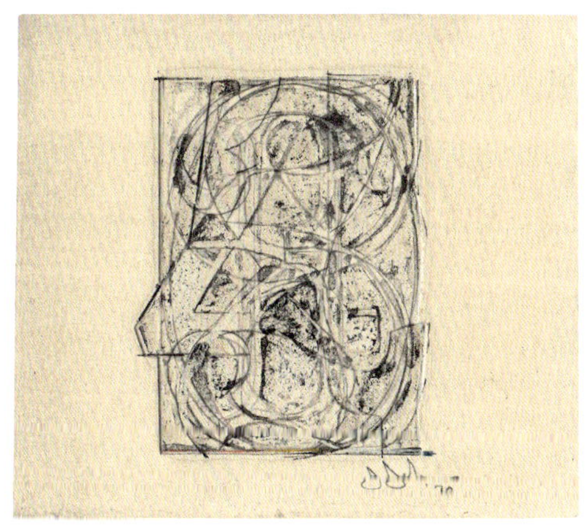

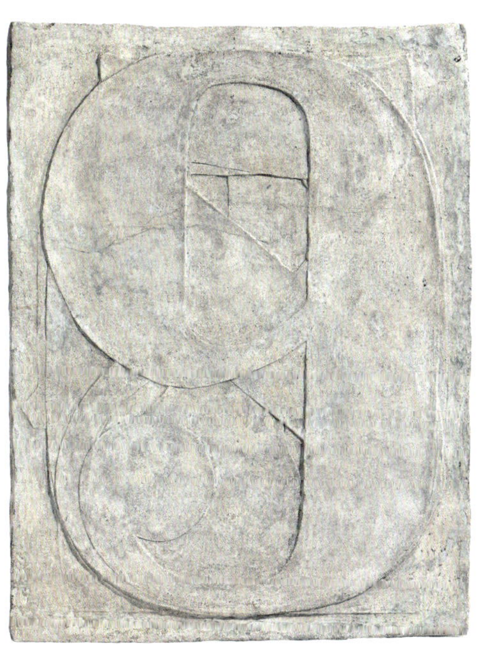

24 ***0 through 9*, 1960**
27 ***0 through 9*, 1965**

25 **Study for *0 through 9*, 1960**
28 ***0 through 9*, 1970**

26 ***0 through 9*, 1961 (cast 1964)**
29 ***0 through 9*, 1961**

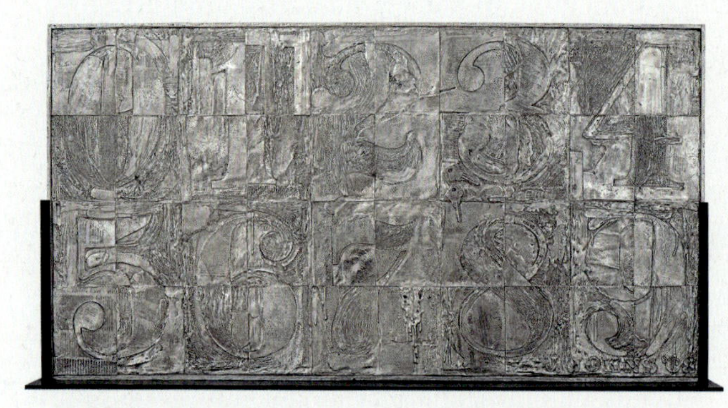

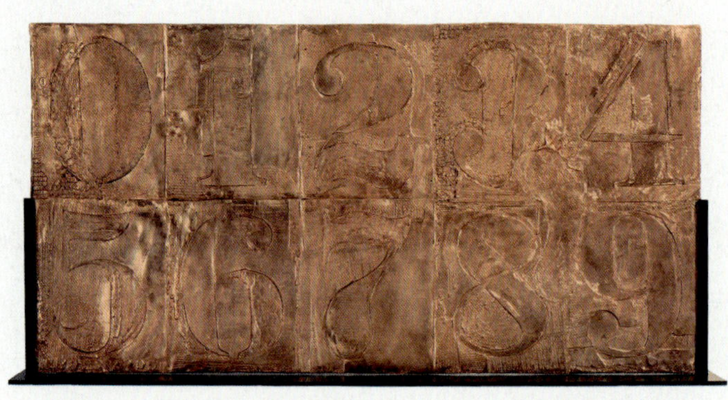

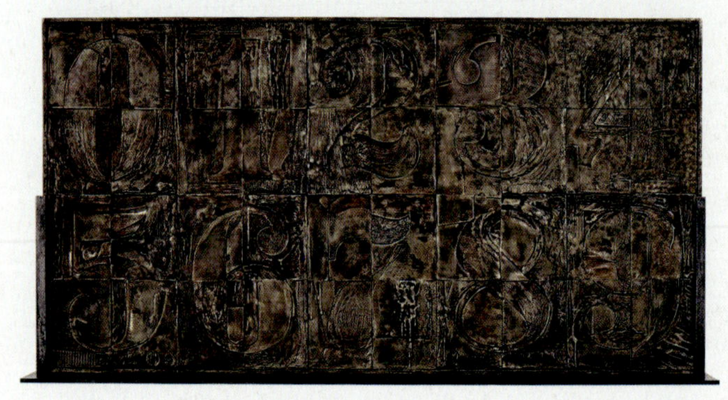

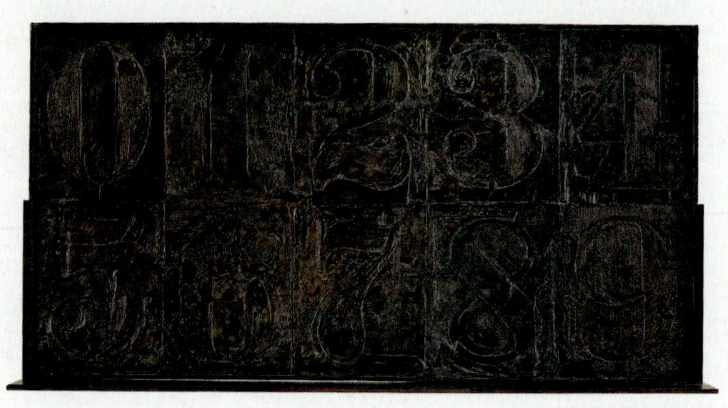

30 ***0–9***, 2008 (cast 2009)
32 ***0–9***, 2009

31 ***0–9***, 2009–12
33 ***0–9***, 2008

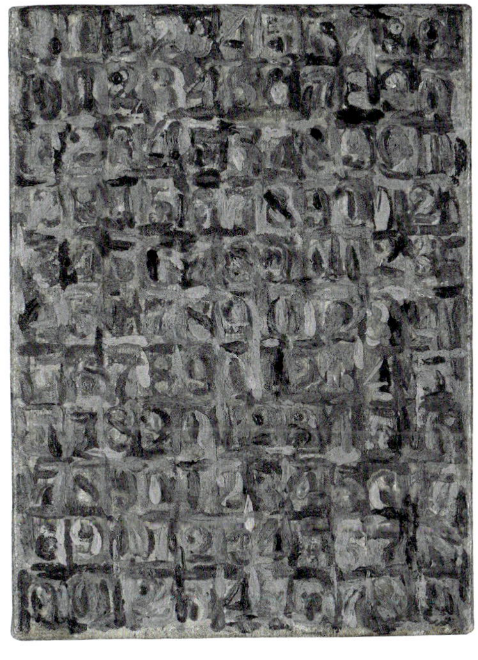

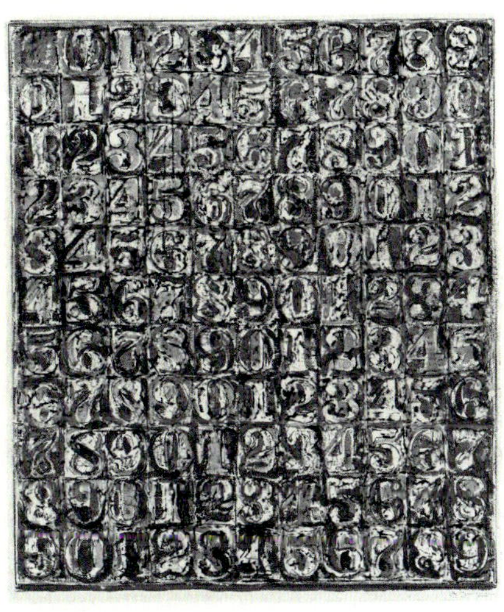

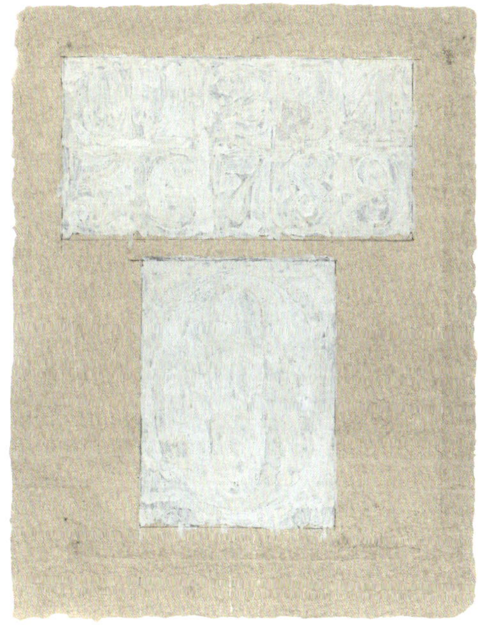

34 ***Gray Numbers*, 1959–61**
37 ***0–9*, 1962**

35 ***Numbers*, 2006**
38 ***Numbers*, 1963 (cast 1968)**

36 ***0–9*, 1958**
39 ***Numbers*, 1963**

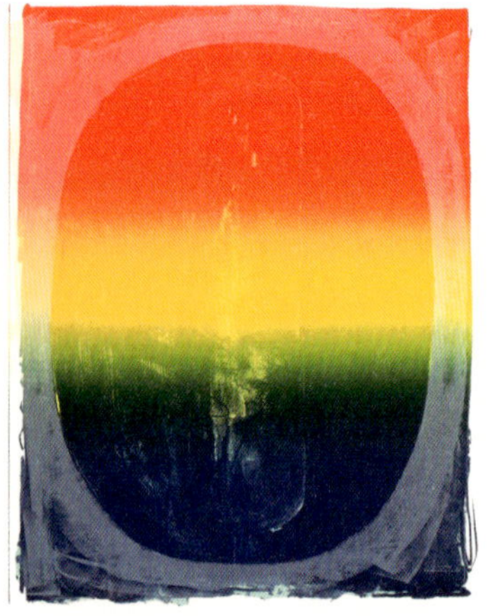

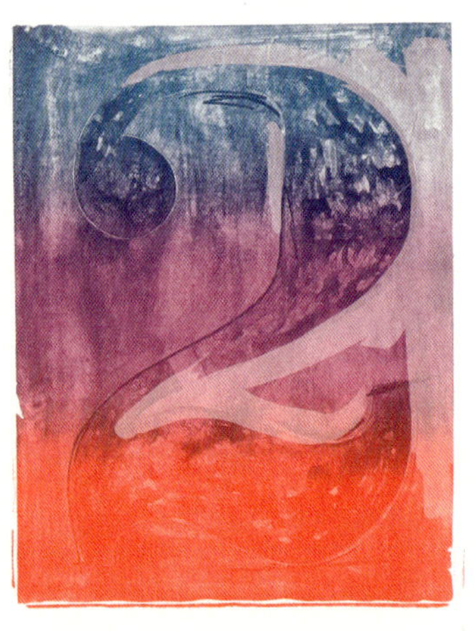

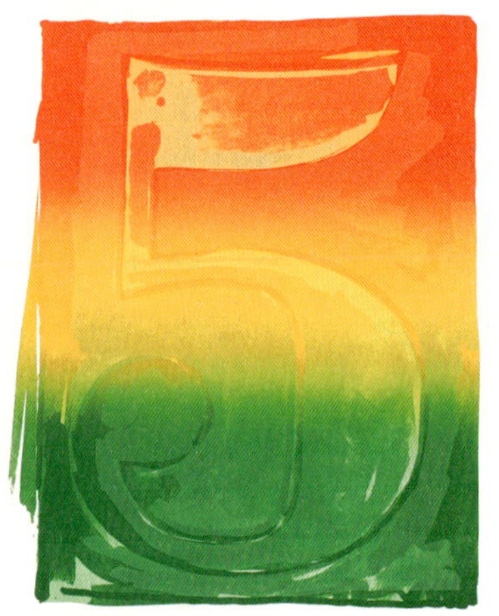

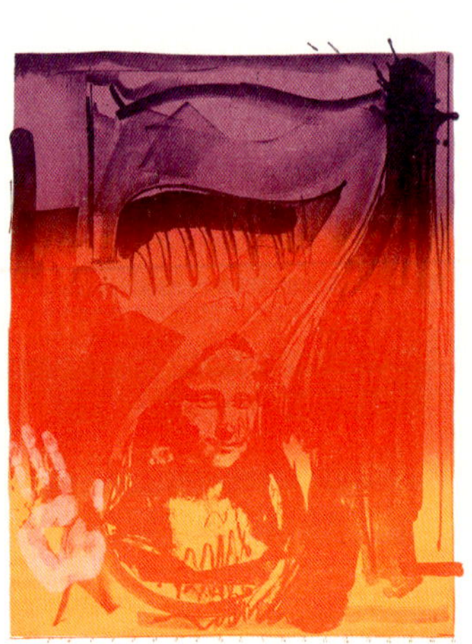

40 ***Figure 0*, from Color Numeral Series, 1969**
45 ***Figure 5*, from Color Numeral Series, 1969**

41 ***Figure 1*, from Color Numeral Series, 1969**
46 ***Figure 6*, from Color Numeral Series, 1969**

42 ***Figure 2*, from Color Numeral Series, 1969**
47 ***Figure 7*, from Color Numeral Series, 1969**

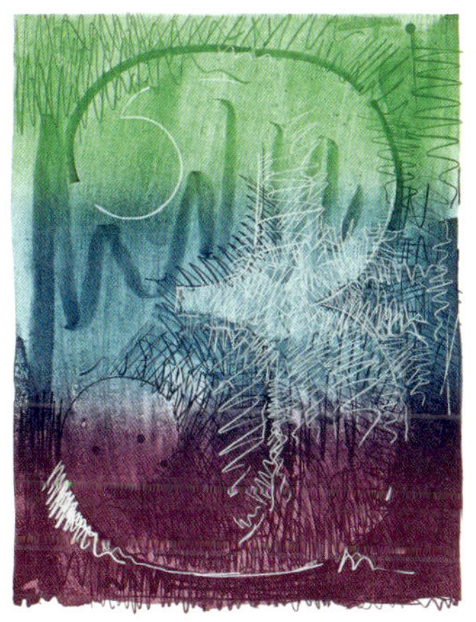

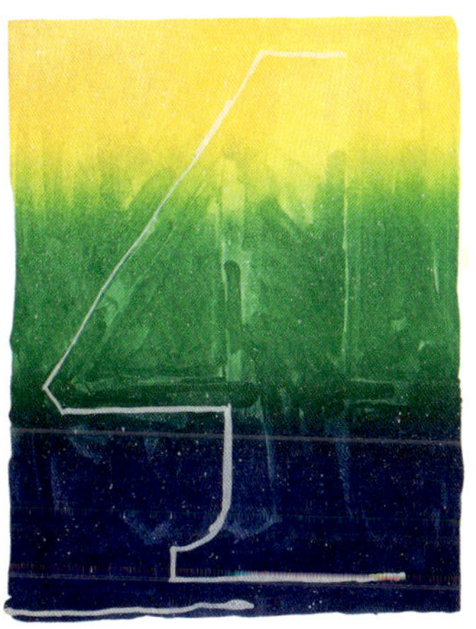

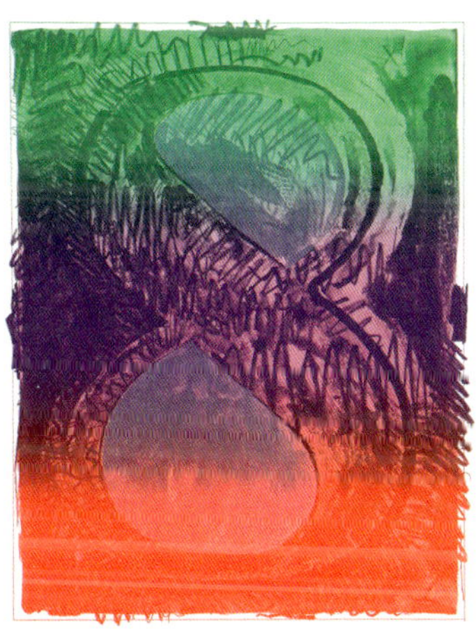

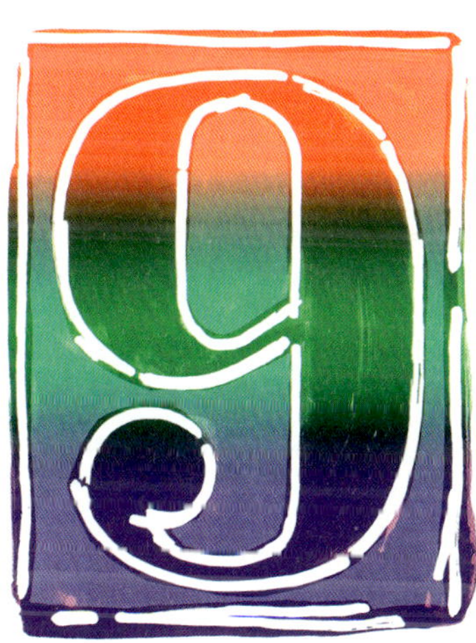

43 ***Figure 3*, from Color Numeral Series, 1969**
48 ***Figure 8*, from Color Numeral Series, 1969**

44 ***Figure 4*, from Color Numeral Series, 1969**
49 ***Figure 9*, from Color Numeral Series, 1969**

The Historic Home Makeover Audio Guide for the White House Jasper Johns Flags Exhibition

Terrance Hayes

Welcome, Friend. Thanks for selecting this handheld audio guide for the White House Jasper Johns Flags Exhibition. This exhibition is underwritten by citizens so desperate for change, they let the recently foreclosed Executive Mansion be reappropriated by a riot of artists. A selection of Johns's celebrated American flag paintings hang throughout rooms that have been transformed into dynamic art installations. Visitors are presented with colorful interactive choices throughout the tour. WARNING: Before entering you must attach a red button to your kisser, a white button to your whiffer, and a blue button to your third eye. Should you enjoy this audio guide, that for the new Thomas Jefferson Monticello Mark Rothko Exhibition is also highly recommended.

—

Jasper Johns's 1958 *Flag* in encaustic on canvas (p. 72, pl. 31) is displayed on T-shirts stacked on a wobbly table in the White House Lobby, which an urban Proto-Pop artist has converted into a gift shop. The actual Johns painting is displayed behind the checkout counter. Note how much this sensational painting favors the quixotic texture of an actual flag. Postcards as well as doormats, table mats, bath mats, loincloths, bobby socks, baby bibs, and Bibles bearing the image are also sold in the shop. Framed replicas ship within forty-eight hours. Should you have the opportunity, be sure to visit the gift shop of Frank Lloyd Wright's Fallingwater, where the innovative quilts of Faith Ringgold hang beside Sam Gilliam's draping, lyrical unstretched canvases. Visit Ernest Hemingway's historic Key West home, where packs of six-toed cats tiptoe below the soup cans of Andy Warhol.

—

Jasper Johns's 1969 *Two Flags* in graphite and collage on paper (p. 68, pl. 17) is displayed in the Roosevelt Room. Cleared of its officious officials and official decor, the space has been changed into a teleportation chamber by a brilliant ethnographic graphic artist. Two adjacent doorways are covered by two large American flags, one gray, the other gauzy. Stepping through the shaded door, you are transported to the Presidential Emergency Operations Center, where the ghosts of schoolchildren cut countless stars from newspaper. Stepping through the doorway behind the second flag, you are transported to the mouth of a manhole in the middle of the Oval Office. Please press the red button if you'd like to be transported to the Rose Garden from here. Press the white button if you'd like to be transported to the Lincoln Bathroom. Press the blue button to be transported to the Secret Attic.

—

Jasper Johns's 1957 *Flag* in pastel, graphite, and collage on gesso board (p. 67, pl. 10) is displayed in a closet of the Cabinet Room. Fifty stars float above dusky delphiniums fenced in by thirteen rows of blood and snow. The Cabinet Room holds a winding queue of visitors waiting to stand in the closet with the painting. The distinguished environmental artist behind this installation instructs you to pull a red lever to transform the closet into a military coffin draped in the flag; a white lever to make the closet a phone booth and the flag Superman's cape; or a blue lever to stand inside the mouth of a blue whale. Please press the red button if you know what this painting says about fear, the white button if you know what it says about the cost of living, or the blue button if what it says changes the longer you look at it.

—

Jasper Johns's 1958 *Flag* in graphite and graphite wash on tracing paper (p. 72, pl. 33) hangs in the James S. Brady Press Briefing Room. The room is filled with the mechanical contraptions of a master animatronic portrait artist. On the left side of the space, a pair of robot boys-in-blue white-knuckle a red-handed robot Izola Curry, the black woman who stabbed Martin Luther King Jr. at a 1958 book signing. In the right corner, you may take a selfie with a leaking robot MLK. Blood stains the ivory handle of Curry's letter opener and King's dark-blue suit. Do spend a few minutes with your nose close to Johns's remarkable flag. One critic remarked that the marks evoke Vincent van Gogh's handwriting in his letters from the Saint-Rémy asylum. Another compared them to the slashing shorthand of Cy Twombly.

—

Jasper Johns's 1959 *Untitled (Envelope)* in watercolor and graphite on a paper envelope (p. 73, pl. 38) can be viewed at a desk in the Palm Room. A pair of cartoon flags glow amid nonchalant scribbles, underscoring Johns's genius even when doodling or reading mail. Press the red button for the envelope's contents. Or sit at the desk for a palm reading by the acclaimed topiary artist who curated the space. Press the white button if you would prefer to write a love letter to the eagle in Robert Rauschenberg's *Canyon*. Press the blue button to make the room a nineteenth-century glass conservatory overgrown with palm trees. For an actual outdoor experience, consider the Georgia O'Keeffe Ghost Ranch Retrospective, where the audio guide leads you on a hiking scavenger tour of paintings displayed across all 21,000 acres of O'Keeffe's New Mexico home. We continue to expand our exhibitions of American women artists in historic homes owned by women. Plans are in development to show Agnes Martin in the childhood home of Amelia Earhart and Judy Chicago somewhere in Chicago.

—

Jasper Johns's 1960 *Flag* in plaster (p. 71, pl. 30) was hung at the top of the Grand Staircase by an unseen guerrilla artist. Its texture recalls the interior of a skull. It must be viewed quickly, as a line often forms down the stairs. Bare, the stairs are painted a somber crimson that recalls both Kennedy assassinations. Press the red button if you think Johns's flag covers bullet holes. The painting leaves the impression of stucco, a wrinkled plaster of paris. A dozen sketchy self-portraits drawn by the last president to inhabit the residence hang along the stairs. Press the white button to hear a brief podcast on the complete history of plaster. The painting's texture recalls the feel of an orthopedic Minerva cast. Press the blue button for the trapdoor at the top of the staircase.

—

Jasper Johns's 1957 *Flag* in oil on paper mounted on cardboard (p. 72, pl. 34) is displayed in the White House Basement. A conceptual martial artist celebrated for his prison installations has converted the space into a mid-century suburban man cave. The painting is displayed on a wood-panel wall above a black-and-white floor-model television. A news broadcast of Governor Orval Faubus of Arkansas marshaling truckloads of soldiers to keep nine Black kids out of high school loops on-screen. Critics debate whether the encaustic technique is intended to stir questions of America's caustic behaviors. Little rocks and cotton balls cover the floor.

—

Jasper Johns's 1957 *Flag on Orange Field* in fluorescent paint, watercolor, pastel, and graphite on paper (p. 67, pl. 11) is displayed in the Situation Room, where paintbrushes and buckets of orange paint have been placed. You are instructed to paint the walls of the room the same orange as in the Johns painting while music composed by a Grammy-winning ambient-sound artist trumpets from boom boxes. Smells of rubber and road, exhausted machines, gasoline, and metal condition the air. A woman stands on a soapbox repeatedly whispering, "Orange, you tired!" and "Aren't you tired?" into a megaphone. Please press the red button to paint the town red, the white button to paint picket fences, or the blue button to paint yourself into a corner. This viewing experience may last as long as you desire.

—

Jasper Johns's *Flag*, made of silver and worked on from 1960 to 1987 (p. 66, pl. 9), is displayed on the second floor in the Lincoln Bedroom, where a Minimalist spoken word artist dressed as a bearded female Lincoln impersonator recites an erasure of the Gettysburg Address. The central feature of the Lincoln Bedroom remains the Lincoln bed, a nearly eight-by-six-foot rosewood Victorian-style dream machine. Its enormous headboard displays Johns's flag of silver, which brings to mind an aerial map of an uproar. It is possible Johns worked on this flag during dry spells and bouts of insomnia. It is certain he worked on it for as long as it took Jean-Michel Basquiat to live and die. Visit the Basquiat exhibition at Graceland if you have the opportunity.

—

Jasper Johns's 1958 *Three Flags* in encaustic on three panels (p. 62, pl. 2) is displayed in the White House Family Elevator at the instruction of a reclusive escape artist. Its three tiers evoke the floors of the building. Only one rider is allowed in the elevator at a time. Lovers, families, tour groups, and field trippers who arrive together must wander the red and blue floors of the White House alone after this room. Your audio guide is here to help you get lost. Please press the red button if you'd like to rise up, the white button if you'd like to stay put, or the blue button if you'd like to back down. Please press the red button to back up, the white button to stay the course, or the blue button to break down. Please press the red button to wake up, the white button to stay the execution, or the blue button to bear down. Study *Three Flags* during your elevator ride. You are on your own when the doors part.

Thank you, Friend, for listening to this Historic Home Makeover Audio Guide.

2019

A Letter to Johns

R. H. Quaytman

January 29, 2020

Dear Johns,

I thought for a long while about what to write and how. Your work has been in my landscape forever. I was invited to write because, like you, my painting has been defined as conceptual or intellectual. Do you have a problem with those definitions? I know I do. But it seems to me that we both make paintings about painting. I keep coming back to a brief conversation you recount between yourself and Willem de Kooning in which he defines himself as a house painter and you as a sign painter. You understood what he meant about being a sign painter, but you weren't so sure what he meant by calling himself a house painter.[1] One thing he meant, it seems to me, was that he painted with his whole body/spirit while you paint with your mind/language. And it's true, out of all the body parts connected with painting, your mind seems the one most present. There is no apparent sexuality. This is what attracted me to your work in the beginning. It set up a closed circuit between the viewer and the painting, giving one the uncanny feeling that the painting is not only looking but almost speaking back. The painting literally starts a conversation by providing the word that defines the common—often banal—image, goading me to try to see something not banal. It works!

This vernacular form of speech I chose, of a "Dear John" letter, seems better equipped than an essay to express the emotional way I tend to think about art. Objective truth is neither assumed nor sought. Understanding what your work gives and what it does not is what interests me. A "Dear John" letter is a breakup letter that can express both love and departure. I follow your lead with perhaps a Critic's Smile in response to your provocation. The viewers and their mouths (sigh). The fact that my words could anger or hurt you concerns me, and to be honest I had to rewrite this several times, cutting back a winding vine of criticality that threatened to overtake admiration. I connect this to my newly acquired 2020 vision, which perhaps changes my thoughts about American art history in unexpected ways. It's difficult to know from a picture if the sun is setting or rising, but either way you are an American painting anthem, Jasper Johns.

The impeachment proceedings drone on in the background as I write from my eastern Connecticut studio to yours in the west. Praise drips, lines are drawn, doubt splatters, drying too quickly to correct. I'm tasked with writing about your numbers—your single digits 0–9. I draw a blank, as you knew I would when you made them. They are abstract like an Ad Reinhardt painting. So all I can do is the math, which I never could do. Does this vaunted and voluminous lifetime of work + or − or × or ÷ and, if so, does it eventually = something that changes painting? The books need to be balanced between common complicity and individual self-expression—between word and spirit, between painting dead or alive. I can't believe how deeply your paintings force me to think about what a painting is! I wish I were doing it now instead of being stuck in thoughts about your painting. Something feels, at once, uncomfortably close and yet deliciously elusive. You cite Duchamp as your model. From my perspective, your masterly touch seems perhaps closer to Picasso. The paintings wave in processional grandeur like Kennedy in his motorcade—keeping a presidential distance, ready to take the American bullet straight to the target, the real, the individual. I hate this word, but your entire oeuvre seems more important than individual works. And now is a perfect vantage point to see the longevity and connectedness of your ideas. I like the serial quality so much that I may unconsciously have stolen it. Those first seven years, as Leo Steinberg convincingly delineates, you introduced the characters that would go on to play leading roles all the way to now: flags, targets, rulers, mouths, numbers, letters, and ducks and rabbits. BRILLIANT! I also draw from that playbook. And the drama was no False Start. The start had its roots firmly connected to its ground. But as the decades passed, it seemed to grow into something not so connected, skirting the eccentric edge. Between your American flags hammered onto the walls of my art history, continuing unabated (unlike some artists I know) through the 1960s, '70s, '80s, '90s, all the way to 2020, and ending with, I suppose, zero, a human skull—presumably yours. But no, it's mine too, I must admit—by painterly implication, that is—a memento mori.

But back to basics. We share an interest in printmaking. To my mind, changes in the history of painting have always followed on the heels of changes in printing technology, ending with the photograph, which became its biggest headache. Having barely survived the invention of the printing press, it seemed reasonable that painting could also survive the photograph. Honestly, though, I have my doubts. Don't you? The computer's seamless integration of the photographic via the 0 + 1 seems to have trumped my pathetic painterly fairy tales. You were onto it, though, weren't you, with your single digits? Painters began to imitate and use the particular mechanical look of printing in an attempt to metabolize or inoculate photography's lethal perspective pull and autocratic rule. The silkscreen dot and delicious squeegee pull were incorporated as painterly marks and quickly colonized by your friends Rauschenberg, Warhol, and Lichtenstein. But listening (as it seems you did) to the chatter, your quick mind alighted on this idea: the hatch, *hachure* in French, the drawing technique developed by printers to reproduce paintings. It was a kind of mark making understood by everyone, even more common than the halftone dot. This idea brought with it the grid of Minimalism, the gesture of Expressionism, and the sign of Conceptualism. By putting the hatch marks into a grid, you turned the shadows into signs. BRAVO! Sometimes it seems painting can win every battle. The drawing of shadows on a grid is also what a photograph does. Your paintings were in sync with your time and demographic, and really, what else can we ask?

Ralph Waldo Emerson wrote, "I now require this of all pictures, that they domesticate me, not that they dazzle.... Nothing astonishes men so much as common-sense and plain dealing. All great actions have been simple, and all great pictures are."[2] Thank you, Jasper, for being an American painting anthem to that bracing American sentiment. I needed a familiar song to sing back in the twentieth century—something communal, natural, and piercing. The American flags repeat, thanks partly to you, endlessly onto my outer and inner space. One-quarter of my blood is American blue, but the red and white not so much. Maybe that's my problem with your American flag—its politics are literally enCaustic. You weren't even thinking about it that way, were you? It was a Cold War. I click on a random YouTube video and learn that your particular Americanness started in your youth, with being raised for a time with your paternal grandfather, "the largest grower of cotton and tobacco in South Carolina."[3] After brief interludes in the academy and in the military (where you picked up your graphic-art chops), you headed to New York, where you hooked up with Rauschenberg. From there, your career's growth coincided with an era of American expansionism. You and your work became icons. Obama awarded you the Presidential Medal of Freedom in 2011. You even had a cameo on *The Simpsons*! Your voice-over calling, "So long, suckers!," as you drive off leaving Homer behind.[4]

I'll never forget how good you looked then, as you metabolized so brilliantly all those complex avant-garde theories and techniques washing up on our shores. No one thought painting could handle it until you came along and managed to show how American pragmatism + realism can also = the sign/word and resonate. I mean, the way a painting can—echoing thoughts and desires like a target between a duck and a rabbit. Jasper, I was thinking, it might help our relationship if you painted another American flag now. Time is running out! If I were to paint the flag, I would first have to do research. Google, uh-huh—Betsy Ross has attracted a lot of bad press lately. (There goes the only female connected to the American Revolution.) I sigh. According to historians, she was such a skillful seamstress that she convinced George Washington to change what had previously been a six-pointed (Masonic, I assume) star to the more Christian five-pointed one. It was just easier to make, she said. The Critic Smiles: one could change the stars back to the six-pointed version, perhaps, in homage to all those Judaic thoughts—especially ones about lethal idolatry, doubt, memory, and abstraction.

I began to depart from American art history like it was a house on fire the day I left college. I never felt at home in it. I like New York, the world's only subway stop, but America in general, not so much. Most famous American artists, I always say, come from and reference America's lower middle class. The results, from Warhol to Koons, often seem to magically negotiate economic inequality in the structure of the art world. The few artists I felt inexplicable urges to follow were either from somewhere else or recognized as important only after leaving the States. I mean important like you. But being the feminist that, despite myself, I am, I do have to credit Betsy Ross. She showed us how important it is to have a pattern, a job, and an opinion. There are so many chatterers around the quilt—around the painting. Back then, around your painting, were mostly brilliant, gay white men. When I imagine what it must have felt like to be you—painting under the blazing eternal sun of the American dream—I remember. No need for a response, though. Your response is your painting. Your reticence is so attractive in its moody defiance because, let's get real, it's the way you and I both like it. Most people don't care much about an artist's intentions—they seem only to care, justifiably, in confirming what they already know and only then what they see. They love it when they can repeat the word that the painting seems to say. I know I do. Anyway, thank you for thinking of that. I did miss a distant horizon though, and maybe you did too, because what followed seems to enact a short story of yourself as a painter with only a few tools. Nothing sexual but very psychological. Luckily, I had a copy of Samuel Beckett's *Complete Short Prose* handy, because I saw in one late-night image search that you had illustrated a book of Beckett's short-and-sweet "Fizzle" stories.[5] So I read them and realized that they explain something about the spirit of your paintings, which have the aura of language being tested or asked over and over to someone whom they suspect will never hear it. They fizzle, as if knocking against the picture plane over and over to communicate something, and I see it, I see the history, the references, the self-imposed rules. "He will never say I, because of me."[6] But before those days, around the quilting/painting, you were listening. And it's a good thing, too, because how wonderfully brilliant for a moment New York was. All those Jewish intellectuals and nonheterosexuals racing to escape every other place on earth, bringing their ideas that flared so hot. I honor it, I do. Maybe it is you who is the simple house painter—or, better yet, like Ross, a stitcher. But that can't be right because, as a painter, I have been guided by your signs, internally, at the edges of outlines, where words end.

That's all she wrote,

R. H. Quaytman

1 Jasper Johns, statement on Willem de Kooning (January 1983), *Art Journal* 48, no. 3 (Fall 1989): 232; reprinted in Kirk Varnedoe, ed., *Jasper Johns: Writings, Sketchbook Notes, Interviews* (New York: Museum of Modern Art, 1996), 23.
2 Ralph Waldo Emerson, "Art," https://emersoncentral.com/texts/essays-first-series/art/ (accessed February 3, 2020).
3 South Carolina Hall of Fame, Myrtle Beach, "1989 Inductee: Jasper Johns," https://youtu.be/H51N8J45UrA (accessed February 3, 2020).
4 Johns voiced the character of himself in the episode "Mom and Pop Art," which first aired April 11, 1999.
5 Samuel Beckett and Jasper Johns, *Foirades/Fizzles* (London: Petersburg Press, 1976).
6 Samuel Beckett, "Fizzle 3: Afar a Bird," in *The Complete Short Prose, 1929-1989*, ed. S. E. Gontarski (New York: Grove, 2007), 233.

Display

Throughout his nearly seventy-year career, Jasper Johns has focused more on making art than on making exhibitions. This might seem unremarkable were it not for the fact that soon after he began showing publicly, many of the artists in his milieu—indeed, even in the stable of his New York gallery—began to treat the exhibition itself as a calibrated mise-en-scène in which to premiere precisely interrelated works. In the decade following Johns's 1958 debut at Manhattan's Leo Castelli Gallery, that venue hosted, for example, Frank Stella's tightly orchestrated presentations of permutational paintings (first notched, then angled, then shaped); James Rosenquist's wraparound mural *F-111* (1964–65); and Andy Warhol's show of canvases printed with the same flower image in various sizes and colors, hung in a modular grid like so much merchandise. The series and its display nearly trumped their constituent parts, and the trend toward visual or thematic unity and architectural integration has only since intensified.

Johns's works, by contrast, betray an air of self-containment, even if their recurring motifs and often sculptural treatment stress their interconnectedness to one another and to the world beyond. Each object—if not necessarily its subject—feels particular and considered, rather than a version of a type. Yet they also frequently participate in larger bodies of work that can themselves be hard to define, given that Johns's series tend to unfold prolongedly with overlaps and interruptions, rather than as successive, circumscribed campaigns. He frequently emphasizes as much in shows of his new work, which usually eschew cohesive imagery and organization. As far back as his very first solo outing at Castelli in 1958, one would have encountered various motifs, media, and scales. In subsequent exhibitions, he wedged disparate paintings atop one another, mixed abstraction and figuration, and included dissimilar images from the same moment. Accordingly, curators working with the artist are often surprised by his apparent indifference to the installation process, his blinkered attention seemingly focused more within a work's bounds than on its company or disposition in space.

Johns is, however, keenly attuned to the display of his works, and two of his early Castelli shows are notable in terms of the striking interdependence of their parts and lucidity of design. In these installations—staged in 1960 and 1968 and re-created, respectively, at the Philadelphia Museum of Art and the Whitney Museum of American Art—Johns articulated refined pictorial statements on his own work, making explicitly legible his artistic methods and conceptual concerns. Located on the second floor of a townhouse at 4 East Seventy-Seventh Street, the space was intimate by contemporary standards, measuring roughly 25 ½ by 21 ½ feet, with ceilings just 12 ½ feet high. Johns used this compressed volume to immerse visitors in a dramatic cohesive set piece. The 1960 exhibition featured eight paintings in collage and oil or encaustic on canvas, all visually united by their busy brushwork in palettes of either black, white, and gray, or the primary colors plus orange, gray, and white. Only his second show at the gallery, it must have seemed like a rebuttal to the first. As Hannah Yohalem notes in this volume, Johns supplanted his quotidian motifs with the seamless "look" of Abstract Expressionist pictures.[1] Yet closer inspection revealed objects and signs embedded within the painted surfaces. Words emerge from or dissolve into the skittish fields of *Out the Window* and *Device Circle* (both 1959; p. 100, pls. 3, 7); the temperature of *Thermometer* (1959; p. 100, pl. 6) awaits being read; stenciled labels name or misidentify colors; and a painted window shade reveals as much as it obscures. If each canvas acts as a meditation on visual perception and its limits, so too did the exhibition as a whole. The works were carefully choreographed around the gallery in a play of repetition and variation, so that their compositional and linguistic gambits ricocheted and reverberated around the space. The polychrome *False Start* (1959; p. 99, pl. 2) and *Out the Window*, for example, were hung kitty-corner to their grisaille cognates *Jubilee* and *Reconstruction* (both 1959; p. 98, pl. 1; and p. 100, pl. 4). Through their installation, Johns paradoxically posited his paintings as both totalities in themselves and part of an evolving series, the definitive utterance of a perpetually inconclusive statement that beguiled the eye and mind.

In 1968, Johns presented an even more holistic ensemble of six paintings, this time with architecture itself operating as a meta-theme within the works and across the show. The overall impression was lighter and more atmospheric than those of his previous Castelli solos, with open expanses, broad gestures, hard whites, and luminous bursts of lemon and pink. No doubt influenced by the serial structures and repeating silkscreens employed by other artists of the period, Warhol most conspicuously, Johns repurposed motifs and modes of making from one work to the next. Four paintings bear the imprint of the same silkscreen with an inscription indicating that the fork in the source image should be reproduced "7" long," presumably at actual size, although in fact the image is twice that length, wryly pointing to the disconnect between real and pictorial space. Yet Johns also sutures the two with the image of a ruler at scale that recurs throughout the paintings. Its insistence on "actual size" is emphasized in the direct impressions of window frames in *Studio II* (1966; p. 106, pl. 2) and *Harlem Light* (1967; pp. 104–5, pl. 1). They play on the trope of painting as an illusionistic portal onto other realms while simultaneously referencing the actual built environment. The motif of flagstones in *Harlem Light* and *Wall Piece* (1968; p. 106, pl. 3) reinforces the sense that these expansive canvases operate as quasi-architectural elements. Rendered from Johns's memory of a wall in Harlem painted to look as if it were made of stones, the shapes are built up with thick impasto in contrast to the thinly applied adjacent passages. Throughout all these works, airy color and open brushwork tense against orthogonal borders and interior elements. Figuring sky within frames and walls within canvases, the paintings redouble and disrupt their own structural logic, as well as that of the gallery that physically contains them.

—Scott Rothkopf, with Carlos Basualdo, Sarah B. Vogelman, and Lauren Young

1 Hannah Yohalem, "On Display: Jasper Johns's Castelli Exhibitions," in this volume, 108.

Display

Leo Castelli, 1960

PHILADELPHIA MUSEUM OF ART

1 ***Jubilee*, 1959**
Oil and collage on canvas
60 × 44 in. (152.4 × 111.8 cm)
Private collection

2 ***False Start*, 1959**
Oil on canvas
67 ½ × 53 ⅛ in. (171.5 × 134.9 cm)
Private collection

3 ***Out the Window*, 1959***
Encaustic and collage on canvas (three panels)
54 ½ × 40 ⅛ in. (138.4 × 101.9 cm) overall
Private collection of David Geffen, Los Angeles

4 ***Reconstruction*, 1959**
Encaustic and collage on canvas
60 × 44 ½ in. (152.4 × 113 cm)
The Cleveland Museum of Art; purchase, Accessions Reserve Fund, and Andrew R. and Martha Holden Jennings Fund, 1973.28

5 ***Highway*, 1959**
Encaustic and collage on canvas with objects
75 ½ × 61 ½ in. (191.8 × 156.2 cm)
Private collection

6 ***Thermometer*, 1959**
Oil on canvas and wood with objects (two panels)
52 ⅛ × 39 ¼ in. (132.4 × 99.7 cm) overall
Seattle Art Museum; gift of the Virginia and Bagley Wright Collection, in honor of the museum's 50th year, 91.97

7 ***Device Circle*, 1959**
Encaustic and collage on canvas with objects
40 × 40 in. (101.6 × 101.6 cm)
Collection of Andrew and Denise Saul

8 ***Shade*, 1959***
Encaustic and collage on canvas with objects
52 ⅛ × 39 in. (132.4 × 99.1 cm)
The Ludwig Museum in the Russian Museum, Saint Petersburg; Ludwig Donation

Leo Castelli, 1968

WHITNEY MUSEUM OF AMERICAN ART

1 ***Harlem Light*, 1967**
Oil and collage on canvas (four panels)
85 × 172 ⅛ in. (215.9 × 437.2 cm) overall
Seattle Art Museum; partial and promised gift of Jon and Mary Shirley, in honor of the 75th Anniversary of the Seattle Art Museum

2 ***Studio II*, 1966**
Oil on canvas
70 ½ × 125 ⅜ in. (179.1 × 318.5 cm)
Whitney Museum of American Art, New York; gift of the family of Victor W. Ganz in his memory, 92.4

3 ***Wall Piece*, 1968**
Oil and collage on canvas (three panels)
72 × 110 ¼ in. (182.9 × 280 cm) overall
Collection of the artist; on long-term loan to the San Francisco Museum of Modern Art, 1978

4 ***Screen Piece*, 1967**
Oil on canvas
72 × 50 in. (182.9 × 127 cm)
Private collection

5 ***Screen Piece 2*, 1968**
Oil on canvas
72 × 50 in. (182.9 × 127 cm)
Collection of Barbara and Richard S. Lane

6 ***Screen Piece 3 (The Sonnets)*, 1968**
Oil on canvas
72 × 50 in. (182.9 × 127 cm)
Nerman Family Collection

Leo Castelli, 1960

PHILADELPHIA MUSEUM OF ART

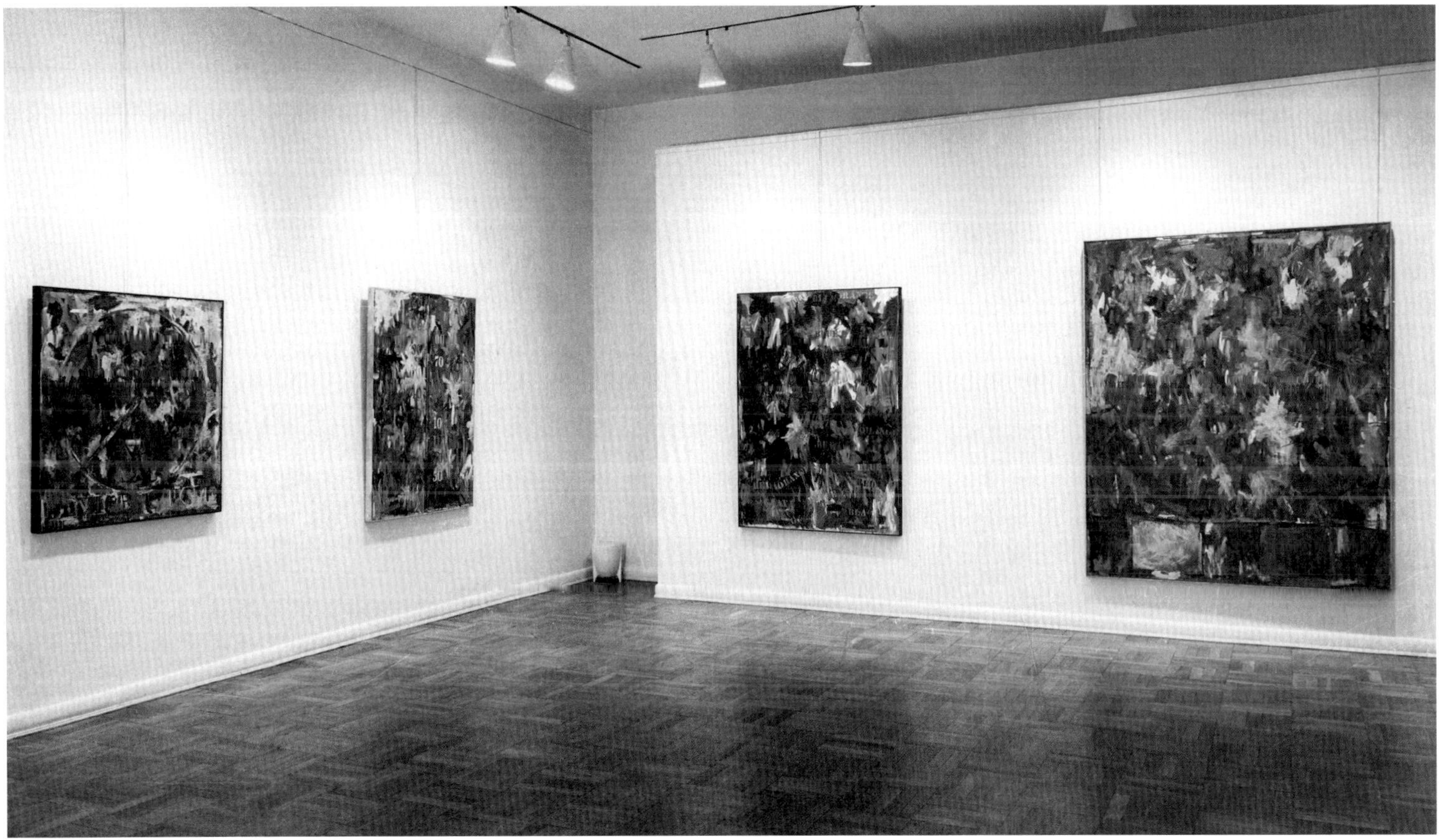

Installation view, Leo Castelli Gallery, New York, 1960

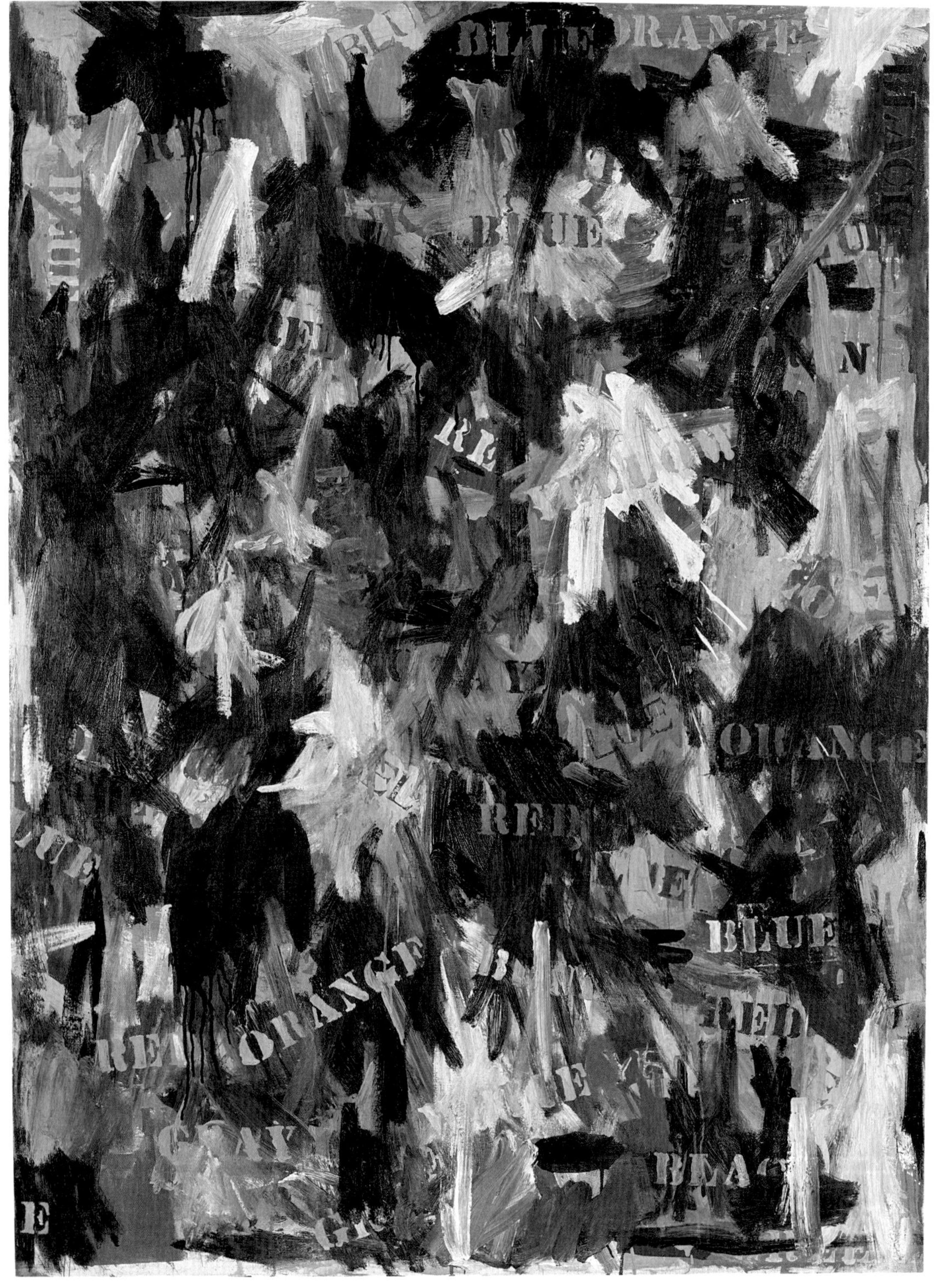

1 ***Jubilee***, **1959**

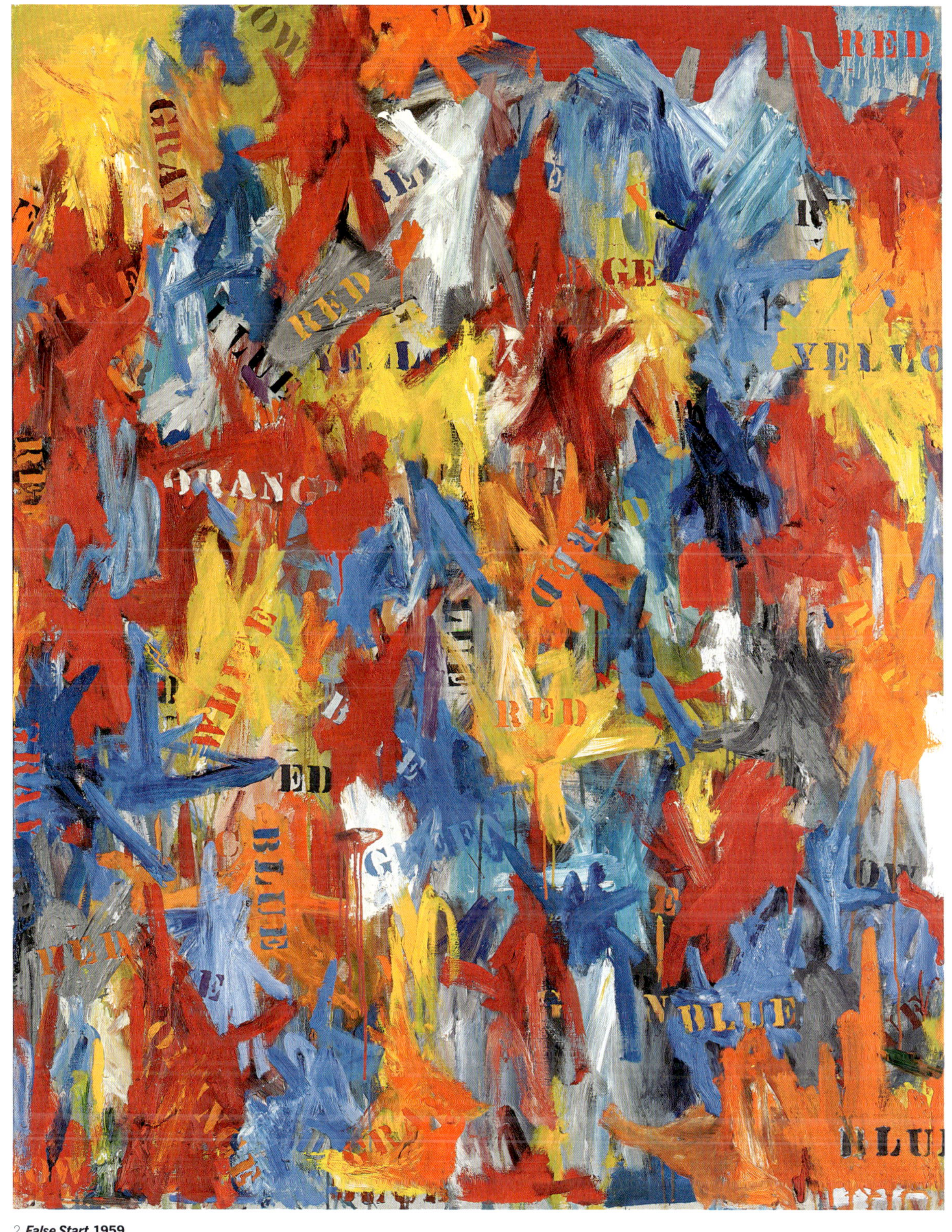

2 ***False Start***, 1959

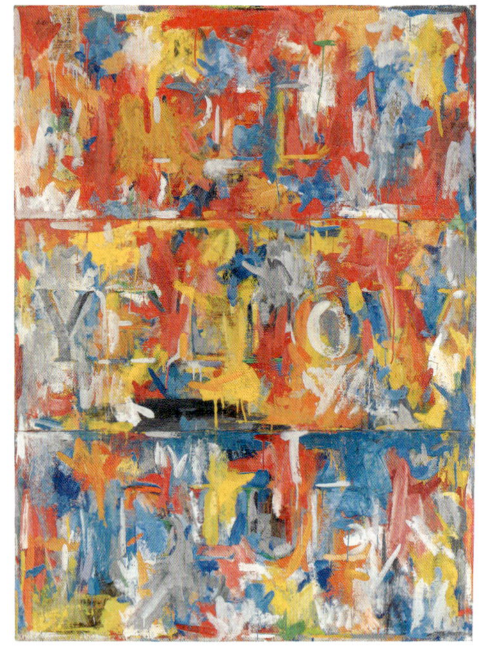

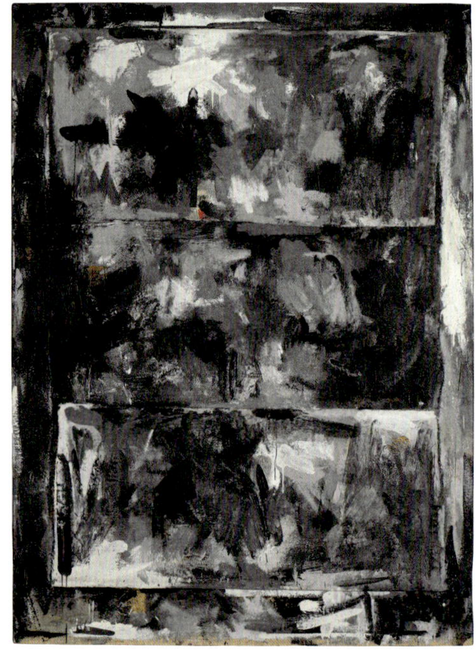

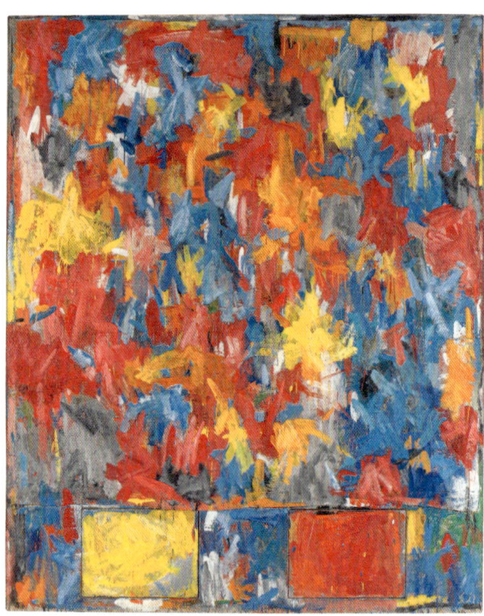

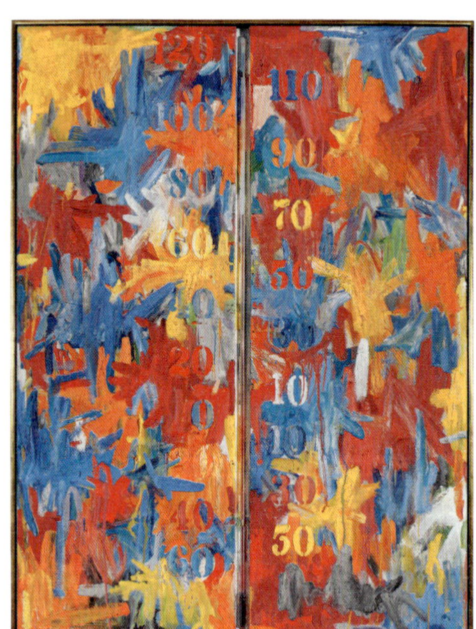

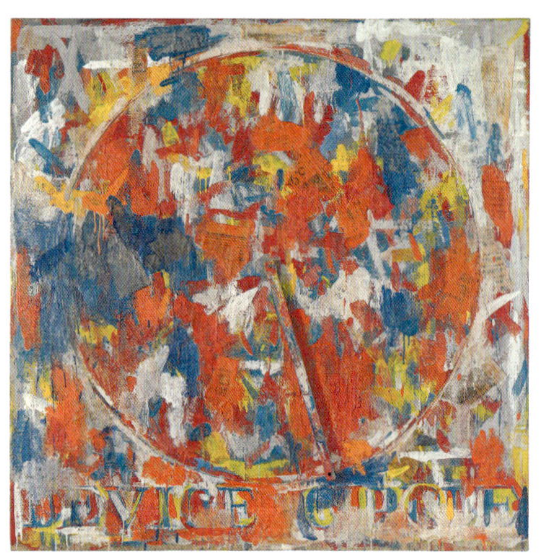

3 ***Out the Window***, **1959**

4 ***Reconstruction***, **1959**

5 ***Highway***, **1959**

6 ***Thermometer***, **1959**

7 ***Device Circle***, **1959**

8 ***Shade***, **1959**

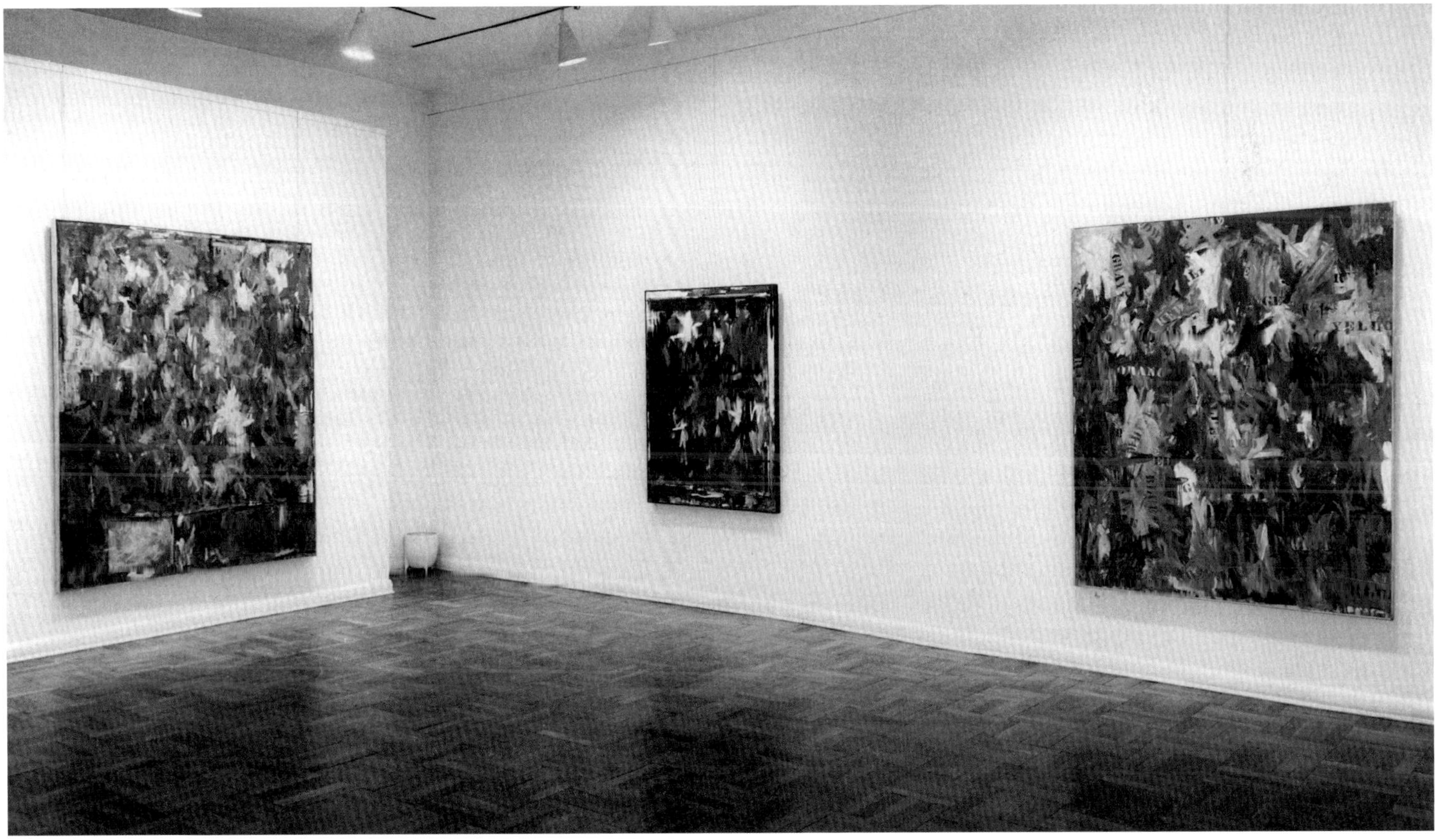

Installation view, Leo Castelli Gallery, New York, 1960

Leo Castelli, 1968

WHITNEY MUSEUM OF AMERICAN ART

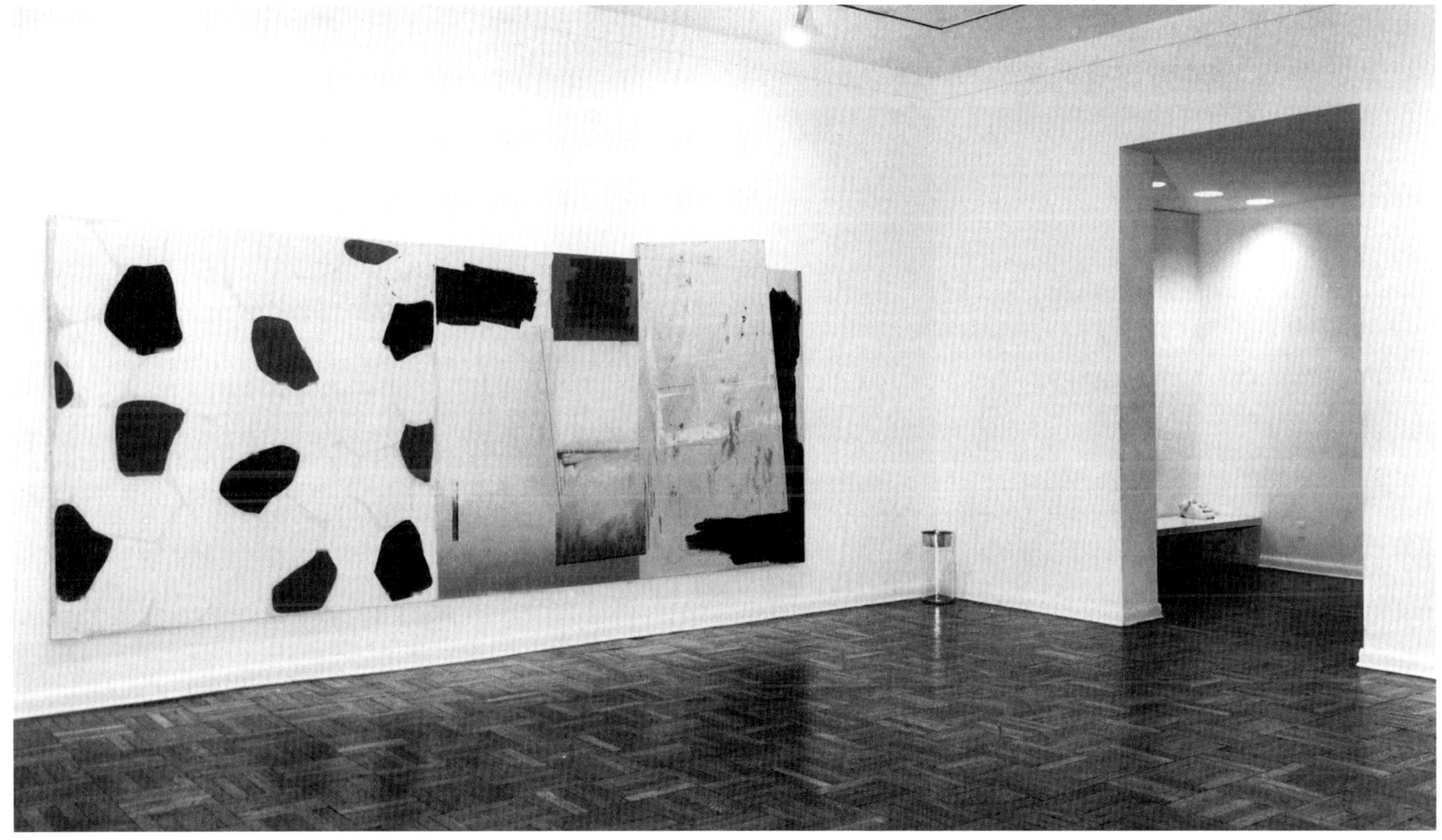

Installation view, Leo Castelli Gallery, New York, 1968

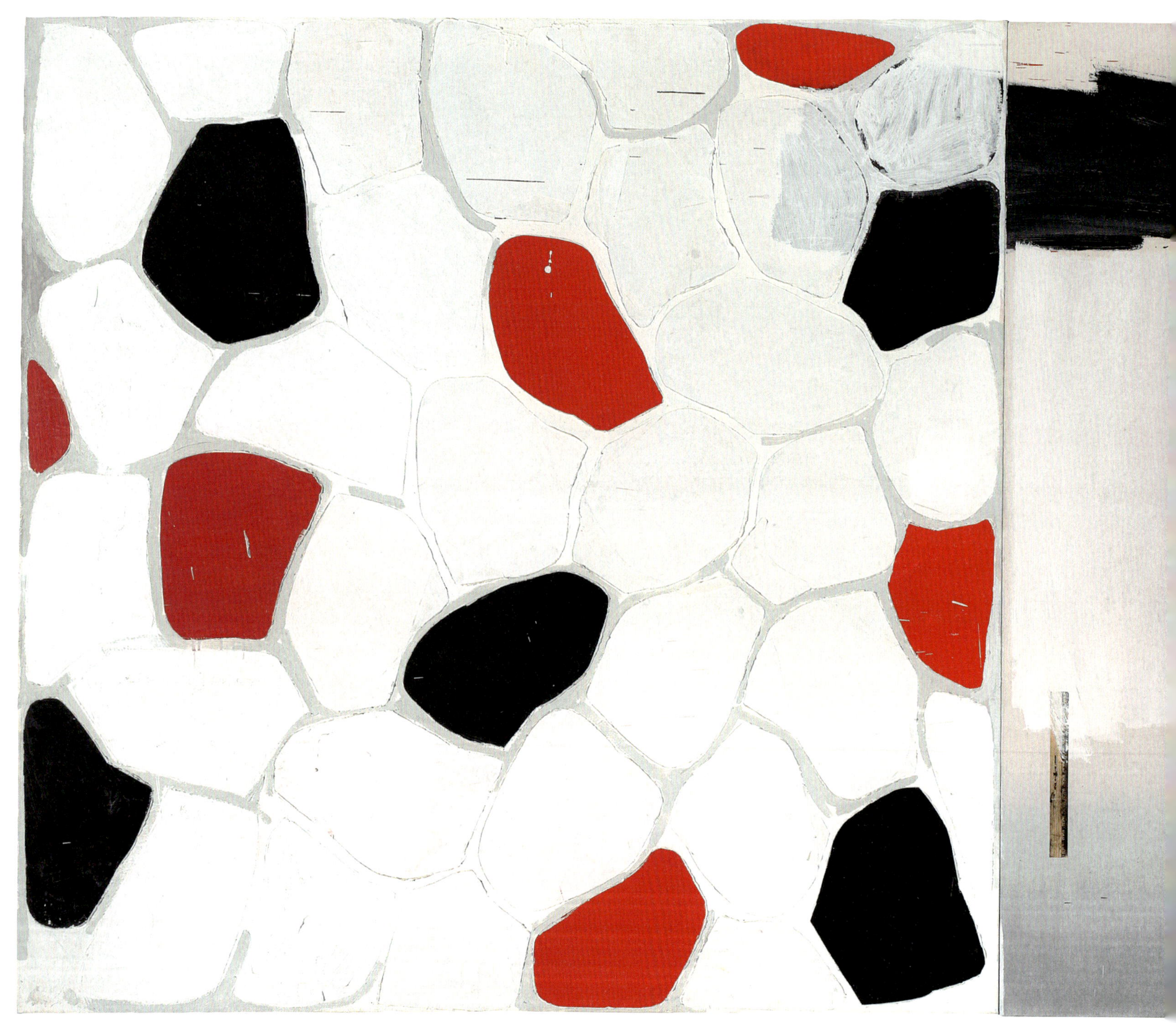

1 *Harlem Light*, 1967

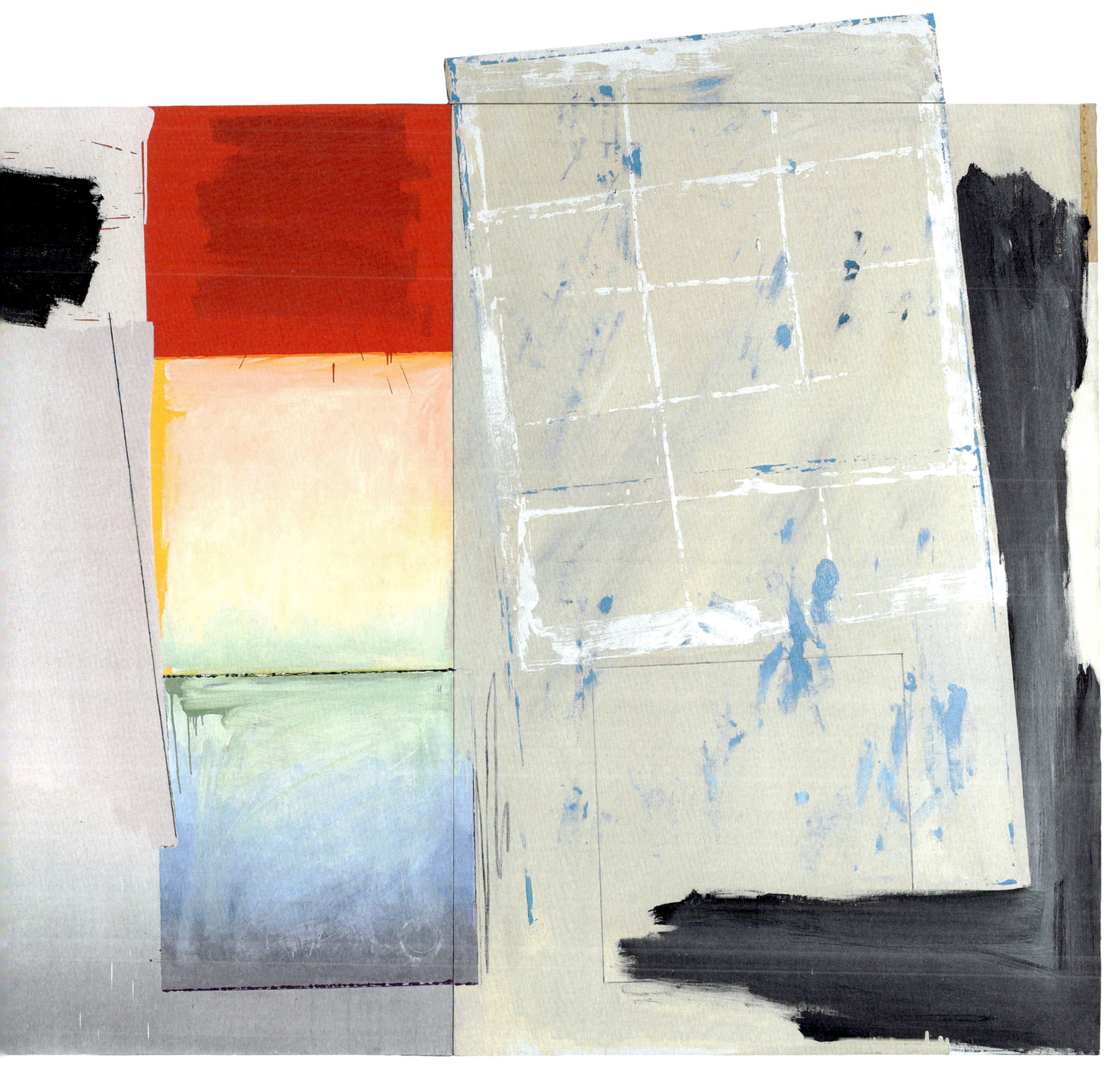

LEO CASTELLI, 1968

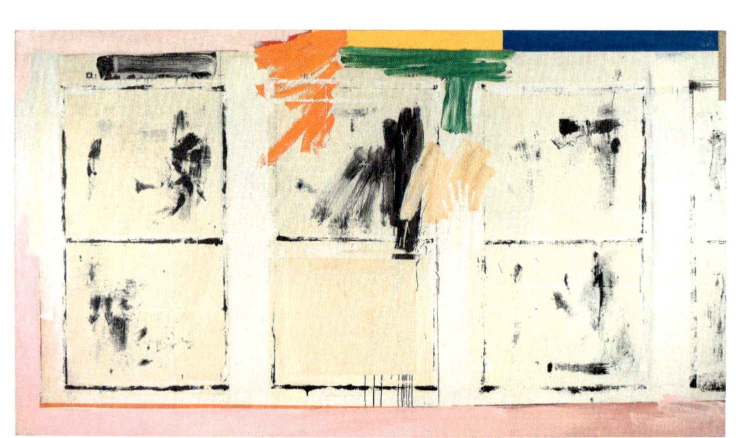

2 ***Studio II*, 1966**

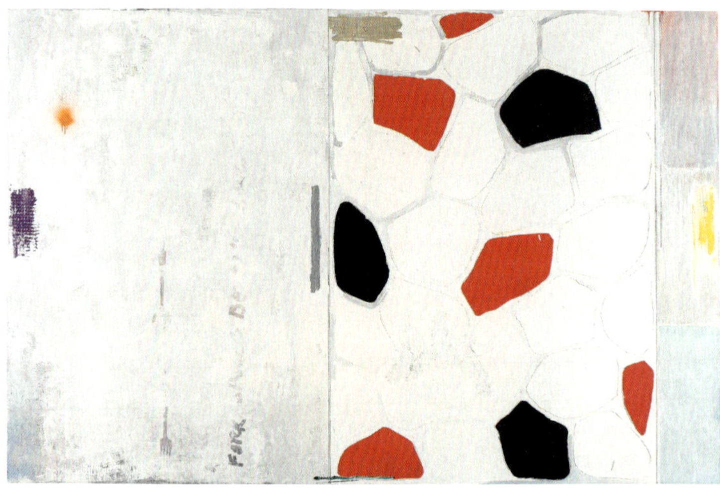

3 ***Wall Piece*, 1968**

4 ***Screen Piece*, 1967**

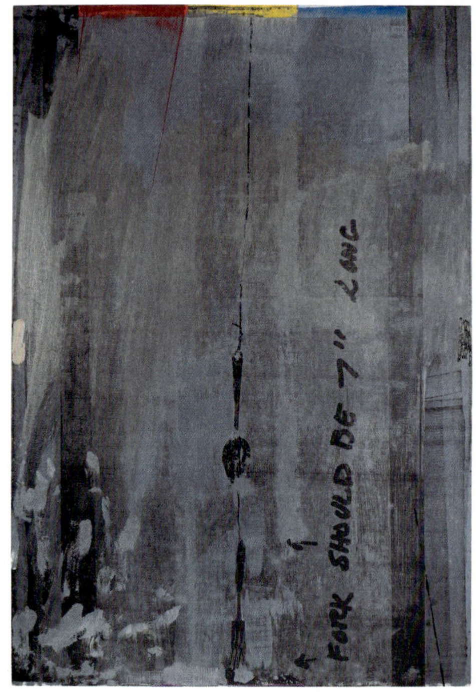

5 ***Screen Piece 2*, 1968**

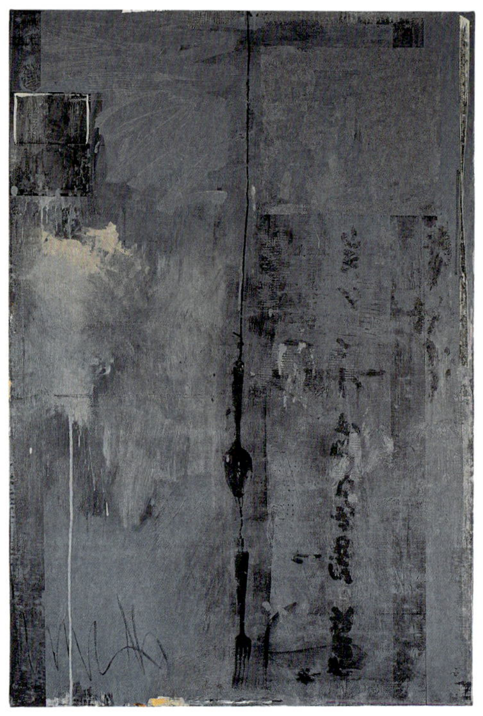

6 ***Screen Piece 3 (The Sonnets)*, 1968**

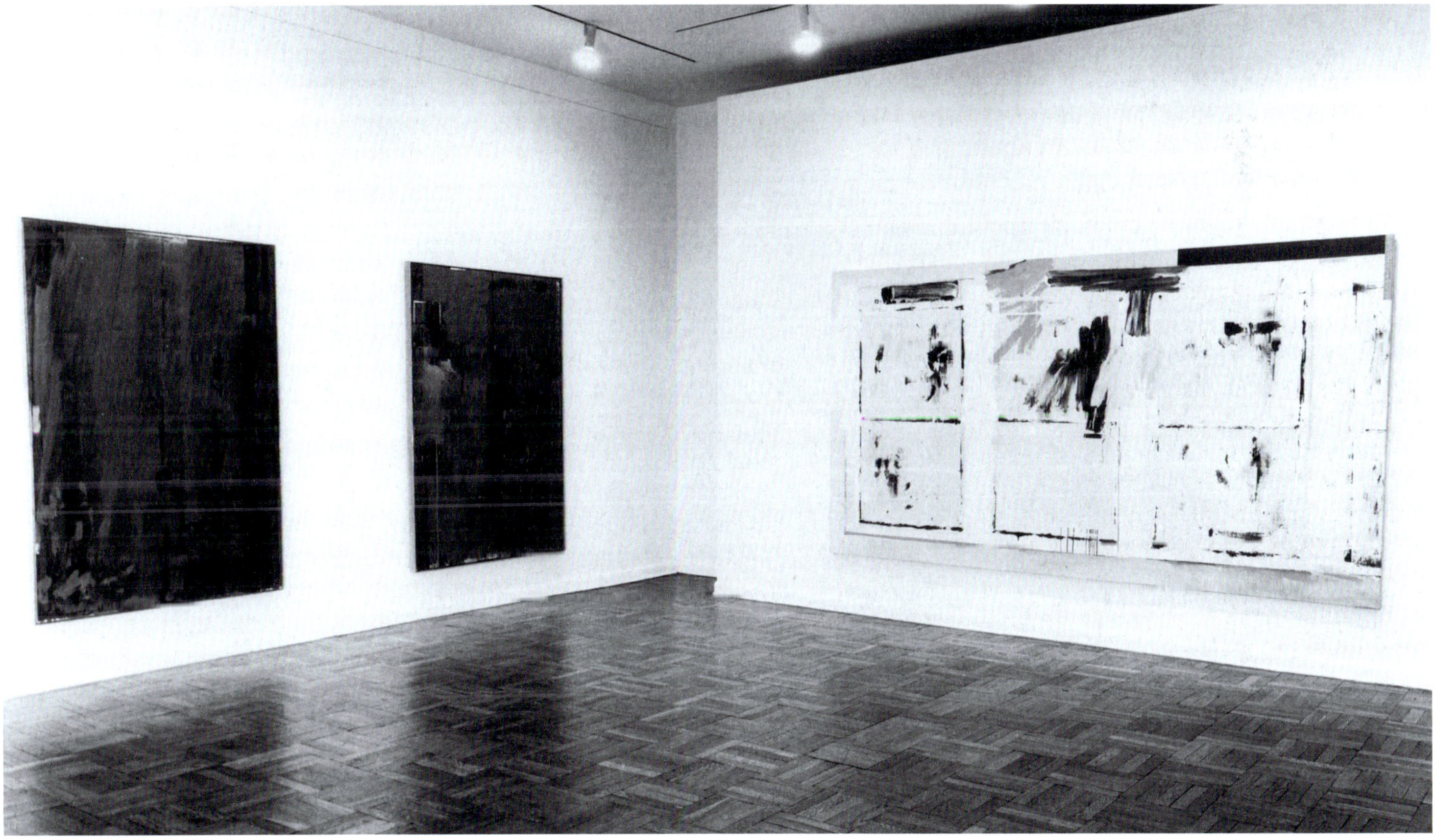

Installation view, Leo Castelli Gallery, New York, 1968

On Display: Jasper Johns's Castelli Exhibitions

Hannah Yohalem

Jasper Johns's first solo exhibition, on view at the Leo Castelli Gallery in New York from January 20 to February 8, 1958, catapulted this little-known artist, whose work had appeared in a few small group exhibitions, to nearly instantaneous international recognition. The Museum of Modern Art (MoMA) expressed an immediate interest: Director Alfred H. Barr and curator Dorothy Miller purchased three paintings from that first exhibition for the museum's collection and arranged for the architect Philip Johnson to purchase a fourth to donate in the future; curator Frank O'Hara invited Johns to be one of three "young American artists" exhibited in the Central Pavilion at the 1958 Venice Biennale; and Miller included Johns in MoMA's exhibition *Sixteen Americans* in 1959-60.[1]

The Castelli exhibition garnered significant press coverage for Johns as well. *Target with Four Faces* (1955; p. 42, pl. 2) appeared on the cover of *ARTnews*. An article in *Newsweek* on Johns and Robert Rauschenberg crowed that both young artists "now live on their sales."[2] Indeed, Johns sold everything in the Castelli show except *Target with Plaster Casts* (1955; p. 168, fig. 1), which Castelli subsequently purchased himself, and *White Flag* (1955; p. 64, pl. 4), which Johns kept.[3] Within six years of this breakout solo exhibition, New York's Jewish Museum would hold the first of Johns's career retrospectives.

The works that prompted this extraordinary reception included now-iconic Johnsian images such as American flags, targets, and numbers. Installation photographs of that first Castelli show (figs. 1, 2) reveal their repetitions and variations: *Flag* (1954-55; p. 66, pl. 7), with its traditional red, white, and blue, hung diagonally across from the larger *White Flag*, while a small *White Target* (1957; p. 46, pl. 6) appeared next to the much larger *Green Target* (1955). Each work stood alone as a complete image simultaneously bound to the others by what was then, in the face of Abstract Expressionism's dominance, a shocking iconicity paired with the meticulous application of graphite or encaustic paint and torn paper.

If visitors came to Johns's second solo exhibition at the Castelli Gallery, in February 1960, expecting to see more of the push and pull between familiar images and their painstaking rendering on canvas and paper, they were sorely disappointed. No flags, numbers, or targets—indeed, no "images" at all—appeared among the large paintings. Instead, clusters of muddy primary and secondary colors or grays, blacks, and whites covered the surface of each work. Johns, who selected and arranged the show himself, surrounded viewers with these painterly gestures at once random and uniform, the same technique applied to work after work throughout the gallery.[4] While it diverged from Johns's previous solo show, the exhibition would have announced itself at first glance as a return to the type of monographic display of abstract painting familiar to the New York art world. Most of the Abstract Expressionists had developed what art historian Yve-Alain Bois calls a "signature style," a trademark "look" and paint handling that not only belied the supposed spontaneity of their gestures but also generated gallery shows full of intimately related

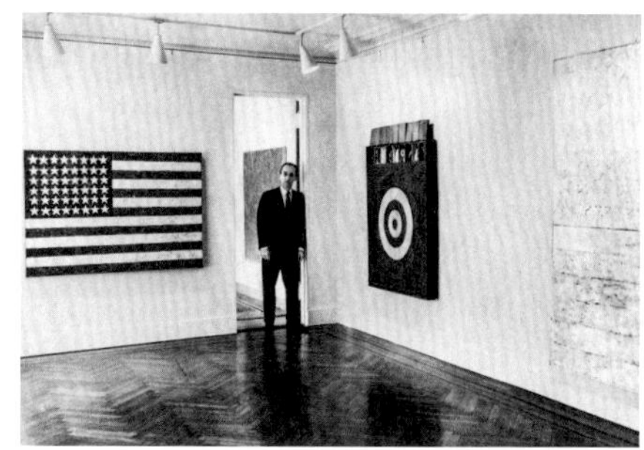

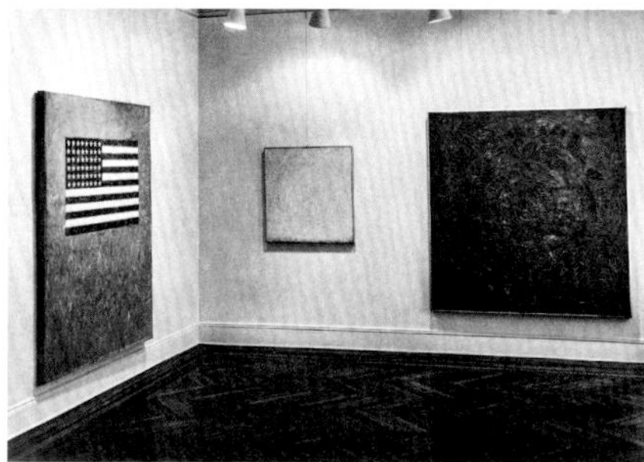

Figs. 1, 2 **Installation views, *Jasper Johns*, Leo Castelli Gallery on East Seventy-Seventh Street, New York, January 20–February 8, 1958**
Archives of American Art, Smithsonian Institution, Washington, DC; Leo Castelli Gallery records, c. 1880-2000, bulk 1957-99, box 48, folder 69

works.[5] Entering Robert Motherwell's 1952 exhibition at the Samuel M. Kootz Gallery, Jackson Pollock's in 1955 at the Sidney Janis Gallery, or Willem de Kooning's at Janis in 1959, viewers would have encountered rooms full of stylistically united works: respectively, floating asymmetrical shapes on white grounds, skeins, or thick slashes of paint (figs. 3-5). The repetition of paint clusters within and across every work in Johns's second Castelli show fits this model.

The familiar exhibition format thus cued visitors to look at Johns's new group of works *as paintings*, to return to a type of looking not predetermined by the immediate recognizability of his earlier images. Accepting this invitation, visitors to Johns's exhibition would have found that the firework-like explosions of pigment covering these 1959 canvases in fact embed disparate objects, numbers, and words within and atop their surfaces. The stenciled names of colors emerge from behind or overlay the gestural strokes in *Jubilee* (p. 98, pl. 1), *False Start* (p. 99, pl. 2), and *Out the Window* (p. 100, pl. 3). For *Device Circle*

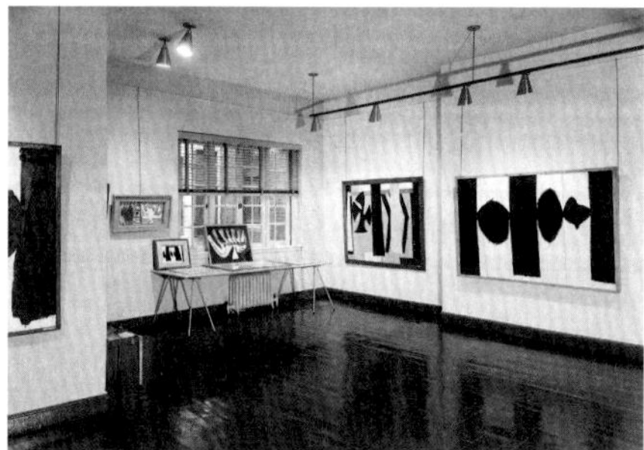

Fig. 3 **Installation view, *Robert Motherwell: Paintings, Drawings, and Collages*, Samuel M. Kootz Gallery, New York, April 1–19, 1952**

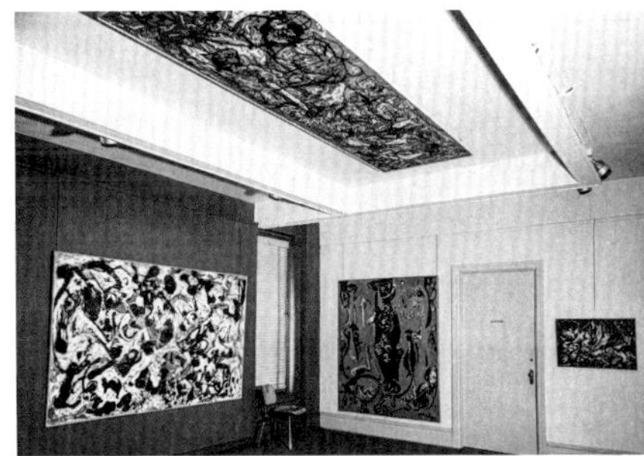

Fig. 4 **Installation view, *Jackson Pollock*, Sidney Janis Gallery, New York, November 28–December 31, 1955**
Archives of American Art, Smithsonian Institution, Washington, DC; Jackson Pollock and Lee Krasner papers, c. 1905–84

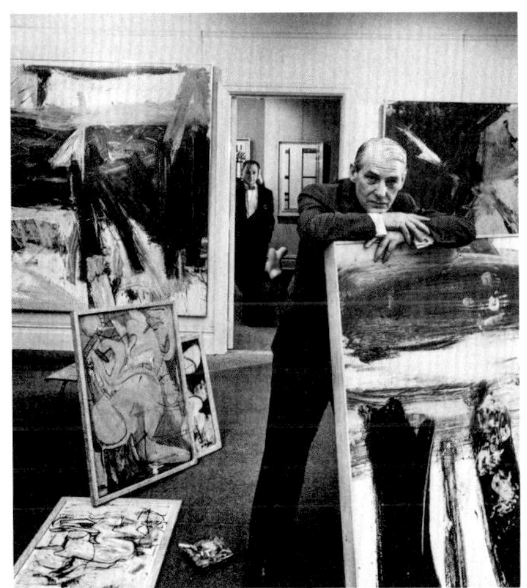

Fig. 5 **Willem de Kooning at the Sidney Janis Gallery, New York, 1959, with Janis in the background**
Photograph by Arnold Newman (American, 1918–2006)

(p. 100, pl. 7), Johns affixed a wooden slat to the surface of the canvas, rotated it to create an incised line, and then left it there after the paint dried. The text "Device Circle" captions the form and object above it.[6] The stenciled numbers in *Thermometer* (p. 100, pl. 6) make legible the movement of the mercury within the instrument, which Johns inserted into a groove between two stretched canvases. He even included pins along the painting's inner edges, their minute round heads marking the temperature more precisely than the large numerals. The two small, stretched rectangular canvases in the lower portion of *Highway* (p. 100, pl. 5), their dirty yellow and orangey red evoking the blur of head- and taillights from a moving car, are harder to see because Johns inserted them flush with the surface of the painting. Similarly, in *Reconstruction* (p. 100, pl. 4) and *Shade* (p. 100, pl. 8), the paint nearly camouflages the folded canvas and closed shade; only the edges differentiate these objects from the underlying painting.

As a group, the works in Johns's 1960 Castelli show communicate that in addition to being painted surfaces full of visual interest, paintings are objects in space that can, for example, measure and respond to changes in the room. For Johns, paintings include and can therefore expand into the narrow depth created by the stretcher bars between the surface of the canvas and the wall, as well as into the space directly in front of the canvas. As objects in their own right, Johns argues, paintings can serve as a support for heavier objects, not just paint or collage. Since paintings have a surface on which words can be stenciled, they can be read as well as looked at. As a record of their making, they can include not just paint but also the tools used in their production.

Unlike Rauschenberg, who moved fully into the third dimension with the Combines he was creating at the time, Johns continued to adhere to the basic material limits of traditional easel painting. If modernist painting, as famously articulated by the critic Clement Greenberg, was understood to have whittled away all unnecessary connections to the world beyond the canvas, Johns incorporated everyday objects and text to emphasize painting's place in the world of things and thereby posit a more expansive and active role for the medium.[7] The paintings Johns made through the 1960s, which were often multipaneled with stenciled text and rulers, cups, paintbrushes, and cutlery attached to them, further developed this vision of painting freed from the conventions of the medium while still contained by its material limits.

While the works in the second solo Castelli exhibition functioned as a series of engagements with painting writ large, they were also interrelated. Depending on the criteria, one could create different groupings among them. For example, *Reconstruction* echoed *Shade* in format and palette, while it shared its tripartite structure with *Out the Window*, whose text, in turn, linked it to *Jubilee* and *False Start*. The play of similarity and difference, most obvious in the way Johns's new painterly style appeared sometimes in gray scale and at other times in color, would have prompted visitors to draw comparisons. *Device Circle*'s encaustic and collage must have looked particularly encrusted and textural hung alongside *Thermometer*'s fluid oil paint. *Jubilee* and *False Start*, displayed so they could not be seen simultaneously, both raised and stymied the question of replication, testing viewers' memories by tempting them to compare the works word for word and stroke for stroke. Together, the two paintings also heightened the complexity of the misalignment between the color names and the shades over which they are layered, as well as the often-conflicting colors and referents of the words themselves.

In interviews and published sketchbook notes from throughout his career, Johns has acknowledged his interest in this type of shifting focus, stating it perhaps most clearly in 1978: "One assumes that one's relationship to the work is the correct or only possible one. But with a slight reemphasis of elements, one finds that one can behave very differently toward it, see it in a different way. I tend to focus upon a relationship between oneself and a thing that is flexible, that can be one thing at one time and something else at another time. I find it interesting, although it may not be very reassuring."[8] Through the selection and arrangement of his paintings in 1960 to highlight similarities and differences across the works, Johns allowed visitors to experience this type of perceptual and conceptual flexibility at the level of the installation.

He selected a similarly cross-referential group of paintings for a solo exhibition at the Castelli Gallery eight years later, in late February 1968. Johns hung only six works in the show. Their production spanned the years 1966 to 1968, and the works shared a limited selection of motifs. Most obvious is an image of a hanging spoon and fork accompanied by the handwritten text "fork should be 7" long," which appears in varying color saturations in the three versions of *Screen Piece* from 1967 and 1968 (p. 106, pls. 4–6) and again as a ghostly rendering in *Wall Piece* (1968; p. 106, pl. 3). *Wall Piece*, in turn, shares its abstract pattern of red, black, and white forms with *Harlem Light* (1967; pp. 104–5, pl. 1) and the imprint of a screen door with *Studio II* (1966; p. 106, pl. 2). Smaller shared elements proliferate as well. A screenprinted ruler measures the top corner of *Studio II*, *Harlem Light*, and *Screen Piece*, becoming the image of a twisted yardstick in *Screen Piece 3*. An even more washed-out version of the blocks of red, yellow, and blue that draw attention near the center of *Harlem Light* flanks the right side of *Wall Piece*; a narrow band of the primary colors peeks out at the top of *Screen Piece 2*; and a muted red, mustard yellow, and deep midnight blue form the top border in *Studio II*. These repetitions, always with significant variation, provide insight into an essential element of Johns's practice: how he arranged and rearranged images or compositional fragments over time while also testing them out in relation to different materials, forms, and actions.

In this group of six works, Johns displayed how he played with the material possibilities of screens of various types—ranging from the window screens and screen doors of his studio to silkscreens traditionally used in printmaking—to explore and blur the distinction between image and object and to experiment with imprinting as an operation.[9] In *Studio II*, which faced visitors as they entered the Castelli Gallery, a handprint is barely visible to the right of the central window frame. It is both a direct mark left by a hand covered in wet paint and an image of a hand.[10] Similarly, the repeated grids are at once images of windows with nothing visible through them and the highly physical traces left by the direct impression of window screens covered with wet paint and pressed onto the canvas.[11]

The three versions of *Screen Piece* come at and undermine the image/object divide from another direction. Johns used an oversize silkscreen to transfer the images of the hanging spoon and fork to the canvas. Photo silkscreens like the one he used are fine-mesh cloths stretched taut on a frame, much like the canvas and stretcher bars that support a painting. The cloth is then soaked in a light-sensitive emulsion and an image on a transparent support is pressed against the screen. Both are then exposed to light, which hardens the emulsion, filling in all the spaces in the mesh except for where the image blocks the light, leaving that part permeable to ink or paint and creating, in effect, a very exact stencil.

The image of the spoon and fork comes from a photograph Johns took of the actual cutlery that hangs from a hook in his painting *Voice* (1964–67; p. 47, pl. 13). He intended to use the photograph to produce a lithographic plate. The size specifications he wrote along the edge of the photo indicated his desired enlargement of the fork from its photographic reduction back to life-size. The person producing the plate misunderstood and included the text within the field of the plate, a mistake that Johns relished and incorporated into the silkscreen he had produced for the *Screen Pieces*.[12] The text asserts the spoon and fork's passage from one material to the next: first, from hanging in a painting to appearing in a photograph (which is itself simultaneously a material object, a representation, and the result of the direct impression of light); then to the silkscreen (whose materiality Johns evoked by leaving gridded impressions of another screen in the paint that are particularly visible in *Screen Piece 3*); and, finally, to appearing seemingly dematerialized—rendered flat and reproduced four times—within the space of the exhibition.

Wall Piece juxtaposes the same screenprint of fork, spoon, and text with a looser pattern, at once mesh-like and utterly solid, which Johns made by inverting the screenprinting process. Johns called this pattern the "flagstone motif."[13] To make it, he pressed paper templates of the irregular "stone" shapes into the surface rather than pushing paint through selective openings in a screen. This produced, as curator Kirk Varnedoe writes, "a new kind of surface articulation, with slick, smooth areas amid a network of interstices edged in raised paint."[14] The two sides of the work thus play with the imprint in relation to positive and negative space: the ghostly imprint of text, fork, and spoon creating a positive image made by pushing paint through the negative openings in a screen while the flagstone templates flatten and recess the interior space between their raised white outlines. *Harlem Light* closes the loop, connecting the flagstones back to the window motif. The grid, off-kilter and irregular, takes center stage here as a visual pattern that is shared by the window and the flagstones and also structures the off-primary color blocks.

In the 1968 Castelli Gallery exhibition, the viewer's ability to compare the paintings to one another, in some cases directly as they hung on the same wall and in others mediated by memory as one moved through the space, would have further complicated the already complex series of oppositions and possibilities raised by any one of the works. Johns has long expressed an interest in complexity. In 1963 he described his paint handling in relation to the flag image as a "very complex set of corrections."[15] Later he distinguished between those flags and targets and the "more complex subjects" in his more recent work; and later still, he talked about how he sought "a different type of complexity, one in which the eye no longer focuses on the flatness of the colors and the sharpness of the edges" in his screenprints.[16] Perhaps most tellingly, he described the choreographer Merce Cunningham as his "favorite artist in any field," justifying the high praise by stating, "Sometimes I'm pleased by the complexity of a work I paint. By the fourth day I realize it's simple. Nothing Merce does is simple."[17] Where in Cunningham's work might Johns have found greater complexity than in his own?

For each dance, Cunningham chose a movement vocabulary and then turned fragmentary phrases, single positions, and even separate gestures originating in various body parts into units. These he recombined using chance operations such as flipping coins or throwing *I Ching* sticks—confounding any preexisting, logical, or even anatomical sequence for their arrangement. This process generated discontinuities and transitions that challenged both the performers' and audience members' ability to follow the works' progression even as each piece maintained a sense of rhythmic clarity. Cunningham derived his chance operations from John Cage, but his use of the method differed significantly. He was not so much trying to distance himself as an author as to arrive at complicated transitions. In a 1954 article in *Dance Magazine*, Remy Charlip, a dancer with Cunningham's company, described the choreographer's chance-based method and added, "There are familiar and unfamiliar movements, but what is continuously unfamiliar is the continuity, freed as it is from usual cause and effect relations."[18] The complexity in Cunningham's dances thus centers on unexpected and unfamiliar transitions between movements and phrases.

"Complexity," as a technical term, applies to systems and both relates to and differs from Cunningham's departure from predictable causality. Complex systems tend to include the interaction of many elements, to continuously change and develop in a nonlinear way, and to contain feedback loops while also remaining open to the broader environment. As the computer scientist Melanie Mitchell writes, these factors generate "hard-to-predict macroscopic behavior," even as one can plot or model certain properties of the system and retrospectively trace limited causal relationships.[19] Because Cunningham depended on chance to (dis)organize his movements, his dances are truly unpredictable and thus not complex systems in this technical sense. Regardless, the general experience of watching one of Cunningham's pieces, with their looping regressions and repetitions, interweaving sections, and sudden shifts of direction, captures the feeling of a complex system.

Johns, in turn, sought out unpredictable, nonlinear developments within his artistic process through negation. In a 1963 interview, he said, "If you are in, say, woods where there are certain areas, known paths or landmarks, which you know, and you can move this way, then one can either move along these ways, which is to say, one does what one knows; or one can, at every moment one comes upon one of these things one knows, go a different direction. And if one does that, it seems to me, then one will know more than one knew if one followed the known situation."[20] While some of this refusal and give-and-take is visible in the juxtaposition of motifs or the layering of gesture in individual works, Johns was correct that, compared to the continuous flow of unpredictable movements in a piece by Cunningham, a single painting could not possibly visibly register every time Johns turned away from the known path while painting.

Complexity thus resides in two places in Johns's work: For the artist, it is in his own experience of making the work as he shifts focus and refuses what he knows. For the viewer, it resides less at the level of individual works and more across Johns's oeuvre. It's there in the way each work connects to many possible predecessors and progeny, with any individual connection always remaining partial. *False Start*, for example, needs to be seen in relation to *Jubilee* and *Out the Window* as well as *Periscope (Hart Crane)* (1963; p. 182, pl. 6), *Scent* (1973–74; p. 139, fig. 2), and any other number of paintings, drawings, and prints. Therefore, Johns's work not only lends itself to retrospective exhibitions and catalogues like this one, but almost mandates this type of comprehensive gathering while refusing any single overarching interpretive rubric. His exhibitions in 1960 and 1968 at the Castelli Gallery made some small portion of this complexity visible in the interactions among the works on display, as Johns posited a materially constrained but expansive definition of painting and experimented with printing in paint and the resulting entanglement of image and object.

1 The Museum of Modern Art purchased *Green Target* (1955), *White Numbers* (1957), and *Target with Four Faces* (1955; p. 42, pl. 2). Johnson purchased *Flag* (1954–55; p. 66, pl. 7) and donated it to the museum in 1973. See Lilian Tone, "Chronology and Plates," in *Jasper Johns: A Retrospective*, ed. Kirk Varnedoe, exh. cat. (New York: Museum of Modern Art, 1996), 128; International Council at the Museum of Modern Art, "U.S. Representation at the XXIX Biennale Includes Paintings by Tobey and Rothko and Sculpture by Smith and Lipton" (June 1, 1958), 6–7, MoMA Press Release Archives 1958_0072; and Dorothy C. Miller, ed., *Sixteen Americans*, exh. cat. (New York: Museum of Modern Art, 1959).

2 "Trend to the 'Anti-Art,'" *Newsweek*, March 31, 1958, 96.

3 Barr was also interested in *Target with Plaster Casts* but passed on it out of concern about reactions to the plaster cast of the penis in one of the boxes. See Tone, "Chronology," 128.

4 Johns told David Sylvester in 1965 that "all the brushmarking [Johns's neologism], other than paint put on through stencils, was arbitrary, and had to do with my arm moving." See "Jasper Johns (1965)," in David Sylvester, *Interviews with American Artists* (New Haven: Yale University Press, 2001), 163.

5 Yve-Alain Bois, "1947b," in *Art Since 1900: Modernism, Antimodernism, Postmodernism*, vol. 2, *1945–2010*, by Hal Foster et al. (New York: Thames and Hudson, 2011), 381–84.

6 Harry Cooper gives an extended and thoughtful account of how the text in *Device Circle* functions as both caption and calligram. He draws on Michel Foucault's discussion of the limited distance and formal similarity between the text "Ceci n'est pas une pipe" (This is not a pipe) and the image of the pipe in René Magritte's *Treachery of Images* (1929). He argues that Johns attempts, and inevitably fails, to reunify his own text and image—bringing the caption up against the circle and stating, in effect, "This *is* a device circle." See Harry Cooper, "Speak, Painting: Word and Device in Early Johns," *October* 127 (Winter 2009): 49–76.

7 Greenberg's most literal and strident understanding of medium specificity appears in "Towards a New Laocoön" (1940), in *The Collected Essays and Criticism*, vol. 1, *Perceptions and Judgments, 1939–1944*, ed. John O'Brian (Chicago: University of Chicago Press, 1986), 23–41. He would later modulate this view somewhat: "The essential norms or conventions of painting are at the same time the limiting conditions with which a picture must comply in order to be experienced as a picture. Modernism has found that these limits can be pushed back indefinitely before a picture stops being a picture and turns into an arbitrary object; but it has also found that the further back these limits are pushed the more explicitly they have to be observed and indicated." See Clement Greenberg, "Modernist Painting" (1960), in *The Collected Essays and Criticism*, vol. 4, *Modernism with a Vengeance, 1957–1969*, ed. John O'Brian (Chicago: University of Chicago Press, 1993), 89–90.

8 Jasper Johns, "Interview mit Jasper Johns / Interview with Jasper Johns," interview by Christian Geelhaar, in *Jasper Johns: Working Proofs*, ed. Christian Geelhaar, exh. cat. (Basel: Kunstmuseum Basel, 1979); reprinted in Kirk Varnedoe, ed., *Jasper Johns: Writings, Sketchbook Notes, Interviews* (New York: Museum of Modern Art, 1996), 193 (hereafter abbreviated Varnedoe, *WSI*).

9 Over the course of the 1960s, Johns became a prolific and adept printmaker, working in a wide variety of media. Jennifer Roberts has argued for the centrality of printmaking, understood as a series of operations, to Johns's practice more broadly. See Jennifer L. Roberts, "The Printerly Art of Jasper Johns," in *Jasper Johns / In Press: The Crosshatch Works and the Logic of Print*, exh. cat. (Cambridge, MA: Harvard Art Museums, 2012), 10–42.

10 In semiotic terms, this is the distinction between an icon and an index. See Charles Sanders Peirce, "Of Reason in General," in *The Essential Peirce: Selected Philosophical Writings*, ed. Nathan Houser and Christian Kloesel (Bloomington: Indiana University Press, 1998), 11–26. For a now-canonical take on the index's importance to postwar art, see Rosalind Krauss, "Notes on the Index: Seventies Art in America," pt. 1, *October* 3 (Spring 1977): 68–81; pt. 2, *October* 4 (Fall 1977): 58–67.

11 Catherine Craft, *Jasper Johns* (New York: Parkstone International, 2012), 116. *Studio II*, like *Shade*, is also a play on the Renaissance tradition of viewing paintings as windows onto the world.

12 Johns did use just the image of the spoon and fork, as planned, in the lithograph *Voice* (1967; p. 296, pl. 37). He discusses this sequence of events in Johns, "Interview mit Jasper Johns," 194.

13 Johns described how he came to this pattern: "The flagstone motif came from a painted wall I saw in Harlem. I was on my way to the airport, and once I saw it, I said, 'Let's put that in my next painting.' But when I came to try to find it, I couldn't even after driving around Harlem for an hour. It wasn't there. So I had to remember or reinvent it. And in a sense, I continue to remember and reinvent it in a number of subsequent works." Johns, quoted in Tone, "Chronology," 233.

14 Varnedoe, *Johns: A Retrospective*, 223.

15 Jasper Johns, interview by Billy Klüver, March 1963, in Varnedoe, *WSI*, 85.

16 Jasper Johns, "I Want Images to Free Themselves from Me" (in Japanese), interview by Yoshiaki Tōno, *Geijutsu Shincho* (Tokyo) 15, no. 8 (August 1964), reprinted in Varnedoe, *WSI*, 98; Johns, "Interview mit Jasper Johns," 188.

17 Jasper Johns, quoted in Hubert Saal, "Merce," *Newsweek*, May 27, 1968, 88. Johns was a longtime supporter of Cunningham, serving as an artistic advisor for his dance company and cofounding the Foundation for Contemporary Performance Arts (now the Foundation for Contemporary Arts) to support the company. For more on this relationship, see Carlos Basualdo and Erica F. Battle, eds., *Dancing around the Bride: Cage, Cunningham, Johns, Rauschenberg, and Duchamp*, exh. cat. (Philadelphia: Philadelphia Museum of Art, 2012); Eric Banks, ed., *Artists for Artists: Fifty Years of the Foundation for Contemporary Arts* (New York: Foundation for Contemporary Arts, 2013); and Fionn Meade and Joan Rothfuss, eds., *Merce Cunningham: Common Time*, exh. cat. (Minneapolis: Walker Art Center, 2017).

18 Remy Charlip, "Composing by Chance," *Dance Magazine*, January 1954, 19.

19 Melanie Mitchell, *Complexity: A Guided Tour* (Oxford: Oxford University Press, 2009), 38. On the difficulty of defining complexity, see also Paul Cilliers, *Complexity and Postmodernism: Understanding Complex Systems* (London: Routledge, 1998), 2–5.

20 Jasper Johns, interview by Billy Klüver, March 1963, complete unpublished transcript, 21–22, in Kirk Varnedoe Papers, Jasper Johns Book Project, Getty Research Institute, Los Angeles.

Place

Jasper Johns has lived and worked in a variety of places that have indelibly shaped his thought and art. From the American South to Asia, these sites have engendered transformative encounters and occasional collaborations with artists, writers, composers, and choreographers, as well as master printers in Paris, Los Angeles, and Long Island. Often the culture, language, and atmosphere of a place obliquely enter his work. Sometimes a locale is named directly on its surface. These sites include Johns's residences in Stony Point, New York; Edisto Beach, South Carolina; the Caribbean island of Saint Martin; and, most recently, Sharon, Connecticut. Apart from New York, where Johns spent most of his adult life, the two places that arguably affected him most are Japan and his native South Carolina.

Japan has loomed large in Johns's experience and imagination since he spent six months of his army service in Sendai in 1952–53. He returned, this time to Tokyo, for two months in 1964 at the invitation of Kusuo Shimizu, director of the Minami Gallery, and art critic Yoshiaki Tōno, who had seen the artist's work at the 1958 Venice Biennale and later met him in New York. Tōno introduced Johns to members of the vibrant Japanese art world, with whom he formed lasting friendships, sharing with many a passion for the work of Marcel Duchamp. In a studio in the Japanese Artists' Hall in the Ginza district, Johns produced nine drawings and four paintings, including *Watchman* (1964; p. 117, pl. 1) and two versions of *Souvenir* (1964; pp. 118–19, pls. 2, 3). The latter works each feature a plate from a tourist shop emblazoned with a blank-faced photo-booth portrait of the artist, ironic mementos that commemorate not some far-off land but the inscrutable traveler himself. As notes in his sketchbooks attest, this was a time of profound self-reflection from a foreign vantage, giving rise to some of his most important works of the 1960s, including *According to What* (1964; pp. 150–51, pl. 2).

Over the following decades, Johns's renown in Japan increased through many exhibitions, and he returned several times, including for a six-week stay in 1966. Yet he maintained his deep fascination with Japanese culture largely at a geographic distance. In 1977, he embarked on a prolific series of crosshatch works titled Usuyuki after an eighteenth-century Kabuki play, a complex love story that Johns described as concerning "the fleeting quality of beauty in the world."[1] The series, whose name means "light snow" in Japanese, includes paintings, drawings, and prints, most notably exquisite silkscreens made with Hiroshi Kawanishi and other Japanese master printers at Simca Print Artists in New York. Their intricate patterning feels, like nature, animated by an appreciable if ineffable order, as parallel marks blossom with high contrast and color or dissolve into the soft tonality of frost or early spring.

During Johns's visit to Japan in 1966, he learned that a fire had destroyed his home and studio at Edisto Beach, along with many of his own works and those by other artists. Johns had grown up in South Carolina, where he lived until he dropped out of college in 1948 and moved to New York. He returned three years later for army service and again in 1961, when he purchased a retreat on Edisto Island, following his breakup with Robert Rauschenberg. The seaside locale was known for its natural beauty but was also the site of particularly painful chapters in the history of the subjugation of African Americans. During Reconstruction, land that had been granted to the formerly enslaved population was soon returned to pardoned plantation owners, and a century later resistance to desegregation remained strong during the final years of the Jim Crow era.

More solitary than his life in New York, his long sojourns there are conjured in the images of Italian photographer Ugo Mulas (pp. 132–35) and in the newly open works Johns made under changing light by the sea. The oceanic grisaille painting *Studio* (1964; pp. 130–31, pl. 2) evokes the sultry southern surrounds through the imprint of a palmetto frond and an askew screen door. Other drawings and paintings bear the names of local places, such as *Edisto* (1962; p. 135, pl. 18) and *Edingsville* (1965), with its appendage of beach trash and a conch shell. This motif recurs in an ink-on-plastic drawing from 1969 (p. 135, pl. 17) and in the lithograph *Pinion* (1966; p. 129, pl. 1), where it lends images of ghostly body parts the sense of impressions in the sand.

During this period, the beach became for Johns a site and symbol of transience, loss, memory, heartbreak, and desire—particularly across a group of works that honor his friendship with the poet and curator Frank O'Hara. He first referenced the writer in one particularly mournful painting, *In Memory of My Feelings—Frank O'Hara* (1961; p. 134, pl. 11), made shortly after his breakup with Rauschenberg and titled after an O'Hara poem. In *Skin with O'Hara Poem* (1965; p. 134, pl. 12), the poet's words merge with disembodied traces of Johns's face and hands, initially produced by rolling his oiled features on a sheet of paper and rubbing it with charcoal. Although O'Hara never visited Edisto, his poem "Dear Jap" intones, "When I think of you in South Carolina, I think of my foot in the sand."[2] O'Hara here references a drawing Johns brought there of the poet's foot, a rubber cast of which figures alongside Edisto Island sand in a sculpture (p. 135, pl. 15) completed after O'Hara's untimely death in an accident on the beach in Fire Island, New York, in July 1966, just months before the Edisto fire.

In the 1990s, Johns began developing a lexicon of imagery from recollections of his youth in South Carolina, where, following his parents' divorce at the age of two, he lived at the homes of his paternal grandfather and, later, an aunt. These disparate motifs from a difficult childhood recur in dazzling combinative compositions like fragments of memory flickering across the mind's eye. Tokens of boyhood appear in the form of piggy banks made from gourds and in the colorful shapes of the homemade lantern in *Untitled (Halloween)* (1998; p. 136, pl. 22), which also features the image of a Chinese costume Johns wore as a child. *Untitled* (1992–94; p. 136, pl. 20) and a group of related works contain floor plans drawn from memory of his grandfather's house. In other series of prints and drawings, his grandparents stare impassively from a family photograph, below which a thin catenary swoops like the fragile thread of life.

—Scott Rothkopf, with Carlos Basualdo, Sarah B. Vogelman, and Lauren Young

1 Jasper Johns, "An Interview with Jasper Johns about Silkscreening," by Katrina Martin, in *Jasper Johns: Printed Symbols*, exh. cat. (Minneapolis: Walker Art Center, 1990); reprinted in Kirk Varnedoe, ed., *Jasper Johns: Writings, Sketchbook Notes, Interviews* (New York: Museum of Modern Art, 1996), 210.

2 Frank O'Hara, "Dear Jap," in *The Collected Poems of Frank O'Hara*, ed. Donald Allen (Berkeley: University of California Press, 1995), 470–71; quoted in Roberta Bernstein, "'You Have One Thing and Make Another Thing': Sculpture, 1958–2012," in *Jasper Johns: Redo an Eye* (New York: Wildenstein Plattner Institute, 2017), 103.

Place

Japan

PHILADELPHIA MUSEUM OF ART

1 ***Watchman*, 1964**
Oil on canvas with objects
(two panels)
80 × 65 ¼ in. (203.2 × 165.7 cm)
overall
The Eli and Edythe L. Broad Collection

2 ***Souvenir*, 1964**
Encaustic and collage on canvas
with objects
28 ¾ × 21 in. (73 × 53.3 cm)
Collection of the artist; on long-term
loan to the San Francisco Museum
of Modern Art, 2000

3 ***Souvenir 2*, 1964**
Oil, charcoal, and collage on canvas
with objects
28 ¾ × 21 in. (73 × 53.3 cm)
Collection of Barbara and Richard S. Lane

4 ***Usuyuki*, 1982**
Encaustic on canvas (three panels)
71 × 113 ¾ in. (180.3 × 288.9 cm)
overall
Sezon Museum of Modern Art,
Nagano, Japan

5 ***Souvenir 2*, 1965**‡
Graphite pencil, graphite wash,
and collage on paper
8 ⅜ × 6 ¼ in. (21.3 × 15.9 cm)
Collection of Mr. and Mrs. Michael D.
Eisner

6 ***Souvenir*, 1964**
Graphite wash and graphite pencil
on paper
19 ½ × 14 ¼ in. (49.5 × 36.2 cm)
Collection of the artist

7 ***Souvenir*, 1964**
Charcoal on paper
35 × 27 ¼ in. (88.9 × 69.2 cm)
Collection of the artist

8 ***Watchman*, 1964**
Graphite pencil and oil on paper
20 ⅜ × 17 ½ in. (51.8 × 44.5 cm)
Private collection

9 ***Watchman*, 1964**
Graphite pencil, graphite wash,
watercolor, and pastel on paper
20 ⅜ × 15 ¼ in. (51.8 × 38.7 cm)
Collection of Gail and Tony Ganz

10 ***For Toru*, 1964**
Oil on paper
12 ⅝ × 9 ½ in. (32.1 × 24.1 cm)
Private collection

11 ***Summer Critic*, 1966**
Cement, wax, and glass
3 ½ × 7 ½ × 2 ⅜ in.
(8.9 × 19.1 × 6 cm)
Private collection

12 ***Untitled (Cut, Tear, Scrape, Erase)*, 1964**
Graphite pencil on paper
11 ⅜ × 11 ⅜ in. (28.9 × 28.9 cm)
Collection of the artist

13 ***No*, 1964**
Graphite pencil and graphite
wash on paper
20 ⅜ × 17 ½ in. (51.8 × 44.5 cm)
Collection of Gail and Tony Ganz

14 ***Summer Critic*, 1966**
Graphite pencil on two sheets
of paper (one folded over the other)
2 ⅛ × 2 ½ in. (5.4 × 6.4 cm)
overall
Toyama Prefectural Museum of Art
and Design, Japan

15 **Atsuko Tanaka (Japanese, 1932–2005)**
Untitled*, 1983
Pencil on paper
10 ¾ × 14 ⅜ in. (27.3 × 36.5 cm)
Collection of Jasper Johns

16 **Shūzō Takiguchi (Japanese, 1903–1979)**
***10 Vicious Circles*, 1964**
Pencil on paper
9 ¾ × 8 ½ in. (24.8 × 21.6 cm)
Collection of Jasper Johns

17 **Jasper Johns with Tōru Takemitsu at a Tokyo gallery, 1964**
Courtesy Jasper Johns

18 **Ushio Shinohara (Japanese, b. 1932)**
***Drink More*, 1964**
Fluorescent paint, oil, plaster,
and Coca-Cola bottle on canvas
18 ⅜ × 14 × 6 ½ in.
(46.7 × 35.6 × 16.5 cm)
Collection of Jasper Johns

19 **Yoshiaki Tōno and Jasper Johns at the Imperial Hotel in Tokyo, 1964**
Photograph by Akira Kanayama
Courtesy Jasper Johns

20 **Shusaku Arakawa (Japanese, 1936–2010)**
War of the Worlde ...*, 1970
Acrylic, pencil, and ink on canvas
49 × 72 in. (124.5 × 182.9 cm)
Collection of Jasper Johns

21 **Tomio Miki (Japanese, 1937–1978)**
***Ear*, n.d.**
Cast aluminum
12 × 8 ½ × 3 ½ in.
(30.5 × 21.6 × 8.9 cm)
Collection of Jasper Johns

22 **Jasper Johns in Kyoto, 1964**
Courtesy Jasper Johns

23 **Yoshiaki Tōno (Japanese, 1930–2005)**
***Self-Portrait*, 1975**
Cast aluminum
8 ½ × 7 ⅜ × 1 ⅜ in.
(21.6 × 18.7 × 3.5 cm)
Collection of Jasper Johns

24 ***Usuyuki*, 1979–81**
Oil on canvas (three panels)
31 × 50 ⅞ in. (78.7 × 129.2 cm)
overall
Allen Family Collection

25 ***Usuyuki*, 1977–78**
Encaustic and collage on canvas
(three panels)
35 ⅛ × 56 ⅝ in. (89.2 × 143.8 cm)
overall
The Cleveland Museum of Art;
Leonard C. Hanna, Jr., Fund, 1993.109

26 ***Usuyuki*, 1979**
Ink, acrylic, and graphite pencil on
plastic
33 ¼ × 51 ½ in. (84.5 × 130.8 cm)
Whitney Museum of American Art,
New York; purchase with funds from
The Lauder Foundation, Evelyn and
Leonard Lauder Fund, 99.13

27 ***Usuyuki*, 1979–95**
Watercolor, black ink, and colored
ink on plastic
33 ⅛ × 51 ½ in. (84.1 × 130.8 cm)
Collection of Zygi and Audrey Wilf

28 ***Usuyuki*, 1995**
Watercolor and graphite pencil on paper
29 ¼ × 46 ½ in. (74.3 × 118.1 cm)
The Broad Art Foundation

29 ***Usuyuki*, 1979**
Screenprint (printed on both sides)
33 × 50 in. (83.8 × 127 cm)
Hiroshi Kawanishi/SPA
TP
National Gallery of Art, Washington, DC;
Patrons' Permanent Fund and Special
Friends of the National Gallery of Art,
2010.116.84

30 ***Usuyuki*, 1981**
Silkscreen: twelve screens
29 ½ × 47 ¼ in. (74.9 × 120 cm)
Kenjiro Nonaka, Hiroshi Kawanishi/
JJ and SPA
Ed. no. 40/85
Philadelphia Museum of Art; purchased
with the Lola Downin Peck Fund,
1983-67-1

31 ***Usuyuki*, 1980**
Screenprint
29 ½ × 47 in. (74.9 × 119.4 cm)
Hiroshi Kawanishi/SPA
TP
National Gallery of Art, Washington, DC;
Patrons' Permanent Fund and Special
Friends of the National Gallery of Art,
2010.116.85

South Carolina

WHITNEY MUSEUM OF AMERICAN ART

1 ***Pinion*, 1966**
Lithograph: two stones, one aluminum
plate
40 × 28 in. (101.6 × 71.1 cm)
Zigmunds Priede/ULAE
Ed. no. 27/36
Whitney Museum of American Art,
New York; gift of Mrs. Volney F. Righter,
66.110

2 ***Studio*, 1964**
Oil on canvas with objects (two panels)
88 × 145 ¾ in. (223.5 × 370.2 cm) overall
Whitney Museum of American Art,
New York; purchase with partial
funding from the Friends of the
Whitney Museum of American Art,
66.1a–c

3 **Ugo Mulas (Italian, 1928–1973)**
***Jasper Johns, Skin, Edisto Beach*, 1965**
Gelatin silver print mounted on
aluminum
26 ⅝ × 19 ¾ in. (67.6 × 50.2 cm)
Ugo Mulas Archive, Milan

4 **Ugo Mulas**
Jasper Johns, Skin, Edisto Beach*, 1965
Gelatin silver print mounted on
aluminum
19 ¾ × 26 ⅝ in. (50.2 × 67.6 cm)
Ugo Mulas Archive, Milan

5 ***Skin*, 1965**
Charcoal and oil on paper
22 × 34 in. (55.9 × 86.4 cm)
The Menil Collection, Houston;
promised gift from the collection of
Louisa Stude Sarofim

6 **Ugo Mulas**
Jasper Johns*, 1964
Gelatin silver print
14 ⅞ × 10 ⅜ in. (37.8 × 26.4 cm)
Ugo Mulas Archive, Milan

7 **Ugo Mulas**
***Jasper Johns, Edisto Beach*, 1965**
Gelatin silver print
13 ¾ × 10 ¼ in. (34.9 × 26 cm)
Ugo Mulas Archive, Milan

8 **Ugo Mulas**
Jasper Johns, Edisto Beach*, 1965
Vintage gelatin silver print
3 ⅞ × 5 ⅛ in. (10 × 13 cm)
Ugo Mulas Archive, Milan

9 **Ugo Mulas**
***Jasper Johns, Edisto Beach*, 1965**
Gelatin silver print
11 ¾ × 15 ¾ in. (29.9 × 40 cm)
Ugo Mulas Archive, Milan

10 **List of items lost in fire at Edisto Beach, S.C., 1966**
Archives of American Art, Smithsonian Institution, Washington, DC; Leo Castelli Gallery Records, box 12, folder 41

11 ***In Memory of My Feelings—Frank O'Hara*, 1961**
Oil on canvas with objects (two panels)
40 × 59 ¾ in. (101.6 × 151.8 cm) overall
Museum of Contemporary Art, Chicago; partial gift of Apollo Plastics Corporation, courtesy of Stefan T. Edlis and H. Gael Neeson, 1995.114.a–d

12 ***Skin with O'Hara Poem*, 1965**
Lithograph: two stones
22 × 34 in. (55.9 × 86.4 cm)
Ben Berns/ULAE
Ed. no. 8/30
Whitney Museum of American Art, New York; purchase with funds from Leonard A. Lauder, 2020.13

13 **Study for *In Memory of My Feelings*, 1967**
Ink and graphite pencil on plastic
14 × 11 in. (35.6 × 27.9 cm)
Collection of the artist

14 **Ugo Mulas**
***Jasper Johns, Edisto Beach*, 1965**
Gelatin silver print
5 ⅞ × 8 ⅝ in. (14.9 × 21.9 cm)
Ugo Mulas Archive, Milan

15 ***Memory Piece (Frank O'Hara)*, 1961–70**
Wood, rubber, Sculp-metal, lead, brass, and sand (four parts)
6 ⅝ × 6 ⅛ × 13 ¼ in.
(16.8 × 15.6 × 33.7 cm)
Collection of the artist; on long-term loan to the Philadelphia Museum of Art, 2015

16 **Ugo Mulas**
***Jasper Johns, Edisto Beach*, 1965**
Gelatin silver print
15 ¾ × 11 ¾ in. (40 × 29.9 cm)
Ugo Mulas Archive, Milan

17 ***From Eddingsville*, 1969**
Ink and graphite pencil on plastic
18 ⅞ × 28 ¾ in. (47.9 × 73 cm)
Ryobi Foundation

18 ***Edisto*, 1962**
Charcoal and graphite pencil on paper
22 × 29 ⅞ in. (55.9 × 75.9 cm)
Collection of the artist

19 ***Untitled*, 1998**
Encaustic on canvas with objects
44 ⅛ × 22 ½ in. (112.1 × 57.2 cm)
Whitney Museum of American Art, New York; promised gift of Emily Fisher Landau

20 ***Untitled*, 1992–94**
Encaustic on canvas
78 × 118 ⅜ in. (198.1 × 300.7 cm)
The Eli and Edythe L. Broad Collection

21 ***Untitled*, 2010**
Ink on plastic
29 × 36 ¼ in. (73.7 × 92.1 cm)
Kravis Collection

22 ***Untitled (Halloween)*, 1998**
Encaustic on canvas with objects
44 × 66 in. (111.8 × 167.6 cm)
Collection of Marguerite and Robert Hoffman

23 ***Untitled*, 2001***
Collage over intaglio
24 ¾ × 32 ⅜ in. (62.9 × 82.2 cm)
Private collection

24 ***Untitled*, 2001***
Watercolor and gouache over intaglio
24 ¾ × 32 ¼ in. (62.9 × 81.9 cm)
Private collection

25 ***Untitled*, 2001***
Acrylic over intaglio
24 ¾ × 32 ½ in. (62.9 × 82.6 cm)
Private collection

26 ***Untitled*, 2001***
Acrylic over intaglio
24 ¾ × 32 ⅜ in. (62.9 × 82.2 cm)
Private collection

Japan

PHILADELPHIA MUSEUM OF ART

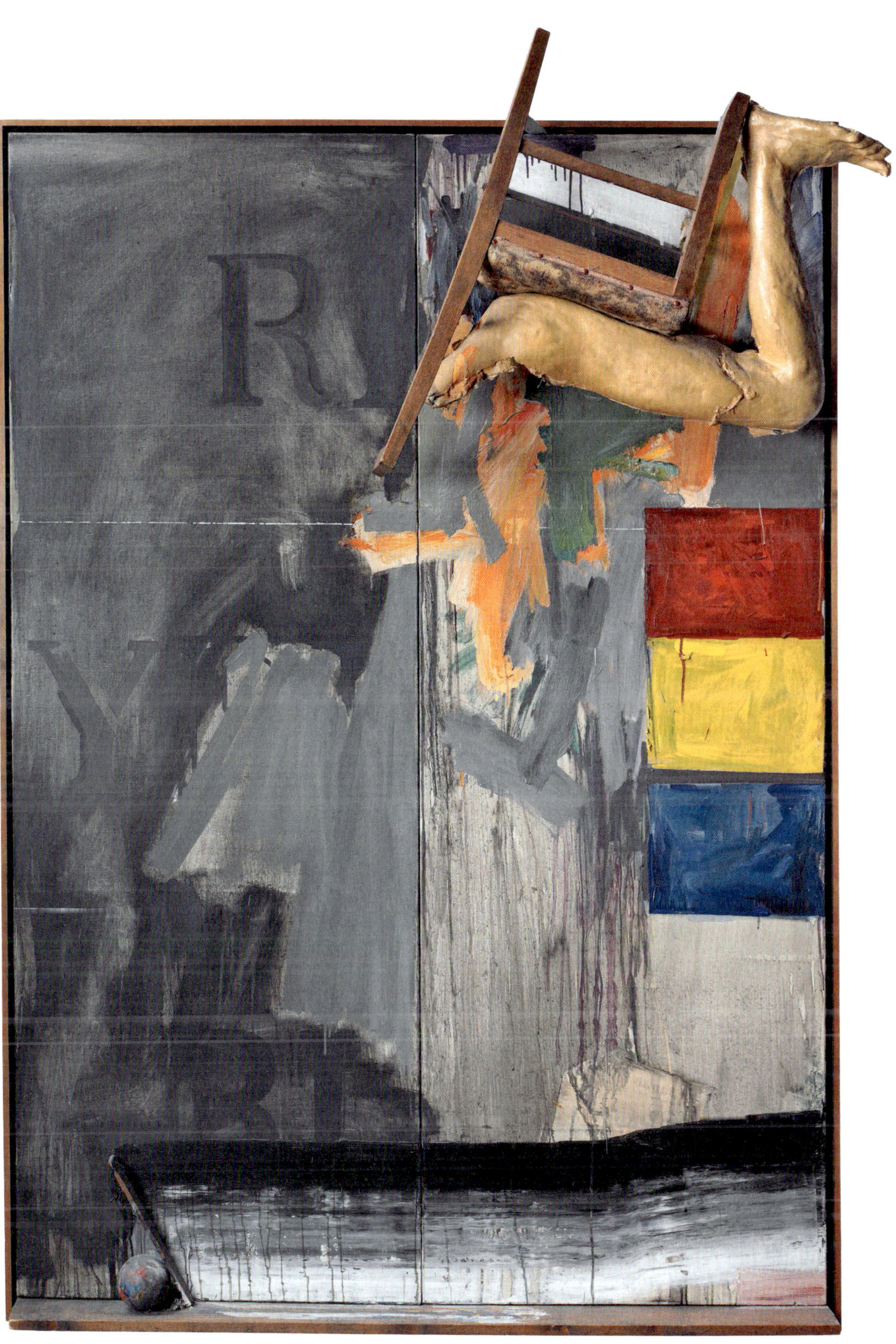

1 ***Watchman*, 1964**

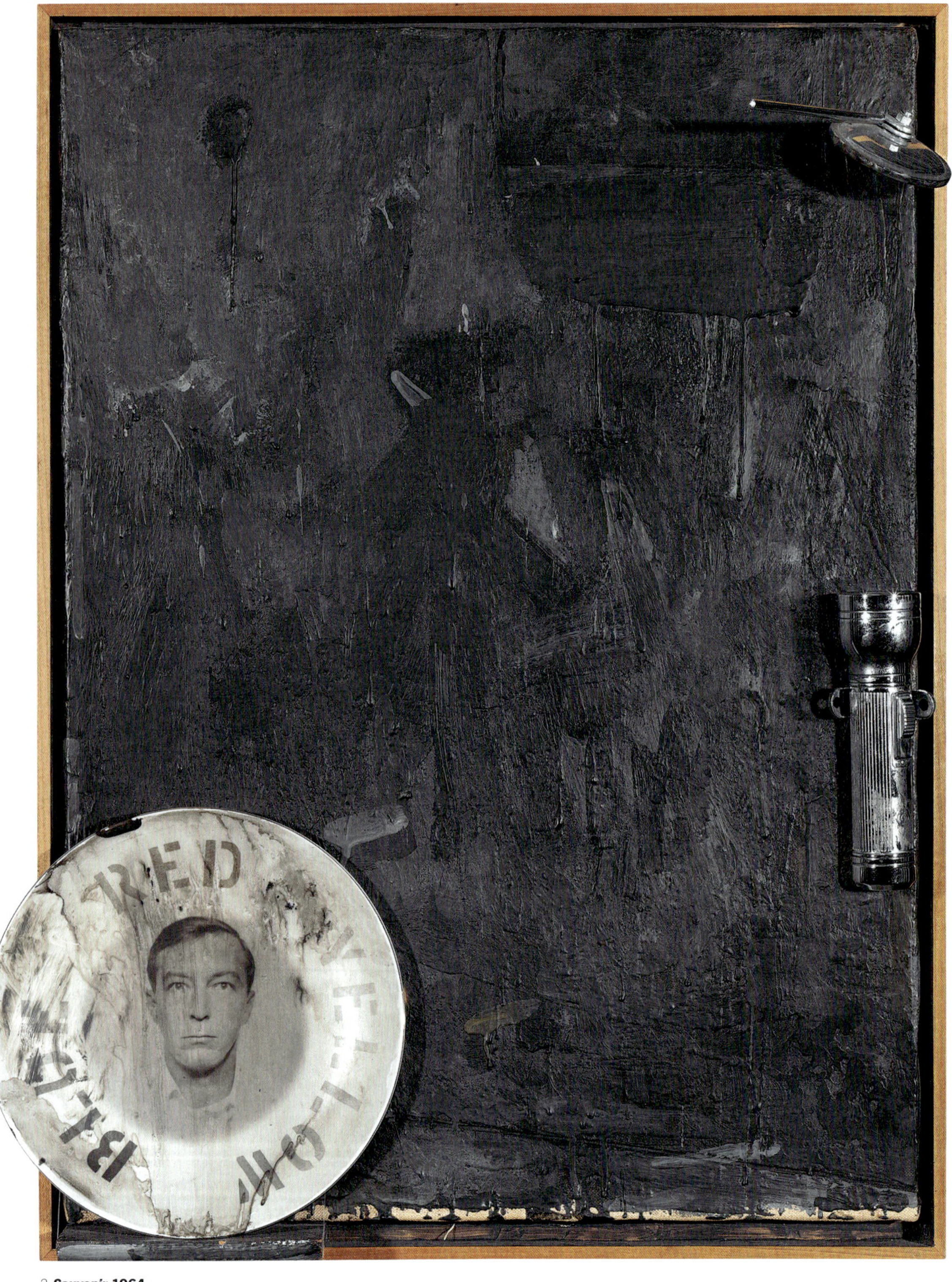

2 ***Souvenir*, 1964**

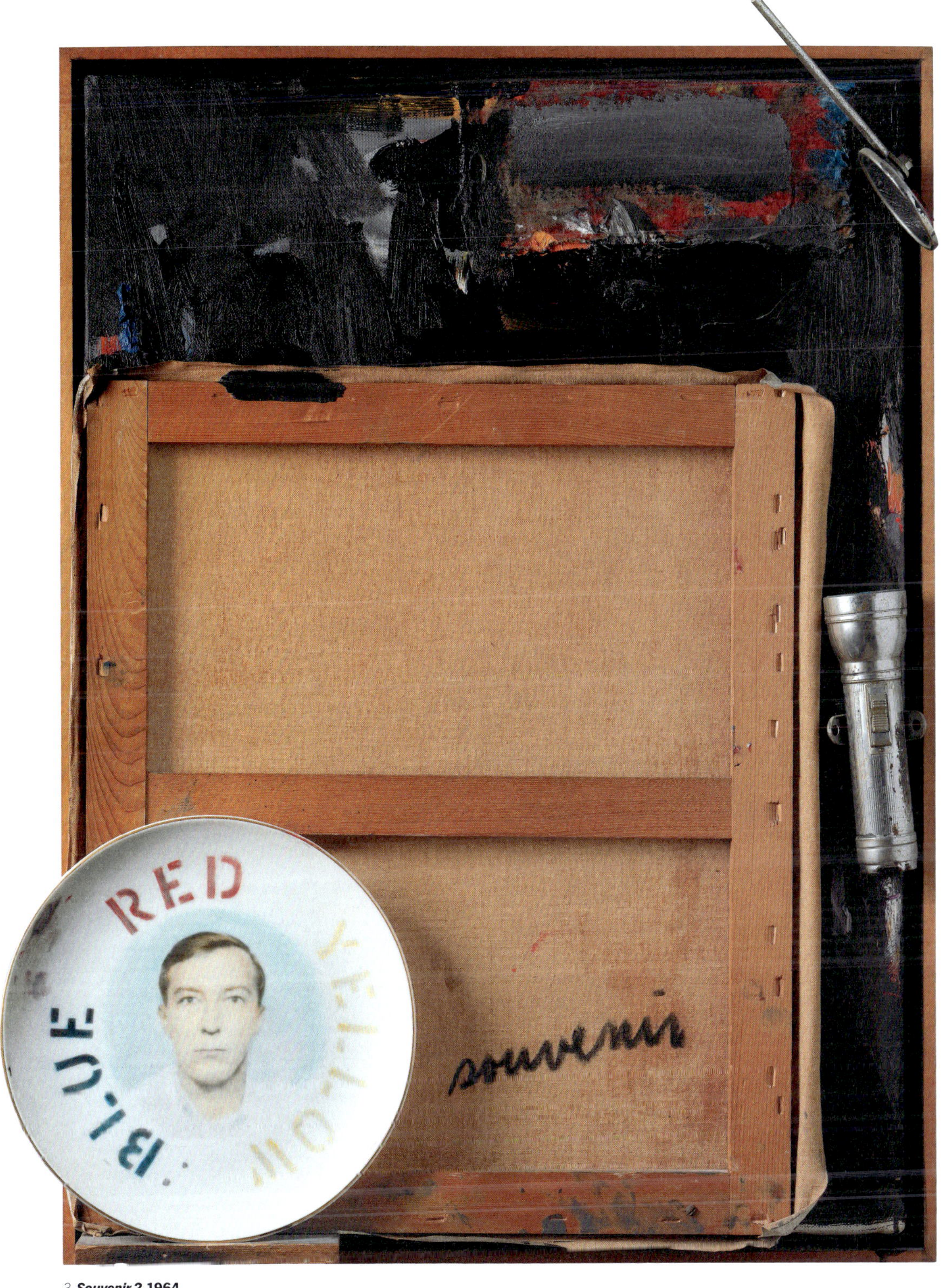

3 ***Souvenir 2***, **1964**

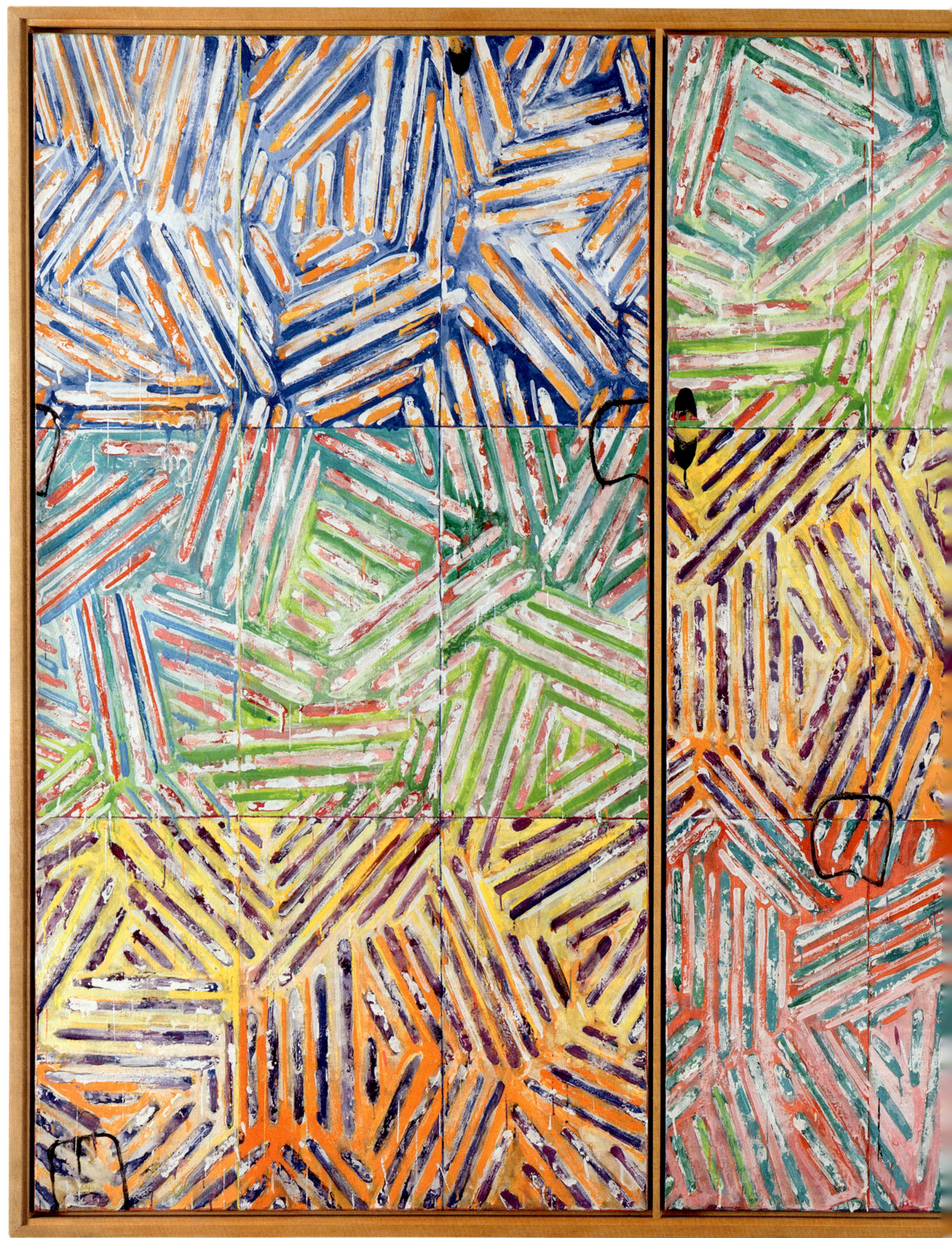

4 ***Usuyuki*, 1982**

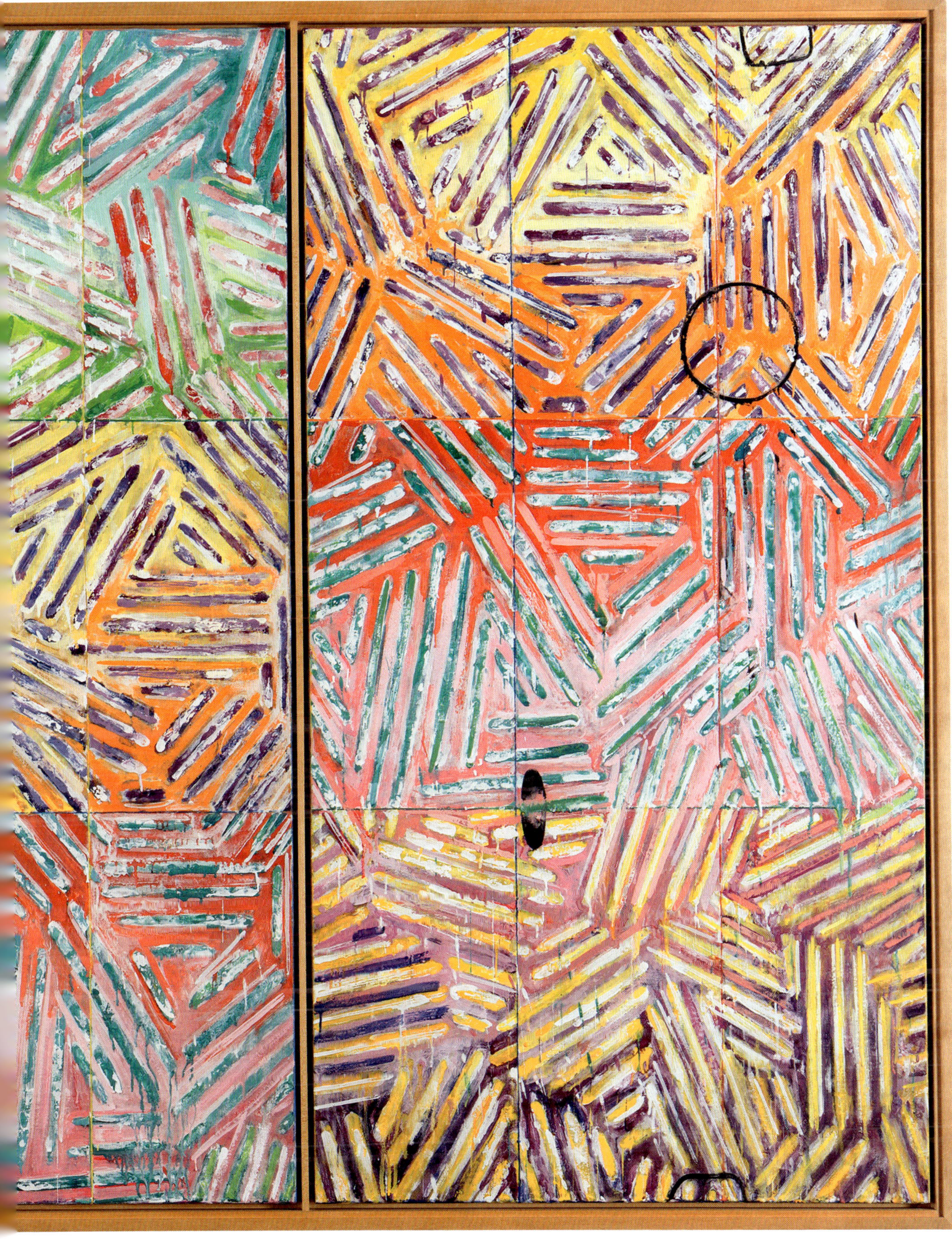

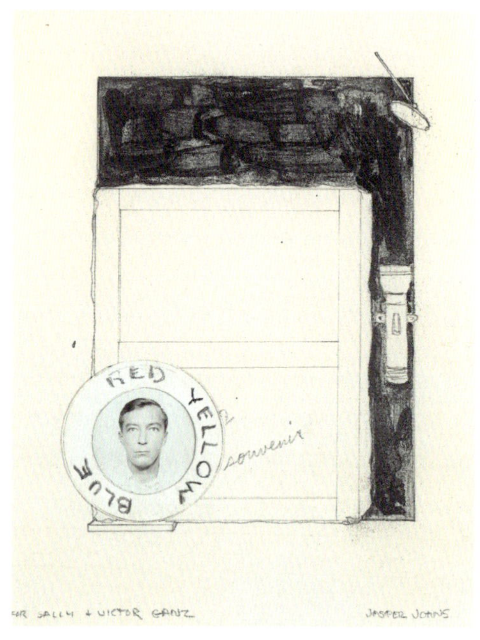

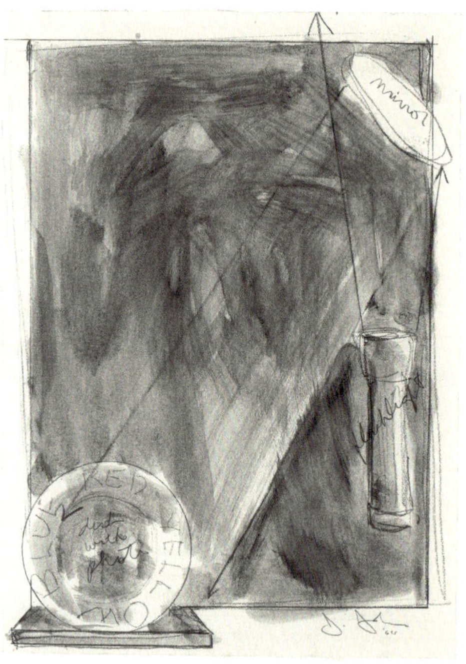

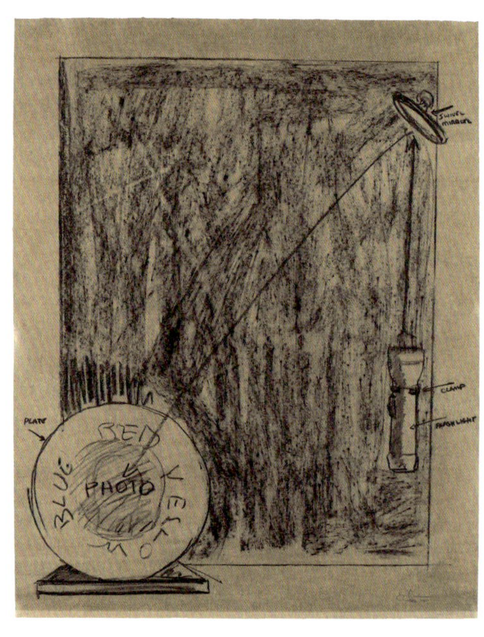

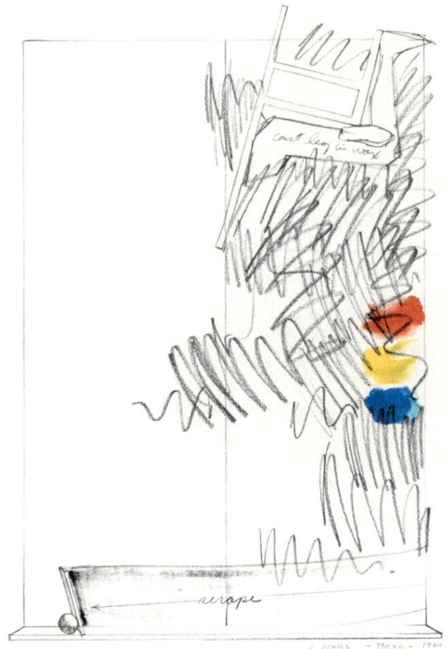

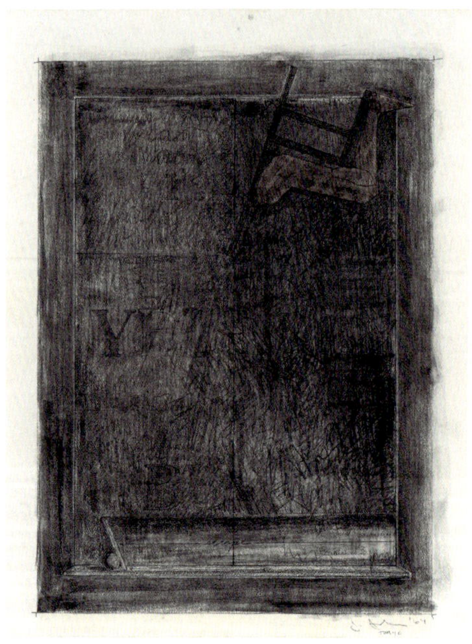

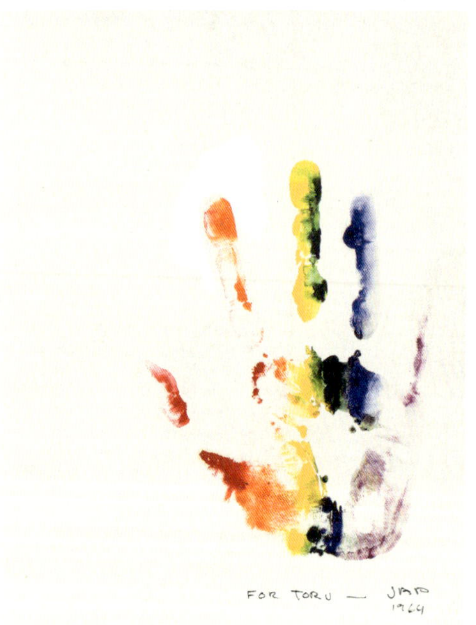

5 ***Souvenir 2*, 1965**
8 ***Watchman*, 1964**

6 ***Souvenir*, 1964**
9 ***Watchman*, 1964**

7 ***Souvenir*, 1964**
10 ***For Toru*, 1964**

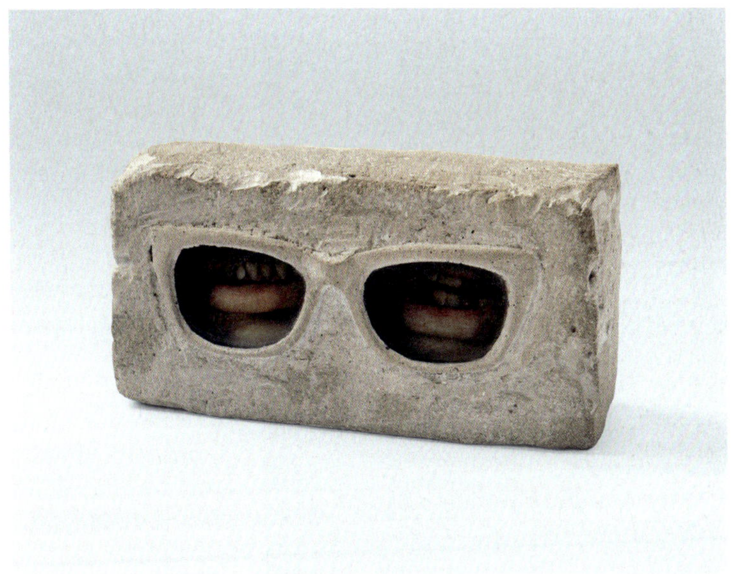

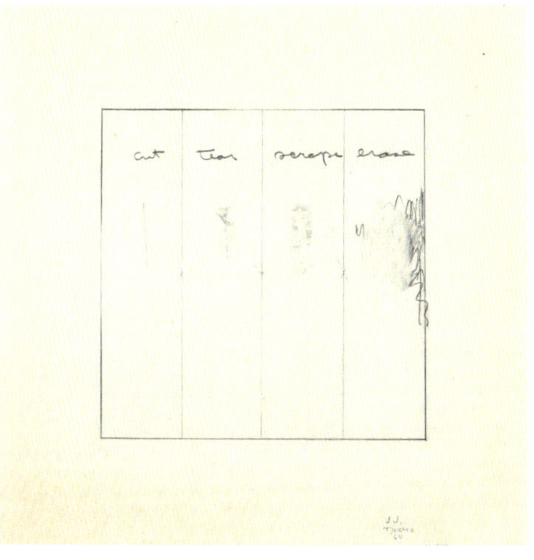

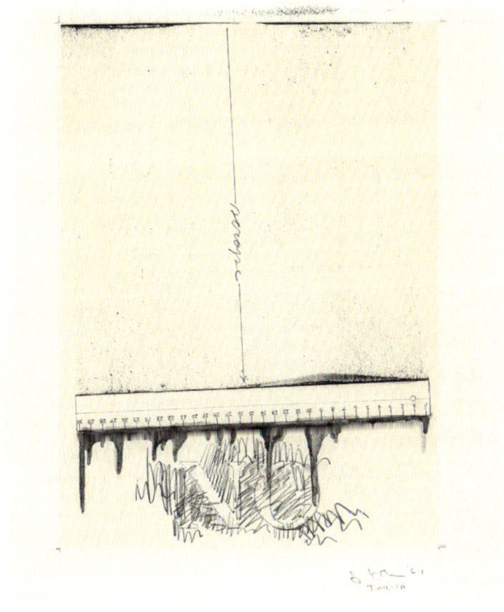

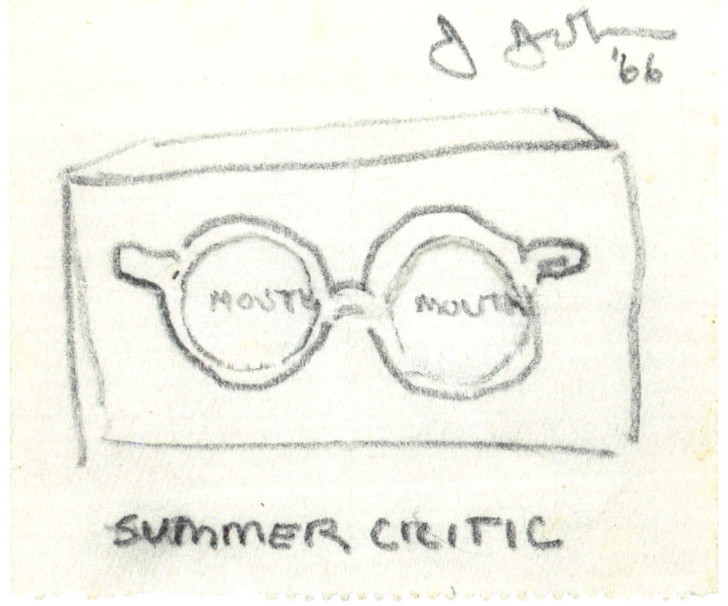

11 ***Summer Critic*, 1966**
13 ***No*, 1964**

12 ***Untitled (Cut, Tear, Scrape, Erase)*, 1964**
14 ***Summer Critic*, 1966**

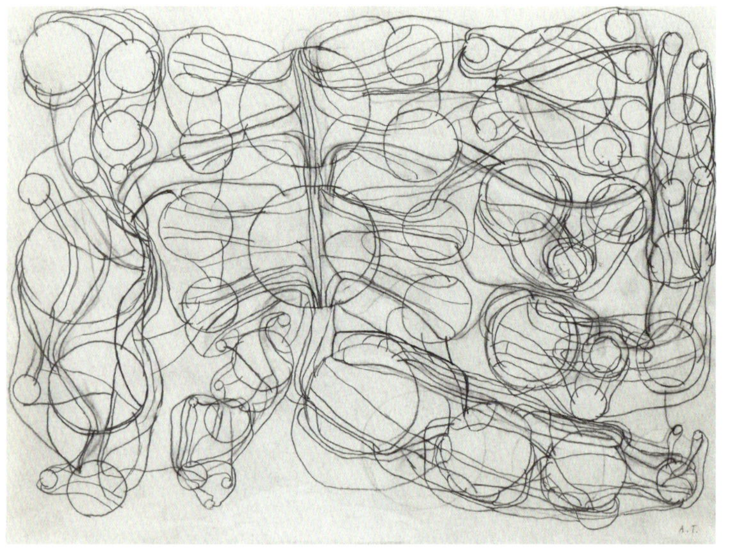

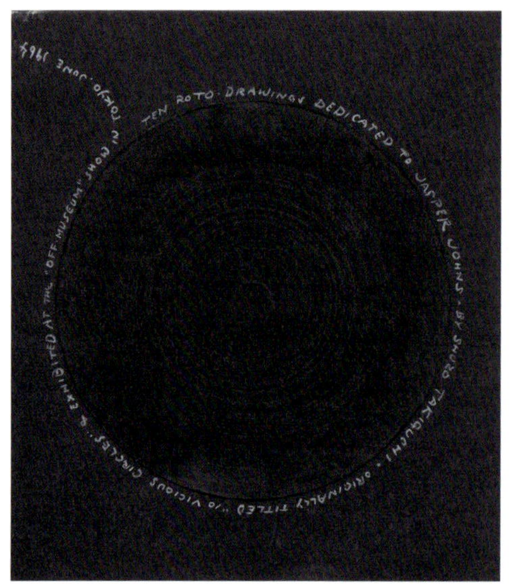

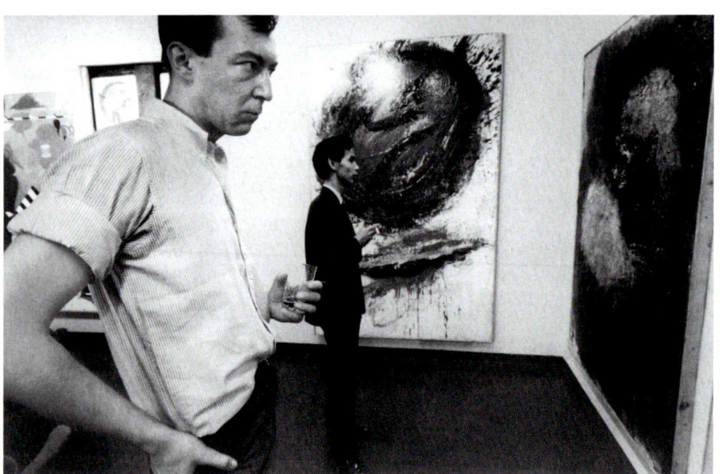

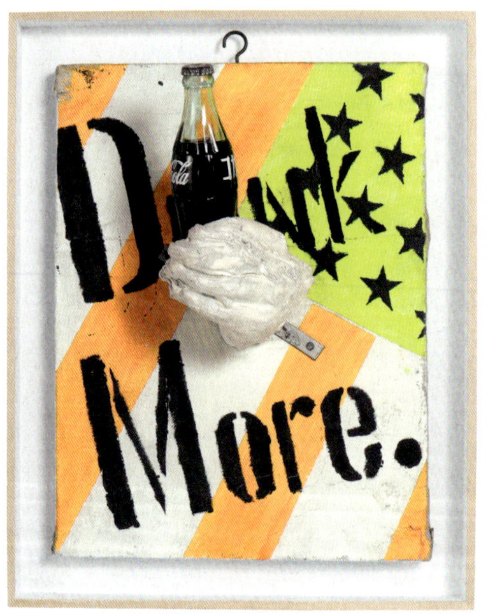

15 **Atsuko Tanaka, *Untitled*, 1983**
17 **Jasper Johns with Tōru Takemitsu at a Tokyo gallery, 1964**

16 **Shūzō Takiguchi, *10 Vicious Circles*, 1964**
18 **Ushio Shinohara, *Drink More*, 1964**

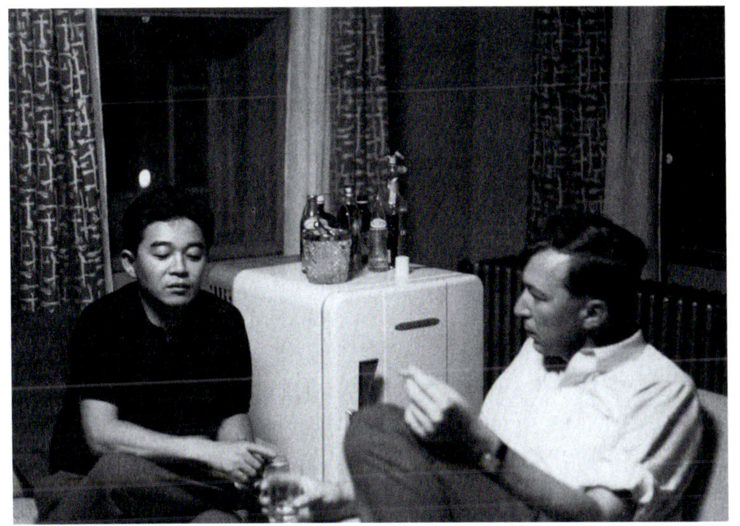

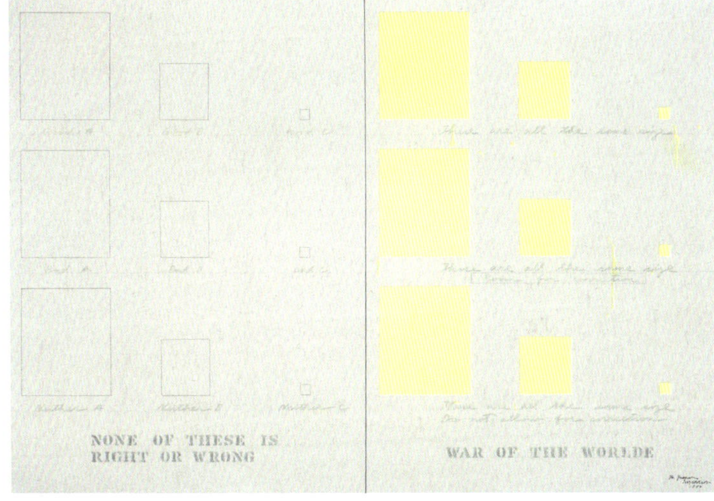

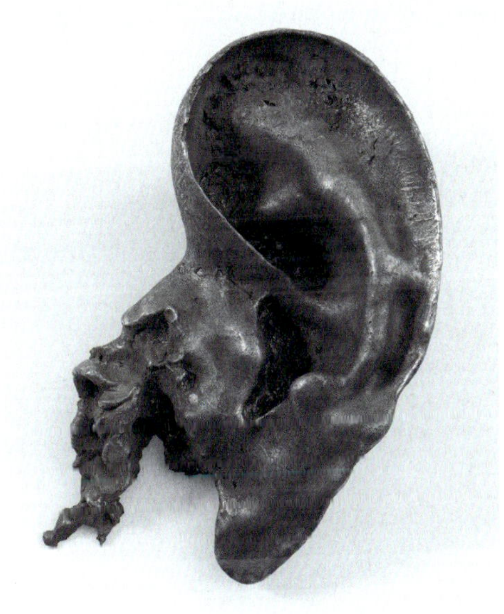

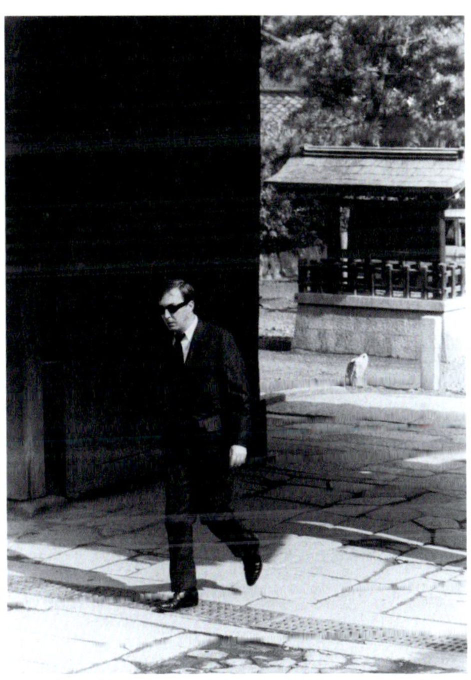

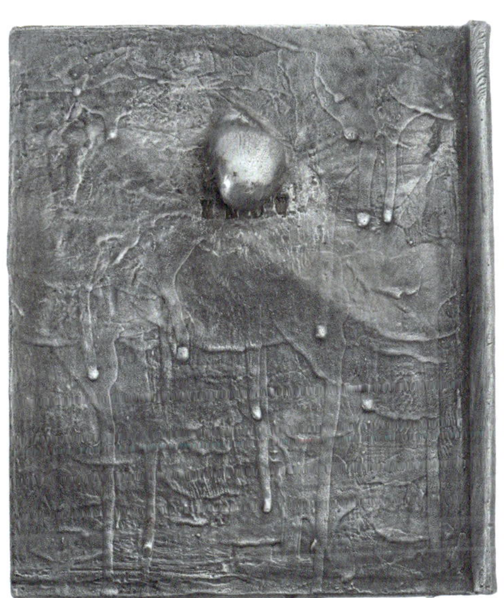

19 **Yoshiaki Tōno and Jasper Johns at the Imperial Hotel in Tokyo, 1964**
21 **Tomio Miki, *Ear*, n.d.**

20 **Shusaku Arakawa, *War of the Worlde ...*, 1970**
22 **Jasper Johns in Kyoto, 1964**

23 **Yoshiaki Tōno, *Self-Portrait*, 1975**

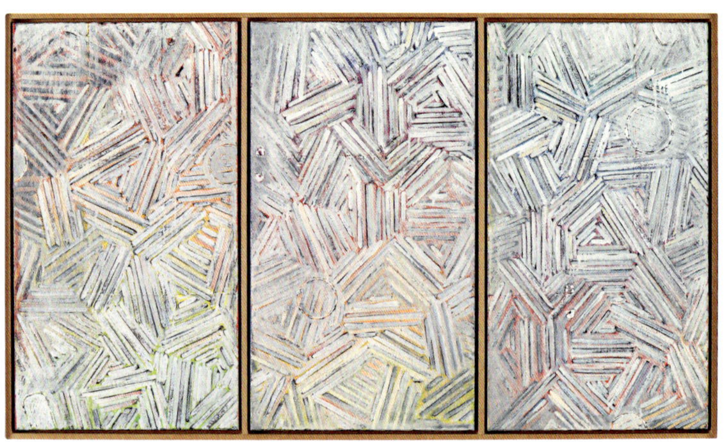

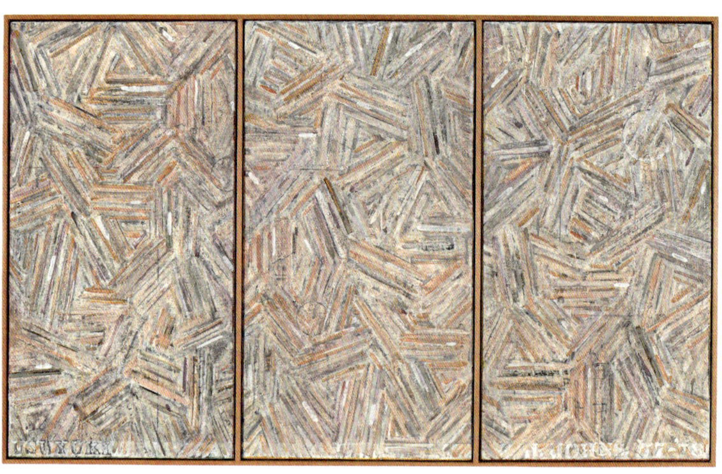

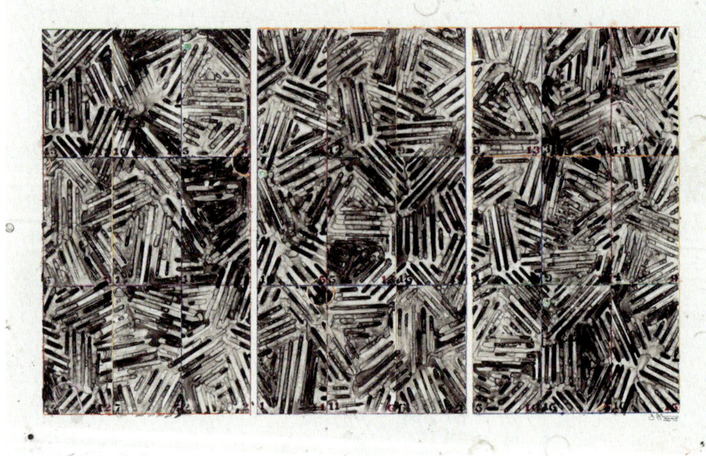

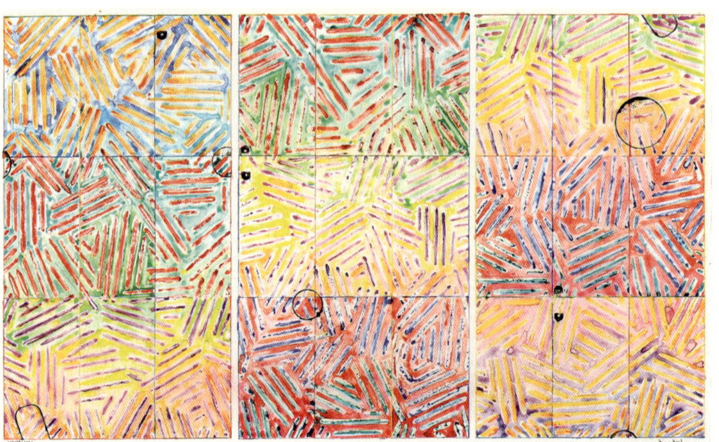

24 ***Usuyuki*, 1979–81**
26 ***Usuyuki*, 1979**

25 ***Usuyuki*, 1977–78**
27 ***Usuyuki*, 1979–95**

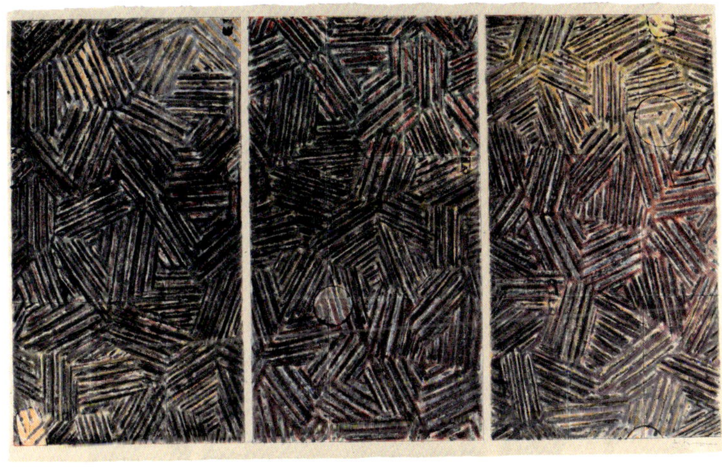

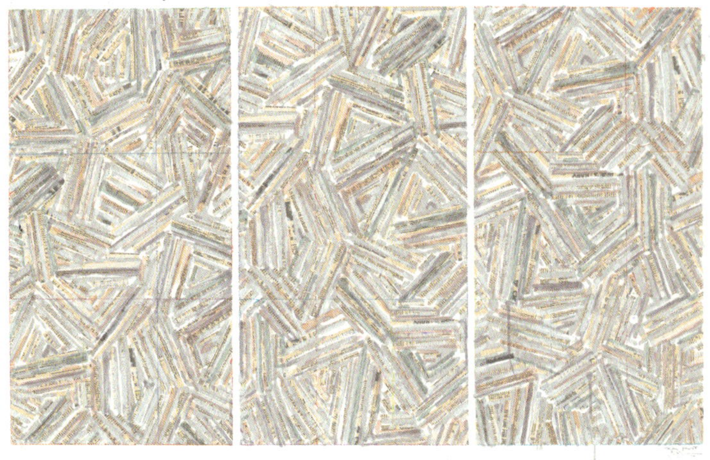

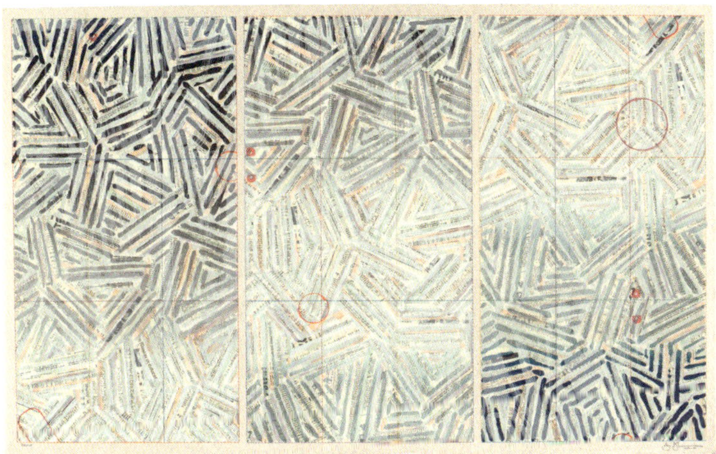

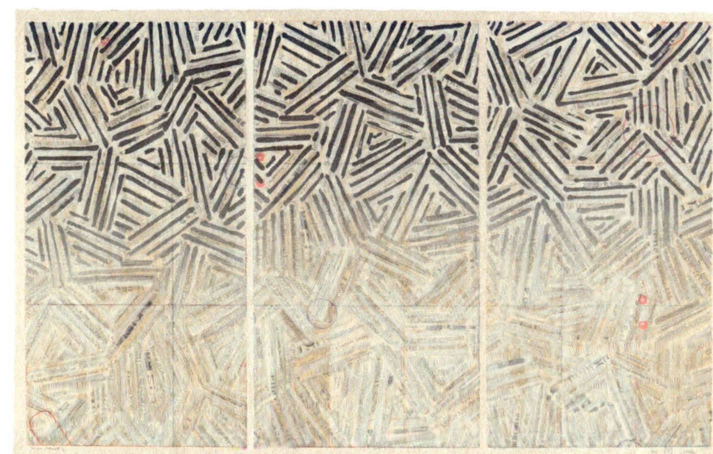

28 ***Usuyuki*, 1995**
30 ***Usuyuki*, 1981**

29 ***Usuyuki*, 1979**
31 ***Usuyuki*, 1980**

South Carolina

WHITNEY MUSEUM OF AMERICAN ART

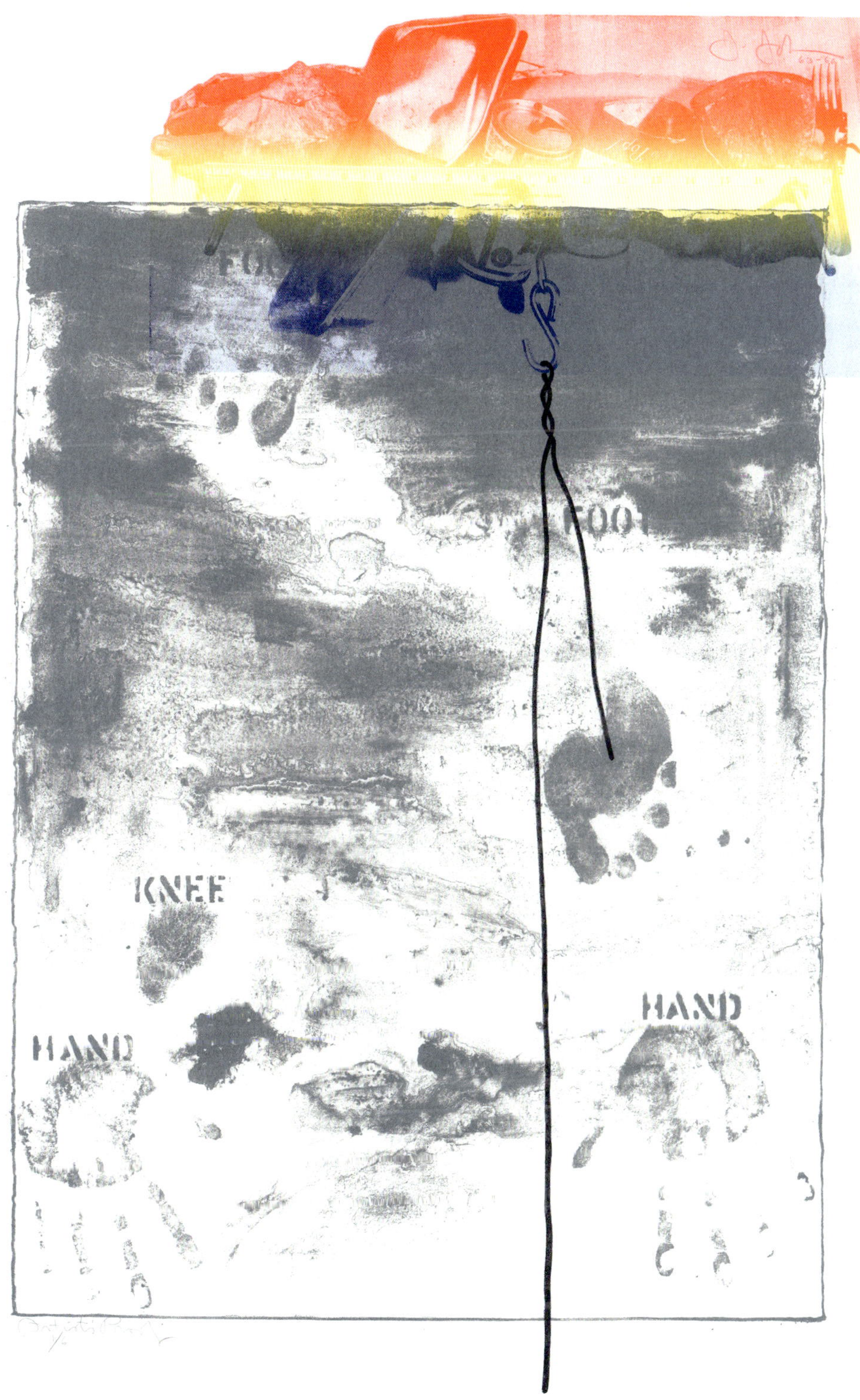

1 ***Pinion*, 1966**

2 *Studio*, 1964

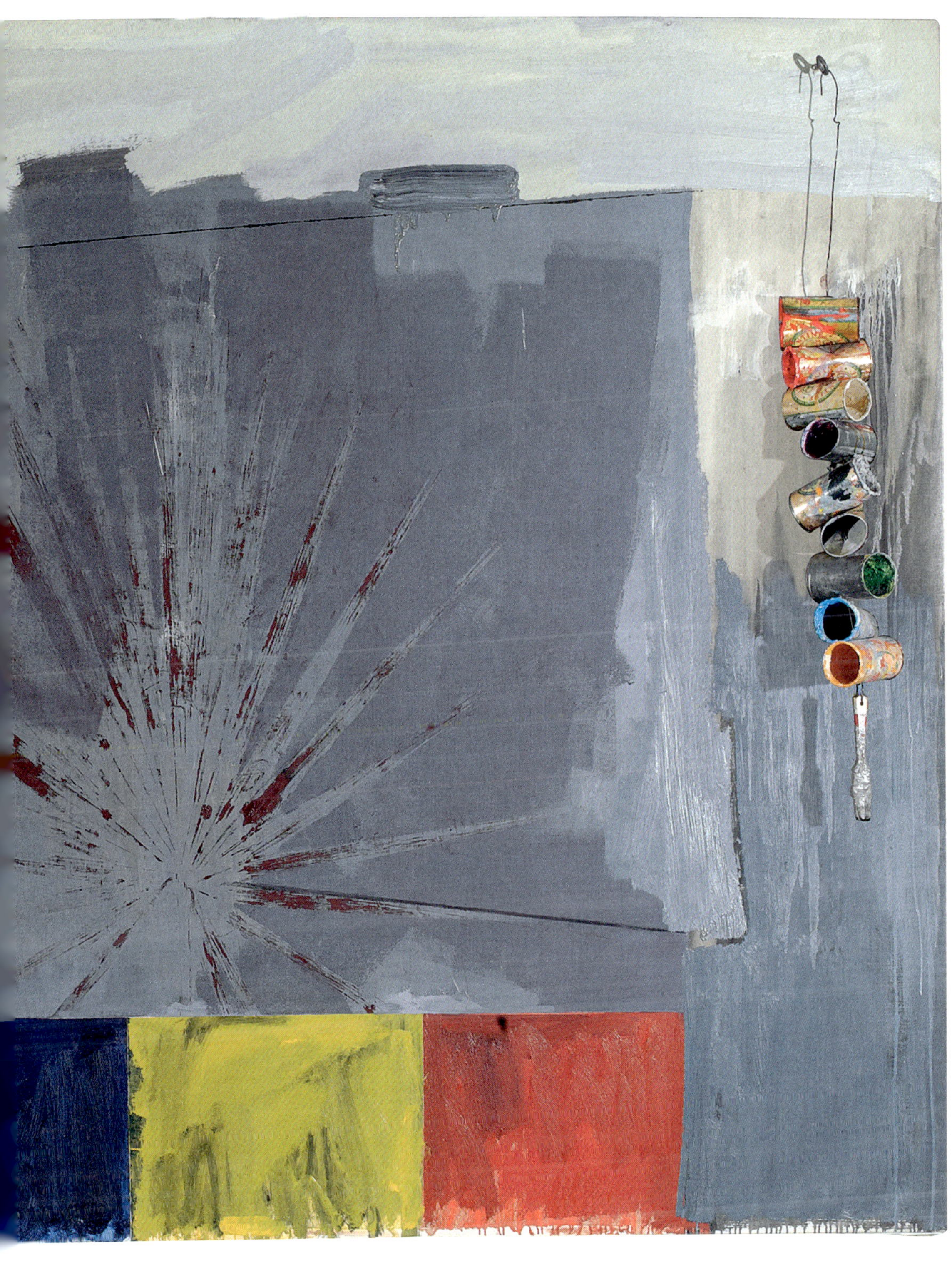

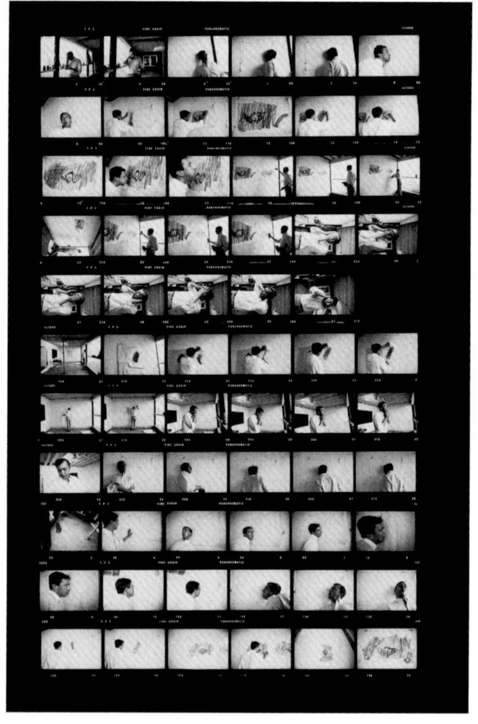

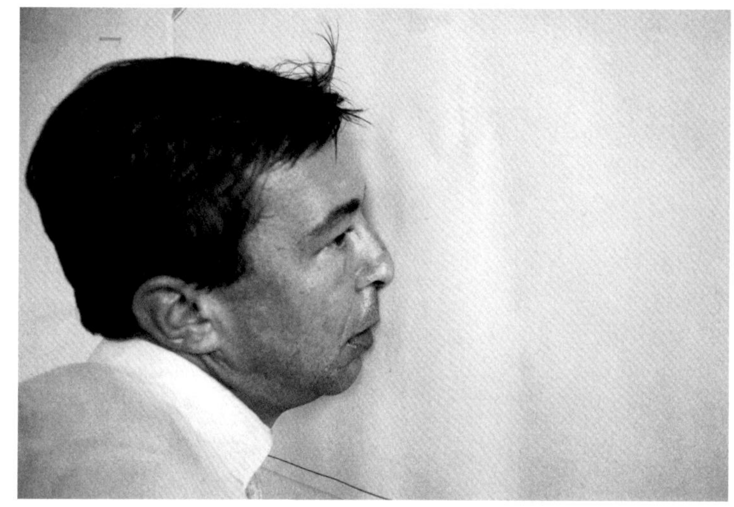

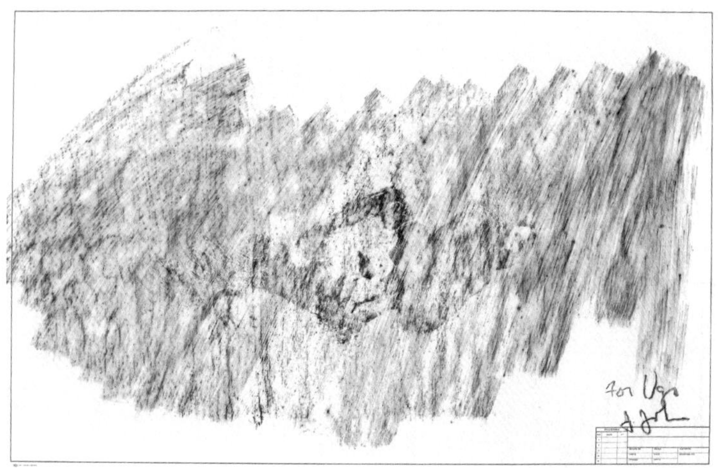

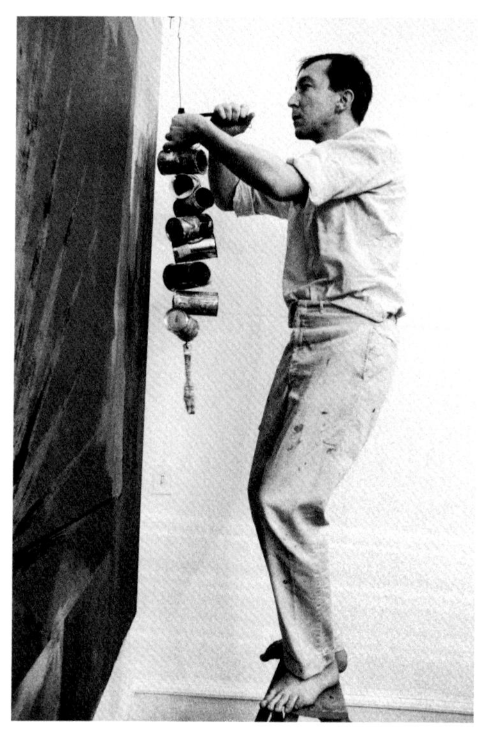

3 **Ugo Mulas, *Jasper Johns, Skin, Edisto Beach*, 1965**
5 ***Skin*, 1965**

4 **Ugo Mulas, *Jasper Johns, Skin, Edisto Beach*, 1965**
6 **Ugo Mulas, *Jasper Johns*, 1964**

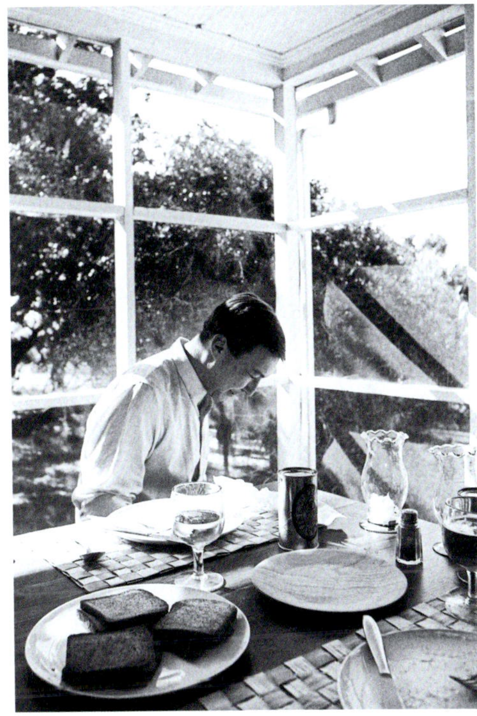

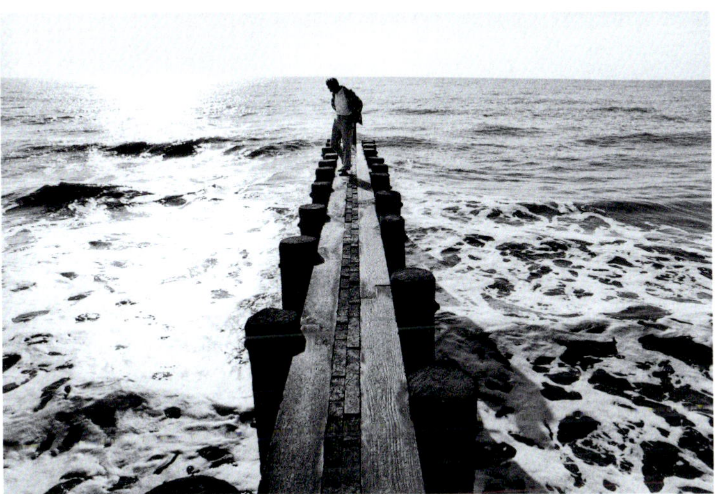

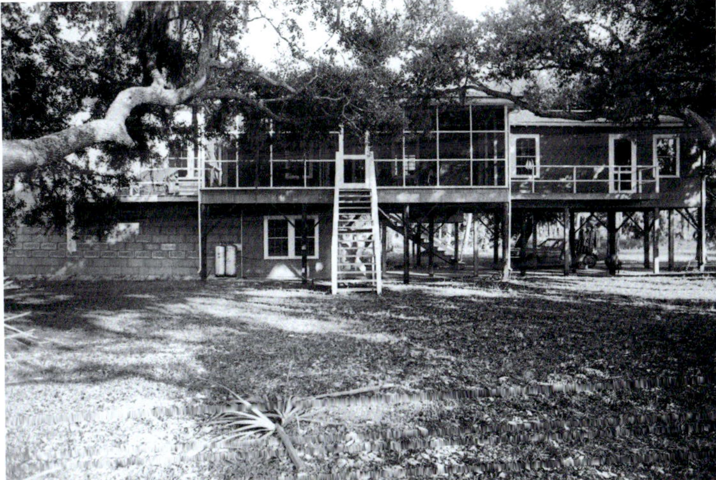

LIST OF BELONGINGS DESTROYED BY FIRE - JASPER JOHNS - EDISTO, S.C.

ARTICLE	DATE OF PURCHASE	COST	PRESENT VALUE
5 Beds	1960	[illegible]	$400.
5 Chests of drawers	1960	$450.	$400.
1 Desk	1960	$275.	$250.
1 Card Table	1960	[illegible]	$35.
1 Table	1960	$60.	$50.
2 Sofas - custom made	1961	$1000.	$800.
1 Table - custom made	1961	$300.	$275.
Antique marble table	1963	$350.	$300.
18 Chairs	1960	$600.	$500.
2 Chairs- overstuffed	1963	$400.	$300.
1 Hammock	1964	$25.	$20.
Picnic table and benches	1962	$125.	$100.
4 Stools- bar	1960	$120.	$100.
4 Lamps	1960	$100.	$80.
Fur rug	1963	$175	[illegible]
300 Books - some rare and some art books	1960- 1966	$	$1,200.
4 Suitcases	1960-1965	[illegible]	[illegible]
2 Attache cases	1964, 1965	$100.	$80.
1 Floor Polisher	1964	[illegible]	[illegible]
1 Vacumn Cleaner	1966	$100.	$90.
Refrigerator	1966	$500.	$500.
Stove	1964	$450.	$350.
Washing Machine	1966	$400.	$400.
1 Television	1964	$300.	$250.
1 Waffle Iron	1966	$60.	$60.
3 Radios	1960, 1963, 1961	[illegible]	$175.
			7,335

7 Ugo Mulas, *Jasper Johns, Edisto Beach*, 1965
9 Ugo Mulas, *Jasper Johns, Edisto Beach*, 1965

8 Ugo Mulas, *Jasper Johns, Edisto Beach*, 1965
10 List of items lost in fire at Edisto Beach, S.C., 1966

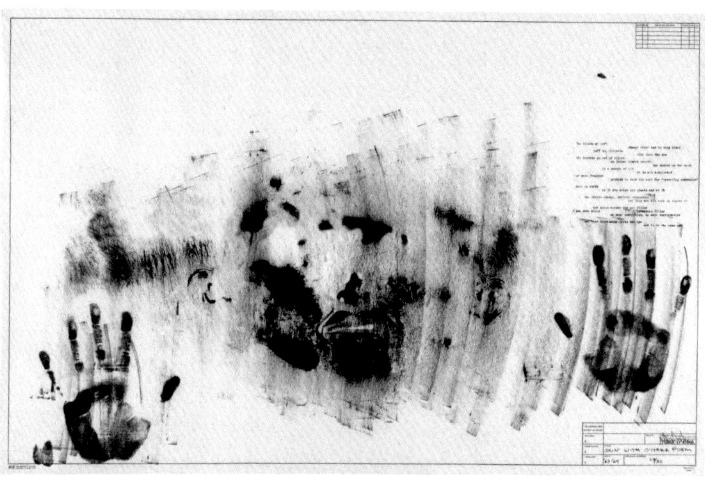

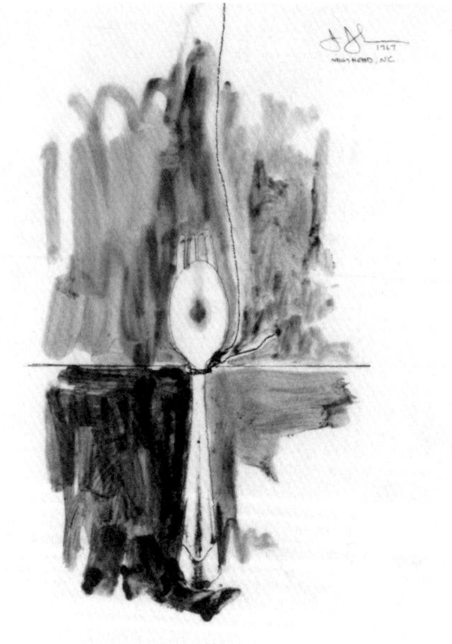

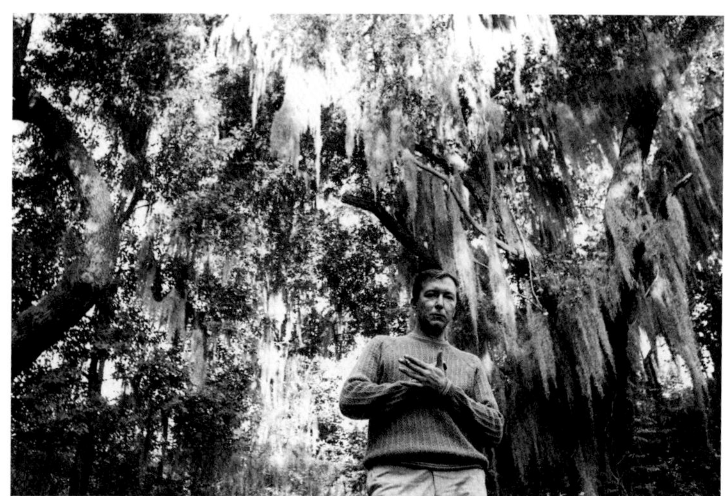

11 ***In Memory of My Feelings—Frank O'Hara*, 1961**
13 **Study for *In Memory of My Feelings*, 1967**

12 ***Skin with O'Hara Poem*, 1965**
14 **Ugo Mulas, *Jasper Johns, Edisto Beach*, 1965**

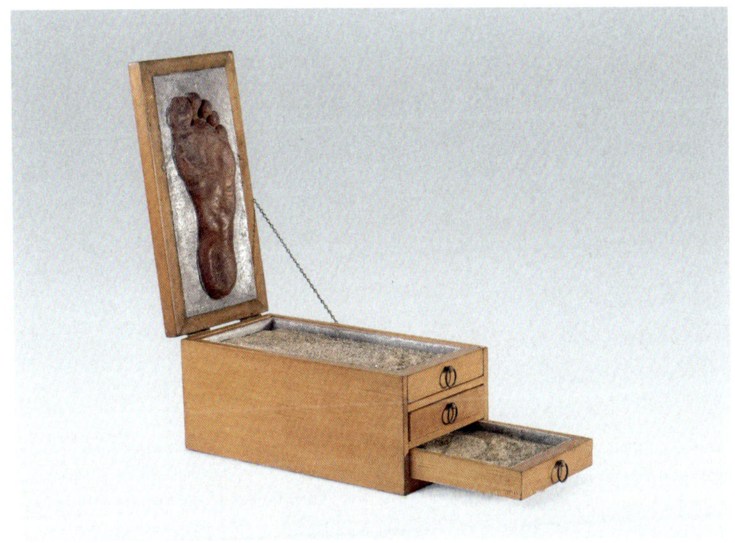

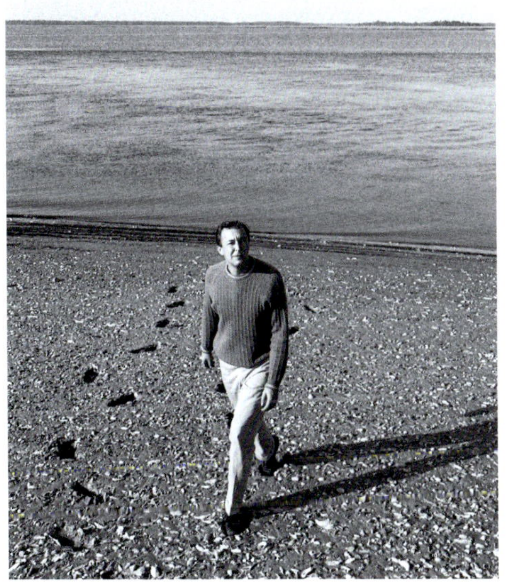

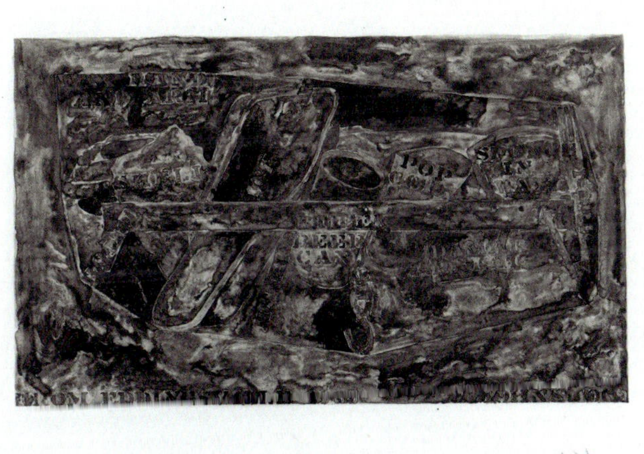

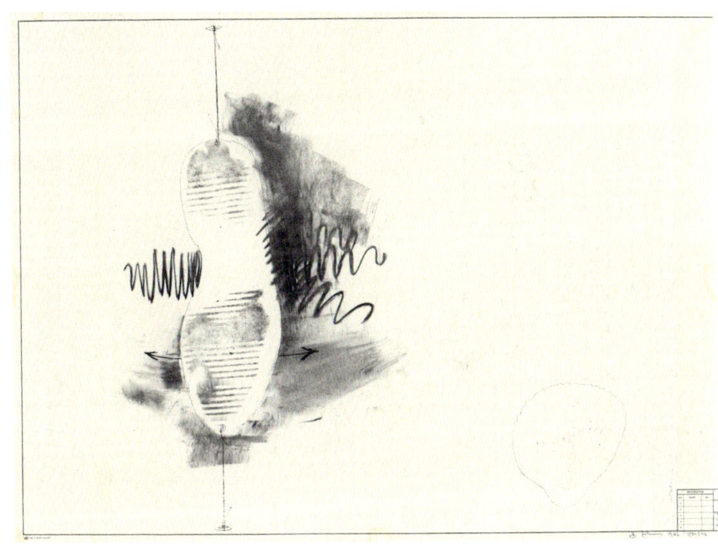

15 ***Memory Piece (Frank O'Hara)*, 1961–70**
17 ***From Eddingsville*, 1969**

16 **Ugo Mulas, *Jasper Johns, Edisto Beach*, 1965**
18 ***Edisto*, 1962**

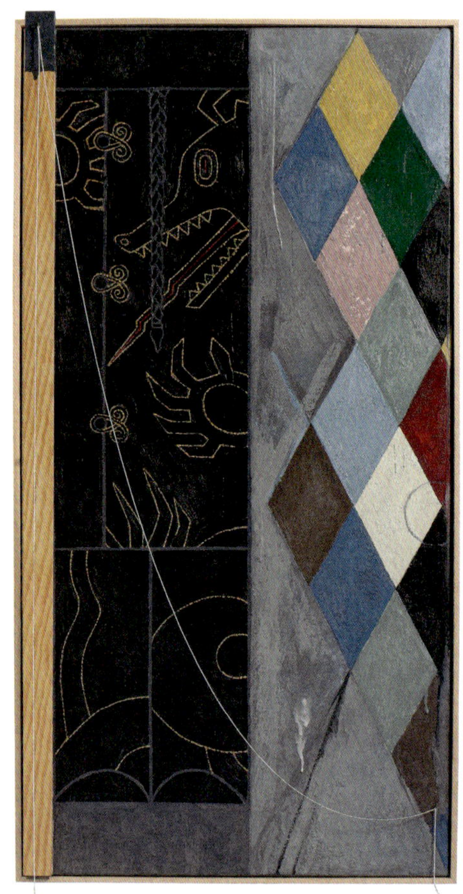

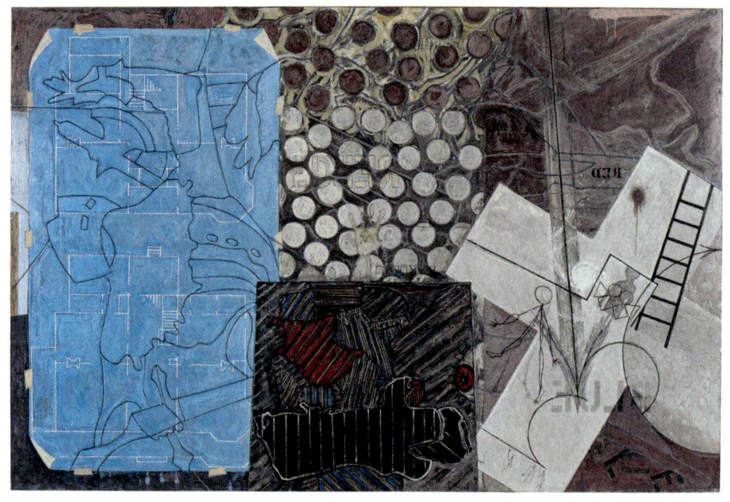

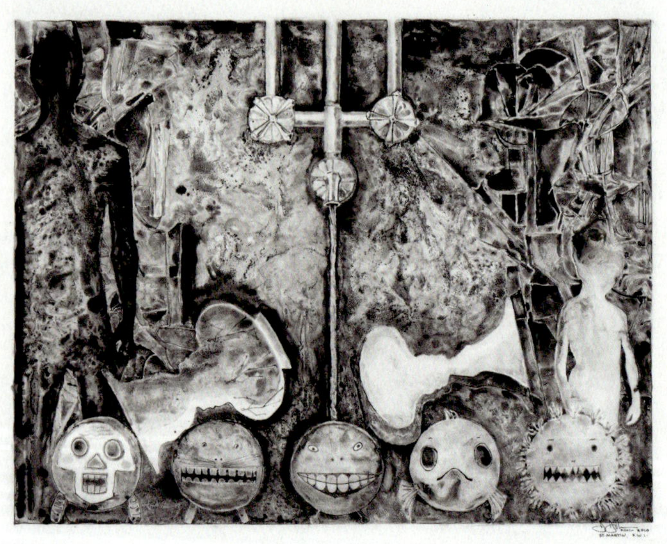

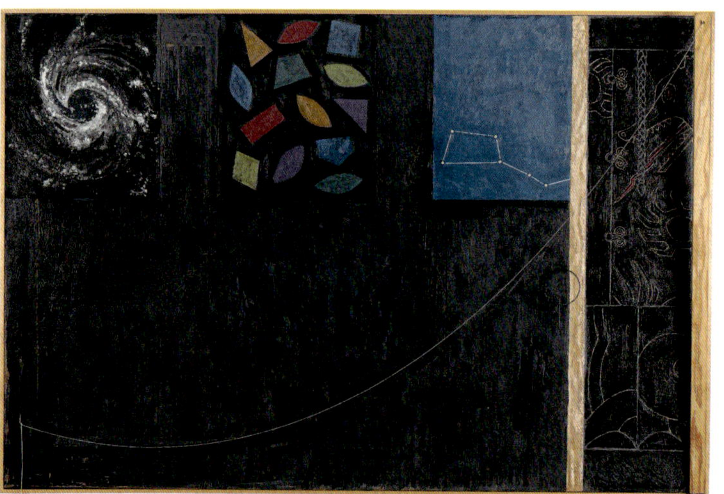

19 ***Untitled*, 1998**
21 ***Untitled*, 2010**

20 ***Untitled*, 1992–94**
22 ***Untitled (Halloween)*, 1998**

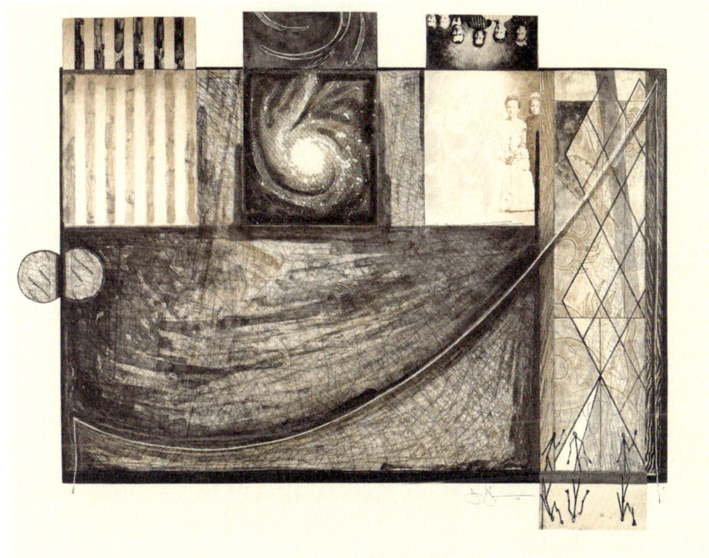

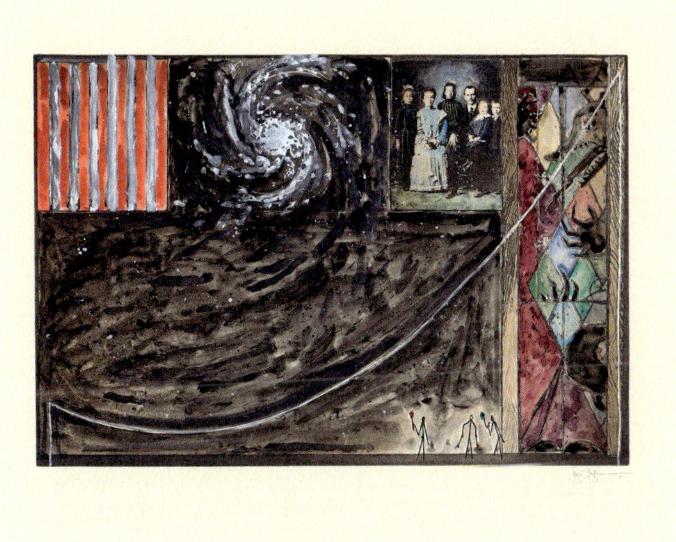

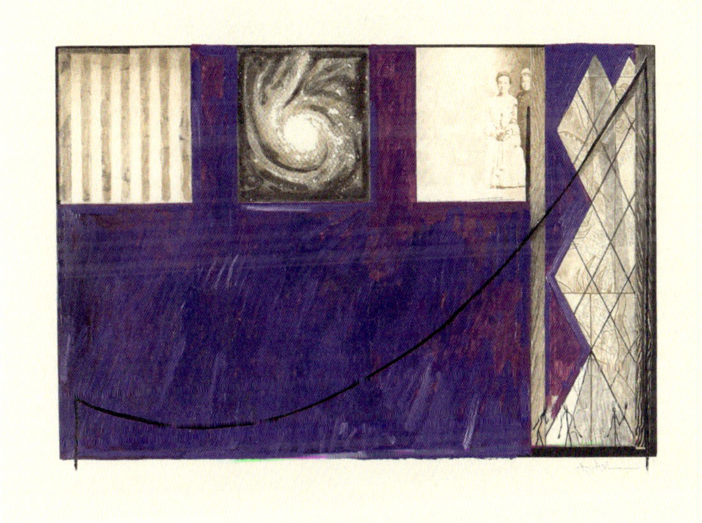

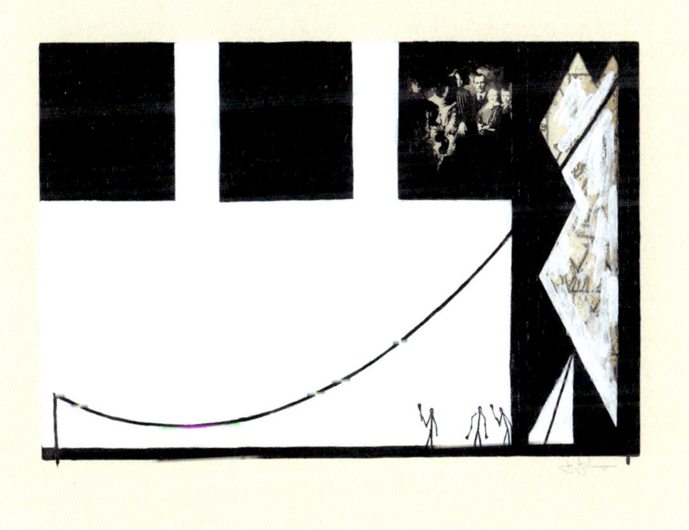

23 ***Untitled***, 2001
25 ***Untitled***, 2001

24 ***Untitled***, 2001
26 ***Untitled***, 2001

Delay as Medium: Jasper Johns and Japan
Michio Hayashi

Any discussion about the relationship between Jasper Johns and Japan must consider his friendship with the art critic Yoshiaki Tōno, who, after first meeting Johns and Robert Rauschenberg in New York in 1959, played an essential role in Johns being offered a two-month residency in Tokyo in 1964.[1] Prior to this, Tōno's essays on Nouveau Réalisme had helped shift the collective focus of the Japanese art world from Paris to New York.[2] Although Johns had previously been to Japan while serving in the United States Army in 1952–53, his return in 1964 was decisive for his ensuing artistic relationship with the island country. Of particular significance to the present essay are the four paintings—*Souvenir* (p. 118, pl. 2), *Souvenir 2* (p. 119, pl. 3), *Watchman* (p. 117, pl. 1), and *Gastro*—and related drawings (p. 122, pls. 6–9) that he produced during this stay, from April 30 to early July.[3]

According to Tōno's memoir-essay, "J. J. in Tokyo," Johns was inspired to include in *Souvenir* a plate with his own photograph on it after seeing a similar plate with a photographic transfer in a gift shop in Tokyo.[4] While the painting's title refers to the shop, it also carries a broader connotation of "memory," from the French *souvenir*. Gary Garrels has suggested another possible connection, to Marcel Duchamp, by pointing to Johns's earlier note on Duchamp that contains the word "souvenir" and to Duchamp's use of a photographic self-portrait that bears some resemblance to that on Johns's plate.[5] This connection resonates with a curious episode in Tokyo in which Johns was described as "the only son of Marcel Duchamp" by Duchamp's friend the poet and art critic Shūzō Takiguchi.[6] Impressed by Johns's work, Takiguchi gave the American artist *10 Vicious Circles* (1964; p. 124, pl. 16), a work that was inspired by Duchamp's *Rotoreliefs*.

Souvenir's multivalent, ambiguous title resonates with the overall structure of the work, which consists of four basic elements: a gray monochrome surface covered with encaustic and collage, a flashlight at the canvas's right edge, a bicycle mirror at upper right, and the aforementioned plate at lower left. The objects are positioned on the canvas in such a way that the light from the flashlight, if it could be turned on, would be deflected by the mirror and illuminate the plate. This imaginary movement of light across the canvas complicates our perception in two ways: first, it introduces temporality, or "delay," to use the Duchampian term, onto the otherwise synchronic existence of the objects within the work;[7] second, it reminds us of the epistemological interdependence of insight and blindness, as the flashlight would illuminate some objects while sinking others into darkness. The additional inclusion of a reversed canvas in *Souvenir 2*, in that regard, might be seen as a material demonstration of the invisibility (or delayed visibility) as a constitutive fact of vision. Although Johns had been using a similar motif from the 1950s, here the overlapping placement of the plate in front of the reversed canvas seems to redouble this query and tries to tempt the viewer into flipping over (and back) not only the canvas but also the plate.

In addition, it is interesting to consider that Tōno reported in 1979 that he had discovered the Japanese character の collaged onto the surface behind the plate of the first *Souvenir*.[8] That character is a possessive preposition, similar to "of" in English, and is pronounced like the English "no." Tōno speculates that Johns might have found this slippage—wherein the same sound signifies completely different things—interesting enough to hide the letter behind the plate (entertaining the possibility that "souvenir of" can easily be turned to "no souvenir"). The validity of Tōno's claim aside, what is important to note is that a delayed discovery such as this endlessly (re)starts our interpretive game and, in this particular case, lures the viewer into wanting to search the same spot of *Souvenir 2*. Or is it the case that the redoubling structure of *Souvenir 2* was intended as a retroactive clue to what is hidden in the first version? In any case, "delay," encoded already in the very title *Souvenir*, seems to function as a medium on its own.

Watchman, the largest work Johns created in Tokyo, has a structure somewhat similar to *Souvenir*. The placement of the former's rectangular shape composed of the three primary colors and the upside-down wax-cast leg on a chair mimics that of the latter's flashlight and bicycle mirror, respectively. Furthermore, in *Watchman* the strong diagonal movement suggested by the bluish-gray painterly marks and the back of the chair echoes the imaginary trajectory of light in *Souvenir*.[9] But the similarity stops there. Johns's portrait-plate is absent from *Watchman*. The horizontal band of various grays scraped along the bottom edge with a stick that is stopped in place by a small ball ends just short of where the plate is positioned in *Souvenir*. The artist's portrait is omitted, and the names of the primary colors that encircle the plate have been dispersed into the canvas's dark gray background.

The wax-cast leg in *Watchman* marked the first return of cast body parts in Johns's work since 1955, when they appeared in such pieces as *Target with Four Faces* (p. 42, pl. 2) and *Target with Plaster Casts* (p. 168, fig. 1).[10] But we also should consider a number of works that Johns produced before his trip to Tokyo; these include the paintings *Land's End* and *Periscope (Hart Crane)* (both 1963; p. 182, pls. 5, 6), and several drawings made in 1962 titled *Study for Skin 1–4*.[11] These works reveal that Johns was developing a keen interest in incorporating indexical traces of the human body (his own included) in his work.[12] *Watchman* can be understood as a pivotal work in this development and as a hinge toward *According to What* (1964; pp. 150–51, pl. 2), produced after Johns's return to the United States.

In fact, the wax-cast body parts in both *Watchman* and *According to What* form a mirror image, mediated by Johns's experience in Japan. When he invited Japanese friends to look at *Watchman* in his studio in Ginza, some of them tried to look at the back of the wax-cast leg by peering at the painting from the side. This unexpected reaction inspired Johns to turn the cast around, inside out so to speak, in *According to What*. According to Johns, it was a "gift" and the "only influence I received in Japan (laughs)."[13] This use of the flipped-over cast added a material dimension to the already-existing conceptual relationship between the two paintings, as the latter's title, *According to What*, derived from a preparatory note by Johns about *Watchman* (fig. 1).

Beginning "The watchman falls 'into' the 'trap' of looking. The 'spy' is a different person," this note has been the source of various interpretations of *Watchman*. Its content revolves around the incommensurable relationship between two kinds of looking, that of the "watchman" and that of the "spy": the former predicated on clear reciprocity and the other on an asymmetrical visibility-invisibility

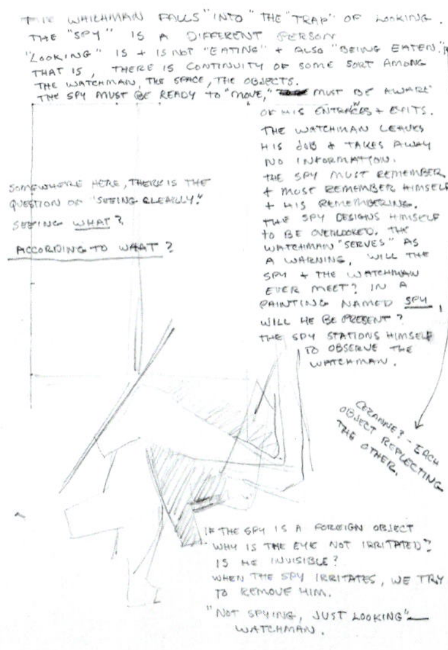

Fig. 1 **Sketchbook page, Book A, 1964**
Courtesy of the artist

relationship. As Hiroko Ikegami argues, the reflective interrogation of the act of looking remains at the core of this note and provides us with an important clue for the reading of the painting, especially in its possible reference to the Cold War, during which the figure of the spy circulated prominently in mass culture.[14] But what confounds the matter is the way in which Johns, rather abruptly in the third sentence, introduces an anti-optical dimension into the text: "'Looking' is + is not 'eating' + also 'being eaten.'"

This invocation of "eating" reminds us of Johns's earlier work *Painting Bitten by a Man* (1961; p. 44, pl. 4), but also resonates with *Souvenir*, where the artist's face is served on a plate.[15] Is the upside-down "watchman" sitting at the table, ready to eat? Or was his absent upper body eaten by a monster? In any case, the indexical tactility emphasized by the wax casting in *Watchman*, when combined with the gushing downflow of paint, seems to imply more than simple touch. A similar observation can be made, in fact, regarding Johns's later sculptural piece *Summer Critic* (1966; p. 123, pl. 11), believed to be modeled on Tōno. The mouths behind the sunglasses are often understood to be tongue-in-cheek sarcasm about how critics "see" an artwork with words. But the mouth is more than an organ for speaking. It is, after all, the most versatile anti-optical organ and has multiple functions: eating, biting, kissing, spitting, and so on. Johns's investigation into the nature of looking somehow ends up spilling over into the realm of the anti-optical, foregrounding the fact that the membrane of visuality is always porous.

Johns's interest in indexical marks with bodily evocations continually informs his production, often in tension with programmed structural transparency. A seminal example of this can be found in his series of crosshatch works known as Usuyuki, to which a number of paintings, prints, and drawings produced between 1977 and 2002 belong (see, for example, pp. 120–21, pl. 4; and pp. 126–27, pls. 24–31).

In this series, shuttling back and forth between media while defying the traditional hierarchy between them, Johns experimented with a variety of compositional strategies, "including repetition, mirroring, rotating, cropping, and scrolling" of preconceived sections of crosshatchings.[16] Although those strategies are employed according to premeditated rules, they are often too complicated to be grasped at once, as if perceptual *delays* are embedded into the material surface of each work. The Usuyuki series is arguably the most sophisticated series-within-a-series that embodies this incongruous dovetailing of instantaneous intelligibility and ever-deferring perceptual density. Its title means "thin or light snow" in Japanese and "is the name of a female character in a play written for traditional Japanese Jōruri, which is popularized as a Kabuki play."[17] According to Johns, he encountered the word in a translated text, and this "triggered" his thinking.[18] Although there are no clear thematic correlations, "the fleeting quality of beauty" implied by the title and the female character's ultimately tragic fate seem to resonate with the ever-shifting impression of this series.[19]

Especially notable are, on the one hand, the combination of multicolored grid patterns over the compositions, and on the other, the complex overlay of thin layers of pigment. The grid has two contradictory functions: it dictates the composition as a static totality but also divides the picture into (dis)junctive rectangular sections that are flipped over, repeated, or rotated across the surface. In addition, gradational colorings often move diagonally across the divided sections—see, for example, the encaustic piece in the collection of the Sezon Museum of Modern Art (pp. 120–21, pl. 4)—adding another layer of rhythm or movement.

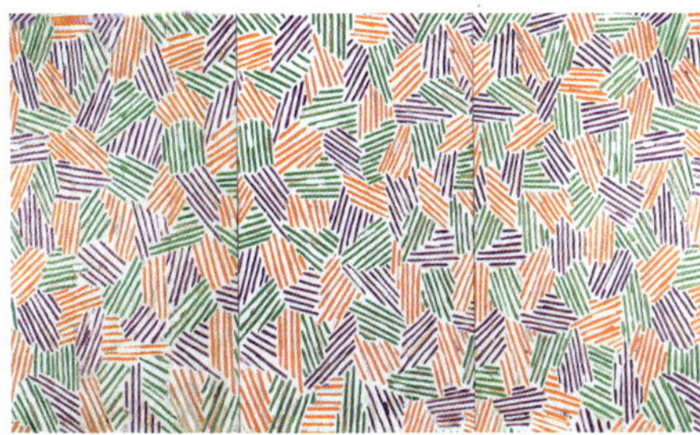

Fig. 2 ***Scent*, 1973–74**
Oil and encaustic on canvas, 72 × 126 ¼ in. (182.9 × 320.7 cm). Ludwig Forum für internationale Kunst, Aachen, Germany

These lateral movements are counterpointed by the agglomeration of thin layers of soft-hued pigments that imbue the whole surface with an atmospheric quality in keeping with the title. A remark Johns made on his earlier crosshatch piece *Scent* (1973–74; fig. 2) is also relevant to the Usuyuki series: "I thought there would be something that couldn't be identified but would be sensed in a certain way."[20] For these prints also engage with this "something" that eludes conceptual grasp. Just as the ontological frailty of thin snow makes us hypersensitive to the multitude of passing sensory effects, Usuyuki variations never stop generating subtle, transient, but sharp sensations that come (fall) and go (melt) in a fleeting moment. And here, too, *delay* is the medium of incessant perceptual revelations.

1 Johns singled out Tōno as "one of the most important people who connected me to Japan." Johns, "Ima Yatte Irukoto o Tsuzukete Ikitai [I Would Like to Continue What I Am Doing Now]," interview by Keiji Usami, *Herumesu*, no. 48 (1994): 87.

2 See especially Yoshiaki Tōno, "Nyū Riarisumu: Nyū Yōku Repōto [New Realism: New York Reports]," *Geijutsu Shinchō*, April 1963, 44–54.
3 *Gastro* is no longer extant.
4 Yoshiaki Tōno, "Tokyo no J. J. [J. J. in Tokyo]," *Bijutsu Techō*, August 1964, 5–8.
5 Gary Garrels, "Souvenir," in *Jasper Johns: Seeing with the Mind's Eye*, ed. Gary Garrels, exh. cat. (San Francisco: San Francisco Museum of Modern Art, 2012), 100–105.
6 See Yoshiaki Tōno, *Tsukurite Tachi to no Jikan: Gendai Geijutsu no Bōken* [Chatting with Artists] (Tokyo: Iwanami Shoten, 1984), 142.
7 *Delay in Glass* was a suggested subtitle for Duchamp's *Large Glass* (1915–23; p. 198, fig. 3), as it appears in one of the notes contained in his *Green Box* (1934; p. 155, pl. 14), a collection of the artist's preparatory notations and diagrams relating to his masterwork. For a reproduction of the note, see Marcel Duchamp, *The Bride Stripped Bare by Her Bachelors, Even: A Typographic Version by Richard Hamilton of Marcel Duchamp's "Green Box,"* trans. George Heard Hamilton (New York: Jaap Rietman, 1976), 1.
8 Yoshiaki Tōno, "Johns no Uragawa [The Backside of Johns]," in *Jasupā Jōnzu: Soshite/Aruiwa* [Jasper Johns: And/Or] (Tokyo: Bijutsu Shuppan-sha, 1979), 181–86. Johns alluded to this in a sketchbook note; see "Book A, p. 53, 1964," in *Jasper Johns: Writings, Sketchbook Notes, Interviews*, ed. Kirk Varnedoe (New York: Museum of Modern Art, 1996), 58 (hereafter abbreviated Varnedoe, *WSI*).
9 These diagonal positionings should also be considered in relation to the frequent appearance of diagonality in Johns's work, as discussed in Jennifer L. Roberts, "The Printerly Art of Jasper Johns," in *Jasper Johns / In Press: The Crosshatch Works and the Logic of Print*, exh. cat. (Cambridge, MA: Harvard Art Museums, 2012), 31.
10 According to the artist, his use of wax-cast body parts was inspired by his visit to Madame Tussauds in London in 1962. See Tōno, "[J. J. in Tokyo]," 8.
11 For illustrations of *Study for Skin 1–4*, see Kirk Varnedoe, ed., *Jasper Johns: A Retrospective*, exh. cat. (New York: Museum of Modern Art, 1996), 212–13, pls. 91–94.
12 Johns's encounter with works by Ushio Shinohara (b. 1932) and Nobuaki Kojima (b. 1935)—including examples employing a plaster cast of a hand and standing figures made of fiber-reinforced plaster, respectively—might have provided another stimulus for him to explore the use of a wax-cast body part in *Watchman*. On Johns's relationship with these artists, see Hiroko Ikegami, "Looking Deeper: Jasper Johns in an International Context of the 1960s," in *Jasper Johns*, ed. Roberta Bernstein, exh. cat. (London: Royal Academy of Arts in collaboration with the Broad, 2017), 46–57.
13 See Jasper Johns, "Sekai wo Hitotsu no Shiten de Hyogen Dekitara! [What If I Can Express the World by One Dot!]," interview by Yoshiaki Tōno, in Tōno, [Johns: And/Or], 200. Obviously, his use of the word "only" should not be taken at face value.
14 Ikegami, "Looking Deeper."
15 See Garrels, "Souvenir," 105.
16 For a detailed account of the formal strategies and the genealogy of the Usuyuki series, see Roberta Bernstein, *Jasper Johns: Usuyuki*, exh. cat. (New York: Fergus McCaffrey, 2019); for the quotation, see page 20. For the importance of the print medium to Johns, see Roberts, "Printerly Art," 10–42.
17 Bernstein, *Johns: Usuyuki*, 86.
18 Jasper Johns, "An Interview with Jasper Johns about Silkscreening," by Katrina Martin, in *Jasper Johns: Printed Symbols*, exh. cat. (Minneapolis: Walker Art Center, 1990), 60.
19 Johns, "Interview with Jasper Johns."
20 Jasper Johns, interview by David Bourdon, October 11, 1977, in Varnedoe, *WSI*, 156.

In My Mother's Voice
Ralph Lemon

I've been asked to write about the American South, to look for it in Jasper Johns's resolute (and, I would say, innocent) early work. My imagined American South, or how I manipulate it.

It might be there:

The heat-induced encaustic (unreliably sublime surfaces)
The body prints (left-behind skin)
Spoons, knives, and forks (some kind of service)
The numbers (counting how long it will take)
The charcoaled (blackened) maps of the United States of America
The targets (on the backs of some folk)
The (white) flags
The photographs (his solitude, confinement, silence)
Anything else ...

By choice, I know the South, before and now, as a Black folk place—that nature, posture, flesh, those images—more than I know it as any other kind of place. My mother, Ruth Evelyn Satterwhite Lemon, grew up in Lancaster, South Carolina, in the 1930s and 1940s. It was the Jim Crow South, and the Depression. It was also about a two-hour drive from Allendale, where Jasper Johns spent his early life. My mother is one year older than Johns, born in 1929. She knew of no lynchings in South Carolina, but she heard about the ones in Georgia (where Johns was born, in Augusta). "I never wanted to go there, that far south," she says. "Lancaster was kind of liberal, if legally segregated." My mother, like her mother, is high yellow, so they didn't treat her like they did the darker kids. Still, she couldn't socialize with white folk. Her all-colored school used old books from the white schools, with lots of pages ripped out ("on purpose," my mother is certain). Colored schools in the state at the time only went to eleventh grade. Most of the classes were training courses: cooking, sewing, and housecleaning for the girls; carpentry, plastering, welding, bricklaying, and cooking for the boys. There were no art classes. White people lived nearby in her "little part" of Lancaster. They got along separately but fine, as long as she and her family and friends used the back doors and alleys and stayed off Main Street. They could go to the ice-cream parlor on Main, but not the hamburger place. She can't really explain why. There were odd, unpredictable incongruities in how the law was supposed to work. Nearby white folk would barter to let their cattle graze on my grandfather's land. He was William Isom Satterwhite, called W.I., and those few acres were given to him by his grandfather Isom Caleb Clinton, who acquired them after the Civil War from his cotton-planter slave master, Irving Clinton. That land held the house where my mother was born. (Johns's grandfather was also called W.I., William Isaac Johns. He was a cotton farmer/producer, a founder of Allendale County, and Johns's caretaker after his parents divorced when he was two. W.I. Johns lived on Main Street.)[1] When my mother went to the movie theater, she could buy popcorn in the main-entrance lobby, but then had to go around to the back-door entrance and up the stairs to the balcony to watch the movie. (She and her friends would throw popcorn on the white kids down below.) In the summertime, she and her brother would take W.I. his lunch at the cotton mill where he worked. "There were lots of poor white trash who lived in little shacks near the mill, and their kids would throw rocks at us as we passed by," she recalls. W.I. told them that the rich white people paid the poor white trash to do their dirty work—to fight the people of color. When my mother crossed the Mason-Dixon Line and moved to Cincinnati in 1949, in an assumed escape, she found a different kind of segregation—not Jim Crow, but one more insidious: "Black people could move into neighborhoods that Jews had left, but not into neighborhoods that white people left behind. I didn't really live and work with white people until we moved to Minneapolis in 1963—a truly integrated place, for the first time in my life.... But I couldn't relax, the damage was done." The tyranny was deeply embedded in her body. My mother keeps no secrets to herself or her family of her South; it is unobscured. She will die with the nightmare of that time and the place still scratching at her skin. She returned in 1971—after it had changed, a little—and to Georgia this time, of all places. She missed some things.

There were also no art classes in any of young Johns's southern schools, he has said. He escaped the South, also in 1949, though for different reasons than my mother. He, too, returned (in 1961, as a celebrated artist), for perhaps similar reasons, culture disorientation above all. He missed some things.

Johns said that going to Edisto changed his life.[2] (A temporary refuge, until his home and studio there burned to the ground in 1966 and Johns went back north.) Edisto Island, South Carolina, is some three-hours' drive from Lancaster, and nearly two hours from Allendale. It was originally home to the Edisto people, a Native American subtribe of the Cusabo, who lived along the Atlantic coast in what is now South Carolina. The Spanish arrived in the sixteenth century, followed in the early seventeenth century by the English, who took over large tracts of land for rice, indigo, and cotton plantations. The Edisto people had disappeared by the early 1700s, and Edisto became a sea-island slave culture. (The 1790 census reported a population of 223 whites and 1,692 Black slaves; the 1860 census indicated 329 whites and 5,082 slaves.) After the Civil War, the planters/slavers abandoned the island but maintained ownership of large tracts of its land. Free Black people created Geechee/Gullah communities, different from those on the mainland, and maintained them for a time. Since the twentieth century, the island has been redeveloped as a tourist destination with resorts. (In 2010 the island's population was 63.7 percent white, 34 percent black.)

I know little about Johns's early life in the South. I do know that he was afforded the emphatic advantages of southern white primacy and Black segregation. (This is not an indictment, just fact.) How extreme, pervasive, and visible it was. When I look at any Johns painting, with its complex layering, curated art history, masterful craft, and virtuosity, I find no traces of that southern world of Jim Crow in which he was born, grew up, and became (or unbecame) the man he is. How is that possible? Is it a purposeful cultural negation, amnesia, and/or an innocent ontological relationship to the South and its horrific legacy of slavery and all the other trauma that followed? Where in his work is the cultural body memory of the South that I know, grew up with (my mother's shrieks), imagine? I would like to believe that the monster is there, if only in a color, surface texture, a geometrical rhythm. Because it is human for the body to hold, somewhere, the inescapable trauma of what happened there (if only in hearsay and living-room parlance). But where is it, really, beyond the absence of the violently oppressed Black body, which obviously does not belong in his paintings? Most likely it is a meaningless concern that, like the best of his work, has nothing to do with anything other than what one is looking at. They are ultimately "paintings about paintings," and in this there is some kind of enlightenment, floating above something else closer to gravity.[3]

In the summer of 1936, Birda Satterwhite, my grandmother, sent her seven-year-old daughter to a butcher and grocery store on Main Street with a note for groceries. "Do not look him in the eye," she cautioned her daughter. The owner, a sweaty, red-faced white man in his forties or fifties, filled the order and, as my mother turned to exit the store through the back door, lifted up her dress and placed one of his hands inside her panties, patting her on the butt. "Have a nice day," he said. My mother hurried home and told her mother, but not W.I., her father, "who surely would have gone to the store, through the front door, and killed the white, sweaty, red-faced man, and then been killed himself, or worse." Soon after, my grandmother took my mother out of her local school and sent her to a coed colored boarding school (with white teachers) founded by the Women's Home Missionary Society of the Methodist Episcopal Church to educate slaves and their descendants, in Camden, thirty-seven miles south of Lancaster. Here she was able to study physics, French, Langston Hughes, and Shakespeare, and play on the girls' basketball team. It was a school they couldn't afford. It was also my mother's first assumed escape.

Trauma is relative, depending on the body traumatized. I see in Johns's ambitious early work of the 1950s and 1960s something of a muse, like Frank O'Hara: full of 1950s–60s queer asymmetrical thinking, with its well-kept secrets, its presentness and futurity—a different kind of trauma. Johns appropriated some things, perhaps as a way to deflect from the southern debacle, both private and national. Southern, white, middle-class, and queer, he was a fugitive of sorts. A different kind of blackness, oppression, aliveness, resistance? No, certainly not—something else.

O'Hara and the Dada-Duchamp-Cage-Cunningham-Rauschenberg mash-up were significant. This white, male, mostly queer creative container, with its own thinking, politics, and exclusive culture, was relatively free of the burden of southern whiteness. Contrast this with, say, the provincial modernist William Faulkner, who never left the South, who devoured southern racist whiteness as food for literary genius. Faulkner's South was one of ongoing land hunger and race hatred, of fraught grace in the face of white culture in decay (with *niggers* everywhere). Its nostalgic locus was the post–Civil War South, before which the place had been paradisiacal, with all that free, Black subservient labor. In the culturally aestheticized delirium of his novels, a strange truth resides in the air and dust of the place: the southern gothic nightmare of the past. A brutally broken land, defeated, outraged—romanticizing its centuries-old terror—made fictionally profound.

Johns's South Carolina had the second-fewest Black lynching victims in the South, with 156 from 1876 to 1947. Willie Earle was the last Black person lynched there, in 1947, in Greenville, two-and-a-half hours from Sumter, where Johns was then finishing high school. Faulkner's Mississippi had the most, with 539 victims. When I look at all those blissful white bodies surrounding a brutalized Black body hanging in a tree or on top of a burning pyre in photographs from the 1800s to the 1940s, do I see any kind of (body) grace? No. I see human obscenity, madness, evil. So, yes, one must try to escape this place psychically, physically, and/or fictionally, and then miss it because it was home. All that one knows before knowing more, how achingly inattentive (and effectively dysfunctional) that lingering process can be.

Johns's early paintings hold some emphatic cultural inattention. They are attentive to so much else that avoids that culture, and therefore also harmless (as paintings). The harmless part is their biggest secret. They are harmless but determinedly not naïve. I would like to believe (because I want to believe) that the outrage of the place and the time is right there, in the layers (the darkness, the erasures, the left-behind skin, a mourning). *Flashlight III* (1958; p. 169, fig. 2), *Flag* (1959; p. 68, pl. 18), *No* (1961; p. 47, pl. 12), *Painting Bitten by a Man* (1961; p. 44, pl. 4), *Hand* (1963; p. 190, pl. 10), *Skin* (1965; p. 132, pl. 5), *Flag* (1965; p. 71, pl. 27), *Two Flags* (1969; p. 68, pl. 17), and nearly every version of *White Flag* (p. 64, pl. 4) have a visceral quality that activates something I find retributionally fulfilling, something I fabricate to justify the time I spend looking at the work. (I don't have the freedom, of late, to look at the work purely or abstractly; there is too much cultural resistance.) Not unlike reading Faulkner (a different white-southern art greatness I'm trying to make sense of, especially *Absalom, Absalom!*). Faulkner also immaculately layered refractions of a particular reality, though he always clearly posed his dominant whiteness, his evolved racism, without obfuscation. His denial was in how utterly wrongheaded it all was. He maintained some social and aesthetic shame/gratification/pleasure (and societal acknowledgment) in the diabolical—a disturbance I find perfectly clarifying.

Where is Johns's social pleasure or displeasure in his southern inheritance? If he had been a writer, maybe he would have had no choice but to deal with the race nightmare and its madness more directly, like Faulkner, Erskine Caldwell, Carson McCullers, and maybe Eudora Welty. Or a musician, since the music of the South (the music of America) is another direct societal consequence of American Blackness. But Johns is a painter, ensconced in that ancient white history (vacuum), who found the appropriated and refined, (sexually) dissident (from the mainstream) pleasure of O'Hara and Hart Crane, as well as Duchamp and company. Beautiful Duchamp, who grew up in a rarefied white French-European world, surrounded by the Western art whose values he sought to negate. Who escaped to America and New York, twice, saying, "There's more freedom here, less remnants of the past."[4] Who knew little if anything about American slavery, I imagine. And who knew that Black people (Africans) have a fantastical visual culture that Westerners now call art. Yes, the sanctified Dada-Duchamp-Cage-Cunningham-Rauschenberg mash-up. That became Johns's salvation, his vehicle out of the South and perhaps out of his racially haunted and oppressed queer white body. Setting up his challenge to the godlike Abstract Expressionists, those hypermasculine native-born and immigrant American white men (Willem de Kooning in particular, with the forward/backward evolution of his insurgency). But Johns's conceptual devotion to the trickster Duchamp and to Rauschenberg's feral (and queer?) art-making qualities seems to have horse-blinded him out of that haunted world, and toward a certain compromised new freedom.

Johns's precise and complex marks deflect any fixed meaning. They're impenetrable—a beautiful escape, it seems: a mediated (negotiated) American flag, a target, a flashlight, a footprint, a borrowed poem about erotic city life and its gracefulness. Never extreme, the geometric tension is always just right. There is a civil balance to the tension in his work—a wish, oneiric, advanced. (While his lover Rauschenberg paid attention to everything, even his own southern past, Johns pays attention to only a few questionably symbolic mundane things, over and over again.)

Suspending, for a moment, what I want to see in a Johns painting (out of much curiosity, because he is an inviolable modern art god, white, of a generation from the South), I think of his early work mostly as iconographic still lifes. A voyeurism. Classical. They offer precise (mis)arrangements of articles perceived as essential to life but mostly independent of people and human narratives. In Johns's words, "All the qualities that interest me—literalness, repetitiveness, an obsessive quality, order with dumbness, and the possibility of complete lack of meaning."[5] People in general, and Johns himself, are missing or obscured, except for the scattered body parts and prints (a universe of perfectly organized death). Is this visual objectification an attempt at obliterating the body, history, nation, self? But unlike the classic still life, his marked (disguised) and arranged flags, maps, targets, and numbers also become a grand burlesque. A trace of human presence, its messiness, is there, if obscured or repressed. There are composed, sudden collapses and eruptions, as in *Jubilee* (1959; p. 98, pl. 1), *Night Driver* (1960; p. 48, pl. 21), *Disappearance II* (1961; p. 48, pl. 19), and *Liar* (1961; p. 45, pl. 5). Some things—many things—are important. The rigor demands it. But what things exactly, I doubt Johns fully knows. Part of the work's intention is to know as little as possible, so as not to fall into the traps of particular knowledge. For us (and him) it's ultimately about the surface, like the flags, marking where one is, a national iconography, a facade, leaving out all the terrible things that flags have wrought. They become banal, but don't disappear (the colors!). They haunt us and are also free. What, then, do we look at, see? What I mostly see and then do not see is a psychically charged geographic shift, the valiant indeterminacy of his work from a body born in a very determined racist Jim Crow South. His particular body escaped and did not fail, did not fall into a river chased by a bunch of bloodhounds. In fact, his fugitive whereabouts were celebrated.

Where is Jasper Johns? I see and imagine (desire) some futurity in these early paintings, as well as a notion of some art-historical past. An equipoise. Johns's work is certainly hard-wrought integration, if only of paint and image—and all that it obscures. Why disrupt one's inherent freedom by being fully seen? It is clearly a negotiated absence. It is absence, too, of all the collaged Black bodies, their labor and their suffering, that were embedded in his young (orphaned) middle-class life in the South—Black bodies who for a time may have prepared his food, washed and ironed his clothes, made his bed, swept his floors, brushed his hair, not leaving a trace.[6] The invisibility of the perpetuated cultural terror to the one terrorizing. How remarkable.

My mother speaks of three flags in her colored schools, her Jim Crow South: the US flag, the South Carolina state flag (white palmetto tree on indigo with a white crescent moon in the upper-left corner), and the Christian flag (a white flag with a blue corner square with a red cross in the center). She doesn't remember ever seeing the second edition of the Confederate flag, the "Stainless Banner." "Maybe it flew in Columbia, the capital," she says. "I never saw it in Lancaster." She also doesn't remember seeing the US flag flying about, other than in her colored-school assemblies. It had disappeared. Holding her hand to her heart, pledging allegiance to segregation, her certain oppression, racism, the law, she wasn't thinking about anything. It was a meaningless daily act, more present and disturbing and without the rigor and abundance of what Johns continues to make up. Basically, she was uninterested in flags—an unmarked agency of resistance. I think my mother wanted to be an artist.

Johns offers an expansive, nonlinear look at certain aspects of life, a privileged vision of the world and being in the world. But there is nothing nonlinear about America's history of segregation. About living, growing up amid a Black body culture oppressed by another more brutally dominant white culture. And how easy it was, perhaps, to talk oneself into not seeing it. That Black body culture was invisible, and that dominant white culture was absolute and sovereign. The binary power dynamic meaningless, invisible as well. I imagine this carries over into Johns's paintings, his "order with dumbness." Helping to make him a great painter. A Johns flag image becomes charged while remaining beatifically meaningless, like a re-marked target, light bulb, or map—familiar images that take on metarepresentational qualities while not answering to any "social demand" or contract.[7] Images that are what they are, nothing more (that is possible for some painters)—there is considerable talent but also entitlement in that gesture, and in the opportunity for those careful marks to become more of what they are and are not. Our seeing and not-seeing fills in the profound gap that holds everything else. (Of course, even if he desired, he couldn't go anywhere near American Blackness, then and now, another salvation, all that it represents, alas. And even if he did go near it and it was somewhere, somehow embedded in the work, I have no idea what it would look like—the lens and its refraction having everything to do with what's being seen.) A vast prism, spectrum, specter. Somewhere in Johns's fraught southern body and work is the abject horror of the Jim Crow South and all the inhumanity that came before. In his paintings is a kind of grace. Ultimately, I stop thinking, embrace the generous, meaningless surfaces momentarily, and am utterly impressed, satisfied. (The causality of the force of circumstances, the suspension of time required to look at this work.) A search for that grace, even empathy, is why he painted them, no doubt. This is why almost everyone and every institution that can afford to look at them as monumental paintings about paintings wants one or more to hang on their walls. But they don't really know/see the half of it. It's not possible. How remarkable.

2019

1 Jill Johnston, *Jasper Johns: Privileged Information* (New York: Thames and Hudson, 1996), 68, 241; M. H. Miller, "Jasper Johns, American Legend," *New York Times Style Magazine*, February 18, 2019, 77.
2 Johnston, *Jasper Johns*, 155.
3 Jasper Johns, quoted in Edward J. Sozanski, "The Lure of the Impossible," *Philadelphia Inquirer Magazine*, October 23, 1988; reprinted in Kirk Varnedoe, ed., *Jasper Johns: Writings, Sketchbook Notes, Interviews* (New York: Museum of Modern Art, 1996), 225 (hereafter abbreviated Varnedoe, *WSI*).
4 Marcel Duchamp, quoted in Calvin Tomkins, *The Bride and the Bachelors: Five Masters of the Avant Garde* (New York: Viking, 1974), 60.
5 Jasper Johns, quoted in Sarah Kent, "Jasper Johns: Strokes of Genius," *Time Out* (London), December 5-12, 1990; reprinted in Varnedoe, *WSI*, 259.
6 Johnston, *Jasper Johns*, 78.
7 See Kirk Varnedoe, "Introduction: A Sense of Life," in *Jasper Johns: A Retrospective*, ed. Kirk Varnedoe, exh. cat. (New York: Museum of Modern Art, 1996), 30.

According to What, 1964
Untitled, 1972

Constellations

In the early 1960s, Jasper Johns introduced a new type of work into his practice: a monumental painting that is at once synthetic and generative. Until then, most of his paintings had centered on a singular image or gesture—a flag, say, or a canvas cleaved apart by a ball. He nearly always treated the surface as a unified field, with an allover composition and consistent materials, palette, and facture. This started to shift with *Fool's House* (1961–62; p. 33, pl. 1), where the support began to act more like a pegboard, covered with assorted objects and explicit references to prior works or the thoughts they contained. The new approach related to Robert Rauschenberg's heterogeneous Combines, but those sculptural paintings are less diagrammatic and analytical than Johns's, which grew into expansive self-citational mash-ups of previous elements and techniques. The multipanel *Diver* (1962) conjoins riffs on three or four earlier works across its fourteen-foot breadth, inaugurating a string of anthological paintings that Johns would execute intermittently over the next four decades, such as the Seasons series (1985–86; pp. 180–81, pls. 3, 4; p. 190, pls. 7, 8), *Untitled* (1992–94; p. 136, pl. 20), and *5 Postcards* (2011; p. 263, pls. 19–23). Yet these paintings function not only as provisional compendiums but also as points of departure—springboards for further works on canvas and experiments in other media. Sometimes this activity took place concurrently with the production of the key paintings, while in other instances Johns revisited them years later. As much as he stuffed into these works, there was always more to unpack.

According to What (1964; pp. 150–51, pl. 2) is the greatest early example of Johns's obsessive process of invention through repetition and recombination. Measuring roughly seven by sixteen feet, it is a visual laboratory that gathers incidents found in previous works across its six abutting panels: an inverted chair and cast leg recalling *Watchman* (1964; p. 117, pl. 1); the hinged lettering of *Field Painting* (1963–64; p. 149, pl. 1); and the splashy brushwork and primary rectangles of *Arrive/Depart* (1963–64; p. 153, pl. 4), among other quotations. A latched panel in the lower-left corner conceals an interpretive key, Marcel Duchamp's silhouette copied from his *Self-Portrait in Profile* (1957), an edition of which Johns owned. Duchamp was a powerful role model for Johns, not just for his readymades but for moving art "into a field where language, thought and vision act upon one another," as Johns put it.[1] The younger artist often explored the literal insertion of language into the pictorial realm, as well as more metaphorical inquiries into the languages of abstraction and representation, whether through the juxtaposition of schematic graphic elements and spontaneous brushwork or of real objects and their trompe l'oeil doubles. Many elements of *According to What* relate directly to Duchamp's rebus-like *Tu m'* (1918) and to *The Green Box* (1934; p. 155, pl. 14), a facsimile publication of a selection of his notes for the iconic *Large Glass* (1915–23; p. 198, fig. 3). Johns acquired a copy of *The Green Box* in 1960 and began keeping his own sketchbook notes soon thereafter.

Johns revisited *According to What* on multiple occasions, mining and elaborating on its discoveries to new ends. A minutely rendered 1969 graphite drawing (p. 155, pl. 11) wryly redoubles the painting's semiotic play by transmuting juicy colorful strokes into scratchy grisaille lines and three dimensions into two. This expansion on the original painting's analytic mode continued in a portfolio of seven lithographs, *Fragments—According to What* (1971; p. 152, pl. 3; p. 154, pls. 5–10), each of which homes in on a sculptural passage, now rendered in perspective. Made long after their source, these prints invert the traditional relationship of part to whole in both space and time. As Johns later explained, ordinarily artists "take a detail and study it in preparation for locating it in its proper place in a larger scene. But a lot of modern experience is of an opposite nature: you take a larger situation and extract from it some bit which you examine with great attention."[2]

Untitled (1972; pp. 158–59, pl. 2), like *According to What*, exists as a visual and conceptual knot within a constellation of interrelated works. Johns organized the painting by combining four equally sized panels, each one discretely featuring a specific motif. The leftmost canvas debuts a new pattern of stripes in green, orange, and purple, with white strokes in between. Rendered from Johns's memory of a car he passed while driving, these crosshatches would dominate much of his output for the following decade as he systematically explored the pattern's conceptual, topological, and formal possibilities. This novel set of marks flanks the two canvases at *Untitled*'s center, which are covered with the familiar flagstones that Johns introduced in *Harlem Light* (1967; pp. 104–5, pl. 1). At first glance, the two panels appear very similar, but Johns handled the motif in encaustic and collage on the left and in oil on the right. A portion of each panel reproduces and extends the design of the adjacent one, catching us in a comparative oscillation between the two. *Untitled*'s rightmost panel supports an unsettling array of lifelike cast wax body parts affixed to a rough wooden lattice. The shockingly dismembered elements evoke both eros and violence: a nipple, a mouth, buttocks, the touch of a hand upon a foot.

Johns further unspooled *Untitled* through subsequent paintings, drawings, print series, and unique working proofs that serve as studied translations of the original, as well as of one another. *Four Panels from Untitled 1972* (1974) synopsizes the whole painting in a quartet of lithographs that respond, respectively, to each panel, while the prints in the series Casts from Untitled (1973–74; p. 164, pls. 17–22) zero in on the right panel alone and render the anatomical casts individually in outline amid vivid fields of color. Some of the prints use embossing to add literal depth to otherwise flat depictions of their sculptural source, revealing once again Johns's inquisitive merging of the real and the depicted. Imagery from *Untitled* recurs in *Foirades/Fizzles* (1976; pp. 166–67, pls. 26–33), a book made in collaboration with Samuel Beckett. Throughout the volume, Johns's moody intaglios accompany fragments of Beckett's unnerving prose in a sequence of pages that explodes any standard relationship between part and whole and leaves meaning forever suspended. Comparing his first subjects, such as maps and numbers, to *Untitled*, Johns remarked, "There are kinds of images that make a single impact and there are kinds of images that express themselves as a multiplicity."[3]

—Scott Rothkopf, with Carlos Basualdo, Sarah B. Vogelman, and Lauren Young

1 Jasper Johns, "Marcel Duchamp (1887–1968)," *Artforum* 7, no. 3 (November 1968): 6; reprinted in Kirk Varnedoe, ed., *Jasper Johns: Writings, Sketchbook Notes, Interviews* (New York: Museum of Modern Art, 1996), 22 (hereafter abbreviated Varnedoe, *WSI*).

2 Jasper Johns, "An Interview with Jasper Johns," by Roberta Bernstein, in *Fragments: Incompletion and Discontinuity*, New York Literary Forum 8–9, ed. Lawrence D. Kritzman ([Martinsville, NJ: Analecta Enterprises], 1981); reprinted in Varnedoe, *WSI*, 203–4.

3 Johns, "Interview with Jasper Johns," 200.

Constellations

According to What, 1964

WHITNEY MUSEUM OF AMERICAN ART

1 ***Field Painting*, 1963–64**
Oil on canvas with objects (two panels)
72 × 36 ¾ in. (182.9 × 93.4 cm) overall
Collection of the artist; on long-term loan to the National Gallery of Art, Washington, DC, 1988

2 ***According to What*, 1964**
Oil, charcoal, and graphite on canvas with objects (six panels)
88 × 191 ¾ in. (223.5 × 487.1 cm) overall
The Middleton Family Collection

3 ***Fragment—According to What: Leg and Chair*, 1971**
Lithograph: one stone, six aluminum plates
35 × 30 in. (88.9 × 76.2 cm)
Kenneth Tyler, James Webb/Gemini
Ed. no. 11/68
Philadelphia Museum of Art; purchased with the Lola Downin Peck Fund (by exchange) and gift (by exchange) of the estate of Mrs. Charles M. Lea, 1986-60-1

4 ***Arrive/Depart*, 1963–64**
Oil on canvas
68 × 51 ½ in. (172.7 × 130.8 cm)
Bayerische Staatsgemäldesammlungen, Pinakothek der Moderne, Munich

5 ***Fragment—According to What: Blue*, 1971**
Lithograph: one stone, one aluminum plate
31 ⅛ × 21 ¼ in. (79.1 × 54 cm)
Kenneth Tyler/Gemini
Ed. no. 8/10
Whitney Museum of American Art, New York; purchase with funds from the Print Committee, 2002.557

6 ***Fragment—According to What: Bent "Blue" (Second State)*, 1971**
Lithograph with newspaper transfer: one stone, three aluminum plates, one newspaper
25 ½ × 28 ¾ in. (64.8 × 73 cm)
Kenneth Tyler, Charles Ritt/Gemini
Ed. no. 51/66
Philadelphia Museum of Art; purchased with the Lola Downin Peck Fund (by exchange) and gift (by exchange) of the estate of Mrs. Charles M. Lea, 1986-60-3

7 ***Fragment—According to What: Bent "U,"* 1971**
Lithograph: one stone, three aluminum plates
25 × 20 in. (63.5 × 50.8 cm)
Kenneth Tyler, Ron Adams/Gemini
Ed. no. 47/69
Philadelphia Museum of Art; purchased with the Lola Downin Peck Fund (by exchange) and gift (by exchange) of the estate of Mrs. Charles M. Lea, 1986-60-4

8 ***Fragment—According to What: Bent Stencil*, 1971**
Lithograph: one stone, eight aluminum plates
27 ½ × 20 in. (69.9 × 50.8 cm)
Kenneth Tyler, Ron Olds/Gemini
Ed. no. 11/79
Philadelphia Museum of Art; purchased with the Lola Downin Peck Fund (by exchange) and gift (by exchange) of the estate of Mrs. Charles M. Lea, 1986-60-2

9 ***Fragment—According to What: Coat Hanger and Spoon*, 1971**
Lithograph: two stones, five aluminum plates
34 × 25 ¼ in. (86.4 × 64.1 cm)
Kenneth Tyler, Charles Ritt/Gemini
Ed. no. 56/76
Philadelphia Museum of Art; gift of William Speiller, 1986-37-1

10 ***Fragment—According to What: Hinged Canvas*, 1971**
Lithograph: one stone, seven aluminum plates
36 × 30 in. (91.4 × 76.2 cm)
Kenneth Tyler, Stuart Henderson/Gemini
Ed. no. 21/69
Philadelphia Museum of Art; gift of William Speiller, 1986-37-2

11 ***According to What*, 1969**
Graphite pencil and graphite wash on paper
29 ½ × 41 ¼ in. (74.9 × 104.8 cm)
Collection of the artist

12 ***Untitled*, 1977**
Collage, graphite pencil, charcoal, and acrylic on paper with objects, in a wood frame with an acrylic sheet
43 ¼ × 34 ⅛ × 3 ⅞ in.
(109.9 × 86.7 × 9.8 cm)
Collection of the artist

13 ***M.D.*, 1964**
Collage and graphite pencil on stencil board
22 × 18 in. (55.9 × 45.7 cm)
Collection of the artist

14 **Marcel Duchamp (American, b. France, 1887–1968)**
***The Bride Stripped Bare by Her Bachelors, Even (The Green Box)*, 1934**
Box containing ninety-four collotype reproductions
Box: 13 ⅛ × 11 × 1 in.
(33.3 × 27.9 × 2.5 cm)
Collection of Jasper Johns

Untitled, 1972

PHILADELPHIA MUSEUM OF ART

1 ***Untitled*, 1973**
Charcoal, opaque white, and graphite pencil on paper
41 ¼ × 29 ½ in. (104.8 × 74.9 cm)
Private collection; courtesy of Craig F. Starr Gallery, New York

2 ***Untitled*, 1972**
Oil, encaustic, and collage on canvas with objects (four panels)
72 × 192 ¼ in. (182.9 × 488.3 cm) overall
Museum Ludwig, Cologne, donation Ludwig, 1976

3 ***Four Panels from Untitled 1972 [A Panel]*, 1973**
Lithograph with embossing
42 ¾ × 30 ⅛ in. (108.6 × 76.5 cm)
Ron McPherson, Serge Lozingot, Charles Ritt, James Webb/Gemini
TP
National Gallery of Art, Washington, DC; Patrons' Permanent Fund and Special Friends of the National Gallery of Art, 2008.136.30.1

4 ***Beckett*, 2005**
Encaustic and oil on canvas with objects (two panels)
66 × 44 in. (167.6 × 111.8 cm) overall
Kathy and Richard S. Fuld, Jr.; promised gift to the Museum of Modern Art, New York

5 ***Four Panels from Untitled 1972 [A Panel]*, 1973**
Lithograph and screenprint
42 ¾ × 30 ⅛ in. (108.6 × 76.5 cm)
Ron McPherson, Serge Lozingot, Charles Ritt, James Webb/Gemini
TP
National Gallery of Art, Washington, DC; Patrons' Permanent Fund and Special Friends of the National Gallery of Art, 2008.136.34

6 ***Four Panels from Untitled 1972 [C Panel]*, 1973***
Lithograph with red crayon
42 ¾ × 29 ⅞ in. (108.6 × 75.9 cm)
Ron McPherson, Serge Lozingot, Charles Ritt, James Webb/Gemini
TP
National Gallery of Art, Washington, DC; Patrons' Permanent Fund and Special Friends of the National Gallery of Art, 2008.136.37

7 ***Four Panels from Untitled 1972 [C Panel]*, 1973–74**
Lithograph with debossing
40 ½ × 28 ½ in. (102.9 × 72.4 cm)
Ron McPherson, Serge Lozingot, Charles Ritt, James Webb/Gemini
TP
National Gallery of Art, Washington, DC; Patrons' Permanent Fund and Special Friends of the National Gallery of Art, 2008.136.44

8 ***Four Panels from Untitled 1972 [A Panel]*, 1973–74***
Lithograph with debossing
40 ½ × 28 ½ in. (102.9 × 72.4 cm)
Ron McPherson, Serge Lozingot, Charles Ritt, James Webb/Gemini
TP
National Gallery of Art, Washington, DC; Patrons' Permanent Fund and Special Friends of the National Gallery of Art, 2008.136.35

9 ***Four Panels from Untitled 1972 [C Panel]*, 1973**
Screenprint
42 ¾ × 29 ⅞ in. (108.6 × 75.9 cm)
Ron McPherson, Serge Lozingot, Charles Ritt, James Webb/Gemini
Proof
National Gallery of Art, Washington, DC; Patrons' Permanent Fund and Special Friends of the National Gallery of Art, 2008.136.38

10 ***Four Panels from Untitled 1972 [C Panel]*, 1973–74***
Lithograph with embossing and paint
42 ¾ × 29 ⅞ in. (108.6 × 75.9 cm)
Ron McPherson, Serge Lozingot, Charles Ritt, James Webb/Gemini
TP
National Gallery of Art, Washington, DC; Patrons' Permanent Fund and Special Friends of the National Gallery of Art, 2008.136.41

11 ***Untitled*, 1973**
Oil and graphite pencil on paper
41 ¼ × 29 ⅝ in. (104.8 × 75.3 cm)
The Menil Collection, Houston; bequest of David Whitney

12 ***Four Panels from Untitled 1972 [D Panel]*, 1973**
Lithograph with crayon
42 ⅞ × 30 in. (108.9 × 76.2 cm)
Ron McPherson, Serge Lozingot, Charles Ritt, James Webb/Gemini
WP
National Gallery of Art, Washington, DC; Patrons' Permanent Fund and Special Friends of the National Gallery of Art, 2008.136.47

13 ***Four Panels from Untitled 1972 [D Panel]*, 1973**
Lithograph
42 ½ × 28 ½ in. (108 × 72.4 cm)
Ron McPherson, Serge Lozingot, Charles Ritt, James Webb/Gemini
TP
National Gallery of Art, Washington, DC; Patrons' Permanent Fund and Special Friends of the National Gallery of Art, 2008.136.45

14 ***Four Panels from Untitled 1972 [D Panel]*, 1973**
Lithograph with chalk and ink wash
42 ¾ × 30 in. (108.6 × 76.2 cm)
Ron McPherson, Serge Lozingot, Charles Ritt, James Webb/Gemini
WP
National Gallery of Art, Washington, DC; Patrons' Permanent Fund and Special Friends of the National Gallery of Art, 2008.136.59

15 ***Four Panels from Untitled 1972 [D Panel]*, 1974**
Lithograph with chalk and graphite
42 ¾ × 30 in. (108.6 × 76.2 cm)
Ron McPherson, Serge Lozingot, Charles Ritt, James Webb/Gemini
WP
National Gallery of Art, Washington, DC; Patrons' Permanent Fund and Special Friends of the National Gallery of Art, 2008.136.57

16 ***Four Panels from Untitled 1972 [D Panel]*, 1973**
Lithograph
42 ½ × 30 in. (108 × 76.2 cm)
Ron McPherson, Serge Lozingot, Charles Ritt, James Webb/Gemini
TP
National Gallery of Art, Washington, DC; Patrons' Permanent Fund and Special Friends of the National Gallery of Art, 2008.136.534

17 ***Face*, 1973–74**
Lithograph: one stone, two aluminum plates
30 ¾ × 22 ¾ in. (78.1 × 57.8 cm)
Charles Ritt, Barbara Thomason/Gemini
Ed. no. 3/49
Philadelphia Museum of Art; purchased with the SmithKline Beckman Corporation Fund, 1986-62-1

18 ***Torso*, 1973–74**
Lithograph: one stone, two aluminum plates
30 ¾ × 22 ¾ in. (78.1 × 57.8 cm)
Dan Freeman, Robbin Geiger/Gemini
Ed. no. 3/50
Philadelphia Museum of Art; purchased with the SmithKline Beckman Corporation Fund, 1986-62-4

19 ***Feet*, 1973–74**
Lithograph: one stone, two aluminum plates
30 ¾ × 22 ¾ in. (78.1 × 57.8 cm)
James Webb, Barbara Thomason/Gemini
Ed. no. 3/47
Philadelphia Museum of Art; purchased with the SmithKline Beckman Corporation Fund, 1986-62-5

20 ***HandFootSockFloor*, 1973–74**
Lithograph: one stone, two aluminum plates
30 ¾ × 22 ¾ in. (78.1 × 57.8 cm)
Serge Lozingot, Edward Henderson/Gemini
Ed. no. 3/48
Philadelphia Museum of Art; purchased with the SmithKline Beckman Corporation Fund, 1986-62-2

21 ***Buttocks*, 1973–74**
Lithograph: one stone, two aluminum plates
30 ¾ × 22 ¾ in. (78.1 × 57.8 cm)
James Webb, Barbara Thomason/Gemini
Ed. no. 3/49
Philadelphia Museum of Art; purchased with the SmithKline Beckman Corporation Fund, 1986-62-3

22 ***Leg*, 1973–74**
Lithograph: one stone, two aluminum plates
30 ¾ × 22 ¾ in. (78.1 × 57.8 cm)
Serge Lozingot, Edward Henderson/Gemini
9/10 AP
Philadelphia Museum of Art; purchased with the SmithKline Beckman Corporation Fund, 1986-62-6

23 ***Within*, 2007***
Acrylic over intaglio on paper
37 ¼ × 29 ¾ in. (94.6 × 76.6 cm)
Private collection

24 ***Within*, 2007**
Acrylic over intaglio on paper
38 ⅛ × 29 in. (96.8 × 73.7 cm)
Collection of Marlene Hess and James D. Zirin

25 ***Within*, 2007**
Acrylic over intaglio on paper
39 ¼ × 31 ⅛ in. (99.7 × 79.1 cm)
Susan and Larry Marx; promised gift to the Hammer Museum, University of California, Los Angeles

26–33 ***Foirades/Fizzles*, 1976**
Bound book with thirty-three intaglios: thirty-eight copperplates, four aluminum plates; box with lithograph
13 ½ × 10 ½ × 2 ⅜ in.
(34.3 × 26.7 × 6 cm) overall (closed)
Atelier Crommelynck, Bill Law/Petersburg Press
Ed. no. 103/250
Philadelphia Museum of Art; 125th Anniversary Acquisition; promised gift of Mildred L. and Morris L. Weisberg

According to What, 1964

WHITNEY MUSEUM OF AMERICAN ART

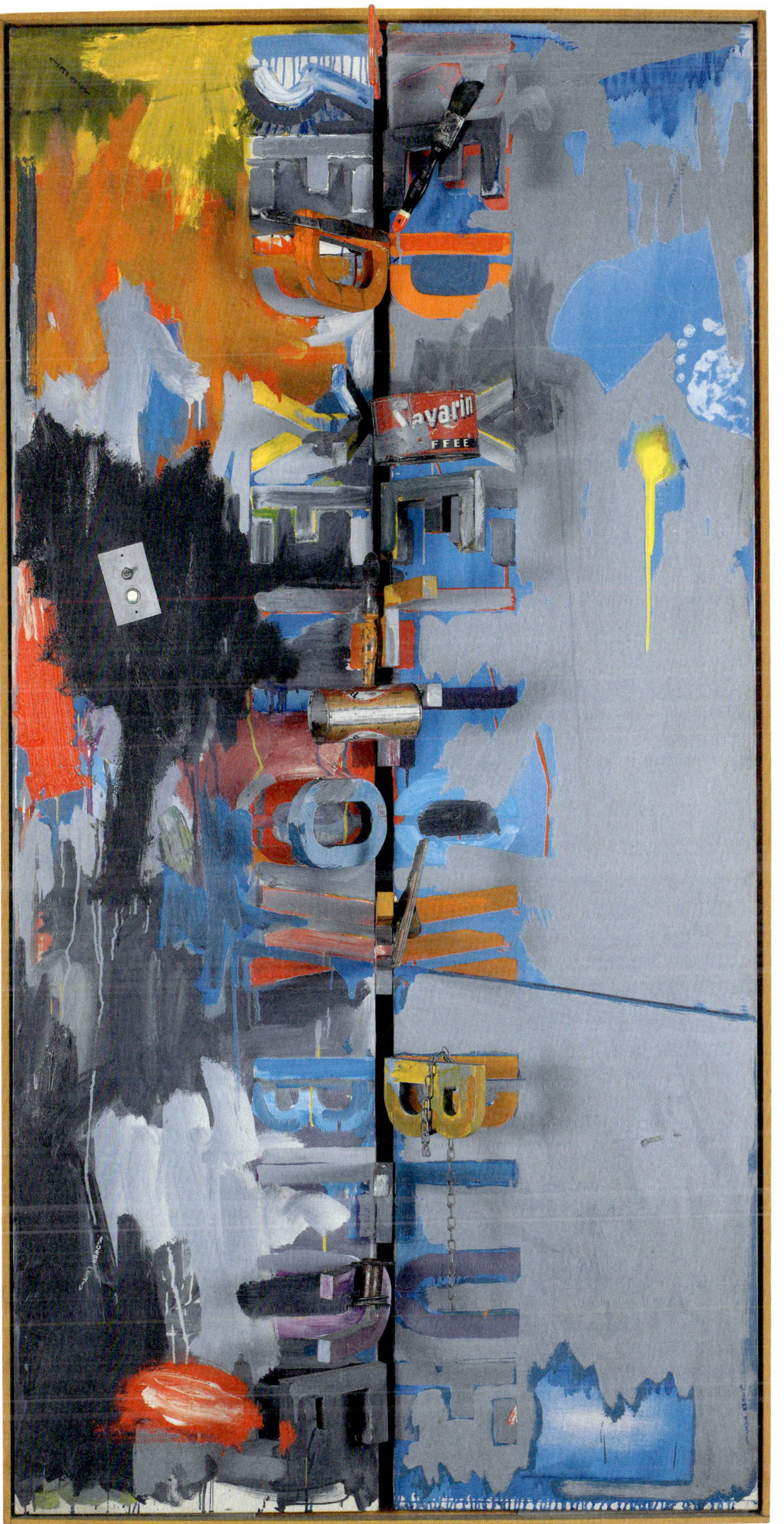

1 *Field Painting*, 1963–64

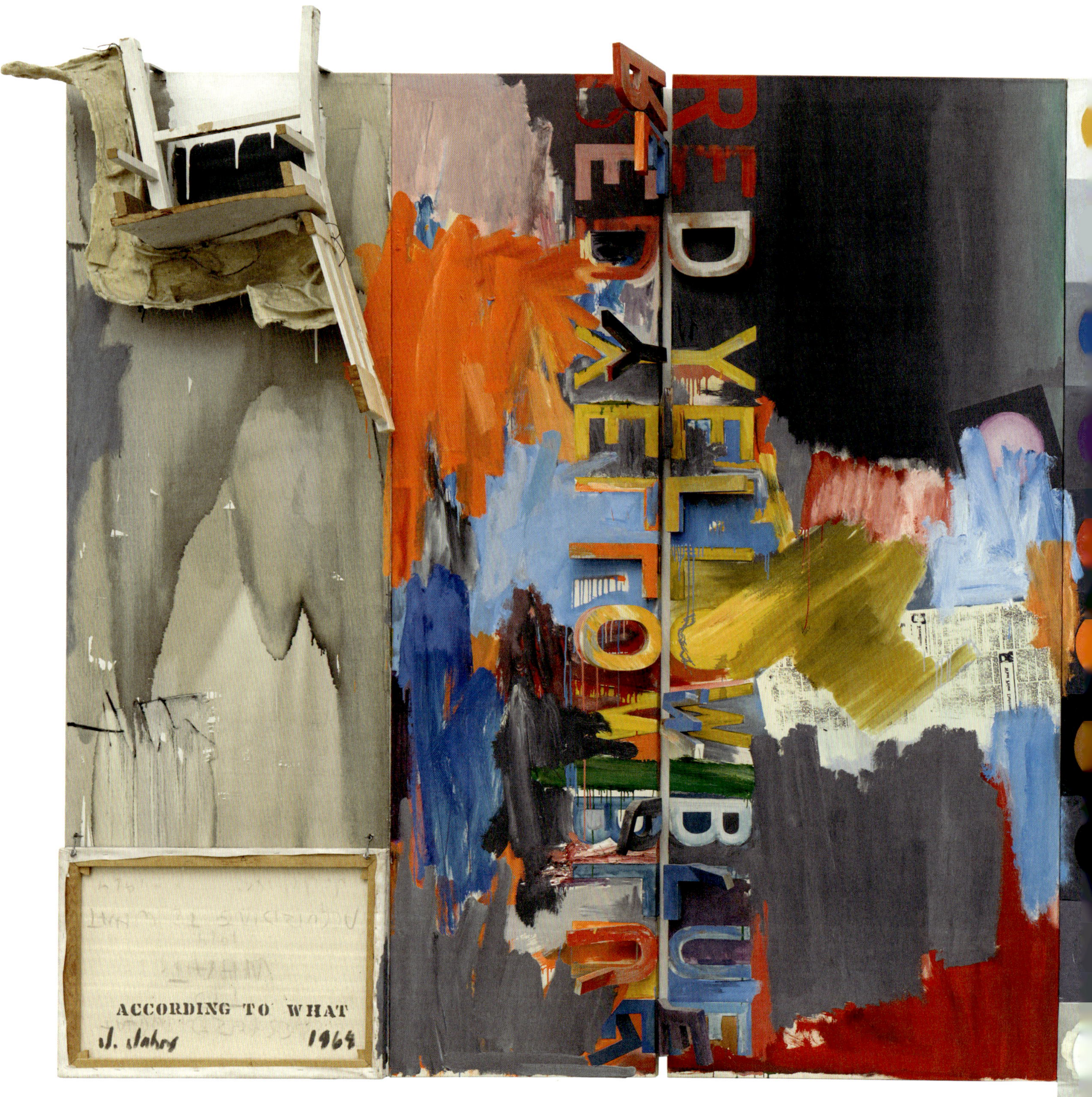

2 ***According to What***, **1964**

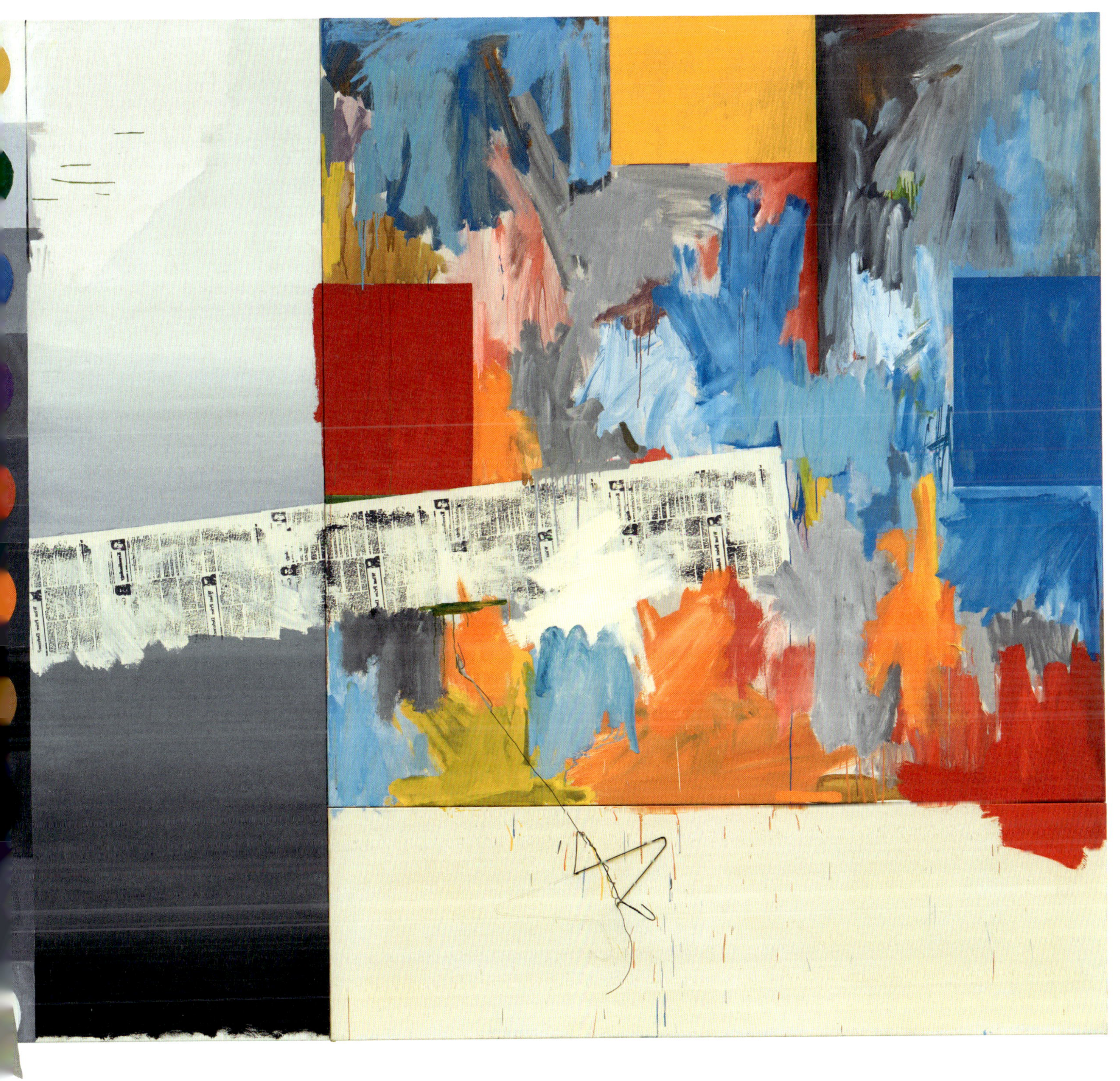

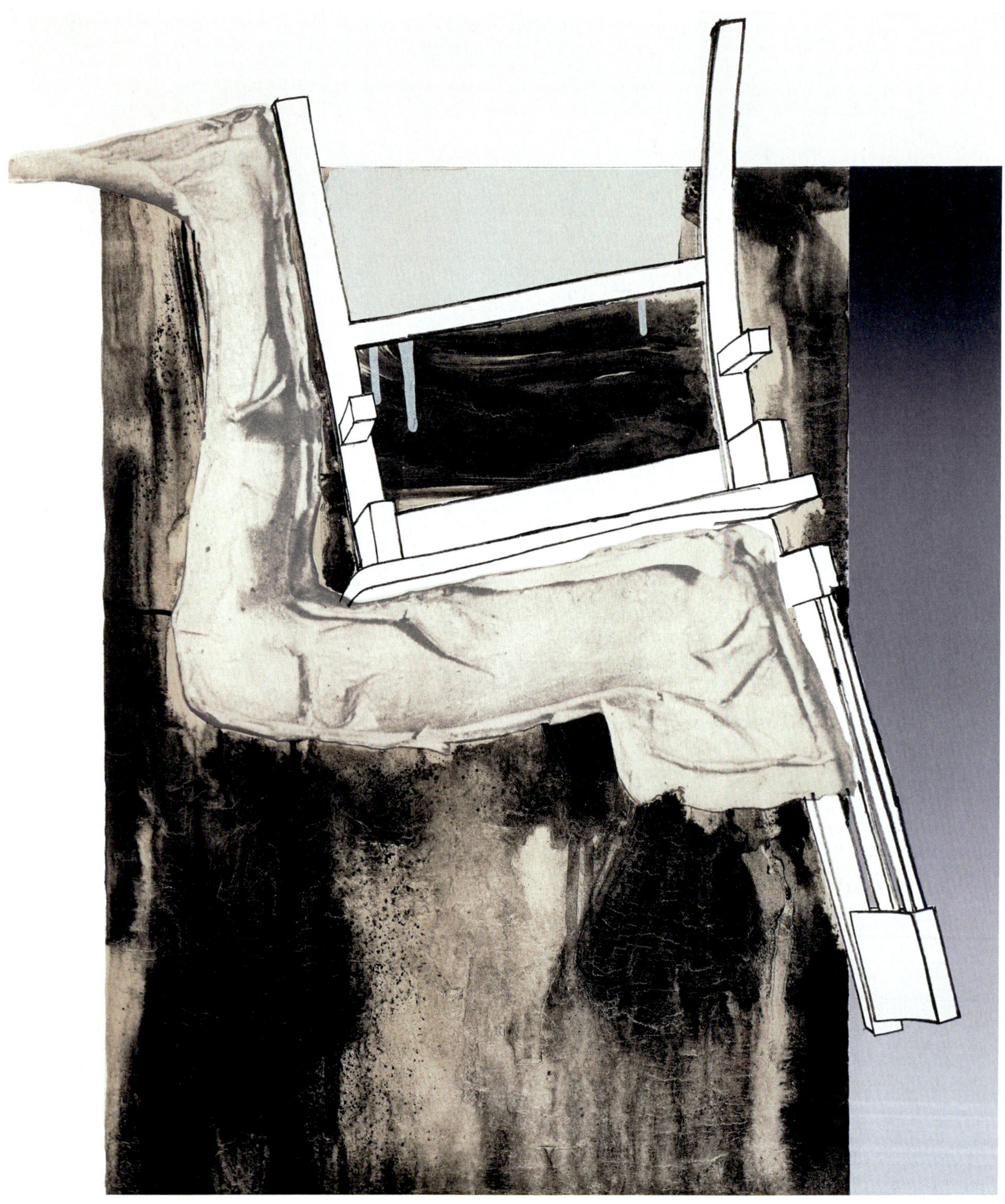

3 ***Fragment—According to What: Leg and Chair*, 1971**

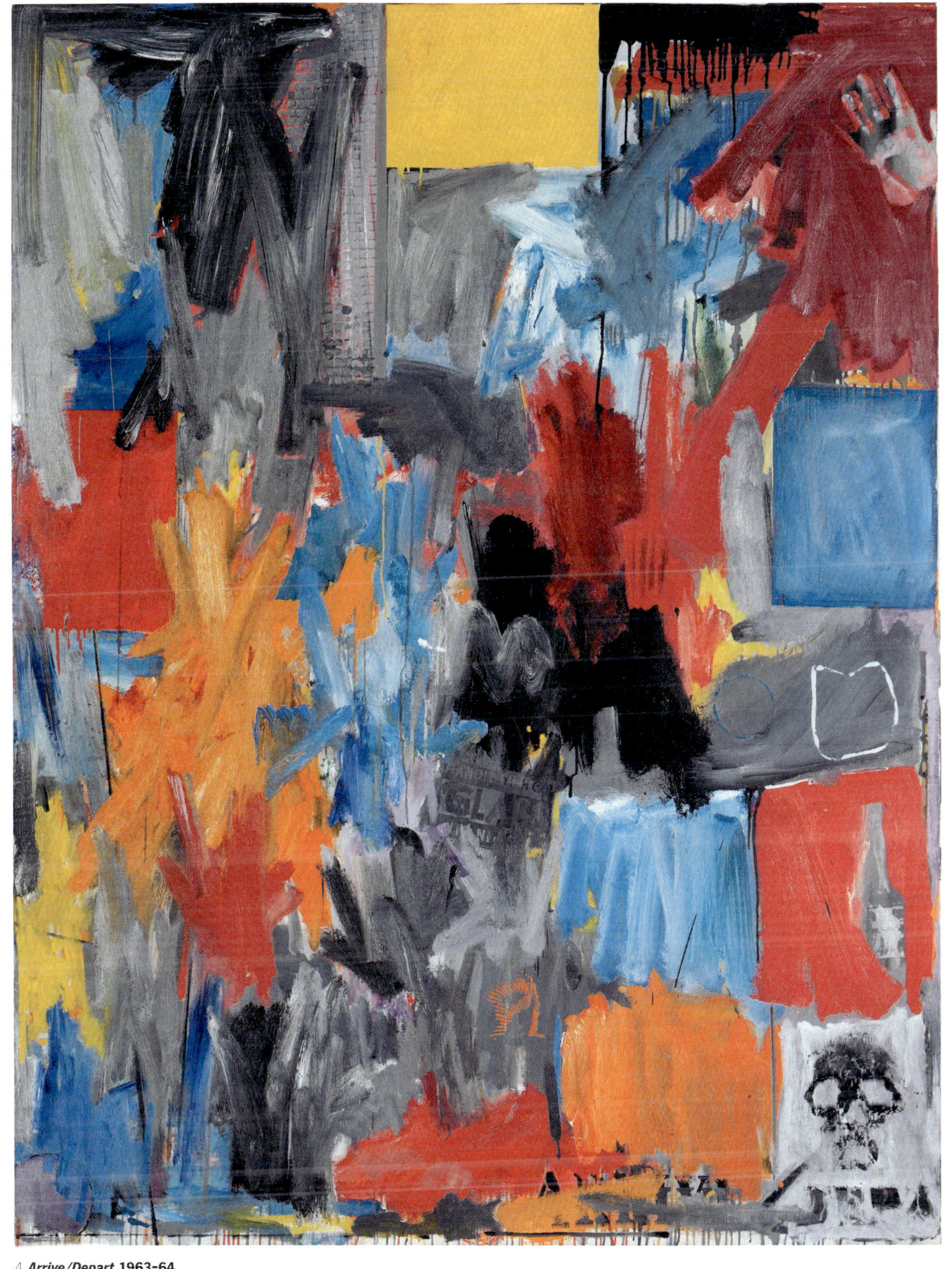

4 ***Arrive/Depart*, 1963–64**

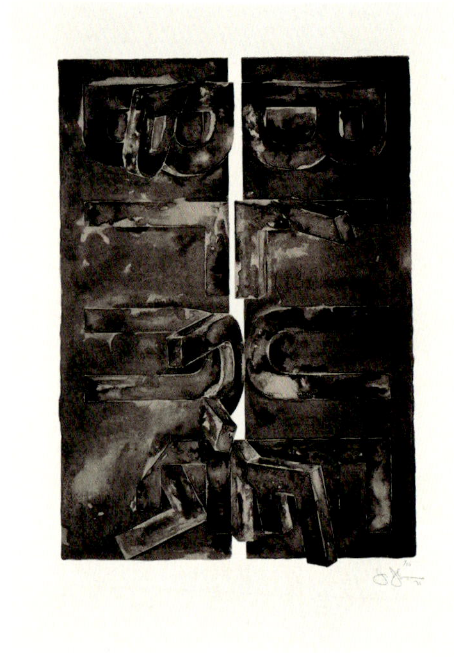

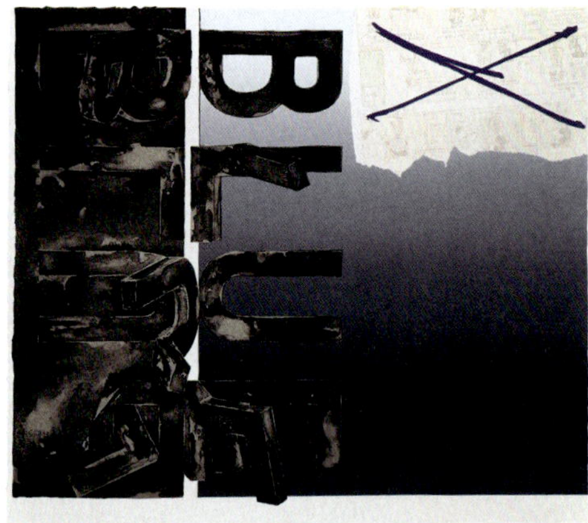

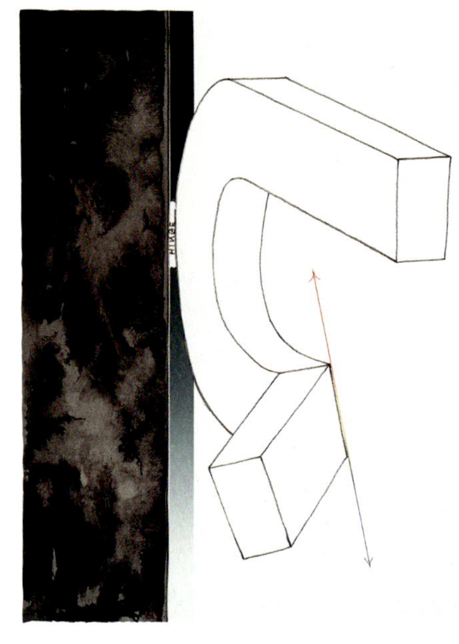

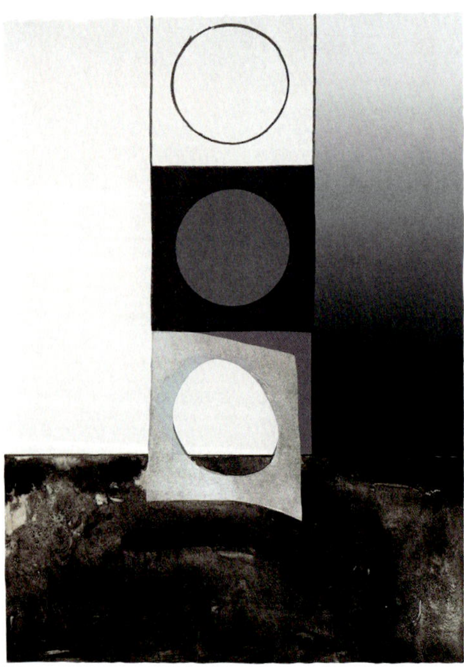

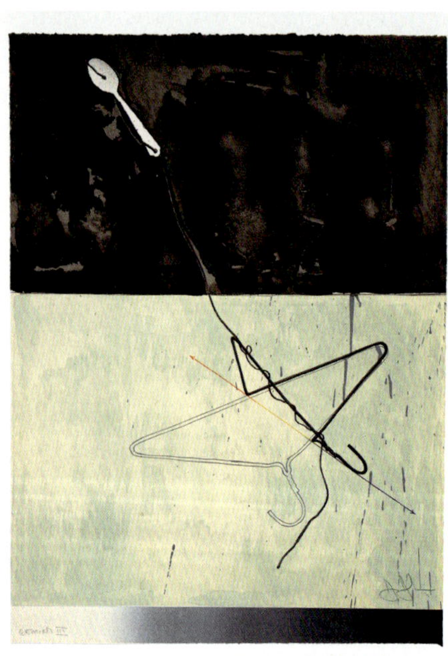

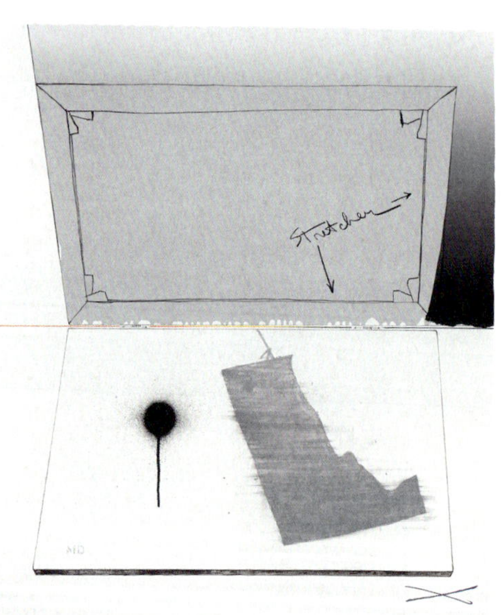

5 ***Fragment—According to What: Blue*, 1971**
8 ***Fragment—According to What: Bent Stencil*, 1971**

6 ***Fragment—According to What: Bent "Blue" (Second State)*, 1971**
9 ***Fragment—According to What: Coat Hanger and Spoon*, 1971**

7 ***Fragment—According to What: Bent "U,"* 1971**
10 ***Fragment—According to What: Hinged Canvas*, 1971**

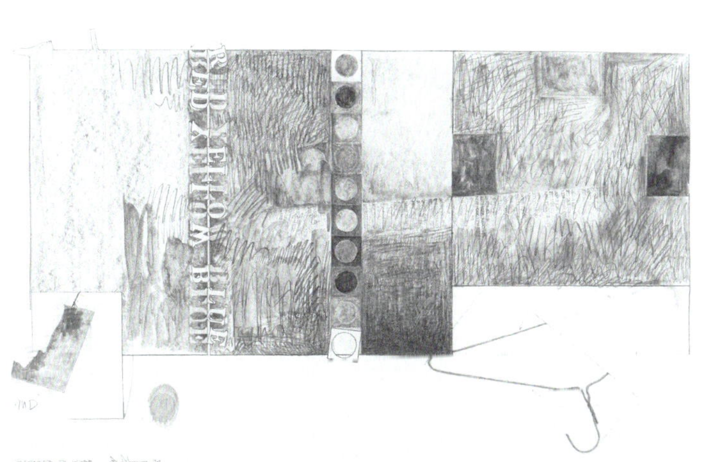

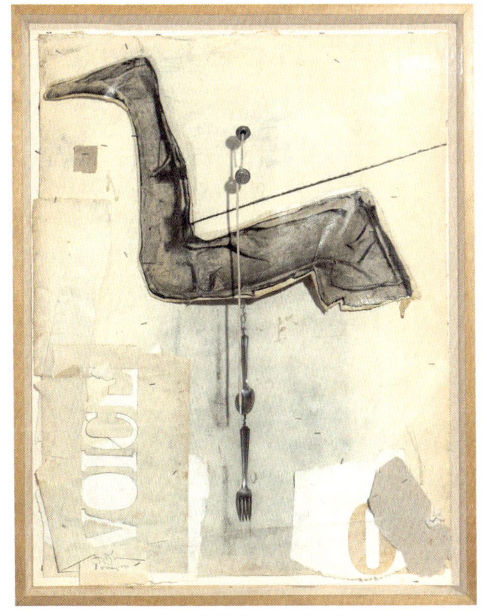

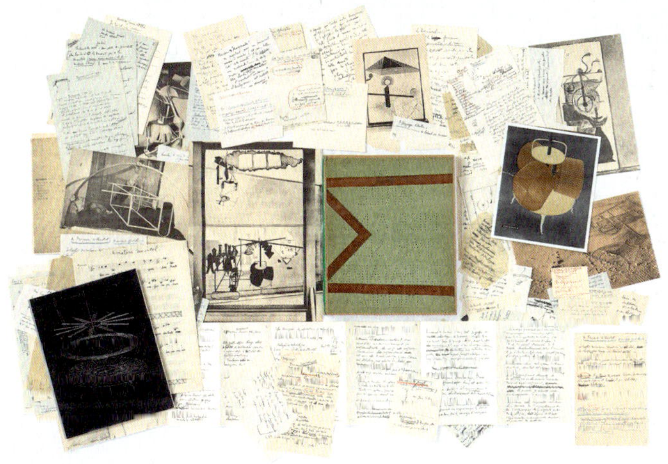

11 ***According to What***, **1969**
13 ***M.D.***, **1964**

12 ***Untitled***, **1977**
14 **Marcel Duchamp, *The Bride Stripped Bare by Her Bachelors, Even (The Green Box)*, 1934**

Untitled, 1972

PHILADELPHIA MUSEUM OF ART

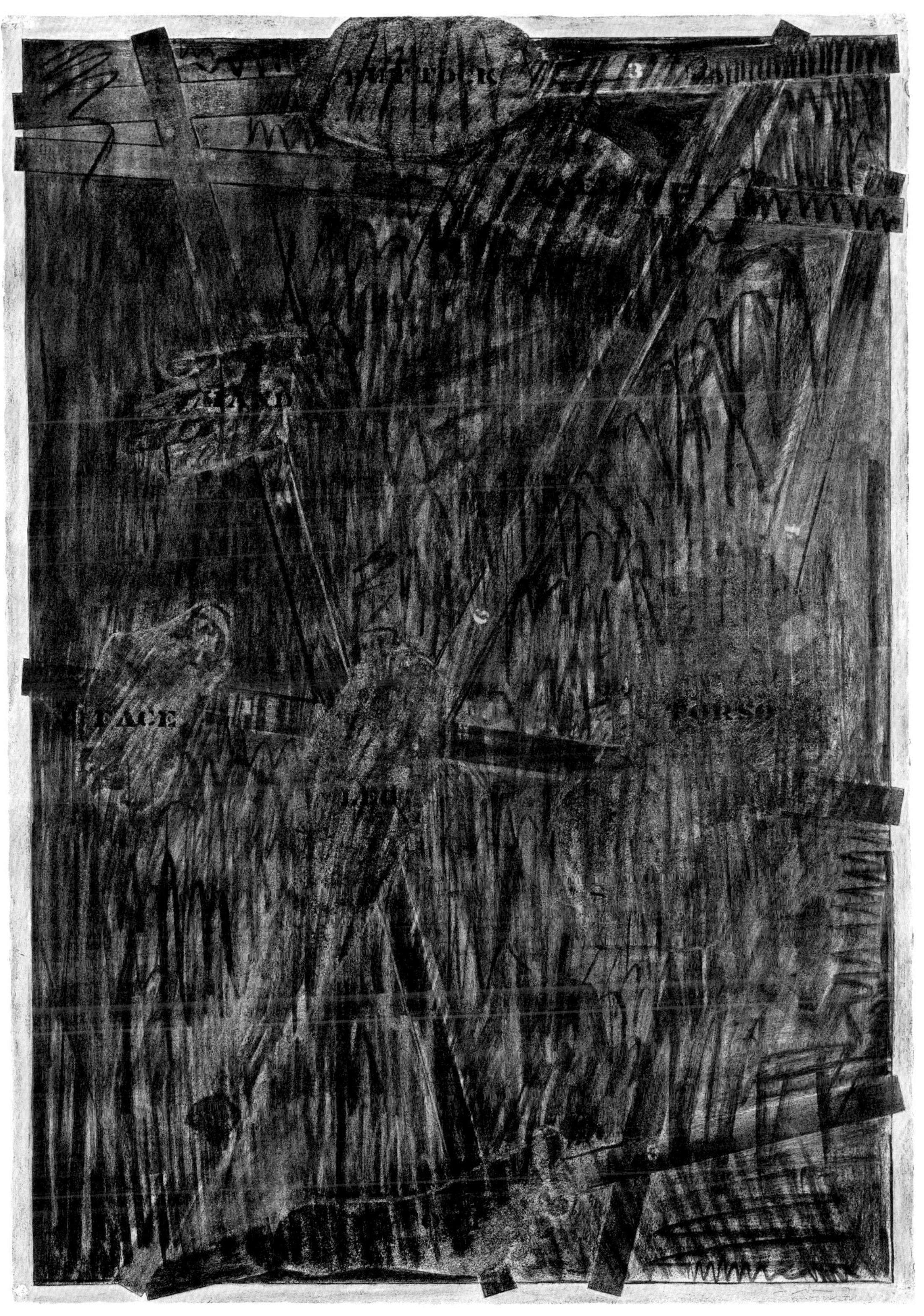

1 *Untitled*, 1973

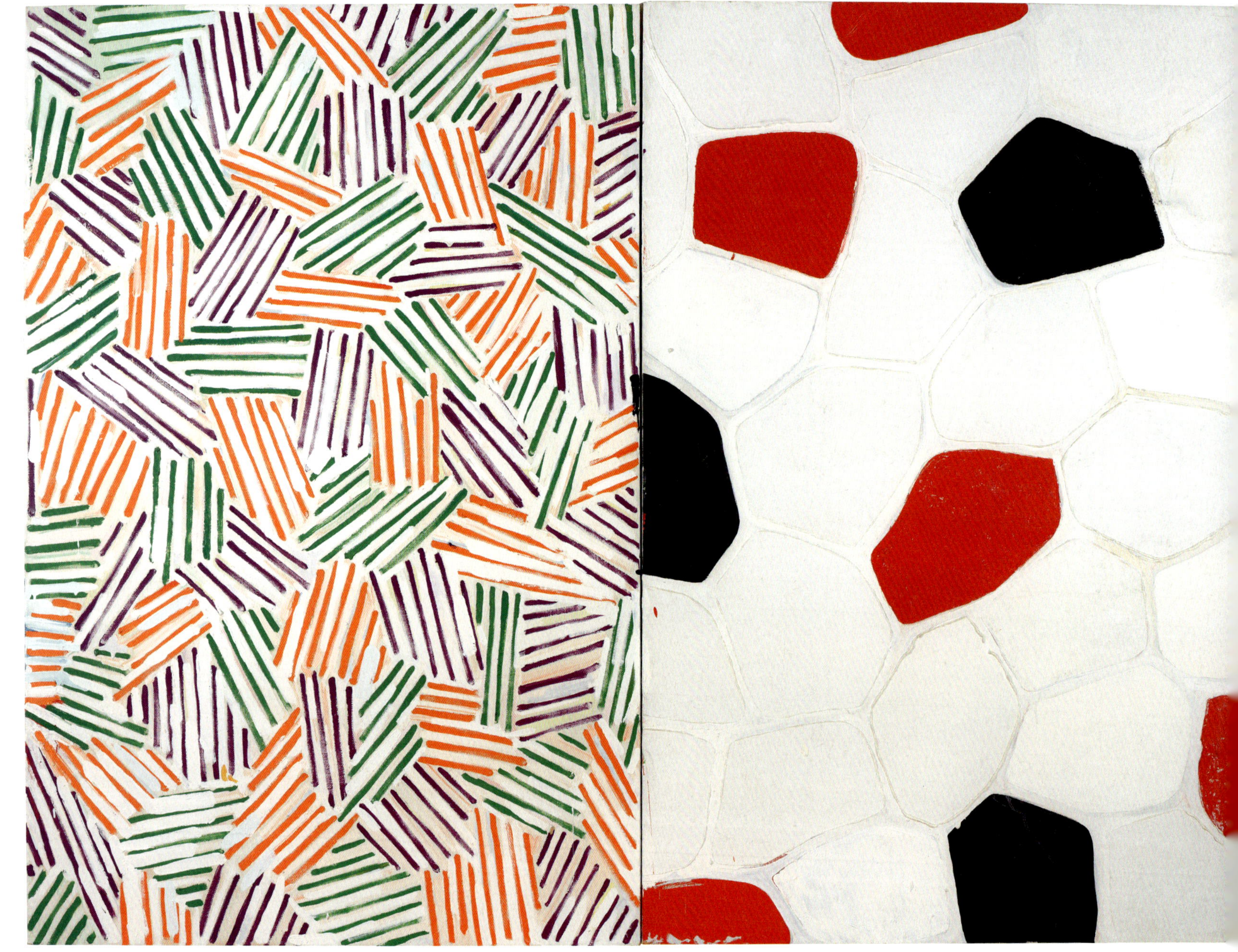

2 *Untitled*, 1972

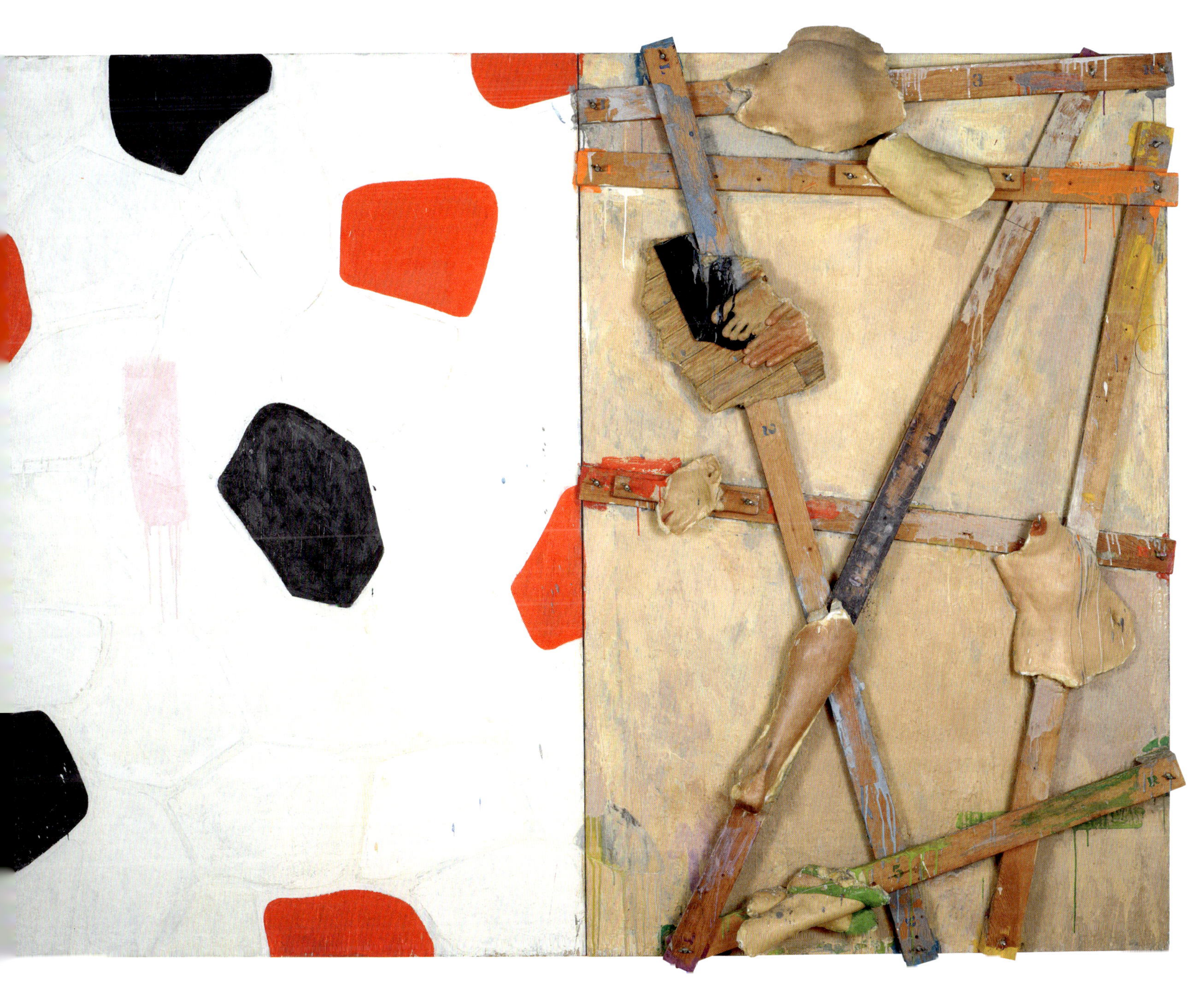

UNTITLED, 1972

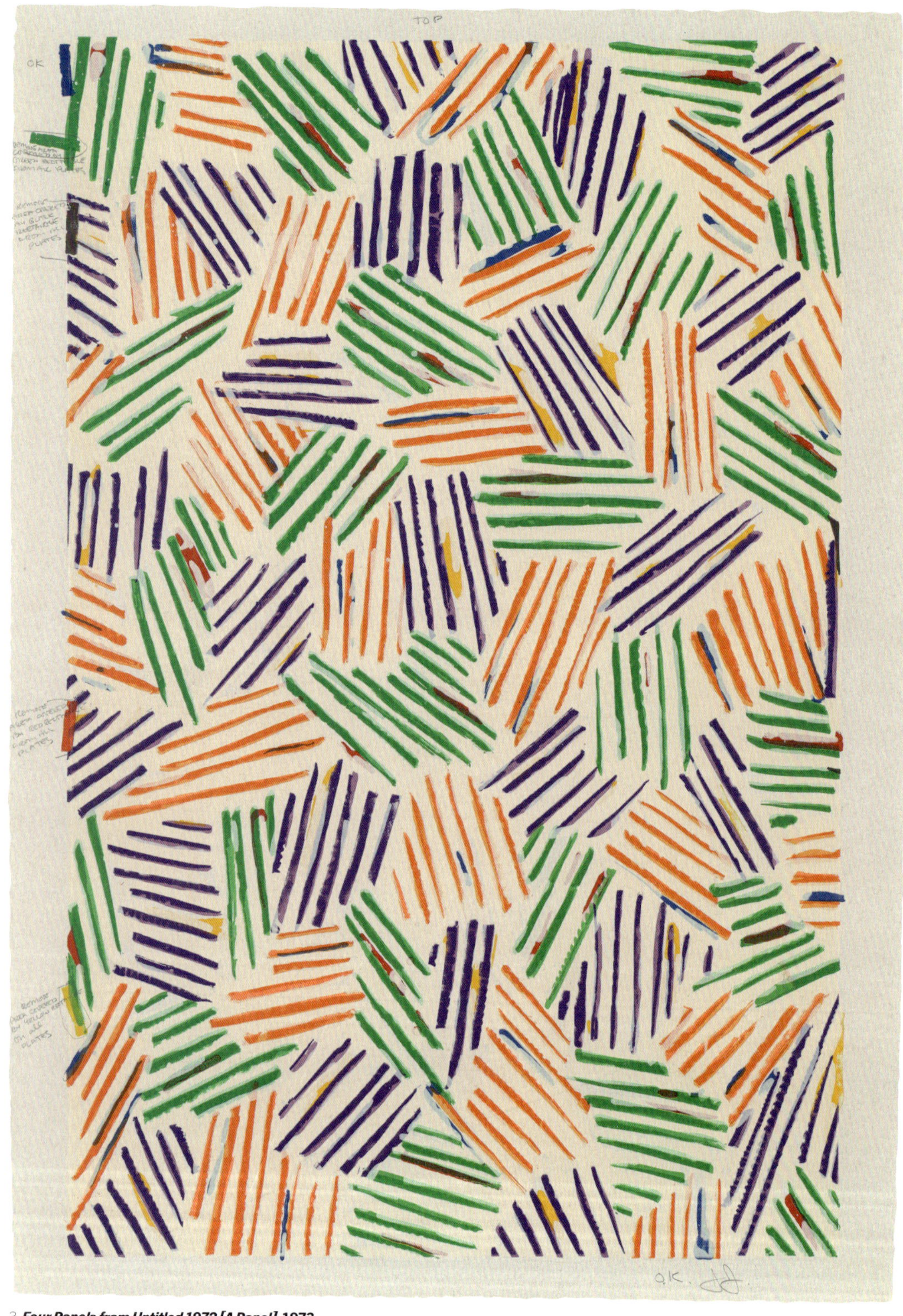

3 ***Four Panels from Untitled 1972 [A Panel]*, 1973**

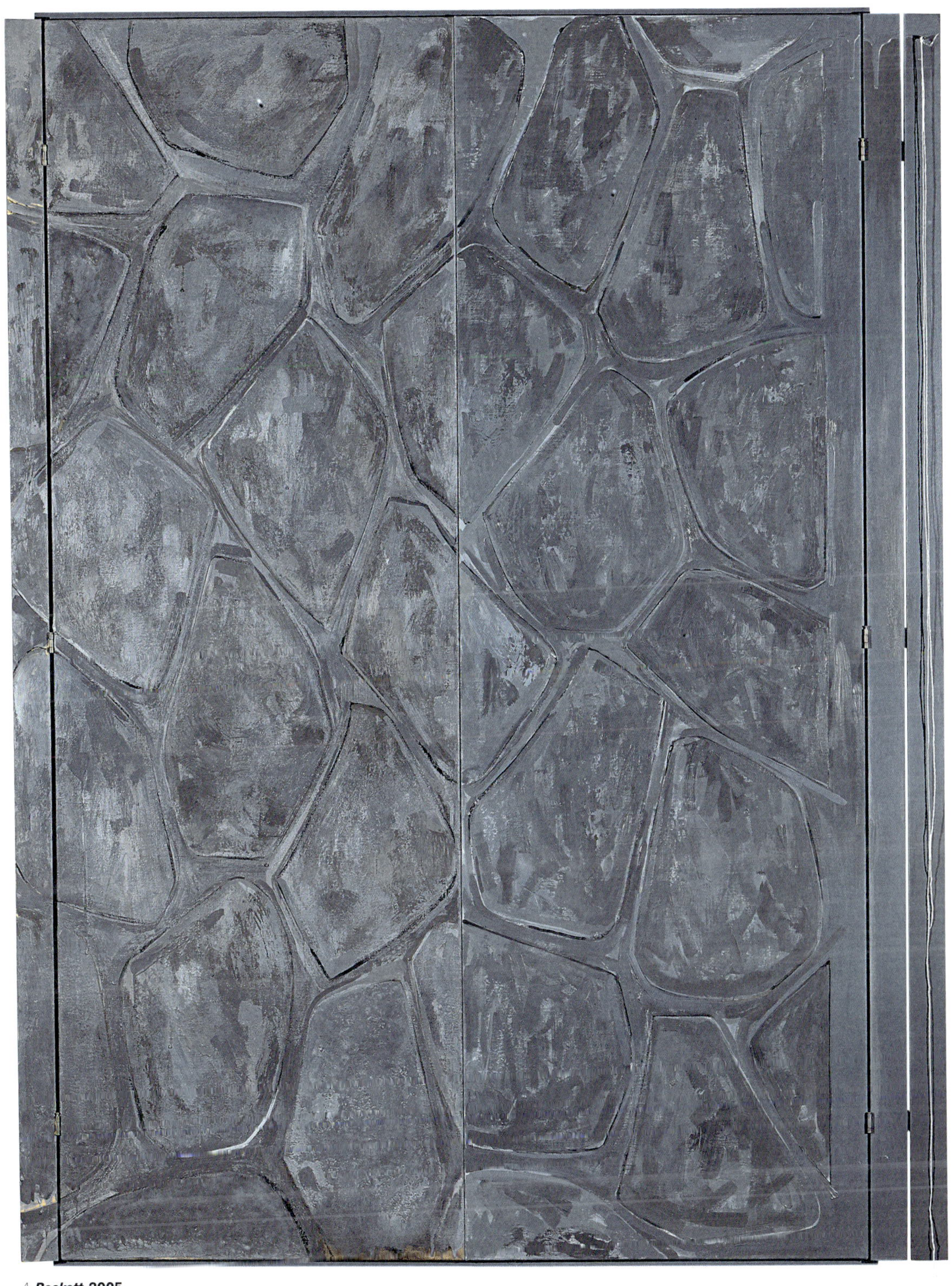

4 ***Beckett*, 2005**

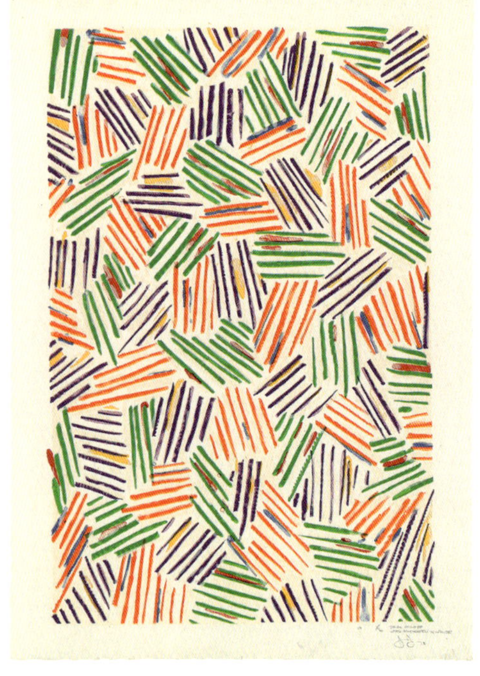
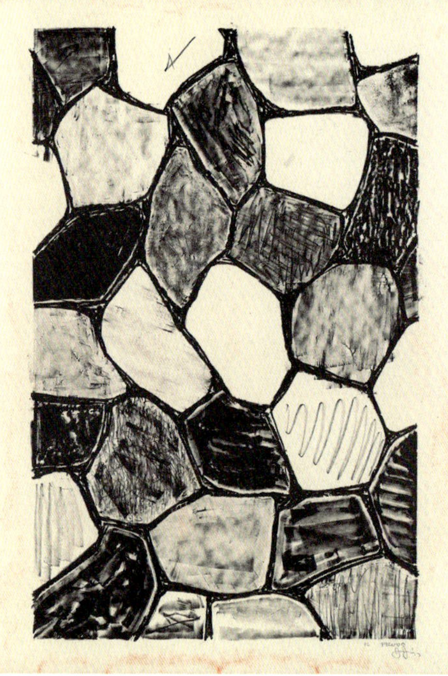
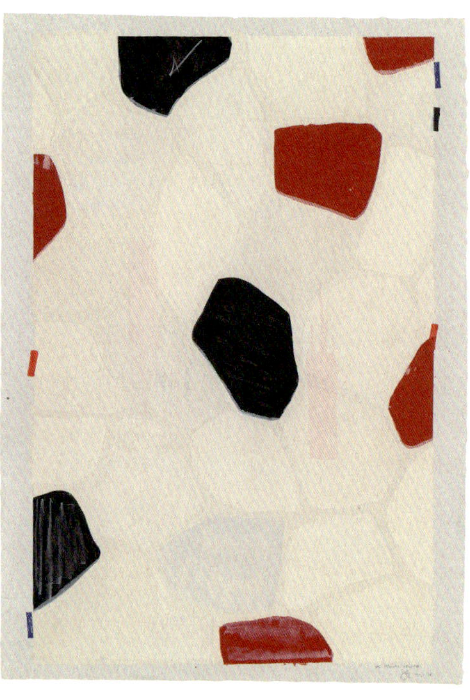
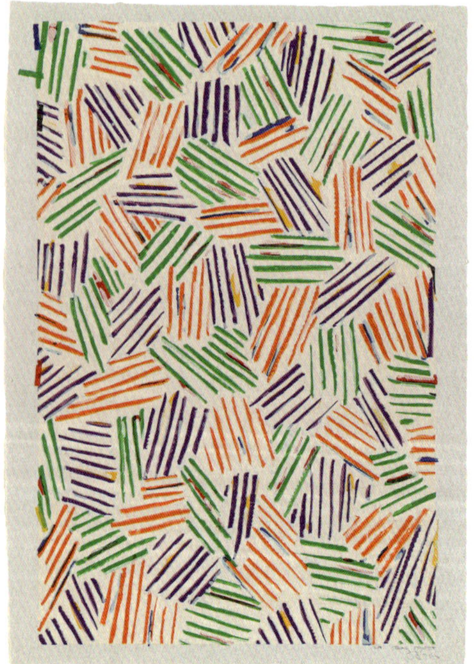

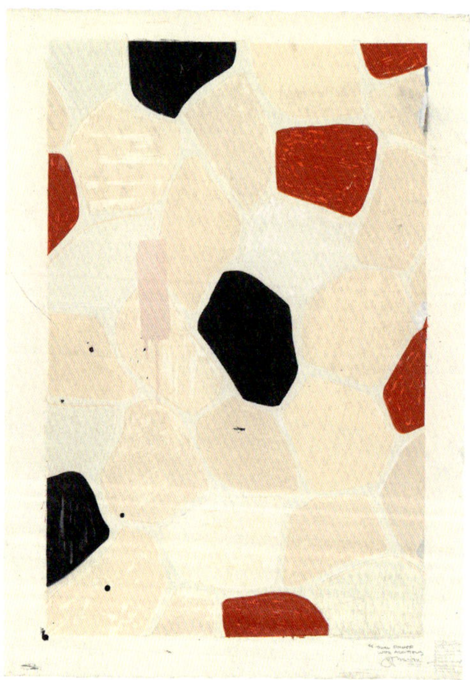

5 ***Four Panels from Untitled 1972 [A Panel]***, 1973
8 ***Four Panels from Untitled 1972 [A Panel]***, 1973–74

6 ***Four Panels from Untitled 1972 [C Panel]***, 1973
9 ***Four Panels from Untitled 1972 [C Panel]***, 1973

7 ***Four Panels from Untitled 1972 [C Panel]***, 1973–74
10 ***Four Panels from Untitled 1972 [C Panel]***, 1973–74

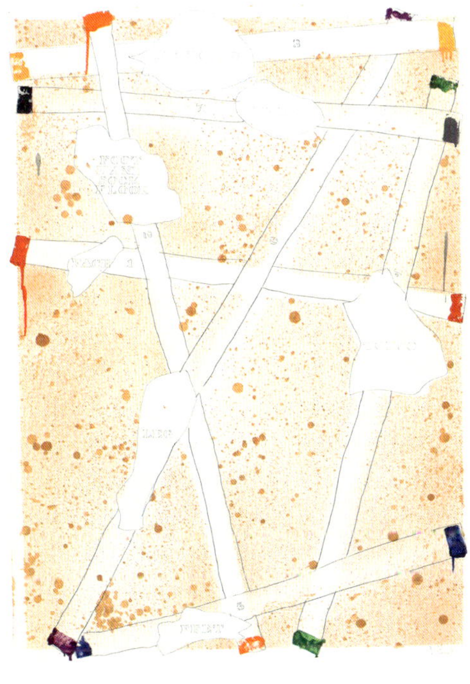
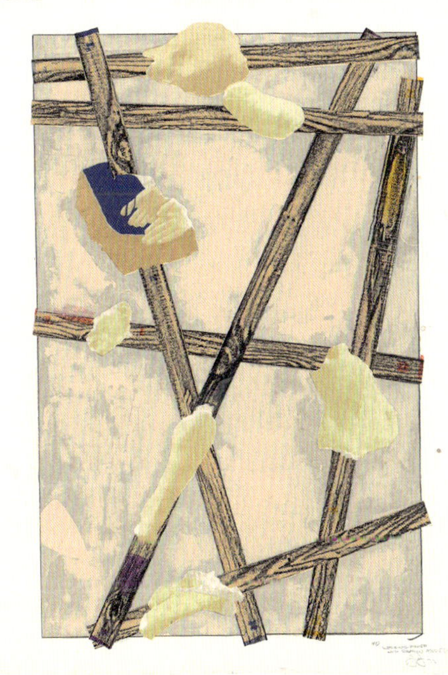
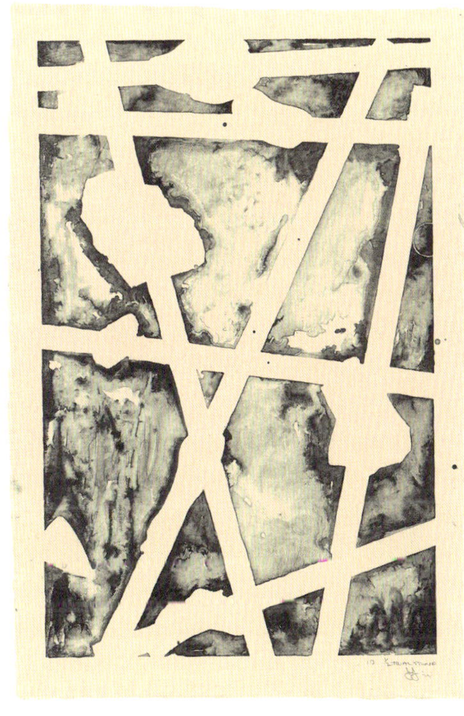
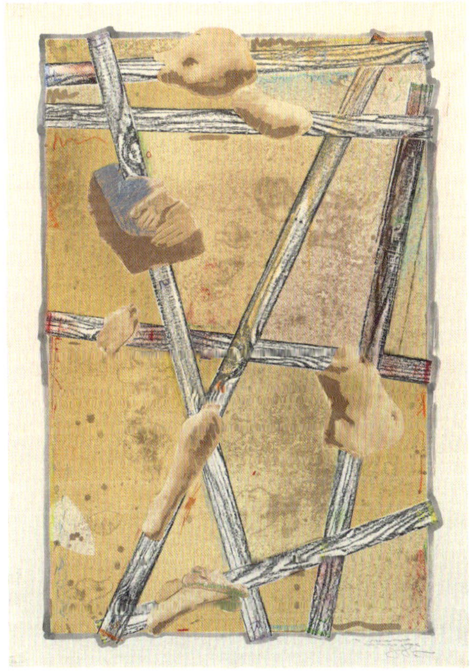

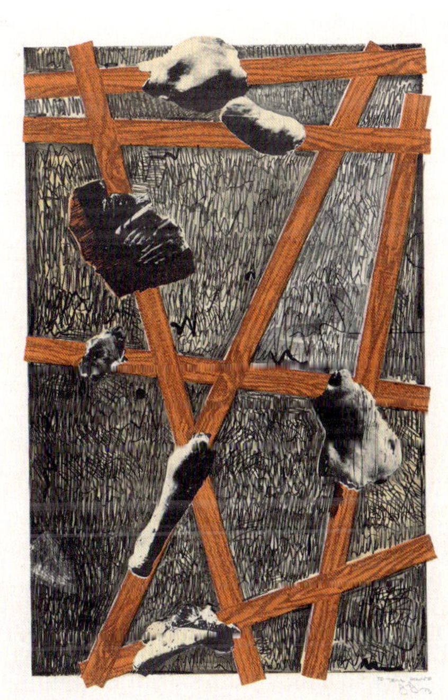

11 ***Untitled***, 1973
14 ***Four Panels from Untitled 1972 [D Panel]***, 1973

12 ***Four Panels from Untitled 1972 [D Panel]***, 1973
15 ***Four Panels from Untitled 1972 [D Panel]***, 1974

13 ***Four Panels from Untitled 1972 [D Panel]***, 1973
16 ***Four Panels from Untitled 1972 [D Panel]***, 1973

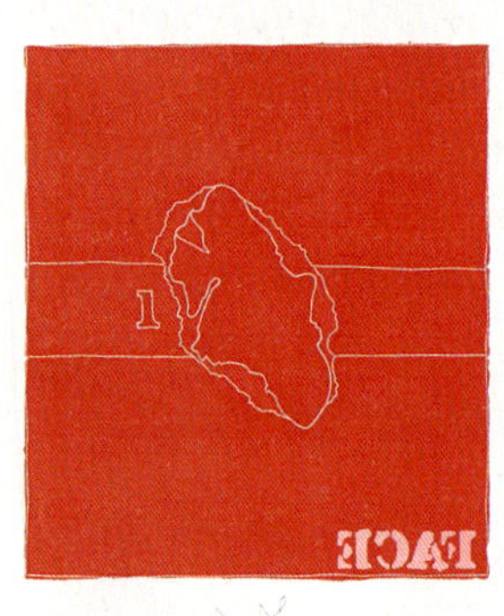
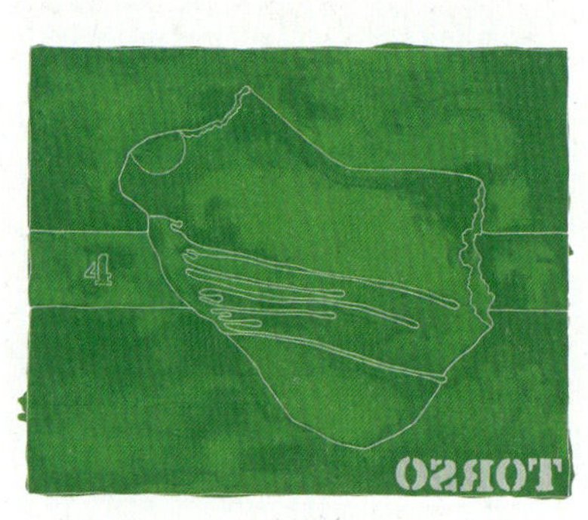
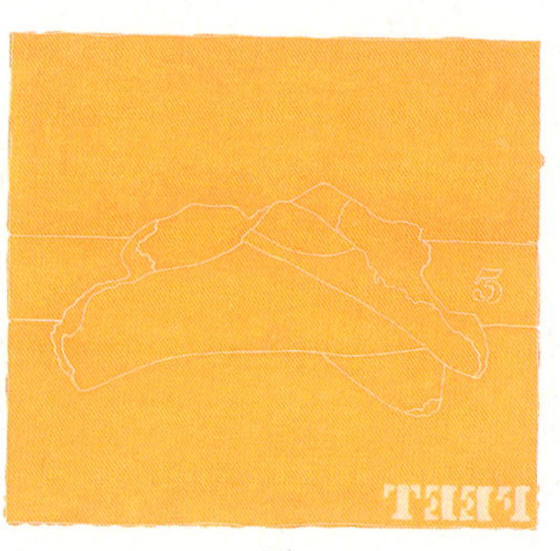

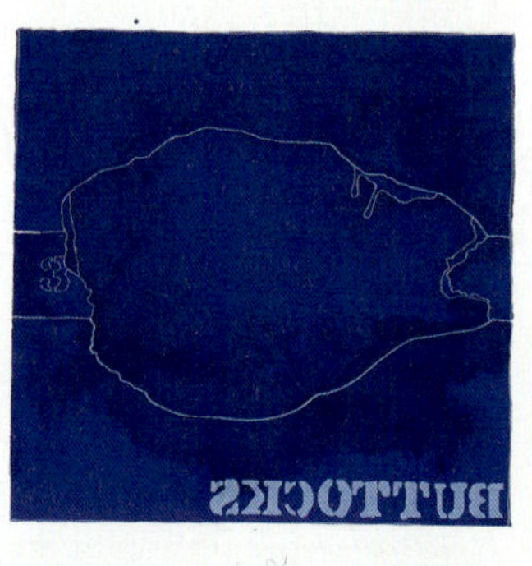
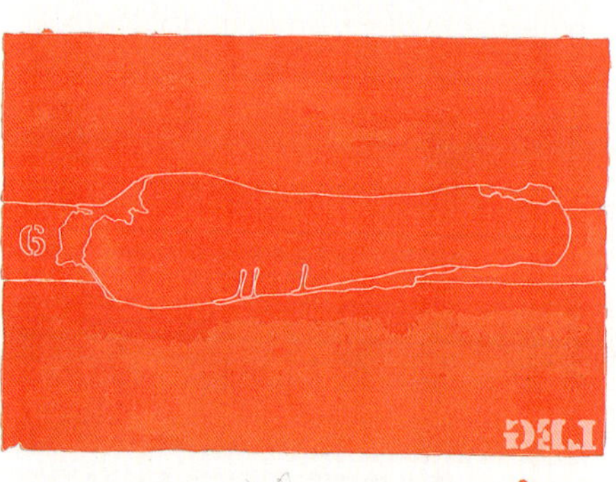

17 ***Face*, 1973–74**
18 ***Torso*, 1973–74**
19 ***Feet*, 1973–74**
20 ***HandFootSockFloor*, 1973–74**
21 ***Buttocks*, 1973–74**
22 ***Leg*, 1973–74**

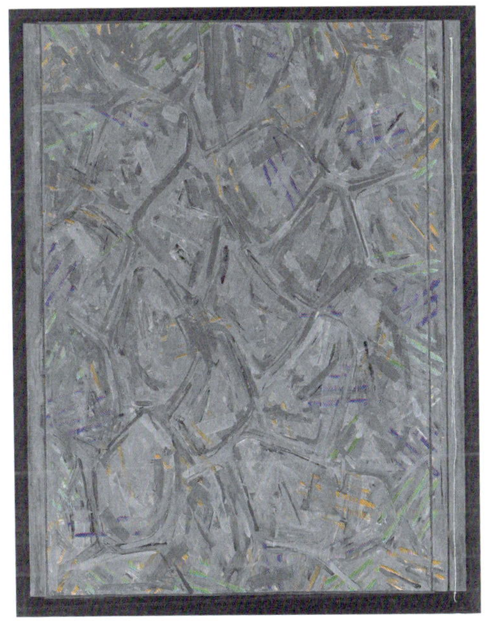

23 *Within*, 2007

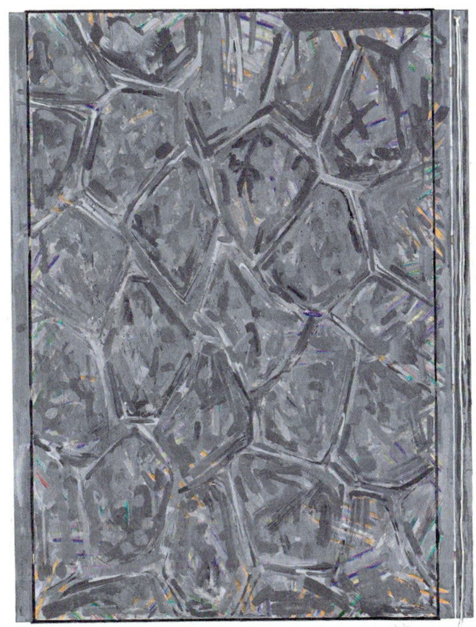

24 *Within*, 2007

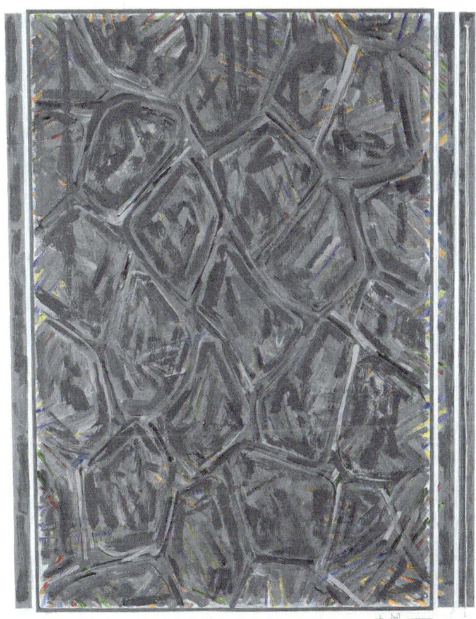

25 *Within*, 2007

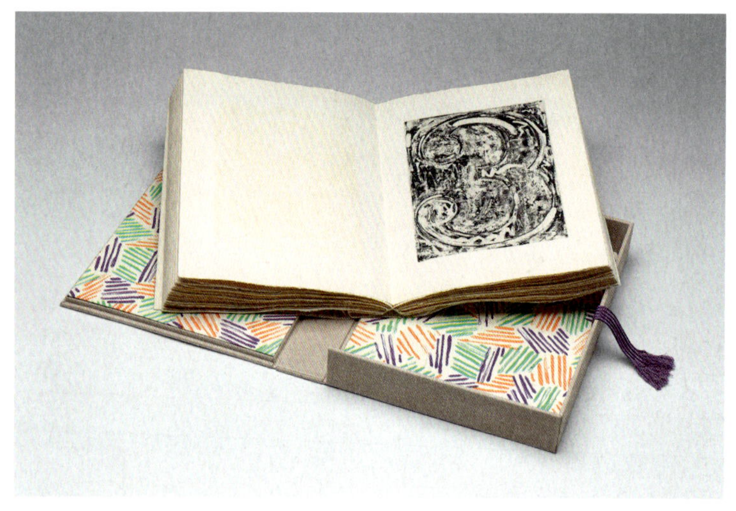

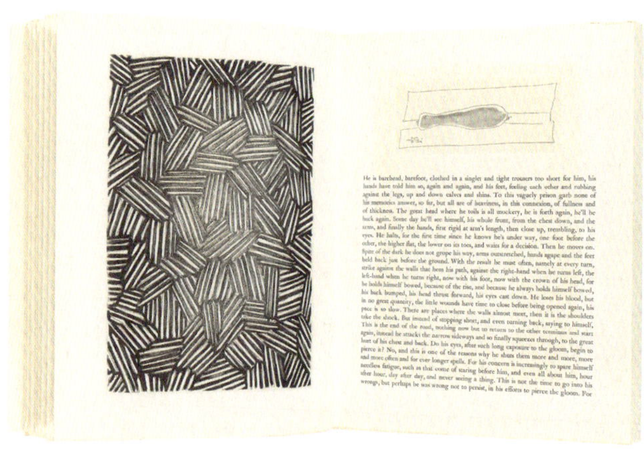

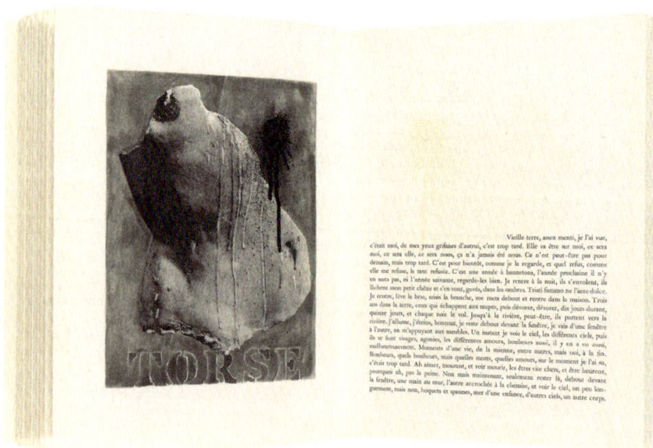

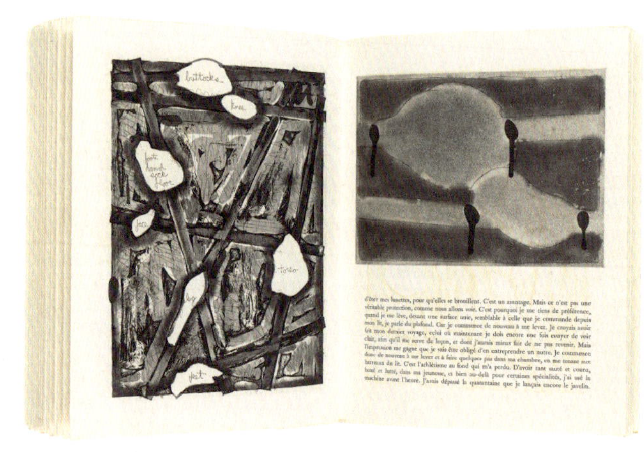

26–33 ***Foirades/Fizzles*, 1976**

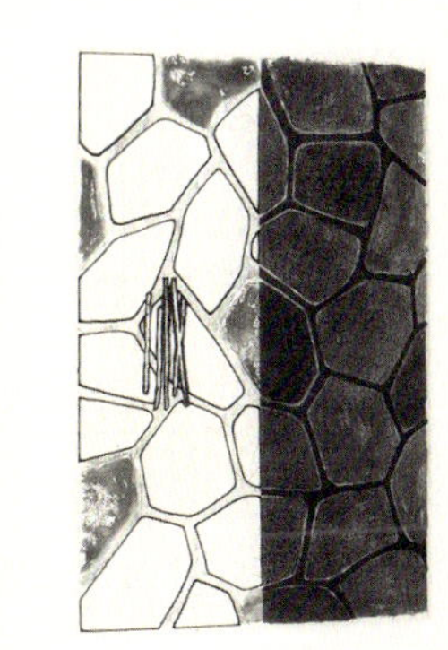

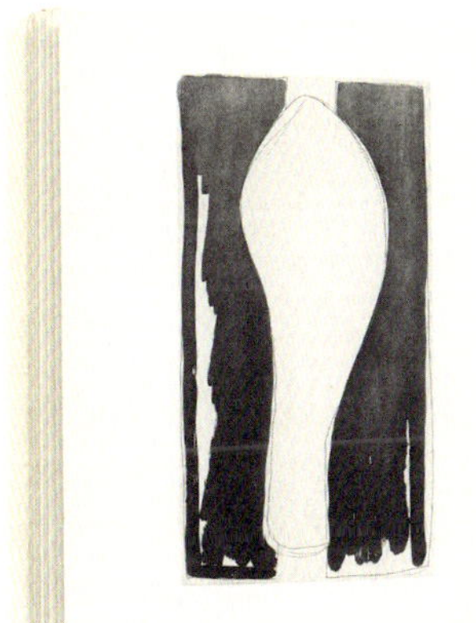

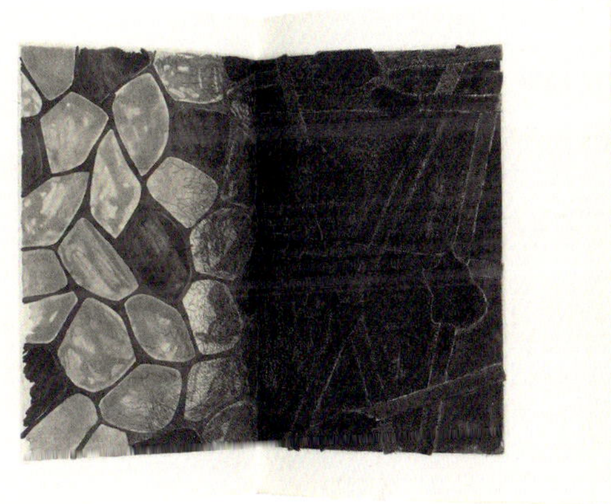

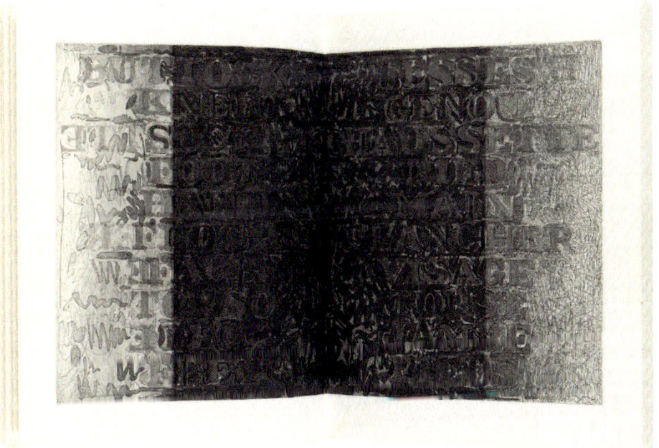

Casting Blind

Jennifer L. Roberts

According to What (1964; pp. 150–51, pl. 2) and *Untitled* (1972; pp. 158–59, pl. 2) are monumental multipanel paintings that serve as touchstones for approaching the first decades of Jasper Johns's career. Both anthologize key elements in Johns's antecedent work, and each foretells the development of work to follow. *According to What* is usually discussed as a compendium of visual rhetoric.[1] Indeed, embedded in its very title, according to a note in Johns's sketchbook, is a question about seeing: "Somewhere here, there is the / question of 'seeing clearly.' / Seeing what? / According to what?"[2] The painting is also linked to Johns's well-known sketchbook meditations on the "watchman" and the "spy," figures that embody various forms of the relationship between seeing and being seen.[3] *Untitled* also concerns itself with visual apprehension; in this case a form of rapid, ephemeral glancing. The painting is best known for having launched Johns upon a decade of recombinative experimentation with the flagstone and crosshatch motifs, both of which originated in a fleeting glimpse from a moving vehicle. The flagstones derive from a wall painted with trompe l'oeil stone patterns that Johns saw while driving through Spanish Harlem on the way to the airport; the crosshatch pattern was painted on a car driving in the opposite direction of Johns on the Long Island Expressway.[4] In *Untitled*, Johns materializes these passing glances and reins them in to the slow roll of the huge panels, each of which echoes the last.

But if these paintings serve as encyclopedic visual tabulations, they are also important for the way they mark the limits of vision in Johns's work: they incorporate radically different, even nonhuman modes of perception into the scene of seeing. An intractable otherness permeates both paintings, and I argue here that this otherness is distilled and distributed by the cast body parts attached to their surfaces. The process of casting gave Johns access to a strange species of perceptive intelligence that he borrowed, here and throughout his work, to interrogate the very notion of painting as a "visual art." *According to What*, together with its immediate precedent *Watchman* (1964; p. 117, pl. 1), marks the return of the cast body part to Johns's work after its initial introduction in key paintings of 1955. *Untitled* marks the last appearance of casts in his work for the next ten years. The paintings remind us of the centrality of casting in Johns's oeuvre and provide us with an opportunity to linger on the topic of casting in his work as a whole.

In the upper-left corner of *According to What*, attached to a canted panel, hangs a wax cast of the outseam portion of a leg and foot. The cast "sits" on a sawed-off cross section of a chair, and the entire assembly is doubly inverted: it hangs upside down, and the hollow inner cavity of the wax cast, rather than the outside (skin side), faces the viewer. The cast is a version of a similar assembly that Johns introduced earlier in 1964 in the painting *Watchman*. The rightmost panel of the 1972 *Untitled* features seven plaster-and-wax casts of body fragments, taken from both male and female subjects, attached to a system of angled, narrow wooden slats.[5] Although these casts might seem to represent an inventory of discrete body parts, in fact each is a quizzical, seemingly arbitrary framing of nameable parts along with nondescript adjacent areas—not a face but the side of a part of a face, not a torso but a portion of the side of a torso stretching from nipple to navel, a tangential buttock with a sliver of another buttock, a knee and its fatty surround, an Achilles view of a heel and calf, a set of crossed ankles along with the tops of the feet, and part of a foot and hand and a portion of flooring.

The body casts in Johns's paintings have generally been interpreted in terms of the psychological unease provoked by their fragmentation of the body.[6] And yet (as always for Johns) there is a relentlessly literal explanation for the way these casts appear. When asked about his motivations for casting the body in such an unsettling way, Johns replied with his typical appeal to the basics of process: "It is simple to cast a part of the body in the way that I do it, but a complete figure would require an enormous amount of time and a technique that I don't have."[7] Johns's appeal to technical "convenience" might appear to close down the possibilities for interpretation of these casts (inasmuch as—in what I have taken to calling "merely-ism"—such matters are often taken to be *merely* material or *merely* technical). But if we take Johns's emphasis on the significance of process seriously (rather than just chalking it up to his laconic communication style), we will find that the simple, direct life-casting methods to which Johns refers bring along entire material philosophies of perception, embodiment, memory, and interdimensional representation. This essay is an experiment in the kind of artisanal analysis that would seem to be required to do justice to Johns's literalism. In working through his casting practice in this short essay, I will refrain from the usual art-historical appeals to his artistic precedents (Marcel Duchamp, Pablo Picasso, etc.) and theoretical informants (Surrealism, psychoanalysis, etc.) in order to attend more fully to what Johns could have learned from the "simple" process of casting itself. Casting is a mode of material intelligence of great importance in Johns's work. Ultimately, of course, it intersects with his theoretical and historical intelligence. But the material intelligence is equally profound and deserves its own account.

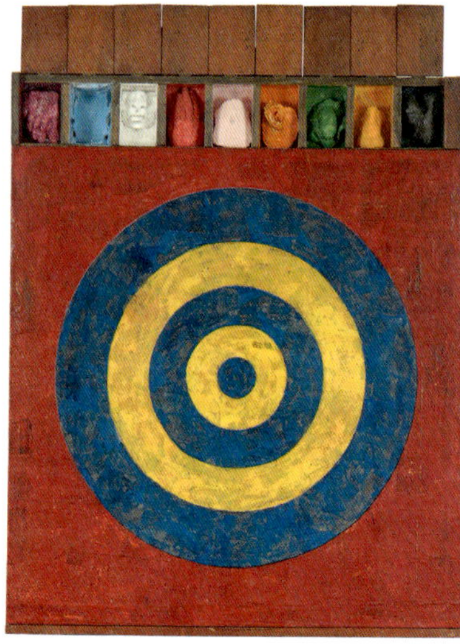

Fig. 1 ***Target with Plaster Casts*, 1955**
Encaustic and collage on canvas and wood with objects, 52 × 44 1/4 in. (132.1 × 112.4 cm). Private collection of David Geffen, Los Angeles

Blind

Casting and molding (its necessary adjunct) have been essentially synonymous with Johns's approach to sculptural form for his entire career, from *Target with Plaster Casts* (1955; fig. 1) through the flashlights and light bulbs and Savarins and Ballantines to his most recent bronze reliefs. (It is important to note that there was nothing self-evident or automatic about Johns's decision to take up casting as a sculptural process in the late 1950s. As Fred Orton has pointed out, heroic dramas of welding and industrial assemblage were the order of the day. Casting was seen as quaint, quiet, and traditional—even, to borrow Orton's memorable characterization, rather "daft.")[8] But if casting is synonymous with Johns's approach to sculpture, it is also inseparable from his approach to painting. He announced as much in 1955, when, after destroying his earlier work, he emerged as a self-conscious artist with two "paintings" that unforgettably conjoined the two practices: *Target with Plaster Casts* and *Target with Four Faces* (p. 42, pl. 2).[9]

Of the partial facial casts in both of these paintings, Roberta Bernstein has rightly pointed out that "the most disturbing aspect of [these] faces is their lack of eyes."[10] Yet there is a practical reason, grounded in the exigencies of life casting, that these faces are eyeless. The disturbances that they provoke derive from the conflict between the pragmatic realities of casting and the illusionistic rhetoric of painting. In these two seminal 1955 paintings, as in all his work incorporating casts, Johns explores a fundamental mismatch between the perceptual habits of the painting's viewer and casting's own mode of "perceiving" its objects.

There is no such thing as a cast eye, if by that we mean a directly molded imprint of a living, seeing eye. To cast a face, plaster or another mold material must be applied directly to the model's (oiled) skin—slumping and creeping, heating up as it cures. Obviously, wet plaster cannot be spread over an open eye. Even casting a closed eye is complicated, not only for technical reasons but because closed-eye casts also cause "disturbances": the model must hold unnaturally still as the mold cures, so life masks are notoriously difficult to distinguish from death masks. In other words, a cast face *with* eyes would arguably be *more* disturbing than Johns's casts that crop out the whole area.[11] Whatever their psychological aftereffects, the facial casts in these two paintings embody the limits of casting as a mode of representing the human eye. And this is one way that body casts interrupt the standard visual logics of representation: the fiction of the reciprocal gaze in painting—the feeling we have that the sitter "looks out at us" from within the scene—is impossible to achieve using the casting process.

Casting is blind in another way as well. The final formation of the cast, which occurs as the liquid material pushes and settles along and against the articulated surface of its matrix and then sets up into its hardened form, is radically invisible to the human observer. The "work" is done darkly, between two surfaces; what happens happens between the model and the mold or the mold and the cast; the artist cannot access or surveil that secret space. This is one of the key qualities that casting shares with printmaking. As I have written in the context of Johns's printmaking practice, in the final analysis prints are made in the dark, tight space of the press, away from the artist's eye.[12] Both casting and printing evoke consummation—physical contact and release coincident with acts of reproduction—but they ultimately exclude the artist from a participatory or even a participant observer's role in this act. All the more appropriate, then, that in his first freestanding sculptures Johns would take light bulbs and flashlights as the objects to be molded and cast: how better to explore the devastating stakes of casting in relationship to visibility? The flashlight, tool of both the watchman and the spy, is smothered in plaster or Sculp-metal—dark, dull, unseeing like the eyeless faces over the target (fig. 2). When it comes to the making of casts, in other words, Johns can be neither watchman nor spy. The cast leg in *According to What* is a blind spot in this painting about watching. It has been "seen" *according to plaster or according to wax*, but human eyes have access only to the fossilized traces of that sequestered material perception.

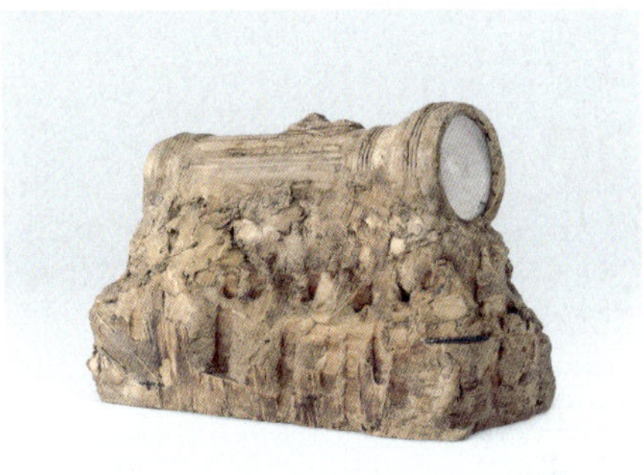

Fig. 2 ***Flashlight III*, 1958**
Plaster and glass, 5 ¼ × 8 ½ × 3 ¾ in. (13.3 × 21.6 × 9.5 cm). Collection of the artist

Every cast object indexes its own prior encasement. The original model or referent is first smothered by the mold, and then the mold is smothered by the casting material. Representation as entombment. What does it mean to adapt this to painting? Here we might recall that Johns's casting and molding materials included wax and Sculp-metal (a synthetic metal paste that hardens after working).[13] His painting materials also included wax (as encaustic) and Sculp-metal (which he sometimes used as if it were paint).[14] Johns famously resuscitated encaustic from historical oblivion because he liked the way each brushstroke quickly hardened, forming a kind of gestural sculpture. To use a casting term, he liked the way the encaustic "set up." There is a thermal affinity between the two processes as well: the warmth of encaustic—the wax/paint mixture is heated before application—echoes the exothermic reaction that accompanies the curing of plaster. This means that, for example, as Johns worked on *Target with Four Faces*, the canvas warmed beneath the encaustic in the same way that the skin of the model for the four faces warmed beneath the plaster.[15] Given this, we might speculate that painting for Johns is, on some level, akin to molding the surface of the canvas (in fact, Johns later made several relief sculptures cast from molds made from the surfaces of his paintings [fig. 3]).[16] To paint, for Johns, is paradoxically both to add and to remove visual incident. Painting blinds and binds the canvas as casting blinds and binds the object. Even as the canvas is of course visible in the vernacular sense, it is also occupied by the remnants of a profoundly proximal and haptic mode of material "knowing" that operates at cross-purposes to the purportedly visual logic of painting. Thus, the "four faces" in *Target with Four Faces* are akin to tutelary figures: they tell us how to understand the paint.

In an interview just a few months before he painted *According to What*, Johns alluded to visual dispossession as one of the goals of his practice: "I ... want an object to be free from the way I see it."[17] Casting performs this freedom. It frees objects (including canvases) from the way the artist sees them because it gives us those objects (including canvases) as perceived instead by matter.

Fig. 3 ***Flag*, 1960**
Bronze, 12 ⅜ × 18 ¾ in. (31.4 × 47.6 cm). Hirshhorn Museum and Sculpture Garden, Smithsonian Institution, Washington, DC; gift of Joseph H. Hirshhorn, 1966, 66.2600

The Inside of the Outside Is Not the Inside

In *According to What*, Johns mounts the cast leg "inside out," so that its "interior" surface faces the viewer. But this interior is just another exterior; it gives us no access to some inner truth of the bodily referent. The original leg was first molded in plaster, producing a hollow form with the impression of the leg on its concave side; Johns then poured and spread wax along that concave surface, transferring the leg impression to a convex (positive) orientation on another hollow form.[18] In *According to What*, we simply see the other side of that wax hollow.

With casting, the inside of the outside is not the inside. Casting remains ever on the outside of forms. It seizes the surface of things; it has no knowledge of their interiors. But even as it remains relentlessly superficial, by flipping impressions in and out of concavity, it hints at cupped, sheltered spaces; it hints at interiority, and triggers a desire for it.[19] With every mold and cast he made, Johns experienced this strange and elusive process of translating a surface between "front" and "back" in such a way that it seems to promise an "inside" but instead provides only the other side of an outside, the outside in reverse. Johns's interest in the relationship between verso and recto in painting is well known.[20] As Max Kozloff put it, for Johns "the front and back of a surface, verso and recto, are understood to be, for all practical purposes, identical."[21] Given that casting and painting emerged together in Johns's art, it is hard to believe that casting did not inform his understanding of reversible surfaces. The vivid, peculiar, and, yes, disturbing spatial and perceptual experience that is specific to casting's way of reversing surfaces must have impressed Johns with the way it could be adapted to painting's own set of similar promises. For a painting, too, is a surface that promises an "interior" (the expressionistic or illusionistic referent "behind" its picture-window plane), but remains, in literal terms, just a surface.

Along with (and unfolding from) its leg cast, *According to What* is filled with other enactments of this principle, in which the viewer is granted access to the other side of objects, only to find a kind of uncanny redundancy: the front side seen from behind. The hinged letters present their backs as their fronts in reverse (the whole idea of the hinge, which Johns takes up from Duchamp as well as the history of trompe l'oeil painting, traffics in this rhetoric of the double-sided surface). The reverse-screenprinted band of newspaper gives us the back side of the front of the paper, with its text reversed, rather than the new page with new information that we would normally expect when turning over a newspaper page (Johns gives us, in other words, the other side of page 1 rather than page 2). The theme of bending or crimping that pervades the painting—the bent letter, the bent color-chart stencil, the bent coat hanger—also deals in peeking behind forms without providing the satisfaction of any "interior" difference.

Undercutting the Body

Casting a complete figure—a figure in the round—is difficult because in casting there is an inherently vexed relationship between surface topology and three-dimensional form. That vexation is expressed in material terms as fragmentation. In the process of molding and casting, the negotiation of form in the round always involves breakage, splitting, piecing, or other forms of partition.

Johns referred to the cast body fragments in the 1972 *Untitled* as "simple" because they could be made using single-piece or "draw" molds. Because he limited himself to small, relatively flat segments of the body, the mold material he applied could easily be lifted up and away from the body after hardening, and the casting material could similarly be "drawn" from the mold after hardening. But if Johns had been working in the round or had attempted to cast a part of the body that had undercuts or indentations, the process would have become much more complicated. For these more complex forms, once casting is complete, it becomes physically impossible to separate the mold from the cast without one of them breaking. In its liquid form, the molding or casting material flows easily around corners, along the surfaces and angles into all the indentations and invaginations of the model, under the "undercuts"—areas of overhang in the model. But once that liquid sets, it locks itself around these topological incidents, gets hung up on them, and cannot be removed intact. The artist must either plan to break the mold apart after it hardens (in which case it becomes a waste mold) or must conceive of the mold in pieces in the first place (a piece mold). The only way to make a full mold of an object without breaking either the mold or the object is to leave the object permanently entombed within its surrounding material, never to be seen again (Johns experimented with this in the sculpture *Flashlight I* [1958; fig. 4], in which he surrounded a flashlight with Sculp-metal and left it there.)[22] For the cast body to "live" in visual representation, to escape this tomb, it must be destroyed. The scattered body fragments in *Untitled* acknowledge the inherent discontinuity imposed upon the body by the casting process—the inherent bodily *cost* of casting that is almost always disavowed in traditional sculpture. The effect of their scatter across the panel lies somewhere between a piece mold and a waste mold: somewhere between a body planned in fragments for assembly and a body violently broken apart.

The fault lines that define the contours of these pieces and fragments in the casting process usually correspond to the areas in the model in which exposed surfaces give way to hidden surfaces. The mold fractures along the turnings or thresholds between the

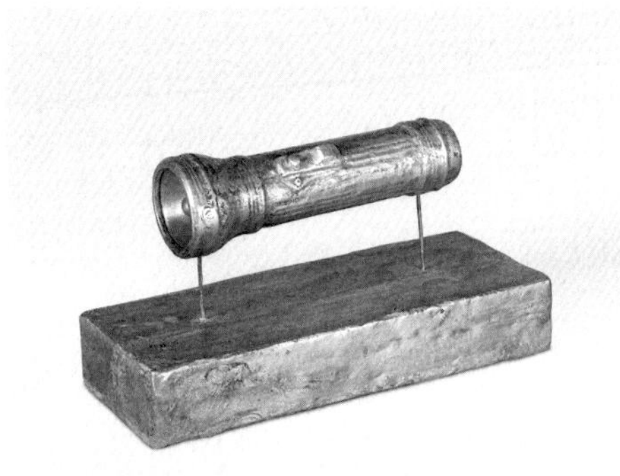

Fig. 4 ***Flashlight I*, 1958**
Sculp-metal on flashlight and wood with wire, 5 ¼ × 9 ⅛ × 3 ⅞ in.
(13.3 × 23.2 × 9.8 cm). Private collection

visible and the invisible. Any hidden surface (an undercut: the back or underside of something) implies fragmentation because it requires (or forces) an act of piecing. It is another way in which casting indexes a form of blindness, since it exacts a physical toll for attempting to see around corners. In its sensitivity to the difference between exposure and occlusion (where occlusion is equivalent to fragmentation), casting is therefore closely related to the interrogation of visibility that is so central to Johns's painting.

And if, as mentioned above, the broken figure embodies the inherently vexed relationship in casting between surfaces and three-dimensional form, Johns's "broken representation of the human physique" speaks to a similarly vexed relationship in painting, which also must somehow reconcile its surfaces with the fulsome world it attempts to represent.[23] Casting's dimensional negotiations gave Johns a strong model for expressing the profundity of the same problems in painting. And casting allowed him to work through this dilemma without resorting (as he refused to do) to illusionistic solutions such as perspective or chiaroscuro. We might say that Johns takes molding rather than modeling as his master concept for the staggering implications of reducing the body to a two-dimensional plane. *Untitled* of 1972 makes this quite clear. The shapes of the cast body fragments clearly echo the shapes of the "stones" in the flagstone panels, as well as the shapes of the hatching clusters in the crosshatch panel. The entire painting meditates upon the way the world must be broken into fragments in order to be flattened onto a surface.

The world according to casting is a blind, thermal, haptic world of eerily reversible fragments born of a perpetual dimensional conflict. Johns brought this way of "seeing" from casting to painting, forever changing both in the process.

1 Francis M. Naumann calls it a "visual compendium of things past" and a "set of visual ideas joined by the common medium of paint." Naumann, *Jasper Johns: According to What & Watchman*, exh. cat. (New York: Gagosian Gallery, 1982), 9.
2 Jasper Johns, "Book A, p. 55, 1964," in *Jasper Johns: Writings, Sketchbook Notes, Interviews*, ed. Kirk Varnedoe (New York: Museum of Modern Art, 1996), 60 (hereafter abbreviated Varnedoe, *WSI*).
3 Johns, "Book A, p. 55," 59–60.
4 Roberta Bernstein, *Jasper Johns: Redo an Eye* (New York: Wildenstein Plattner Institute, 2017), 175, 181.
5 According to Roberta Bernstein (*Redo an Eye*, 187n85), Barbara Rose and Marion Javits "posed" for some of the casts, but the rest of the body parts come from unidentified sources.
6 Even Leo Steinberg (Johns's most perceptive and supportive early critic) called *Target with Plaster Casts* (1955; see fig. 1) a miscalculation: "The attitude of detachment required to make it work on his stated terms is too special, too rare, and pitilessly matter-of-fact to acquit the work of morbidity." Leo Steinberg, "Jasper Johns: The First Seven Years of His Art" (1962), in *Other Criteria: Confrontations with Twentieth-Century Art* (New York: Oxford University Press, 1972), 37. Margaret Iversen has written perceptively about Johns's casts; she reads their unsettling qualities in terms of fossilization and burial. See Margaret Iversen, *Photography, Trace, and Trauma* (Chicago: University of Chicago Press, 2017), 52–56.
7 Jasper Johns, "An Interview with Jasper Johns," by Roberta Bernstein, in *Fragments: Incompletion and Discontinuity*, New York Literary Forum 8–9, ed. Lawrence D. Kritzman ([Martinsville, NJ: Analecta Enterprises], 1981); reprinted in Varnedoe, *WSI*, 201.
8 Fred Orton, *Jasper Johns: The Sculptures*, exh. cat. (Leeds, UK: Centre for the Study of Sculpture, Henry Moore Institute, 1996), 33.
9 See Orton, 12.
10 Bernstein, *Redo an Eye*, 43.
11 Johns's first use of a cast body fragment in his work was the full-facial cast of his friend Rachel Rosenthal inserted in *Untitled* of 1954 (p. 49, pl. 24). This cast does include Rosenthal's closed eyes. The following year, for *Target with Plaster Casts* and *Target with Four Faces*, he cropped the casts below the eyes, arguably in order to reduce their morbidity. As he told Roberta Bernstein in a 1980 interview, "I don't want to say that I didn't understand thoughts that could be triggered by casts of body parts, but I hoped to neutralize, at least for myself, their more obvious psychological impact." Johns, "Interview with Jasper Johns," 202.
12 Jennifer L. Roberts, "The Printerly Art of Jasper Johns," in *Jasper Johns / In Press: The Crosshatch Works and the Logic of Print*, exh. cat. (Cambridge, MA: Harvard Art Museums, 2012), 19; Jennifer L. Roberts, "The Metamorphic Press: Jasper Johns and the Monotype," in *Jasper Johns: Catalogue Raisonné of Monotypes*, by Susan M. Dackerman and Jennifer L. Roberts (New York: Matthew Marks Gallery; New Haven: Yale University Press, 2017), 14–16.
13 For an excellent discussion of Sculp-metal, see Orton, *Johns: Sculptures*, 25: "Sculp-metal is a specious stuff, a complex mixture of tints, fillers, vinyl resin, aluminium powder, toluol and methyl ethyl ketone."
14 *Target* (1958; p. 35, pl. 3), for example, is painted in Sculp-metal, and the Sculp-metal extends around to the back of the painting. Bernstein, *Redo an Eye*, 95.
15 The model was Johns's friend Fance Franck, who, as a poet and ceramicist, would certainly have known a thing or two about the metamorphic power of heat. On her modeling sessions for this painting, see Bernstein, *Redo an Eye*, 64n24.
16 On these cast paintings, see Bernstein, *Redo an Eye*, 96.
17 Jasper Johns, "I Want Images to Free Themselves from Me" (in Japanese), interview by Yoshiaki Tōno, *Geijutsu Shinchō* (Tokyo) 15, no. 8 (August 1964); reprinted in Varnedoe, *WSI*, 100.
18 On the complexities of this concave/convex oscillation, see Patrick R. Crowley, "Roman Death Masks and the Metaphorics of the Negative," *Grey Room* 64 (Summer 2016): 64–103.
19 Johns exposed this side of the cast in response to precisely this desire of viewers to access the "interior" of the cast: "The first time I used this kind of element was in Japan, in a painting called *Watchman* (1964), in which I did a section of figure [*sic*] seated in a chair. It was used with the realistic or imitative surface shown forward. After I finished the painting, I invited various people to come and look at it. My Japanese friends all went up against the painting to look behind to see how it was made. So when I made this painting [*According to What*], which I already had in mind, I turned it the other way to show the back of the cast, as it were, or the inside of the cast rather than the outside." Jasper Johns, "Fragments According to Johns: An Interview with Jasper Johns," interview by John Coplans, *Print Collector's Newsletter* 3, no. 2 (May–June 1972); reprinted in Varnedoe, *WSI*, 139.
20 For a discussion, see James Rondeau and Douglas Druick, *Jasper Johns: Gray*, exh. cat. (Chicago: Art Institute of Chicago, 2007), 45.
21 Max Kozloff, *Jasper Johns* (New York: Harry N. Abrams, 1968), 21, quoted in Rondeau and Druick, *Johns: Gray*, 49.
22 On *Flashlight I*, see Orton, *Johns: Sculptures*, 26.
23 Johns, "Interview with Jasper Johns," 201.

Doubles and Reflections

Mind/Mirror

Jasper Johns has employed so staggering a range of motifs, media, sizes, and formats that it is nearly impossible to synopsize his oeuvre or distill from it a single defining trait. Despite this formal and thematic heterogeneity, the twinned concepts of the mirror and the double—as both image and operation—stand out as perhaps his most abiding preoccupations. The strategy of organizing the picture plane symmetrically emerged from the start as a way of resisting the compositional balancing act of reigning mid-1950s abstraction. Works such as *Canvas* (1956; p. 34, pl. 2), *Drawer* (1957; p. 38, pl. 6), and *Book* (1957; pp. 36–37, pl. 4), among many others, implicitly mirror themselves across their central vertical axes. The symmetrical *Target with Four Faces* (1955; p. 42, pl. 2) amplifies this approach, since the cast plaster visages not only replicate one another but also bear the indexical imprint—or double—of their model in the world. These faces remind us that the bilateral symmetry of all these works echoes that of the human body, thereby implicitly mirroring an essential aspect of their beholders.

Symmetrical structures proliferate across the great diversity of Johns's early paintings and drawings, some divided by a central seam; some using folds or hinges; and some bearing the graphite imprint of the artist's own face and body. Over the following years, Johns would explore this logic with increasing complexity in his crosshatch works, such as *Corpse and Mirror* (1974) and *Corpse and Mirror II* (1974–75; pp. 178–79, pl. 2) and the two versions of *Dancers on a Plane* from 1979 (p. 193, pl. 21) and 1980. In his sketchbooks, Johns mused on the distinction between the frozen image of a corpse and the infinitely changing reflections on a mirror, a tension palpable in these paintings.[1] Poised and precise yet restlessly animated, they play with mirroring not only through their bilateral symmetry (which grows more off-kilter farther from the central seam) but also in the way the hatches partially mirror themselves across the paintings' abutting horizontal panels. In the more recent Regrets series and another based on an image of the grieving marine James Farley, Johns explores similar principles, this time not through abstract marks but through the mirroring of photographs of men in despair. The process yields mysterious apparitions, such as the stark image of a human skull in the Regrets series, which add to the air of anguish.

Symmetrical compositions are but one instantiation of Johns's relentless interest in mirroring and doubling. Sometimes, this strategy unfolds within drawings or canvases that feature a pair of nearly identical motifs or objects, whether stacked, as in the dual-panel paintings *Two Flags* (1962;

p. 183, pl. 10) and *Two Maps* (1989; p. 182, pl. 9), or adjacent, as with the titular spheres of *Painting with Two Balls* (1960; p. 38, pl. 8) and the shimmying dancers of *Big Island Hula* (2014; p. 194, pl. 28). In other cases, Johns explores duality across two different versions of an image or work, executed both in color and black and white, in encaustic and oil, at small scale and large, or as a painting and a work on paper. Often these cognates demonstrate double transpositions, as in the two *Racing Thoughts* (1983–84; pp. 186–87, pls. 2, 3), the first in hefty polychrome encaustic and its copy in grisaille and thinner oil. The relationship between a pair of works grows even more entangled when Johns introduces figure/ground inversions and reverses a composition from left to right or top to bottom. In the Seasons (1985–86), he created cognates that reverse or invert their compositional logic across the calendar, so that *Summer* and *Winter* (pp. 180–81, pls. 3, 4) are variants of each other, as are *Spring* and *Fall* (p. 190, pls. 7, 8). These panels are peppered with dual symbols that are legible in one of two ways, such as the rabbit-duck illusion that can be read as the outline of either animal but never as both at once. A similar perceptual ambiguity occurs in the recurring motif of a vase with contours delineating two opposing profiles, so that we see either a vessel or two faces, depending on which we perceive as figure or ground.

Johns's involvement in prints and sculpture only deepened his engagement with these ideas. Beginning in 1960, his prints often served as a double of a painting or drawing in a different scale, palette, and, of course, medium. But, more important, the repetition and reversal inherent in the process of transferring an image from plate to paper became a fertile field of inquiry and play that reverberated across his entire oeuvre. Casting sculptures and reliefs similarly provides Johns the occasion to scramble the relationships among an "original" object, a negative mold, and a positive metal cast. And actual mirrors have made appearances in several of his works, including the Sculp-metal shoe of *High School Days* (1964) and the polychrome and grayscale versions of *Souvenir* (1964; pp. 118–19, pls. 2, 3). Most recently, Johns included a circular mirror at the center of an untitled drawing from the Catenary series (2007; p. 192, pl. 19), the paper surface of which is shaded as if to emulate the play of light across a reflective piece of glass.

Few, if any of Johns's works encapsulate this turn of mind with, almost paradoxically, greater complexity and concision than the two versions of *Painted Bronze* (1960; p. 177, pl. 1; and p. 185, pl. 1) that depict Ballantine Ale cans resting on a plinth. By casting the original object and minutely rendering its trademark labels, Johns engaged the old saw of art as a mirror of the world, in this case the worldly token being a manufactured product that is itself a single instance of an endless chain of copies. In each version of the sculpture, Johns wryly presents two cans side by side as if to highlight the duplicative function of industry, the artist, and the casting process. And yet the near-perfect similitude of the casting is undone by the imperfect handiwork of the brush, inviting a ricocheting glance as one unpuzzles sameness and difference, both within the sculpture itself and between its two editions. We sense ourselves in the act of perception, and in this regard the device of the mirror or double acutely engenders a self-conscious mode of engagement long hailed as a hallmark of Johns's art.

—Scott Rothkopf, with Carlos Basualdo, Sarah B. Vogelman, and Lauren Young

1 See Jasper Johns, "Book B, c. 1979," in *Jasper Johns: Writings, Sketchbook Notes, Interviews*, ed. Kirk Varnedoe (New York: Museum of Modern Art, 1996), 68.

Mind/Mirror

Doubles and Reflections

PHILADELPHIA MUSEUM OF ART

1 ***Painted Bronze*, 1960**
Bronze and oil paint (three parts)
5 ½ × 8 × 4 ⅝ in. (14 × 20.3 × 11.8 cm)
Ed. no. 1/2
Museum Ludwig, Cologne; loan Peter and Irene Ludwig Foundation, 1986

2 ***Corpse and Mirror II*, 1974–75**
Oil and sand on canvas (four panels)
57 ⅝ × 75 ¼ in. (146.4 × 191.1 cm) overall
Collection of the artist; on long-term loan to the Art Institute of Chicago, 1976

3 ***Summer*, 1985**
Encaustic on canvas
75 × 50 in. (190.5 × 127 cm)
The Museum of Modern Art, New York; gift of Philip Johnson, 506.1998

4 ***Winter*, 1986**
Encaustic on canvas
75 × 50 in. (190.5 × 127 cm)
Private collection

5 ***Land's End*, 1963**
Oil on canvas with objects
66 ⅞ × 48 ⅛ in. (169.9 × 122.2 cm)
San Francisco Museum of Modern Art; gift of Harry W. and Mary Margaret Anderson, 1972

6 ***Periscope (Hart Crane)*, 1963**
Oil on canvas
67 ⅛ × 48 in. (170.5 × 121.9 cm)
Collection of the artist; on long-term loan to the Menil Collection, Houston, 2002

7 ***Ventriloquist*, 1983**
Encaustic on canvas
74 ⅞ × 50 ⅛ in. (190.2 × 127.3 cm)
The Museum of Fine Arts, Houston; museum purchase funded by the Agnes Cullen Arnold Endowment Fund, 84.87

8 ***Regrets*, 2013**
Oil on canvas
50 × 72 in. (127 × 182.9 cm)
Collection of Marguerite Steed Hoffman

9 ***Two Maps*, 1989**
Encaustic on canvas (two panels)
90 × 70 ¼ in. (228.6 × 178.4 cm) overall
The Robert and Jane Meyerhoff Collection

10 ***Two Flags*, 1962**
Oil on canvas (two panels)
98 ⅜ × 72 ¼ in. (249.9 × 183.5 cm) overall
Collection of Irma and Norman Braman

11 ***Green Angel*, 1990**
Encaustic and sand on canvas
75 ⅛ × 50 ¼ in. (190.8 × 127.6 cm)
Collection Walker Art Center, Minneapolis; anonymous gift in honor of Martin and Mildred Friedman, 1990.205

12 ***Untitled*, 1990**
Oil on canvas
75 × 50 in. (190.5 × 127 cm)
Glenn Dubin and Dr. Eva Dubin; promised gift to the Museum of Modern Art, New York

13 ***Flashlight*, 1960**
Plaster, glass, wire, and nails
5 ½ × 8 × 4 ⅜ in. (14 × 20.3 × 11.1 cm)
Collection of the artist

14 ***Flashlight*, 1960 (cast c. 1979)**
Bronze and glass
4 ¾ × 7 ¾ × 4 ¼ in. (12.1 × 19.7 × 10.8 cm)
Ed. no. 2/3
Collection of the artist; on long-term loan to the Philadelphia Museum of Art, 1986

Doubles and Reflections

WHITNEY MUSEUM OF AMERICAN ART

1 ***Painted Bronze*, 1960 (cast and painted 1964)**
Bronze and oil paint (three parts)
5 ½ × 8 × 4 ⅝ in. (14 × 20.3 × 11.8 cm)
Ed. no. 2/2
Whitney Museum of American Art, New York; purchase with funds from the Leonard A. Lauder Masterpiece Fund

2 ***Racing Thoughts*, 1983**
Encaustic and collage on canvas
48 ⅛ × 75 ⅜ in. (122.2 × 191.5 cm)
Whitney Museum of American Art, New York; purchase with funds from the Burroughs Wellcome Purchase Fund; Leo Castelli; the Wilfred P. and Rose J. Cohen Purchase Fund; the Julia B. Engel Purchase Fund; the Equitable Life Assurance Society of the United States Purchase Fund; The Sondra and Charles Gilman, Jr. Foundation, Inc.; S. Sidney Kahn; The Lauder Foundation, Leonard and Evelyn Lauder Fund; the Sara Roby Foundation; and the Painting and Sculpture Committee, 84.6

3 ***Racing Thoughts*, 1984**
Oil on canvas
50 × 75 in. (127 × 190.5 cm)
The Robert and Jane Meyerhoff Collection

4 ***Mirror's Edge*, 1992**
Oil on canvas
66 × 44 in. (167.6 × 111.8 cm)
Esther Grether Family Collection

5 ***Mirror's Edge 2*, 1993**
Encaustic on canvas
66 × 44 ⅛ in. (167.6 × 112.1 cm)
The Robert and Jane Meyerhoff Collection

6 ***Skull*, 1971**
Printing ink on paper towel mounted on board
12 × 12 in. (30.5 × 30.5 cm)
Collection of the artist

7 ***Spring*, 1986**
Encaustic on canvas
75 × 50 in. (190.5 × 127 cm)
The Robert and Jane Meyerhoff Collection

8 ***Fall*, 1986**
Encaustic on canvas
75 × 50 in. (190.5 × 127 cm)
Collection of the artist; on long-term loan to the Philadelphia Museum of Art, 1989

9 **Study for *Regrets*, 2012**
Watercolor, colored pencil, ink, collage, and acrylic on paper
11 ½ × 17 ⅞ in. (29.2 × 45.4 cm)
The Menil Collection, Houston; promised gift from the collection of Louisa Stude Sarofim

10 ***Hand*, 1963**
Lithograph: one stone
22 ½ × 17 ½ in. (57.2 × 44.5 cm)
Zigmunds Priede/ULAE
Ed. no. 18/29
The Metropolitan Museum of Art, New York; Florence and Joseph Singer Collection, 65.674.5

11 ***Ale Cans*, 1975***
Graphite wash on paper
11 ¼ × 18 in. (28.6 × 45.7 cm)
Collection of the artist

12 ***Ale Cans*, from 1st Etchings, 1968**
Intaglio
25 × 20 in. (63.5 × 50.8 cm)
Donn Steward/ULAE
Ed. no. 8/26
Whitney Museum of American Art, New York; gift of Stanley and Renie Helfgott, 71.236.3

13 ***Decoy*, 1971**
Oil on canvas with object
72 × 50 in. (182.9 × 127 cm)
The Newhouse Collection

14 ***Decoy*, 1972**
Oil on canvas with object
41 × 29 ½ in. (104.1 × 74.9 cm)
Ryobi Foundation

15 ***Drawing with Two Balls*, 1957***
Graphite pencil on paper
10 ⅛ × 8 ⅞ in. (25.7 × 22.5 cm)
Collection of Andrew and Denise Saul

16 ***Untitled*, 2006**
Ink on plastic
32 ¾ × 40 in. (83.2 × 101.6 cm)
Collection of the artist

17 ***Ventriloquist*, 1986**
Lithograph: eleven aluminum plates
41 ¼ × 29 in. (104.8 × 73.7 cm)
Keith Brintzenhofe/ULAE
Ed. no. 36/69
Whitney Museum of American Art, New York; purchase with funds from the Print Committee, 86.42

18 ***Untitled*, 1984**
Graphite pencil on green paper
6 ⅝ × 4 ¾ in. (16.8 × 12.1 cm)
Collection of Jack Shear

19 ***Untitled*, 2007**
Graphite pencil on paper with objects, in a wood frame
26 ⅝ × 34 ⅜ × 4 ⅝ in. (67.6 × 87.3 × 11.8 cm)
Private collection

20 ***Device*, 1961–62**
Oil on canvas with objects
72 ⅛ × 48 ⅛ in. (183.2 × 122.2 cm)
Dallas Museum of Art; gift of The Art Museum League, Margaret J. and George V. Charlton, Mr. and Mrs. James B. Francis, Dr. and Mrs. Ralph Greenlee, Jr., Mr. and Mrs. James H. W. Jacks, Mr. and Mrs. Irvin L. Levy, Mrs. John W. O'Boyle, and Dr. Joanne Stroud in honor of Mrs. Eugene McDermott, 1976.1

21 ***Dancers on a Plane*, 1979**
Oil on canvas and partially painted wood frame with objects
77 ⅞ × 64 ⅛ in. (197.8 × 162.9 cm)
Collection of the artist; on long-term loan to the National Gallery of Art, Washington, DC, 2000

22 ***Between the Clock and the Bed*, 1980**
Pastel on paper
33 ½ × 24 in. (85.1 × 61 cm)
Collection of Marsha and Jeffrey Perelman

23 ***Tracing after de Kooning*, 2007**
Acrylic and graphite pencil on paper
19 ¼ × 24 in. (49 × 61 cm)
Collection of the artist

24 ***Painting with Two Balls I*, 1962**
Lithograph: three stones
26 ½ × 20 ½ in. (67.3 × 52.1 cm)
Robert Blackburn/ULAE
Ed. no. 3/39
Whitney Museum of American Art, New York; gift of the family of Victor W. Ganz in his memory, 90.49

25 ***Untitled*, 1968**
Ink and varnish on plastic
13 × 11 in. (33 × 28 cm)
Collection of the artist

26 ***After Paul Gavarni*, 2002**
Ink on paper
12 ⅞ × 10 ⅛ in. (32.7 × 25.7 cm)
Collection of the artist

27 ***After Cézanne*, 1994**
Ink on paper
22 ½ × 17 ⅝ in. (57.1 × 44.8 cm)
Collection of the artist

28 ***Big Island Hula*, 2014***
Ink on plastic
12 × 13 ½ in. (30.5 × 34.3 cm)
Collection of the artist

29 ***The Critic Sees*, 1962**
Graphite pencil on two sheets of paper
10 ½ × 14 ¼ in. (26.7 × 36.2 cm) overall
Private collection; courtesy Castelli Gallery, New York

30 ***Cups 4 Picasso*, 1972***
Lithograph: four aluminum plates
22 × 32 in. (55.9 × 81.3 cm)
Bill Goldston, James W. Smith/ULAE
Edition of 39

31 ***Untitled*, 2000**
Watercolor and graphite pencil on paper
4 ⅞ × 6 ⅜ in. (12.4 × 16.2 cm)
Private collection

32 ***Valentine*, 2010–11**
Acrylic over intaglio on paper mounted on paper
12 ¼ × 17 ¼ in. (31.1 × 43.8 cm)
Collection of Susan Lorence

33 ***Untitled*, 2014**
Monotype
11 ¼ × 15 in. (28.6 × 38.1 cm)
John Lund/Low Road Studio
Collection of the artist

Doubles and Reflections

PHILADELPHIA MUSEUM OF ART

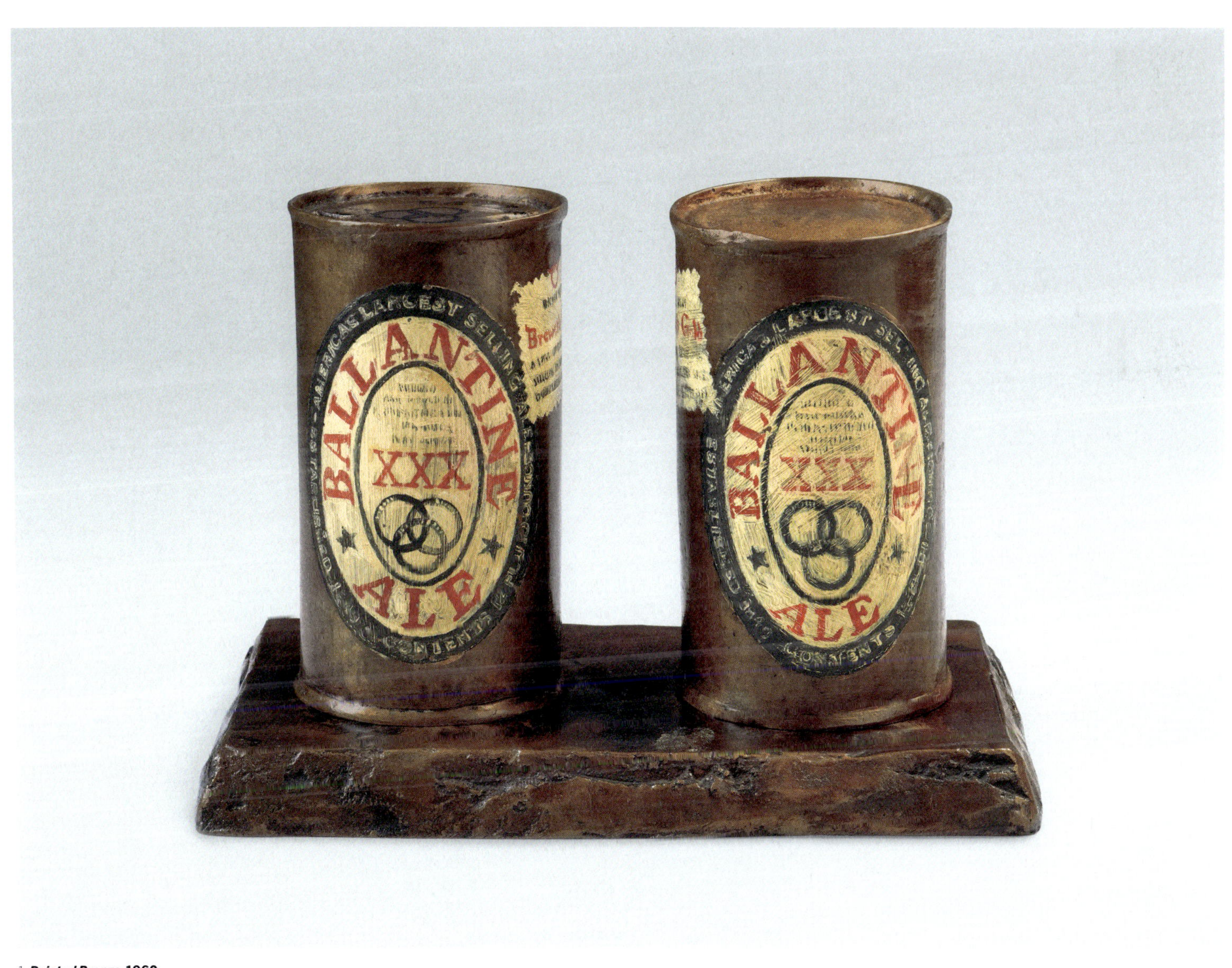

1 ***Painted Bronze*, 1960**

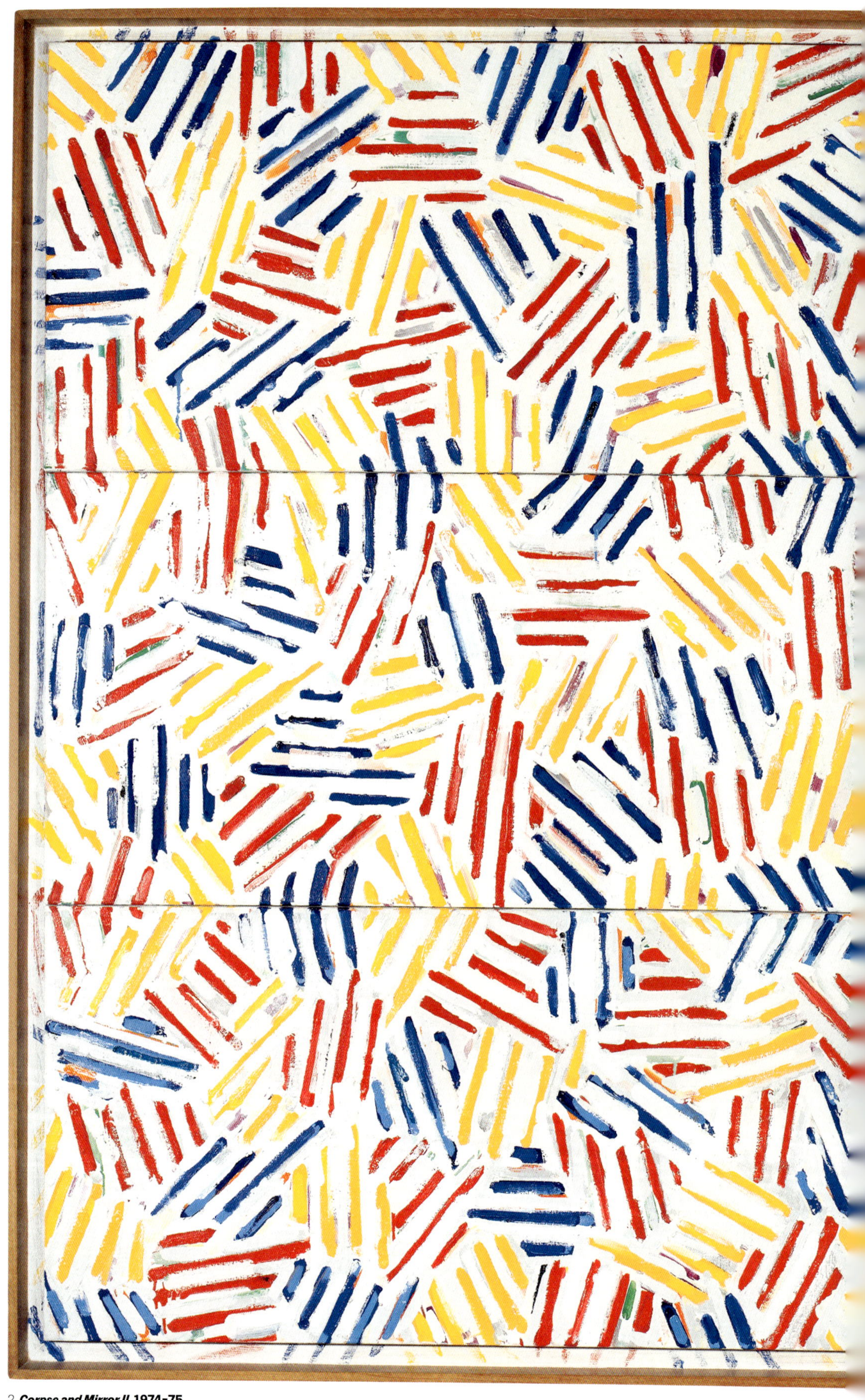

2 ***Corpse and Mirror II*****, 1974–75**

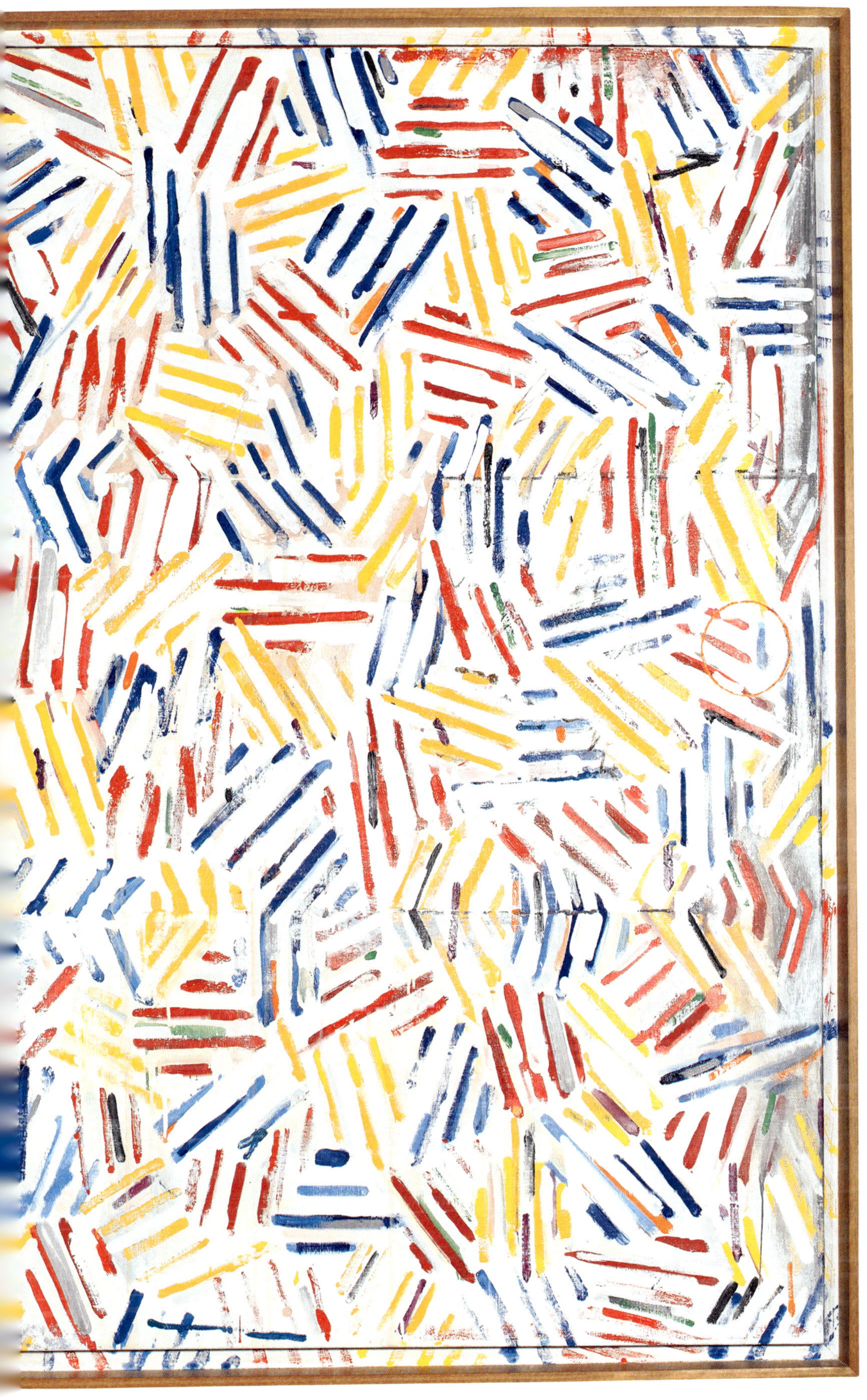

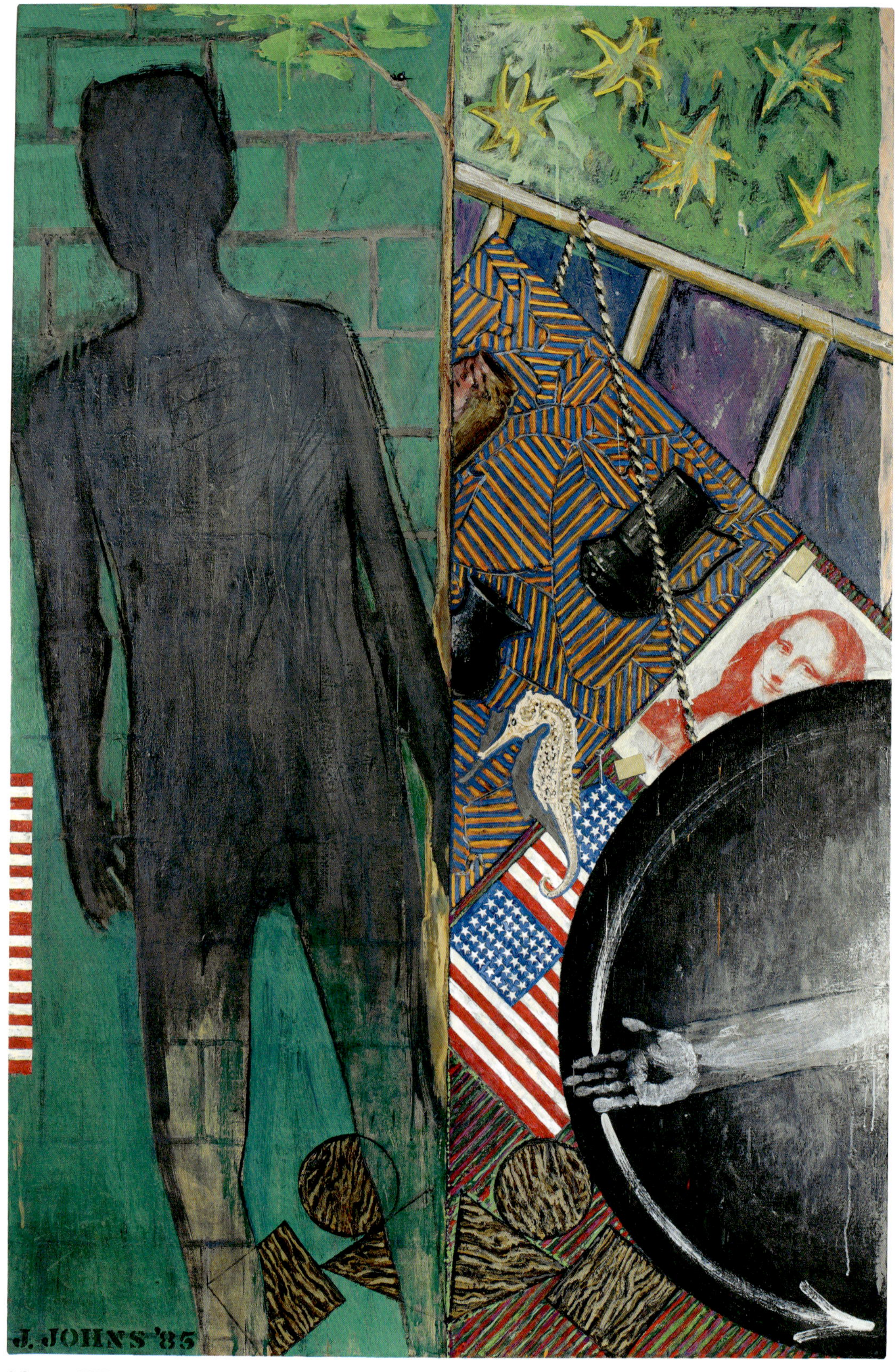

3 ***Summer***, **1985**

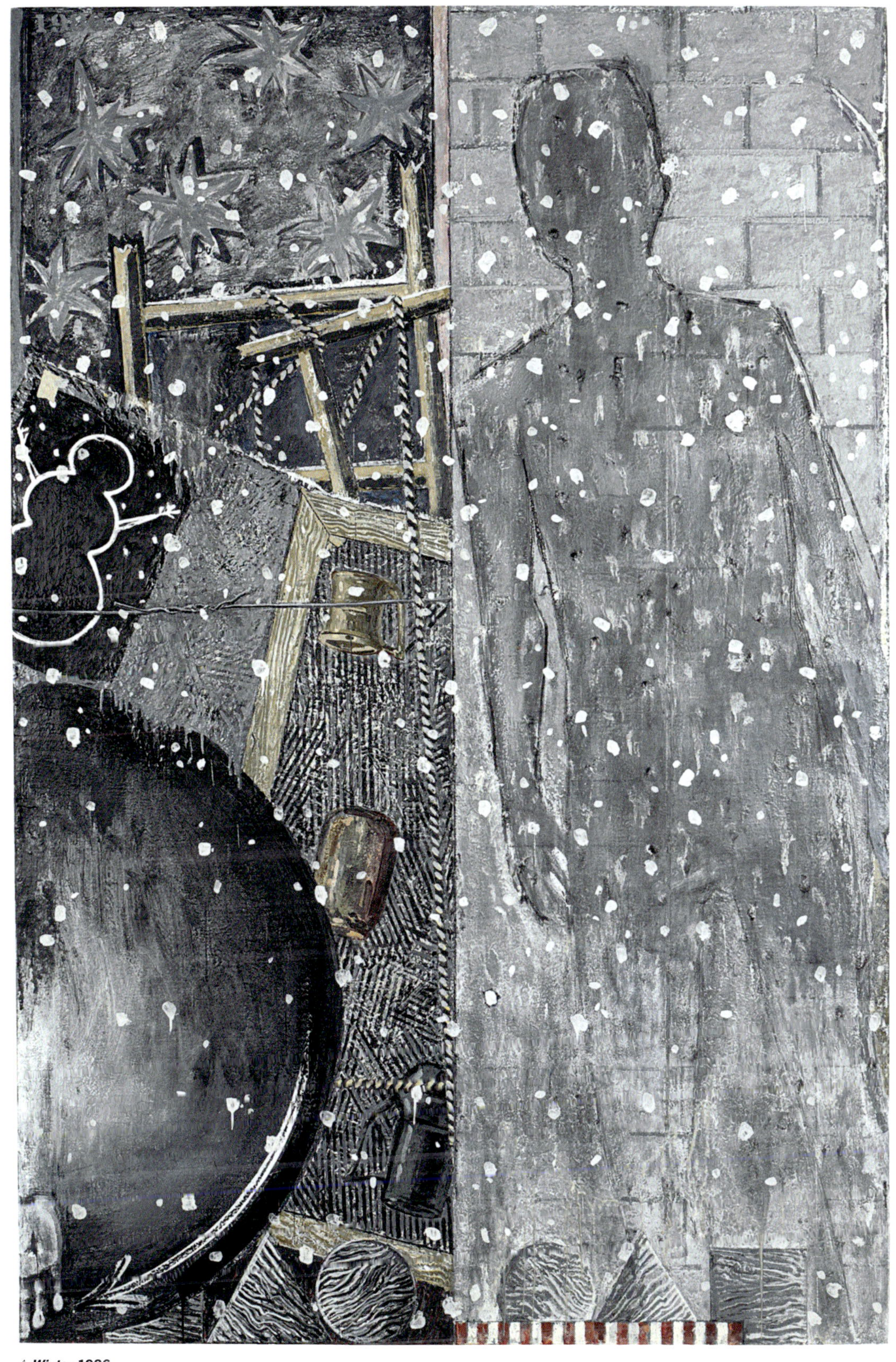

4 ***Winter*, 1986**

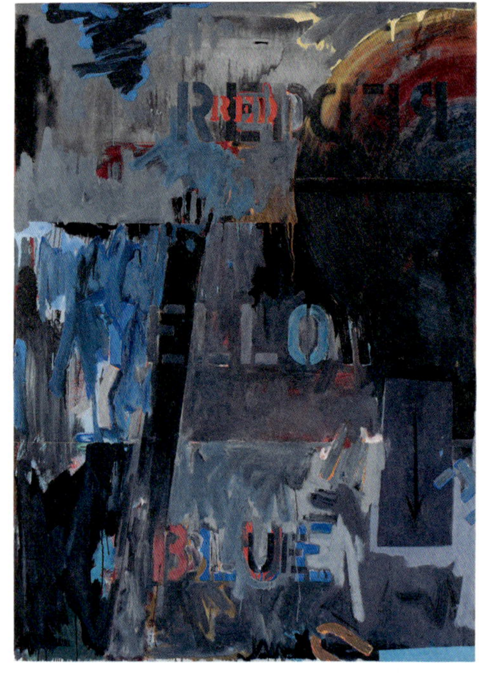

5 ***Land's End*, 1963**

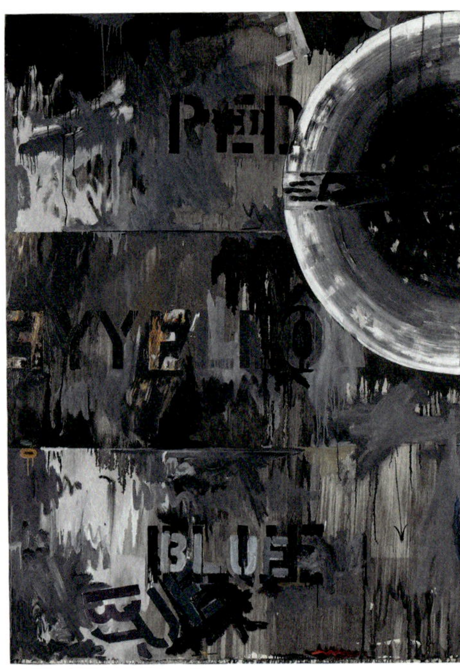

6 ***Periscope (Hart Crane)*, 1963**

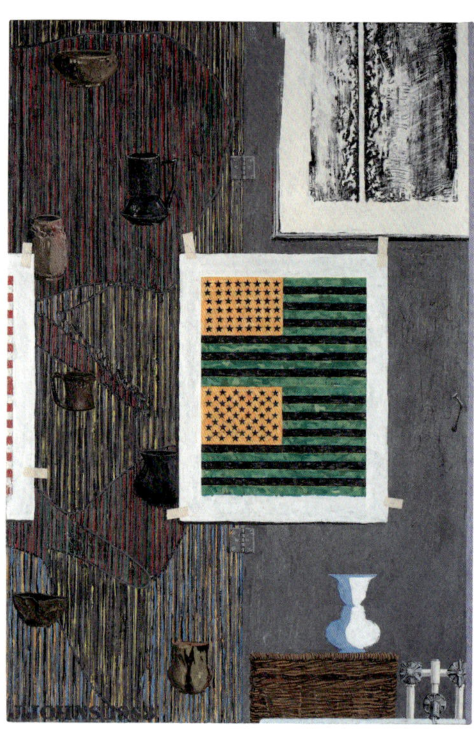

7 ***Ventriloquist*, 1983**

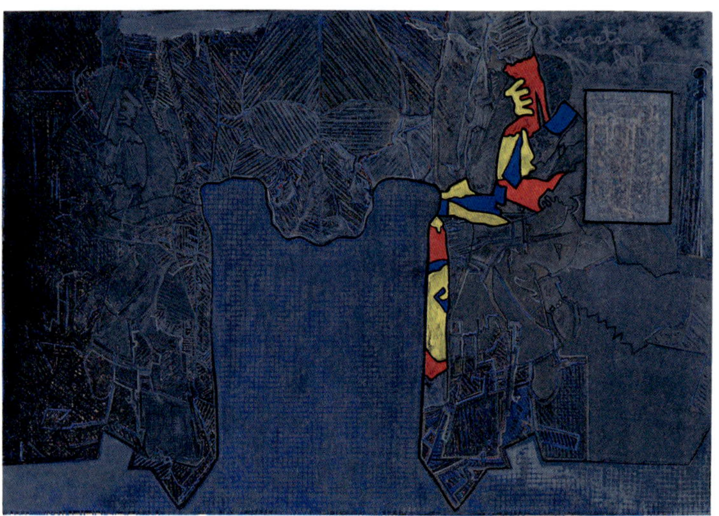

8 ***Regrets*, 2013**

9 ***Two Maps*, 1989**

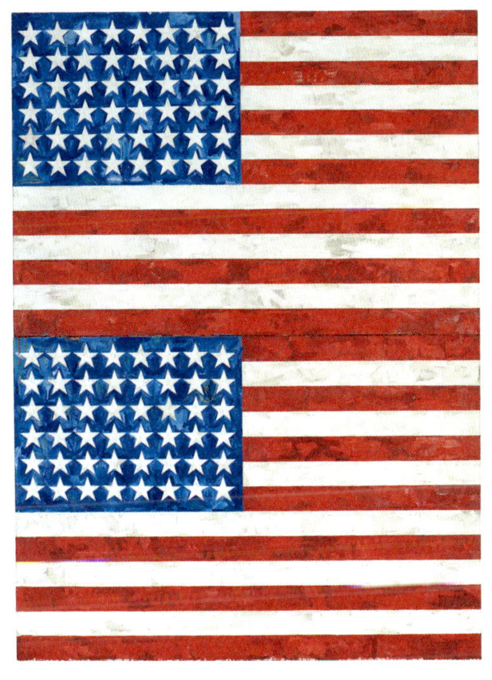

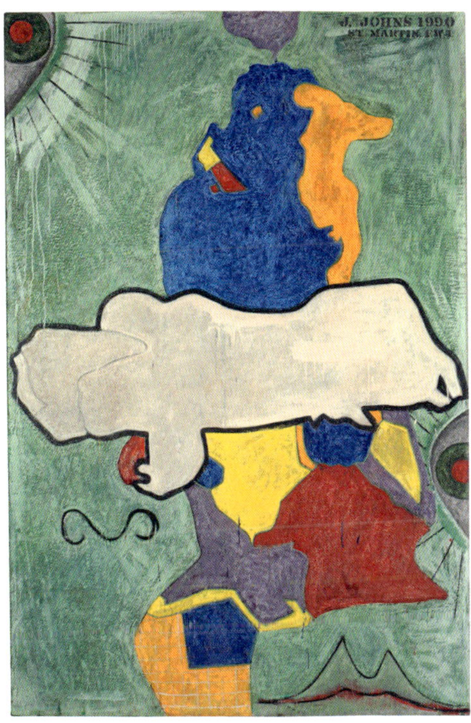

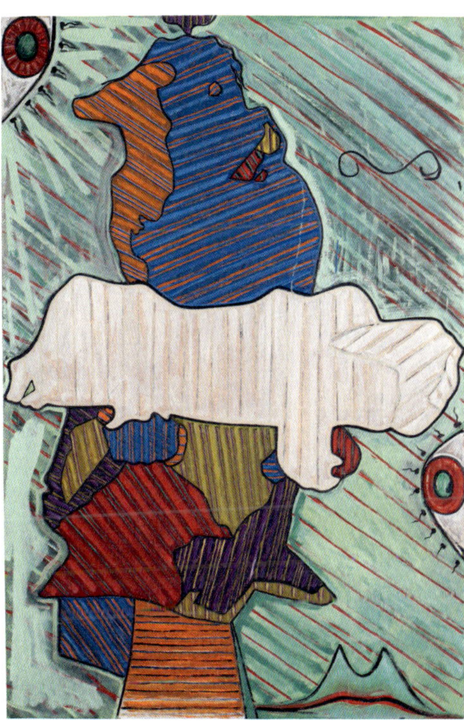

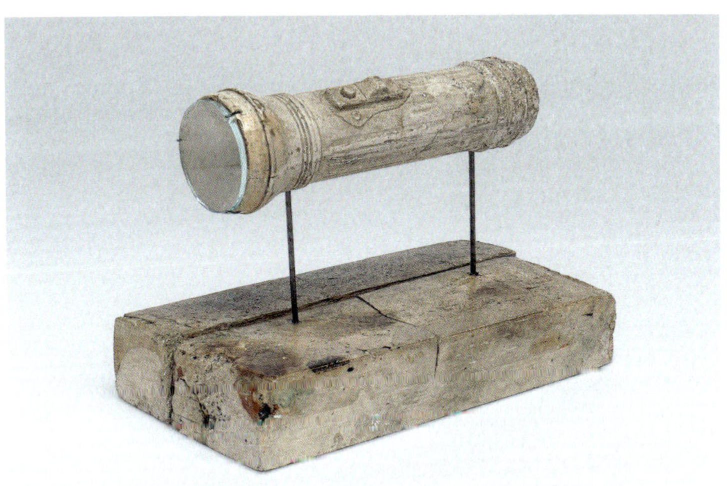

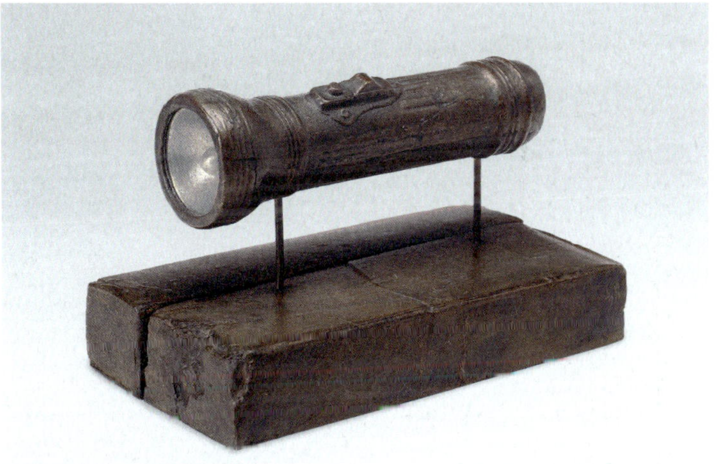

10 ***Two Flags***, 1962

11 ***Green Angel***, 1990

12 ***Untitled***, 1990

13 ***Flashlight***, 1960

14 ***Flashlight***, 1960 (cast c. 1979)

Doubles and Reflections

WHITNEY MUSEUM OF AMERICAN ART

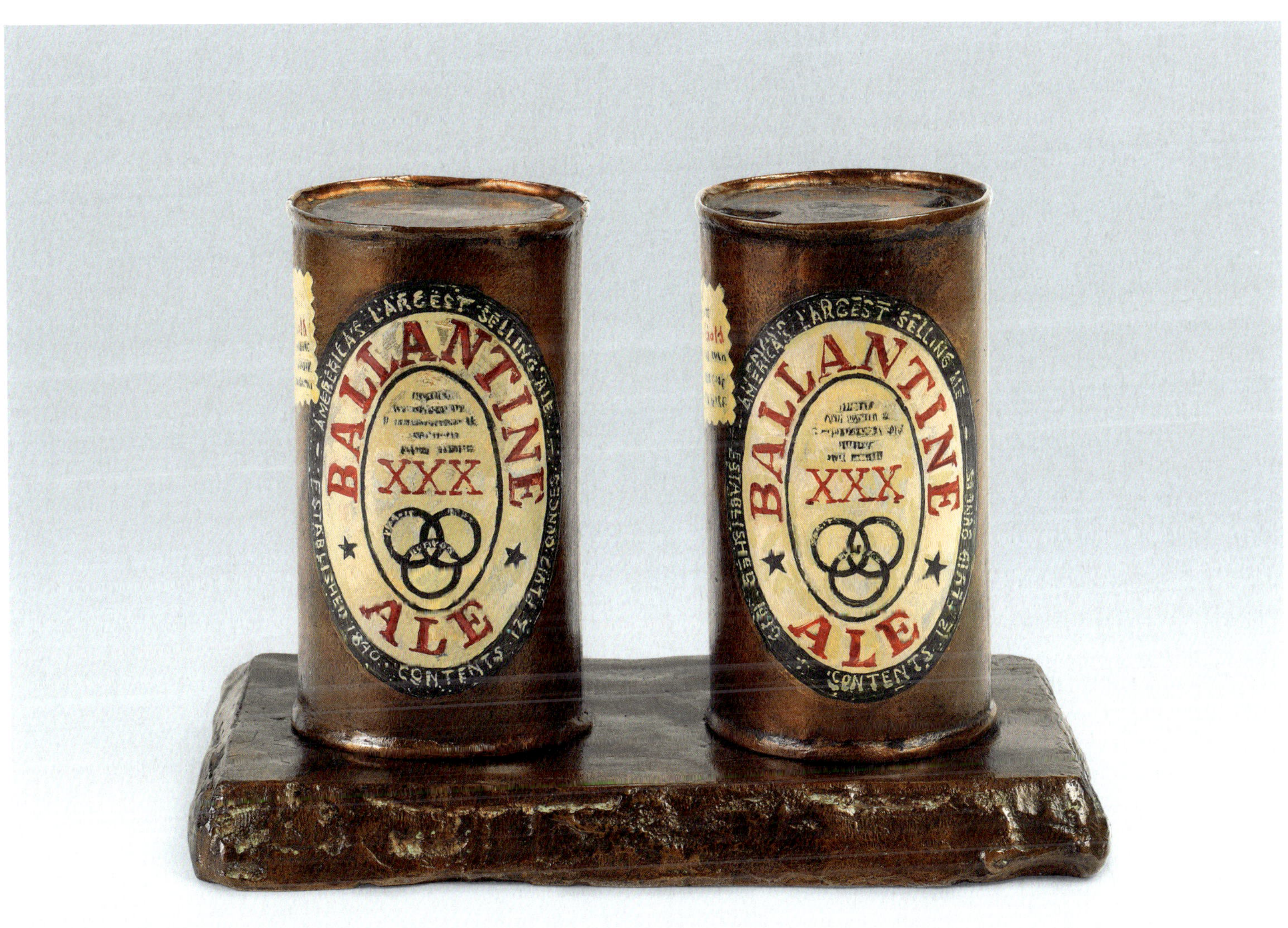

1 *Painted Bronze*, 1960 (cast and painted 1964)

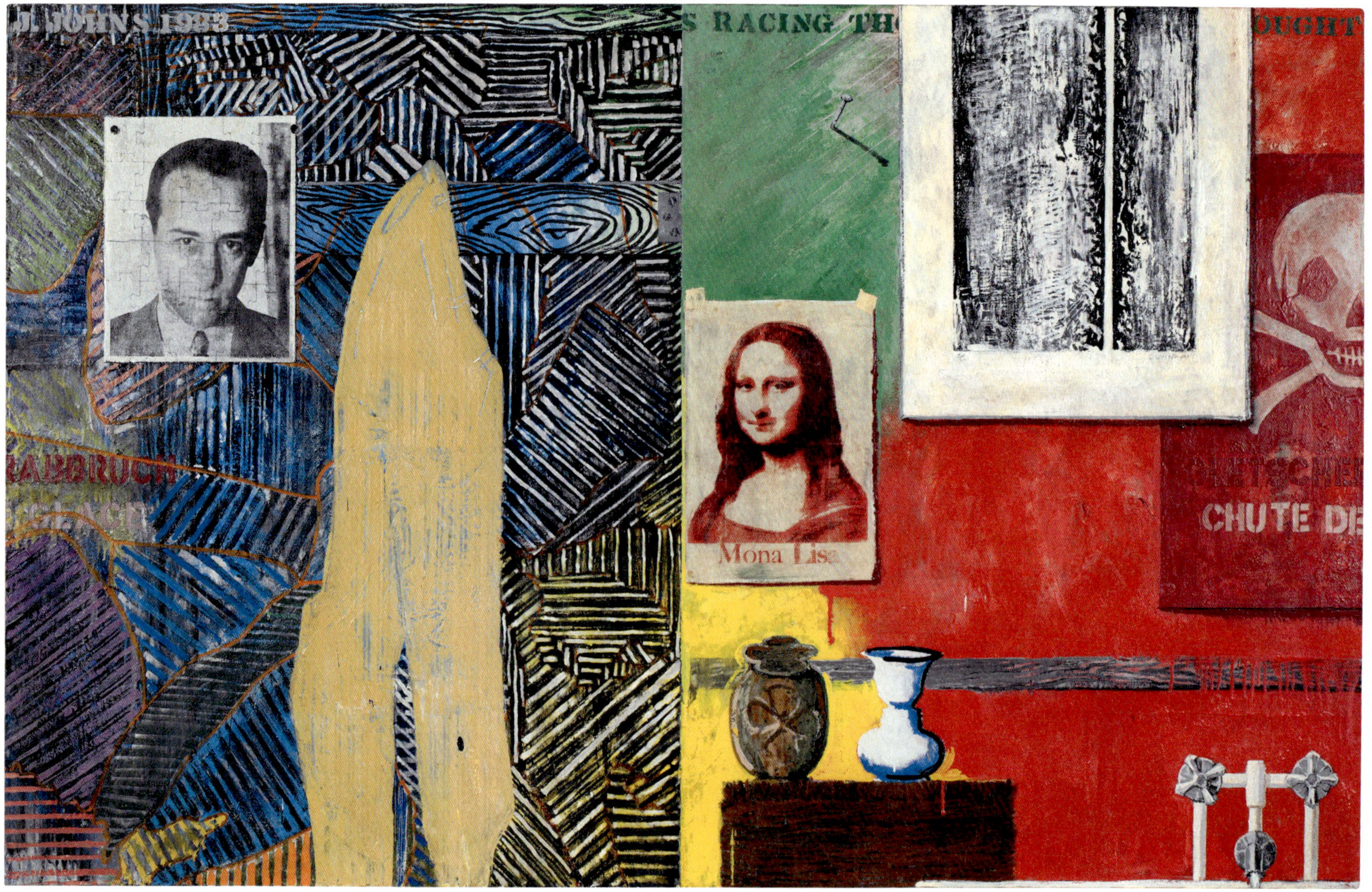

2 ***Racing Thoughts*, 1983**

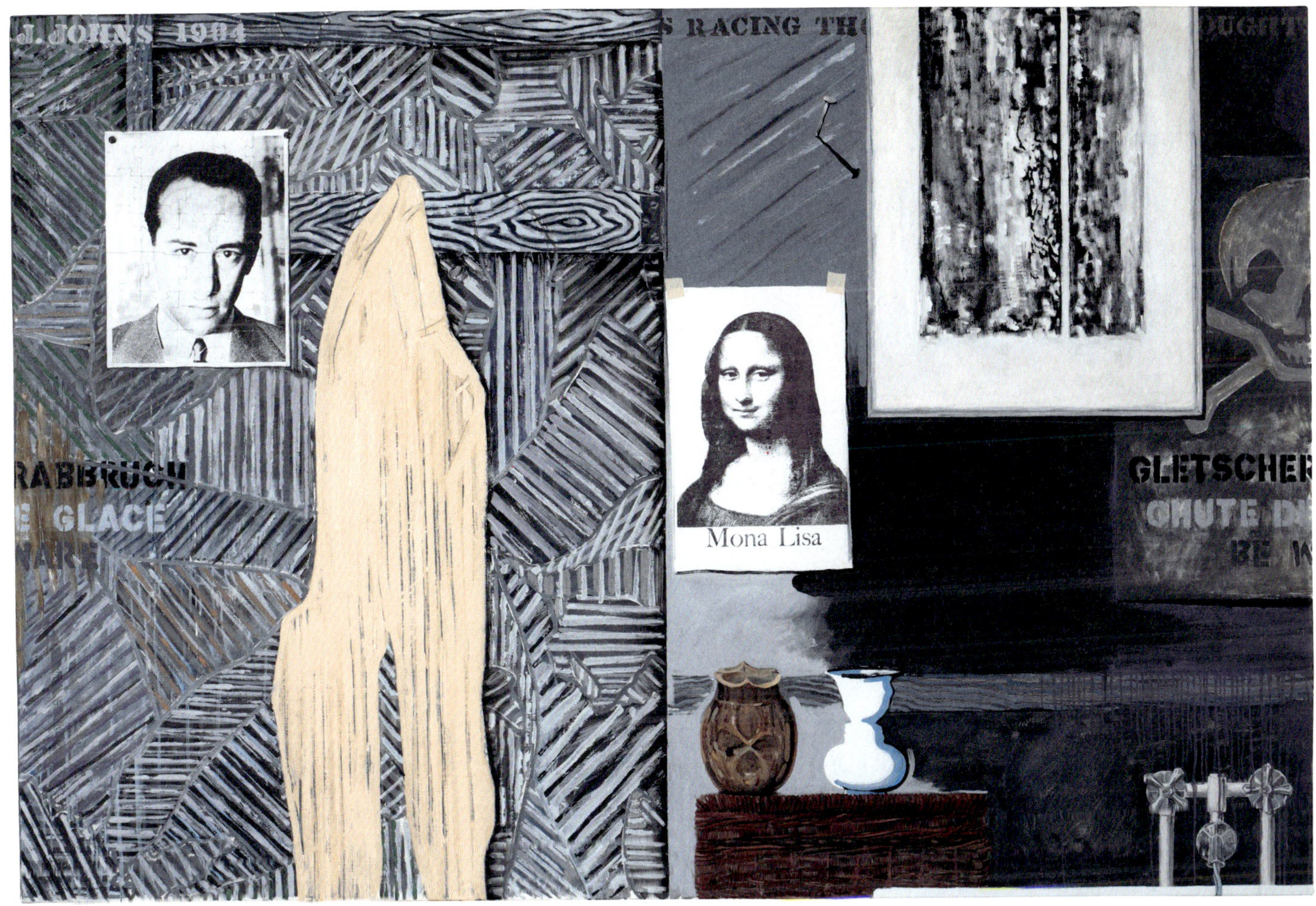

3 ***Racing Thoughts*, 1984**

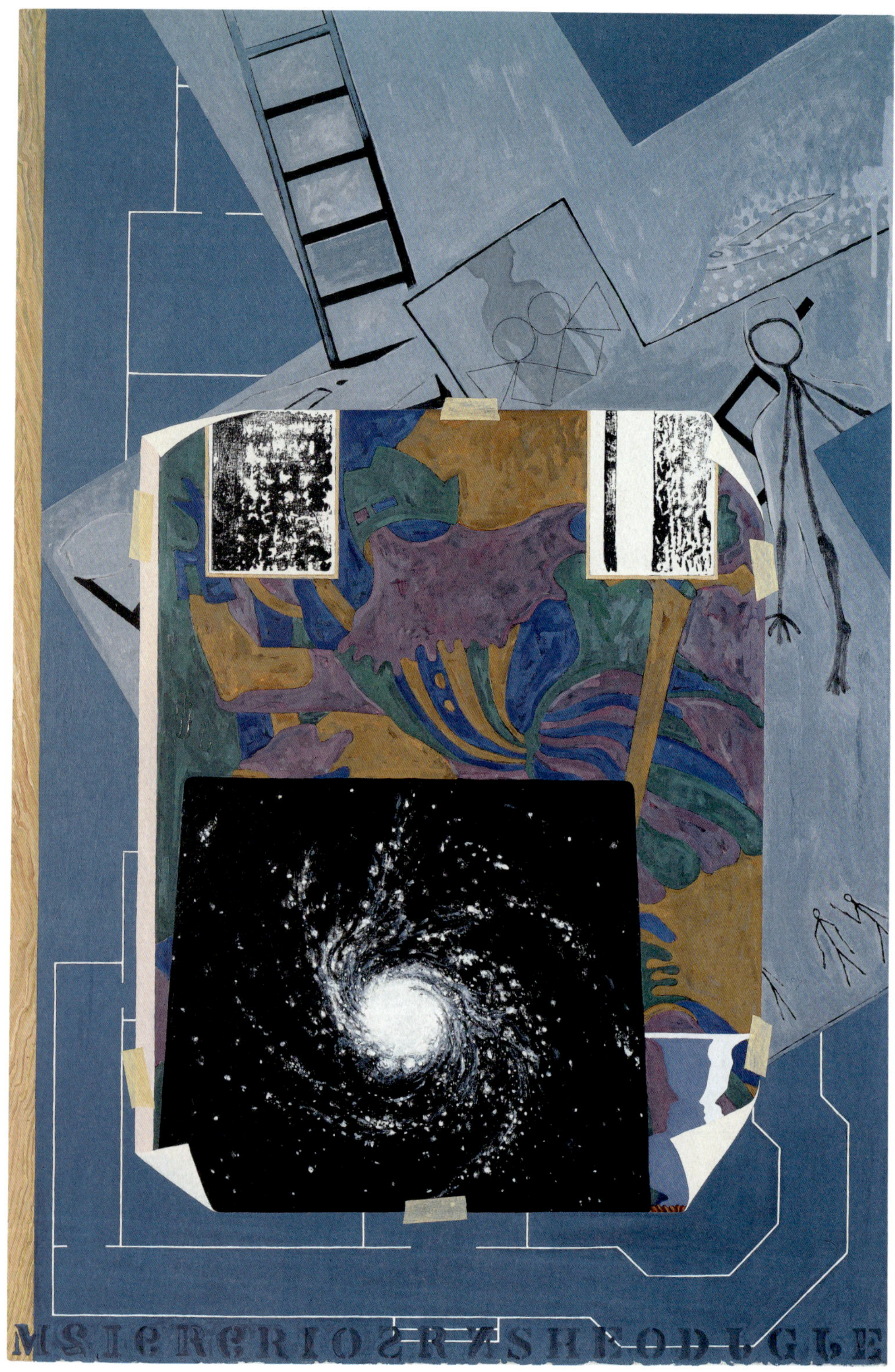

4 ***Mirror's Edge*, 1992**

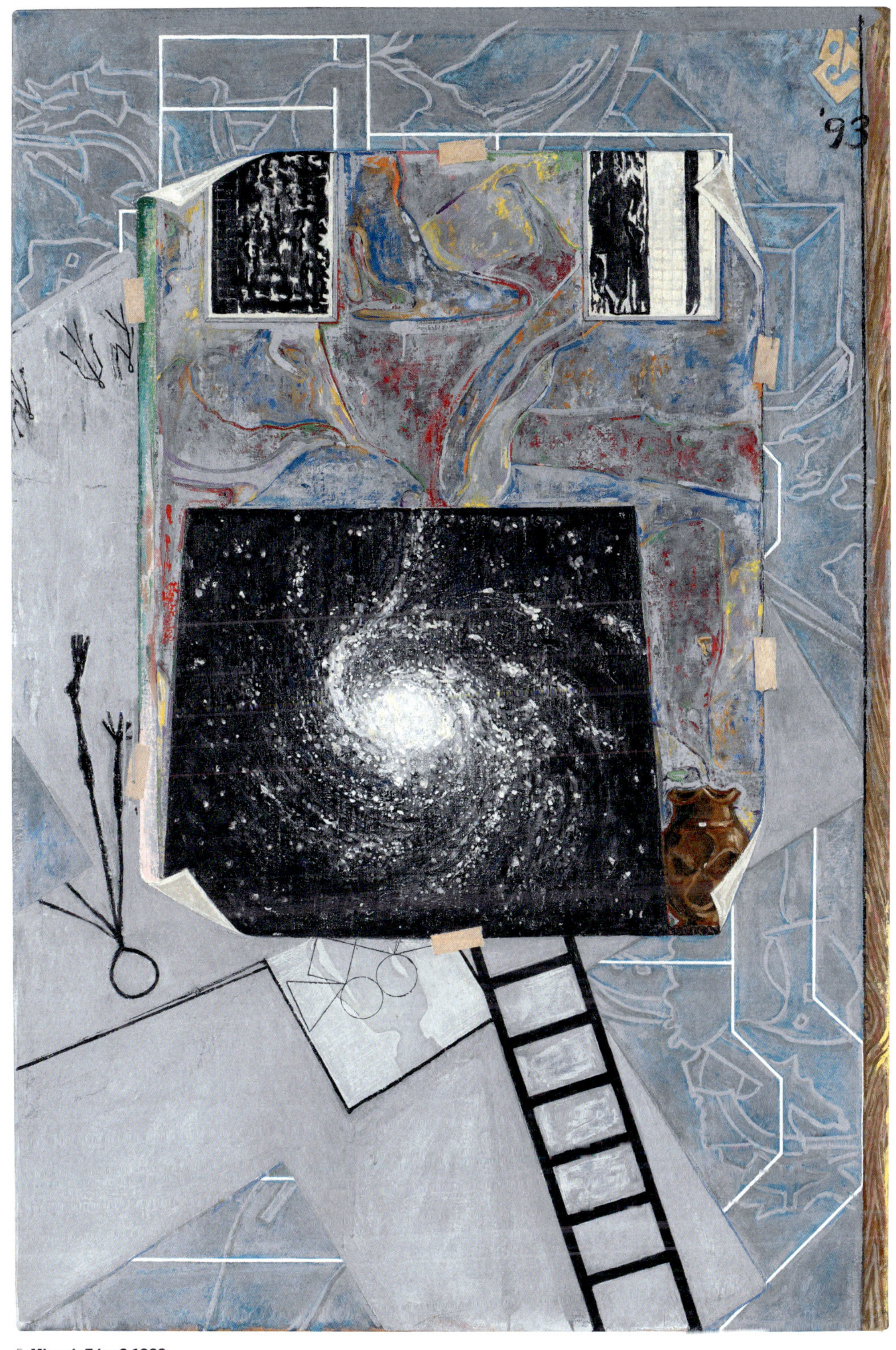

5 ***Mirror's Edge 2*, 1993**

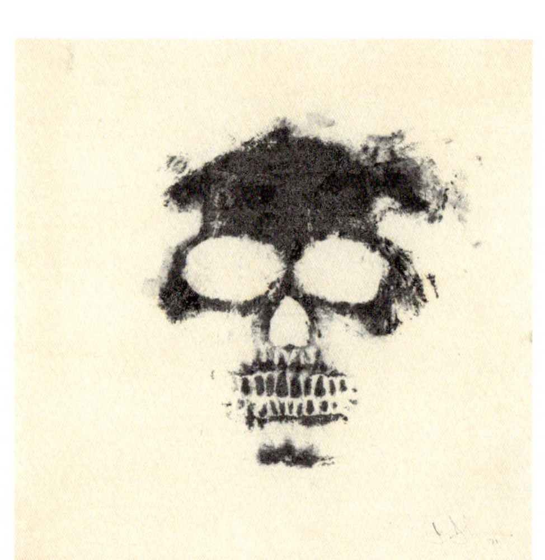

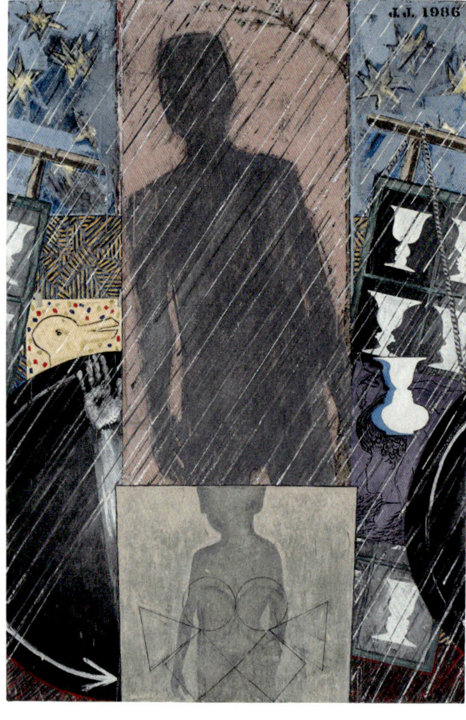

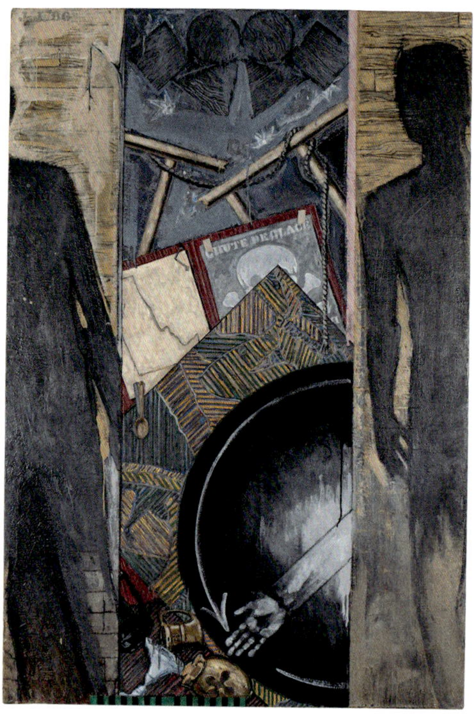

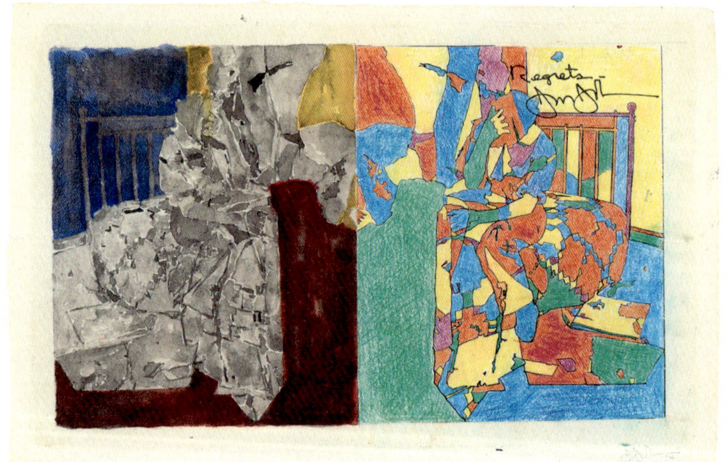

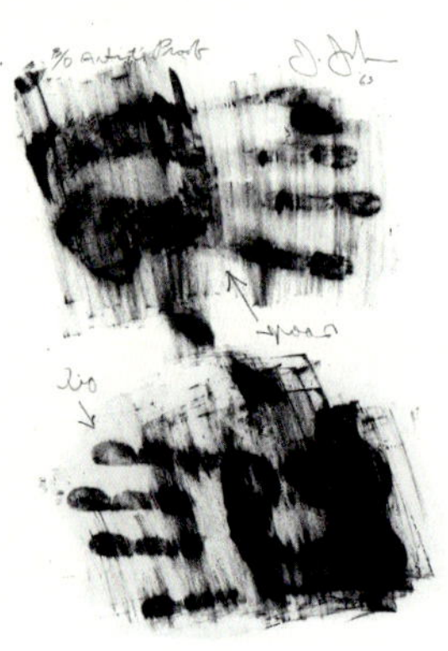

6 ***Skull*, 1971**
9 **Study for *Regrets*, 2012**

7 ***Spring*, 1986**
10 ***Hand*, 1963**

8 ***Fall*, 1986**

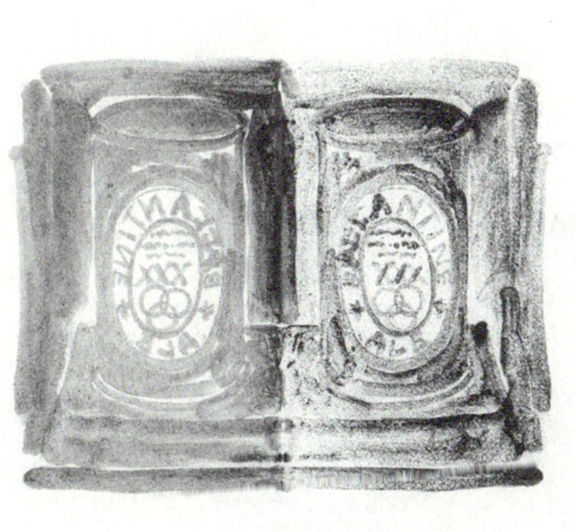

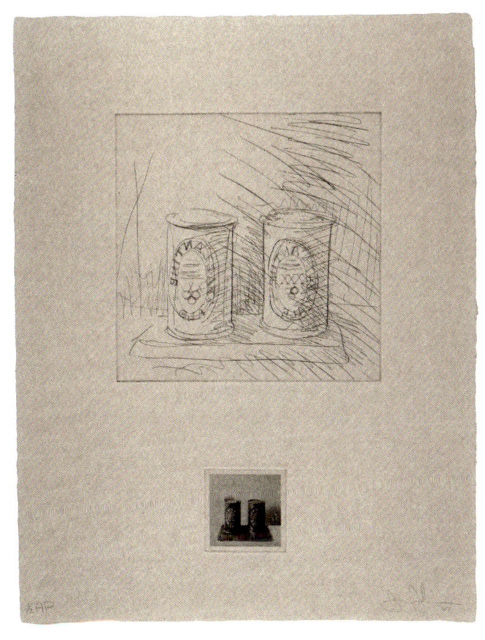

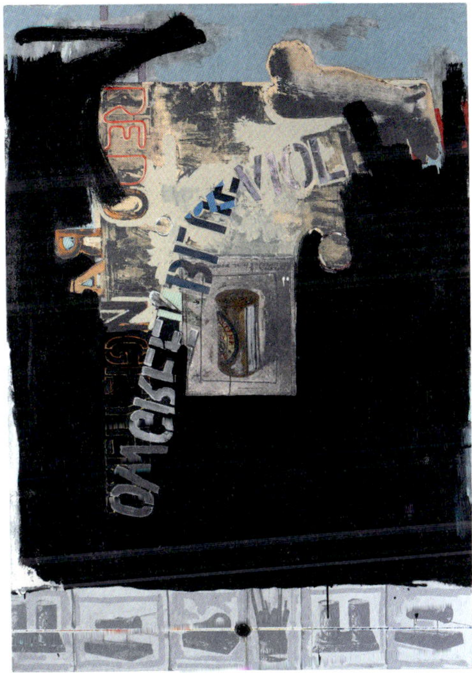

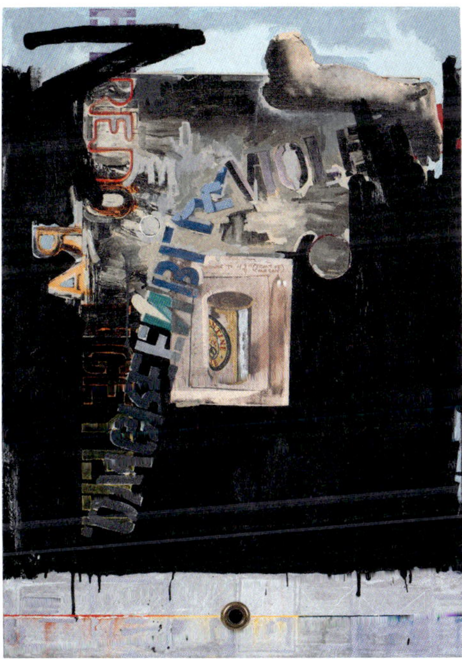

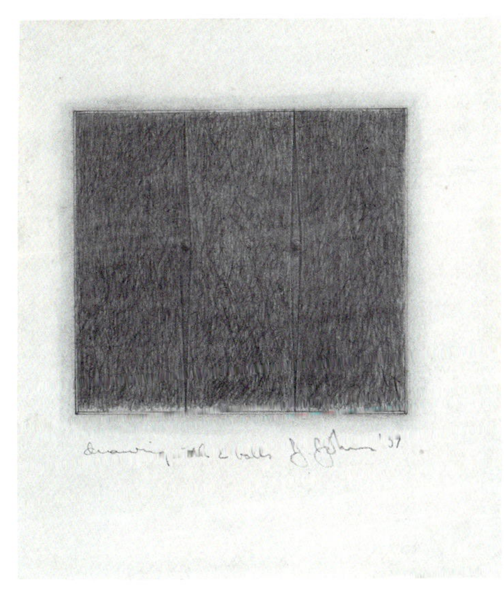

11 ***Ale Cans*, 1975**
13 ***Decoy*, 1971**

12 ***Ale Cans*, from 1st Etchings, 1968**
14 ***Decoy*, 1972**

15 ***Drawing with Two Balls*, 1957**

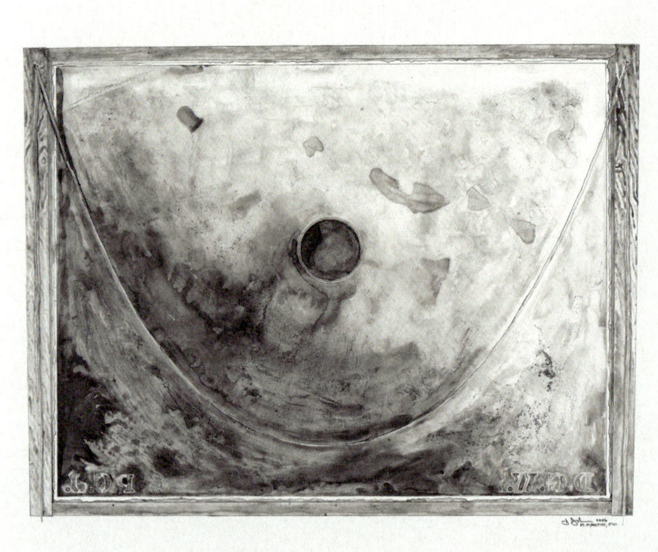

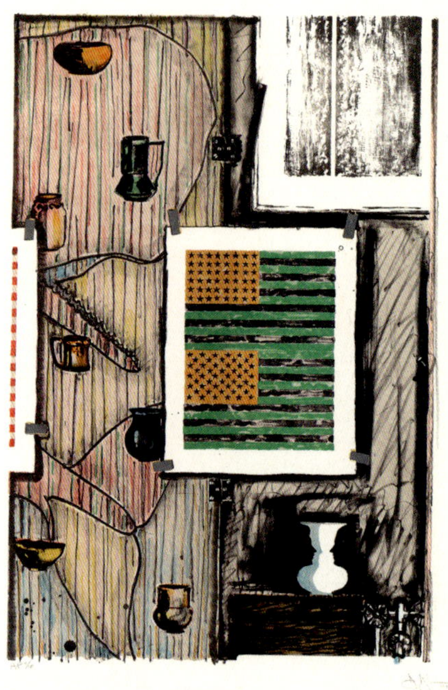

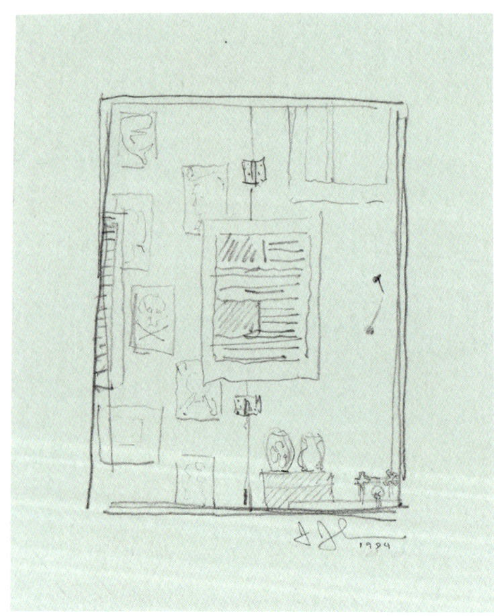

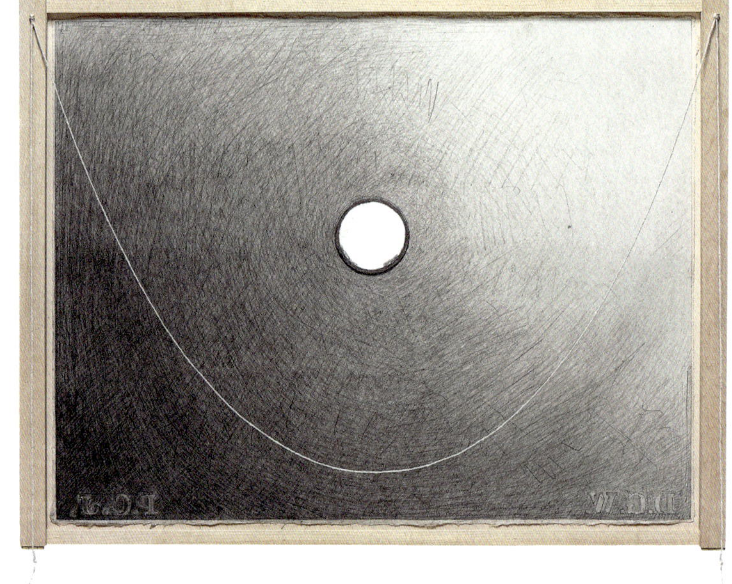

16 ***Untitled*, 2006**
18 ***Untitled*, 1984**

17 ***Ventriloquist*, 1986**
19 ***Untitled*, 2007**

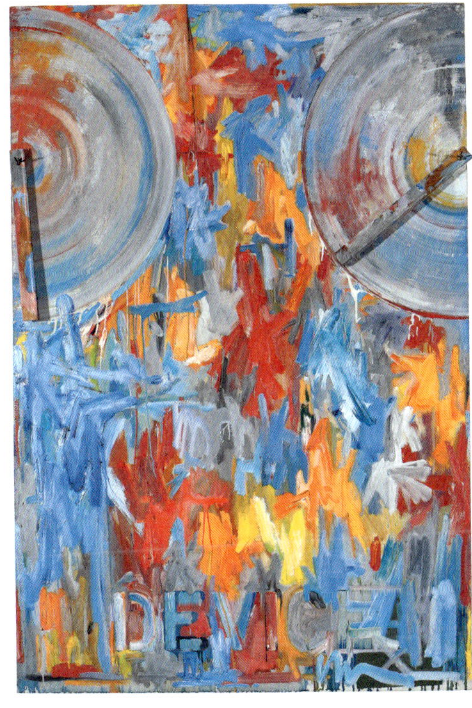

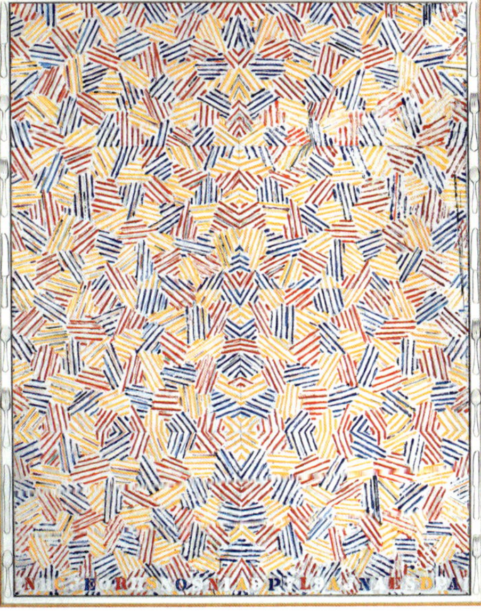

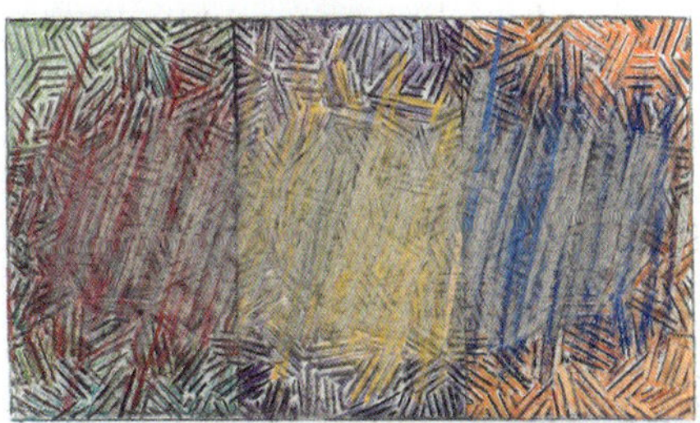

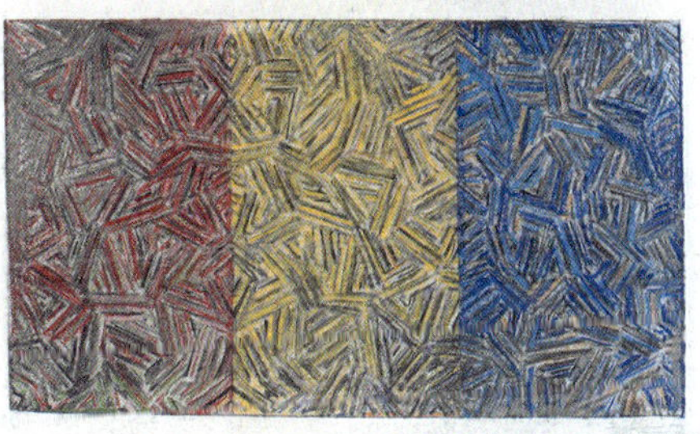

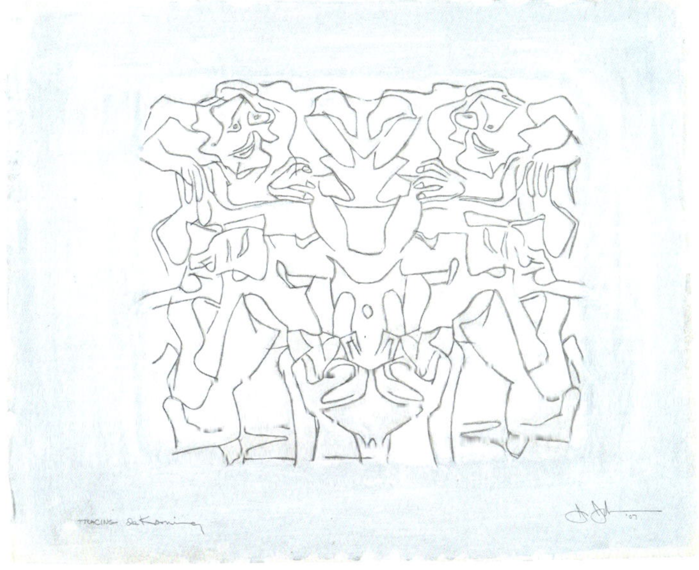

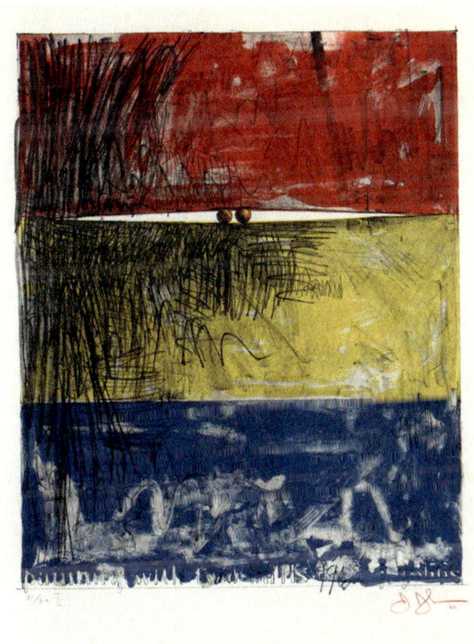

20 ***Device***, 1961–62

21 ***Dancers on a Plane***, 1979

22 ***Between the Clock and the Bed***, 1980

23 ***Tracing after de Kooning***, 2007

24 ***Painting with Two Balls I***, 1962

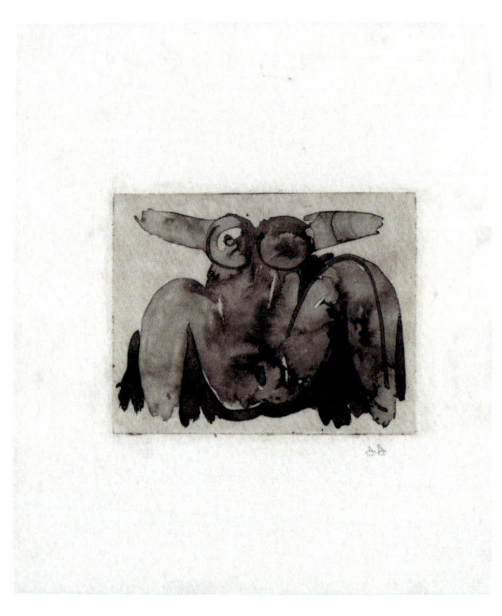

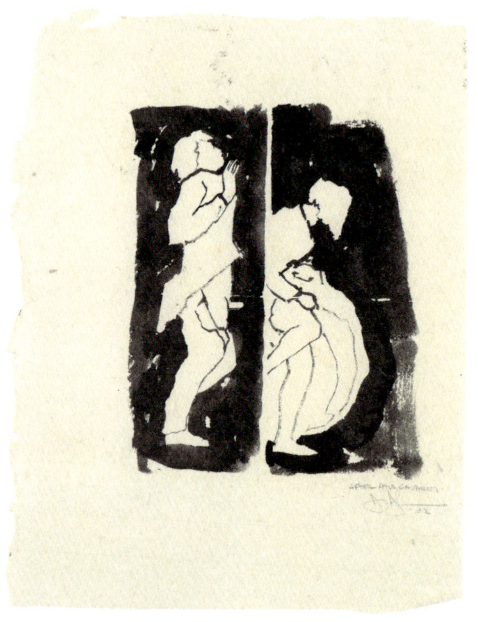

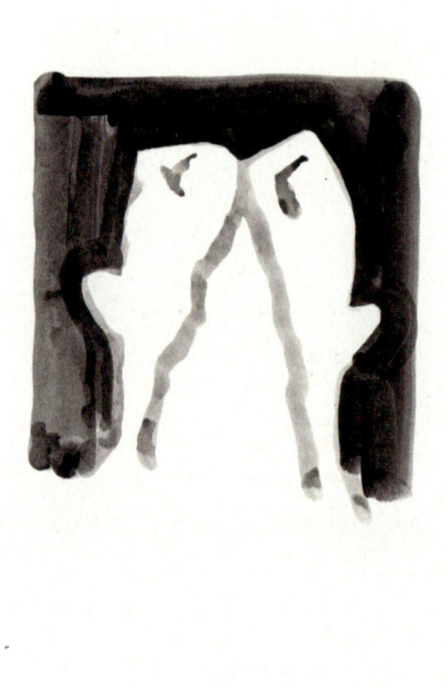

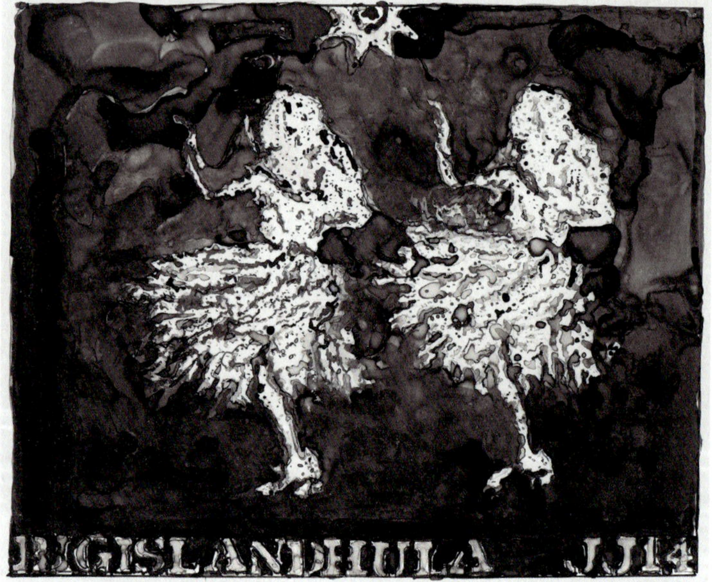

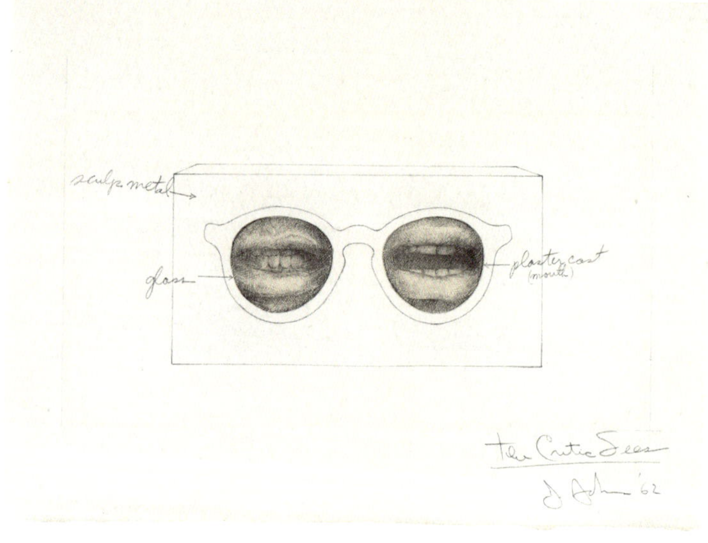

25 ***Untitled*, 1968**
28 ***Big Island Hula*, 2014**

26 ***After Paul Gavarni*, 2002**
29 ***The Critic Sees*, 1962**

27 ***After Cézanne*, 1994**

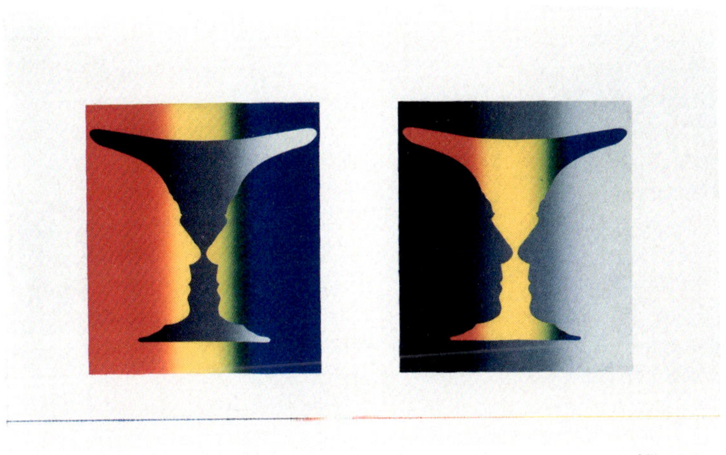

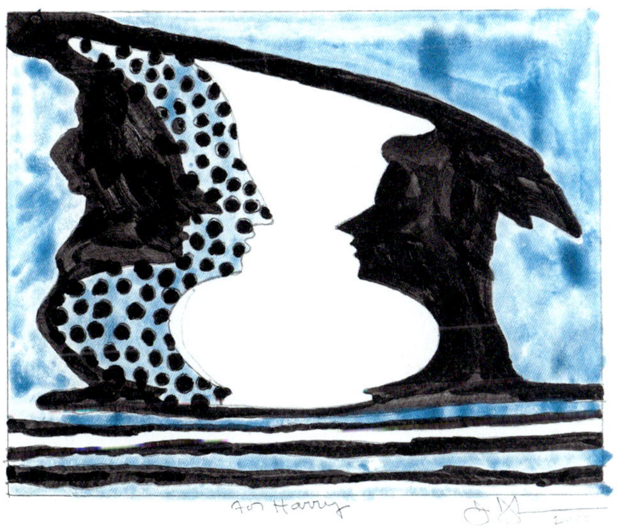

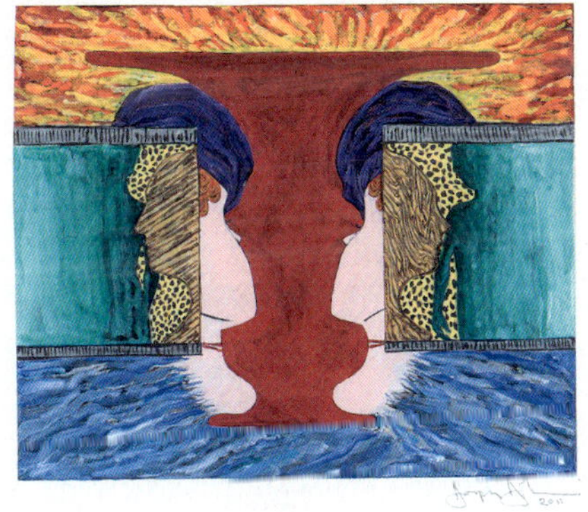

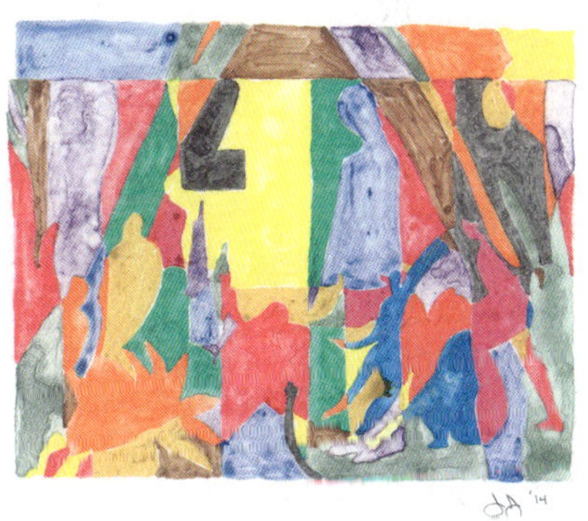

30 ***Cups 4 Picasso*, 1972**
31 ***Untitled*, 2000**
32 ***Valentine*, 2010–11**
33 ***Untitled*, 2014**

Jasper's Dilemma

Emmanuel Alloa

In 1962, Frank Stella started a painting he would call *Jasper's Dilemma* (fig. 1). The piece represents both an homage to his much-admired colleague Jasper Johns's practice and an implicit critique of it. Stella's well-known credo is straightforward: "What you see is what you see."[1] For him, leaving space for ambiguity means leaving space for hidden reserves that must be depleted. Some of Johns's own statements seem to follow a similar vein, especially when celebrating the "possibility of complete lack of meaning."[2] This possibility, however, looms as a promise rather than an easy goal to achieve, and sometimes the claim of flatness turns out to be in itself an uncovered metaphysical check.

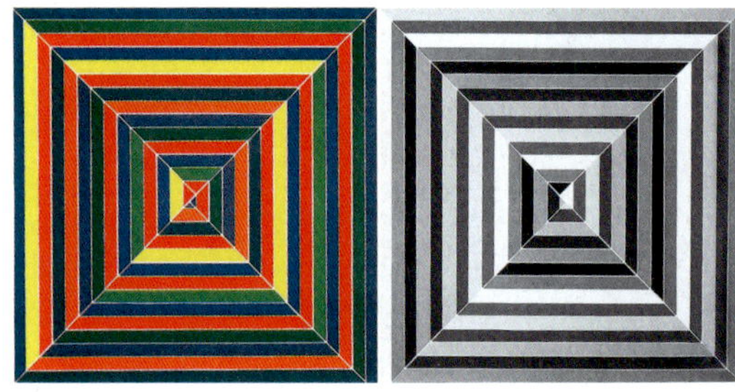

Fig. 1 **Frank Stella (American, b. 1936). *Jasper's Dilemma*, 1962**
Alkyd on canvas, 77 × 154 in. (195.6 × 391.2 cm). Collection of Irma and Norman Braman

Jasper's Dilemma is structured as two mirroring halves, each organized around a respective center from which a square-like structure grows and expands radially. Its double-pyramid shape gives it an almost vertiginous three-dimensionality, a spiraling quality as it were, alternating between an infinite recess and an obtrusive relief. This instability is exacerbated by the fact that the four sides of the pyramid do not quite meet at the center. Whereas the left half is painted in vivid motley tones made of primary and secondary colors, that on the right is realized in scales of gray. The grisaille quadrant refers to Johns's statement that, when painting, after some time, he would start seeing everything in gray.[3]

The difference is striking: whether in value or in hue, the mazes yield a radically different effect. While clairvoyantly circumscribing the profoundly dilemmatic nature of Johns's works, Stella reduces the dilemma to a single one: that between using color or gray scale. In that sense, *Jasper's Dilemma*, which Stella was to explore further in a print series by the same title, is not just a formulation of the problem, but an attempt at solving the riddle: from left to right, its structure is that of either/or. *Either* painting in color *or* with a reduced palette. In his own painting, as we know, Stella opted for the latter. For sure, he formalized the problem by simplifying it. Such a reduction, however, minimizes the extent of the dilemma that, in part, remains ours today.

The Divorce of Saying and Seeing

Beyond the choice between color and its negation, beyond the red and blue flags that eventually give way to almost ethereal white versions and to monochrome ones painted gray on gray, Johns's dilemma in fact increases in complexity the further one looks into his oeuvre. The divorce of saying and seeing, for example, are illuminated in paintings such as *Out the Window* (p. 100, pl. 3), *False Start* (p. 99, pl. 2), and *Jubilee* (p. 98, pl. 1), all from 1959. According to Johns, he began to feel trapped by earlier procedures he had been using, as they had created habits, especially with respect to the attribution of color patterns.[4] *Out the Window* features the names of the three primary colors stenciled in old-fashioned letters; *False Start* and *Jubilee* include the names of all six primary and secondary colors as well as the words "black" and "gray," all stenciled in similar typography. The perceptual impression of these paintings is discomforting, as the names of the colors clearly affect how the colors are apprehended, not to mention the awkward discordance caused by the name of one color being painted in another (such as the word "white" written in red)—a phenomenon of cognitive dissonance known as the Stroop effect.[5]

While he is neither the first nor the last artist to resort to effects of cognitive dissonance in his work (a generation later, one might think of the neon works of Joseph Kosuth or Bruce Nauman that feature the name of one color appearing in another [fig. 2]), Johns has indisputably taken the issue to a very radical level. Between language and affect, between saying and seeing, there cannot be an ultimate match or full transparency. On this matter, Johns—who has been said to downplay the importance of Belgian Surrealism in his oeuvre, especially René Magritte's works, which he discovered as early as 1954—is certainly close to Magritte when it comes to playing on the divorce between words and images (he was familiar with Magritte's 1929 essay "Les mots et les images").[6] Later works highlight this incompatibility even further by their dividing lines. Johns's *Field Painting* (1963–64; p. 149, pl. 1), for example, is made of two vertical panels with color names magnetically drawn toward an empty central space, itself filled with minute objects and letters that work as hinges. What we see is not what we read. Just as Ludwig Wittgenstein saw the task of philosophy as fighting back the "bewitchment of our intelligence by the means of language," one could claim that according to Johns, the aim is to rebuke the bewitchment of our vision by linguistic means.[7]

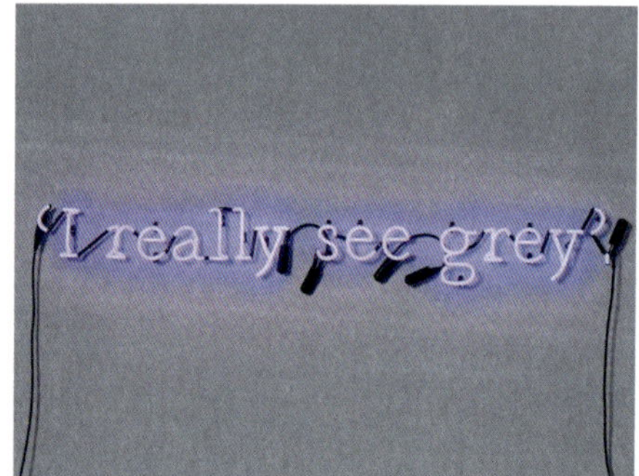

Fig. 2 **Joseph Kosuth (American, b. 1945). *On color #9 (violet)*, 1991**
Neon, 6 ½ × 51 ⅛ × 2 ⅛ in. (16.5 × 130 × 5.5 cm). Hermann and Margrit Rupf Foundation, Bern, Switzerland

The Dilemma of Literalness

"What you see is what you see"—Stella's apothegm is notorious. Although, through the lens of Johns's works, it sounds more like an incantation than a finding. Do we really only see what we see? Following the French phenomenologist Maurice Merleau-Ponty, one might be tempted to disagree and to contend "that to see is always to see more than one sees."[8] Johns's approach is far from being phenomenological, yet he would probably subscribe to such a statement. Reaching the literalness that Stella and so many other artists, including Johns, were looking for is a genuine challenge. Johns's flags, targets, maps, and words from the 1950s boast straightforwardness; they are, as the painter puts it, "things the mind already knows."[9] But knowing and seeing are not the same. Do we see because we know, or do we know because we have seen? Johns has explained that he decided to use everyday, banal shapes because, while well known and recognizable, they are hardly ever looked at. But what does it entail to look at a map, a target, or a flag? "A picture ought to be looked at the same way you look at a radiator" goes a famous admonition by Johns.[10] But who really looks at radiators? Toward the end of the 1960s, Johns started questioning the seeming stability that quotidian objects such as radiators would provide:

> I thought at the time that a radiator is a radiator. We can agree on this. Now, I'm not so sure. At that time, I was willing to take the radiator as a concrete object with definition and spatial characteristics. If you please, as a real object. I was even willing to take it as a reference—something steady and set. Art has so often involved ambiguities and the possibility of ambiguities. I originally thought the radiator was not ambiguous, that it was a basis on which we might agree. I am not sure any longer that I believe or am secure in that type of thinking. I would now question the reference as much as the work.[11]

Simplicity is among the hardest things to achieve in art, and modernism's insistence on literalness, once a response to illusionist virtuosity, turns out to be a trap. Are Johns's Flag paintings objects or images of such objects? All the questions Johns asks are rhetorical. Not because they are not serious to him. But rather because they are inherently unanswerable.

"I've always considered myself a very literal artist," he explains.[12] But when trying to reach to the things themselves, in their very literality, *letters* get in the way, and the strictures of language linger. Johns's *Light Bulb* (1960), comprising a light bulb cast in bronze, suddenly becomes a paradox, as not only does its opaque surface allow for no light to shine through but its new heaviness stands in stark contrast to a "light" bulb. As if in response to this inevitable presence of the discursive in the figurative, Johns resorts to a counterstrategy by figuring discourse in a painterly manner and drawing the letters (and numbers) up to the point of unrecognizability (one might think of his *0 through 9* paintings from 1961 [p. 82, pls. 18–20]). When staring for too long at the letters, their meaning—what they stand for—gets lost; hyperattention turns into distraction, and the other way around: suddenly, the materiality of the form, the specific configuration of the otherwise irrelevant elements of meaning come to the fore. As if the vessels first had to be emptied to appear in their own right. As always, by redoubling literality by the letter, a dissociation takes place, which allows for new openings. A literality it is, but one that always remains ambivalent.

Materialism without Dialectics

Rather than a conceptualist, Johns should be termed a factualist (indeed, in a 1964 interview, he called some of his paintings "facts").[13] As a factualist, he should also be considered, to a certain extent, a materialist. Among Johns's continuous experimentations with matter we find a return to long-forgotten techniques such as encaustic, which was used for centuries, through Giotto and the early Renaissance, before it fell into disuse. When working on his first flags, Johns changed enamel for encaustic, because he had grown increasingly tired of having to wait until the oil pigments dried. The encaustic technique, wherein color pigments are dispersed into wax, has a very peculiar two-sidedness. On the one hand, it allows for discreteness, a value much appreciated by Johns, as the well-contained portions of color preserve the integrity of each. On the other hand, encaustic boasts an amazing plastic quality that was immediately apparent when Johns first used encaustic in his flags. Although solidified, the beeswax that Johns had started using in 1954 kept the record of its initial fluidity and remains extremely tactile. Johns used small irons to heat up the wax to turn it into a receptacle of the pigments before "burning" it into the canvas. It is the ductility of the wax medium that allows it to be fixed in such a pristine way.

Encaustic has a poetic quality—the referral to infinite vitreous plasticity—while also bearing witness to an inherent violence, that of its initial fire. Johns's use of encaustic has very little in common with some of his contemporaries' use of fire (most prominently, Yves Klein in his *Fire Paintings* from the early 1960s) and rather inaugurates another artistic line in American art that can be traced to painters such as Brice Marden and his subtle monochrome encaustics. Be that as it may, even Johns's dispassionate use of encaustic cannot help but refer to the medium's connection to fire and its intrinsically deforming, if not openly destructive, nature. When, in book thirty-five of his *Natural Histories*, Pliny the Elder investigates the putative origins of the encaustic technique, he mentions a certain Lysippus, who was famous for having inscribed on his painting at Aegina the word *enekaen*, which literally means "burnt in." According to Pliny, this is the explanation of encaustics, given that the word *enkaustikos* stems from the verb *enkiaein* (to burn in).

There has been a tendency in recent years to read Johns's work in a more autobiographical fashion, as he was slowly starting to hint at the circumstances of and inspirations for some paintings. For sure, elements of grief and desire were never absent; on the contrary, *Periscope* (*Hart Crane*) (1963; p. 182, pl. 6) has almost elegiac qualities, with its mise-en-scène of the mourning of color, while *The Seasons* (1989–90; p. 230, pl. 2) stages the permanently thwarted desire to attempt a self-portrait through a look in the mirror. Should his oeuvre, therefore, be interpreted in an allegorical way?

Allegory and Tautegory

Johns's use of banal objects—light bulbs, flashlights, beer cans—has had the opposite effect on audiences. Years ago, Stephen Koch noted that if all artists of the twentieth century are somehow heirs of Marcel

Duchamp, they had to choose on which side of the inheritance they wanted to stand.[14] According to Koch, Duchamp opened two parallel paths: the first being "transparent," wherein the artistic operation would be confoundingly simple, such as the musealization of everyday objects that, like the artist's *Fountain* urinal, are now exhibited in all their literalness; the second being "hermetic," obscure and mysterious, accessible to only a few selected minds and culminating in Duchamp's *Large Glass* (1915–23; fig. 3). Following Koch, Andy Warhol supposedly belongs to the transparent path, while Johns would be on the hermetic one.[15] Yet, while such an account might be true to some extent for Warhol (at least in his own intentions), for Johns, one might argue that it misses the full picture. Why is it that the incontestably puzzling nature of many of Johns's works necessarily entails something symbolic, some sort of hidden, cryptic meaning? Is the only alternative exposed by avant-garde artists that between literalism and symbolism? Or, to fall back on a slightly more barbaric-sounding polarity, is art left to choose between *allegory* (expressing something else) and *tautegory* (expressing nothing but itself)? One might doubt that such pure positions are ever attainable, lest that once they are reached, they start to revert to their opposites: absolute metaphoricity and absolute objecthood are hard to find. Johns himself points to this, when remarking that "the object itself is a somewhat dubious concept."[16] And that literalness hardly qualifies as anti-metaphoric. After all, "literalness" itself expresses this ambivalence, given that the pure objecthood is already invaded by letters. In other words, the notion of either absolute transparency or full legibility is yet another chimera of twentieth-century art.

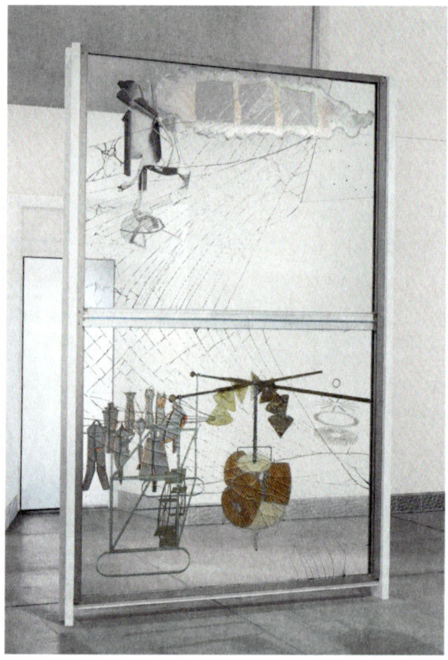

Fig. 3 **Marcel Duchamp (American, b. France, 1887–1968). *The Bride Stripped Bare by Her Bachelors, Even (The Large Glass)*, 1915–23**
Oil, varnish, lead foil, lead wire, and dust on two glass panels, 109 ¼ × 70 × 3 ⅜ in. (277.5 × 177.8 × 8.6 cm). Philadelphia Museum of Art; bequest of Katherine S. Dreier, 1952-98-1

Nonetheless, what remains true is that Johns's works are perplexing because they do not immediately give themselves away, all the while refusing backdoor and second-order levels. Their facticity remains a riddle. In this respect, Johns's works do not hide anything away: they appear exactly as they are. Yet the question remains: how do they appear? A work such as *Painted Bronze* (1960; p. 206, pl. 2) crystallizes this conundrum. Neither found object nor trompe l'oeil, it attracts the attention toward its own making, or rather toward the fact that the brushes are both the medium and the object, all the while thwarting, in their obtrusive factuality, any simple symbolic reading.

Mirrorings: Johns's Hinge Pictures

The binary opposition of allegory and tautegory is steeped into a wider ontological brace, one that divides the world into two kinds of entities: *signs* and *things*. While things exist in and of themselves, signs, in their full presence, exist as representations. In their symbolic dimension, images have usually been subsumed under the general category of signs, as representations of things. One type of image, however, escapes this move toward representational symbolism: natural images such as those seen in mirrors. Mirrors represent only the things that stand before them, and thus undercut the metaphysical alternative of presence and absence, of immediacy and deferral. Beyond referring to some sort of narcissistic symbolism of self-enamorment, the mirror is, before anything else, a specular device that undercuts speculative flights of fancy. Johns started introducing mirroring devices into his work in the 1970s. In works such as *Corpse and Mirror* (1974) and *Corpse and Mirror II* (1974–75; pp. 178–79, pl. 2), an internal division line creates a divisive redoubling of sorts, leaving the beholder with the puzzlement whether she is—or is not—facing a double image or simply one internally divided. Although initially inspired by the Surrealist game of the *cadavre exquis* (exquisite corpse), where the powers of imagination are meant to be released through the aleatory arrangement of verbal or visual signifiers, Johns's painting is decisively more sober. Rather than soliciting the fantasies of what lies elsewhere, Johns's poetics is one of internal self-recursion, uncovering how much more there is in what is deemed stable.

Upon closer inspection, it turns out that Johns's oeuvre, especially the latter part, is traversed by mirroring structures, where the "one" reduplicates into a more-than-one that never fully stabilizes into an oppositional "two." Neither merely a thing nor a representational redoubling, a work by Johns situates itself in a troubled in-between, or rather, it articulates a difference that refuses to be binary coded. Many diptychs—from *Two Flags* (1972; fig. 4) to the Usuyuki prints (see, for example, p. 127, pls. 29–31)—avail themselves of the resources of the mirror device by internally redoubling the artwork and creating incertitude about which is the mirroring half and which the mirrored. Rather than a static line, the dividing segment acts as an articulation or a hinge that keeps the two halves reverting like wings or shutters. *Fragment—According to What: Hinged Canvas*, a lithograph from 1971 (p. 154, pl. 10), alludes to this, by offering the spectator a paradoxical view of both the recto and the verso of a painting. Instead of mechanically replicating equivalences, hinges are in fact translating forces that inaugurate a playful field of tensions. If anywhere, it is in these hinged paintings that Johns comes close to Duchamp's poetics.

Incontestably, Johns has refused many of the watersheds that twentieth-century art established, such as that between abstraction and gesture (in a way, his crosshatch series, produced between 1972 and 1983, consists of an astute combination of both abstractive

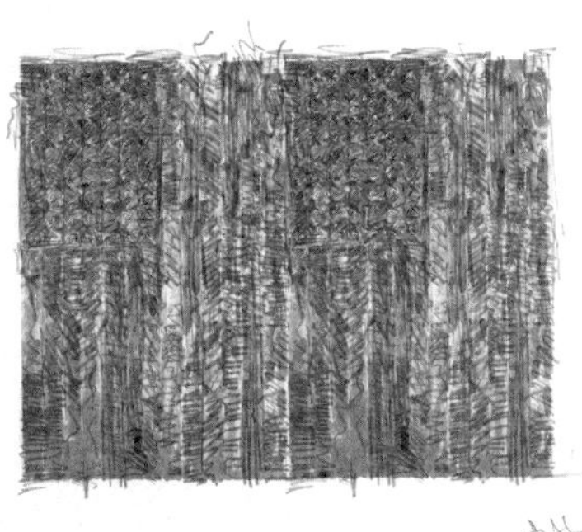

Fig. 4 ***Two Flags*, 1972**
Lithograph: two stones, three aluminum plates, 27 ½ × 32 ¾ in. (69.9 × 83.2 cm). Bill Goldston, James V. Smith/ULAE. Ed. no. 13/36. Whitney Museum of American Art, New York; gift of Arthur and Susan Fleischer, 2013.114

and gestural while avoiding any virtuosity one might find in Abstract Expressionism), just as he has refused to choose between the seductive powers of the color spectrum versus the seduction of rigorous monochromaticity. In this respect, he parts both with the literalist heirs of Duchamp as well as with his hermetic family branch. At best, he retains Duchamp's idea of a pictorial "hinge." "Perhaps make a hinge picture (*tableau de charnière*)" is one of the first notes in Duchamp's *The Bride Stripped Bare by Her Bachelors, Even (The Green Box)* (p. 155, pl. 14), and indeed he repeatedly called for creating devices that would, by folding them back, open onto new perspectives. As in revolving doors, which are never fully open nor fully closed, Johns has adapted these artistic strategies aimed at questioning the logic of identity. Many paintings, indeed, integrate hinges of some sort. In *Target with Four Faces* (1955; p. 42, pl. 2), decidedly one of Johns's most enigmatic works, the upper part of the faces is replaced with a hinged wooden lid. The obstruction of sight—the "closed eyelids"—paradoxically equals the open position of the lid. It becomes clear, however, that closing the lid hardly works as an eye-opener, either.

The Puzzle of Seeing

What, then, does Jasper's dilemma consist of? Stella, although detecting its presence early on, might not have charted all its depth. Wittgenstein astutely observed that "we find certain things about seeing puzzling because we do not find the whole business of seeing puzzling enough."[17] Against this background, it could be claimed that Stella, having identified the dilemmatic nature of Johns's art, also missed the vastness of its quandary. As a well-trained logician would do, he broke down the conundrum to two (and only two) possible solutions. Sometimes, however, there is no easy way out. Johns's dilemma derives from the dilemmatic nature of seeing itself. In a way, rather than a dilemma, in the moral sense of the word, where one has to choose between two (equally awkward) exit options, Johns's work confronts the beholder with an aporia—that is, very literally, with the absence of escape routes.

Whenever sensory perception is involved, there is no straightforward way out; as sensible embodied subjects, we are enmeshed in it—hence the deeply aporetic dimension of this puzzle prompted by seeing itself. As Gerhard Richter, another of the sharpest minds among contemporary painters, put it, painting is all about the "despair, prompted by the dilemma that our sense of sight causes us to apprehend things, but at the same time restricts and partly precludes our apprehension of reality"[18]—thus the need to acknowledge this ambivalence of simultaneous gain and loss, of this permanent instability called perception.

For sure, the mind knows, as Johns often stresses, but too much confidence in it would be misplaced. The task of art, first and foremost, is that of undoing recognition, so as to rivet the gaze to what is far too well known. "Whence no knowing," as Samuel Beckett writes in *Worstward Ho*.[19] Negating requires true art. All in all, "no knowing" sounds exactly as "know no'ing." Johns, whose Beckettian ascendancy is recognized, has described things as follows: "Not knowing exactly is something that I find fascinating. Whatever the basis, it probably moves one to see life in an ambiguous way."[20]

What is at stake is the pursuit of an elusive sense, a shifty, ever-moving sense that can, however, be experienced sensibly. Johns's art is certainly much more than a large gallery of mind games, of speculative snares stimulating our cerebral capacities. His many perplexing artistic devices mirror the puzzles that a sensible reality confronts us with every single day. Becoming aware of the puzzling nature of our own seeing is certainly among the hardest things to achieve. As Émile Zola wrote in the nineteenth century, "The gift of seeing is rarer today than the gift of creating."[21] Johns is, most certainly, among those creators who teach us how not to take as a given what we see.

1 Frank Stella, "Questions to Frank Stella and Donald Judd," interview by Bruce Glaser (1966), in *Minimal Art: A Critical Anthology*, ed. Gregory Battcock (Berkeley: University of California Press, 1995), 158.
2 Jasper Johns, quoted in Sarah Kent, "Jasper Johns: Strokes of Genius," *Time Out* (London), December 5-12, 1990; reprinted in Kirk Varnedoe, ed., *Jasper Johns: Writings, Sketchbook Notes, Interviews* (New York: Museum of Modern Art, 1996), 259 (hereafter abbreviated Varnedoe, *WSI*).
3 "When I worked on it for longer than a minute, the entire painting would turn gray to me. I couldn't see any of the colors, and I would have to stop." Jasper Johns, quoted in Michael Crichton, *Jasper Johns* (New York: Harry N. Abrams in association with the Whitney Museum of American Art, 1994), 39.
4 As Johns noted, he had become aware of "certain limitations in my work, and I had the need to overcome those, to break with certain habits I had formed, certain procedures I had used." Johns, quoted in Crichton, *Jasper Johns*, 39.
5 The Stroop effect is named after the American psychologist J. Ridley Stroop. Stroop's studies demonstrated the difficulties test subjects had in correctly identifying colors when their names were printed in a different color. For example, when the word "orange" is printed in blue, individuals have far greater difficulty in naming the color than if both the word and its printed color match. The Stroop effect is connected with the law of associative inhibition, which states that "if *a* is already connected to *b*, then it is difficult to connect it to *k*; *b* gets in the way." Linus W. Kline, "An Experimental Study of Associative Inhibition," *Journal of Experimental Psychology* 4 (1921): 270. All Johns's works, in a way, could be said to stage and actively promote associative inhibitions, by both connecting what usually isn't and dissociating commonalities.
6 René Magritte, "Les mots et les images," *La révolution surréaliste* 12 (December 15, 1929): 32–33.
7 Ludwig Wittgenstein, *Philosophical Investigations*, ed. P. M. S. Hacker and Joachim Schulte (London: Wiley, 2010), 47.
8 Maurice Merleau-Ponty, *The Visible and the Invisible*, ed. Claude Lefort, trans. Alphonso Lingis (Evanston, IL: Northwestern University Press, 1968), 247.
9 Jasper Johns, quoted in "His Heart Belongs to Dada," *Time*, May 4, 1959; reprinted in Varnedoe, *WSI*, 82.
10 Johns, quoted in "His Heart Belongs to Dada."
11 Jasper Johns, quoted in Joseph E. Young, "Jasper Johns: An Appraisal," *Art International* 13, no. 7 (September 1969), reprinted in Varnedoe, *WSI*, 134.
12 Johns, quoted in Young, "Johns: An Appraisal," 131.
13 Jasper Johns, "What Is Pop Art? Part II," interview by Gene R. Swenson, *ARTnews* 62, no. 10 (February 1964), reprinted in Varnedoe, *WSI*, 93.
14 Stephen Koch, *Stargazer: The Life, World, and Films of Andy Warhol* (New York: Marion Boyars, 1991), v.
15 Koch, *Stargazer*.
16 Jasper Johns, quoted in *Jasper Johns: Drawings*, exh. cat. (London: Arts Council of Great Britain, 1974), 16.
17 Wittgenstein, *Philosophical Investigations*, 212.
18 Gerhard Richter, "Notes, 1971," in *The Daily Practice of Painting: Writings and Interviews, 1962–1993*, ed. Hans-Ulrich Obrist (London: Thames and Hudson, 1995), 64.
19 Samuel Beckett, "Worstward Ho," in *Nohow On* (London: Calder, 1995), 107.
20 Jasper Johns, quoted in W. J. Weatherby, "The Enigma of Jasper Johns," *Guardian* (London), November 29, 1990; reprinted in Varnedoe, *WSI*, 257.
21 Émile Zola, "Le roman expérimental" (1880), in *Oeuvres complètes* (Montreal: Nouveau Monde, 2004), 9:416: "Le don de voir est moins commun encore que le don de créer."

Unique Prints

Printmaking is in essence a means for faithfully reproducing an image, but for Jasper Johns that has never been the point. "A lot of time is taken to make printmaking reproductive," he stated bluntly in 1969, "and that's not very interesting to me."[1] By contrast, he has long shown as much curiosity about the process of creating a print as he has about the editioned result. Along the way, he might make dozens of permutational "trial proofs" to test the same design in various colors or on different papers, as well as "working proofs" that bear additions by his hand. He has signed and carefully archived more than 2,400 of these proofs, suggesting that he considers them not just intermediary steps but artworks in themselves. In addition, he has executed hundreds of monotypes, irreproducible prints made without a fixed matrix by painting or drawing directly on a plate. The sheer volume of all this material vastly exceeds Johns's output in every other medium combined, and its dizzying sense of play contrasts with the sober deliberateness of his paintings and drawings. Yet Johns's unique prints share with his entire oeuvre an iterative logic of repetition and difference: each sheet is at once a fragment of a process and itself a whole.

Johns made his first mature monotypes in 1978, and four years later, he embarked on what remains his most sustained and inventive series of them to date, a group of thirty-three variations on his editioned lithograph *Savarin* (1981).[2] That print features a grisaille depiction of *Painted Bronze* (1960; p. 206, pl. 2), his uncanny trompe l'oeil cast of a Savarin coffee can filled with brushes, meticulously painted to look like his studio tools. An image of the pivotal sculpture had appeared in Johns's prints since the 1960s, most conspicuously in the poster for his 1977–78 retrospective at the Whitney Museum of American Art (p. 311, pl. 7), in which the artist depicted it against a backdrop of his recent crosshatches, merging past and present and affirming its totemic import. Printed with extra plates from the Whitney lithograph, *Savarin* reprised the same composition above a predella containing a red impression of Johns's forearm and hand alongside the initials "E. M.," a nod to Edvard Munch's caliginous lithographic *Self-Portrait* (1895) in which the artist's gaunt face hovers ominously over a skeletal rendering of the same anatomy. Like Munch's print, Johns's is also a self-portrait, substituting his visage with two of his signature motifs, the crosshatch and his iconic portrayal of his studio implements, along with the very hand that wields them.

When editioning *Savarin*, Johns withheld a group of prints due to an inconsistency in the paper, and the 1982 cycle of monotypes developed over four days directly atop these sheets. To make most of them, he applied ink to Plexiglas plates positioned over the lithograph so that he could see the image on which his new marks would be superimposed. The ensuing works present an astonishing sequence of free-flowing pictorial ideas and interrelationships, executed with a spontaneity rare in Johns's oeuvre. In some, he redrew the crosshatch lines in vivid primaries with his fingertips, with which he also daubed the coffee can, making even more intimate the image of his tools. In others, he accentuated the self-portrait conceit by adding an oval frame reminiscent of historical vignettes or by enmeshing the hatches with his handprints in a conflation of two emblems of his art and identity. Five of the monotypes cloak the hatches with fields of dark indigo and gray pocked by drops of emulsifier that dissolved the ink into starry dots on a night sky. And two festive variants proclaim "Hallelujah!" as the series neared its end. While twenty-six of the examples are printed directly on the earlier lithographic outtakes, Johns employed blank paper for the remaining seven, the most luscious and painterly of the suite. The final, ghostly counterproof, made by running a monotype again through the press with another sheet on top, is reversed and almost unrecognizable, dissolving into a torrential haze of celadon, black, and gray.

In 1982, the same year that Johns made the Savarin monotypes, he published the prints *Untitled (Red)*, *Untitled (Yellow)*, and *Untitled (Blue)*, variations of which would occupy him intermittently over the next two decades. Serving as a conceptual hinge between past and present, the trio of prints was made by reworking the three copperplates used in the etching *Land's End* (1979), which was itself based on the 1963 eponymous painting prominently featuring a handprint appended to a rectangular limb (p. 182, pl. 5). In 1984, Johns conjoined the three images of the *Untitled* prints in the monumental painting *Untitled (Red, Yellow, Blue)*, a composition he ultimately funneled back into a tripartite etching when his printer returned the three original plates in 1991.[3]

Throughout the 1990s, Johns frequently revisited the plates in unique trial and working proofs, which together constitute one of the most daring and generative series of his career. If the Savarin monotypes manifest Johns's analytical abandon in the manifold ways he applied ink to plates with no fixed image, the *Untitled* intaglio proofs demonstrate his experimentation with manipulating an etched image through editing, recombination, reorientation, and some of his boldest color combinations ever. Complementary hues such as red and green or yellow and purple sear the prints in optical bursts, which pulse against the black armature of the design like flickering passages of a projected film. Some of the tripartite compositions play out calmer tonal melodies in burnt orange or cool aquamarine, while grayscale versions reveal modulations in contrast or are enlivened by discrete tinted passages. In another group of trial proofs from 1998, Johns again returned to his handprint, this time eschewing an open palm for more contorted arrangements of his aging digits. His hands appear at life size, individually or in pairs, on small sheets or printed from multiple plates in grids on larger paper. Sometimes silhouetted against deep black grounds or by hasty outlines of white paint, they suggest a secret, inquisitive choreography of gestures that unfolds from plate to plate and page to page.

—Scott Rothkopf, with Carlos Basualdo, Sarah B. Vogelman, and Lauren Young

1 Jasper Johns, quoted in Joseph E. Young, "Jasper Johns: An Appraisal," *Art International* 13, no. 7 (September 1969); reprinted in Kirk Varnedoe, ed., *Jasper Johns: Writings, Sketchbook Notes, Interviews* (New York: Museum of Modern Art, 1996), 131.

2 This discussion of the Savarin monotypes relies on the scholarship of Judith Goldman in *Jasper Johns: Seventeen Monotypes* (West Islip, NY: Universal Limited Art Editions, 1982); Susan Dackerman in "The Monotypes of Jasper Johns in Detail," *Jasper Johns: Catalogue Raisonné of Monotypes*, by Susan Dackerman and Jennifer L. Roberts (New York: Matthew Marks Gallery; New Haven: Yale University Press, 2017), 290–93; and Ruth Fine in "What If?," in this volume, 220–23.

3 Wendy Weitman, *Jasper Johns: Process and Printmaking*, exh. brochure (New York: Museum of Modern Art, 1996), 8–14.

Unique Prints

Savarin Monotypes

WHITNEY MUSEUM OF AMERICAN ART

1 ***Savarin*, 1982**
Monotype
50 × 38 in. (127 × 96.5 cm)
Bill Goldston, James V. Smith, Thomas Cox/ULAE
Whitney Museum of American Art, New York; gift of the American Contemporary Art Foundation, Inc., Leonard A. Lauder, President, 2002.223

2 ***Painted Bronze*, 1960**
Bronze and oil paint
13 ½ × 8 in. (34.3 × 20.3 cm)
Kravis Collection; promised gift to the Museum of Modern Art, New York, in honor of David Rockefeller

3 ***Savarin*, 1982**
Monotype
50 × 38 in. (127 × 96.5 cm)
Bill Goldston, James V. Smith, Thomas Cox/ULAE
Whitney Museum of American Art, New York; gift of the American Contemporary Art Foundation, Inc., Leonard A. Lauder, President, 2002.232

4 ***Savarin*, 1982**
Monotype
50 × 38 in. (127 × 96.5 cm)
Bill Goldston, James V. Smith, Thomas Cox/ULAE
Whitney Museum of American Art, New York; gift of the American Contemporary Art Foundation, Inc., Leonard A. Lauder, President, 2002.235

5 ***Savarin*, 1982**
Monotype
50 × 38 in. (127 × 96.5 cm)
Bill Goldston, James V. Smith, Thomas Cox/ULAE
Whitney Museum of American Art, New York; gift of the American Contemporary Art Foundation, Inc., Leonard A. Lauder, President, 2002.228

6 ***Savarin*, 1982***
Monotype
50 × 38 in. (127 × 96.5 cm)
Bill Goldston, James V. Smith, Thomas Cox/ULAE
Whitney Museum of American Art, New York; gift of the American Contemporary Art Foundation, Inc., Leonard A. Lauder, President, 2002.224

7 ***Savarin*, 1982**
Monotype
50 × 38 in. (127 × 96.5 cm)
Bill Goldston, Thomas Cox/ULAE
Whitney Museum of American Art, New York; gift of the American Contemporary Art Foundation, Inc., Leonard A. Lauder, President, 2002.225

8 ***Savarin*, 1982**
Monotype
50 × 38 in. (127 × 96.5 cm)
Bill Goldston, James V. Smith, Thomas Cox/ULAE
Whitney Museum of American Art, New York; gift of the American Contemporary Art Foundation, Inc., Leonard A. Lauder, President, 2002.226

9 ***Savarin*, 1982**
Monotype
50 × 38 in. (127 × 96.5 cm)
Bill Goldston, James V. Smith, Thomas Cox/ULAE
Whitney Museum of American Art, New York; gift of the American Contemporary Art Foundation, Inc., Leonard A. Lauder, President, 2002.231

10 ***Savarin*, 1982**
Monotype
50 × 38 in. (127 × 96.5 cm)
Bill Goldston, Thomas Cox/ULAE
Whitney Museum of American Art, New York; gift of the American Contemporary Art Foundation, Inc., Leonard A. Lauder, President, 2002.233

11 ***Savarin*, 1982**
Monotype
50 × 38 in. (127 × 96.5 cm)
Bill Goldston, James V. Smith, Thomas Cox/ULAE
Whitney Museum of American Art, New York; gift of the American Contemporary Art Foundation, Inc., Leonard A. Lauder, President, 2002.234

12 ***Savarin*, 1982**
Monotype
50 × 38 in. (127 × 96.5 cm)
Bill Goldston, James V. Smith, Thomas Cox/ULAE
Whitney Museum of American Art New York; gift of the American Contemporary Art Foundation, Inc., Leonard A. Lauder, President, 2002.227

13 ***Savarin*, 1982**
Monotype
50 × 38 in. (127 × 96.5 cm)
Bill Goldston, James V. Smith, Thomas Cox/ULAE
Whitney Museum of American Art, New York; gift of the American Contemporary Art Foundation, Inc., Leonard A. Lauder, President, 2002.229

14 ***Savarin*, 1982**
Monotype
50 × 38 in. (127 × 96.5 cm)
Bill Goldston, James V. Smith, Thomas Cox/ULAE
Whitney Museum of American Art, New York; gift of the American Contemporary Art Foundation, Inc., Leonard A. Lauder, President, 2002.230

15 ***Savarin*, 1982**
Monotype
50 × 38 in. (127 × 96.5 cm)
Bill Goldston, James V. Smith, Thomas Cox/ULAE
Whitney Museum of American Art, New York; gift of the American Contemporary Art Foundation, Inc., Leonard A. Lauder, President, 2002.237

16 ***Savarin*, 1982**
Monotype
50 × 38 in. (127 × 96.5 cm)
Bill Goldston, Thomas Cox/ULAE
Whitney Museum of American Art, New York; gift of the American Contemporary Art Foundation, Inc., Leonard A. Lauder, President, 2002.238

17 ***Savarin*, 1982**
Monotype
50 × 38 in. (127 × 96.5 cm)
Bill Goldston, Thomas Cox/ULAE
Whitney Museum of American Art, New York; gift of the American Contemporary Art Foundation, Inc., Leonard A. Lauder, President, 2002.239

Trial and Working Proofs

PHILADELPHIA MUSEUM OF ART

1 ***Untitled*, 1997**
Etching and aquatint
42 ½ × 29 ½ in. (108 × 74.9 cm)
Aldo Crommelynck/Atelier Crommelynck
TP
National Gallery of Art, Washington, DC; Patrons' Permanent Fund and Special Friends of the National Gallery of Art, 2010.116.489

2 ***Untitled*, 1996**
Etching and aquatint
41 ¼ × 75 ¼ in. (104.8 × 191.1 cm)
Aldo Crommelynck/Atelier Crommelynck
TP
National Gallery of Art, Washington, DC; Patrons' Permanent Fund and Special Friends of the National Gallery of Art, 2010.116.514

3 ***Untitled*, 2014**
Unique etching on paper mounted on paper support: six plates
43 ½ × 79 ½ in. (110.5 × 201.9 cm)
Collection of the artist

4 ***Untitled*, 1998**
Intaglio
12 × 7 ¼ in. (30.5 × 18.4 cm)
John Lund/Low Road Studio
TP
Private collection

5 ***Untitled*, 1998**
Intaglio
22 ¼ × 15 in. (56.5 × 38.1 cm)
John Lund/Low Road Studio
TP
Private collection

6 ***Untitled*, 1998**
Intaglio
14 ½ × 8 ½ in. (36.8 × 21.6 cm)
John Lund/Low Road Studio
TP
Private collection

7 ***Untitled*, 1998**
Intaglio
15 × 11 in. (38.1 × 27.9 cm)
John Lund/Low Road Studio
TP
Private collection

8 ***Untitled*, 1998**
Ink on mylar (matrix for laser cuts)
11 ½ × 7 ½ in. (29.2 × 19.1 cm)
John Lund/Low Road Studio
Private collection

9 ***Untitled*, 1998**
Intaglio
15 × 11 in. (38.1 × 27.9 cm)
John Lund/Low Road Studio
TP
Private collection

10 ***Untitled*, 1998**
Intaglio
22 ¼ × 14 ¾ in. (56.5 × 37.5 cm)
John Lund/Low Road Studio
TP
Private collection

11 ***Untitled*, 1998**
Intaglio
20 ½ × 14 ½ in. (52.1 × 36.8 cm)
John Lund/Low Road Studio
TP
Private collection

12 ***Untitled*, 1998**
Intaglio
22 ¼ × 14 ¾ in. (56.5 × 37.5 cm)
John Lund/Low Road Studio
TP
Private collection

13 ***Untitled*, 1998**
Intaglio
20 ½ × 14 ½ in. (52.1 × 36.8 cm)
John Lund/Low Road Studio
TP
Private collection

14 ***Untitled*, 1998**
Intaglio
20 ½ × 14 ½ in. (52.1 × 36.8 cm)
John Lund/Low Road Studio
TP
Private collection

15 ***Untitled*, 1998**
Intaglio
20 ½ × 14 ½ in. (52.1 × 36.8 cm)
John Lund/Low Road Studio
TP
Private collection

Savarin Monotypes

WHITNEY MUSEUM OF AMERICAN ART

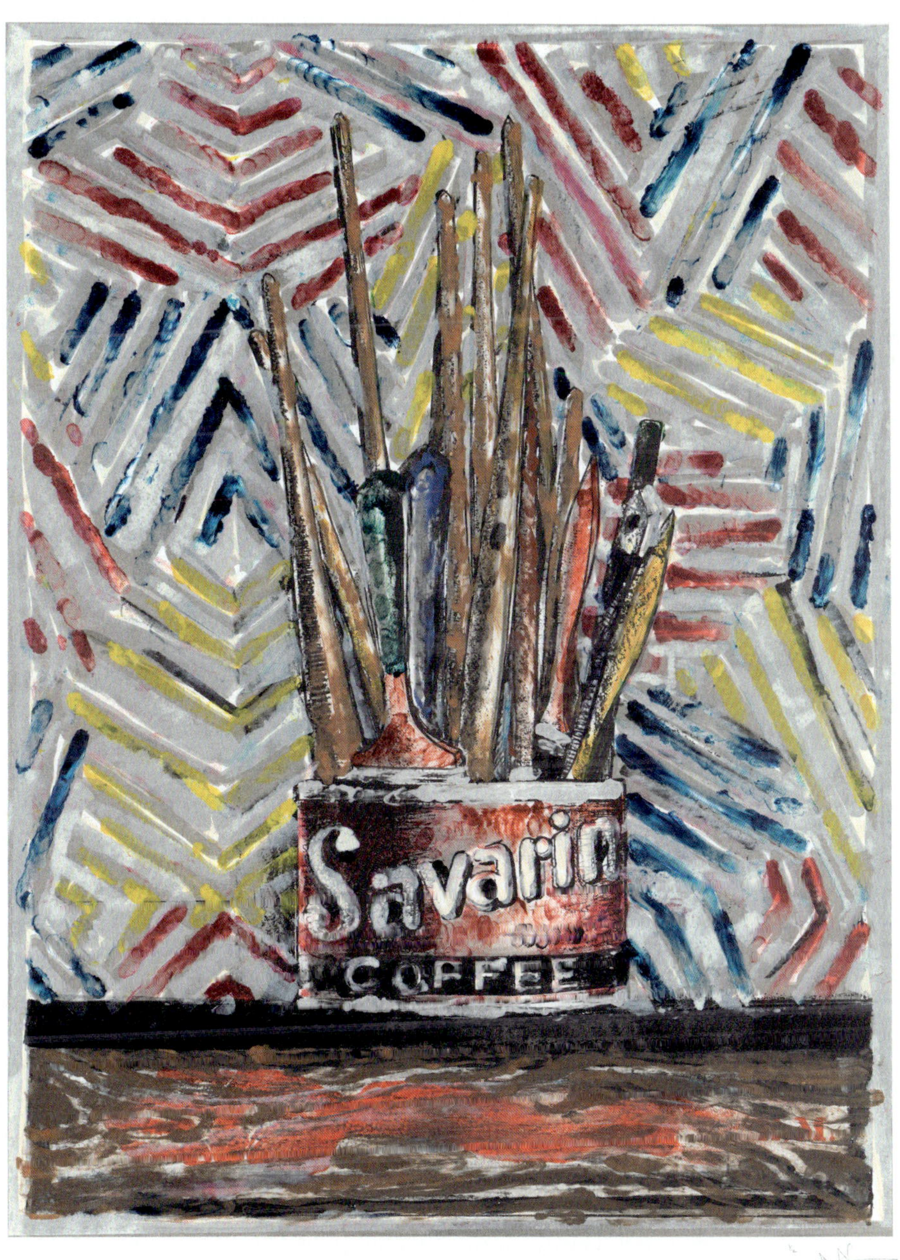

1 ***Savarin*, 1982**

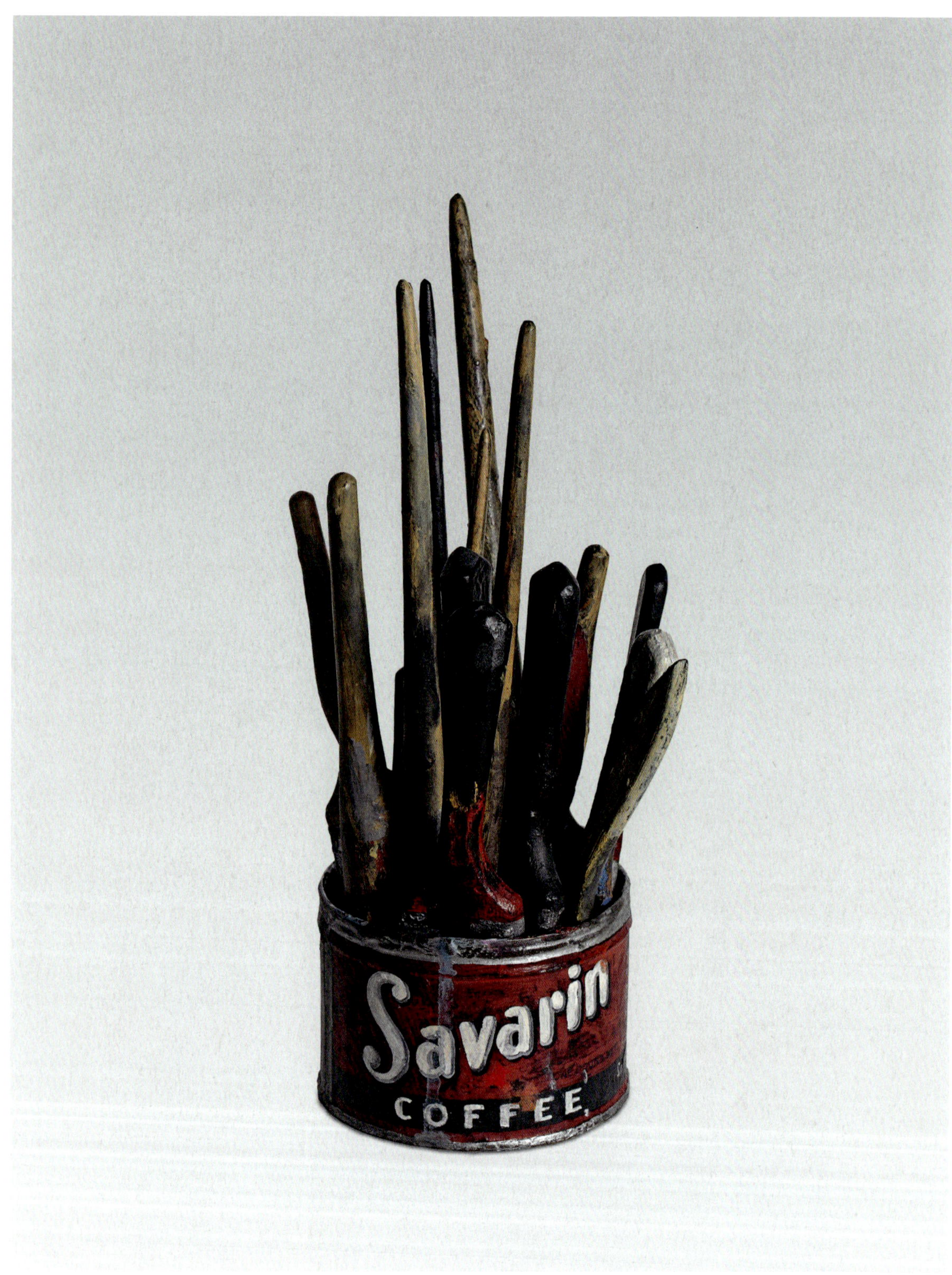

2 ***Painted Bronze*, 1960**

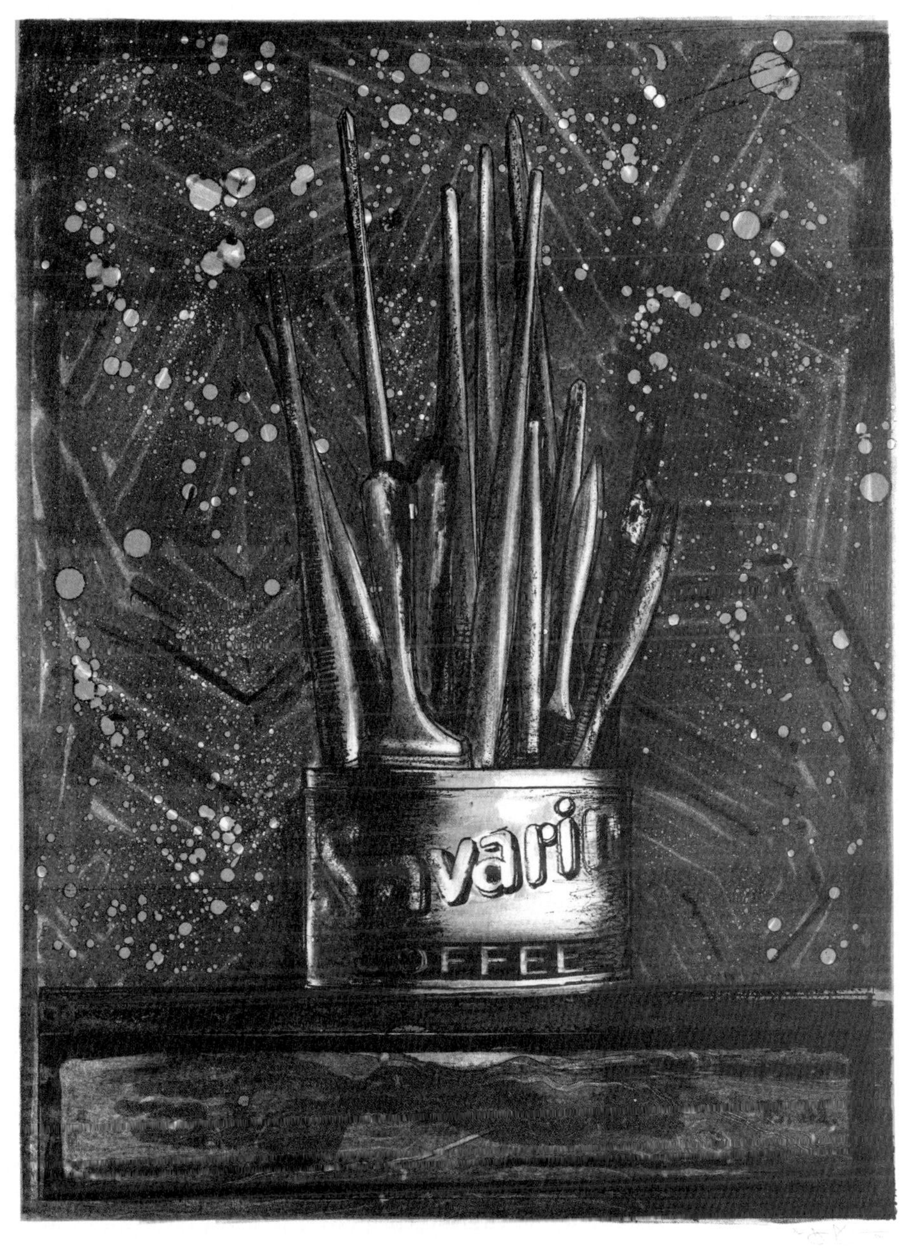

3 ***Savarin***, **1982**

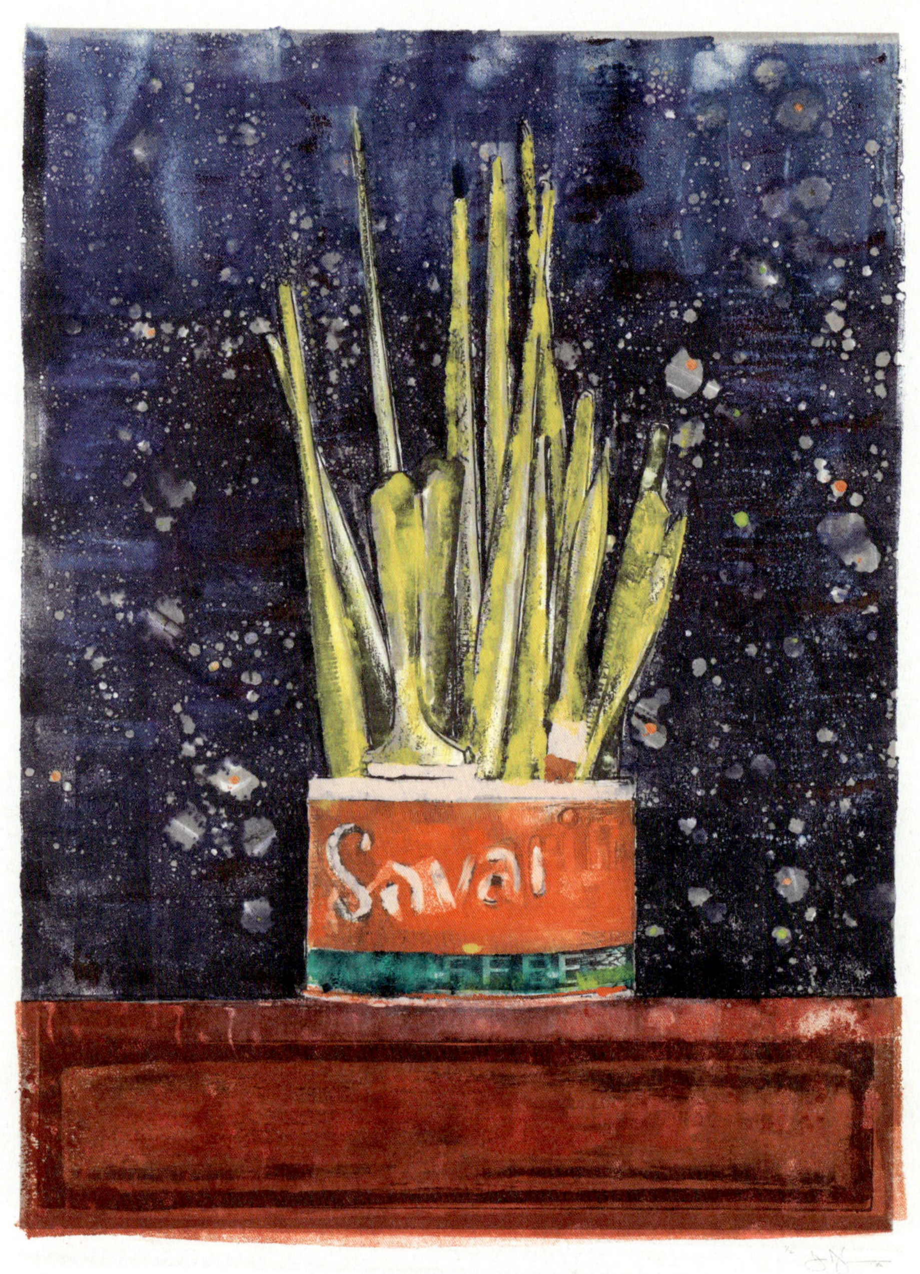

4 ***Savarin*, 1982**

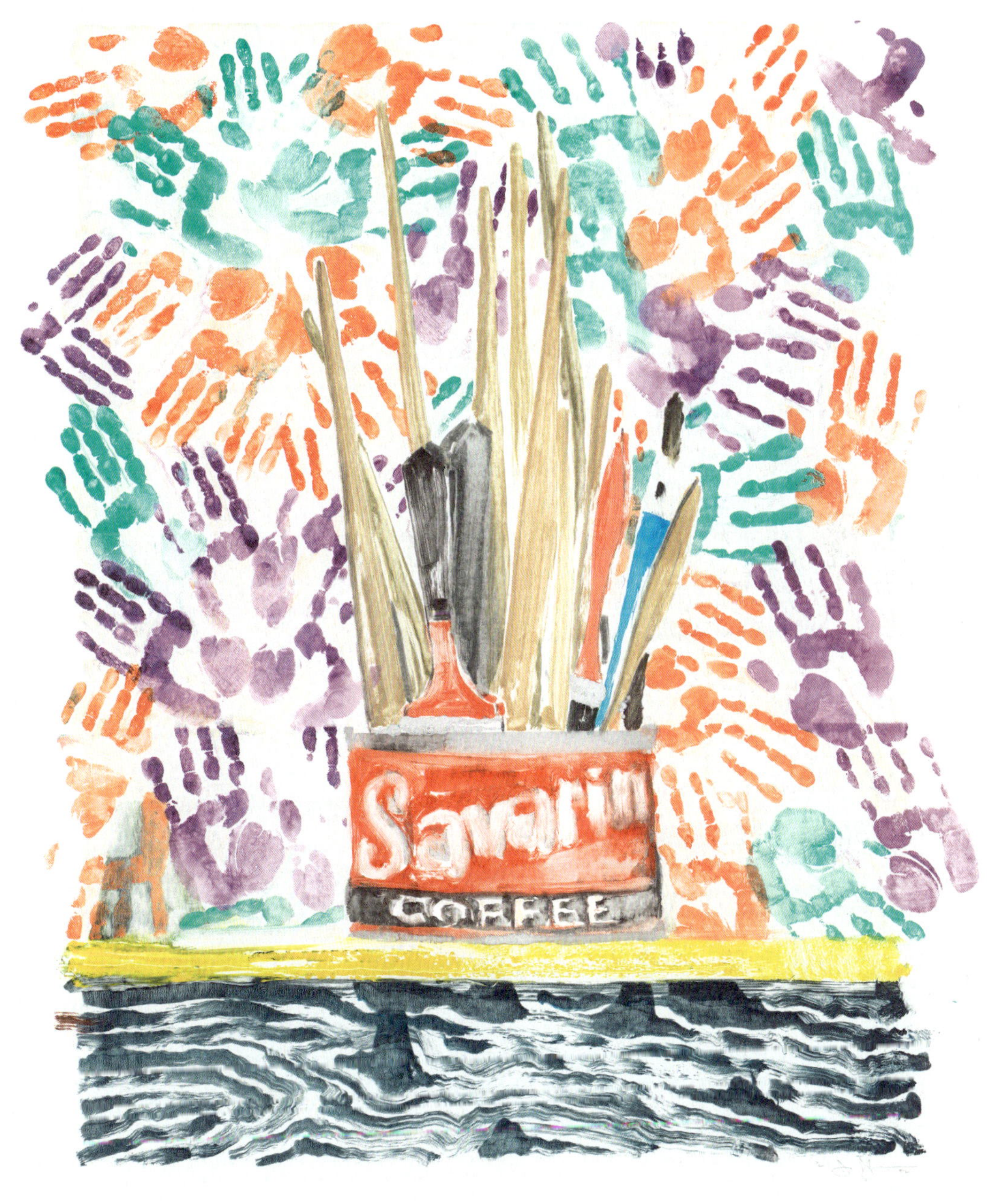

5 ***Savarin***, **1982**

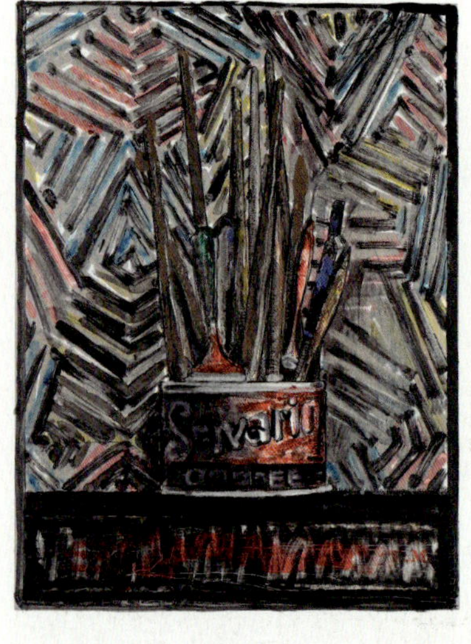

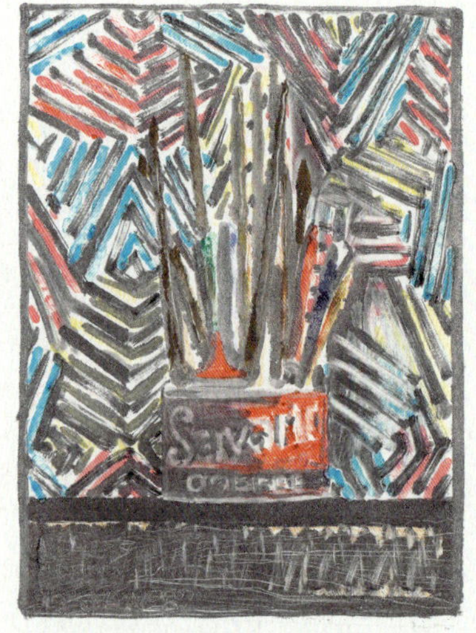

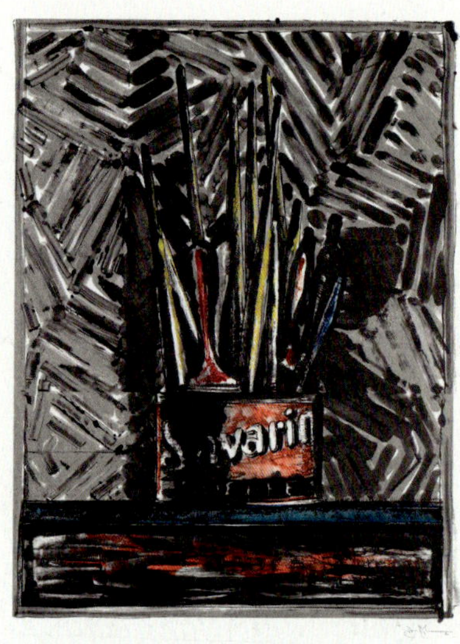

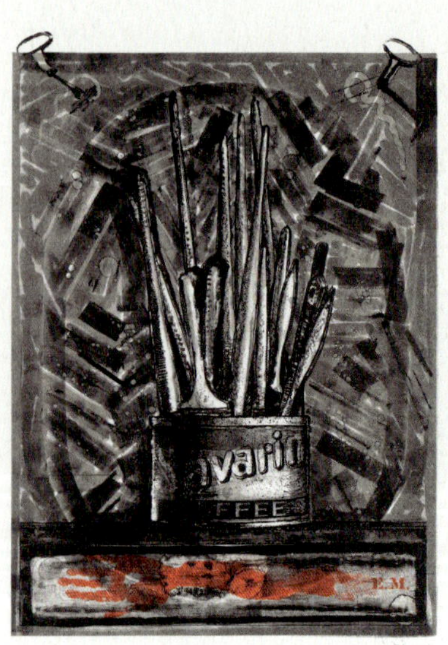

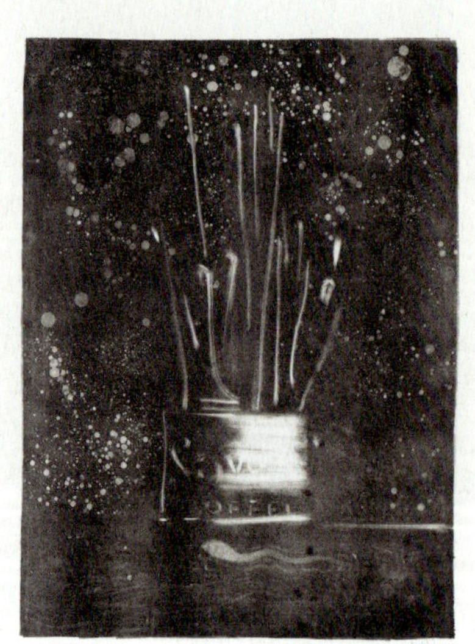

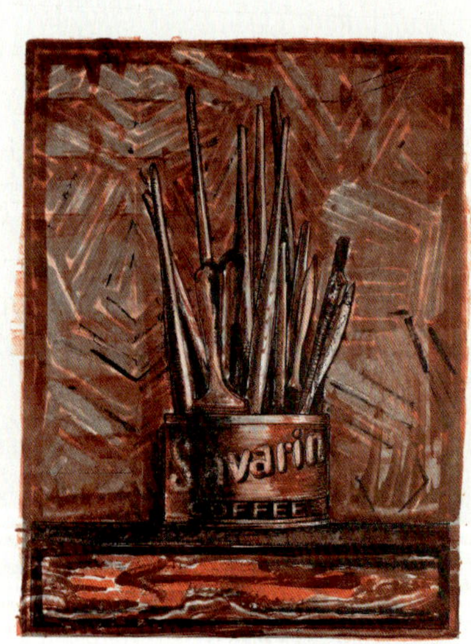

6 ***Savarin*, 1982**
9 ***Savarin*, 1982**

7 ***Savarin*, 1982**
10 ***Savarin*, 1982**

8 ***Savarin*, 1982**
11 ***Savarin*, 1982**

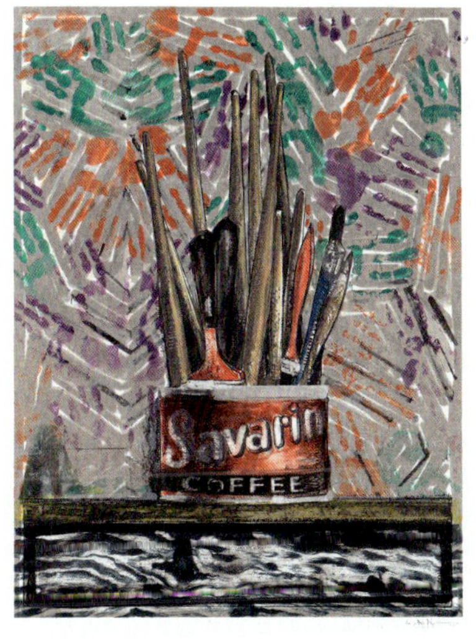

12 ***Savarin*, 1982**

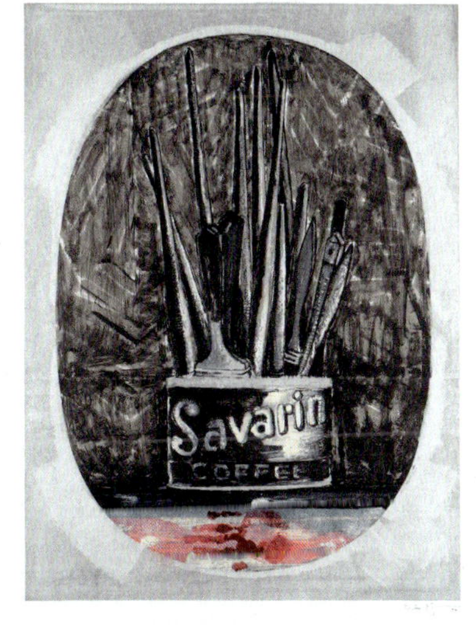

13 ***Savarin*, 1982**

14 ***Savarin*, 1982**

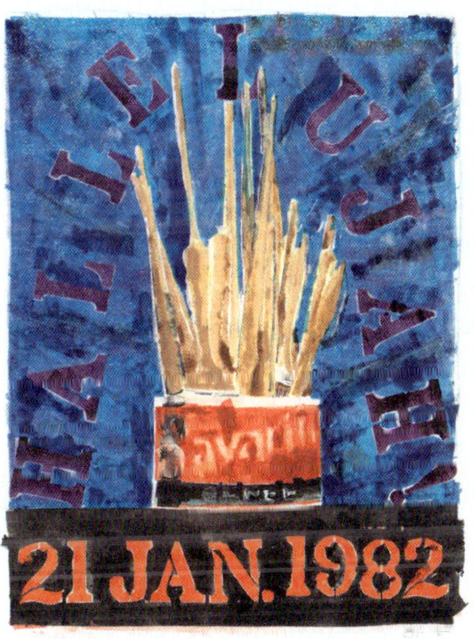

15 ***Savarin*, 1982**

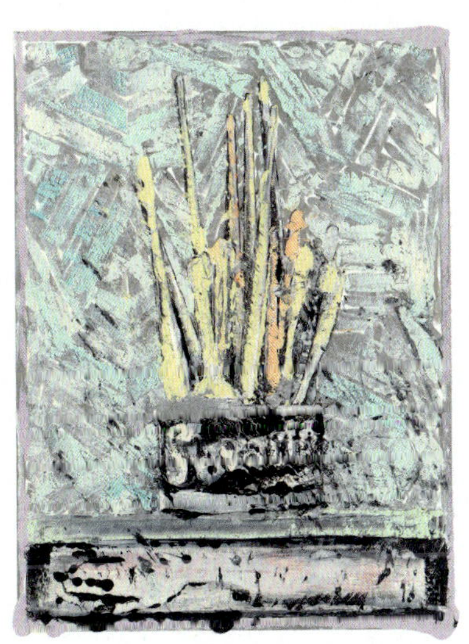

16 ***Savarin*, 1982**

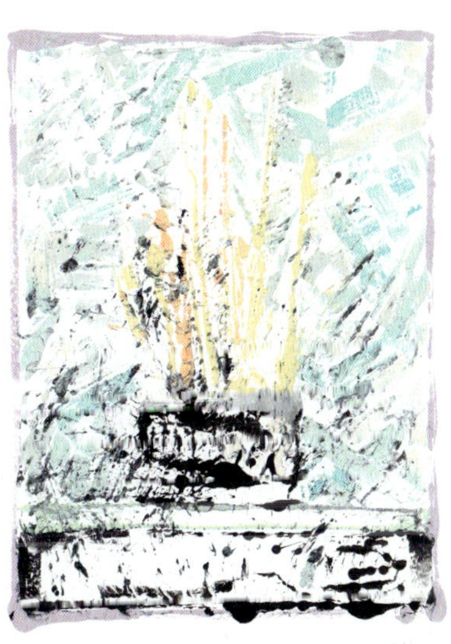

17 ***Savarin*, 1982**

Trial and Working Proofs

PHILADELPHIA MUSEUM OF ART

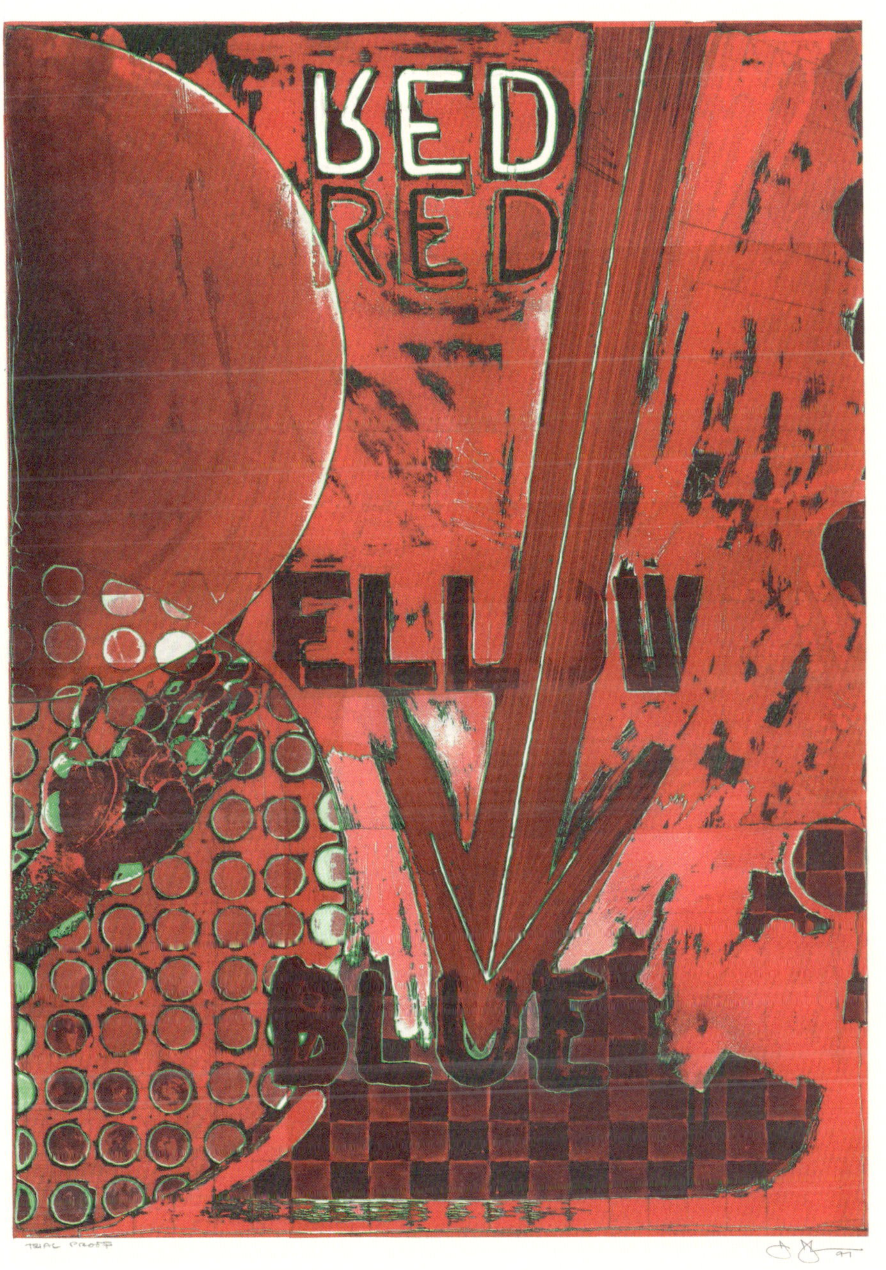

1 ***Untitled*, 1997**

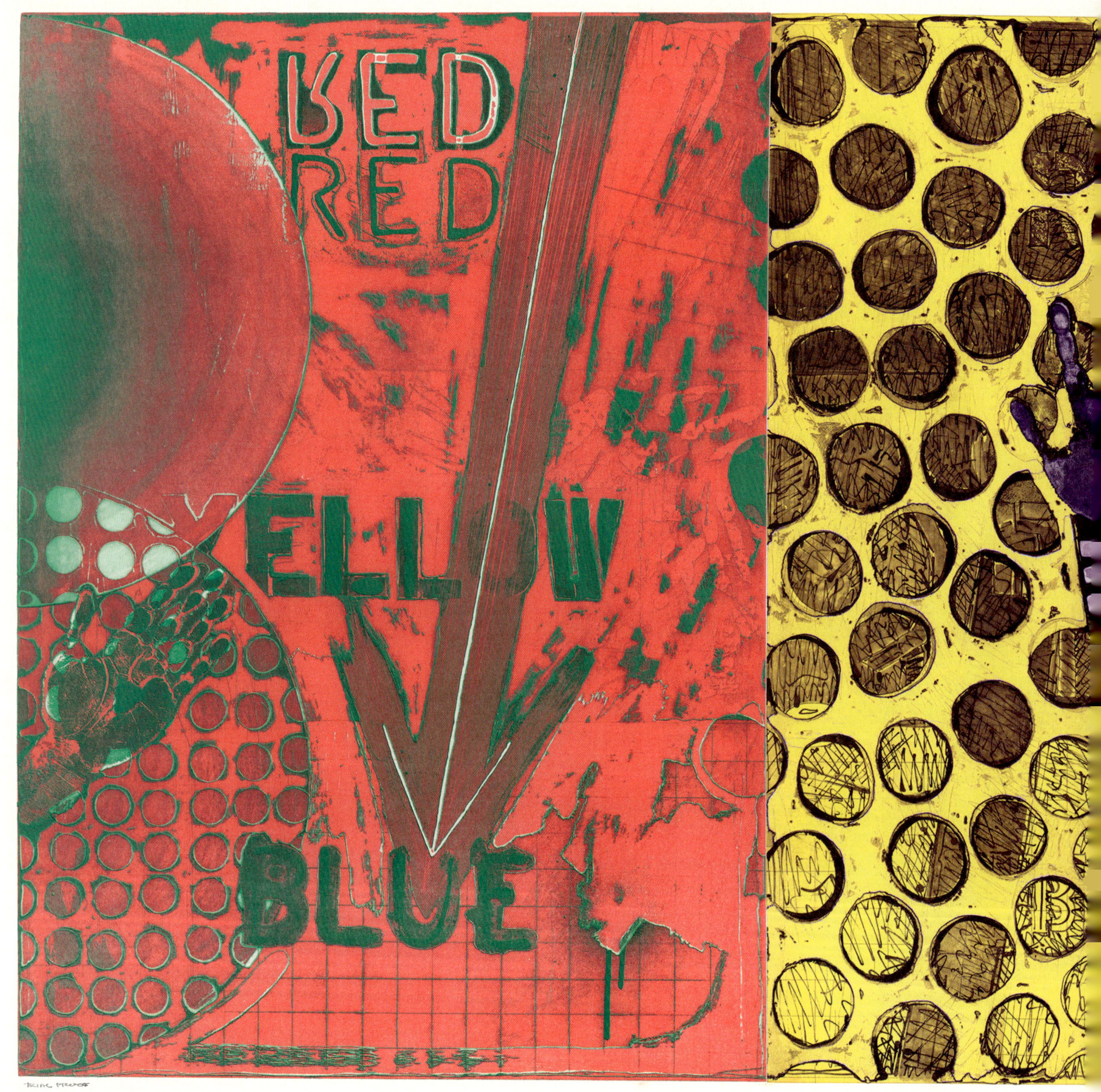

2 ***Untitled*, 1996**

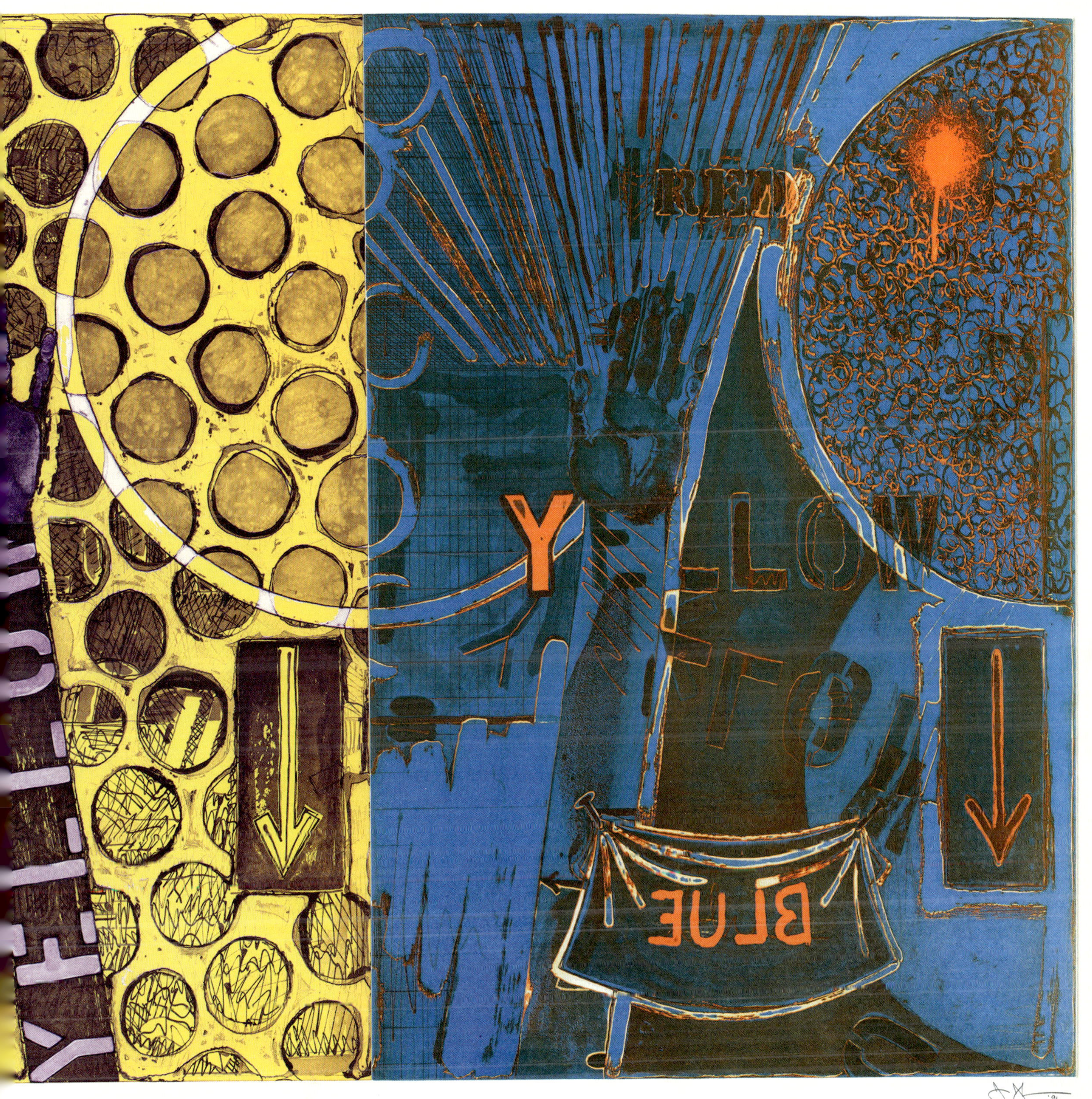
RED
BLUE

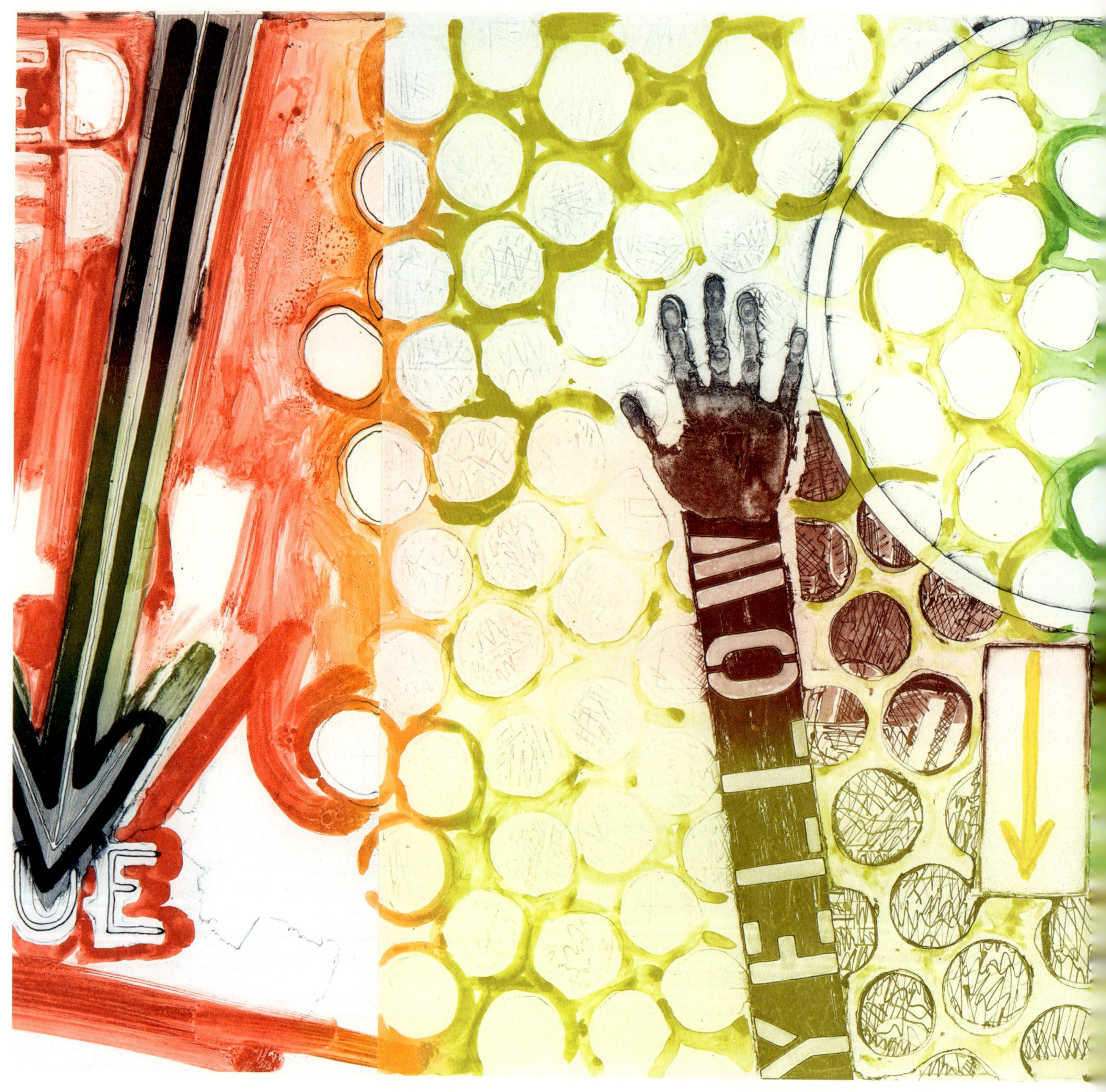

3 ***Untitled*, 2014**

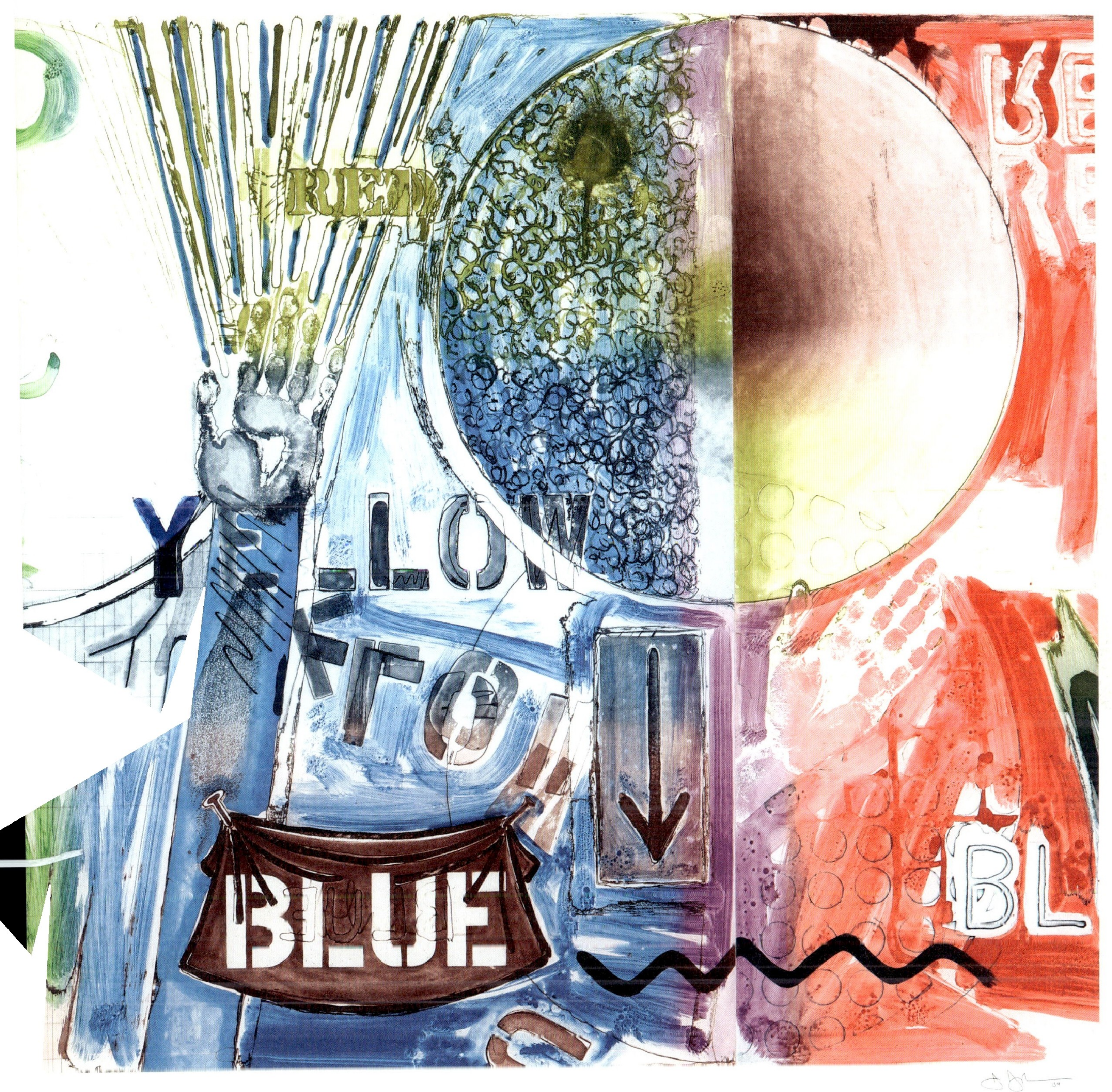
RED
LOW
BLUE
BL

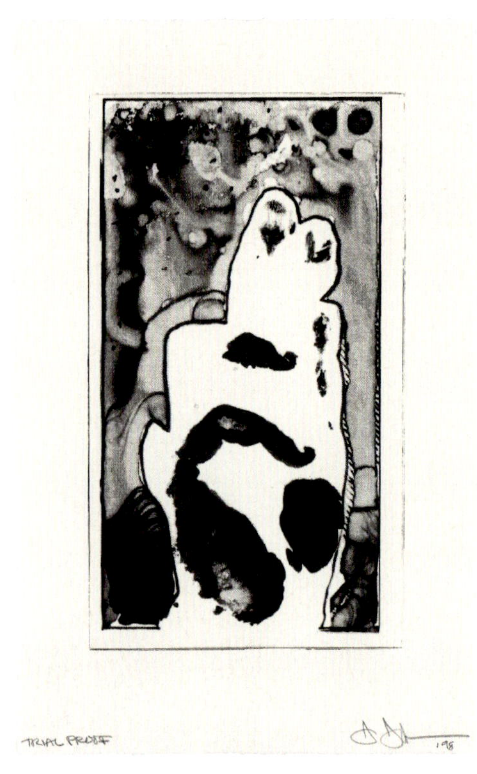

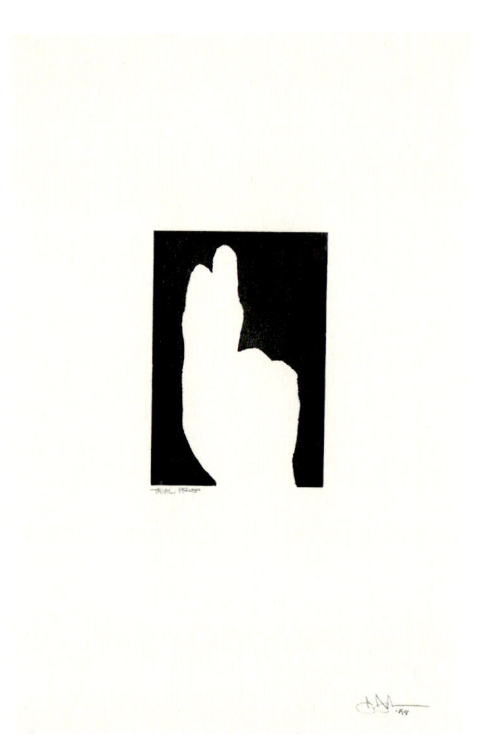

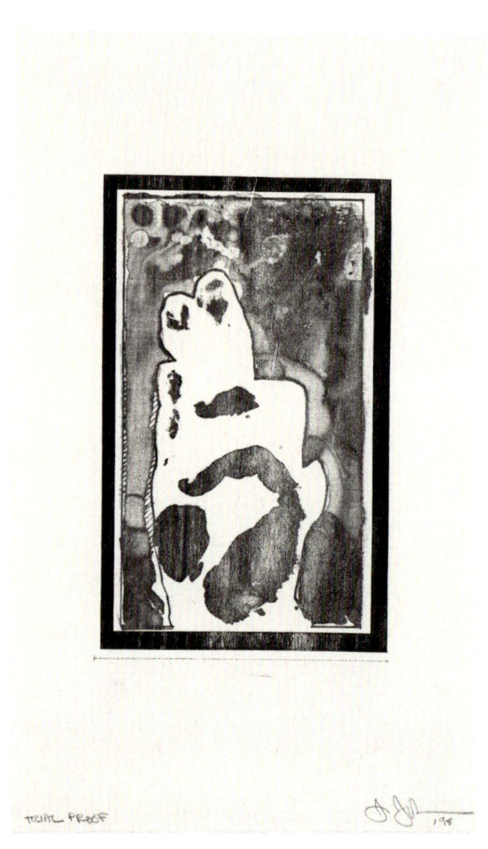

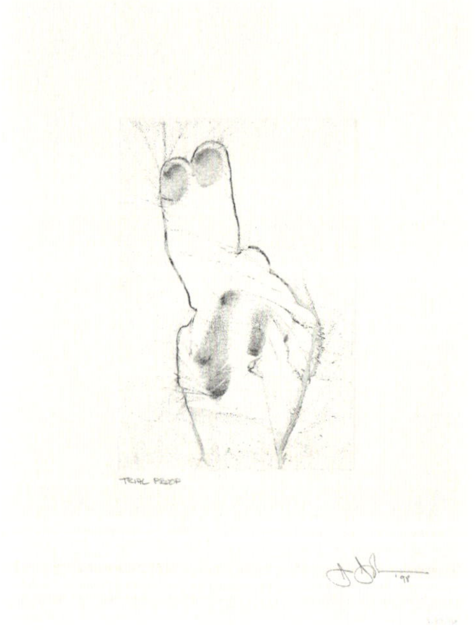

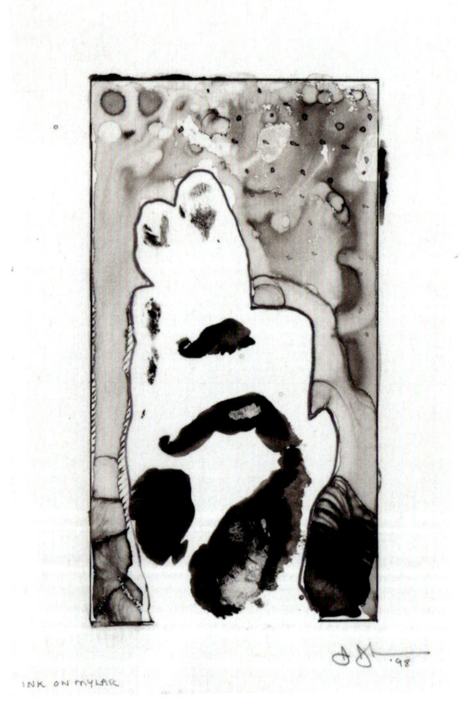

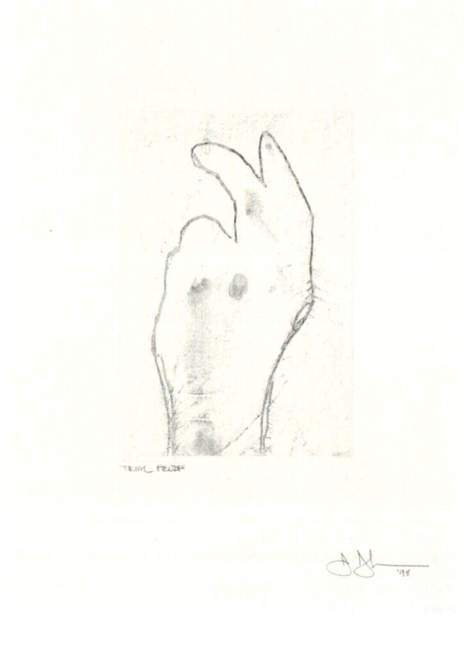

4 ***Untitled*, 1998**
7 ***Untitled*, 1998**

5 ***Untitled*, 1998**
8 ***Untitled*, 1998**

6 ***Untitled*, 1998**
9 ***Untitled*, 1998**

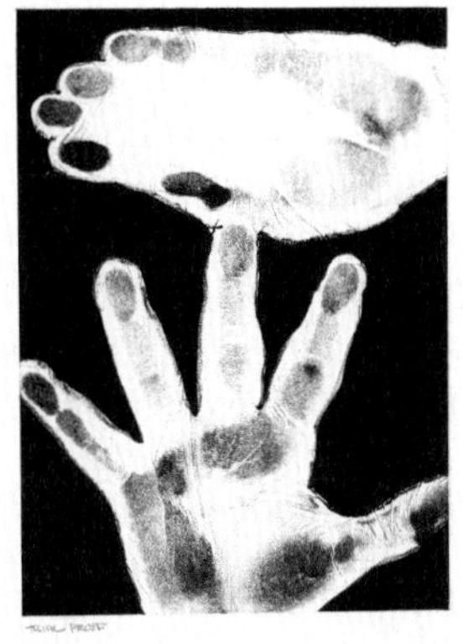
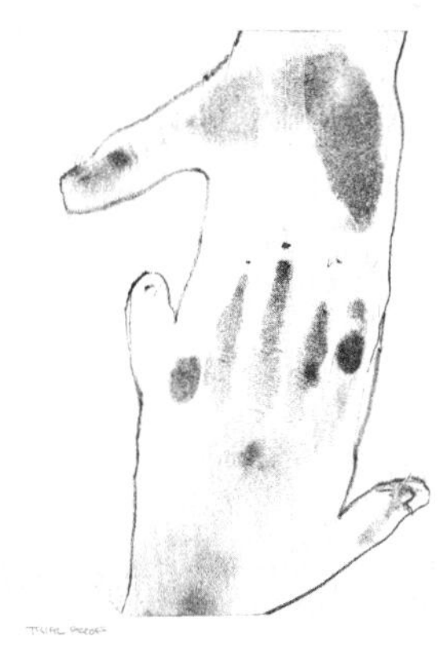
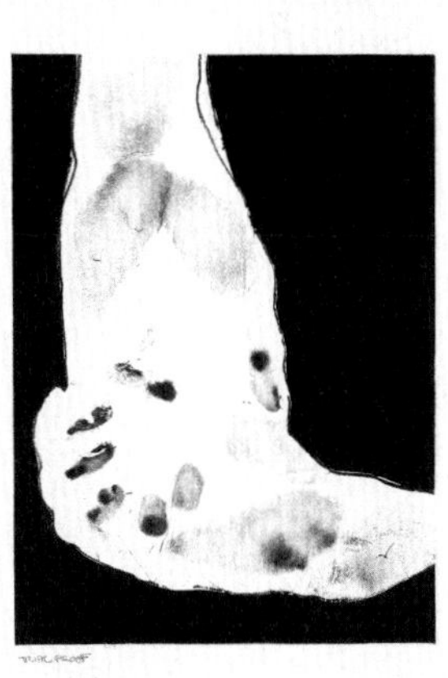
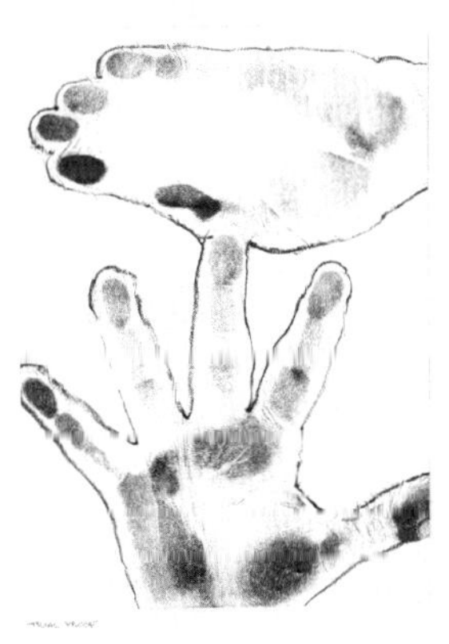
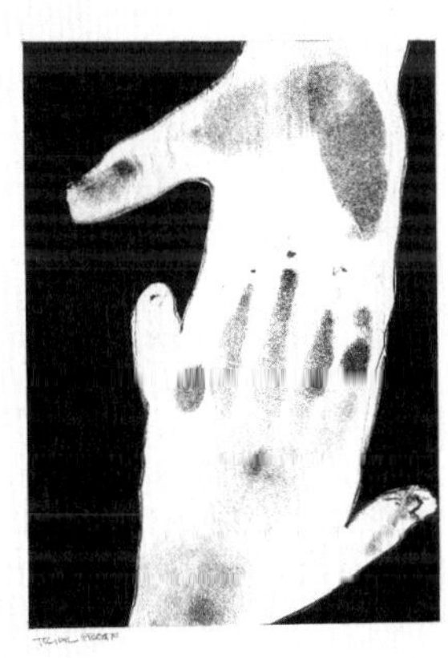
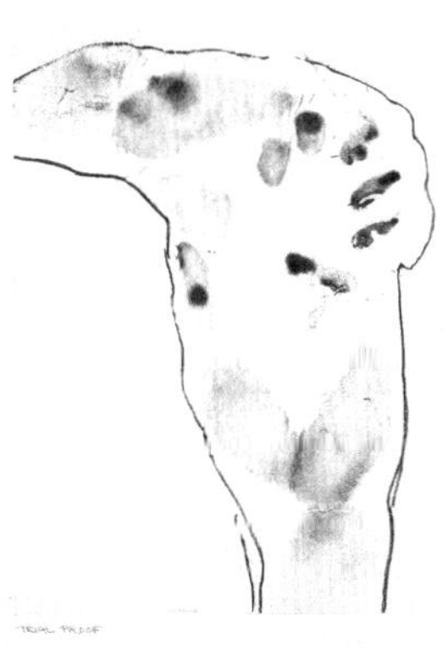

10 ***Untitled*, 1998**
13 ***Untitled*, 1998**

11 ***Untitled*, 1998**
14 ***Untitled*, 1998**

12 ***Untitled*, 1998**
15 ***Untitled*, 1998**

What If?

Ruth Fine

Over the course of some six decades, Jasper Johns has made approximately 340 edition prints, as well as more than 260 non-editioned printed objects, called monotypes.[1] These immensely admired works demonstrate the artist's originality as a printmaker, as well as the ways in which printmaking-related issues, such as image reversals, have contributed to his approach in other media. Indeed, printmaking is fully integrated into his art, as exemplified by the connections between the sculpture *Painted Bronze* (1960; p. 206, pl. 2), the lithograph *Savarin* (1977), and the related *Savarin* monotypes (1982; p. 205, pl. 1; pp. 207–11, pls. 3–17), of which seventeen were documented when they were first published in 1982.[2] Some of these monotypes are unique, while others are part of small variable editions.

Johns's reported inspirational sources for motifs, processes, or tools incorporated in his work include dreams, views on highways, works of art, and gifts of pictures and objects from friends. Some sources became prominent when the artist was considering death caused by the AIDS crisis in the 1980s, others when he was moving houses, and still others by his own aging process marked by loss. This is what makes Johns's art essential to our lives and time: he faces and engages in a highly evocative manner experiences to which we all must personally respond. For those of us who are likewise deeply involved with looking at art, he helps us understand or connect usefully with history as well as with the troubles and pleasures of living in our turbulent times.

Johns's prints insist that we accept their—and their maker's—mysterious nature, embrace of paradox, and refusal to acknowledge any one reading. Even so, sixty years of prints and related proofs confirm consistent threads (intended or intuitive) in the artist's juxtapositions that represent vivid clarity as much as enigma. This is why so many artists, curators, critics, and historians repeatedly reconsider and reevaluate his work. The proofs, in particular, offer viewers a unique opportunity to observe the artist's thought processes as he develops his visual world. Through them, we can trace a print's developmental process, as changes to the matrix or matrices (an umbrella term for stones, plates, or blocks that carry images to be printed) reveal aspects of a work in progress.

For many distinguished artists, past and present, printmaking has been a collaborative activity that involves working with printers in workshops. The 1960s saw the opening of many such workshops, and Johns became a central figure in the decade's printmaking renaissance, reinvigorating the medium by inventing new ways of engaging its possibilities.[3] Artists have discretion over the number and type of proofs produced with their printer-collaborators. In Johns's case, their numbers have been large and their nature probably as diverse as those by any maker of prints in the history of art.[4]

Proofs have played a core role in Johns's printmaking, starting with his earliest lithographs, in 1960, and the variants of an image/idea that reappear throughout his art are particularly refined in the prints and proofs. This is owing to the reuse of matrices over many years and in multiple editions, starting with the limestone slabs on which he drew his early lithographs but also including different kinds of metal plates for lithography and etching, wood and linoleum blocks, and frames stretched with silk or synthetic materials of variable mesh for screenprinting.

Like his edition prints, Johns's proofs have fostered extensive scholarly attention.[5] They are uniquely beautiful as independent objects, as well as parts of the puzzle essential to assembling a complex printed image.[6] As the latter, proofs offer multiple entrances to an enriched understanding of the densely layered concerns throughout Johns's oeuvre.[7] "Densely layered" likewise describes the physicality of many of the proofs, which in this respect closely reflect and echo the artist's metaphysical approach. Proofs and the edition prints that evolve from them flourish from his "what if" attitude, which appears to be as spontaneous as it is measured, and which has always been enhanced by the artist's engagement of the haptic aspects of art making. His sense of touch, remarked upon throughout his career, in recent decades has become increasingly poignant and able to convey and stimulate expressive responses of great variety through a single work. This is especially true in intaglios, which have become a strong focus of the prints. These range from coarse mezzotint fields to delicate aquatint washes and line work that is unparalleled in contemporary etching and drypoint practice.

In Johns's prints, widely shared symbols such as numbers and maps exist alongside highly personal motifs such as diagrams of an ancestral home and family photographs. Other elements are drawn from works of art he has collected and lives with—including many works by his contemporaries and younger practitioners, as well as by Paul Cézanne and Pablo Picasso, masters closely associated with Johnsian motifs, but also art objects from throughout the centuries that suggest no direct impact on his art. Many are known from their inclusion in exhibitions to which Johns generously has lent. They represent the various media in which he creates his own art, but primarily are works on paper. In recent decades, the artist's prints have incorporated specific art-based motifs, including work by Matthias Grünewald and Marcel Duchamp. Johns also has referenced tantric compositions and studied masters of Japanese brushwork and woodcut, as suggested, for example, in the Usuyuki works (see, for example, p. 120, pl. 4; and pp. 126–27, pls. 24–31).

For any artist, making prints presents a range of distinct technical and aesthetic possibilities, the inseparability of which Johns's art celebrates; options vary depending on the process he employs. In terms of the order in which the artist initially explored each of his methods, monotype came first in 1954 (but was not again explored until 1978),[8] followed by lithography (his focus from 1960 to 1967), then etching, and then relief (on the basis of a rubber stamp combined with lithography in the 1970 *Light Bulb*), with screenprinting last. With few exceptions, Johns's prints (like his drawings) are created after the paintings with which they are associated.[9]

Who besides Johns knows what actions he takes in the privacy of his painting studio, or which areas of works he subsequently paints over or scrapes out? Proofs, by contrast, offer him an option of trying out and maintaining for study over time as many responses as he wishes—for example, testing multiple colors and color combinations outside his usual palette choices. Studying these "what if" responses in an assembly of related proofs allows him comparative contemplation of a unique kind (fig. 1).

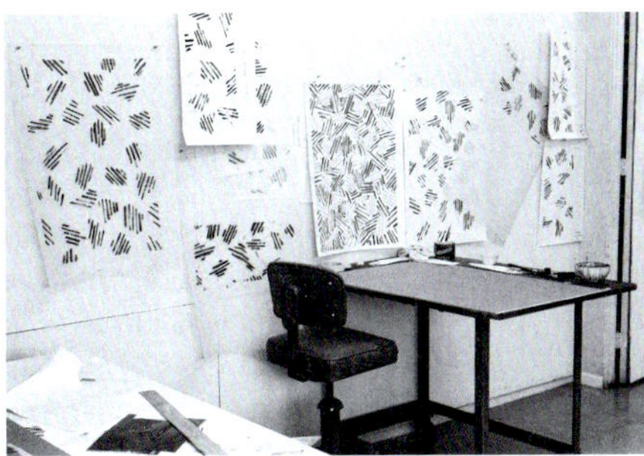

Fig. 1 **Working proofs for Johns's *Four Panels for Untitled 1972 (Grays and Black)* tacked to the wall of the artist studio at Gemini G.E.L., Los Angeles, 1975**
Photograph by Sidney B. Felsen (American, b. 1924)

The creation of most works of art is preceded by some variation of this essay's title question: "What if?" Responses to that question are potentially innumerable, and may shift course as a work develops. In making prints, the exploration is layered with unpredictable areas of potential accident, processes in which it is virtually impossible to assume full control. This is part of printmaking's seductive nature, a consistent element of surprise, encountered every time a sheet of paper is lifted from a matrix after being run through a press (or ink is passed through a screen). At that time the artist and printer discover if it will be suitable as part of the edition, close to all the other impressions printed so far—or, in the case of a monoprint, essentially replicating what the artist envisioned. Each step leading up to the transfer of matrix image to printed paper is marked by chance events. For example, the strength of acids used for etching and for processing lithography plates may vary due to frequency of use or in response to climate changes in the workshop. Differences of color density in batches of ink and absorbency in paper production are also major chance elements. Only when a paper is lifted from a matrix after printing does the artist see the results of his or her work.

Fig. 2 ***Coat Hanger I*, 1960**
Lithograph: one stone, 36 × 27 in. (91.4 × 68.6 cm). Robert Blackburn/ULAE. Edition of 35

Johns's practice of rethinking a motif is evident in some of his earliest lithographs. For example, his 1960 lithograph *Coat Hanger I* (fig. 2), inspired by a 1958 drawing, was extensively reworked that same year to both eliminate and add marks and tones to the original drawing on stone. This additional work led to *Coat Hanger II* (1960; fig. 3), a starkly defined hanger on a dense field, very different from the previous version, in which the hanger was tightly embedded within vertical, diagonal, and horizontal pen-like marks. Respectively, *Coat Hanger I* and *II* exemplify Johns's tendency to alternate between depictions of a motif that feature the marks of their making and those where the image itself is most prominent. This important distinction, which appears throughout his oeuvre, may have originated in the print studio. It also has been part of his practice to create multiple editions of prints by revisiting a single matrix—famously, in two of his three portfolios of ten lithographs each featuring the numbers 0 through 9.[10]

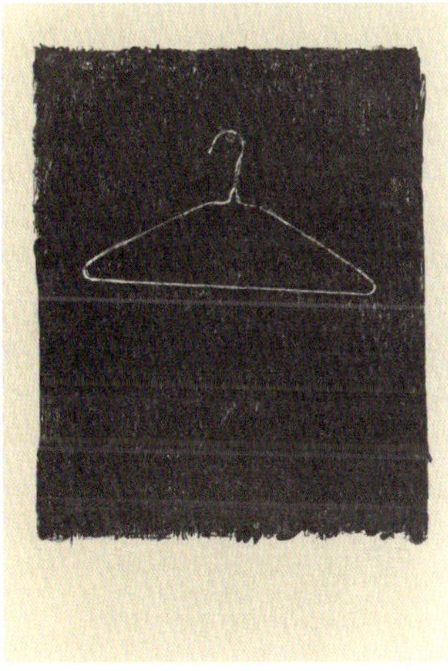

Fig. 3 ***Coat Hanger II*, 1960**
Lithograph: one stone, 35 ½ × 25 in. (90.2 × 63.5 cm). Robert Blackburn/ULAE. Edition of 8

Johns has maintained annotated proofs for almost all his edition prints. These convey the extraordinary diversity of his print processes, but they are also beautiful in their own right. This is as important as the intentional functionality of the proofs in responding to Johns's "what if" inspiration. Documenting the creation of some editions are dozens of variously designated proofs: trial, color trial, working, state (as many as sixteen states for a single image), and cancellation proofs among them.[11]

The Savarin monotypes function similarly to a body of proofs, showing Johns rethinking a subject multiple times in print, with each image related to the others yet also dramatically independent. Together, they reinforce our sense of the immense possibilities a given—but unbounded—set of visual circumstances makes available to this artist, who transforms them repeatedly, each time offering new challenges to himself. Rethinking an image/idea by doing something else to it has long been at the root of Johns's approach, as has his concern with relationships between parts and a related whole. When viewers encounter these assets together in his printed art, whether in the Savarin or other monotype series or in the thousands of proofs for his editions, they incorporate new ways of thinking and seeing into their visual realms, each in as singular a way as the artist.

Some proofs record only a fragment of an image, presumably a detail Johns needed to think about as he moved forward. For edition prints that require several matrices placed atop one another, the proofs may record the evolution of the images on a single matrix, whether plate, block, stone, or screen. Others may show selected matrices printed in layers on a single sheet, rather than all those in play for the edition. Some document reductions to the size or shape of an image, if Johns determined he wanted a matrix cut down. Others are printed from matrices that do not appear in any edition but are closely related to one or more images. Johns presumably created these and then rejected them as not providing his composition with what he had hoped for or imagined (fig. 4). A proof of a 1993 drypoint on pewter, *After Holbein* (fig. 5), documents a test of a potential new metal matrix. While this image was never editioned, it is related to several similarly titled compositions that were. This virtually unknown proof is evidence of Johns trying new surfaces on which to create a rich variety of lines. Some of Johns's proofs explore subtle changes to details of form and space that result, not from alterations to the matrix surfaces or the colors printed, but from changing the order in which the overlaid elements are printed. Some proofs documenting layered matrices record changes to some of the matrices but not others. Embossing and debossing experiments (by which a matrix creates, respectively, raised or lowered areas in the paper) may be evident as well. Because different ink manufacturers yield variant hues for the same color name, printing trial proofs helps determine the desired brand of ink. Printing an image on different presses is a reason for making proofs as well: an offset press reverses the image twice, so that it appears in the same orientation as seen on the original matrix image; when using a direct press, the printed composition is reversed, since the paper is placed facedown on the matrix to be printed.

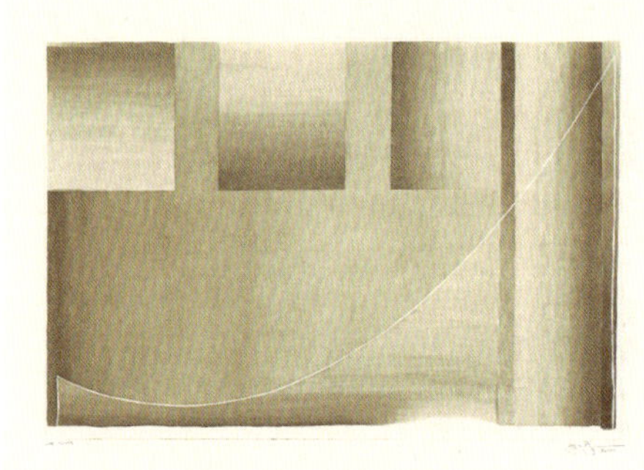

Fig. 4 ***Untitled*, 2001**
Etching and aquatint, 22 ¼ × 33 ¾ in. (56.5 × 85.7 cm). John Lund/Low Road Studio for ULAE. National Gallery of Art, Washington, DC; Patrons' Permanent Fund and Special Friends of the National Gallery of Art, 2010.116.744

Johns's proofs also document differentiations in the thickness, weight, color, and texture of the paper, sometimes without changes to the images themselves. Other paper-related issues Johns explores in his proofs include the size and orientation of the margins, the location of the image on the sheet, and sometimes the location or color of his signature on a sheet. Johns is extremely knowledgeable about the technical aspects of printmaking and pays close attention to such details, according to printers who have worked with him.[12]

Explorations of fine papers, especially handmade sheets, were of particular interest to Tatyana Grosman, founder of Universal Limited Art Editions on Long Island, New York, where Johns first made prints. Papermakers sent their handmade papers—first to her and now to him—for consideration, often in substantial numbers of sheets. Some waited for decades before the appropriate image called for a given sheet, such as a leather paper tried and rejected in 1976 but recently used for an edition. A Fred Siegenthaler "confetti" paper was used for trial proofs of etchings as far back as 1986, and as the mount sheet of an untitled 2011 drawing in acrylic over intaglio.[13] Not until 2016 was this unusual and colorful paper selected for a printed edition in which an especially tall bottom margin highlights the beauty of the sheet (p. 291, pl. 16). Some trials explore a process called *chine collé*, in which a thin sheet, usually of Asian origin, is adhered as part of the image during the printing process, to alter the base paper's hue and texture. Additionally, the subtleties of human touch in inking and printing any matrix produce differences that only a highly refined eye will detect.

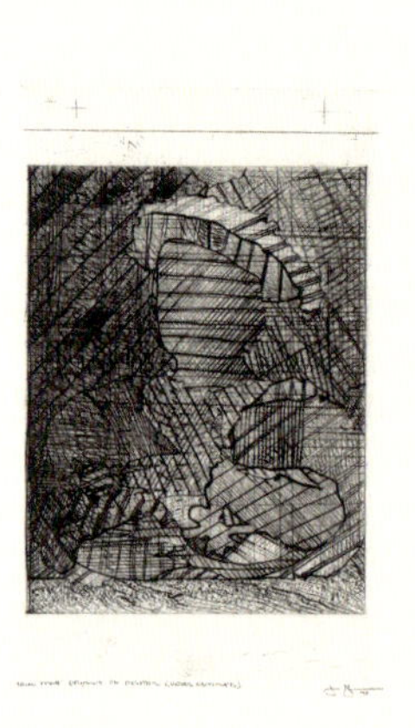

Fig. 5 ***After Holbein*, 1993**
Drypoint, 29 ⅜× 20 ⅞ in. (74.6 × 53 cm). Bill Goldston, Douglas Volle, Bruce Wankel/ULAE. TP. National Gallery of Art, Washington, DC; Patrons' Permanent Fund and Special Friends of the National Gallery of Art, 2010.116.191

Comparing multiple proofs of an image can heighten the details, allowing Johns to reconsider the print's development. Exemplary here are proofs related to three campaigns: the lithograph with embossing *Four Panels from Untitled 1972* (p. 160, pl. 3; p. 162, pls. 5–10; p. 163, pls. 12–16), of which Johns produced a full-color edition as well as one in grays and blacks on handmade gray paper; the screenprint *Usuyuki* (1982), eventually printed on Kurotani Kozo paper, with proofs on other substrates (p. 127, pls. 29, 31); and the vast array of proofs related to the three-panel intaglio *Untitled (Red, Yellow, Blue)*, of which more than sixty reside in the National Gallery of Art archive in Washington, DC (pp. 213–15, pls. 1, 2). The individual panels vary widely not only in hue, but also in the translucency and intensity of each color and whether it was printed in relief (where the surface of the matrix, from which parts of the image are removed, is inked), intaglio (where the lowered areas, bitten away by acid, are inked), or both. Some trial proofs are printed from a single plate, inked both in intaglio and relief. For the edition, where the three segments are printed together, each section is printed from two matrices that are layered onto each other, rather than from one plate as in the proofs. The *Untitled (Red, Yellow, Blue)* motifs reference two paintings from 1963, *Land's End* and *Periscope (Hart Crane)* (p. 182, pls. 5, 6), and print ideas initiated in related works from 1979.[14] Fascinating, too, are Johns's extensions of *Untitled (Red, Yellow, Blue)* made well after the 1998 edition was completed, in which he worked it further with drawing and collage. An example is included in the present exhibition in Philadelphia (pp. 216–17, pl. 3).

Equally provocative, however, is evidence that in 1998, while rethinking the *Land's End* and *Periscope* images from thirty-five years earlier, Johns also was pressing forward, proofing in thirty-two examples a decidedly new motif, American Sign Language (pp. 218–19, pls. 4–15). The signing hands did not take form in finished prints until 2010, however, in a diptych titled *Fragment of a Letter*. It transcribes a fragment from Vincent van Gogh's correspondence, employs hands presenting American Sign Language, and incorporates a handprint that relates to the ones in *Land's End* and *Untitled (Red, Yellow, Blue)*.

The thirty-two untitled proofs, printed from multiple matrices, present large, at times barely recognizable hands, some of them signing, all of them very different from the hand form in *Untitled (Red, Yellow, Blue)*. The edition image to which these proofs are most fully related is *Untitled* of 1998–2015 (p. 293, pl. 25), affirming that Johns's life-long practice of mulling over ideas for periods of many years remains essential to his process.

Johns's working proofs are perhaps the most personal of these records of his printmaking process. These are trials to which the artist has made drawn or painted additions that suggest new thinking about his image. Some may explore options the artist does not necessarily intend to incorporate into the print in progress, but is considering for future work in any medium, including a later edition. Many working proofs convey transformations to areas of paper: additions in collage, areas of the sheet cut away, or the printed image cut from its sheet and mounted on another paper. Media additions include chalk, crayon, colored pencil, charcoal, graphite, ink line and wash, tusche (a greasy liquid used to draw on lithography stones and plates), gouache, acrylic, and watercolor, often in combination.[15] These drawn and painted areas sometimes suggest major changes; other times the additions are technical annotations to aid the printer's work. Like all the proofs, they remain long after an edition is finished, available for the artist to study when he revisits an idea, supported by his long history of retaining plates, stones, and screens for possible reuse at a later time.

Progressive proofs are made when an image is complete, documenting the printing process used to create the edition version. In theory, the first proof in the progression would carry one color, the second two colors, the fifth five colors, and so on. It is possible, however, to print more than one color in a single operation, so the fifth progressive proof might carry six or seven colors. Each progressive state would provide accurate sequencing data.

Johns also has created unique works on paper by layering drawing and painting upon a printed base.[16] More than eighty such works were documented in 2010, with, in some instances, more than two decades separating the creation of the print and Johns's additions to it by hand. The materials employed in these works are collage, oil, encaustic, acrylic, gouache, pastel, chalk, crayon, pigment stick, carborundum wash, watercolor, ink, and graphite, often in combination, as is true for his working proofs. The printed base sheets may have been impressions he decided not to publish as an edition (or perhaps rejected because of flaws in the printing), trials using paper different from the one selected for the edition, or abandoned for other reasons. These drawings over prints function, however, as another way printmaking plays a critical under-heralded role in Johns's complex and magnificent oeuvre of works on paper. They also celebrate an additional means by which the artist responds to the question "What if?" when making prints.

As artist Mel Bochner recently commented, "Johns has made up more ways of making prints than any one else I can think of."[17]

1 I am grateful to Maureen Pskowski and John Lund in Jasper Johns's studio for their immense assistance; and to Mel Bochner, Jack Cowart, Margo Dolan, Shelley Langdale, and Susan Lorence for conversations while writing this essay. The edition prints to 1993 are documented in Richard S. Field, *The Prints of Jasper Johns, 1960–1993: A Catalogue Raisonné* (West Islip, NY: Universal Limited Art Editions, 1994), with a selection of monotypes included in the supplement. Monotypes through 2015 are documented in Susan Dackerman and Jennifer L. Roberts, *Jasper Johns: Catalogue Raisonné of Monotypes* (New York: Matthew Marks Gallery; New Haven: Yale University Press, 2017). The artist completed an additional 121 monotypes after Dackerman and Roberts went to press, one hundred of which were exhibited at the Museum of Fine Arts, Houston, from September 29, 2019, through February 16, 2020, as *Jasper Johns: 100 Variations on a Theme*, with an eponymous catalogue. For introductory information on printmaking processes, see Anthony Griffiths, *Prints and Printmaking: An Introduction to the History and Techniques* (London: British Museum, 1980).

2 Judith Goldman, *Jasper Johns: Seventeen Monotypes* (West Islip, NY: Universal Limited Art Editions, 1982). Jennifer Roberts affirms that monoprints, printed uniquely from a manipulated matrix, are distinct from monotypes, printed from an image that is painted and/or drawn on a flat surface. Roberts, "The Metamorphic Press: Jasper Johns and the Monotype," in Dackerman and Roberts, *Johns: Catalogue Raisonné of Monotypes*, 26n2. If more than one monotype is made without reworking the surface, those that follow the first are referred to as "ghost images." Dackerman and Roberts do not distinguish between monoprint and monotype, indicating that the distinction is not important to Johns, although many print scholars and most print curators do attend to it.

3 Johns started working at Universal Limited Art Editions (ULAE) in 1960, followed by several other publishing shops, including Gemini G.E.L., Petersburg Press, Simca Print Artists, and Johns's Connecticut-based Low Road Studio, where printer John Lund has worked with the artist since 1995. At each of these studios, craftsmen and craftswomen have transferred Johns's marks from the matrices to the paper. Throughout history, many artists have printed their own matrices. Those of Johns's generation follow in the footsteps of Stanley William Hayter and Robert Blackburn, whose Atelier 17 and Printmaking Workshop, respectively, were community shops where artists both created matrices and printed them. Blackburn was the first printer at ULAE, collaborating with Johns on his first dozen lithographs.

4 Another figure of Johns's generation of landmark importance in this regard is Helen Frankenthaler, who produced hundreds of proofs for more than three hundred editions and monotypes. However, proofs functioned very differently for her than they do for him.

5 Two exhibition catalogues by Richard Field—*Jasper Johns: Prints, 1960–1970* (Philadelphia: Philadelphia Museum of Art, 1970) and *Jasper Johns: Prints, 1970–1977* (Middletown, CT: Wesleyan University, 1978)—are landmarks in the field of print scholarship. The Wesleyan exhibition circulated to venues throughout the United States. Christian Geelhaar's *Jasper Johns: Working Proofs*, exh. cat. (London: Petersburg, 1980) was the first of many useful studies; Elizabeth C. DeRose, *Jasper Johns: From Plate to Print*, exh. cat. (New Haven: Yale University Art Gallery, 2006) documents *Untitled* (1999) and its related proofs and the copperplates from which they were printed, all in Yale's collection.

6 During the 2000s, when the National Gallery of Art in Washington, DC, acquired Johns's archive of approximately 1,700 proofs, the artist indicated to this writer that he viewed each sheet both individually and as a part of and contribution to the related edition.

7 Two exhibitions of proofs have been held at the National Gallery of Art in the 2000s, one of them accompanied by a brochure: Ruth Fine, *States and Variations: Prints by Jasper Johns* (Washington, DC: National Gallery of Art, 2007).

8 For Johns's first *Untitled* monotype, see Dackerman and Roberts, *Johns: Catalogue Raisonné of Monotypes*, 32, 33, and 287. Its process encompassed folding, incising, blotting, and impressing, all of which later became essential to Johns's art.

9 Notable exceptions are *Decoy* (1971; p. 291, pl. 14), *Decoy II* (1971–73); and *Untitled (Red, Yellow, Blue)* (1998).

10 See Field, *Prints of Jasper Johns, 1960–1993*, nos. 17–19 (one entry for each portfolio of ten lithographs). The third portfolio incorporates a second stone in some of the prints.

11 A cancellation proof implies that a matrix will not be used again.

12 Interviews by Susan Lorence with printers who worked extensively with Johns are published in Susan Brundage, ed., *Technique and Collaboration in the Prints of Jasper Johns*, exh. cat. (New York: Leo Castelli Gallery, 1996).

13 The drawing is currently in the artist's collection. See Menil Collection, ed., *Jasper Johns: Catalogue Raisonné of Drawing* (Houston: Menil Collection, 2018), 5:254, no. D777.

14 These include a *Land's End* etching (ULAE 197) published by Petersburg Press and a lithograph of that title (ULAE 199; p. 296, pl. 36) published by Gemini G.E.L., as well as the *Periscope I* (ULAE 200; p. 297, pl. 43) and *II* (ULAE 201) lithographs, both published by Gemini G.E.L.

15 Media designations here and in the discussion of drawings over proofs below echo the artist's annotations.

16 See Pepe Karmel, *Jasper Johns: Drawing Over*, exh. cat. (New York: Leo Castelli, 2010). Karmel's essay, "Cancellation/Creation, Jasper Johns: Drawing over Prints," addresses the artist's proofs as well.

17 Mel Bochner, telephone conversation with the author, December 28, 2019.

Reveries

At the start of the 1980s, something broke loose in Jasper Johns's art. He had spent much of the previous decade systematically exploring the visual and conceptual possibilities of his abstract crosshatches in primary and secondary colors or in muted pastels and foggy grisaille. Suddenly, a profusion of perplexing images and heightened emotion flooded his works. In contrast to his earlier found objects and common motifs, this imagery derived from disparate art histories and popular sources, including fragments of Matthias Grünewald's and Barnett Newman's art, a Nepalese tantric gouache, George Ohr's ceramics, perceptual diagrams, a reproduction of the *Mona Lisa*, and a vase commemorating Queen Elizabeth II's Silver Jubilee. The references were the most overtly personal of Johns's career to date, their combination suggesting an enigmatic form of self-portraiture. Some, such as the Newmans and Ohrs, are objects he collected, while a photograph of his art dealer Leo Castelli points to a lifelong friendship. Johns's own spectral shadow enters the paintings, prints, and drawings related to the Seasons (1985–86; pp. 180–81, pls. 3, 4; p. 190, pls. 7, 8), while other canvases, including *In the Studio* (1982; p. 235, pl. 13) and *Untitled* (1983; p. 243, pl. 12), are set in the intimate interiors in which he worked and even bathed. Now in his fifties and sixties, Johns seemed confident in breaking the rules he had set for himself decades prior and also alive to the work of younger artists associated with appropriation and the referential postmodernism of the day.[1]

To hold his motley new lexicon, Johns opened the space of his canvases as never before, and, for the first time in his painting, rendered three-dimensional images directly rather than imprinting or transposing them from the world. Perspectival illusionism, previously restricted almost exclusively to his graphic work, along with chiaroscuro and stark shadows create a newfound, if equivocal, sense of depth. Harking back to the semiotic inquiries of his 1960s paintings, he counterposed disparate techniques and sign systems but now within a unified gestalt that is all the more uncanny for the multitude it contains. Sometimes found images pile atop the canvas or paper as though tacked to a board. These pictures within pictures appear to be painted on swaths of fabric or printed on a page, an illusion heightened by trompe l'oeil nails and bits of masking tape. But often faint schematic tracery, watercolor bleeds, and encaustic drools dissolve an image into the picture plane, which itself gives way to emptiness or celestial whorls. The merging of identifiable and indecipherable imagery within improbably coherent spaces that likewise straddle the real and the irrational lends these works a sense of unconscious imagining.

If the rebus-like mash-ups of elements in Johns's earlier agglomerative paintings invite us to unpuzzle modes of making, looking, and thinking, his hybrid compositions of the 1980s and 1990s conjure a realm of symbolic association and reverie. Physiognomic features and dismembered limbs, rendered or cast in wax, dangle and drift across grounds that evoke the heavens, speckled with galaxies and stars. The woman's profile from Pablo Picasso's *Straw Hat with Blue Leaves* (1936; p. 248, fig. 4) appears repeatedly, as do her disembodied eyes, which attach themselves to the edges of a painting or drawing, so that it becomes a goofy face peering in on itself. A talismanic form dubbed the Green Angel recurs in precise contours that suggest a specific but mysterious source, which Johns has refused to identify in a rebuff to iconologists and an invitation to our imaginative projection. The invocation of a spiritual being in the figure's name alone brings the specters of religion and the occult to these works. They also betray a Surrealist fascination with the unconscious, evident in their irrational space and imagery, which in some cases prominently includes an off-kilter face copied from a drawing by a schizophrenic child. Color takes on a new dimension with richly saturated hues in often jangly combinations. In related pastels, watercolors, and monotypes, Johns's semitransparent materials allow light to reverberate off the paper support, suffusing his surfaces with a dreamy effulgence.

Johns's rekindled expressionism of this period could also turn nightmarish. He treated many of the same motifs in a fuliginous palette, irradiated by caustic lines and passages of purple, red, and green. Black handprints anxiously impress some surfaces, while simplified skulls appear as deracinated emblems of mortal peril or in the motif of a poster warning of falling ice. References to John Cage's composition for prepared piano *The Perilous Night* (1944)—an ode, in Cage's words, to the "loneliness and terror" of unhappy love—amplify the grisliness of cast wax forearms afflicted with splotchy ailments.[2] This air of pestilence reverberates in the repeated presence of a tracing of a diseased creature from the Temptation of Saint Anthony in Grünewald's *Isenheim Altarpiece* (1512–16). Although Johns first used tracings from this source in 1981, before the advent of the AIDS crisis, commentators have read the persistence of this motif over the following years as a reference to the pandemic, which ravaged the arts community throughout the 1980s and 1990s and persists today.[3] This contemporary plague tested the bounds of reason and hope, science and faith, and tragically seeped into the lives and art of many of Johns's contemporaries. In other nocturnes, he returned to his most iconic images—ale cans, targets, crosshatches, American flags, and the Savarin can stabbed with his brushes—rendered in dark daubs, slashes, and tempestuous puddles of black ink. In the context of Johns's work from this troubled time, these signature images might be taken as symbolic self-portraits of an artist at middle age, reflecting on his youthful iconography with greater awareness of his own advancing years.

—Scott Rothkopf, with Carlos Basualdo, Sarah B. Vogelman, and Lauren Young

1 Fiona Donovan, *Jasper Johns: Pictures within Pictures, 1980–2015* (London: Thames and Hudson, 2017), 94.

2 John Cage, quoted in Calvin Tompkins, *The Bride and the Bachelors: Five Masters of the Avant-Garde* (New York: Viking, 1968), 97; quoted in Roberta Bernstein, "'A Conversation with Other Paintings': Paintings, 1982–90," in *Jasper Johns: Redo an Eye* (New York: Wildenstein Plattner Institute, 2017), 222.

3 Bernstein, "'Conversation with Other Paintings,'" 227.

Reveries

Dreams

WHITNEY MUSEUM OF AMERICAN ART

1 ***Untitled*, 1987**
Watercolor, ink, and graphite pencil on paper
30 1/8 × 22 1/8 in. (76.5 × 56.2 cm)
Collection of the artist

2 ***The Seasons*, 1989–90**
Acrylic over intaglio on paper
26 1/4 × 57 1/4 in. (66.7 × 145.4 cm)
Collection of Marlene Hess and James D. Zirin

3 ***A Souvenir for Andrew Monk*, 1987**
Pastel, charcoal, graphite pencil, and collage on paper
41 7/8 × 28 in. (106.4 × 71.1 cm)
Collection of Andrew Monk

4 ***Untitled*, 1997**
Oil on canvas
44 × 66 in. (111.8 × 167.6 cm)
Collection of the artist

5 ***Untitled (Leo Castelli)*, 1984**
Encaustic on canvas
13 1/4 × 10 1/2 in. (33.7 × 26.7 cm)
Collection of the artist

6 ***Untitled*, 1991**
Watercolor and graphite pencil on paper
27 1/2 × 41 3/8 in. (69.9 × 105.1 cm)
The Jewish Museum, New York; gift of The Barnett and Annalee Newman Foundation, New York, 2018-39

7 ***Untitled*, 1983–84**
Black ink and colored ink on plastic
24 × 34 3/4 in. (61 × 88.3 cm)
Private collection

8 ***Perilous Night*, 1990**
Watercolor and ink on paper
30 1/2 × 23 1/8 in. (77.5 × 58.7 cm)
Collection of the artist

9 ***The Bath*, 1988**
Encaustic on canvas
48 1/4 × 60 1/4 in. (122.6 × 153 cm)
Kunstmuseum Basel, Switzerland; acquired with a contribution from the Friends of the Kunstmuseum Basel and the Museum of Contemporary Art, G 1988.21

10 ***Montez Singing*, 1989**
Encaustic and sand on canvas
75 × 50 in. (190.5 × 127 cm)
Collection of Marguerite Steed Hoffman

11 ***Untitled*, 1990**
Oil on canvas
18 × 18 in. (45.7 × 45.7 cm)
Collection of the artist

12 ***Untitled*, 1982**
Pastel and graphite pencil on paper
19 7/8 × 10 1/4 in. (50.5 × 26 cm)
Collection of the artist

13 ***In the Studio*, 1982**
Encaustic, crayon, and collage on canvas with objects
72 × 48 in. (182.9 × 121.9 cm)
Collection of the artist; on long-term loan to the Philadelphia Museum of Art, 1984

14 ***Untitled*, 1988***
Watercolor, ink, and graphite pencil on paper
28 × 39 in. (71.1 × 99.1 cm)
The Robert and Jane Meyerhoff Collection

15 ***Untitled*, 1996***
Monotype
39 × 25 in. (99.1 × 63.5 cm)
Collection of Barbara Bertozzi Castelli

16 ***Untitled*, 1991**
Encaustic and sand on canvas
50 7/8 × 35 1/2 in. (129.2 × 90.2 cm)
The Eli and Edythe L. Broad Collection

17 ***Untitled*, 1996**
Watercolor and charcoal on paper
37 × 30 in. (94 × 76.2 cm)
Collection of the artist

18 ***Untitled*, 1990**
Pastel on paper
28 × 21 in. (71.1 × 53.3 cm)
Collection of the artist

19 ***Untitled (Bruno Bettelheim)*, 1995**
Acrylic over mezzotint mounted on canvas and acrylic on wood frame
20 1/4 × 13 3/4 in. (51.4 × 34.9 cm)
Collection of Marlene Hess and James D. Zirin

20 ***Untitled*, 1989**
Pastel and graphite pencil on paper
15 1/8 × 14 1/2 in. (38.4 × 36.8 cm)
Collection of the artist

21 ***Untitled*, 1990**
Watercolor and graphite pencil on paper
31 × 22 1/2 in. (78.7 × 57.2 cm)
Collection of the artist

22 ***Untitled*, 1988***
Watercolor, ink, and graphite pencil on paper
31 1/2 × 47 1/2 in. (80 × 120.7 cm)
Collection of Julie and Edward J. Minskoff

23 ***Untitled*, 1990***
Watercolor and graphite pencil on paper
28 × 19 3/8 in. (71.1 × 49.2 cm)
Collection of the artist

Nightmares

PHILADELPHIA MUSEUM OF ART

1 ***Céline*, 1978**
Oil on canvas (two panels)
85 × 48 1/4 in. (215.9 × 122.6 cm) overall
Kunstmuseum Basel, Switzerland; acquired with a contribution from the Max Geldner Foundation in 1979, G 1979.15

2 ***Perilous Night*, 1982**
Encaustic on canvas with objects
67 1/4 × 96 1/8 in. (170.8 × 244.2 cm)
National Gallery of Art, Washington, DC; Robert and Jane Meyerhoff Collection, 1995.79.1

3 ***Untitled*, 1980–84**
Ink, acrylic, and graphite pencil on plastic
21 × 16 in. (53.5 × 40.6 cm)
Collection of the artist

4 ***Untitled*, 1979–84**
Ink, oil, and pastel on plastic
30 × 18 in. (76.2 × 45.7 cm)
Collection of the artist

5 ***Perilous Night*, 1990**
Watercolor and ink on paper
31 × 22 1/2 in. (78.7 × 57.2 cm)
Margaret Leng Tan

6 ***Perilous Night*, 1982**
Black ink and colored ink on plastic
33 5/8 × 43 1/4 in. (85.4 × 109.9 cm)
The Art Institute of Chicago; through prior gift of Mary and Leigh Block; Harold L. Stuart Endowment, 1989.82

7 ***Untitled*, 1983–84**
Watercolor, charcoal, and crayon on two adjoined sheets of paper
45 1/8 × 66 in. (114.6 × 167.6 cm) overall
Aaron I. Fleischman Collection

8 ***Untitled*, 1982**
Ink on paper
17 7/8 × 11 1/8 in. (45.4 × 28.3 cm)
Collection of the artist

9 ***Tantric Detail I*, 1980***
Oil on canvas
50 × 34 in. (127 × 86.4 cm)
The Museum of Modern Art, New York; gift of Donald L. Bryant, Jr., and promised gift of Marie-Josée and Henry R. Kravis, 2008

10 ***Tantric Detail II*, 1981***
Oil on canvas
50 × 34 in. (127 × 86.4 cm)
The Museum of Modern Art, New York; gift of Donald L. Bryant, Jr., and promised gift of Marie-Josée and Henry R. Kravis, 2008

11 ***Untitled*, 1983**
Encaustic on canvas (two panels)
30 1/2 × 45 1/4 in. (77.5 × 114.9 cm) overall
Collection of the artist; on long-term loan to the Montclair Art Museum, New Jersey, 2014

12 ***Untitled*, 1983**
Encaustic and collage on canvas with objects
48 1/8 × 75 1/8 in. (122.2 × 190.8 cm)
Kravis Collection

13 ***Two Flags*, 1985**
Ink on plastic
26 3/4 × 22 in. (68 × 55.9 cm)
Whitney Museum of American Art, New York; gift of the American Contemporary Art Foundation, Inc., Leonard A. Lauder, President, 2002.240

14 ***Target*, 1992**
Encaustic and collage on canvas
55 × 54 1/8 in. (139.7 × 137.5 cm)
Larry Gagosian

15 ***Savarin*, 1977**
Ink and graphite pencil on plastic
36 1/4 × 26 1/8 in. (92.1 × 66.4 cm)
The Museum of Modern Art, New York; gift of The Lauder Foundation, 1979, 103.1979

16 ***Untitled*, 1984***
Ink and graphite pencil on plastic
28 3/4 × 36 1/4 in. (73 × 92.1 cm)
The Menil Collection, Houston; promised gift of Janie C. Lee

17 ***Ale Cans*, 1978**
Black ink and colored ink on plastic
15 × 16 1/2 in. (38.1 × 41.9 cm)
Collection of the artist

18 ***End Paper*, 1976**
Oil on canvas (two panels)
60 × 69 1/2 in. (152.4 × 176.5 cm) overall
The Museum of Modern Art, New York; gift of Philip Johnson, 1979, 505.1998.a–b

19 ***Usuyuki*, 1981**
Black ink, colored ink, and graphite pencil on plastic
49 1/4 × 18 1/8 in. (125.1 × 46 cm)
Collection of the artist

20 ***Untitled*, 1988**
Ink on plastic
26 1/2 × 19 1/2 in. (67.3 × 49.5 cm)
Collection of the artist

21 ***Untitled*, 1988***
Ink on plastic
26 1/2 × 19 1/2 in. (67.3 × 49.5 cm)
Collection of the artist

22 ***Periscope*, 1977***
Ink, watercolor, and graphite pencil on plastic
36 ⅜ × 27 ⅞ in. (92.4 × 70.8 cm)
The Menil Collection, Houston; bequest of David Whitney

Dreams

WHITNEY MUSEUM OF AMERICAN ART

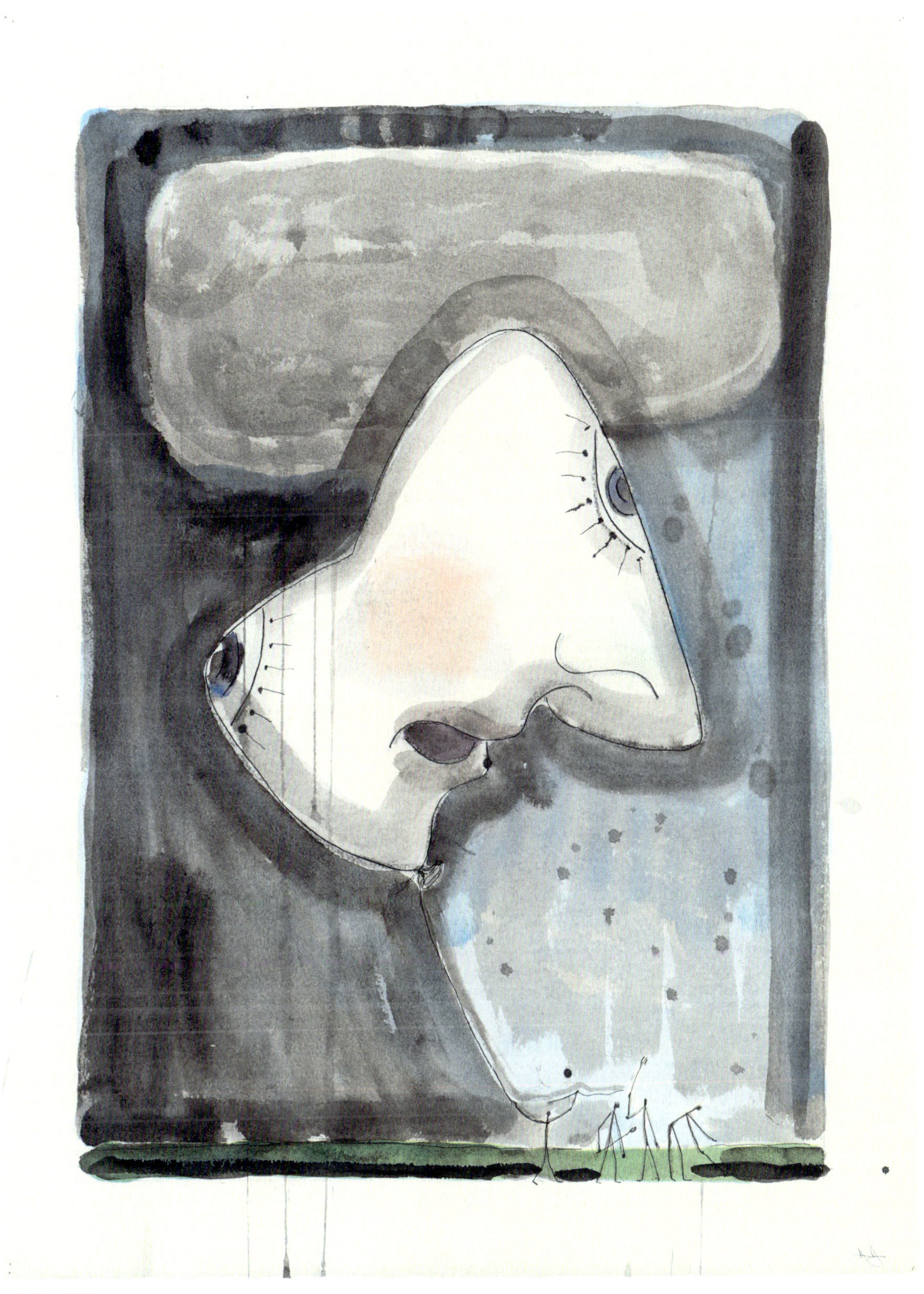

1 *Untitled*, 1987

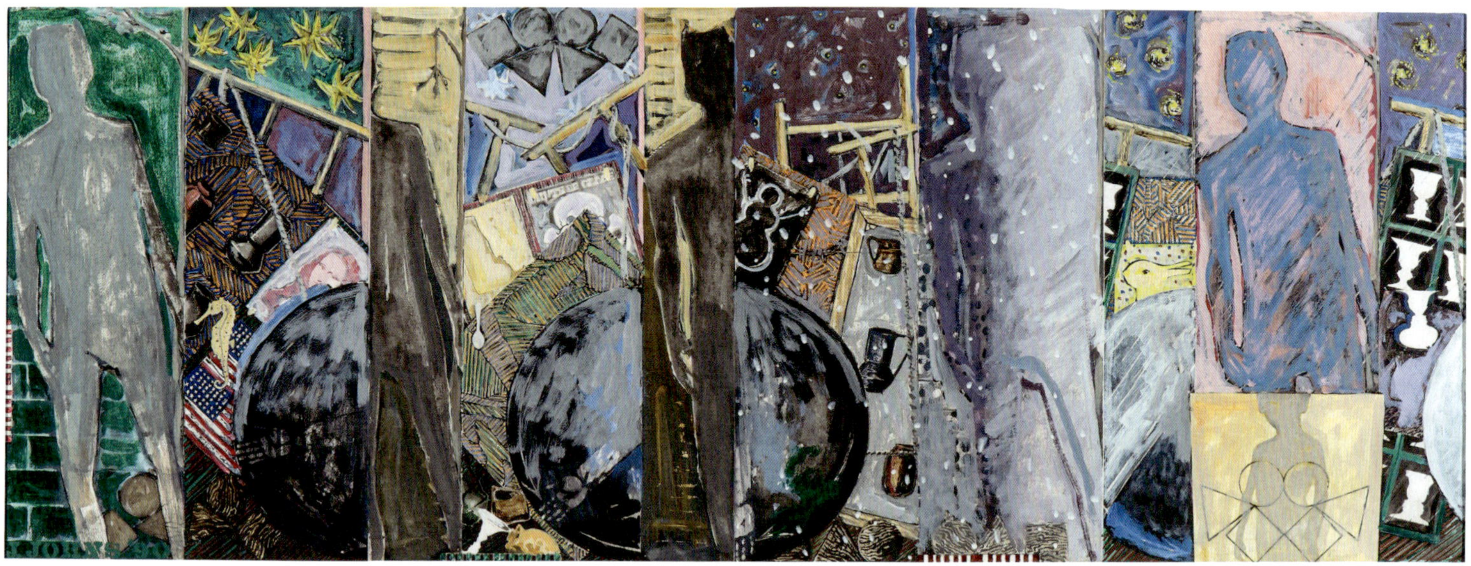

2 *The Seasons*, 1989–90

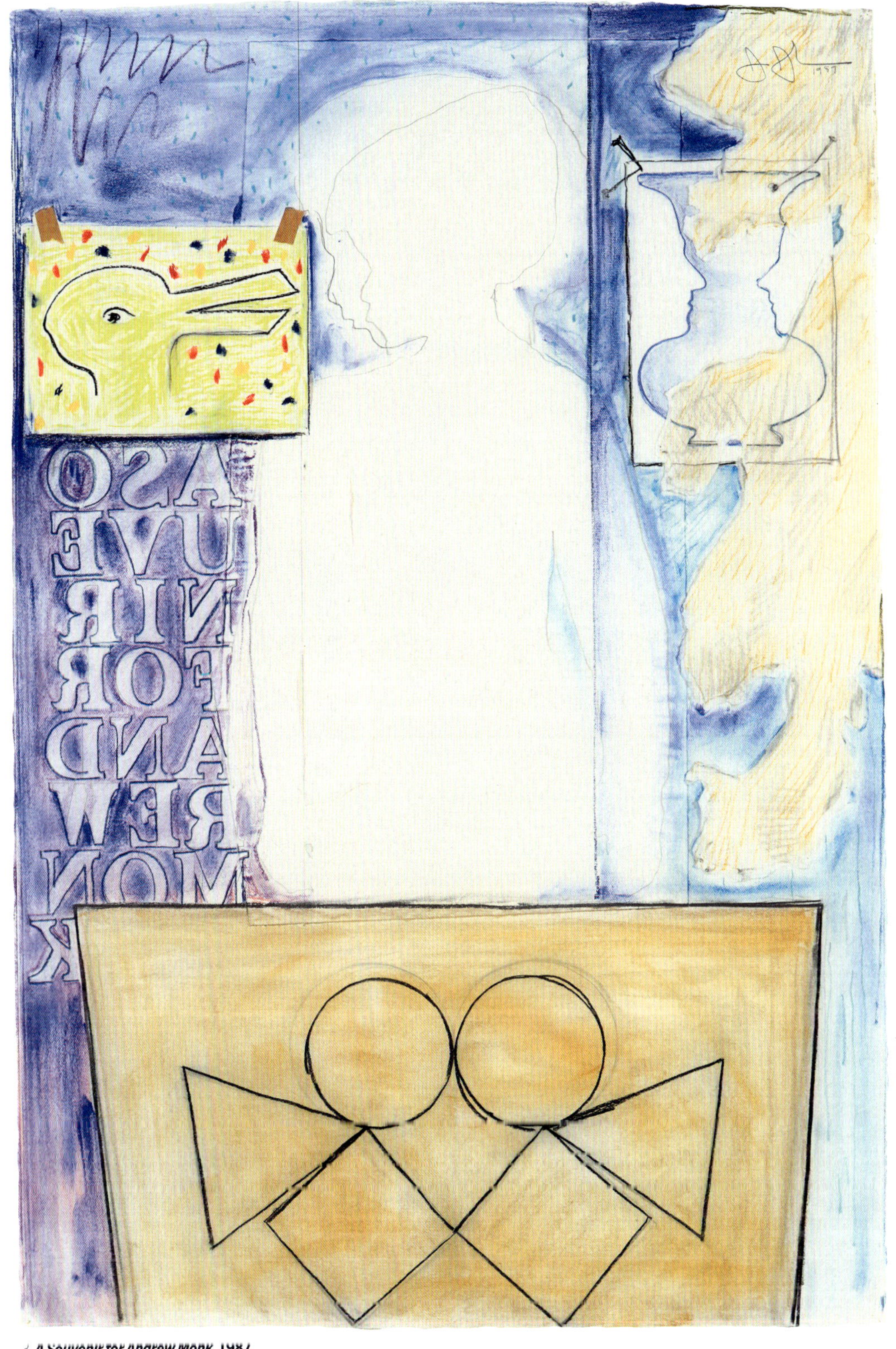

3 ***A Souvenir for Andrew Monk*, 1987**

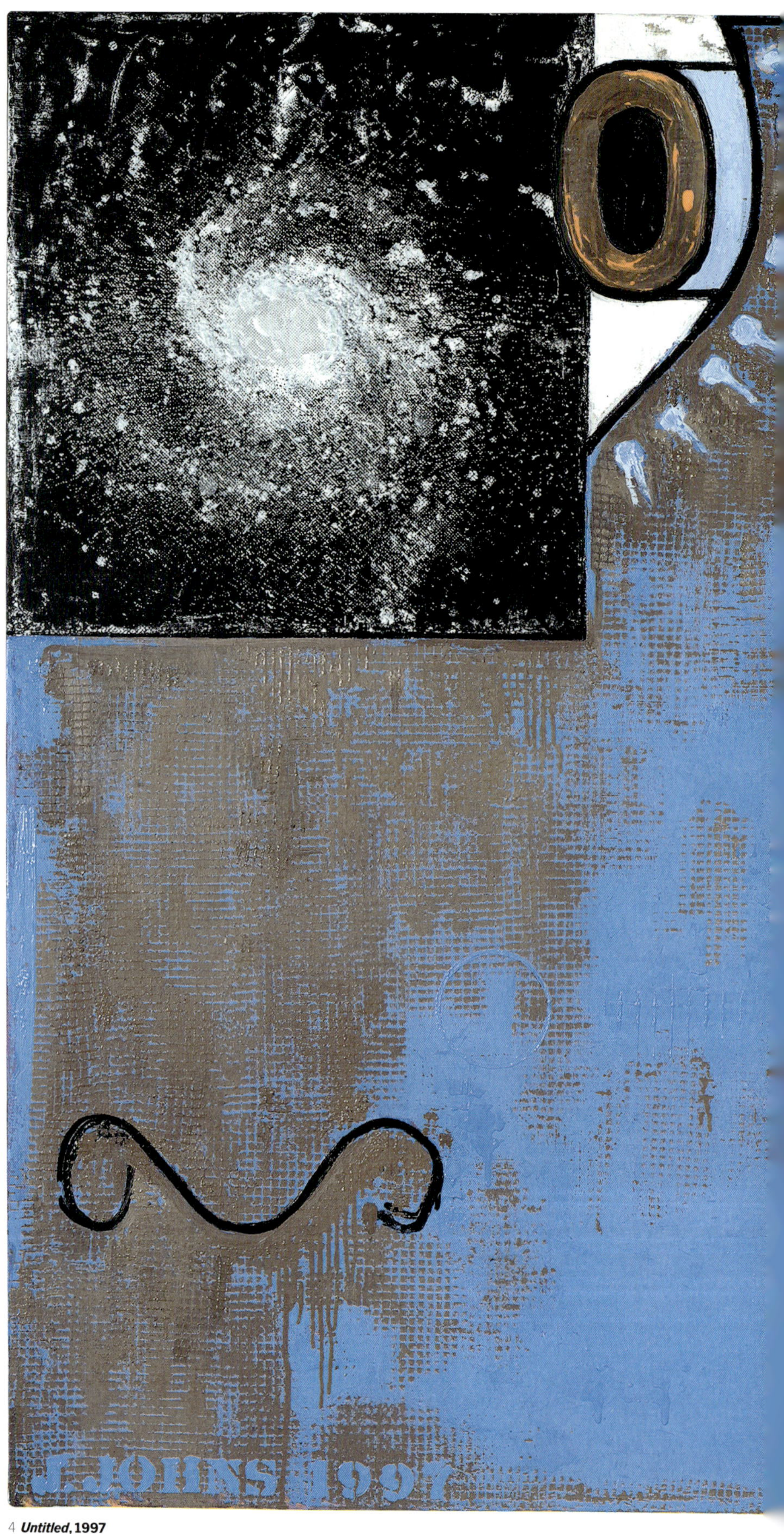

4 ***Untitled***, **1997**

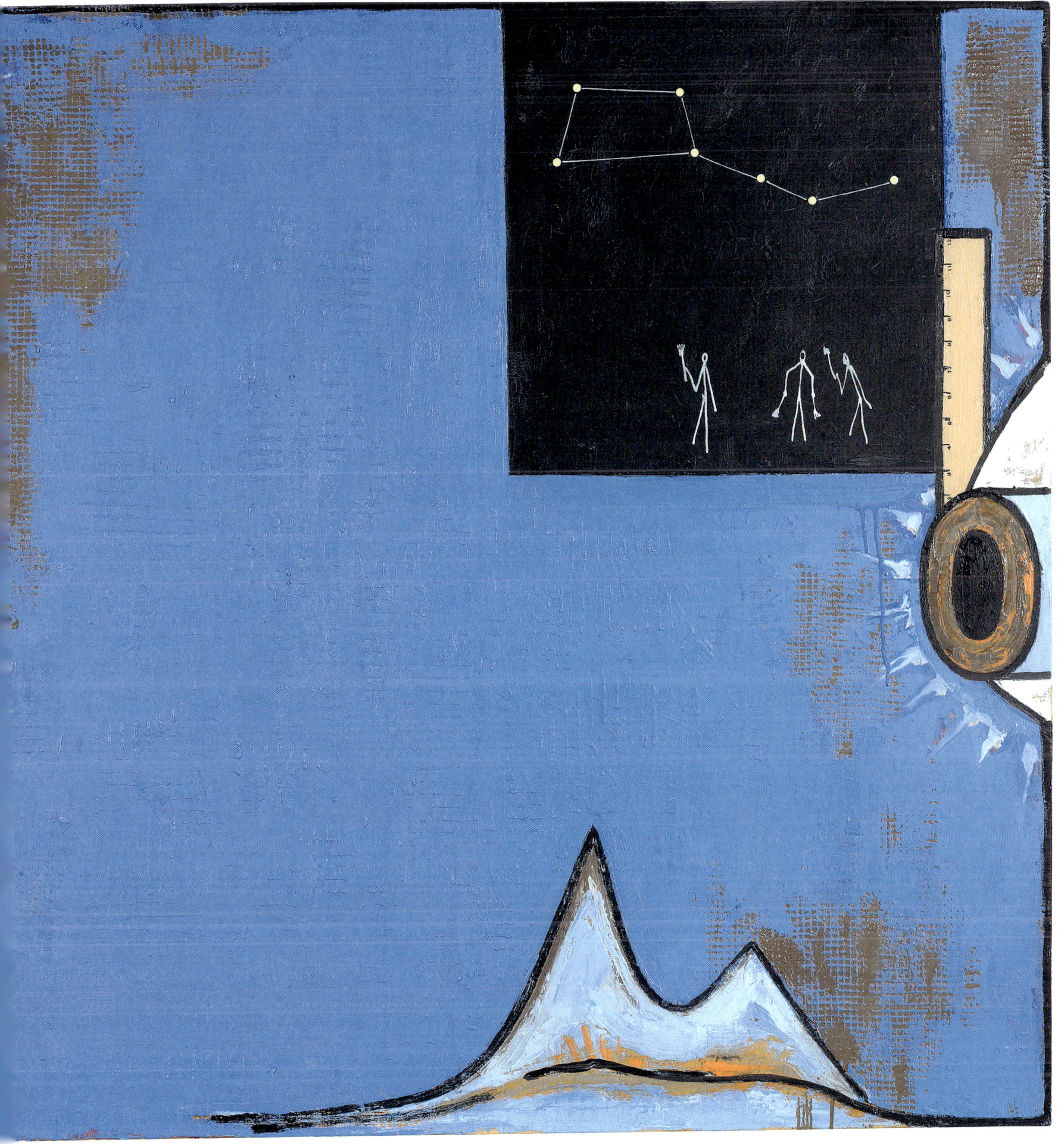

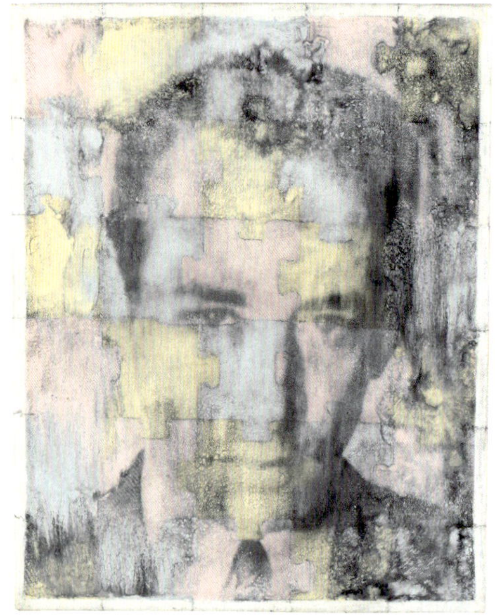

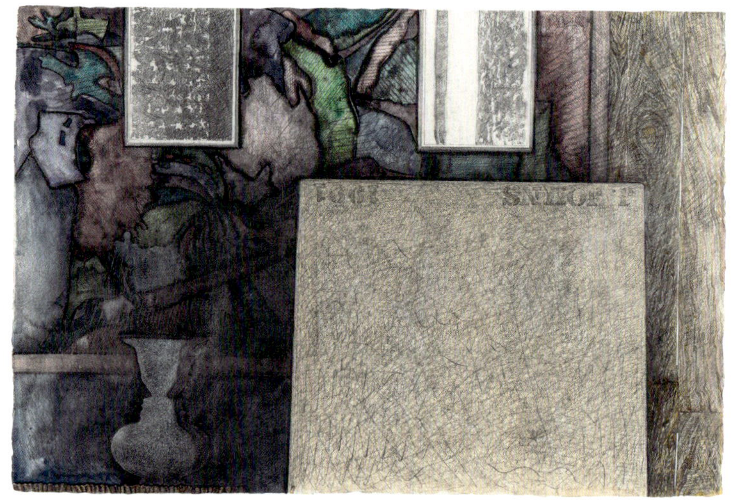

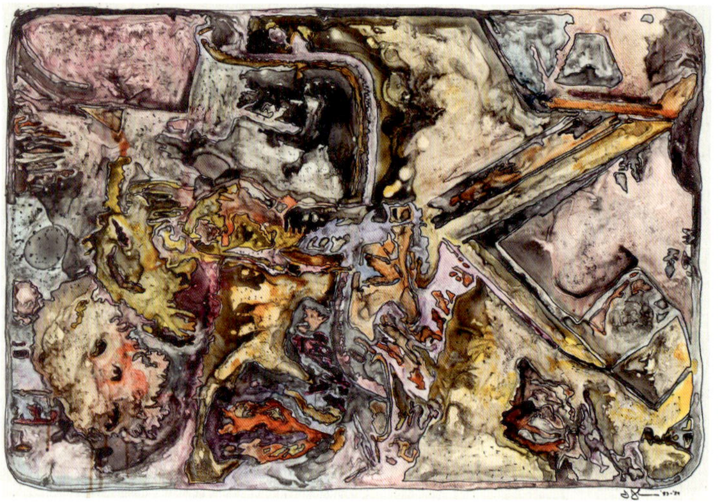

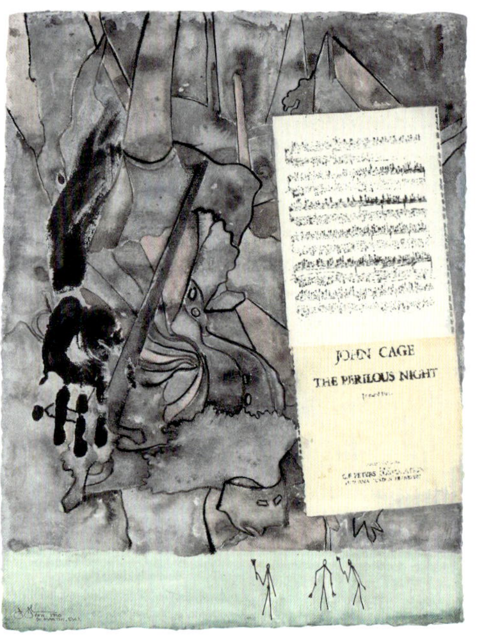

5 ***Untitled (Leo Castelli)*, 1984**
7 ***Untitled*, 1983–84**

6 ***Untitled*, 1991**
8 ***Perilous Night*, 1990**

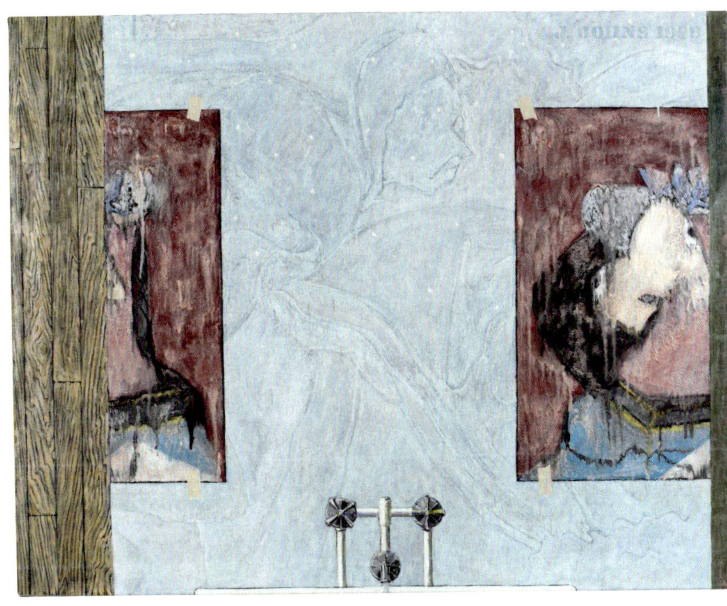

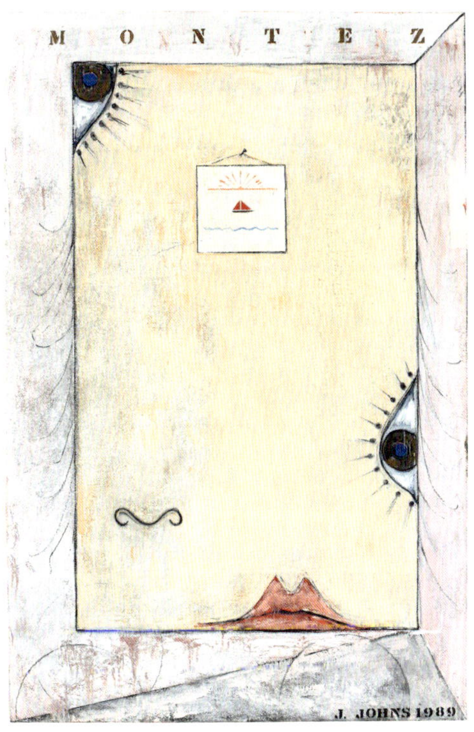

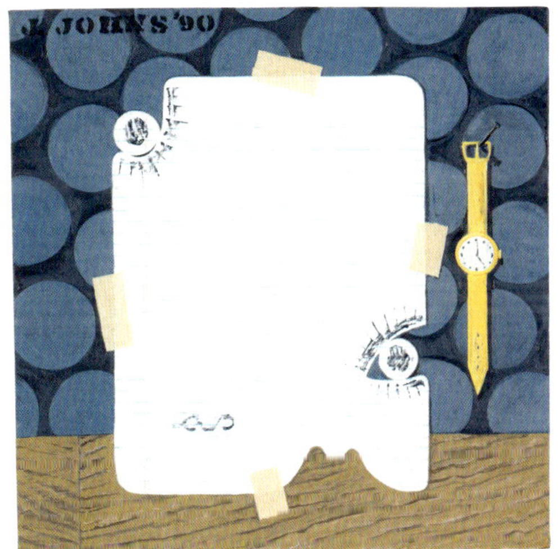

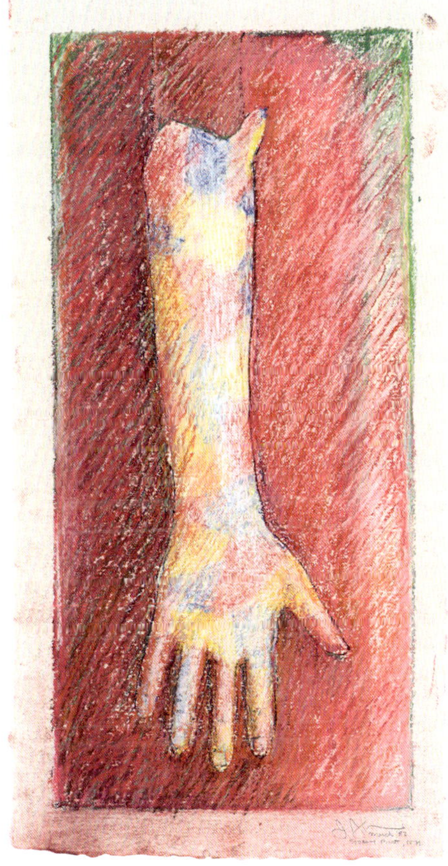
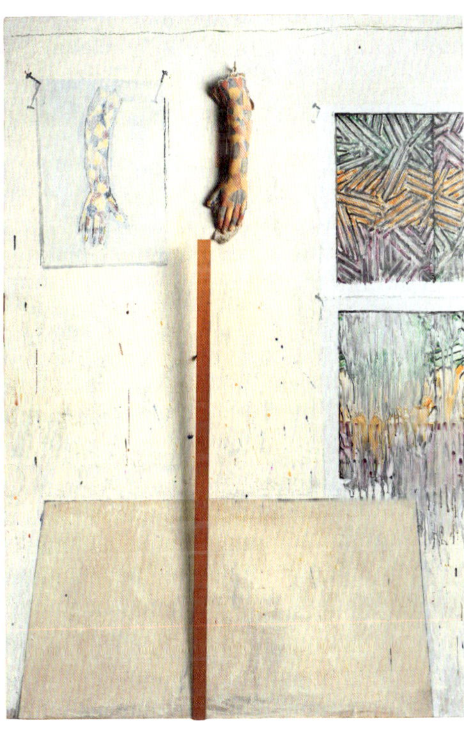

9 *The Bath*, 1988
11 *Untitled*, 1990

10 *Montez Singing*, 1989
12 *Untitled*, 1982
13 *In the Studio*, 1982

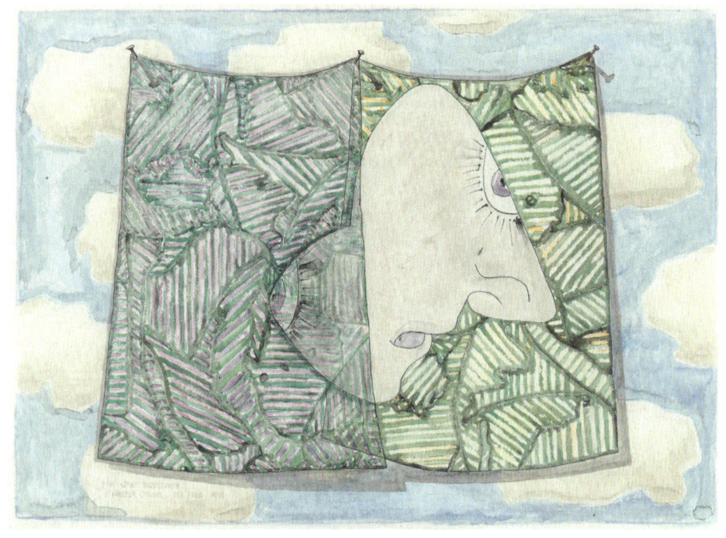

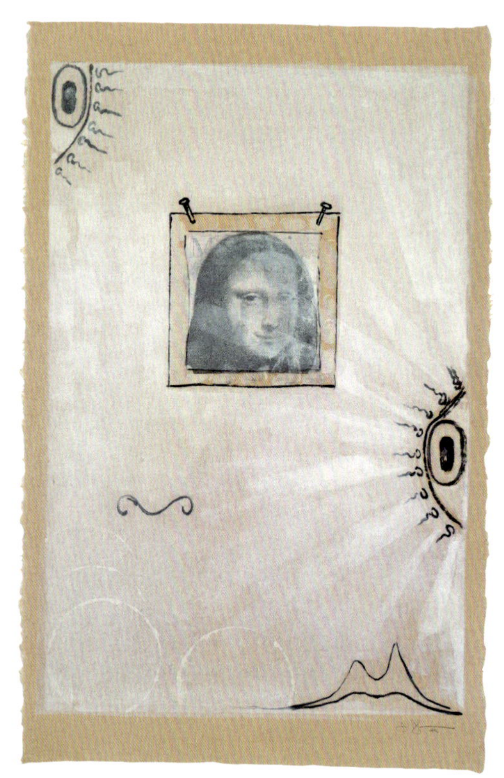

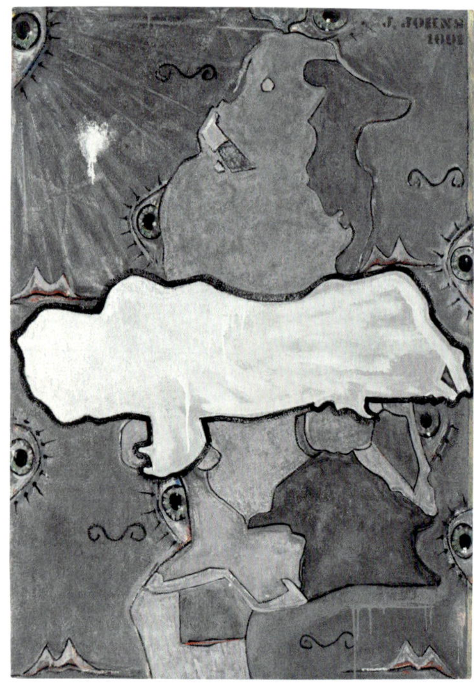

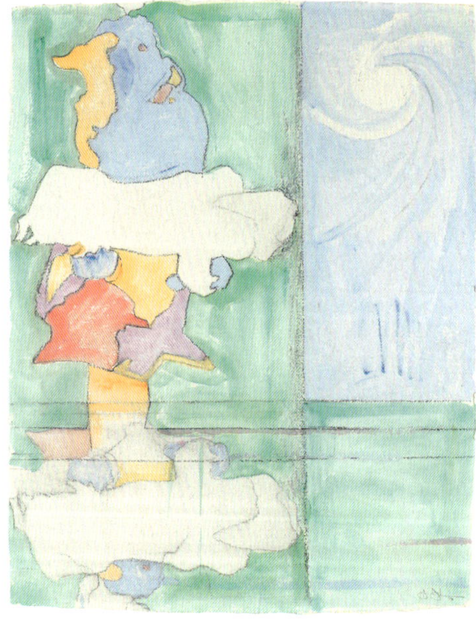

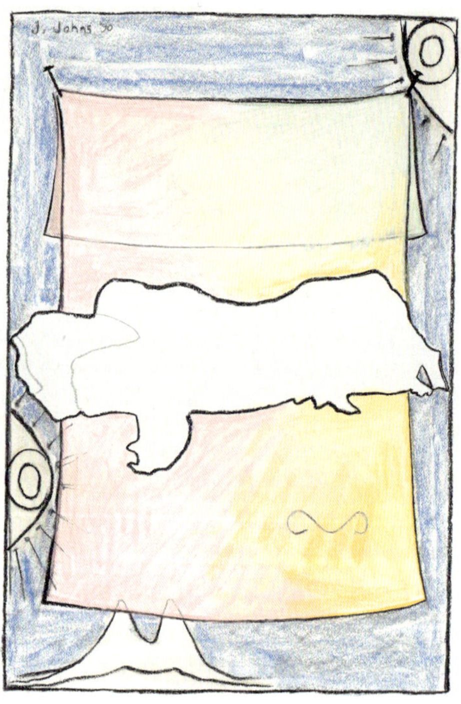

14 ***Untitled*, 1988**
16 ***Untitled*, 1991**

15 ***Untitled*, 1996**
17 ***Untitled*, 1996**

18 ***Untitled*, 1990**

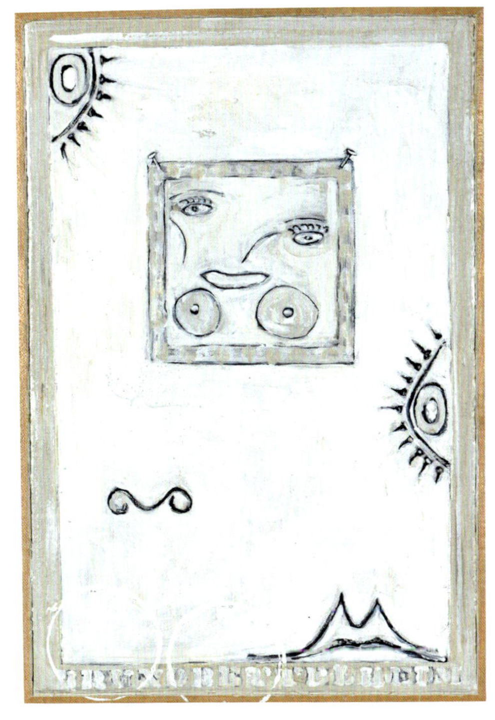

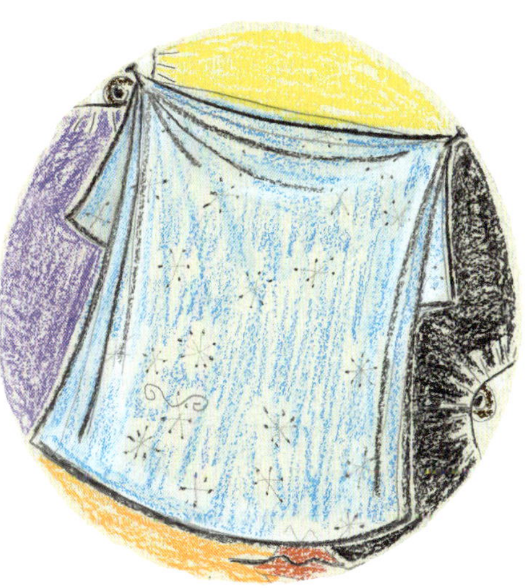

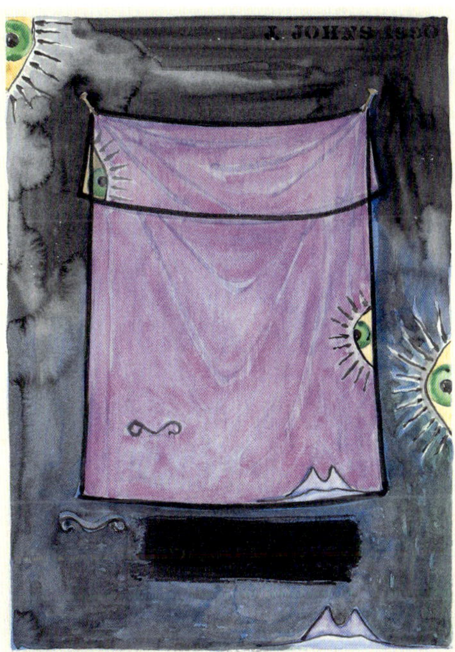

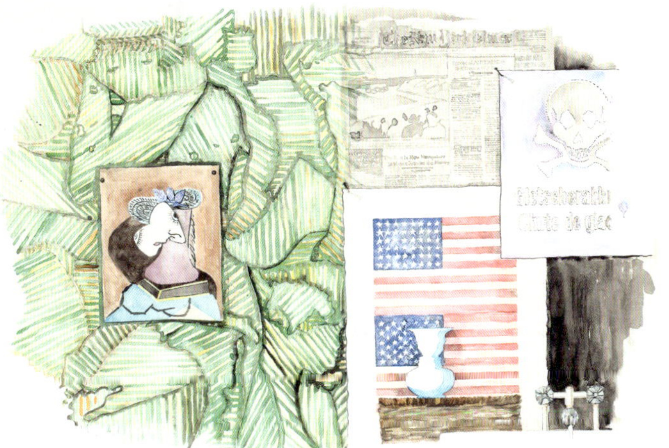

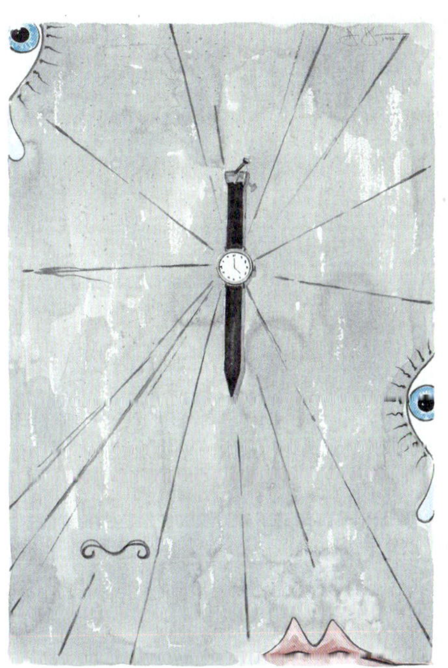

19 ***Untitled (Bruno Bettelheim)*, 1995**
22 ***Untitled*, 1988**

20 ***Untitled*, 1989**
23 ***Untitled*, 1990**

21 ***Untitled*, 1990**

Nightmares

PHILADELPHIA MUSEUM OF ART

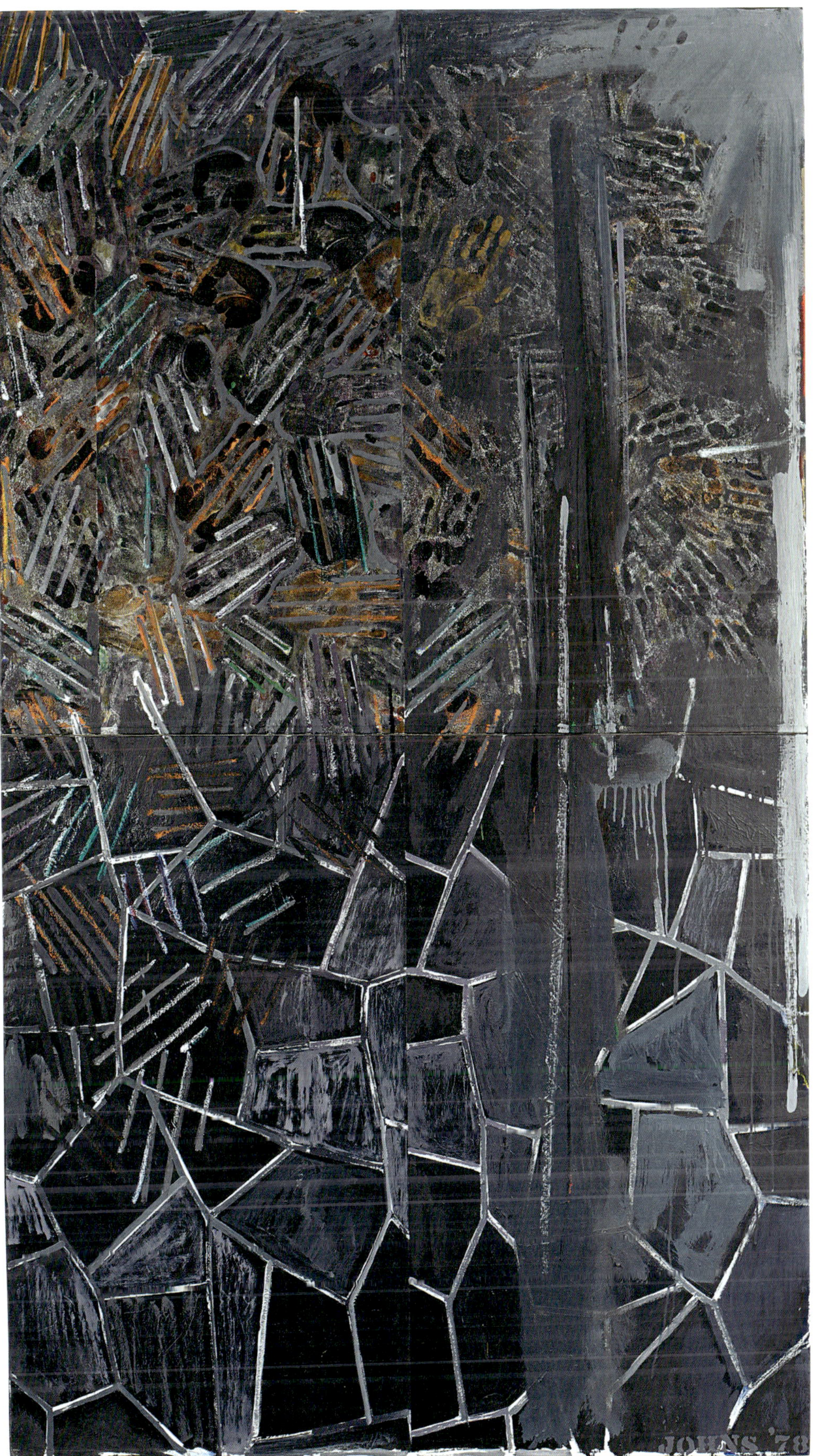

1 ***Céline*, 1978**

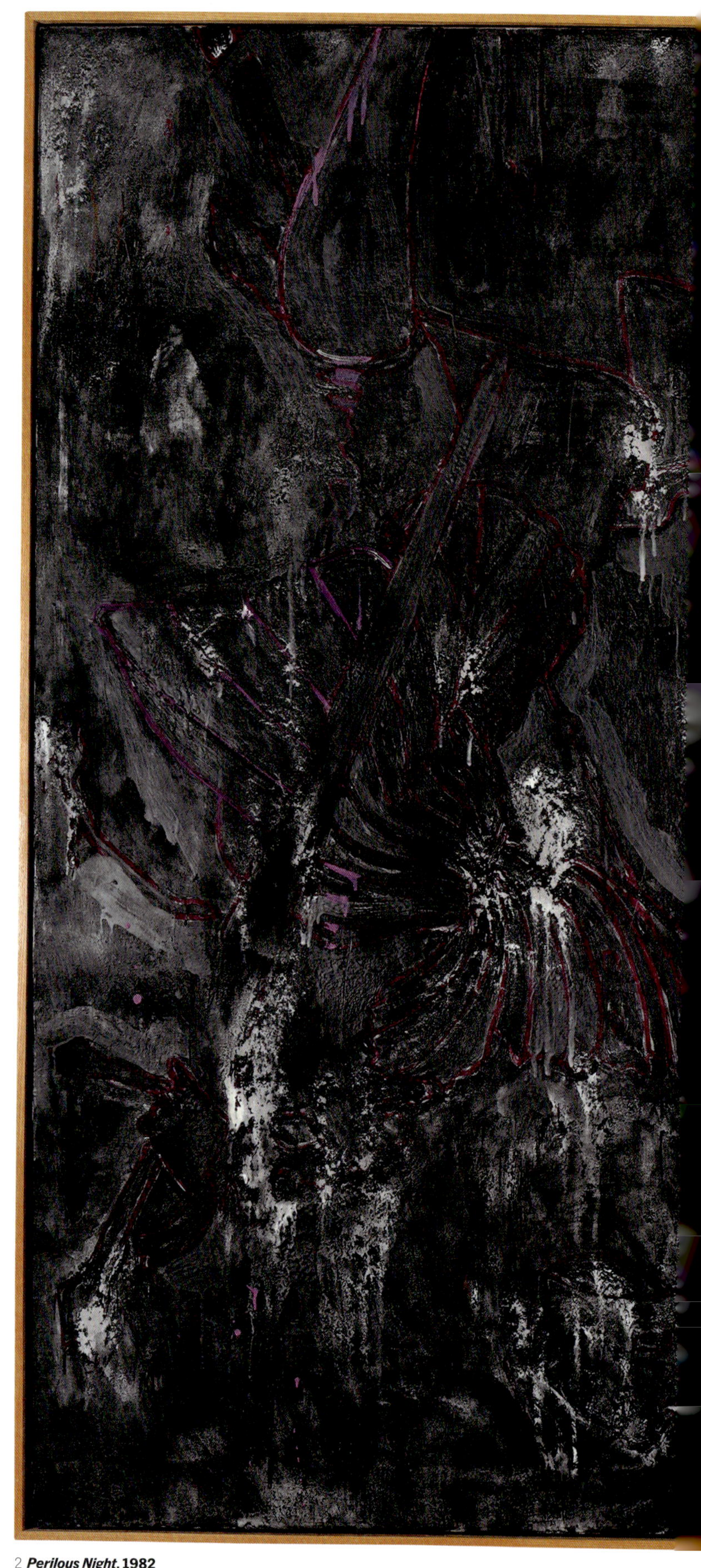

2 ***Perilous Night*, 1982**

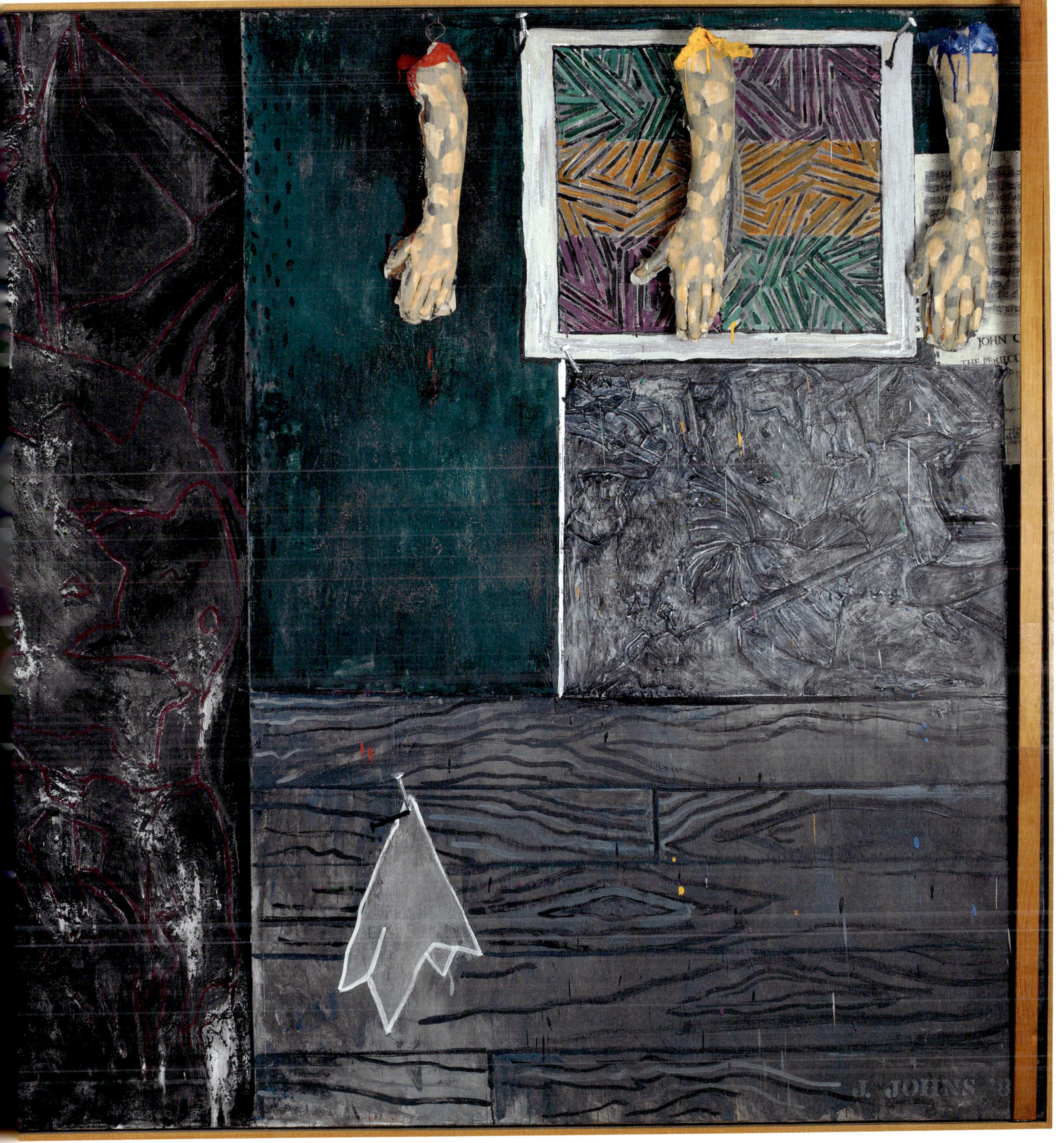
J. JOHNS

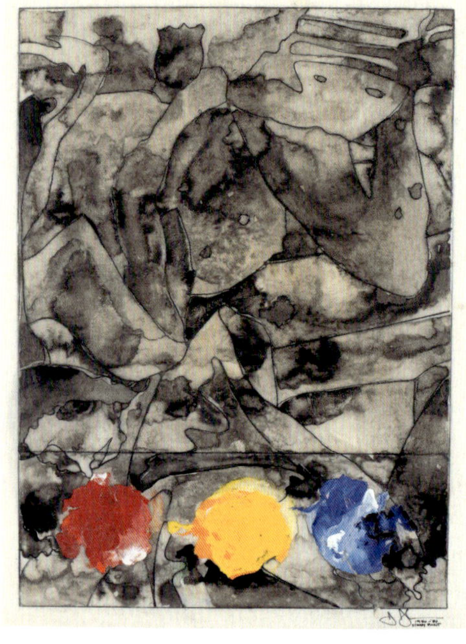

3 ***Untitled***, **1980–84**

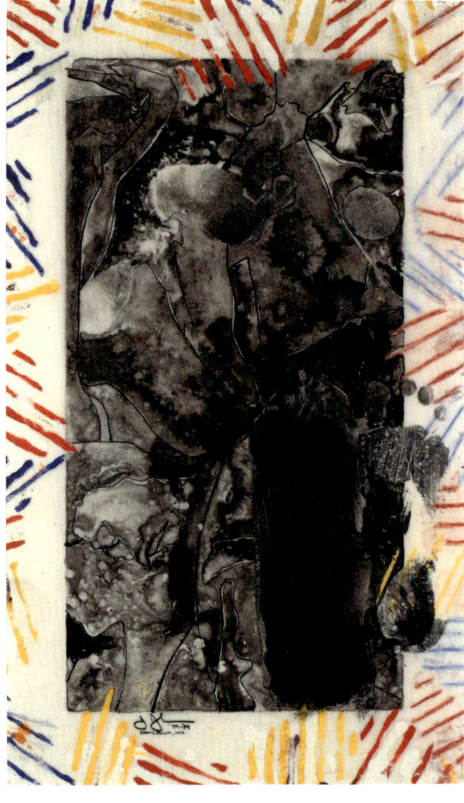

4 ***Untitled***, **1979–84**

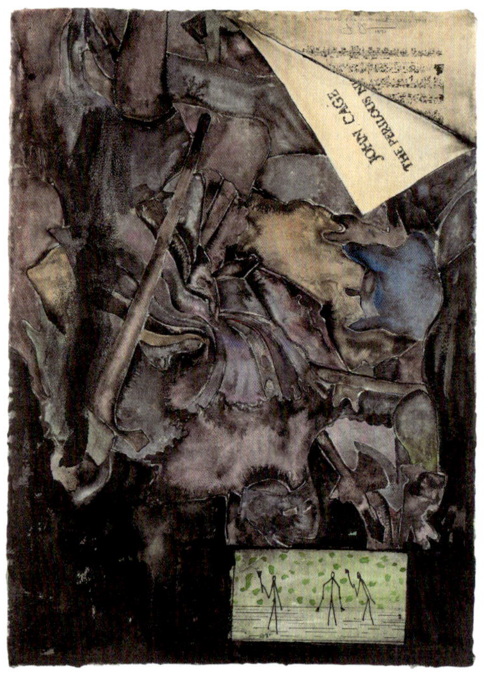

5 ***Perilous Night***, **1990**

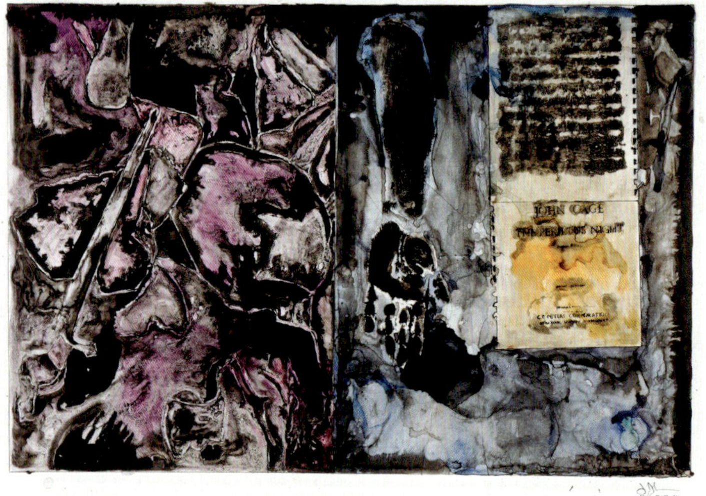

6 ***Perilous Night***, **1982**

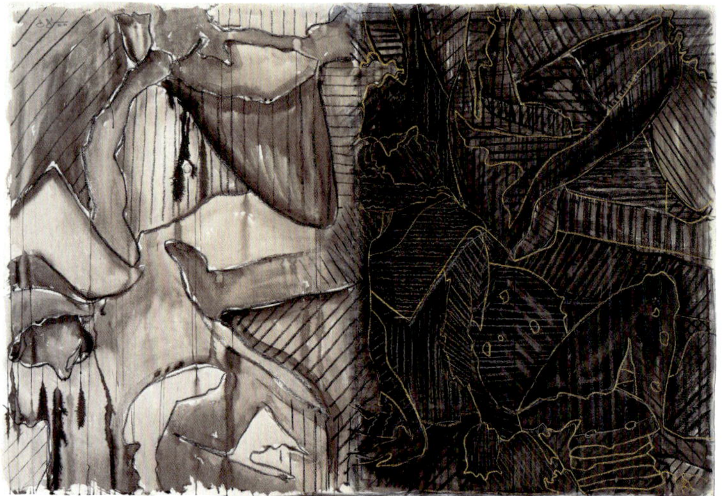

7 ***Untitled***, **1983–84**

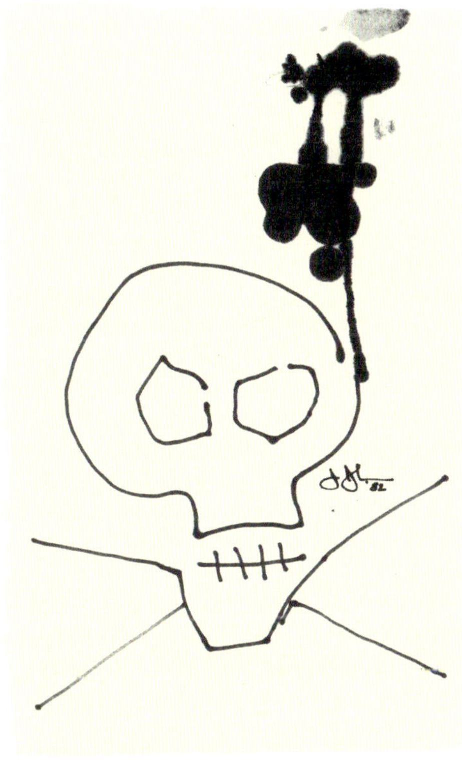

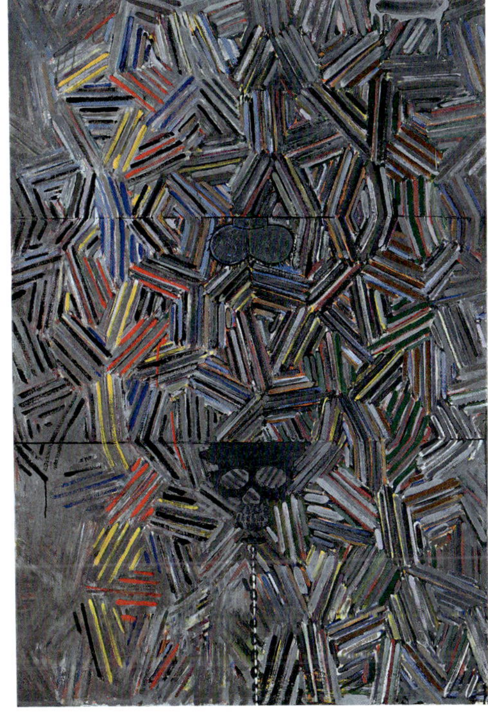

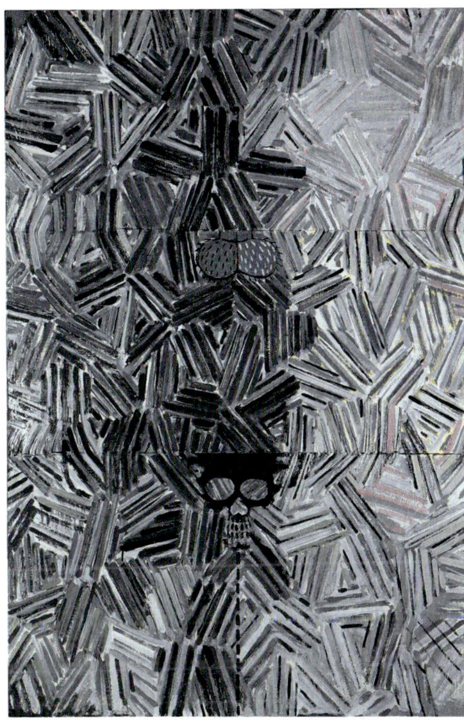

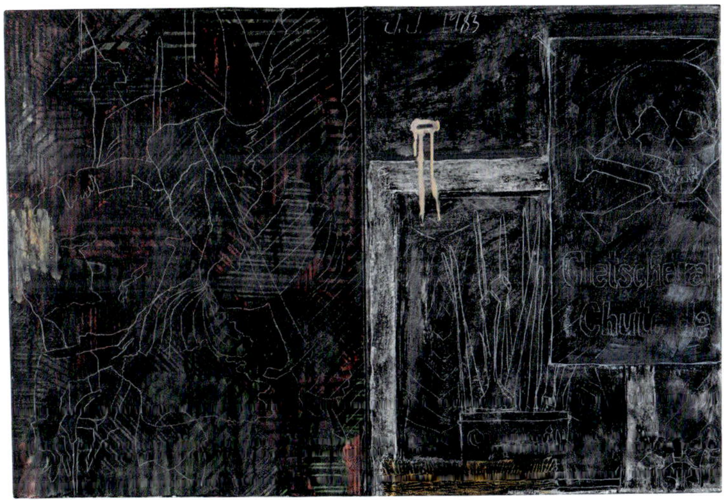

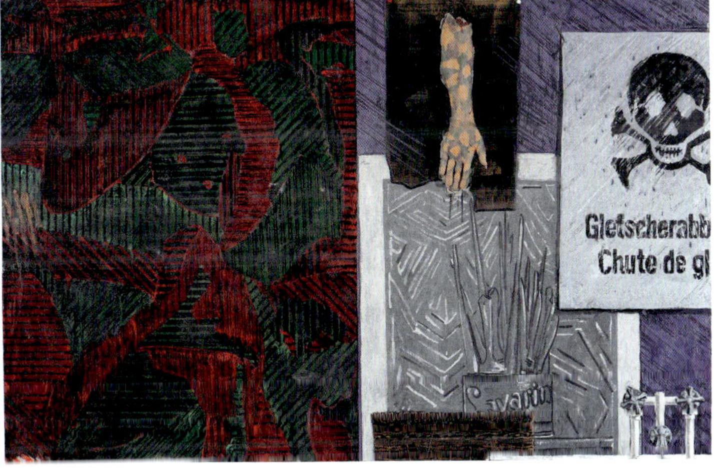

8 ***Untitled*, 1982**
11 ***Untitled*, 1983**

9 ***Tantric Detail I*, 1980**
12 ***Untitled*, 1983**

10 ***Tantric Detail II*, 1981**

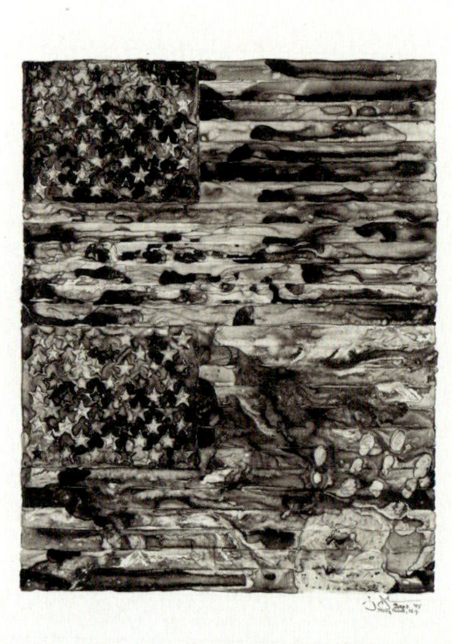

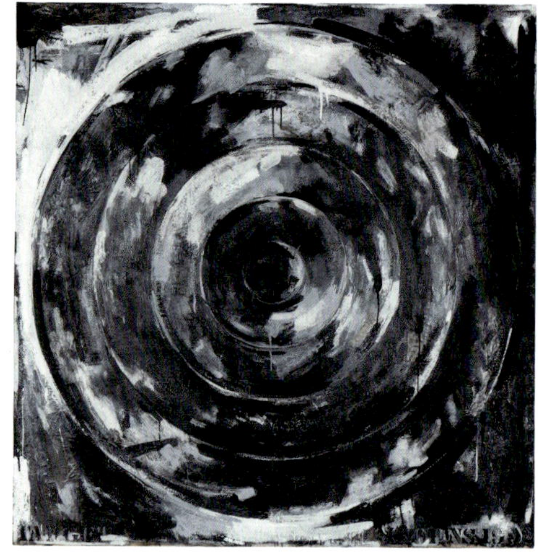

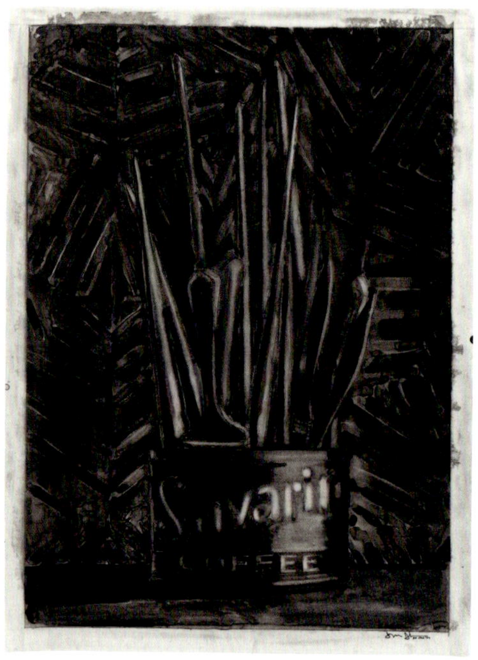

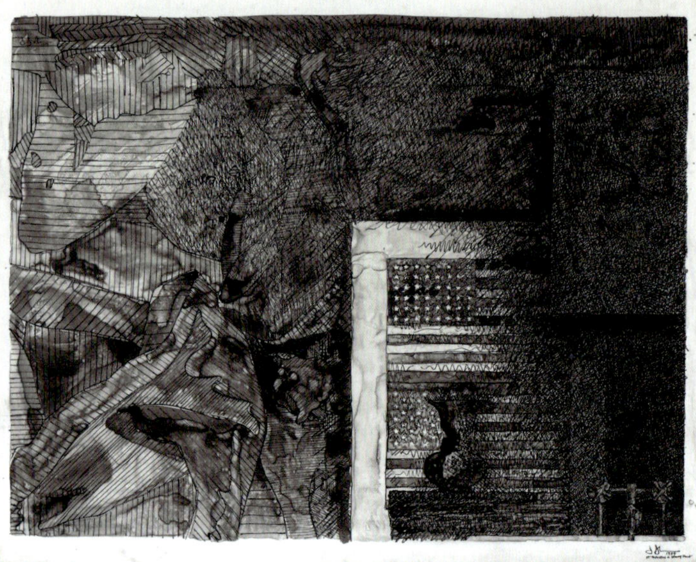

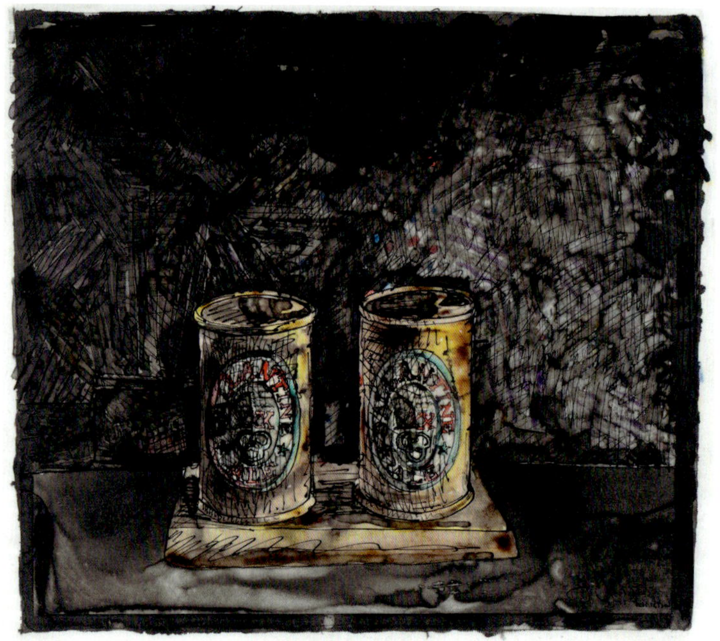

13 ***Two Flags*, 1985**
16 ***Untitled*, 1984**

14 ***Target*, 1992**
17 ***Ale Cans*, 1978**

15 ***Savarin*, 1977**

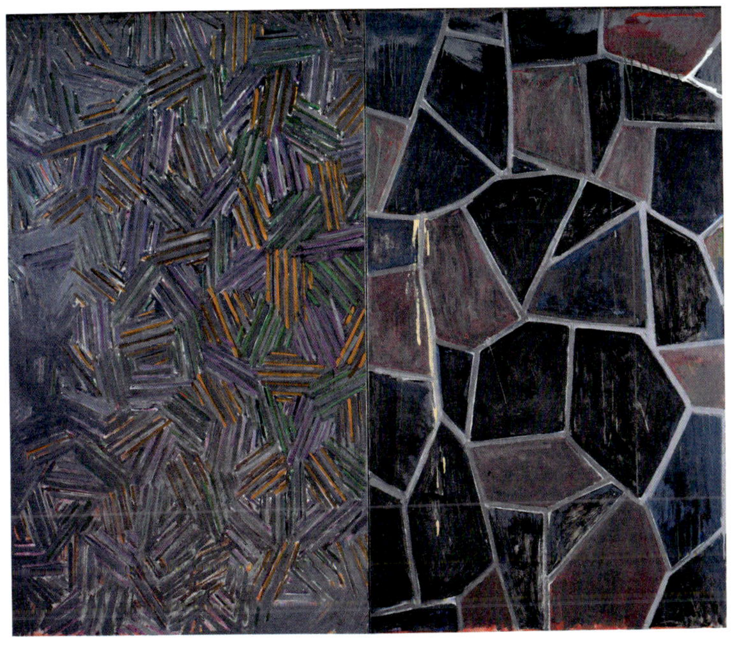

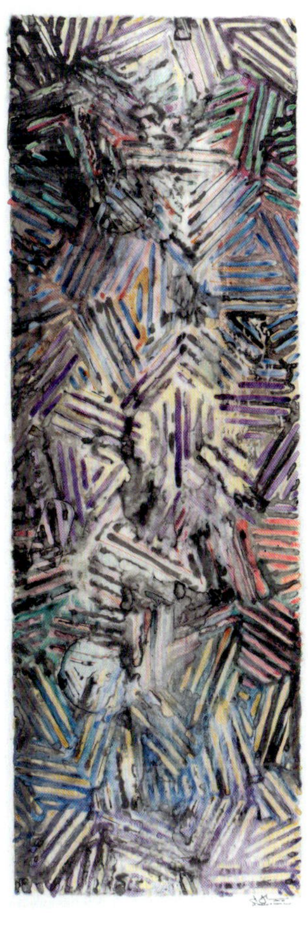

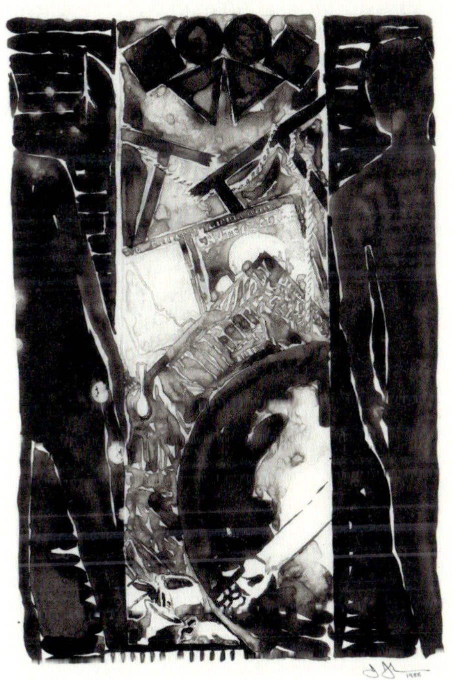

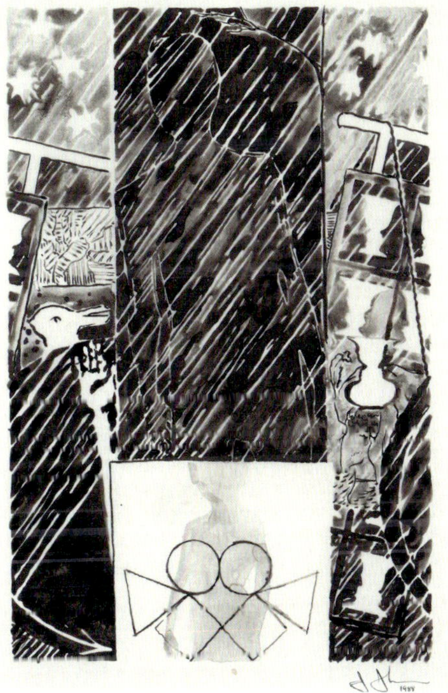

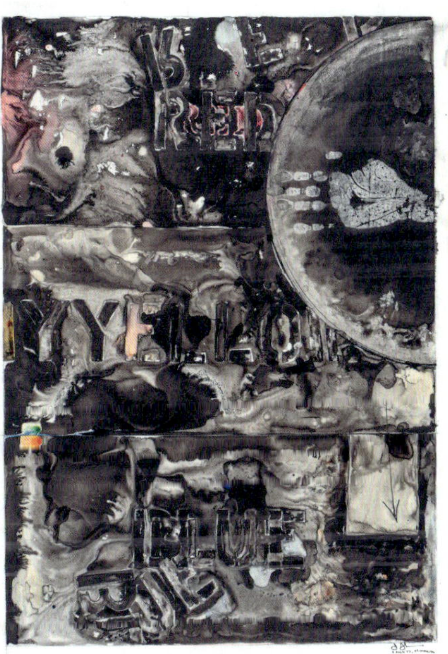

18 ***End Paper***, **1976**
20 ***Untitled***, **1988**

19 ***Usuyuki***, **1981**
21 ***Untitled***, **1988**

22 ***Periscope***, **1977**

Face Time

Carroll Dunham

In the mid-1980s, a new subject appeared in Jasper Johns's work, a human face represented by detached, schematically rendered facial features held together by a pictorial rectangle and deployed around its edges. Once this motif inserted itself into the artist's vocabulary, it joined the oceanic churn of subjects and procedures in his work, recycling and recombining, migrating from drawing to painting to prints and back through the various media the artist has long explored. Johns has a unique ability to see possibility where others might see redundancy. The original appearance of a thing in his work may feel jarring, even nonsensical. (This was as true of his early flags as it is of his recent drawings of a skeleton in vaudeville attire.) Then, through extreme repetition and diverse material incarnations, the subject matter becomes "his."

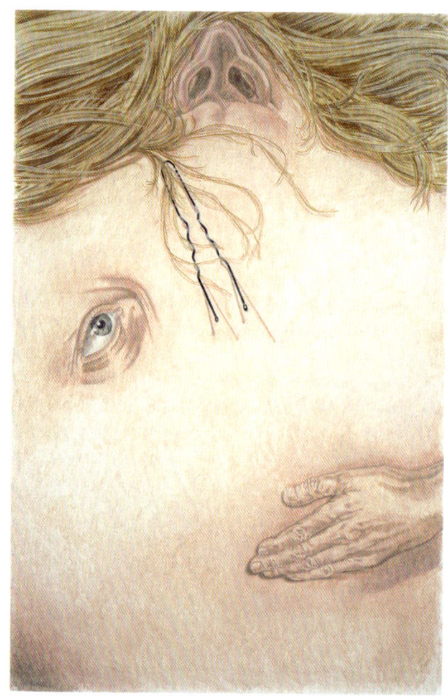

Fig. 2 **Alan Turner (American, 1943–2020). *Hairpin*, 1989**
Oil on canvas, 60 × 40 in. (152.4 × 101.6 cm). The Rosenblum Family

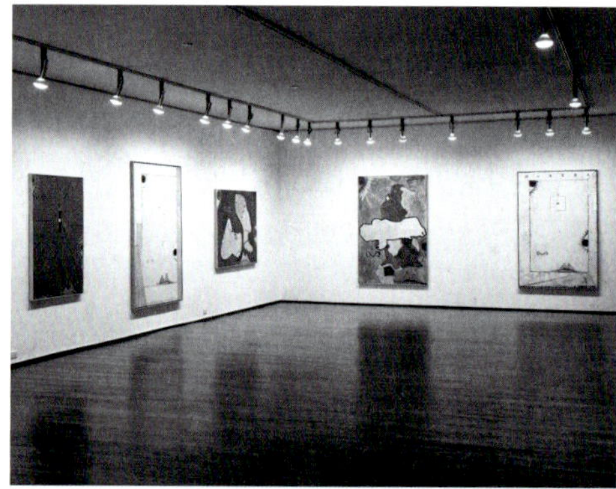

Fig. 1 **Installation view, *Jasper Johns*, Leo Castelli Gallery on West Broadway, New York, February 6–March 9, 1991**
Archives of American Art, Smithsonian Institution, Washington, DC; Leo Castelli Gallery records, c. 1880–2000, bulk 1957–99, box 48, folder 86

I Never Forget a Face

The first time I saw the motif was in an exhibition of the artist's recent work at the Leo Castelli Gallery in New York in 1991 (fig. 1). At least I think it was ... While doing research for this text I realized that my memory of the experience was selective if not completely inaccurate. Gallery installation photographs reveal paintings and drawings in the show, most if not all of them employing this new device to bracket a lot of the artist's other subjects (some previously familiar, some not). I remember finding the entire exhibition confusing and somewhat off-putting, but the only work I remembered seeing that employed the facial motif was the painting *Montez Singing* (1989; p. 235, pl. 10); for some reason this creamy, dreamy masterpiece had differentiated itself from its companions and taken up residence with surprising clarity in my visual memory. I think this painting may have stayed with me because its palette and use of redistributed facial features reminded me of Alan Turner's paintings (fig. 2), with which I was quite engaged at the time, and I knew that he and Johns were acquainted.

Also, *Montez Singing* was emptier than the other work around it, and actually more "naturalistic," making it easier to focus on and to hold in one's memory. The canvas was painted with encaustic and sand, giving the richly varied, warm off-white surface a cozy scratchiness somewhat at odds with the cartoonishness of the primary subject. A margin was delineated around the edges of the canvas, a layout common in printmaking, against which clung two bulging eyeballs with lashes like little sperm attacking an egg, and a rosy, mountainous mouth sat along the bottom edge. A little curlicue indicating the tip of a nose drifted in the field, completing the inventory of features necessary to reach the threshold where a "face" could be said to appear—not so much a "person" as a general notion of personhood. In the upper middle of the inscribed area was a rendering of a little painting, hanging on a nail and string, simplistically depicting a sailboat with red sails drifting on the water at sunset. The margins of the canvas were filled with incident: across the upper margin the words "Montez" and "singing" were intertwined in dark brown and pale pink, respectively. Who the hell was Montez (the name sounds like that of a character in a spaghetti western), and why "singing"? "Red Sails in the Sunset" (a pop song recorded by many artists from the late 1930s onward)? Really?

The painting was jarring and a bit uncanny. It felt like a conscious thing, and nothing in my knowledge or understanding of Johns's concerns up to that point had prepared me for the possibility of his work looking back at me as I looked at it. That face always watched from the threshold of legibility, mute yet seemingly about to announce itself (perhaps about to sing). I'm not sure I "liked" the painting at the time, but the peculiarity of the sensation has remained vivid with time. I think the tension between the apparent dumbness of the face and its straightforward humanism must have deeply appealed to me, because my fascination with the motif has deepened with its episodic and persistent reappearance in Johns's work.

Face the Facts

I was eight years old in 1958, when Johns had his first one-person exhibition at the Castelli Gallery, so I have never inhabited an art scene where he wasn't a dominant or at least prominent figure. By the time I moved to New York in the early seventies, there was already an image of *Flag* (1954–55; p. 66, pl. 7) in every history of postwar American art. The older artists I met, and whose concerns became influential to my cohort (all roughly a generation younger than Johns), were to some extent responding to ideas and strategies that he had put into play in his early work. Their understanding of Johns's concerns trickled down to us and structured our youthful modeling of the recent art history that was incumbent upon us to understand and respond to. In an entirely natural example of confirmation bias, these older artists were focused on the more materialistic and philosophical elements of Johns's investigations; there was much attention paid to the targets, numbers, alphabets, and maps that populate his paintings (subjects the artist had described in one of his infrequent, gnomic utterances as "things the mind already knows"[1]), and to the physical specificity of the encaustic-and-collage technique Johns had developed. Ludwig Wittgenstein and Marcel Duchamp were invoked frequently. The iconic Flag paintings were understood primarily in structural/theoretical terms, focusing on the coextensiveness of subject and support, largely bypassing more pedestrian "Pop" interpretations. Johns's influence had diverse effects. Mel Bochner's drawings and sculptures employing measurement, numbers, and language (fig. 3) and Brice Marden's adaptation of encaustic paint in his early monochromatic canvases were understood to consciously acknowledge Johns as the key precedent.

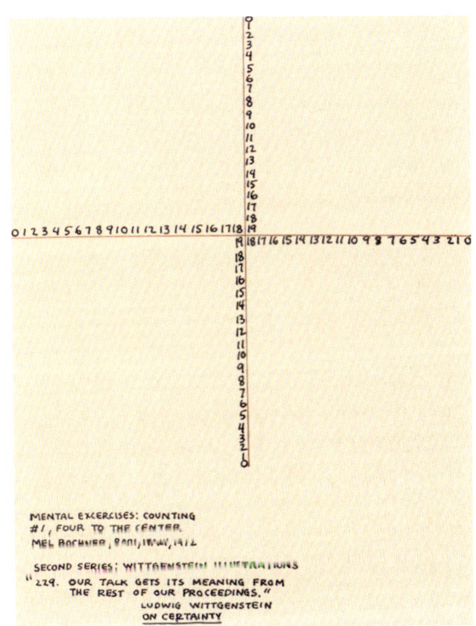

Fig. 3 **Mel Bochner (American, b. 1940). *Mental Exercises: Counting (#1, Four to the Center)*, 1972**
Ink on paper, 12 × 9 in. (30.5 × 22.9 cm). Private collection

Other ways of thinking about Johns's work were always hiding in plain sight (for example, no one I talked to was saying much about the cropped faces or male genitals that appeared as small reliefs along the top edge of some of the early paintings of targets), but I didn't have enough direct experience of his work to really interrogate the consensual reading of his significance until the Johns retrospective at the Whitney Museum of American Art in 1977–78, which provided masses of new data to chew on. That show revealed a mind and sensibility far rangier than one was entirely prepared for. Subjects as diverse as philosophy and flatware were there for the unpacking, as well as an inspiring array of approaches to the physical craft of painting. That was the first time I saw *Fool's House* (1961–62; p. 33, pl. 1), from what we might now call the artist's "late early" period, which, while checking all the boxes for a linguistic and "Duchampian" interpretation, had an obviously used household broom and white china coffee cup attached to its brushy gray surface, conveying a powerful sense of ghostly human presence and emotional loss rooted in solitary quotidian reality.

If the sheer range of the Whitney exhibition made it impossible to continue seeing Johns as purely a patron saint of Conceptual art, the most recent works in that exhibition, the earliest of the so-called crosshatch paintings, could be understood to reinforce Marden's understanding of Johns's work as a sensuous yet self-aware variant of reductive abstraction. But any survey of a living artist's work creates a false sense of closure; in the three *Tantric Detail* paintings of 1980–81 (p. 243, pls. 9, 10; p. 251, fig. 1), first shown in a group exhibition with Ellsworth Kelly and Richard Serra at New York's Blum Helman Gallery in 1982, images of disembodied human skulls and rather hairy scrotums are embedded along the central axes in fields of hatch marks, making it clear that in Johns's thinking the details and indignities of life in and as a human body were inextricably intertwined with the aspects of abstraction he was exploring.

The enormous Johns retrospective at the Museum of Modern Art (MoMA) in 1996–97 ended on a very different note, with work that could be seen by the unsympathetic as self-absorbed, obsessive, and obscure. Many trains of thought were revealed, and a lot of apparent loose ends. By the mid-nineties, his subject matter had become both more obviously personal (floor plans of the house he lived in as a child, intimate bathroom scenes) and inscrutably historicist (the apparently abstract forms derived from Matthias Grünewald's *Isenheim Altarpiece* [1512–16] and direct tracings from Hans Holbein and Paul Cézanne). The tightening of facture and dense spatial layering in some of these paintings chilled their surfaces and made the works feel somewhat clogged and diagrammatic (for example, the Seasons cycle of 1985–86 [pp. 180–81, pls. 3, 4; p. 190, pls. 7, 8] or the pair of *Mirror's Edge* paintings of 1992–93 [pp. 188–89, pls. 4, 5]). But this was also the first opportunity to reconsider *Montez Singing* and related material within the maze of Johns's other then recent preoccupations.

The facial motif emerged close in time to other subjects of a more inscrutable and personally referential nature ("things the mind already knows" had evolved into things *his* mind already knows), and seems to have been derived in part from the eyes in the distorted head in Pablo Picasso's *Straw Hat with Blue Leaves* (1936; fig. 4), which Johns had been appropriating extensively. The paintings that employ this device as a primary formal event have a structural clarity that sets them apart from his other activity. As Johns became increasingly interested in a dense aggregation of subjects reminiscent of both nineteenth-century American trompe l'oeil painting (John F. Peto, William Harnett) and a computer screen with too many folders left open, the facial motif had the effect of returning fragmentation to wholeness. However complicated the internal relations in the field, the face surrounds and contains the various elements, allowing the picture to be apprehended as one thing.

Like *Montez Singing*, some works utilize an internal framing margin to contain the face, as in three nominally monochromatic untitled paintings of 1991 and 1991-94 (fig. 5) within which the portrayal of a child's scrambled drawing of a face and breasts nailed to the plane in the center of the frame invokes yet another level of self-referential disconnect embedded in the oscillating balance of the subject and its material realization.[2] In others, such as *Untitled* of 1991, the facial features are pushed to the edges of the canvas.[3] I remember experiencing this painting as if for the first time at the 1996-97 MoMA retrospective, although I now realize that I must have seen it at Castelli in 1991. Its poppy-red field, acidic color contrasts, and bluntness of touch must make it the most obnoxious (in a good way) painting Johns has ever made. In other works, the face is part of an accumulation of subjects—found lurking, for instance, in the dense mood board-like space of the two large, quantumly entangled *Untitled* paintings of 1992-94 (p. 136, pl. 20) and 1992-95.

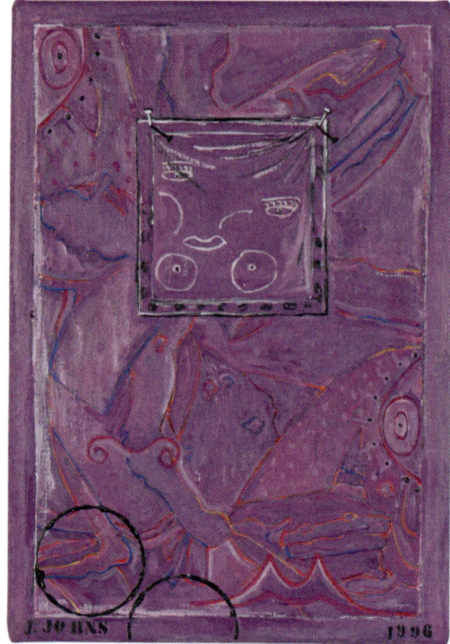

Fig. 5 ***Untitled*, 1991-94**
Oil on canvas, 60 1/8 × 40 1/8 in. (152.7 × 101.9 cm). Collection of the artist

An untitled oil painting from 1997 (pp. 232-33, pl. 4) has the face with its icy blue lips presiding over and around secondary subjects of "cosmic" scale and implication (the Milky Way, little stick figures under the Big Dipper). The eyeballs seem to be bugging out of their surroundings (one is pushing up against a painted wooden ruler), as though the looming entity can't absorb the implications of what it is contemplating. Johns has returned to this construction in recent years; his exhibition at Matthew Marks Gallery in 2019 included a 2017 restating/repainting of the same themes and structure on a squarer canvas.

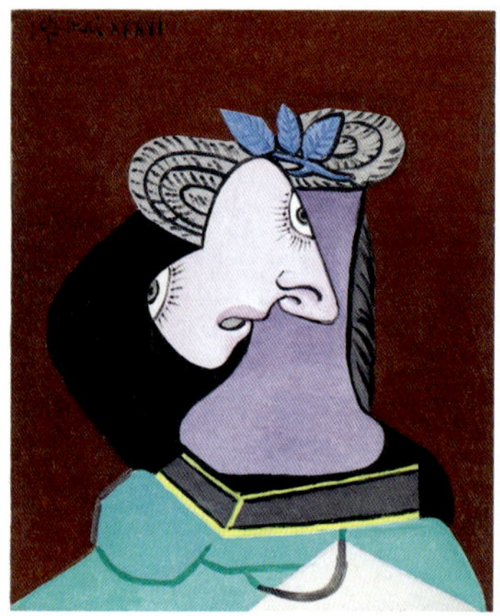
Fig. 4 **Pablo Picasso (Spanish, 1881–1973). *The Straw Hat with Blue Leaves*, 1936**
Oil on canvas, 24 × 19 in. (61 × 48.3 cm). Musée Picasso, Paris

The present exhibition(s) will no doubt deepen our understanding of the facial motif's relationship to the artist's overall project. In addition to paintings, drawings and watercolors illustrate Johns's compulsion to drill relentlessly into the implications of virtually every aspect of his work, each material incarnation striking its own emotional tone. In a beautiful untitled watercolor from 1990 (p. 237, pl. 21), the whites of the eyes have turned yellow, and the face appears both at the edges of the sheet and rendered as cloth nailed to the center of the field like the Shroud of Turin. Another watercolor from the same year (p. 237, pl. 23) has the eyes dripping with pendulous teardrops around the central image of a wristwatch, again hanging from a nail and surrounded by radiating lines. The narrative flat-footedness of these works is so direct it disguises itself: in the former, the face is a mask of projection trapped in a potentially endless series of formal regressions; in the latter, a worldly symbol of time radiates from the center of a field literally defined by sadness.

At Face Value

Unpacking the iconography in Johns's work over the years has been a cottage industry within Johns scholarship and fandom. More knowledge is usually a less dangerous thing, and a deeper understanding of references can certainly enrich one's appreciation of both content and intent in an artist's work. For example, from my reading I am now aware that the Montez in *Montez Singing* refers, not to a character in a movie, but to Johns's step-grandmother, Montez (Bramlett) Johns, with whom he lived as a child, and that the little painting within the painting is indeed meant to invoke "Red Sails in the Sunset," a popular song during that time.[4] This poignant information deepens one's empathetic response to the painting, but these connections should not be confused with the apprehension of "meaning" in the work, any more than one is prevented from having an authentic response to a masterpiece of the Northern Renaissance without a thorough understanding of the Christian symbolism of that time. Since the beginning of his career, Johns has been interested in, for lack of a better word, the "obvious." I think this was the original notion behind "things the mind already knows."

Johns's work offers so much physical and pictorial specificity, and his use of subject matter is so repetitive, that it can seem almost like a misunderstanding to overly rely on traditional notions of interpretation when engaging with it.

Like his earliest chosen subjects of numbers and the American flag, the face motif is immediately comprehensible. It is impossible to parse whether the recognition of faces is biologically or culturally encoded, but most of us rely on facial cues as the signal manifestation of personal individuation and identity. We dote on the features of our friends and loved ones as the flowering of their inner beauty, and find the aspect of people we dislike to be proof of their inner repugnance. An ability to distinguish specific faces is crucial to an infant's early development of emotionally (and nutritionally) supportive relationships. We are always dealing with faces at the center of an infinitely complex environment of visual and other physical cues, every face the same yet every one unique. We are on both sides of the face at all times, throughout life. You are reading this page through holes in your face. From behind our own faces we mount an offensive projection of a self that (hopefully) accomplishes the tasks we require of it in the matrix of perceptions and agendas we inhabit, and we extrapolate from the faces of others a similar set of clues to the central character and intentions assumed to be "inside" another person.

Johns's use of the facial motif literalizes the idea of an inner life wearing a face as a mask. The ancillary subjects that drift around and through the work frame the subjects within in a way quite analogous to how we imagine human personalities to cohere, with what Wassily Kandinsky called the "Basic Plane" standing in for the biological organism of the human body.[5] This face has no obvious gender, and could as easily stand for the artist himself as for his step-grandmother. Indeed, it is open to debate whether the entity one imagines "behind" the face is experiencing the other subjects or is itself another subject (or both).

Shit Faced

The asymmetry of the eye placement in Johns's face motif is noteworthy. The eyes are never level with each other, which activates the rectangular field formally while imparting an almost cartoonish imbalance or intoxication to the "person" in the artwork.

Most of us start the day looking in the mirror (at least I do), checking the condition of our external presentation before rejoining the dimension of intersubjectivity. These mirrors are usually rectangular, and we see our own features framed and drifting in a pictorial field in all their asymmetrical inadequacy, while "inside" we deal with the lingering detritus of dreams and our morning apprehensions about "reality." This seems to me an almost literal parallel to the construction Johns developed in his work.

Our identity is formed at the intersection of deep personal memory and our sense of the nation, world, or universe we feel we inhabit. We might all prefer to think that as a signifier of identity our face operates on a deeper level than the flag to which we swear allegiance, or the galaxy within which we travel the universe. In our present cultural climate, the desire to imagine a separation from the confusing schizophrenia of the collective is gathering urgency, while our reality principle tells us this is increasingly impossible. These are things the mind probably already knows, but might wish it did not.

1 Jasper Johns, quoted in "His Heart Belongs to Dada," *Time*, May 4, 1959; reprinted in Kirk Varnedoe, ed., *Jasper Johns: Writings, Sketchbook Notes, Interviews* (New York: Museum of Modern Art, 1996), 82.

2 See the paintings *Untitled (Bruno Bettelheim)* (1991) and *Untitled* (1991). For illustrations, see Roberta Bernstein, *Jasper Johns: Catalogue Raisonné of Painting and Sculpture* (New York: Wildenstein Plattner Institute, 2017), 3:198, no. P2275; and 200, no. P276. For a similar composition, see page 237, plate 19, in this volume.

3 For an illustration of *Untitled* (1991), see Bernstein, *Johns: Catalogue Raisonné*, 3:196, no. P274.

4 Bernstein, *Johns: Catalogue Raisonné*, 1:247–55.

5 See Wassily Kandinsky, *Point and Line to Plane: Contribution to the Analysis of Pictorial Elements*, trans. Howard Dearstyne and Hilla Rebay (New York: Solomon R. Guggenheim Foundation for the Museum of Non-Objective Painting, 1947); and Fiona Donovan, *Jasper Johns: Pictures within Pictures, 1980–2015* (London: Thames and Hudson, 2017), 107–21.

Jasper Johns: The Hurt Imagination
Colm Tóibín

Poems take pleasure in night-sounds, in night-thoughts; they relish the small creak in the woodwork that makes you shiver, or a distant rustling in the trees, or a memory of someone who has passed into shade, or the sudden thought of death and all that it means. Poems are hospitable to ghosts. In a sonnet written in 1658, John Milton describes seeing his dead wife, who "came vested all in white," only to register, in ten stark one-syllable words in the last line: "I wak'd, she fled, and day brought back my night."[1]

In his poem "The Reassurance," Thom Gunn summons up a friend who had died of AIDS in cadences that appear as simple as speech itself:

> About ten days or so
> After we saw you dead
> You came back in a dream.
> I'm all right now you said.[2]

And in a chilling poem from the early 1860s, Emily Dickinson imagined herself dead and then dreamed, as the seasons went on, of coming back to earth to visit her loved ones until she thought it would be better instead if they "should come to me."[3] She was willing them to join her in death. The poem's stanzas are a way of marking time until the living become the dead.

In his sequence of poems *Caelica*, written in the early seventeenth century, the English poet Fulke Greville teased out what happens to "hurt imaginations" once darkness falls, "In night when colors all to black are cast, / Distinction lost, or gone down with the light," and the mind "doth forge and raise impossibility." He writes about seeing "inward evils" under the canopy of "thick depriving darknesses."[4]

I have a memory of the road between Ballyferriter and Dunquin on the Dingle Peninsula in the southwest of Ireland in a summer when I was in my late teens. I had walked into the village on my own. The late August evening was calm and windless. I sat in a pub, knowing that the walk home would take less than an hour.

I had not bargained for the sheer darkness that enveloped everything once I stepped out into the night. There were no stars and no moon, no remnant of the day. Instead, there was a thickness in the air, a heaviness. It was not the loss of visibility that comes with fog or mist, but rather it was a dry darkness, brittle, severe, absolute. I was sure, really sure, there were other people on the road, people standing still, hovering, or crossing and recrossing in front of me. As I went on, I became desperately afraid of them. But I continued walking. There was no choice.

At the end of his story "The Dead," James Joyce found a way of shifting his imaginative gaze from the mere mortals, whose attendance at a party had given him his drama, to a landscape reaching out from the city across Ireland, a landscape in winter, changing from substance to spirit, gradually becoming peopled by the dead. Gabriel, the protagonist, finds that "his own identity was fading out into a grey impalpable world: the solid world itself which these dead had one time reared and lived in was dissolving and dwindling."[5]

In all these texts, there is a sense that the literary tone itself is easily lured down roads that lead into some vast unknown place, into some realm where life has been distilled and darkened and where death's melody, rising and becoming dominant, seems the most fitting sound.

The novelist Henry James was concerned mostly with material things, with felt life. He liked writing about style and money and the intricacies of human behavior. He specialized in dramatizing desires and knotted treacheries that were acutely human. His world was almost fully secular.

In some of his best fiction, however, he released an energy that was infused with the pull between light and dark. He became concerned with his characters as yearning souls. He saw his art as a way of making humans, in all their waywardness and frailty, more complete, as if he were a kind of god. In a letter to his friend Grace Norton about his novel *The Portrait of a Lady*, he wrote, "In truth everyone, in life, is incomplete, and it is [in] the work of art that in reproducing them one feels the desire to fill them out, to justify them, as it were."[6]

In both his novella "The Aspern Papers" and his late novel *The Golden Bowl*, James tempts us to look beyond the merely human toward some other space. In "The Aspern Papers," this occurs in the last two pages, when our protagonist returns to the Venetian palace having rejected an offer of marriage from Miss Tita. He notices, on seeing Tita, "an extraordinary alteration" in her: "She stood in the middle of the room with a face of mildness bent upon me, and her look of forgiveness, of absolution made her angelic.... This optical trick gave her a sort of phantasmagoric brightness." When he says goodbye to her, and she replies that she won't see him again, and does not want to, "she smiled strangely, with an infinite gentleness.... And now she had the force of soul."[7] She had the force of soul because she had been despised and rejected. This force could emerge only after darkness and pain; it was something lurking beneath the veneer of the social self in the material world.

There is a scene in chapter two of book five of *The Golden Bowl* in which Maggie Verver's father is playing a game of bridge with three others. Maggie quietly steps outside and begins to observe them through a window. Slowly things shift in her perception until, without anything visibly changing in the room, Maggie experiences "the horror of finding evil seated all at its ease where she had only dreamed of good; the horror of the thing hideously *behind*, behind so much trusted, so much pretended, nobleness, cleverness, tenderness."[8]

Later in the book, Maggie hears her mother-in-law give a guided tour of the treasures of the house to neighbors: "The high voice went on; its quaver was doubtless for conscious ears only, but there were verily thirty seconds during which it sounded, for our young woman, like the shriek of a soul in pain."[9]

—

The force of soul; the soul in pain. A gray impalpable world. A sort of phantasmagoric brightness. Thick depriving darknesses.

Jasper Johns's 1981 painting *Tantric Detail III* (fig. 1) includes the outline of a skull in the lower third and, higher up, the outline of a pair of testicles. The painting appears at first to be deliberately incomplete. Even the left-hand side, with its crosshatching, has areas that are unsettled, smudged, shadowy. The right-hand side has lines and traces of marks, but there is much that has petered out, as though land has given way to sea, or noise to silence, or body to soul.

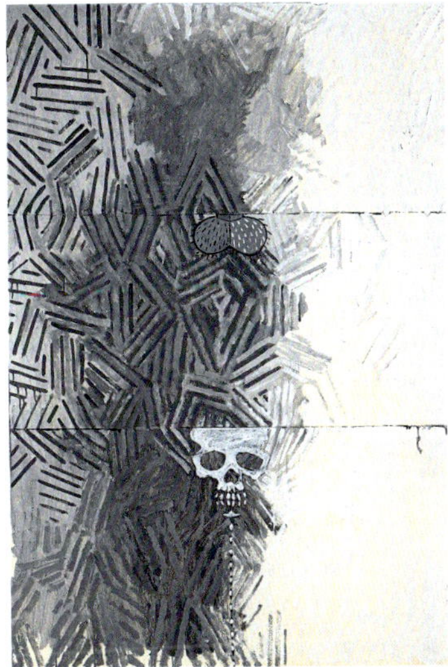

Fig. 1 ***Tantric Detail III*, 1981**
Oil on canvas, 50 × 34 in. (127 × 86.4 cm). The Museum of Modern Art, New York; promised gift of Donald L. Bryant, Jr. and Marie-Josée and Henry R. Kravis

The closer you look, the more haunting the painting becomes, and the more total and complete the image is. Like Joyce in "The Dead" and James in his fiction, Johns has summoned up the soul while paying close attention to the body, or parts of the body.

The left-hand side of the painting deals with the solid world; it has lines and shapes that form a sort of pattern. The skull and the testicles belong to this sense of substantial things. They hang in the air between territory that is inhabited and explored and territory that is unknown. As sex and death, they guard the portal into the place of spirit, and of phantasmagoria, and of the impalpable, and of the luminous realm from which there is no return.

Johns is allowing paint to represent pure shadow, to conjure the invisible, the spectral, the liminal. He works as alchemist as much as painter, inflecting the canvas with the shimmering idea of soul.

If *Tantric Detail III* dramatizes the line between the substantial and the ethereal, literally having the painting itself enact the dividing space, then Johns's 1992 *Target* (p. 244, pl. 14) plays light and dark not as opposites but as uneasy companions. In this painting, Johns explores the possibilities around circle and spiral, and the gap between inner and outer zones and between clear line and dynamic texture. The title appears almost ironic. In this work, there can be no real, clear target, only something that takes on the guise of target, but is more spiritual than actual, more journey than destination. In this painting, in Fulke Greville's words, distinction has been lost, or gone down with the light.

Light in these works by Johns further emphasizes depth and innerness. He uses white or off-white not merely to contrast with black lines or black brushwork, but to suggest soul or space that has shifted beyond the solidity of darker colors into an impalpable world, into death, nonbeing, transcendence.

Johns is interested in paintings in states of transformation. No image for him is single or stable. His diptychs force the eye to move between the images, making sure that each has a competing strength. While the two sides compete, there is no possibility that one will win or that some form of visual synthesis will emerge. The process is more dynamic than that; it thrives on uncertainty, disruption, irony.

In *Perilous Night* (1982; pp. 240–41, pl. 2), for example, Johns uses elements of white in the right-hand panel to pull the eye in past the purples and grays. Instead of suggesting an opening or the possibility of light, the white offers depth to the image. It is mysterious rather than comforting. It is mixed in with the dark tones all around it, as they swirl at will. This is dream territory, turbulent, unsatisfied, suggesting the soul in a state of unrest or a looming chaos from which nothing, nobody, will return unscathed.

In creating two panels, Johns is more interested in distinction than connection. He has no easy affinities to propose. The images on the right of the painting are in sharp conflict with the more abstract tones on the left. While the painting on the left side can stretch inward and outward toward infinity, the one on the right allows angles to create a structure; it uses the shape of a room, the image of an enclosed space—with floorboards and a wall on which a crosshatch painting by Johns hangs—as well as three disembodied arms, with strange spots on them, and a page from a composition by John Cage.

While the image on the left is out of time, the image on the right—with its veiled references to Matthias Grünewald and Pablo Picasso, and its use of moments from Johns's own work—pays homage to art history and to tangible space. Nonetheless, the power of the work does not emerge from simple binaries such as eternity and time, infinity and space, or mystery and memory. The image on the right explores darkness and fear with as much energy and determination as the one on the left. The tone of both is somber, uncomforting, anguished.

In these paintings by Johns, there is never any need to ask why an object is placed where it is, or why certain colors are used or textures placed in opposition to each other. It is not as though Johns works with an easy symbolism or a set of signs that can simply be read. It is more that he responds to pictorial needs. He notes what is missing or examines what is empty and then seeks to fill the space with a mark or the outline of an object that will satisfy the eye, or pull the viewer's gaze in further, without offering a quick or glib solution.

This does not mean that Johns makes images that are random, images that were created for no reason at all. We are entitled to feel that some of his imagery and many of his colors have deep private resonance, but a resonance that has all the more power for holding onto its mystery, resisting any temptation to be explicit.

The question, then, is not what a painting means, but what it does. In some paintings, Johns invites culture to take a bow, allowing his images to include references to other images; or he paints objects, like still lifes, against a swirling, abstract background. In other paintings, he makes interesting use of shapes within nature. In *Untitled* (1980–84;

p. 242, pl. 3), for example, the shapes made with ink and graphite pencil could easily come from rocks impacted on each other, desperately trying to hold onto their form and sovereignty. The work is all competing masses and lines, resisting easy pattern until a more hard-won pattern slowly emerges.

Johns loves artifact, and thus the ink and pencil serve to move the scene away from a depiction of something observed in nature toward something created by the mind, giving the materials as much autonomy as possible. To emphasize that he is concerned to disrupt nature or transform it into something in art's likeness, he has placed three colors—red, yellow, and blue—at the bottom of the drawing. These bright, acrylic daubs trap the eye, hold it in thrall, so that, having been sharpened, it can see the more muted shapes and lines above the three colors.

Johns explores darkness with considerable subtlety. The moments in his work when he leaves himself open to the spiritual, the ethereal, the impalpable, the sinister, are not times when he gives in to vagueness, or to some abstract notion of what fear and suffering might look like. He has, in the words of Emily Dickinson, made his "soul familiar—with her extremity."[10] Out of this come images that are pure and stark, that emerge from knowledge, experience, struggle, insight.

1 John Milton, "Sonnet 23: Methought I saw my late espoused saint," https://www.poetryfoundation.org/poems/44746/sonnet-23-methought-i-saw-my-late-espoused-saint (accessed December 11, 2019).
2 Thom Gunn, "The Reassurance," in *The Man with Night Sweats* (London: Faber and Faber, 1992), 67.
3 Emily Dickinson, "'Twas just this time, last year, I died," in *The Complete Poems of Emily Dickinson*, ed. Thomas H. Johnson (Boston: Little, Brown, 1960), 217.
4 Lord Brooke Fulke Greville, "Sonnet 100," https://poets.org/poem/sonnet-100 (accessed December 11, 2019).
5 James Joyce, "The Dead," in *Dubliners* (London: Grant Richards, 1914), 277.
6 Henry James to Grace Norton, December 28, 1880, in *Henry James: Letters*, vol. 2, *1875–1883*, ed. Leon Edel (Cambridge, MA: Belknap Press of Harvard University Press, 1975), 324.
7 Henry James, "The Aspern Papers," in *The Aspern Papers, Louisa Pallant, The Modern Warning* (London: Macmillan, 1888), 135–36.
8 Henry James, *The Golden Bowl* (London: Macmillan, 1923), 2:209.
9 James, *Golden Bowl*, 257.
10 Emily Dickinson, "I read my sentence steadily," in *The Complete Poems of Emily Dickinson*, ed. Thomas H. Johnson (London: Faber and Faber, 1970), 196.

Recent Work

If the first forty years of Jasper Johns's protean art resist any claims to thematic coherence, the past twenty-five demonstrate a remarkably consistent leitmotif: mortality and its attendants, sorrow, loss, and death. This specter had, of course, haunted his work since the beginning, whether in the suicidal reverberations of *Diver* (1962–63; p. 41, pl. 1), the recurring images of skulls, the abstract X-ray *Corpse and Mirror* (1974), or the allegorical life cycle of the Seasons (1985–86; pp. 180–81, pls. 3, 4; p. 190, pls. 7, 8). But as Johns entered his late sixties, this preoccupation grew more focused, even as the modes through which he explored it widened. In 1996–97, the Museum of Modern Art in New York presented a major retrospective, an occasion in the life of any artist that is infamously both celebratory and fraught. Faced with the measure of his career to date, Johns turned the page on the frantic fantasies of the previous fifteen years and began the stark and solemn Catenary series, named for the tenuous curve of humble string that hangs across these works' broad surfaces. Over the ensuing years, Johns reintroduced a few familiar motifs as well as disparate new sources and denser surfaces. Yet nearly all are tinged with elegy and exist along a tonal spectrum that ranges from pallid dissolution to the darkest cloak of night.

With their moody gray grounds and delicate threads, Johns's Catenary paintings evoke an air of stately sadness. *Catenary (Manet-Degas)* (1999; p. 272, pl. 5) comprises collaged rectangles of canvas that correspond to pieces of a dismembered version of Édouard Manet's *Execution of Maximilian* (about 1867–68), which were lovingly collected and reconstituted by Edgar Degas. Although Johns's rainy grisaille strokes betray no hint of the original violent scene, the painting is suffused with a sense of loss—Manet's eviscerated canvas and the murder it depicted—and of tender homage in the hands of Degas and Johns. Spanning the bottom of *Catenary (I Call to the Grave)* (1998; p. 267, pl. 1), the painting's title cites the Book of Job's tale of suffering, while the addendum of the stenciled signature "JOHNS" makes the pronoun "I" vacillate ambiguously between the biblical prophet and the artist himself. The moody duskiness of these paintings gives way to a creamy softness in related drawings and prints, including monotypes such as *Catenary* (2001; p. 260, pl. 8), which bears the ghostly trace of a prior work impressed upon the page. In the sole white canvas of the group, *Untitled* (2003; p. 257, pl. 1), the string sways gently, casting erratic shadows across a pasty, scabrous surface. Because they are alive to the contingencies of air, light, gravity, and our regard, the threads that traverse and dangle alongside the voids of these paintings also summon, conversely, frailty and undoing.

During this period, Johns matched the mournful abstraction of the Catenary works with a range of imagery that played along a similar emotional register. He pried the outlines of the man and boy loose from the busy grounds of the Seasons paintings and deployed them in sparer compositions that signal the somber passage of time, as in *5 Postcards* (2011; p. 263, pls. 19–23). Sometimes the boy appears small and solitary, his hollow nightmarishly inhabited by Pablo Picasso's tortured *Reclining Nude* (1938). Ladders abound, with their traditional symbolism of the bridge between earth and heaven, and shrouds, crosses, and a pedestaled urn become funereal markers. A priapic male figure copied after a print by Henri Monnier peers at lovers through a screen that keeps him at a lonely distance, while photographs of men in grimmer solitude inspired two of Johns's most powerful recent series. The Regrets series derived from a posed image of painter Lucian Freud perched on a bed, his anguished head in his hands. When Johns mirrors the fragment of this photograph across these compositions, an ominous skull emerges. Slightly later he would return to an image he had adopted years before, a 1965 photograph by Larry Burrows of Marine Lance Corporal James Farley crumpled in grief at the loss of a comrade in the Vietnam War (p. 277, fig. 3). Johns treats nearly all these images in both light and dark. In the paler variants, figures and symbols fade softly away or dissolve, as in *5 Postcards* and *Untitled* (2012; p. 262, pl. 16), into refulgent fields of white striated with bright color. In the darker versions, such as the flickering drawing *Regrets* (2013; p. 275, pl. 25), Johns obscures his images under black skeins or puddles of ink that entangle his figures and materials in a twisted, tenebrous embrace. Rarely in history do we find such passionate examples of a great artist making work about the end of life so late in it.

In 2018, the FBI returned to Johns a group of works furtively stolen from him over many years by his longtime assistant. In one of these, an unfinished canvas related to the Seasons, Johns memorialized the painful betrayal by inscribing a skeleton within the silhouette originally traced from his own shadow (p. 274, pl. 18). At once fearsome and funny, the skeleton grins menacingly beneath a shrunken top hat and wisps of hair. In related drawings, prints, and Sculp-metal paintings, he holds a second skull at his crotch, skips rope, and leans jauntily on a cane as if about to crack a joke or break into dance (pp. 264–65, pls. 24–34). Made as Johns neared ninety, these works might be both laughing in the face of death and laughing at it. His own aging body appears in prints made by applying his arthritic hand directly to the plate more than three decades after he first pressed it to his drawings—a lapse of time unmistakable in the gathering skin. He alludes more obliquely to his ailing body in *Slice* (2020; pp. 270–71, pl. 4), a painting imprinted with an anatomical diagram of a knee, which he first spied in his orthopedist's office, drawn and signed by a high school student named Jéan Marc Togodgue. Bones and ligaments exposed, the specimen floats on a map of galaxy positions in a slice of the universe by astrophysicists Valérie de Lapparent, Margaret Geller, and John Huchra, with graphics by Michael Kurtz. In the darkness behind them unfurls an intricate radial pattern derived from one of Leonardo da Vinci's knot drawings. The intimate and the vast, the evanescent and the eternal, and the human and the cosmic, all hold balance, and the art goes on. "You don't normally plan the length of your life," Johns remarked in an interview published in late 2020. "Occasionally, I have thought that I was working on the last thing I would do, but so far I've been wrong."[1]

—Scott Rothkopf, with Carlos Basualdo, Sarah B. Vogelman, and Lauren Young

1 Jasper Johns, "Wir werden nicht entzweibrechen!," interview by Georg Imdahl, *Frankfurter Allgemeine Zeitung*, November 3, 2020, https://www.faz.net/aktuell/feuilleton/kunst/jasper-johns-und-frank-stella-ueber-die-us-wahl-und-ihre-kunst-17032360.html.

Recent Work

Elegies in Light

PHILADELPHIA MUSEUM OF ART

1 ***Untitled*, 2003**
Encaustic and collage on canvas with objects
34 ¾ × 50 ⅛ in. (88.3 × 127.3 cm)
Private collection

2 ***Untitled*, 2018**
Encaustic on canvas
78 × 60 in. (198.1 × 152.4 cm)
Glenstone, Potomac, Maryland

3 ***Untitled*, 2014**
Graphite pencil, ink, and watercolor on paper
23 ⅞ × 19 ¾ in. (60.6 × 50.2 cm)
Collection of the artist

4 ***Untitled*, 2002**
Ink on paper
43 ⅞ × 30 ¼ in. (111.4 × 76.8 cm)
Private collection

5 ***Bushbaby*, 2004–5**
Collage over intaglio on paper
43 ⅝ × 30 ½ in. (110.8 × 77.5 cm)
Susan Lorence

6 ***Bushbaby*, 2005**
Graphite wash and watercolor on paper
40 ½ × 27 ½ in. (102.9 × 69.9 cm)
Private collection

7 ***Catenary (Manet-Degas)*, 1999**
Graphite pencil, watercolor, acrylic, and ink on paper
24 ⅜ × 33 ⅝ in. (61.9 × 85.4 cm)
Whitney Museum of American Art, New York; gift of the American Contemporary Art Foundation, Inc., Leonard A. Lauder, President, 2002.281

8 ***Catenary*, 2001**
Monotype
25 ⅜ × 35 ⅝ in. (64.5 × 90.5 cm)
John Lund/Low Road Studio
Collection of the artist

9 ***Farley Breaks Down—After Larry Burrows*, 2014**
Ink on plastic
31 ⅞ × 24 in. (81 × 61 cm)
The Keith L. and Katherine Sachs Collection

10 ***Untitled*, 2017**
Monotype
35 ⅛ × 30 in. (89.2 × 76.2 cm)
John Lund/Low Road Studio
Forman Family Collection

11 ***Untitled*, 2017**
Ink on plastic
33 ¾ × 29 ½ in. (86.7 × 74.9 cm)
Forman Family Collection

12 ***Untitled*, 2014**
Ink on paper
22 ⅜ × 30 ½ in. (56.8 × 77.5 cm)
Private collection

13 ***Untitled*, 2012**
Monotype
30 ⅞ × 22 ⅝ in. (78.4 × 57.5 cm)
John Lund/Low Road Studio
Collection of the artist

14 ***Untitled*, 2005‡**
Ink on paper
8 ½ × 5 ¼ in. (21.6 × 13.3 cm)
Collection of Matthew Marks

15 ***After Larry Burrows*, 2014**
Water-soluble encaustic and graphite pencil on paper
20 ⅜ × 15 ⅝ in. (51.8 × 39.7 cm)
Collection of the artist

16 ***Untitled*, 2012**
Watercolor and graphite pencil on paper
22 ¾ × 15 ½ in. (57.8 × 39.4 cm)
The Menil Collection, Houston; promised gift from the collection of Louisa Stude Sarofim

17 ***Untitled*, 2013**
Watercolor and ink on paper
22 ¼ × 31 in. (56.5 × 78.7 cm)
Anne Dias Griffin

18 ***Untitled*, 2014**
Acrylic on canvas
20 ½ × 29 ½ in. (52.1 × 74.9 cm)
Private collection; courtesy Matthew Marks Gallery

19–23 ***5 Postcards*, 2011**
Encaustic on canvas, 36 × 24 in. (91.4 × 61 cm); oil on canvas, 36 × 27 in. (91.4 × 68.6 cm); oil on canvas, 36 × 27 in. (91.4 × 68.6 cm); oil and graphite on canvas, 36 × 27 in. (91.4 × 68.6 cm); encaustic on canvas, 36 × 24 in. (91.4 × 61 cm)
Philadelphia Museum of Art; promised gift of Keith L. and Katherine Sachs

24–29 ***Untitled*, 2018**
Ink on paper or plastic (twenty-four sheets)
11 ⅝ × 8 ⅛ in. (29.5 × 20.6 cm) each (approx.)
Collection of Marguerite Steed Hoffman

30–34 ***Untitled*, 2019**
Sculp-metal on canvas with Sculp-metal on wood frame in five parts
12 ⅝ × 8 ¾ × 1 ⅜ in. (32.1 × 22.2 × 3.5 cm) each
Forman Family Collection

Elegies in Dark

WHITNEY MUSEUM OF AMERICAN ART

1 ***Catenary (I Call to the Grave)*, 1998**
Encaustic on canvas with objects
78 × 118 in. (198.1 × 299.7 cm)
Philadelphia Museum of Art; 125th Anniversary Acquisition; purchased with funds contributed by Gisela and Dennis Alter, Keith L. and Katherine Sachs, Frances and Bayard Storey, The Dietrich Foundation, Marguerite and Gerry Lenfest, Mr. and Mrs. Brook Lenfest, Marsha and Jeffrey Perelman, Jane and Leonard Korman, Mr. and Mrs. Berton E. Korman, Mr. and Mrs. William T. Vogt, Dr. and Mrs. Paul Richardson, Mr. and Mrs. George M. Ross, Ella B. Schaap, Eileen and Stephen Matchett, and other donors, 2001-91-1a–d

2 ***Farley Breaks Down*, 2014**
Ink and water-soluble encaustic on plastic
42 × 29 ⅛ in. (106.7 × 74 cm)
Whitney Museum of American Art, New York; promised gift of Monique H. and Gregg G. Seibert

3 ***Untitled*, 2018**
Oil on canvas
38 × 25 ½ in. (96.5 × 64.8 cm)
Whitney Museum of American Art, New York; purchase with funds from the Leonard A. Lauder Masterpiece Fund, 2019.310

4 ***Slice*, 2020**
Oil on canvas
51 ½ × 67 ½ in. (130.8 × 171.5 cm)
Private collection

5 ***Catenary (Manet-Degas)*, 1999**
Encaustic and collage on canvas with objects
38 × 57 ⅜ in. (96.5 × 145.7 cm)
The Newhouse Collection

6 ***From Henri Monnier*, 2000**
Ink on plastic
23 ¾ × 18 in. (60.3 × 45.7 cm)
Private collection

7 ***Untitled*, 2002**
Ink on plastic
41 ⅛ × 28 in. (104.5 × 71.1 cm)
Collection of Kate Ganz

8 ***Untitled*, 1998**
Ink on paper mounted on paper
41 × 25 ¼ in. (104.1 × 64.1 cm)
Collection of the artist

9 ***Untitled*, 2010**
Ink and graphite pencil on paper
31 ⅝ × 24 ½ in. (80.3 × 62.2 cm)
Collection of the artist

10 ***Untitled*, 2010**
Black ink and colored ink on paper
22 × 30 ⅞ in. (55.9 × 78.4 cm)
Collection of the artist

11 ***Untitled*, 2017**
Acrylic on canvas
19 ¾ × 23 ¾ in. (50.2 × 60.3 cm)
Collection of Jeffrey Seller and Josh Lehrer

12 ***Untitled*, 2013–14**
Acrylic on canvas
36 × 27 in. (91.4 × 68.6 cm)
Collection of Lisa and Steven Tananbaum

13 ***Untitled*, 2010**
Black ink and colored ink on plastic
4 × 3 ¼ in. (10.2 × 8.3 cm)
Collection of Matthew Marks

14 ***Untitled*, 2012**
Monotype
42 × 28 ¾ in. (106.7 × 73 cm)
John Lund/Low Road Studio
Kravis Collection; promised gift to the Museum of Modern Art, New York, in honor of Merrill C. Berman

15 ***Untitled*, 2016***
Ink and watercolor on plastic
34 ¾ × 23 ⅞ in. (88.3 × 60.6 cm)
The Menil Collection, Houston; promised gift from the collection of Louisa Stude Sarofim

16 ***Untitled*, 2015**
Ink and watercolor on plastic
37 × 29 ⅝ in. (94 × 75.3 cm)
The Menil Collection, Houston; promised gift from the collection of Louisa Stude Sarofim

17 ***Untitled*, 2018**
Oil on canvas
39 × 30 ⅛ in. (99.1 × 76.5 cm)
Private collection

18 ***Untitled*, 2018**
Oil on canvas
50 ¾ × 34 ⅛ in. (128.9 × 86.7 cm)
Private collection

19 ***Untitled*, 2018**
Unique etching on papyrus
31 ⅝ × 20 ⅛ in. (80.3 × 51.1 cm)
Whitney Museum of American Art, New York; promised gift of Donna Perret Rosen and Benjamin M. Rosen

20 ***Untitled*, 2010–11**
Ink over intaglio on paper
13 ½ × 14 in. (34.3 × 35.6 cm)
Collection of the artist

21 ***Untitled*, 2014**
Ink and water-soluble encaustic
on plastic
16 × 12 in. (40.6 × 30.5 cm)
Collection of the artist

22 ***Untitled*, 1998**†
Intaglio
24 × 18 in. (61 × 45.7 cm)
John Lund/Low Road Studio
TP
Private collection

23 ***After Picasso*, 1998***
Oil on canvas
34 ½ × 28 ½ in. (87.6 × 72.4 cm)
Collection of the artist

24 ***Regrets*, 2013**
Oil on canvas
67 × 96 in. (170.2 × 243.8 cm)
Kravis Collection; promised gift to
the Museum of Modern Art, New York

25 ***Regrets*, 2013***
Charcoal, watercolor, and pastel
on paper
31 ½ × 47 ¼ in. (80 × 120 cm)
Kravis Collection; promised gift to
the Museum of Modern Art, New York

Elegies in Light

PHILADELPHIA MUSEUM OF ART

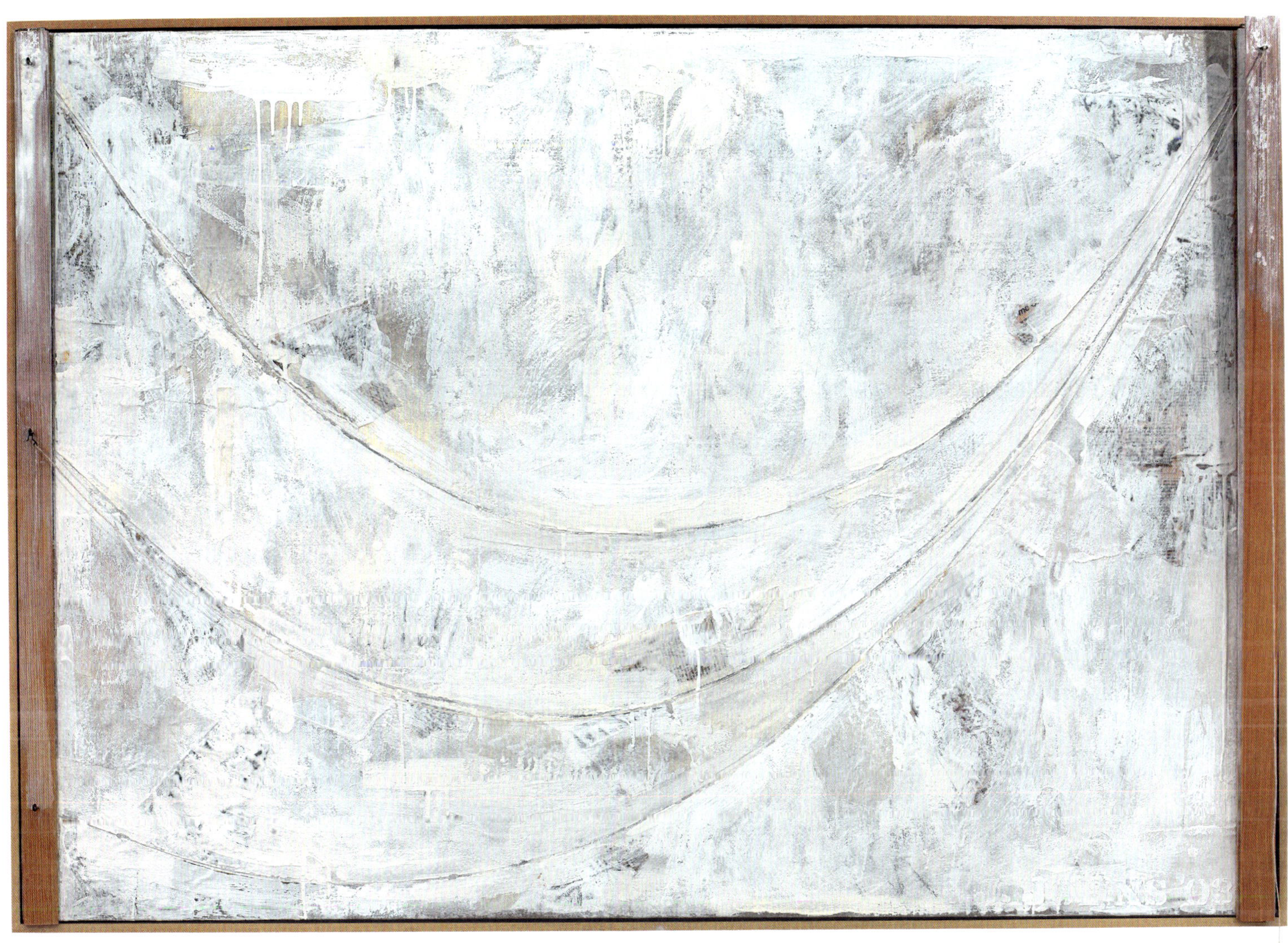

1 ***Untitled*, 2003**

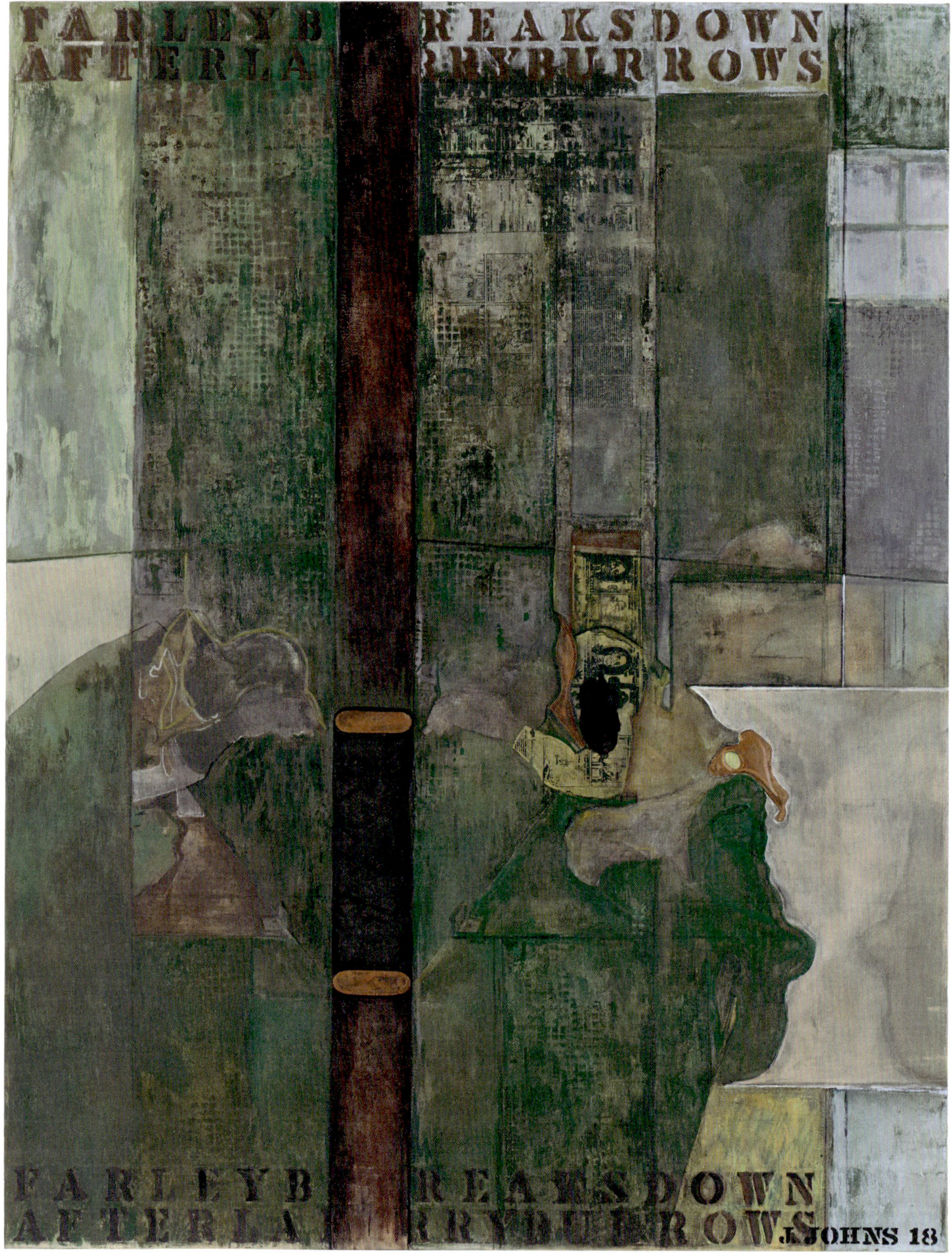

2 ***Untitled*, 2018**

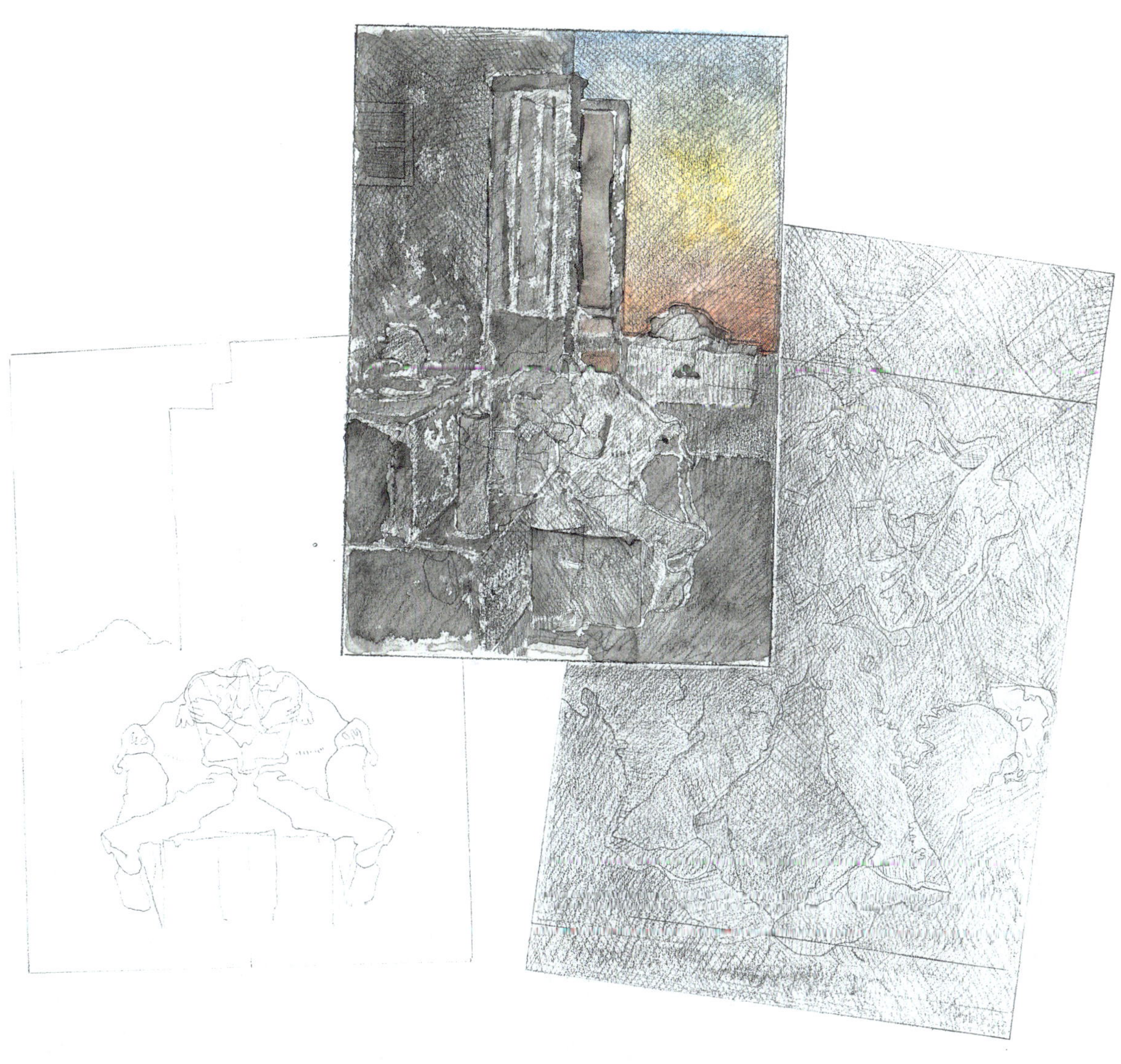

3 *Untitled*, 2014

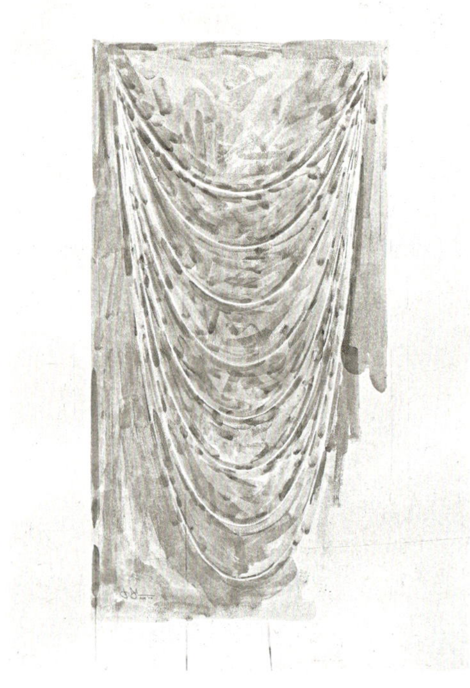

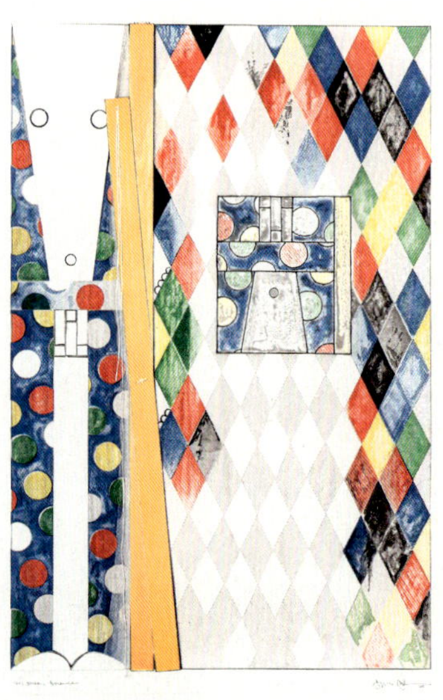

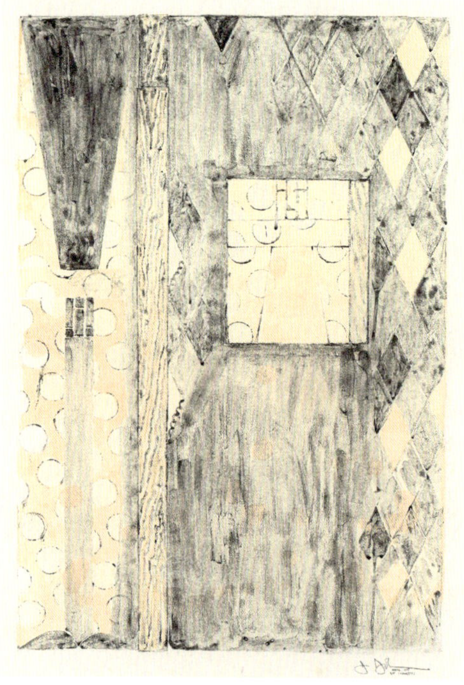

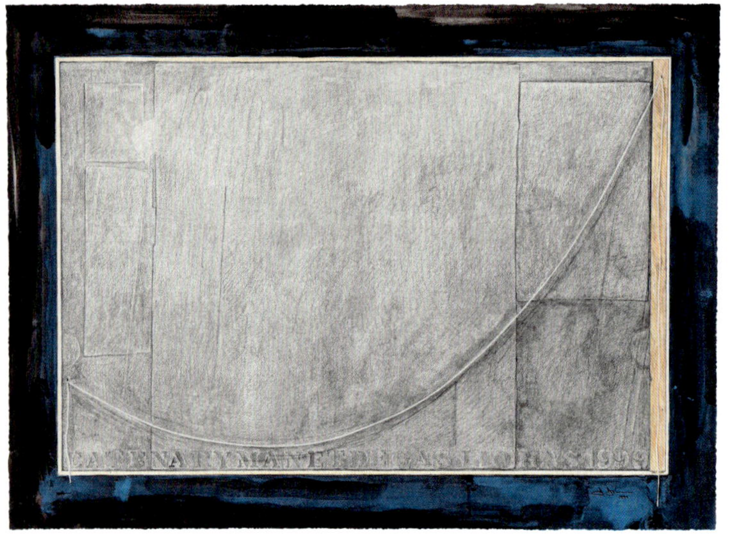

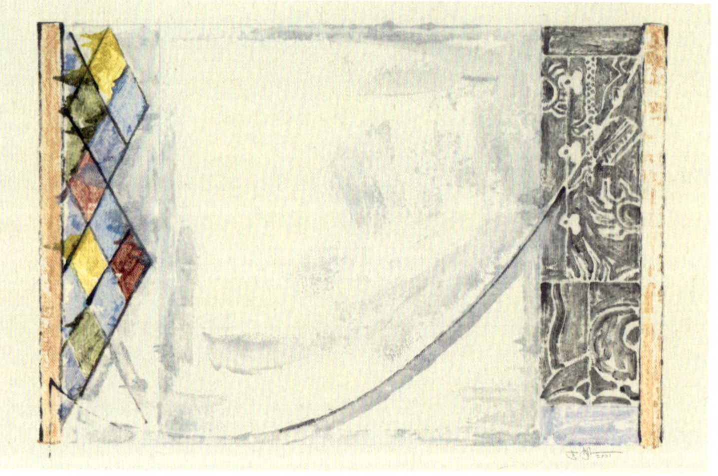

4 ***Untitled*, 2002**

5 ***Bushbaby*, 2004-5**

6 ***Bushbaby*, 2005**

7 ***Catenary (Manet-Degas)*, 1999**

8 ***Catenary*, 2001**

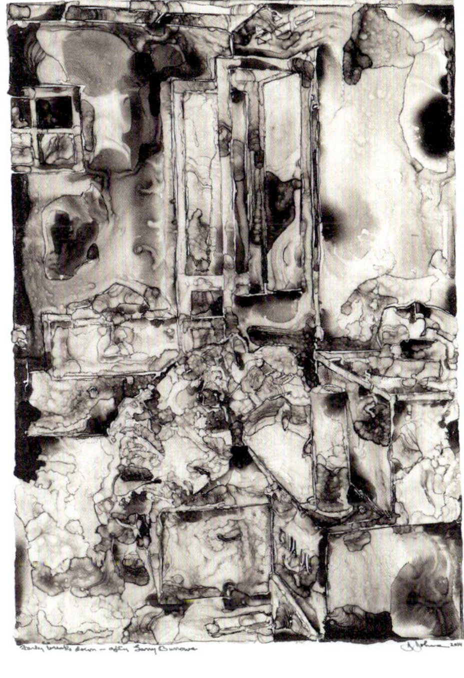

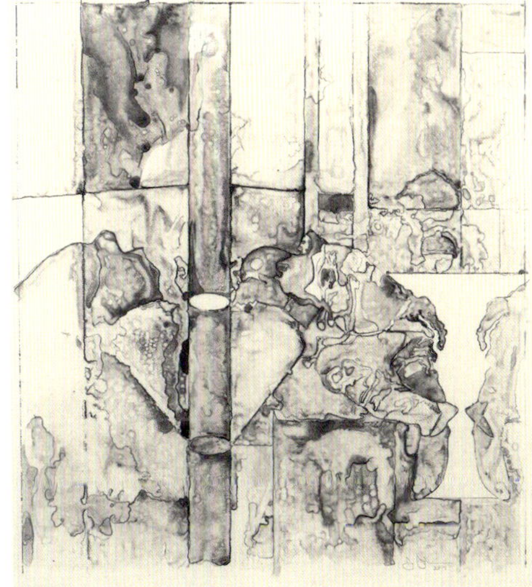

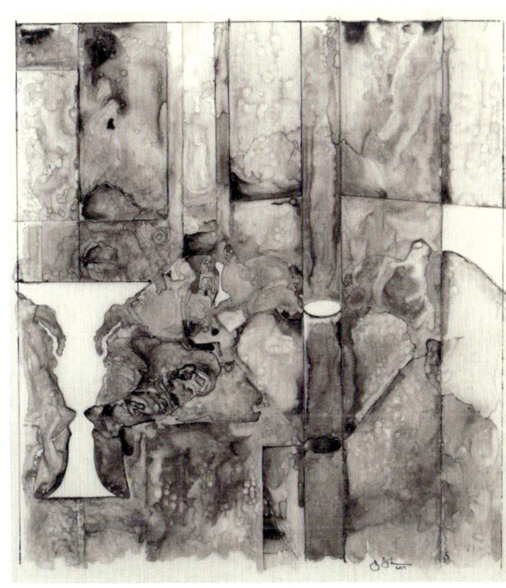

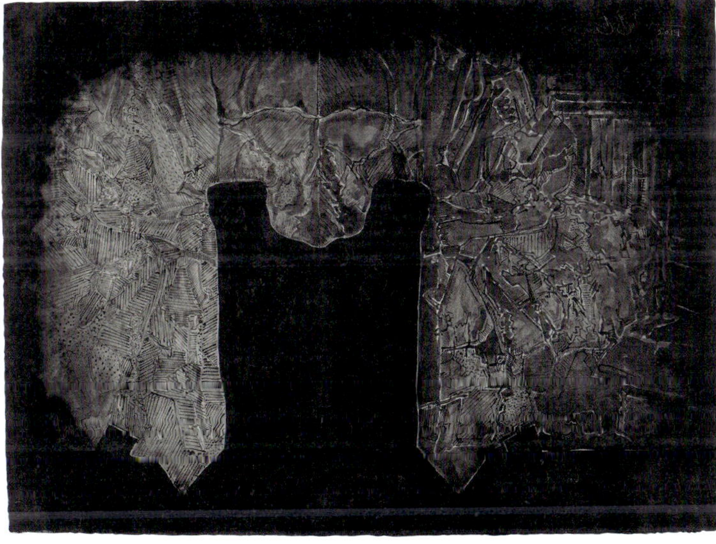

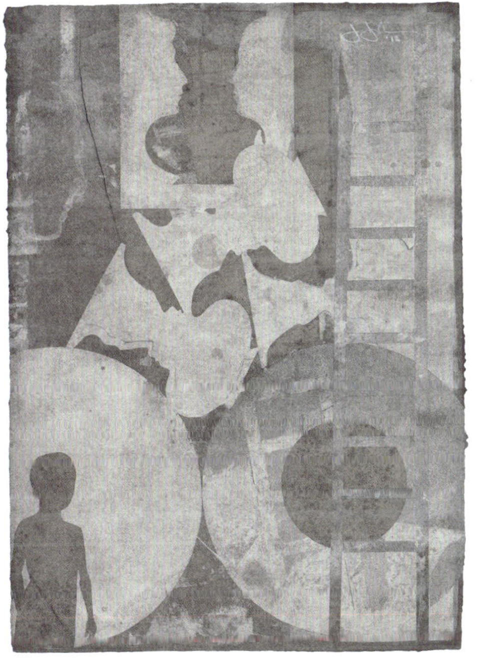

9 ***Farley Breaks Down—After Larry Burrows*, 2014**
10 ***Untitled*, 2017**
11 ***Untitled*, 2017**
12 ***Untitled*, 2014**
13 ***Untitled*, 2012**

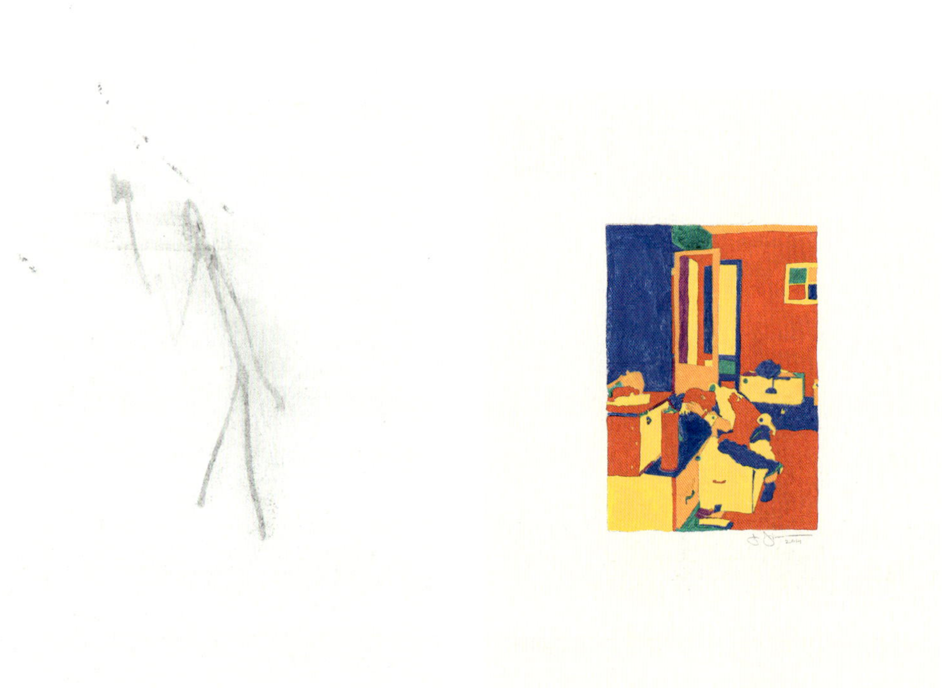

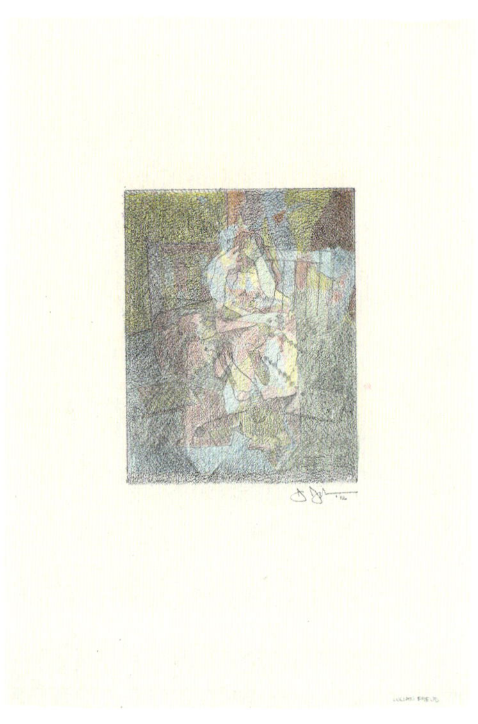

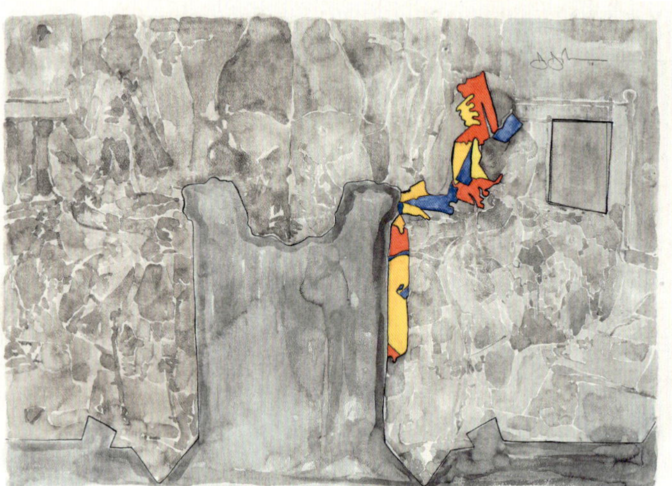

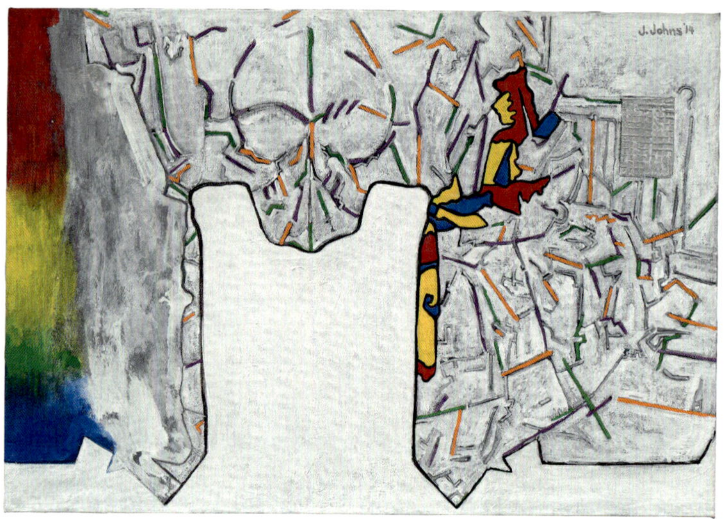

14 ***Untitled***, **2005**
17 ***Untitled***, **2013**

15 ***After Larry Burrows***, **2014**
18 ***Untitled***, **2014**

16 ***Untitled***, **2012**

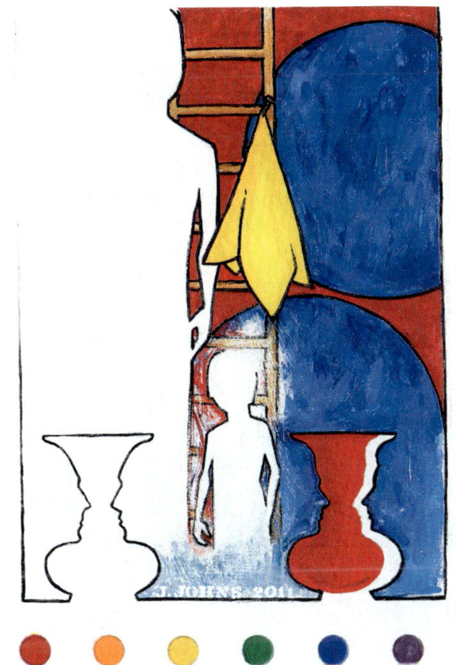

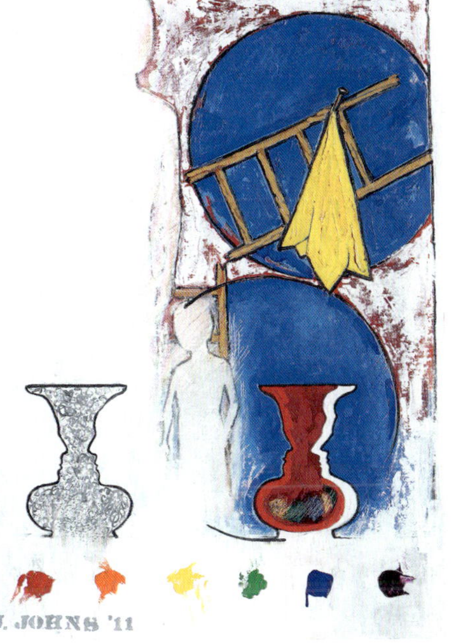

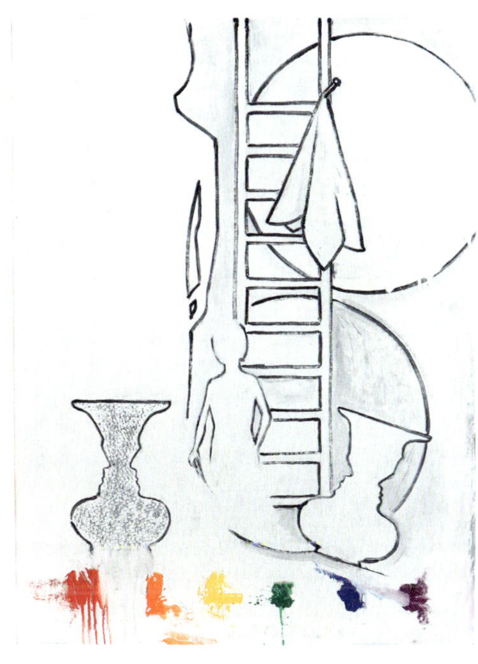

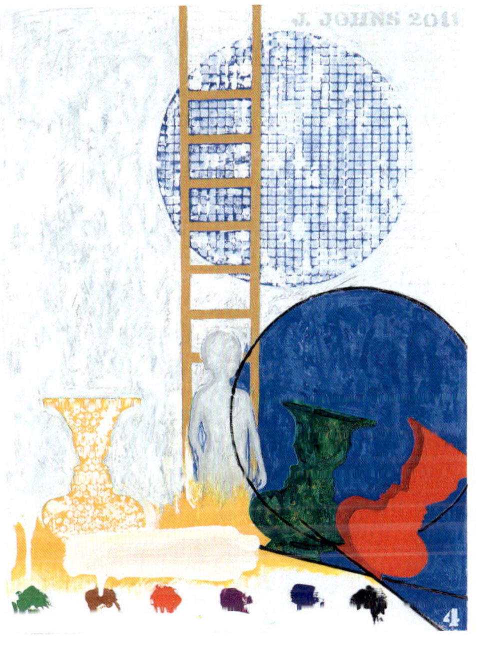

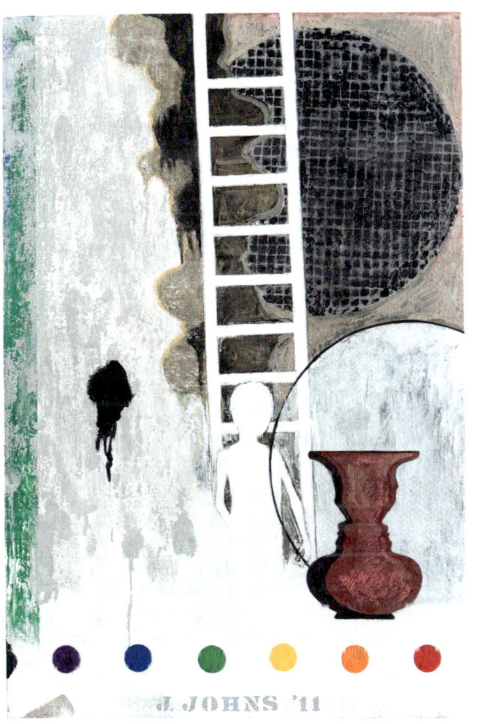

19–23 ***5 Postcards*, 2011**

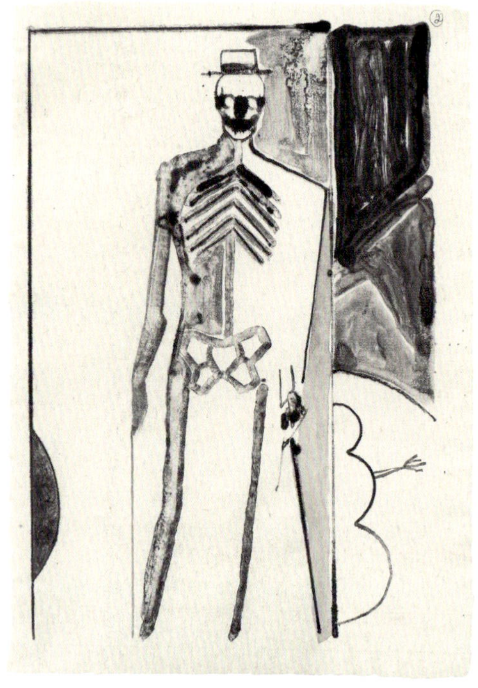

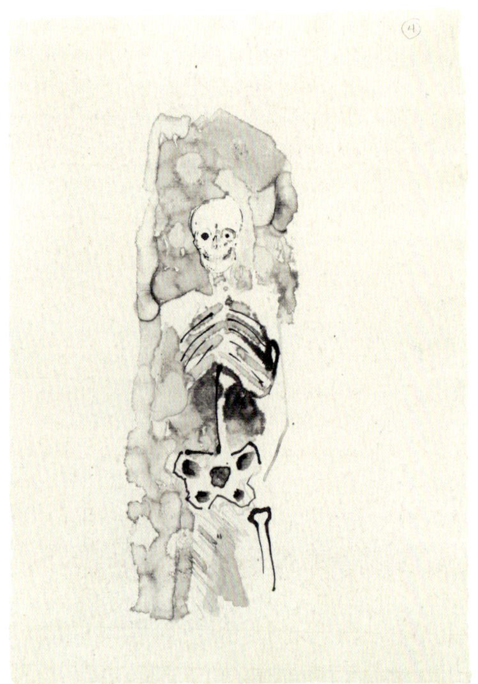

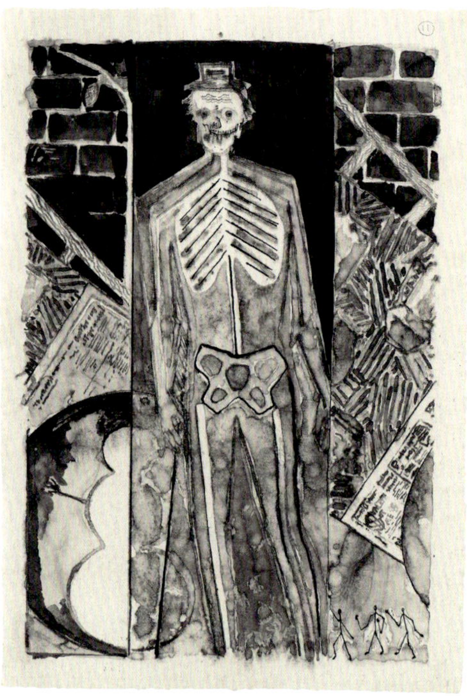

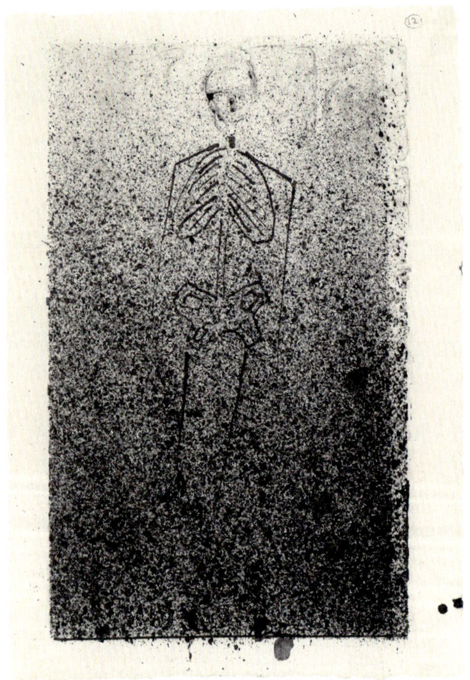

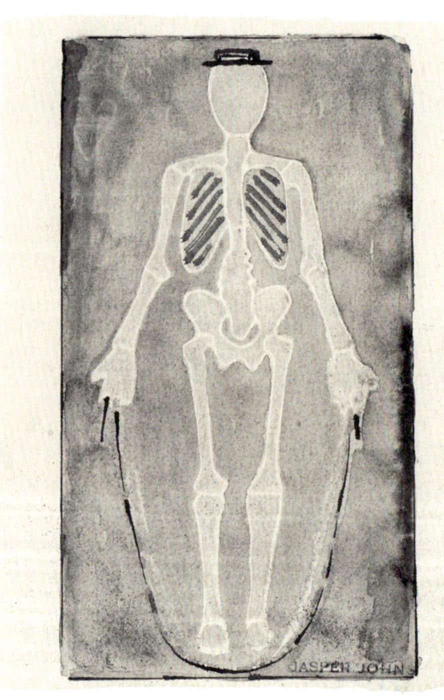

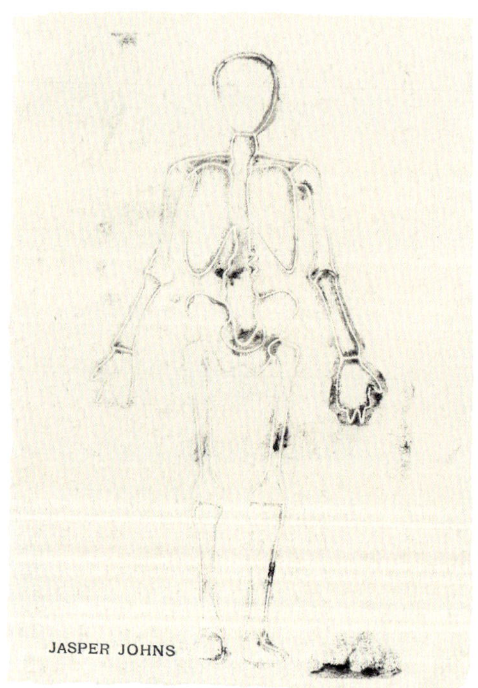

24-29 ***Untitled*, 2018**

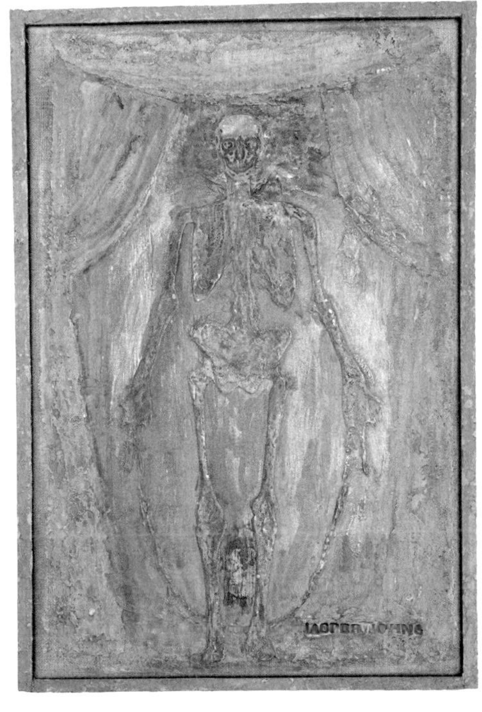

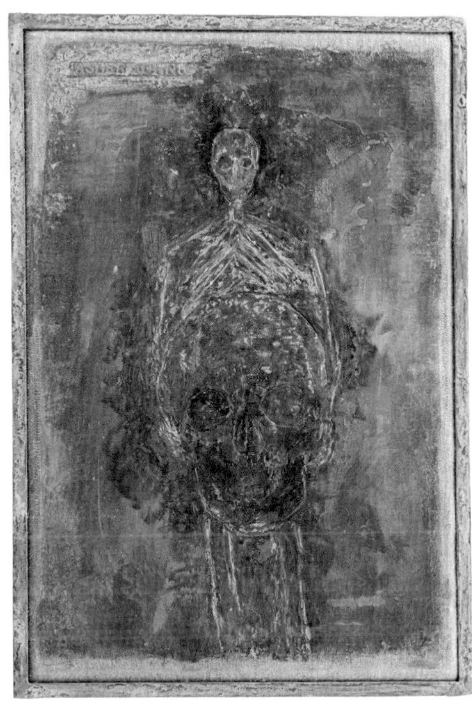

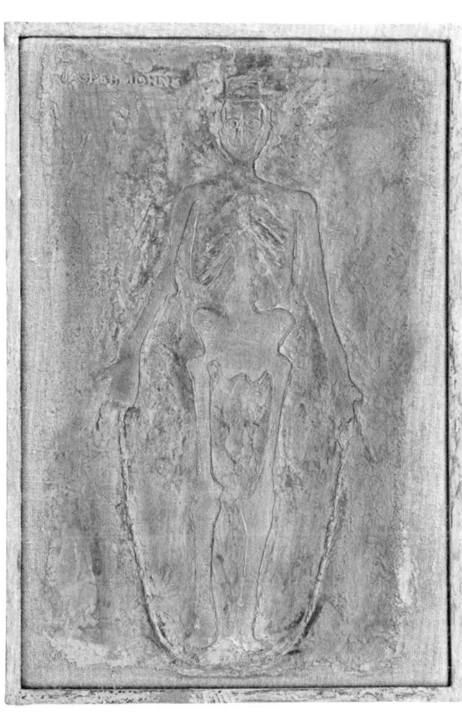

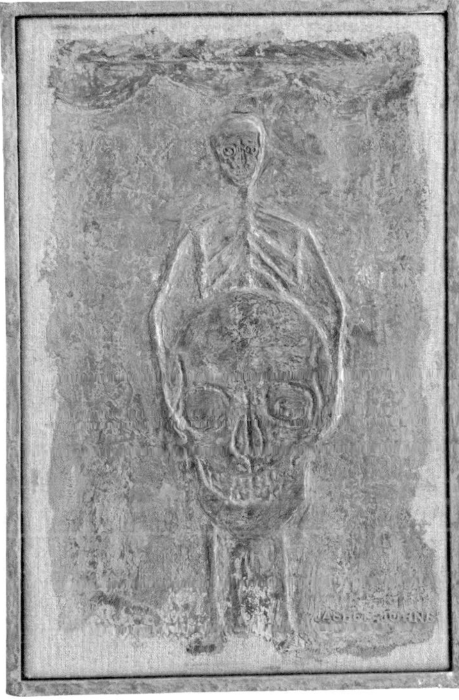

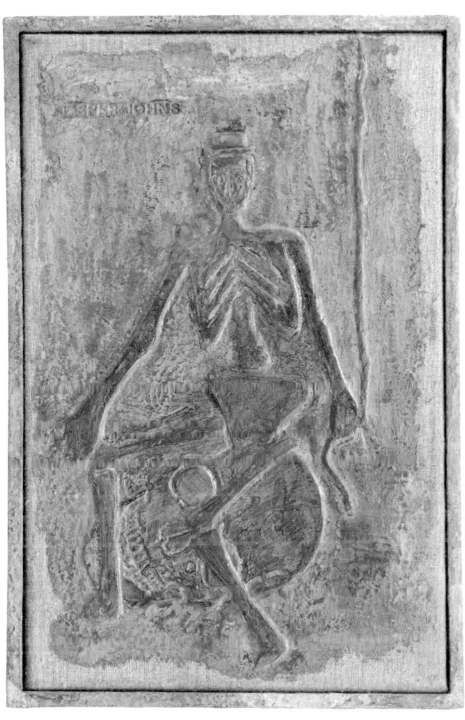

30–34 ***Untitled*, 2019**

Elegies in Dark

WHITNEY MUSEUM OF AMERICAN ART

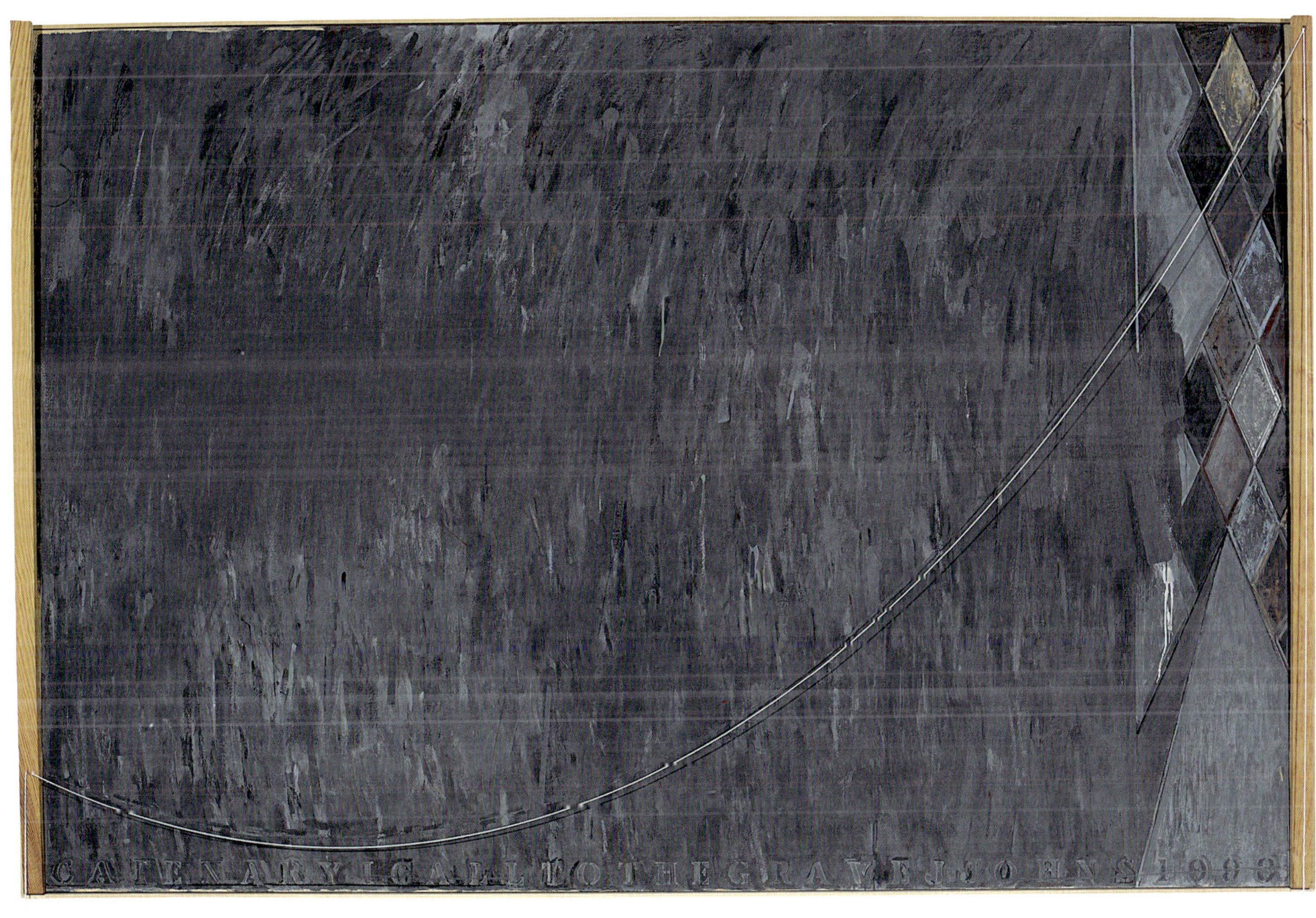

1 ***Catenary (I Call to the Grave)***, **1998**

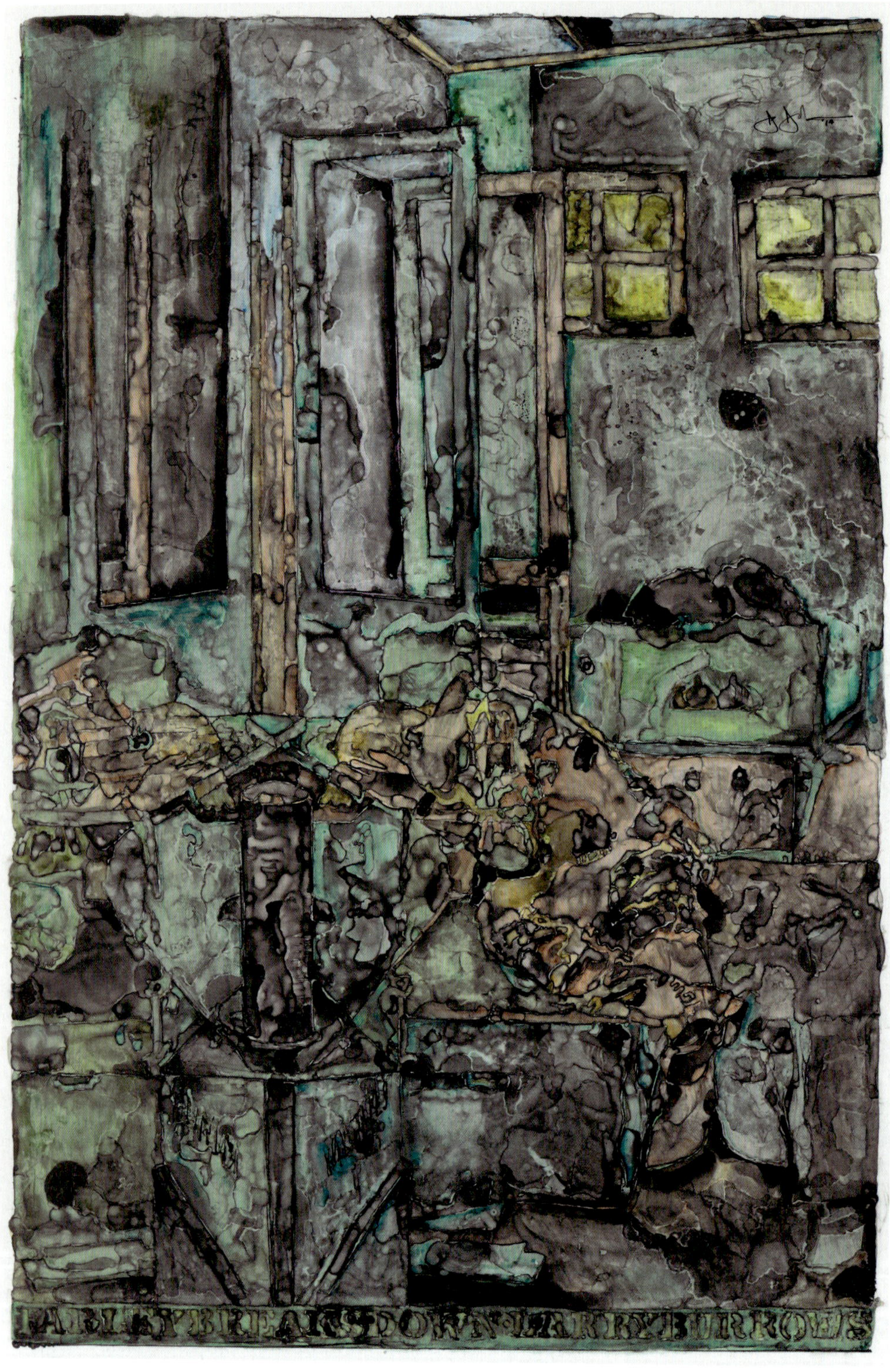

2 *Farley Breaks Down*, 2014

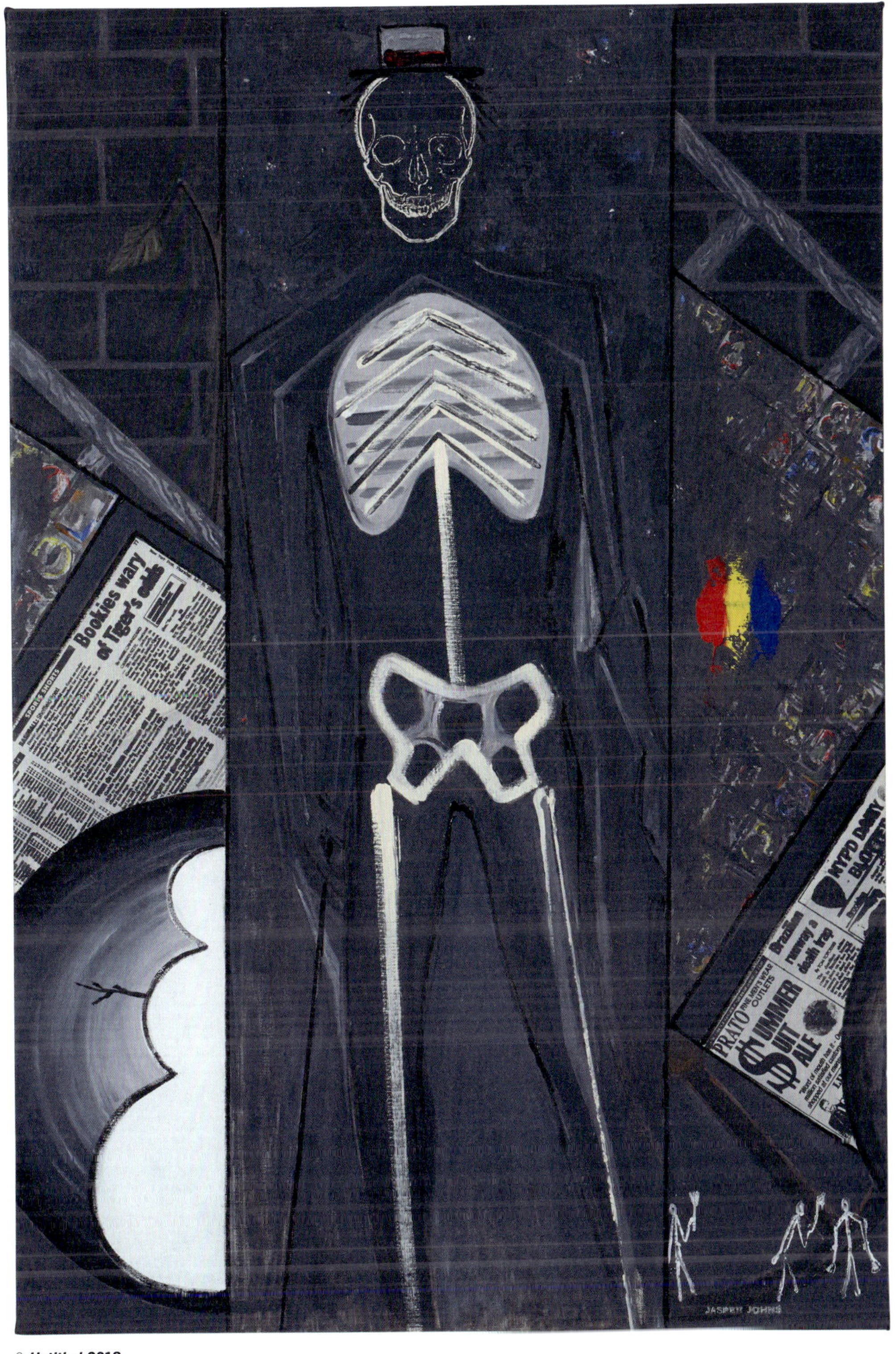

3 ***Untitled*, 2018**

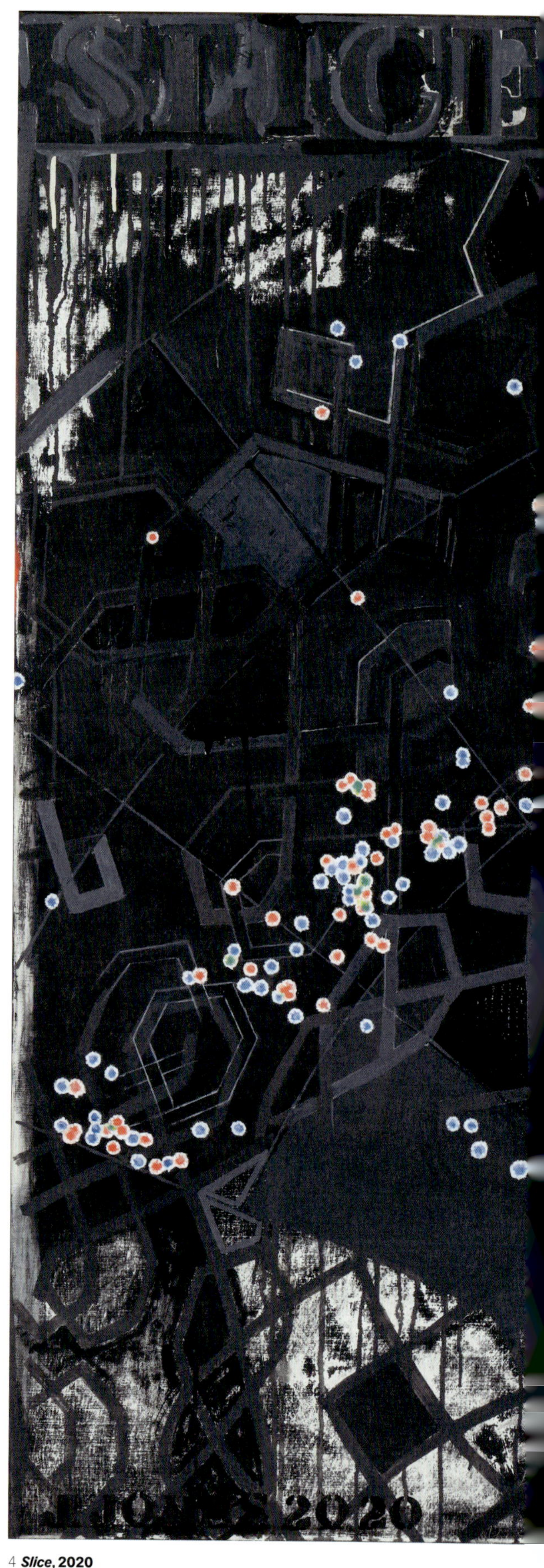

4 ***Slice*, 2020**

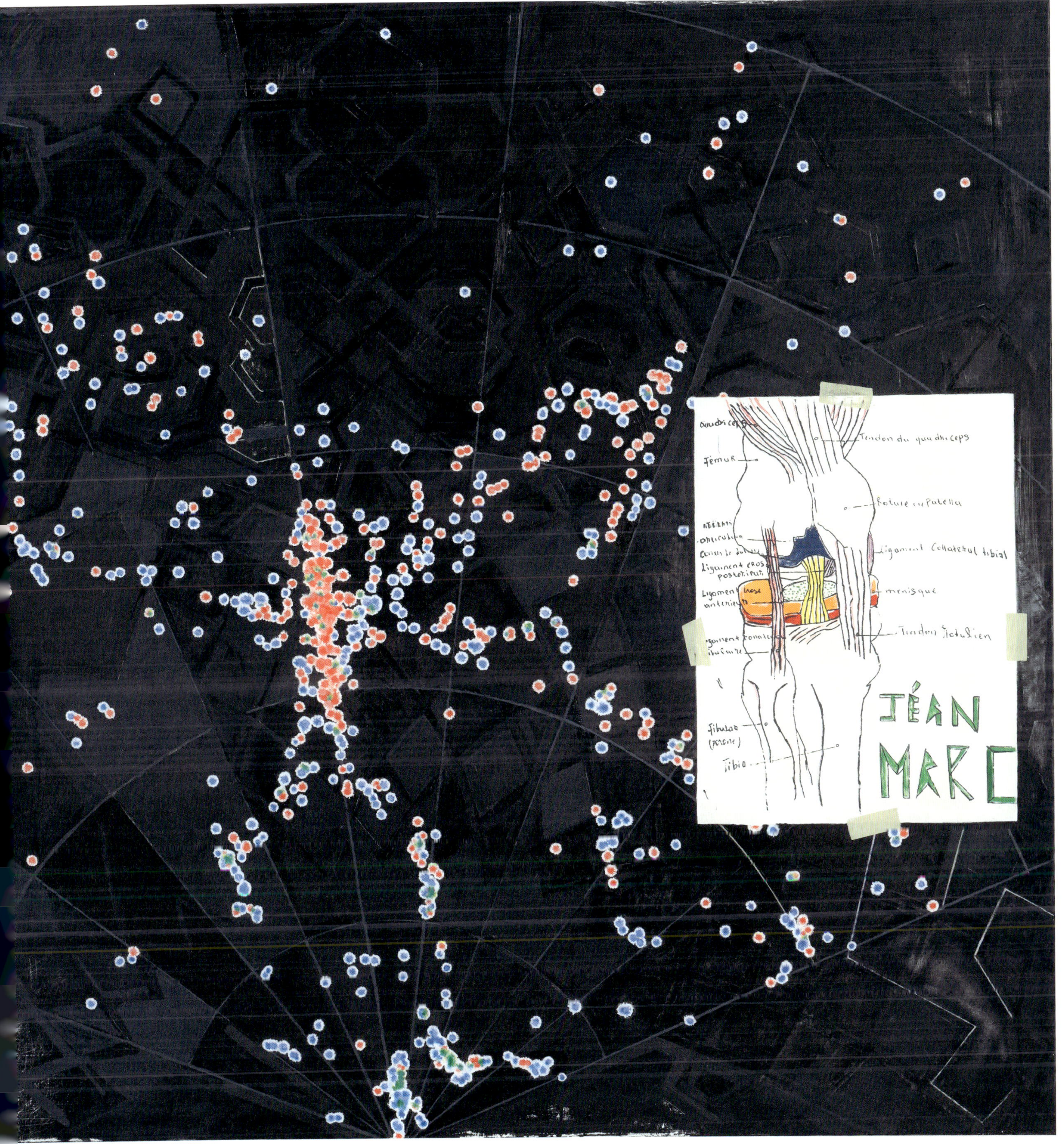
Femur
Rotule ou Patella
menisque
JÉAN
MARC

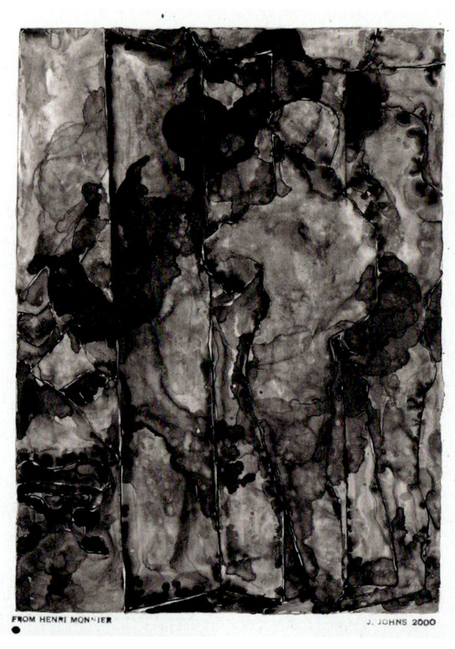

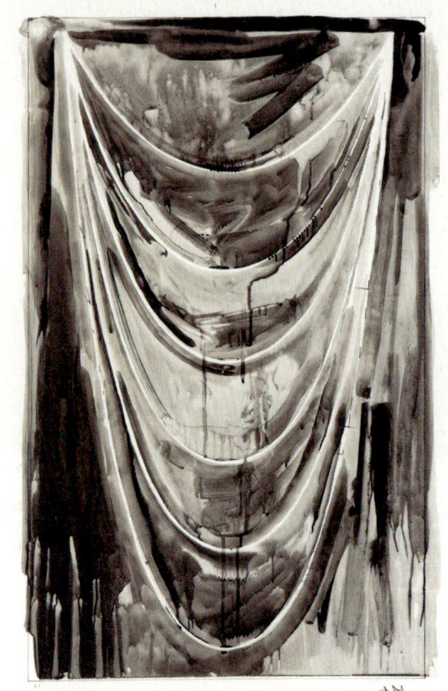

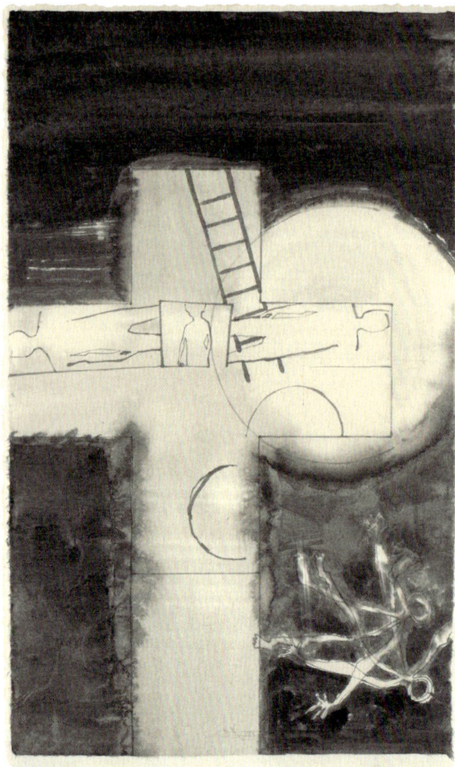

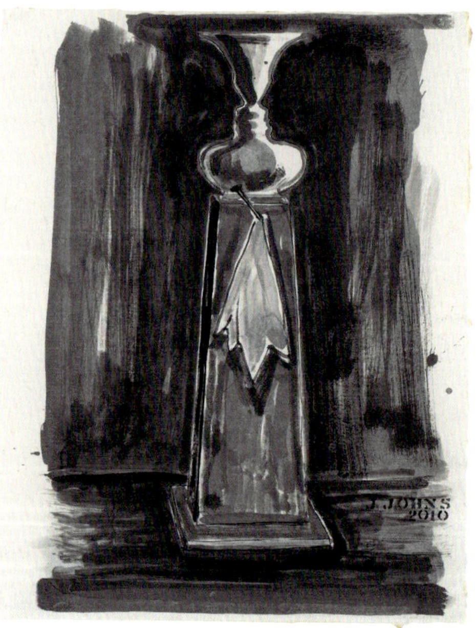

5 ***Catenary (Manet-Degas)***, 1999
7 ***Untitled***, 2002

6 ***From Henri Monnier***, 2000
8 ***Untitled***, 1998

9 ***Untitled***, 2010

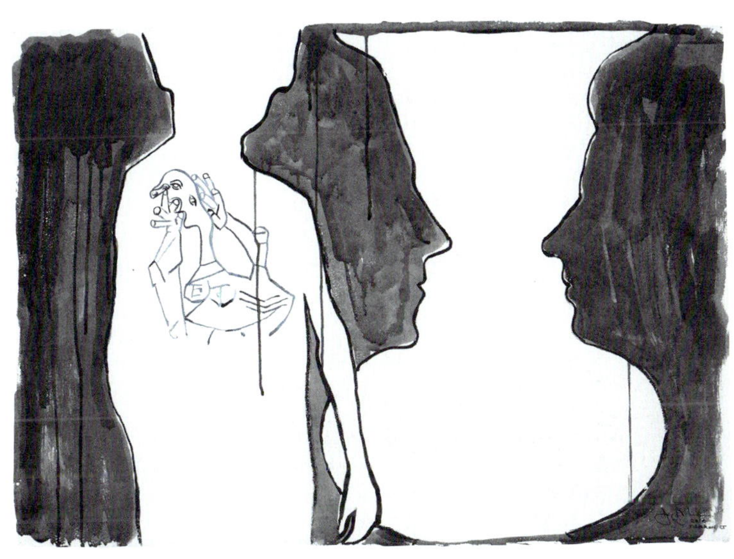

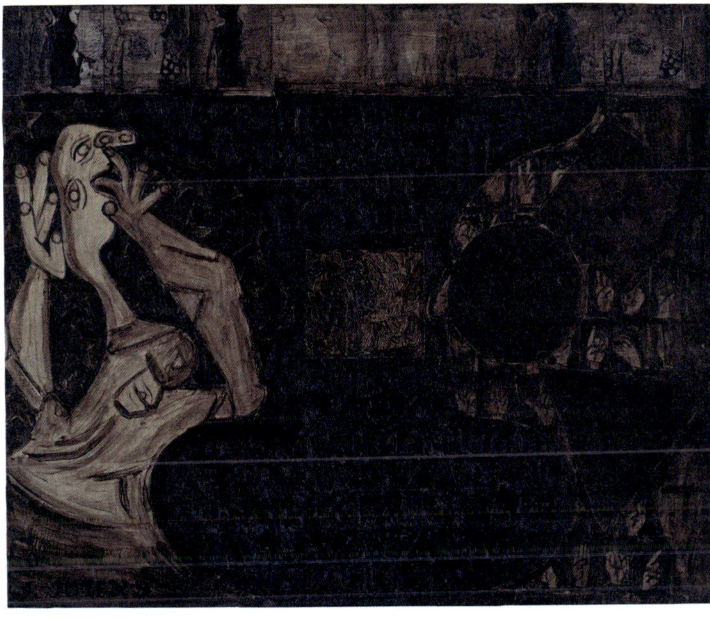

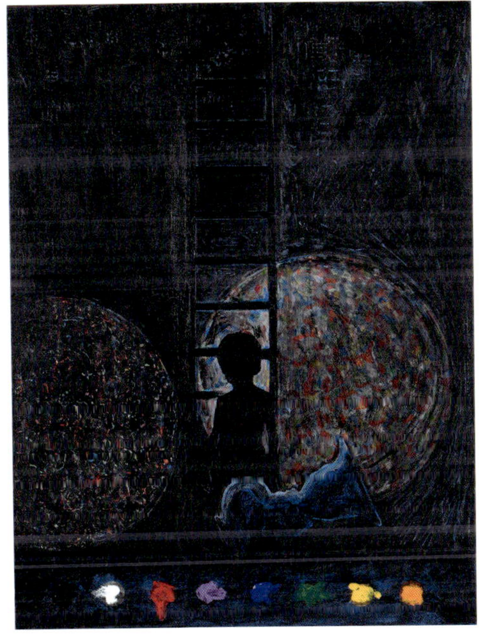

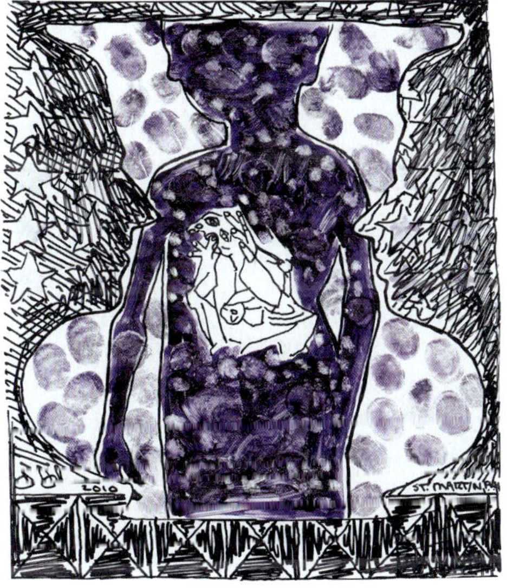

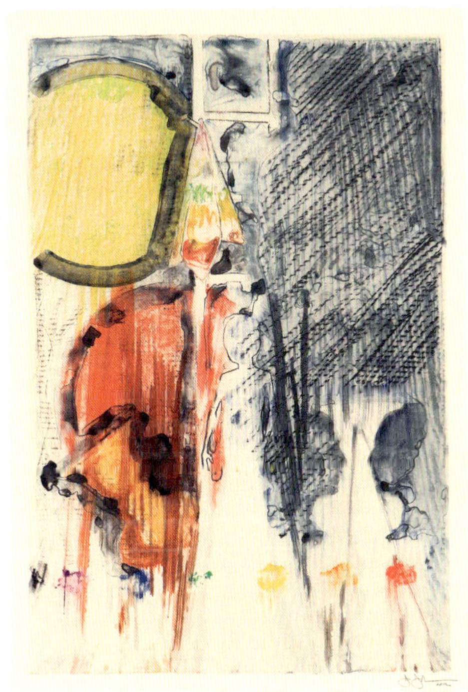

10 ***Untitled*, 2010**
12 ***Untitled*, 2013–14**

11 ***Untitled*, 2017**
13 ***Untitled*, 2010**

14 ***Untitled*, 2012**

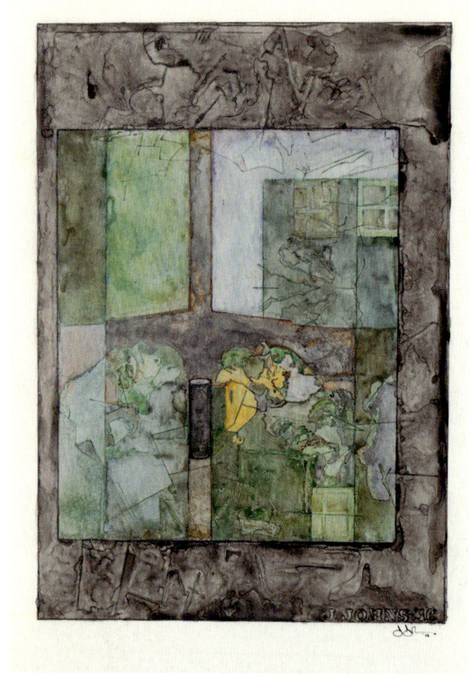

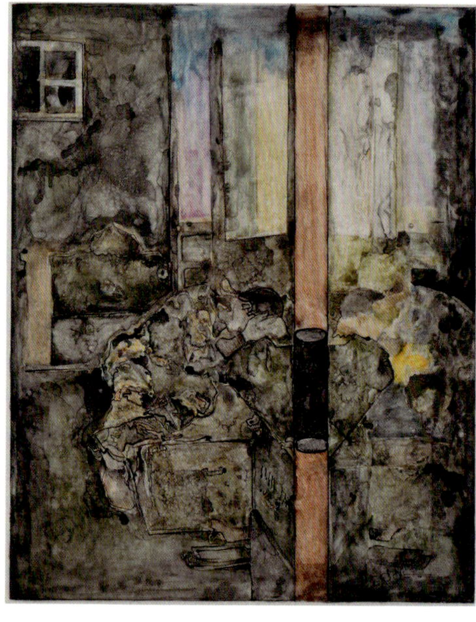

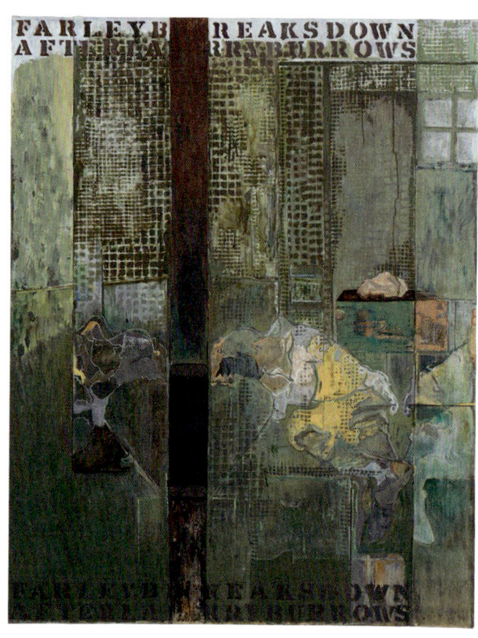

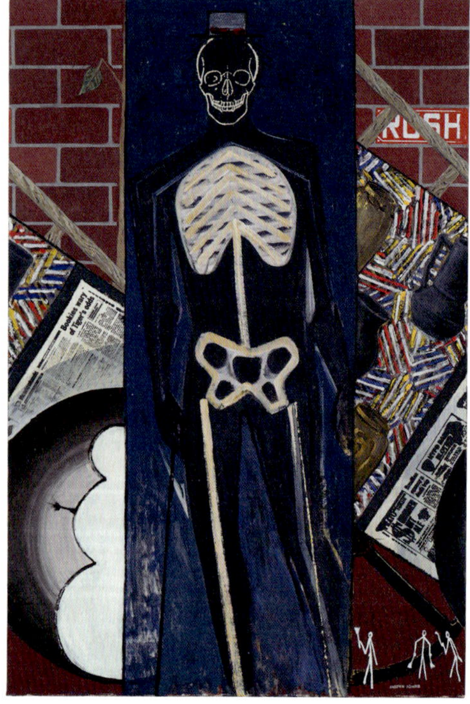

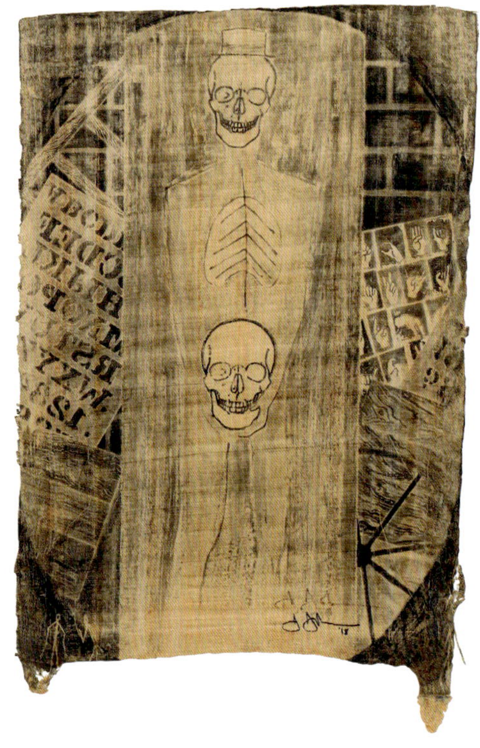

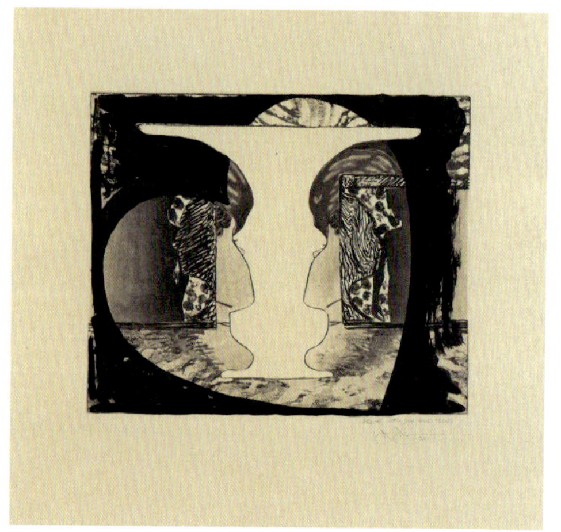

15 ***Untitled*, 2016**
18 ***Untitled*, 2018**

16 ***Untitled*, 2015**
19 ***Untitled*, 2018**

17 ***Untitled*, 2018**
20 ***Untitled*, 2010–11**

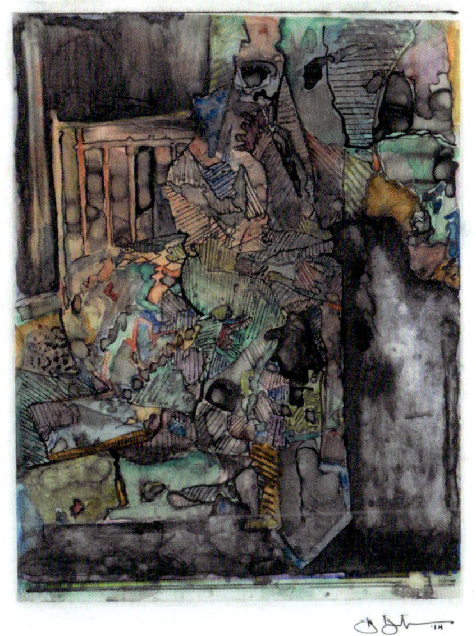

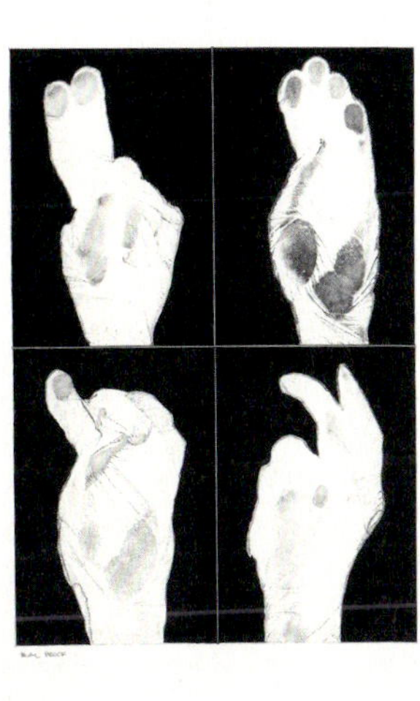

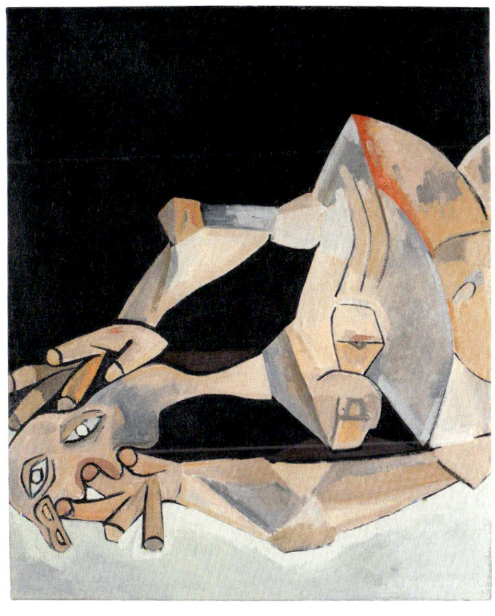

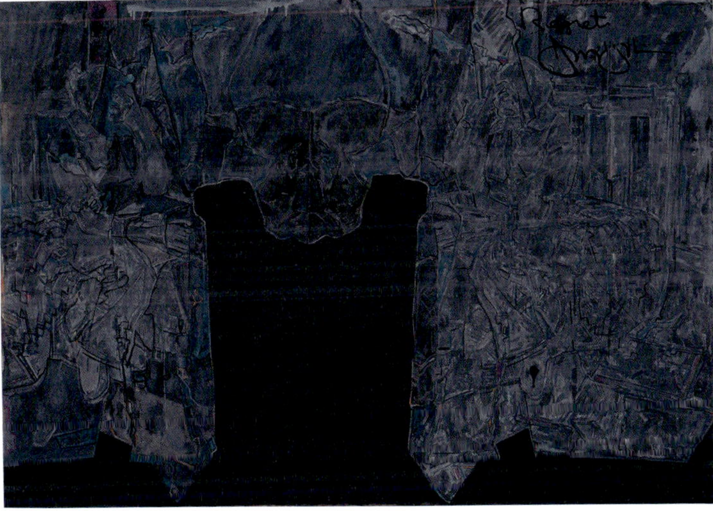

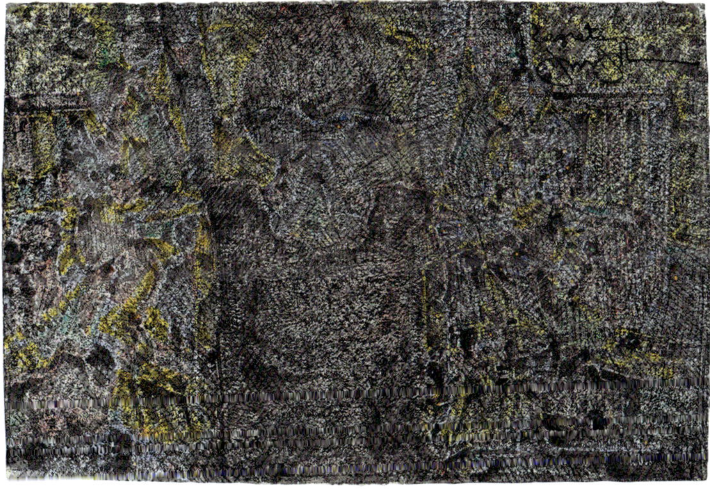

21 ***Untitled*, 2014**

22 ***Untitled*, 1998**

23 ***After Picasso*, 1998**

24 ***Regrets*, 2013**

25 ***Regrets*, 2013**

Of Late
Michael Ann Holly

> The owl of Minerva spreads its wings only with the falling of the dusk.
> —G. W. F. Hegel, *The Philosophy of Right* (1821)

> This is the prerogative of late style: it has the power to render disenchantment and pleasure without resolving the contradiction between them. What holds them in tension, as equal forces straining in opposite directions, is the artist's mature subjectivity, stripped of hubris and pomposity, unashamed either of its fallibility or of the modest assurance it has gained as a result of age and exile.
> —Edward Said, "Thoughts on Late Style" (2004)

Disenchantment and pleasure, melancholy and joy, death and beauty—these are contradictions not easily resolved. What artists shed in youthful vitality, they gain in sagacity. Wisdom, however, comes in many shapes and guises. Like Theodor Adorno before him, Edward Said describes "intransigence, difficulty, and contradiction" as the signature of brilliant late styles in musical masterpieces.[1] To be sure, some artists find serenity as they heroically approach the end of their creative lives, but others, as it were, struggle to hold two ends of the rope bridge of contradiction swinging over the abyss. The latter trait marks Jasper Johns's sublime paintings as he approaches the tenth decade of his life. "Late" in this sense refers not only to his age or his works' place in a chronological evolution but to his recent grappling with themes of mortality and an impending sense of an ending. Nevertheless, there is no clear beginning to Johns's "late style," for some of these animating principles have been present throughout his career. They simply have become more intense, plentiful, and present "of late."

Back to *early* beginnings for a moment. Leo Steinberg, in his classic 1962 essay "Jasper Johns: The First Seven Years of His Art," claims that "Johns puts two flinty things in a picture and makes them work against one another so hard that the mind is sparked. Seeing them becomes thinking."[2] This insight is echoed by Robert Hughes in 1980: in the wake of Abstract Expressionism, Johns is forcing "his viewers to think about representation and the paradoxes it entails."[3] Painting as thought; visual art as a kind of painted philosophy: in these fundamental premises, Johns's works alter very little over the course of sixty years, even if their iconography differs wildly. Not the *last* seven years of his art (to parallel Steinberg), but recent work—Johns's so-called late style—is the subject of this essay.

Consider the suggestively subtitled *Catenary (I Call to the Grave)* (1998; p. 267, pl. 1) from Johns's Catenary series (1997–2003). Is it too much of a critical cliché to say that the lone string attached to the upper right and falling in a graceful swerve to the lower left, before it briefly escapes the wooden frame, has something to do with the arc of life in this quiet, transcendent painting? The right-hand strip of the painted encaustic background harks back to Johns's youth by bequeathing an afterlife to his harlequin motifs, with the remaining three-quarters sensuously painted in subtle shades of silvery gray. The palest of lights barely flickers through a nowhere wall streaked with—tears? fog? rain? Johns, as silent as his work, does not say and professes not to know (although, according to John Cage, he was captivated by Leonardo's deluge drawings in Windsor Castle).[4] A similar Catenary painting, which now hangs in Johns's kitchen in Connecticut, has the curvature of the string, after its fall, ascend again to the opposite upper corner. A cheerier resolution to the arc of life, perhaps? The thickly painted encaustic once in a while reveals the barest hint of color (maroon and especially light blue, as the paint beneath mirrors the actual string in front of it) peeking through the gray impasto, but in this case the deliberately shaky wooden frame is "hanging on," loosely attached by hooks to the canvas beneath.

In the catalogue accompanying the 2007–8 show *Jasper Johns: Gray* at the Art Institute of Chicago (followed by a similar exhibition at the Metropolitan Museum of Art in New York), the curators characterize Johns's palette of grays as the "look of thought" by invoking an aphorism from Hegel: "When philosophy paints its grey in grey, then has a shape of life grown old. By philosophy's grey in grey it cannot be rejuvenated but only understood."[5] Collectively, these late works no doubt constitute a visual meditation on frailty, aging, death, and mortality. Encaustic, a painterly technique used by ancient Egyptians to portray effigies of the mummified dead on their coffins (fig. 1), is also resurrected by Johns for his recent somber and fragmented multiple portraits of Lance Corporal James Farley and Lucian Freud (more about them in a moment). It has been rumored that Johns keeps a small, bubbling cauldron of wax nearby when painting in his studio. A kind of alchemy at work?

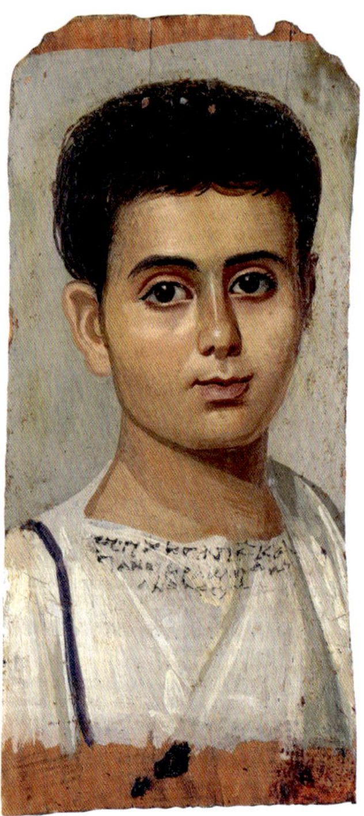

Fig. 1 ***Portrait of the Boy Eutyches*, 100–150 CE**
Egypt, Roman period. Encaustic on wood, paint, 15 × 7 ½ in. (38.1 × 19 cm). The Metropolitan Museum of Art, New York; gift of Edward S. Harkness, 18.9.2

A melancholic shadow is thrown over Johns's late works; on this nearly all his many contemporary critics would agree. Their time, their place, is located somewhere between dying and death. One critic declares that underlying the works exhibited at Matthew Marks Gallery in early 2019 is "a deeply felt, intellectual inquiry into what it means to exist, to live with one's memories, to grow old, and die." Another refers to "a tangible weight of melancholy [that] infuses his palette and surfaces," and a third cites the "melancholic finality of recent works."[6] In her 2017 book about Johns, Fiona Donovan echoes Said and Adorno when she speaks about the "brooding clarity" that characterizes Johns's "late style" as "disenchantment and beauty coexist[ing] without the impulse to resolve the contradiction."[7] It requires a look back at the Renaissance notion of this saturnine temperament, what rhetoricians of that age characterized as "artist's melancholy," to imagine why this is neither a dispirited nor a harmonious resolution to a long life, but instead a productive paradox.

Although there are probably thousands of depictions of Melancholy in the West from the ancient to the contemporary world, one of the most famous is Albrecht Dürer's *Melencolia I*, an engraving from 1514 (fig. 2). Here the personification sits, almost but not quite a fallen angel, a saturnine genius surrounded by all the instruments of earthly knowledge and human initiative—scale, mathematical equations, compass, saw, ladder, hammer, discarded nails, and so on—accompanied by a chubby cupid and an emaciated dog. A comet illuminates the sky at twilight, and a "squeaking bat" unfurls a banner announcing the subject of the scene. Melancholy's eyes glow eerily in the crepuscular light, as she rests her head disconsolately against her hand, perhaps aware of all the secrets of the universe that, even with all our instruments of knowledge, we will never comprehend. She seems mired in "gloomy inaction," a state of mind reflected in the paraphernalia strewn about her in bewildering disarray. The scene of unrest underscores its familiar etiology as one of the four Renaissance temperaments coursing through bodily fluids: in this case, black bile is dry, autumnal, and connected to evening and old age.[8]

This compendium of melancholic traits can nevertheless be turned inside out, as it sometimes was by humanists and, perhaps,

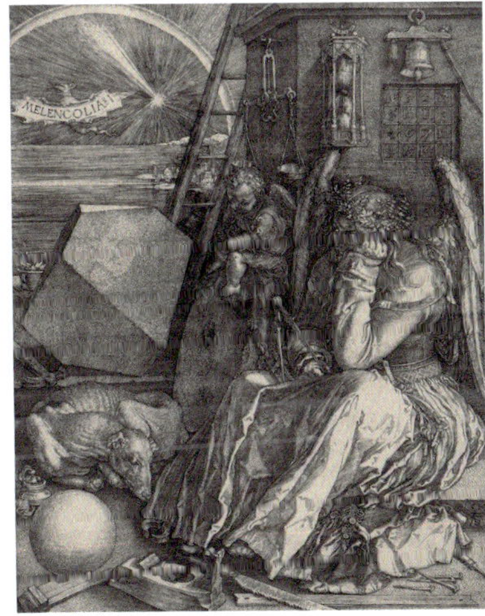

Fig. 2 **Albrecht Dürer (German, 1471–1528). *Melencolia I*, 1514**
Engraving, 9 ½ × 7 ⅜ in. (24.1 × 18.7 cm). Philadelphia Museum of Art; purchased with the Lisa Norris Elkins Fund, 1951-96-5

by Dürer himself. Divine inspiration—*furor melancholicus* as induced by Saturn—was reputed to be the origin of genius, in visual art, in literature, in the mechanical arts, even in the arts of statehood. Viewed as the source of an ecstasy capable of awakening a sleeping, disheartened soul, artist's melancholy carries with it another kind of unrest, but this one spurs active creation rather than passive despair. In the psychoanalyst Melanie Klein's theory, the creation of art cures the suffering soul by generating, above all, a sense of reparation.[9] Paradox and perplexity drive the melancholic forward. Contradictions abound: aspiration and failure, serenity and anguish, euphoria and despair (akin to what Said characterizes as the creative imbalances of a certain "late style"). By the nineteenth century, the personification of Melancholy had persuasively braided together seemingly contradictory attributes, such as neurasthenic suffering and bursts of creative brilliance, and thereby served as a coveted standard for the Romantic sensibility.[10]

Looking at Johns's multiple renditions of Lance Corporal Farley and Lucian Freud in a variety of media, one cannot help musing how the ghost of Renaissance melancholy still haunts not only their formal characteristics but also their content, their subjects' postures as well as the artist's urge to press onward, to repeat again and again. As the critic Christopher Knight describes, "Death, the specter of mortality, is here essential to making art that lives."[11]

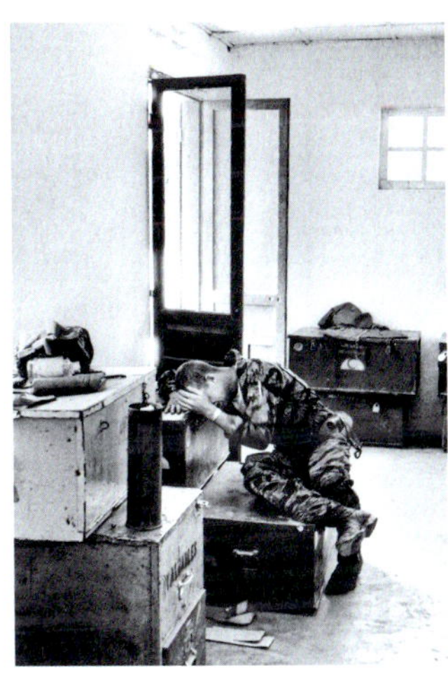

Fig. 3 **Marine Lance Corporal James C. Farley crying in an office over the death of fellow soldiers during the Vietnam War, Vietnam, March 31, 1965**
Photograph by Larry Burrows (English, 1926–1971)

Published in 1965 during the Vietnam war, the *Life* photograph of Lance Corporal Farley by Larry Burrows captures the desolation suffered by the young gunner after the death of other marines in a failed helicopter mission (fig. 3). It is a picture of all-consuming grief far beyond the state of artist's melancholy. Alone in an office, head in hands, collapsed into himself, the inconsolable Farley has been a photographic subject preoccupying Johns ever since the 1960s, but never so much as in the last melancholic decade. His 2014 *Farley Breaks Down* (p. 268, pl. 2), executed with ink and encaustic on nonabsorbent plastic, literally breaks down the barely recognizable soldier in the photograph, who is himself breaking down. His camouflage uniform bleeds outward into exquisite mineralized puddles of green and gray and yellow and pink (not the blood red that might remind us of Sigmund Freud's definition of melancholy as "the wound that will not heal"[12]). Abject hurt is dissolved into unrecognizable agate-like shapes as old as the rock itself. Broken and distorted forms, stunning in their sensuousness, contribute to the very indeterminacy that the drawing courts. As Peter Schjeldahl writes, "As always, his beautiful touch—as patient as solitaire, as unpredictable as roulette—simultaneously establishes and etherealizes the image. You can seek to make out the figure or contemplate how Johns painted it."[13] But you cannot do both simultaneously, a visual trick that Johns adopted from his frequent reading of Ludwig Wittgenstein and especially the philosopher's intriguing rabbit-duck riddle, deployed in works such as *Spring* (1986; p. 190, pl. 7).[14] The artist himself has long been a trickster of sorts with his intricate visual interplay of showing and concealing: a skeleton as joker, listing off-kilter in a darkened doorway and sporting a silly Buster Keaton hat (see, for example, p. 274, pl. 18), or a shadowy silhouette of a man or a child seemingly just passing through. Some great artists confront "the end" courageously, bathed in a feeling of peace (as Said intimated), but Johns faces it with both "a grin and a grimace."[15]

The artist's Regrets series, titled prosaically after a rubber stamp, is anything but commonplace, offering a sustained meditation on art and death. As Robert Storr notes, "Embedded in all those signs and in every layer of their background or support is an ineffable sorrow and a dull ache that cannot be mistaken for anything but what they are."[16] The origin of the series, which comprises two paintings, ten drawings, and two prints, can be traced to a 1964 photograph of Lucian Freud that formally relates to the Farley "portraits," provoked as it is by a figure in a similar melancholic pose. This torn and tattered photograph, once owned by Francis Bacon (and found by Johns in a Christie's catalogue), depicts a contorted Freud on a patterned quilt haphazardly thrown atop a simple single bed with an iron bedstead, newspapers scattered on the floor (fig. 4). Again, his tortured pose and dejected mood set the pictorial tone of the many renditions to follow.

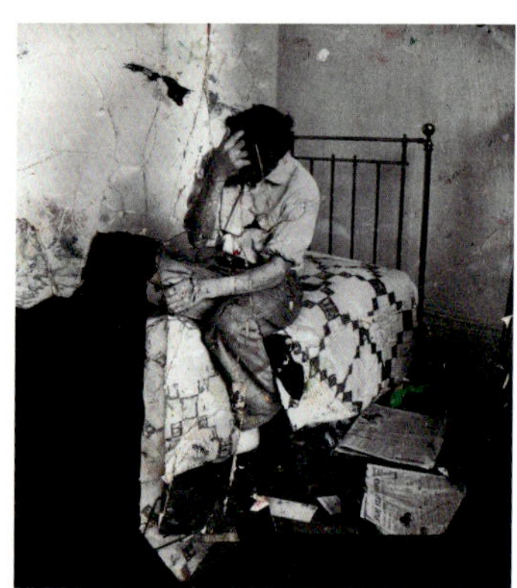

Fig. 4 **Lucian Freud on a bed, 1964**
Photograph by John Deakin (English, 1912–1972)

When Johns "replicates" the photograph, he expands and reduces the details, fills in the missing corner, and adds (or do we only imagine it?) particulars not in the original (see p. 261, pl. 12; and p. 262, pls. 17, 18). Distressed cracks and folds are filled in as strange shapes and colors entangle Freud "in complex, cubistic gatherings of lines and voids, blacks and greys, reflections and imaginings."[17] Bits and pieces of recognizable forms dissolve, like honey in hot tea, into unrecognizable puddles. The doubling of motifs causes the work to read like a Rorschach test. "It's spooky," according to one critic. "The absence of the photograph comes to form a presence in the painting,"[18] kind of like a shadowy ghost in Johns's untitled 2013–14 painting (p. 273, pl. 12). In the middle of several versions of *Regrets* looms a giant death's head (shades of the anamorphic skull in Hans Holbein's *Ambassadors* of 1533), often not recognized at first glance, topping what might be a tombstone, a cenotaph, an age-old monument to the dead and dying, or simply a reminder of the shape of what's torn away in the original photograph, now doubled (see p. 182, pl. 8; p. 275, pls. 24, 25; and p. 295, pl. 34). It is a curious doubling of what's not there in the first place—what's gone missing, what will never return, nearly always aspects of Johns's private pictorial syntax. The dark grays appear crystallized on the wintry surface, like a frozen pond exuding fantastic icy patterns. An isolated and silent secret seems to lie deep within.

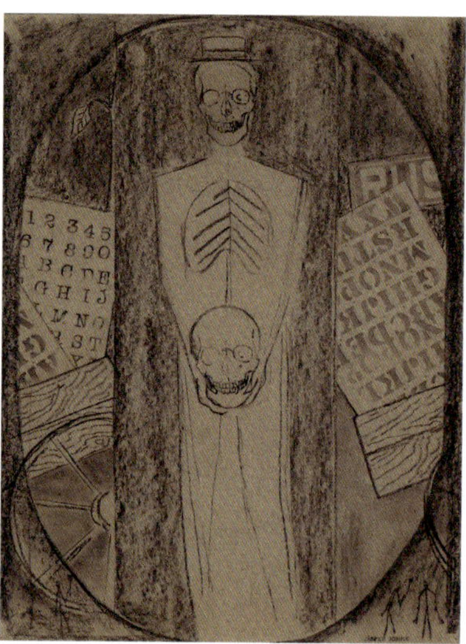

Fig. 5 ***Untitled*, 2018**
Charcoal on paper mounted on paper, 32 ⅛ × 24 in. (81.6 × 61 cm).
Private collection

A complicated, not exactly tortured, visual silence marks Johns's "late style," a questioning mood that accepts yet resists the silence that comes from what cannot be seen. It is almost as though he is harboring, or lending artistic shape and form, to the phenomenologist Maurice Merleau-Ponty's quandary about his own attentiveness to particularly significant objects: "I always feel [*éprouve*] that there is still some being beyond what I currently see, and not merely more visible being.... There is always an horizon of unseen or even invisible things around my present vision," resulting in a work of art's "irrecusable presence and ... perpetual absence into which it withdraws."[19] Johns's late style? Smiling skeletons (fig. 5), sinister skulls, stick figures, snowmen, dissolving figures—not so much a style as a constellation of elegiac subjects that face us with intransigence and difficulty. Visual valedictions to an art of contradiction: absence and presence, seen and unseen, disenchantment and pleasure, incompleteness and sublimity, melancholy and joy, agitation and silence, death and beauty.

A conclusion to Jasper Johns's late style? Mercifully, it's too early to tell.

1 Edward Said, "Thoughts on Late Style," *London Review of Books*, August 5, 2004; Theodor Adorno, "Late Style in Beethoven" (1937), in *Essays on Music*, ed. Richard Leppert, trans. Susan H. Gillespie et al. (Berkeley: University of California Press, 2002), 564–68. On late style, see also Kenneth Clark, "The Artist Grows Old" (1970), *Daedalus* 135, no. 1 (Winter 2006): 77–90.

2 Leo Steinberg, "Jasper Johns: The First Seven Years of His Art" (1962), in *Other Criteria: Confrontations with Twentieth-Century Art* (New York: Oxford University Press, 1972), 54.

3 Robert Hughes, *The Shock of the New: Art and the Century of Change* (London: British Broadcasting Corporation, 1980), 340.

4 See Christopher Knight's review of the 2018 exhibition *Jasper Johns: "Something Resembling Truth"* at the Broad Museum, Los Angeles, "Does the Broad's New Jasper Johns Exhibition Hit the Bull's Eye? It Gets Darn Close," *Los Angeles Times*, February 9, 2018. The anecdote about Johns and Leonardo comes from John Cage, "Jasper Johns: Stories and Ideas," in *Jasper Johns*, by Alan R. Solomon, exh. cat. (New York: Jewish Museum, 1964), cited by Max Kozloff in *Jasper Johns* (New York: Harry N. Abrams, 1967), 38.

5 G. W. F. Hegel, quoted in James Rondeau and Douglas Druick, *Jasper Johns: Gray*, exh. cat. (Chicago: Art Institute of Chicago, 2007), 32.

6 John Yau, "Jasper Johns's Messengers of Aging and Mortality," *Hyperallergic*, February 17, 2019, https://hyperallergic.com/484848/jasper-johns-recent-paintings-and-works-on-paper-matthew-marks-gallery/ (accessed February 27, 2020); Robert Storr, "Bewitched, Bothered and Bewildered," in *Jasper Johns*, ed. Roberta Bernstein, exh. cat. (London: Royal Academy of Arts in collaboration with the Broad, 2017), 27; Isabel Loring Wallace, *Jasper Johns* (London: Phaidon, 2014), 14.

7 Fiona Donovan, *Jasper Johns: Pictures within Pictures, 1980–2015* (London: Thames and Hudson, 2017), 17.

8 My description of Dürer's print is indebted to Erwin Panofsky, *The Life and Art of Albrecht Dürer* (1943; Princeton: Princeton University Press, 1955), 156–71. See also my book *The Melancholy Art* (Princeton: Princeton University Press, 2013).

9 Julia Kristeva, *Melanie Klein*, trans. Ross Guberman (New York: Columbia University Press, 2001), 80.

10 For many thinkers, the era of melancholy runs from the fourteenth century to the "end" of modernism in the late twentieth century. See Jennifer Radden, ed., *The Nature of Melancholy: From Aristotle to Kristeva* (Oxford: Oxford University Press, 2000). Panofsky earlier had claimed that Dürer's engraving is a "spiritual self-portrait," but in 2017 Mitchell Merback went so far as to assert that the picture has a "therapeutic goal": as a work good to think with, *Melencolia I* "is complete in its incompleteness, perfect in its studied imperfections. Perplexity is the picture's therapeutic gift, its diagnosis and its cure." See Mitchell Merback, *Perfection's Therapy: An Essay on Albrecht Dürer's "Melencolia I"* (Brooklyn, NY: Zone, 2017), 261.

11 Knight, "Broad's New Jasper Johns Exhibition."

12 Sigmund Freud, "On Mourning and Melancholia" (1917), in *Freud: The Standard Edition of the Complete Psychological Works of Sigmund Freud*, ed. and trans. James Strachey (London: Hogarth, 1973), 14:253.

13 Peter Schjeldahl, "Jasper Johns and the Question of Meaning," *New Yorker*, February 25, 2019, https://www.newyorker.com/magazine/2019/03/04/jasper-johns-and-the-question-of-meaning (accessed February 27, 2020).

14 For more on Johns's indebtedness to Wittgenstein's "language games," see Storr, "Bewitched," 35–37.

15 Jonathan Jones, "Jasper Johns's Regrets Review: Love and Loss as Death Comes Knocking," *Guardian* (London), September 12, 2014.

16 Storr, "Bewitched," 37.

17 Jones, "Jasper Johns's Regrets."

18 Noelle Bodick, "How to Understand Jasper Johns's Haunting 'Regrets' at MoMA," *Artspace*, April 26, 2014, https://www.artspace.com/magazine/interviews_features/in_depth/jasper_johns_regrets_walk_through-52234 (accessed February 27, 2020).

19 Maurice Merleau-Ponty, *Phenomenology of Perception*, trans. Donald A. Landes (1945; London: Routledge, 2012), 224–25, 242.

Editioned Prints

Jasper Johns's sixty-year involvement with printmaking has been so profound that it is hard to say whether the medium was a natural extension of his turn of mind or what shaped it. In 1964, he wrote in his sketchbook, "Take an object / Do something to it / Do something else to it / [repeat]."[1] This oft-quoted precept aptly describes Johns's painterly investigations of a motif such as a target or a flag, but it even more perfectly epitomizes the process of making a print. In that instance, the "object" is an image on a plate, which the artist and printers subject to myriad possible revisions before proofing and printing with various inks and papers. Working with a matrix necessarily allows—even frees—Johns to experiment intuitively with the formal and expressive possibilities of an image, as does the collaborative nature of the printshop, the alchemy of the half-blind procedures, the ease of testing variations, and the chance outcomes of the press. Since his first lithograph in 1960, made at the invitation of Tatyana Grosman, founder of Universal Limited Art Editions on Long Island, New York, he has made 343 editioned prints and more than two thousand unique proofs and monotypes in collaboration with master printers at studios on two continents. Nearly all feature motifs found in his most important paintings and sculptures or elaborate on those works themselves. Yet Johns's prints are never mere reproductions. They expand on ideas latent in his work in other media and constitute a labyrinthine parallel corpus that both summarizes his oeuvre and pressures it into new directions.

Printmaking inherently involves reversal and reproduction, two hallmarks of Johns's art. Throughout his paintings and drawings, he often flips compositions left to right or top to bottom. He mirrors patterns around a seam or impresses surfaces with implements he sometimes leaves stuck to them. All this happens more easily, if not automatically, in printmaking, and over the years his work in that medium has amplified his fascination with these operations on canvas. Without the aid of an offset press, the image on the matrix necessarily mirrors what is printed on the paper, and a plate can just as effortlessly be rotated before the next proof is pulled. But the greater conceptual correspondence between Johns's printmaking and the rest of his art lies in its essentially systematic and iterative procedures. Johns often works recursively from one painting to the next to the one after that. An image frequently returns—sometimes years and even decades later—in a different size, medium, or palette. Prints both collapse and extend this modality. On the one hand, an individual image may develop over successive discrete campaigns on a matrix, sometimes followed by the sequential superimposition of multiple plates. On the other hand, printmaking allows for the easy unfurling of permutational thinking in contrast to a suite of paintings or drawings, each of which must be started afresh. After a print's final state is reached and editioned, Johns's inquisitive temperament often leads him to "do something else" with the matrix. He might try it again in different colors or invert its values, transforming a black image on light paper into its X-ray correlate. Johns tends to avoid the customary practice of canceling a plate after an edition is complete (to ensure no more examples are made), preferring instead to use that matrix as the launchpad for another work. His mind keeps on turning and so does the press.

Unlike the story of his paintings, Johns's printmaking is a narrative of technical development. Within the first few years of his work on canvas, he had already mastered nearly all the materials he would continue to use there—encaustic, oil, assemblage, Sculp-metal, and eventually silkscreen. The work developed less through the introduction of new techniques than through new images and ideas. Johns's prints, by contrast, have undergone a decades-long evolution of means, from lithography and etching to silkscreen, monotype, and linocut. "What interests me is the technical innovation possible for me in printmaking," he remarked in 1969, well before that journey of discovery was complete.[2] For Johns, each technique suggests its unique quality and possibility. Lithography allows "great facility"; the etching plate can "store multiple layers of information"; and silkscreen is "best used for images which require sharp edges and smooth-textured, flat, clear areas of color."[3] These techniques are not rote instruments for realizing a preconceived end but instead "make up the life of the work really," as Johns has said. "They are real concerns and make the working process a very lively activity, something other than the reproduction of an image; they alter what 'image' is."[4]

Curiosity about what image is impels Johns's heuristic approach to printmaking. It is the place in his work where the literalism of three dimensions most conspicuously gives way to the illusionism of two. If a painted flag, coterminous to its support, can be both that very thing and its picture, one printed on a page, surrounded by a margin, can only be an image of a flag or an image of a painting of one but never the thing itself. It makes sense, then, that Johns's prints, like his drawings, contained perspectival and volumetric illusionism some three decades before his paintings: they are all involved in the work of representation, if not exactly reproduction. Indeed, Johns's prints comprise an auto-anthology of familiar motifs, iconic paintings and sculptures, and details of them, all metamorphosed by their transposition from one medium into another. Surveyed chronologically, as they are in the portion of this exhibition presented at the Whitney, they present entwined timelines of Johns's motifs, means, and ideas. Yet the effect is by no means linear, given how images recur and recombine, far more promiscuously in his prints than in his paintings. (Johns hasn't painted a target in nearly thirty years, but he has printed one in the past three.) In the spirit of this nonlinearity, the prints exhibited at the Philadelphia Museum of Art are arranged according to chance with the aid of ROVER, a computer program developed by Andrew Culver and John Cage, who used it to install and reshuffle his exhibition *Rolywholyover A Circus for Museum by John Cage* at the same venue in 1995. ROVER also organized the images in the pages that follow, creating, like the prints themselves, an aleatory index of familiar images and fresh encounters.

—Scott Rothkopf, with Carlos Basualdo, Sarah B. Vogelman, and Lauren Young

1 Jasper Johns, "Book A, p. 42, c. 1963–64," in *Jasper Johns: Writings, Sketchbook Notes, Interviews*, ed. Kirk Varnedoe (New York: Museum of Modern Art, 1996), 54 (hereafter abbreviated Varnedoe, *WSI*).

2 Jasper Johns, quoted in Joseph E. Young, "Jasper Johns: An Appraisal," *Art International* 13, no. 7 (September 1969); reprinted in Varnedoe, *WSI*, 131.

3 Jasper Johns, quoted in Mark Stevens with Cathleen McGuigan, "Super Artist: Jasper Johns, Today's Master," *Newsweek*, October 24, 1977, reprinted in Varnedoe, *WSI*, 165; Jasper Johns, "Interview mit Jasper Johns / Interview with Jasper Johns," interview by Christian Geelhaar, in *Jasper Johns: Working Proofs*, ed. Christian Geelhaar, exh. cat. (Basel: Kunstmuseum Basel, 1979), reprinted in Varnedoe, *WSI*, 188.

4 Johns, "Interview mit Jasper Johns," 195.

Editioned Prints

Rolywholyover

1 ***Figure 7*, 1968**
Lithograph: one stone, one aluminum plate
37 × 30 in. (94 × 76.2 cm)
Kenneth Tyler/Gemini
Ed. no. 41/70
Whitney Museum of American Art, New York; gift of Robert Simons, 85.46.8

2 ***Leo*, 1997**
Intaglio
37 × 27 in. (94 × 68.6 cm)
John Lund, Lothar Osterburg/Noblet Serigraphie, Inc.
Ed. no. 45/90
Philadelphia Museum of Art; gift of Jean-Christophe Castelli and tribute from the artist in honor of Leo Castelli, 1999-16-1a–i

3 ***Bread*, 1969**
Embossing with object: one relief; sheet lead, oil paint, and paper, with aluminum frame
23 × 17 × 1 ⅝ in. (58.4 × 43.2 × 4.1 cm)
Kenneth Tyler/Gemini
Ed. no. 28/60
Whitney Museum of American Art, New York; purchase with funds from the Howard and Jean Lipman Foundation, Inc., 69.86a–b

4 ***False Start I*, 1962**
Lithograph: eleven stones
31 ½ × 22 ½ in. (80 × 57.2 cm)
Robert Blackburn/ULAE
Ed. no. 15/38
Whitney Museum of American Art, New York; purchase with funds from the Leonard A. Lauder Masterpiece Fund, 2020.99

5 ***Ocean*, 1996**
Lithograph
27 ⅞ × 36 ¾ in. (70.8 × 93.4 cm)
John Lund, Douglas Bennett, Bruce Wankel, Craig Zammiello/ULAE
3/4 PP
Whitney Museum of American Art, New York; purchase with funds from the Print Committee, 99.41

6 ***The Seasons*, 1990**
Intaglio: eight copperplates
50 ¼ × 44 ½ in. (127.6 × 113 cm)
John Lund, Keith Brintzenhofe, Shi Ji-Hong, Craig Zammiello, Hitoshi Kido/ULAE
Ed. no. 47/50
Whitney Museum of American Art, New York; gift of Arthur and Susan Fleischer, 2014.279

7 ***0 through 9*, 1967**
Lithograph: three stones
25 × 20 in. (63.5 × 50.8 cm)
Donn Steward/ULAE
Ed. no. 50/50
Philadelphia Museum of Art; Print Club of Philadelphia Permanent Collection, 1968-55-9

8 ***Untitled*, 2018**
Intaglio with chine collé
37 ¼ × 26 ½ in. (94.6 × 67.3 cm)
John Lund, Brian Berry, Bruce Wankel/ULAE
Ed. no. 20/36
Whitney Museum of American Art, New York; purchase with funds from Leonard A. Lauder, 2019.311

9 ***Untitled*, 2019**
Intaglio
16 ½ × 12 in. (41.9 × 30.5 cm)
John Lund/Low Road Studio
Ed. no. 10/15
Collection David R. Baum and Tilly Macalister-Smith

10 ***Untitled*, 1973**
Silkscreen: three screens
24 × 33 in. (61 × 83.8 cm)
Adolph Rischner and family at Styria Studio/Multiples, Inc.
16/25 AP
Whitney Museum of American Art, New York; promised gift of Emily Fisher Landau

11 ***The Critic Sees*, 1967**
Embossing with silkscreen: one relief, one screen
23 ⅞ × 20 in. (60.6 × 50.8 cm)
Joan Farrar/Tanglewood Press
Ed. no. 119/200
Philadelphia Museum of Art; purchased with the Elizabeth Wandell Smith Fund, 1967-140-7

12 ***Targets*, 1968**
Lithograph with stamp: nine stones, two aluminum plates, one rubber stamp
34 × 25 in. (86.4 × 63.5 cm)
Zigmunds Priede, Fred Genis/ULAE
Ed. no. 32/42
Whitney Museum of American Art, New York; gift of Dr. and Mrs. Harley Shands, 77.103

13 ***Fool's House Black State*, 1972**
Lithograph: one stone, six aluminum plates
44 × 26 in. (111.8 × 66 cm)
Kenneth Tyler/Gemini
Ed. no. 12/18
Whitney Museum of American Art, New York; gift of Stephen Dull, 2015.259

14 ***Decoy*, 1971**
Lithograph with die cut: eighteen aluminum plates, one stone, one die
41 × 29 in. (104.1 × 73.7 cm)
Bill Goldston, James V. Smith, Zigmunds Priede, Steve Anderson/ULAE
AP for an edition of 55
Philadelphia Museum of Art; gift of Barbara Bertozzi Castelli, 2015-135-1

15 ***Spring*, from the Seasons, 1987***
Intaglio: five copperplates
26 × 19 in. (66 × 48.3 cm)
John Lund, Hitoshi Kido, Craig Zammiello, Keith Brintzenhofe/ULAE
Ed. no. 2/73
Whitney Museum of American Art, New York; purchase with funds from the friends of Victor Ganz in his memory, 88.10.1

16 ***Untitled*, 2016**
Intaglio: three plates
19 × 12 in. (48.3 × 30.5 cm)
John Lund/Low Road Studio
Ed. no. 6/30
Collection of Barbara Bertozzi Castelli

17 ***Summer Critic*, 1968**
Embossing with silkscreen: one relief, one screen
9 ¾ × 12 ½ in. (24.8 × 31.8 cm)
Mizue Kano/Shūzō Takiguchi
10/10 AP
Whitney Museum of American Art, New York; gift of the artist, 69.124

18 ***Ruler*, 1966**
Lithograph: two stones
28 × 20 in. (71.1 × 50.8 cm)
Zigmunds Priede/ULAE
Ed. no. 5/25
Philadelphia Museum of Art; gift of Dr. Joseph Singer, 1971-171-1

19 ***Untitled (Ruler)*, 1968**
Silkscreen: four screens
35 ⅞ × 24 ¾ in. (91.1 × 62.9 cm)
Aetna Printing Co./[illegible]
Ed. no. 50/110
Whitney Museum of American Art, New York; gift of the artist, 69.123

20 ***Within*, 2007**
Intaglio
42 ¼ × 32 ½ in. (107.3 × 82.6 cm)
John Lund, Brian Berry, Bill Goldston, Kyle Gruber, Jason Miller, Bruce Wankel/ULAE
6/12 AP
Whitney Museum of American Art, New York; gift of Universal Limited Art Editions, Inc., in honor of Emily Fisher Landau and in memory of Richard L. Fisher, 2007.100

21 ***Fall*, from the Seasons, 1987***
Intaglio: five copperplates
26 × 19 in. (66 × 48.3 cm)
John Lund, Hitoshi Kido, Craig Zammiello, Keith Brintzenhofe/ULAE
Ed. no. 2/73
Whitney Museum of American Art, New York; purchase with funds from the friends of Victor Ganz in his memory, 88.10.3

22 ***Between the Clock and the Bed*, 1989**
Lithograph: ten aluminum plates
29 × 42 in. (73.7 × 106.7 cm)
Bill Goldston, Douglas Volle, Bruce Wankel/ULAE and Friends of the Philadelphia Museum of Art
Ed. no. 1/32
Philadelphia Museum of Art; gift of the Friends of the Philadelphia Museum of Art, 1989-3-3

23 ***Hatteras*, 1963**
Lithograph: one stone
41 × 29 in. (104.1 × 73.7 cm)
Zigmunds Priede/ULAE
Ed. no. 29/30
Philadelphia Museum of Art; gift of an anonymous donor, 1964-87-1

24 ***Watchman*, 1967**
Lithograph: five stones
36 × 24 in. (91.4 × 61 cm)
Zigmunds Priede/ULAE
Ed. no. 13/40
Whitney Museum of American Art, New York; gift of the artist, 69.119

25 ***Untitled*, 1998–2015**
Intaglio
42 × 30 in. (106.7 × 76.2 cm)
John Lund/Low Road Studio
Ed. no. 3/16
Collection David R. Baum and Tilly Macalister-Smith

26 ***Numbers*, 1967**
Lithograph: one stone, one aluminum plate
28 × 23 ½ in. (71.1 × 59.7 cm)
Zigmunds Priede, Fred Genis/ULAE
Ed. no. 15/35
Whitney Museum of American Art, New York; gift of the artist, 69.120

27 ***Art in America*, 2013**
Offset lithograph
16 ⅞ × 12 ½ in. (42.9 × 31.9 cm)
Official Offset under the supervision of Bill Goldston/*Art in America* and Sharon Coplan Hurowitz
Edition of 50,000
Philadelphia Museum of Art; purchased with Museum funds, 2016-47-1

28 ***Light Bulb*, 1966**
Lithograph: two stones
19 ½ × 24 ½ in. (49.5 × 62.2 cm)
Ben Berns/ULAE
Ed. no. 39/45

Philadelphia Museum of Art; gift of Leonard B. Friedman, 1967-112-2

29 ***Gray Alphabets*, 1968**
Lithograph: four aluminum plates
60 × 42 in. (152.4 × 106.7 cm)
Kenneth Tyler, Charles Ritt/Gemini
Ed. no. 13/59
Philadelphia Museum of Art; gift of Barbara Bertozzi Castelli, 2015-135-3

30 ***Target with Four Faces*, 1979**
Intaglio: four copperplates
30 × 22 in. (76.2 × 55.9 cm)
Atelier Crommelynck/Petersburg Press
13/13 AP
Philadelphia Museum of Art; gift of Barbara Bertozzi Castelli, 2015-135-5

31 ***Winter*, from the Seasons, 1987**
Intaglio: five copperplates
26 × 19 in. (66 × 48.3 cm)
John Lund, Hitoshi Kido, Craig Zammiello, Keith Brintzenhofe/ULAE
Ed. no. 2/73
Whitney Museum of American Art, New York; purchase with funds from the friends of Victor Ganz in his memory, 88.10.4

32 ***Corpse and Mirror*, 1976**
Silkscreen: thirty-six screens
42 ¼ × 53 in. (107.3 × 134.6 cm)
Kenjiro Nonaka, Hiroshi Kawanishi, Takeshi Shimada/JJ and SPA
Ed. no. 17/65
Whitney Museum of American Art, New York; gift from the Emily Fisher Landau Collection, 2020.142

33 ***Painting with Two Balls*, 1971**
Silkscreen: proof with three of seven screens
39 ¼ × 27 ½ in. (99.7 × 69.9 cm)
Studio Heinrici, Ltd./JJ
2/2 for an edition of 59
Whitney Museum of American Art, New York; promised gift of Emily Fisher Landau

34 ***Regrets*, 2014**
Intaglio
26 ¼ × 34 ⅛ in. (66.7 × 86.7 cm)
John Lund, Brian Berry/ULAE
Edition of 10
Collection of the artist

35 ***Summer*, from the Seasons, 1987**
Intaglio: five copperplates
26 × 19 in. (66 × 48.3 cm)
John Lund, Hitoshi Kido, Craig Zammiello, Keith Brintzenhofe/ULAE
Ed. no. 2/73
Whitney Museum of American Art, New York; purchase with funds from the friends of Victor Ganz in his memory, 88.10.2

36 ***Land's End*, 1979**
Lithograph: one aluminum plate
52 × 36 in. (132.1 × 91.4 cm)
Charles Ritt, Serge Lozingot/Gemini
Ed. no. 15/70
Philadelphia Museum of Art; gift of the Committee of Prints, Drawings, and Photographs in honor of Muriel and Philip Berman, 1986-1-1

37 ***Voice*, 1967**
Lithograph: one stone, two aluminum plates
48 ½ × 32 in. (123.2 × 81.3 cm)
Zigmunds Priede, Donn Steward, Timothy Huchthausen/ULAE
3/5 AP
Whitney Museum of American Art, New York; gift of Stephen Dull, 2015.258

38 ***Flashlight I*, from 1st Etchings, 2nd State, 1969**
Etching over photoengraving
25 ¾ × 19 ¼ in. (65.4 × 48.9 cm)
Donn Steward/ULAE
Ed. no. 12/40
Philadelphia Museum of Art; gift of William M. Speiller, 1972-270-2

39 ***Voice 2*, 1982**
Three lithographs: twenty aluminum plates
35 ¾ × 24 ¼ in. (90.8 × 61.6 cm) each
Bill Goldston, James V. Smith, Thomas Cox, Keith Brintzenhofe/ULAE
5/5 AP
Philadelphia Museum of Art; gift of Barbara Bertozzi Castelli, 2016-221-1a–c

40 ***Target with Four Faces*, 1968**
Silkscreen: seven screens
41 ½ × 29 ¾ in. (105.4 × 75.6 cm)
Aetna Printing Co./JJ
4/10 AP
Whitney Museum of American Art, New York; gift from the Emily Fisher Landau Collection, 2018.296

41 ***0 through 9*, 1960**
Lithograph: one stone
30 × 22 in. (76.2 × 55.9 cm)
Robert Blackburn/ULAE
Ed. no. 35/35
Philadelphia Museum of Art; Print Club of Philadelphia Permanent Collection, 1962-78-17

42 ***Cicada*, 1979***
Silkscreen: sixteen screens
22 ¼ × 18 ¼ in. (56.5 × 46.4 cm)
Kenjiro Nonaka, Hiroshi Kawanishi, Takeshi Shimada/JJ and SPA
Ed. no. 68/100
Whitney Museum of American Art, New York; promised gift of Emily Fisher Landau

43 ***Periscope I*, 1979***
Lithograph: seven aluminum plates
50 × 36 in. (127 × 91.4 cm)
Serge Lozingot, Anthony Zepeda/Gemini
12/12 AP
Whitney Museum of American Art, New York; gift of David Bolger and Mark Lancaster

44 ***Untitled*, 1995**
Mezzotint
29 ¾ × 22 ½ in. (75.6 × 57.2 cm)
John Lund/Low Road Studio
Ed. no. 25/48
Philadelphia Museum of Art; purchased with funds from the bequest of Drs. Maxwell and Sondra Nemser Scarf, 1996-165-1

45 ***Painting with Two Balls (Exhibition Poster)*, 1971**
Screenprint (poster)
39 ¼ × 27 ½ in. (99.7 × 69.9 cm)
Albin Uldry/Kunsthalle Bern
Unknown edition
Philadelphia Museum of Art; gift of an anonymous donor, 1971-195-1

46 ***Figure 5*, from Black Numeral Series, 1968**
Lithograph: one stone, one aluminum plate
37 × 30 in. (94 × 76.2 cm)
Kenneth Tyler, James Webb/Gemini
Ed. no. 51/70
Philadelphia Museum of Art; purchased with funds contributed by the Women's Committee and the Craft Show Committee of the Philadelphia Museum of Art, 1969-72-1

47 ***Untitled*, 2012**
Intaglio
21 × 16 in. (53.3 × 40.6 cm)
Doug Bennett/LeRoy Neiman Center for Print Studies, Columbia University in the City of New York
Ed. no. 10/30
Whitney Museum of American Art, New York; purchase with funds from the Director's Discretionary Fund, Vanessa and Henry Cornell, Beth Rudin DeWoody, Katja Goldman, Brooke Garber Neidich and Daniel Neidich, Nancy and Fred Poses, Jane Dresner Sadaka and Ned Sadaka, Fern and Lenard Tessler, and Carol and Michael Weisman, 2013.95

48 ***Untitled*, 1999**
Intaglio
29 ½ × 17 ¾ in. (74.9 × 45.1 cm)
John Lund, Jihong Shi, Craig Zammiello/ULAE
Ed. no. 2/46
Whitney Museum of American Art, New York; promised gift of Emily Fisher Landau

49 ***Target*, 1960**
Lithograph: one stone
22 ½ × 17 ½ in. (57.2 × 44.5 cm)
Robert Blackburn/ULAE
Ed. no. 10/30
Whitney Museum of American Art, New York; purchase with funds from the Print Committee, 85.62

50 ***Untitled*, 1988**
Carborundum: three plates
35 ⅝ × 47 in. (90.5 × 119.4 cm)
Maurice Payne/JJ
Ed. no. 9/36
Whitney Museum of American Art, New York; purchase in honor of Charles Simon, with funds given by his friends from Salomon Brothers on the occasion of his 75th birthday, 90.14

51 ***Untitled*, 2010**
Intaglio
19 × 21 ½ in. (48.3 × 54.6 cm)
John Lund, Brian Berry/Low Road Studio to benefit the Museum of Modern Art Department of Prints and Illustrated Books
Ed. no. 40/50
Whitney Museum of American Art, New York; purchase with funds from an anonymous donor in honor of Emily Fisher Landau, 2011.8

52 ***Recent Still Life*, 1966**
Lithograph: one stone, one aluminum plate
35 × 20 in. (88.9 × 50.8 cm)
Ben Berns/ULAE
Ed. no. 2/100
Philadelphia Museum of Art; purchased with the Print Revolving Fund, 1966-208-24

53 ***Passage II*, 1966**
Lithograph: four stones, one aluminum plate
28 × 36 in. (71.1 × 91.4 cm)
Zigmunds Priede, Donn Steward/ULAE
Ed. no. 12/20
Philadelphia Museum of Art; purchased with the Elizabeth Wandell Smith Fund, 1967-201-3

54 ***Souvenir*, 1970**
Lithograph: nine stones
30 ½ × 21 ½ in. (77.5 × 54.6 cm)
Frank Akers/ULAE
Ed. no. 23/50
Whitney Museum of American Art, New York; gift of Stanley and Renie Helfgott, 74.124

55 ***Bushbaby*, 2004**
Intaglio
43 × 30 in. (109.2 × 76.2 cm)
John Lund, Bill Goldston, Phil Sanders, Jason Miller, Bruce Wankel/ULAE
Edition of 55
Collection of Beth Rudin DeWoody

56 ***Untitled*, 2020***
Intaglio
14 × 14 in. (35.6 × 35.6 cm)
Edition of 35

Rolywholyover

WHITNEY MUSEUM OF AMERICAN ART & PHILADELPHIA MUSEUM OF ART

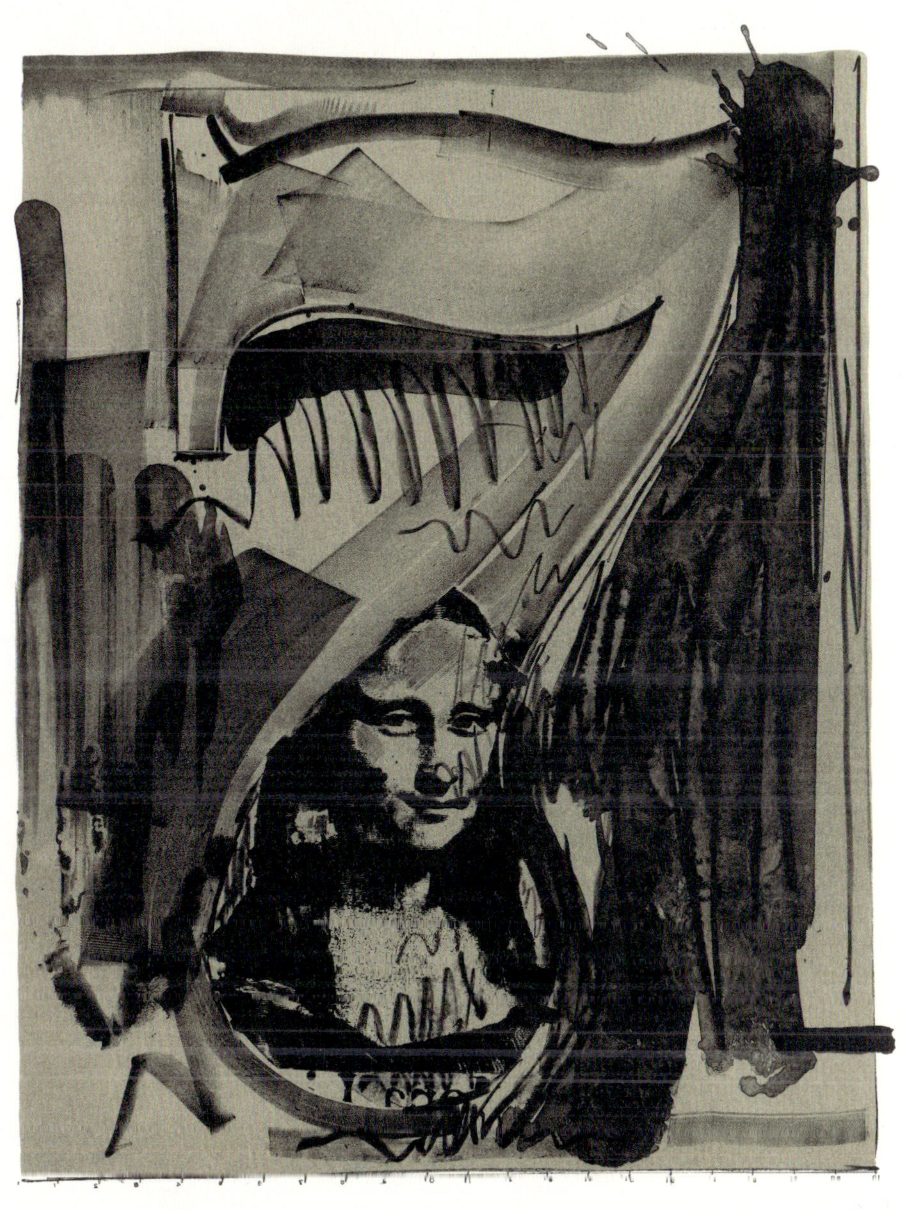

1 ***Figure 7*****, 1968**

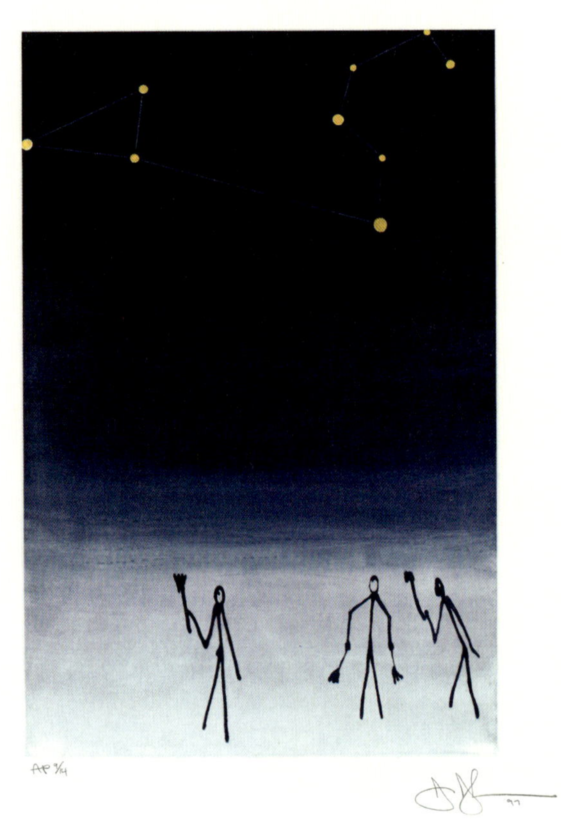

2 *Leo*, **1997**

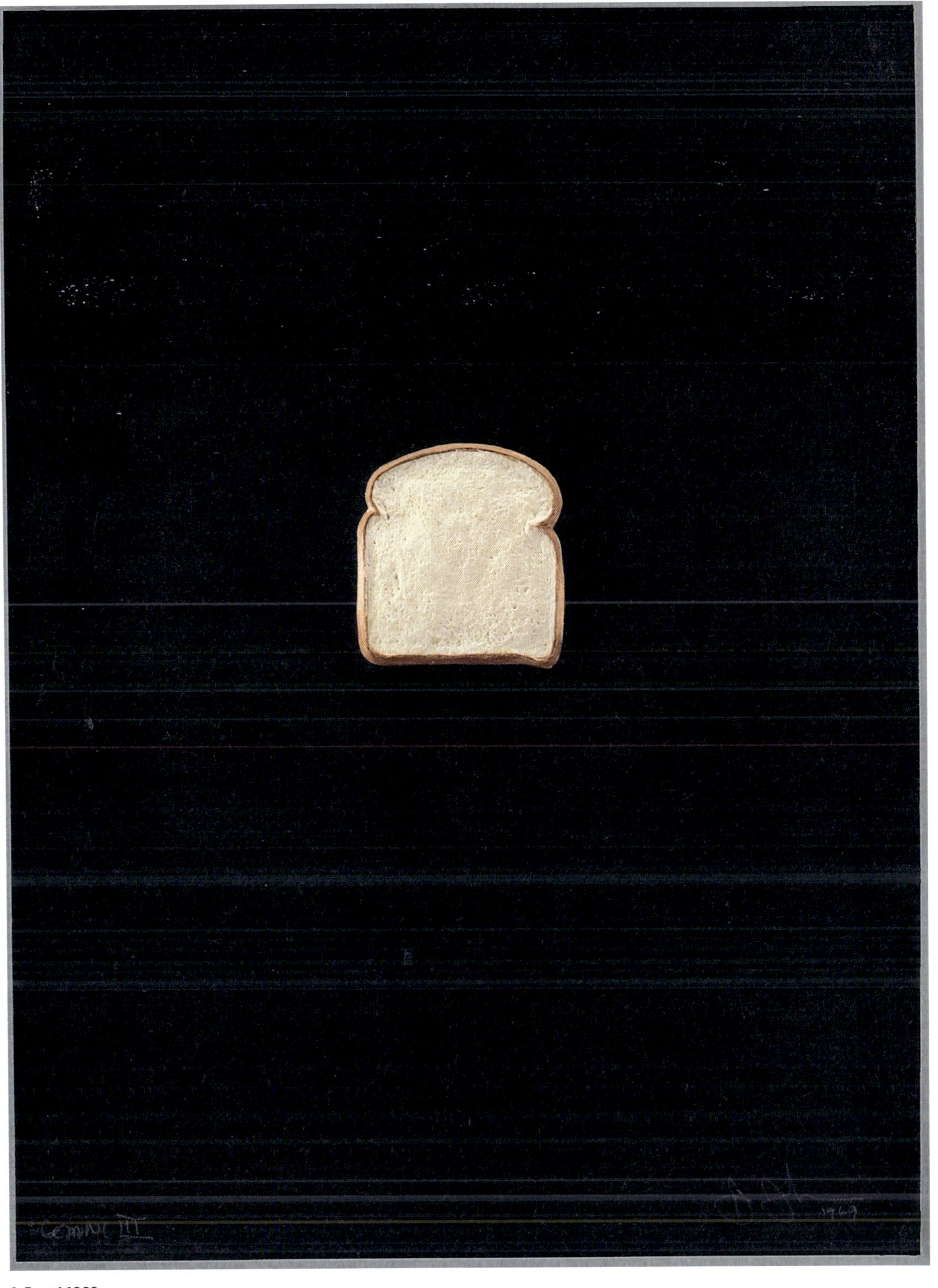

3 ***Bread***, 1969

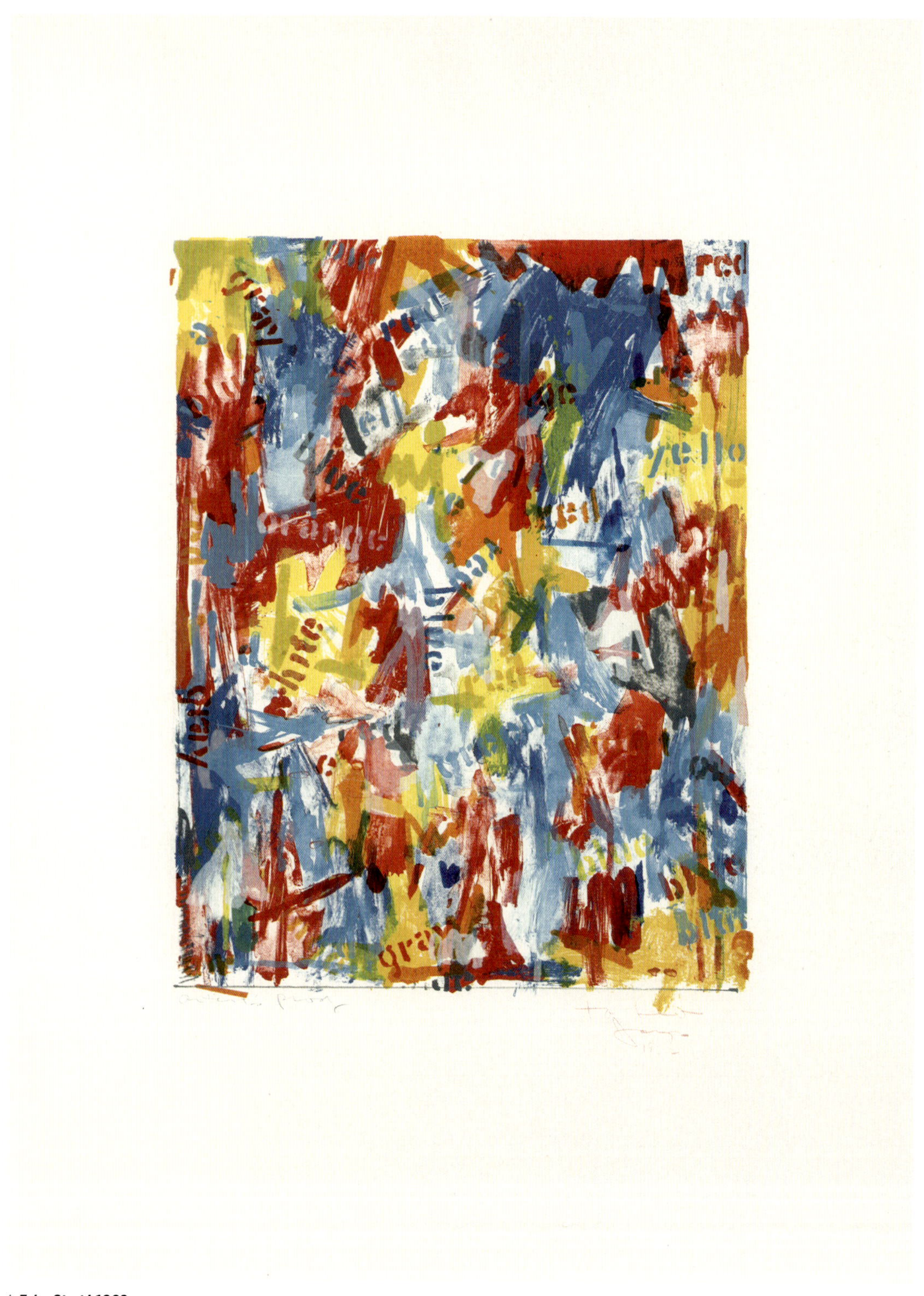

4 ***False Start I*, 1962**

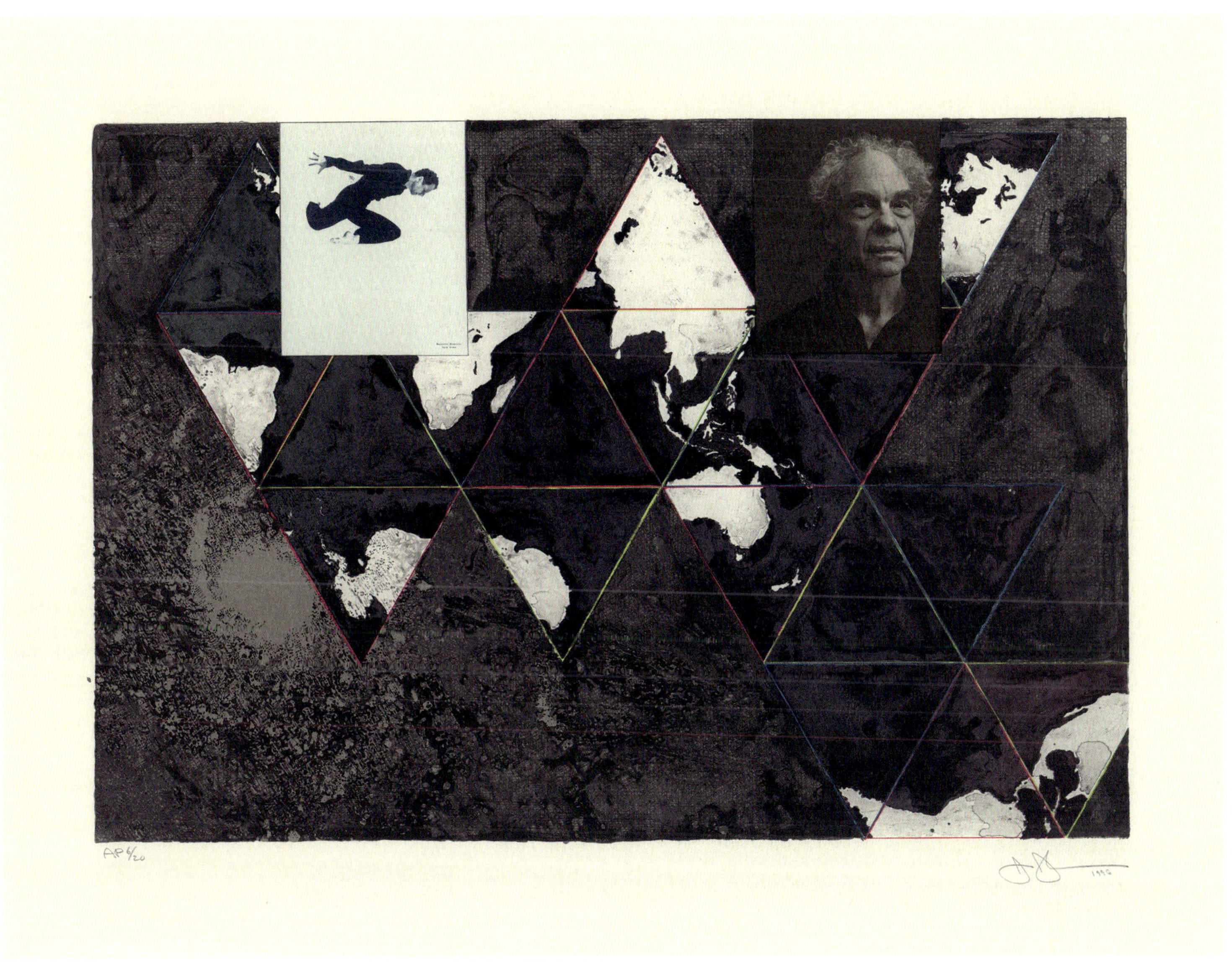

5 ***Ocean*, 1996**

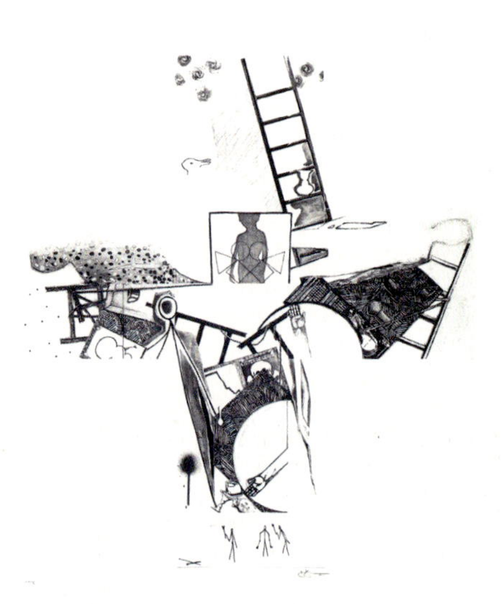

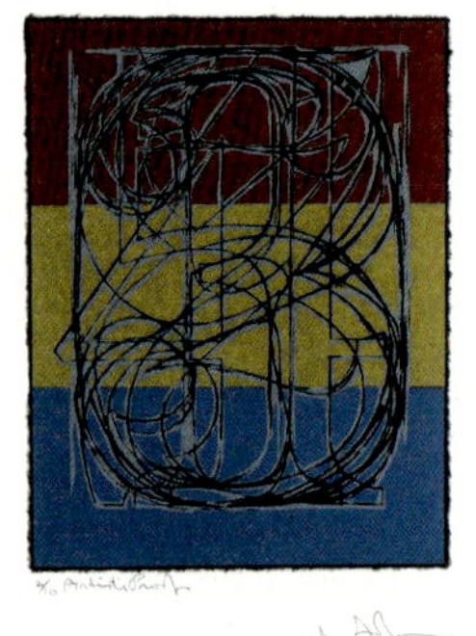

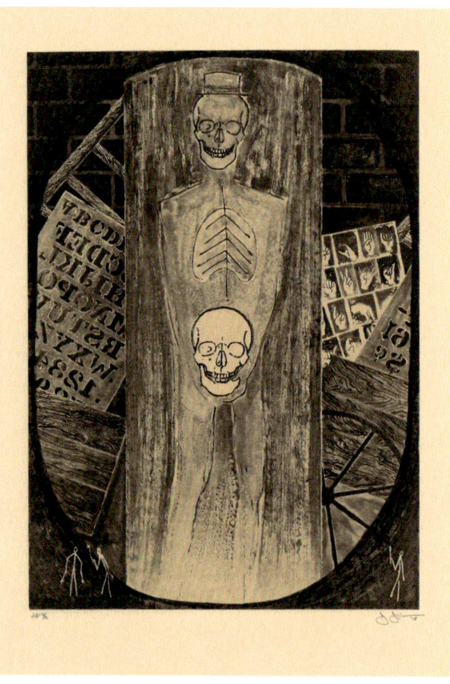

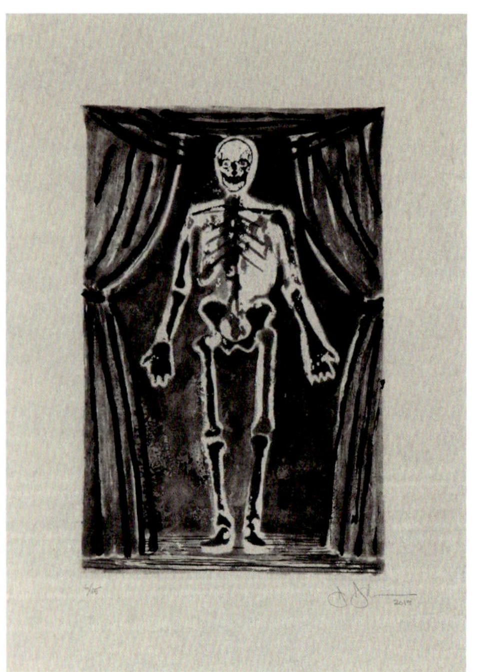

6 ***The Seasons*, 1990**
9 ***Untitled*, 2019**

7 ***0 through 9*, 1967**
10 ***Untitled*, 1973**

8 ***Untitled*, 2018**

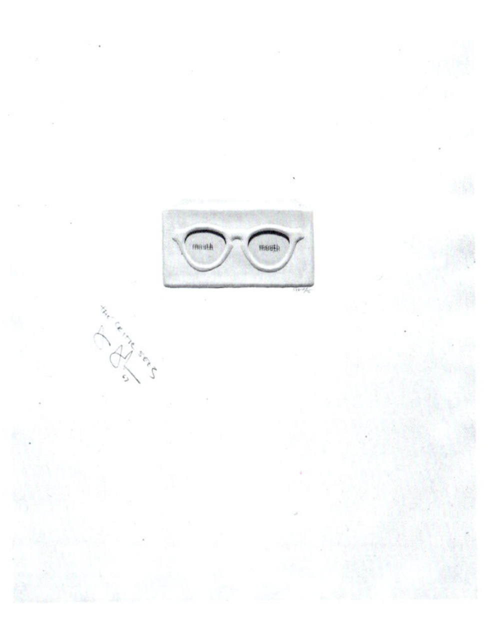

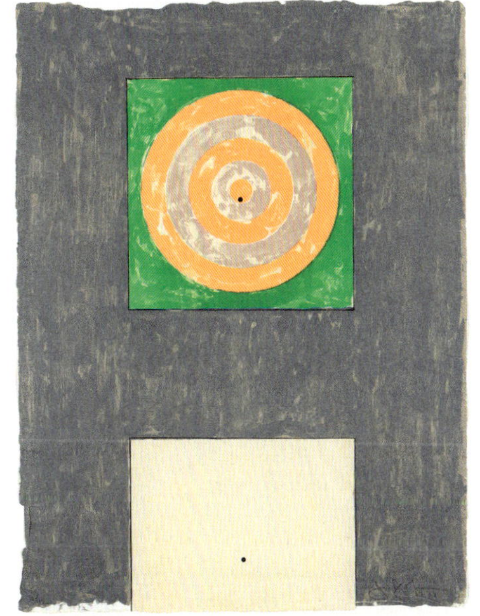

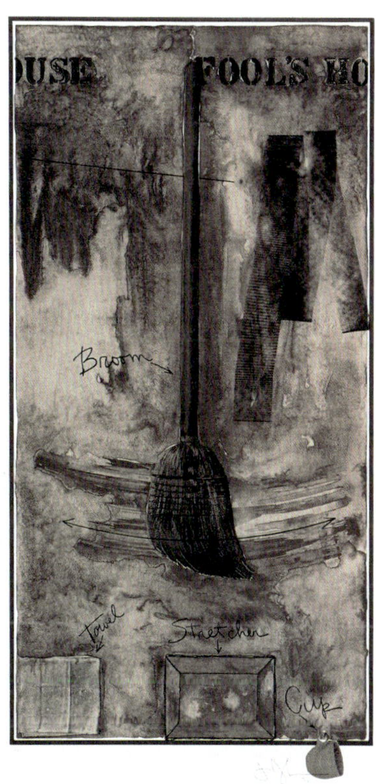

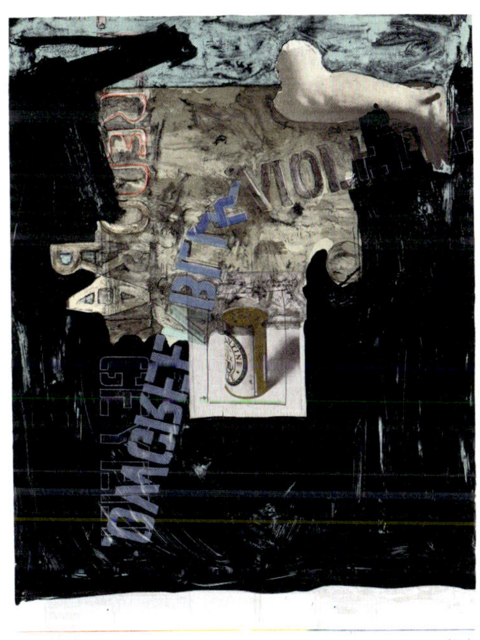

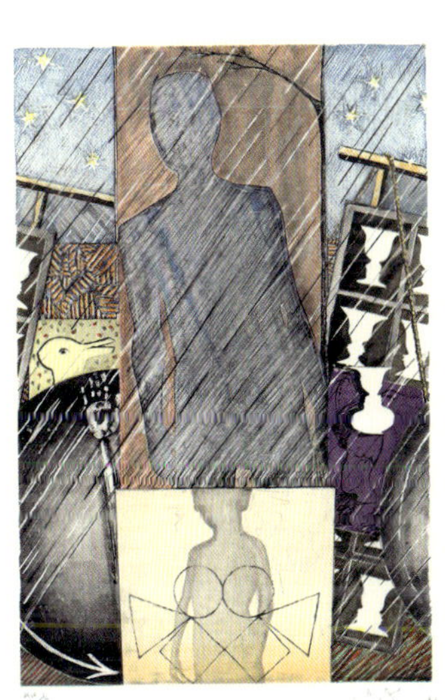

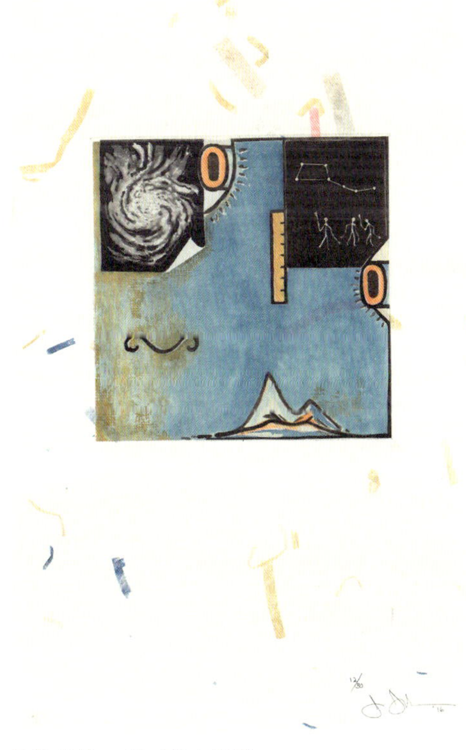

11 ***The Critic Sees***, **1967**

14 ***Decoy***, **1971**

12 ***Targets***, **1968**

15 ***Spring***, **from the Seasons, 1987**

13 ***Fool's House Black State***, **1972**

16 ***Untitled***, **2016**

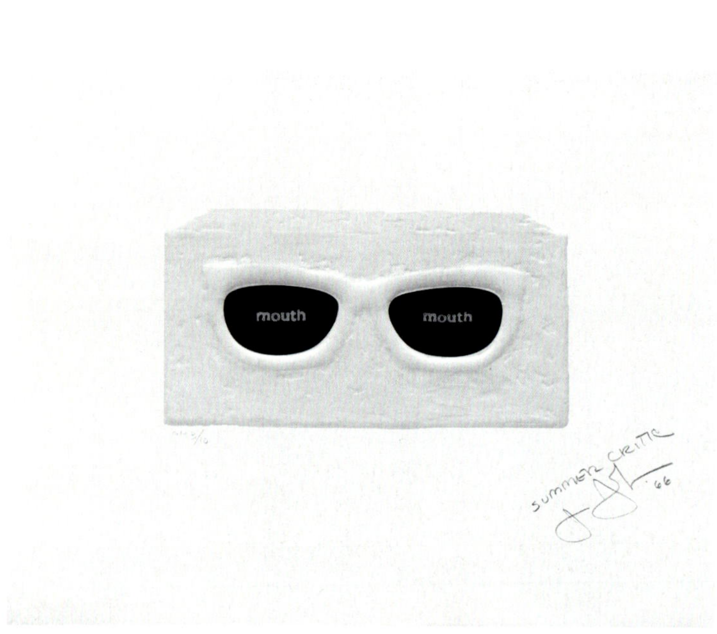

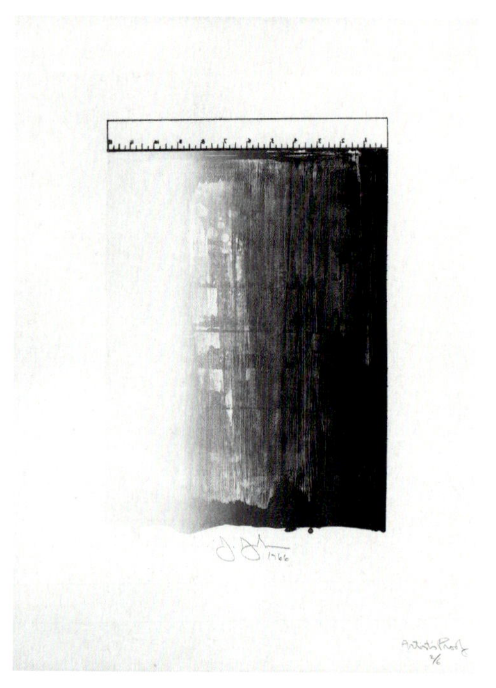

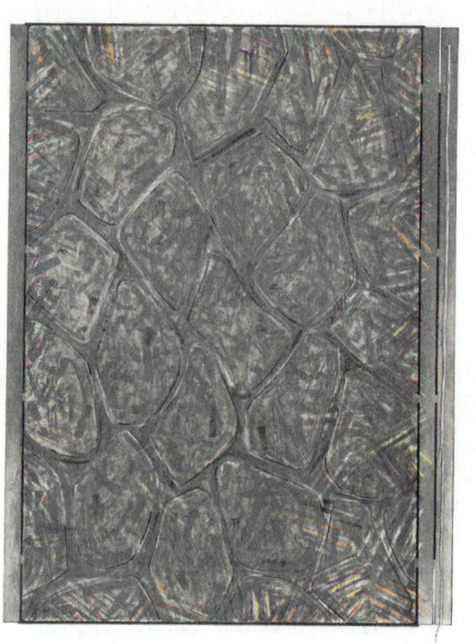

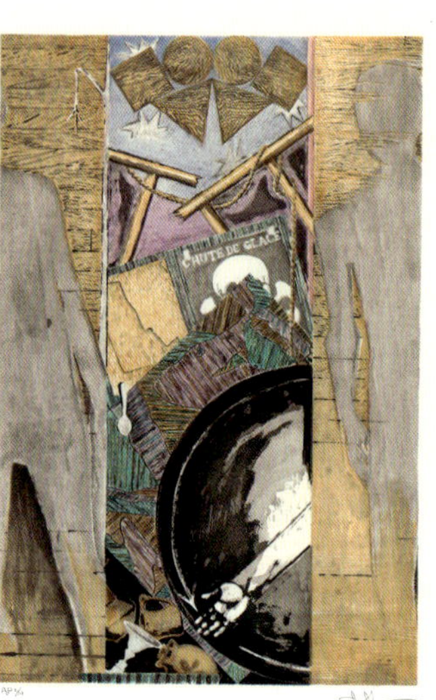

17 ***Summer Critic*, 1968**
19 ***Untitled (Ruler)*, 1968**

18 ***Ruler*, 1966**
20 ***Within*, 2007**

21 ***Fall*, from the Seasons, 1987**

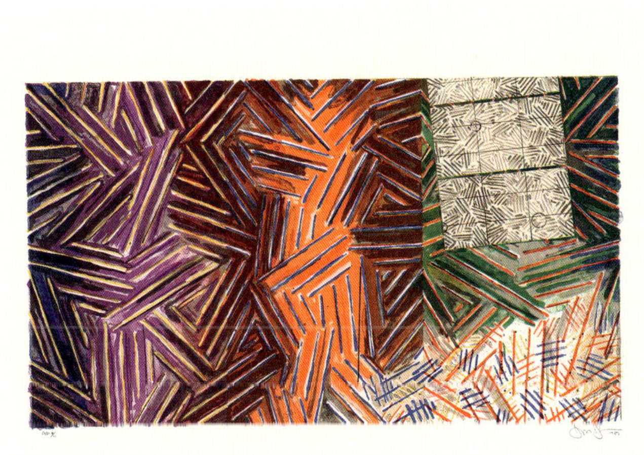

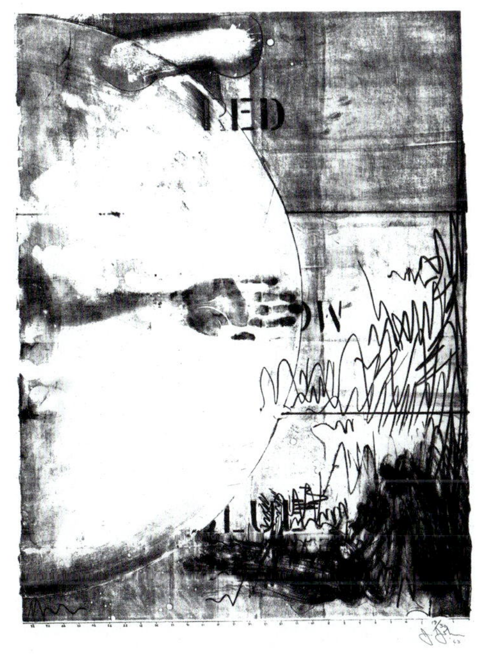

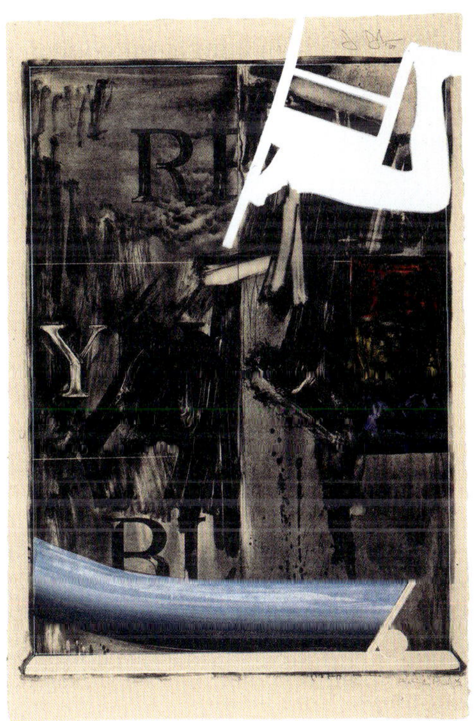

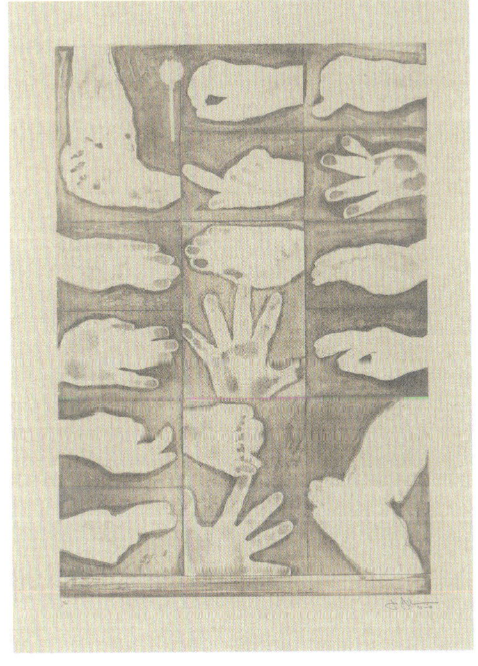

22 ***Between the Clock and the Bed*, 1989**
24 ***Watchman*, 1967**

23 ***Hatteras*, 1963**
25 ***Untitled*, 1998–2015**

26 ***Numbers*, 1967**

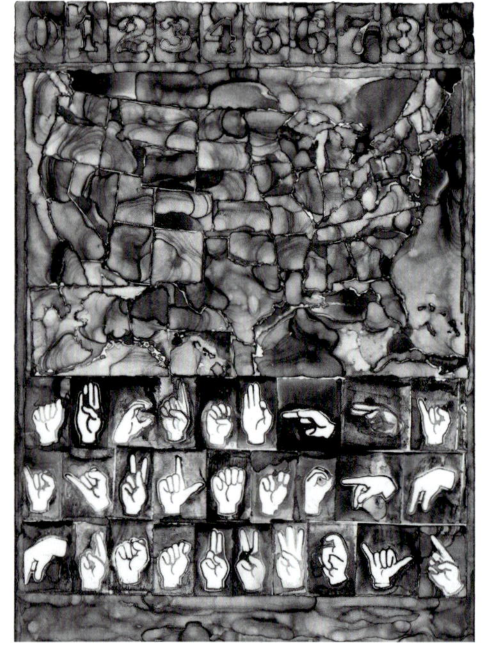

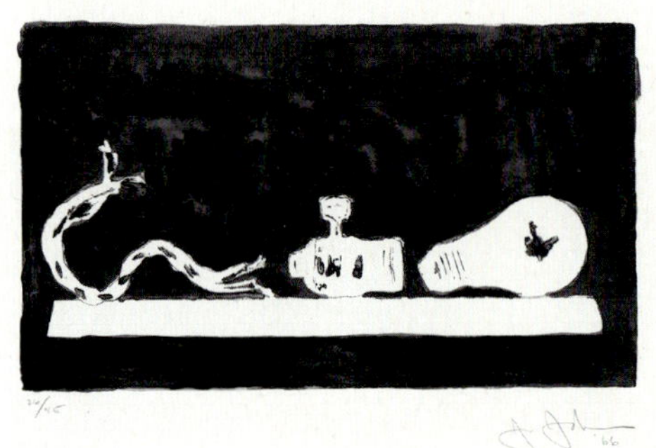

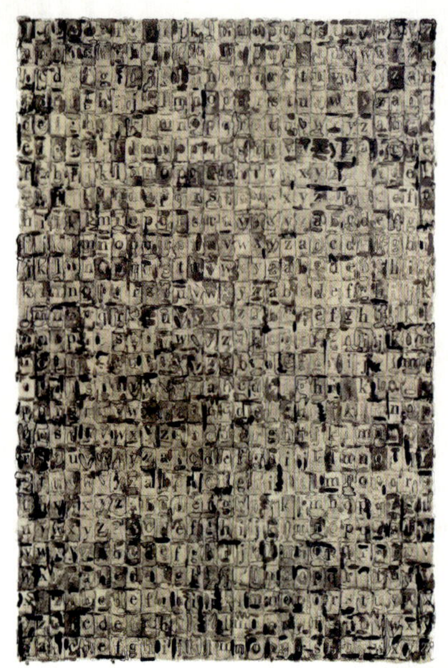

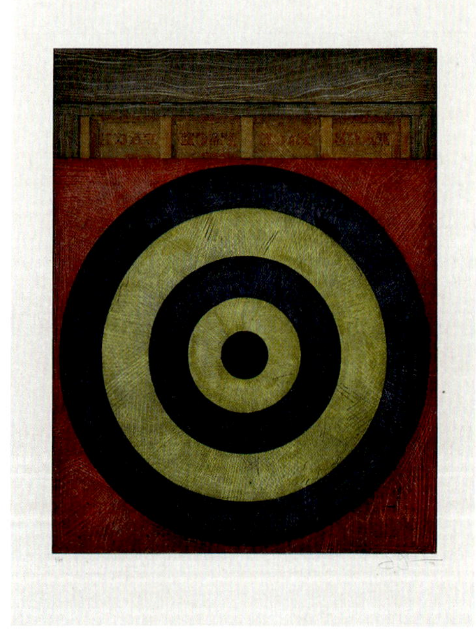

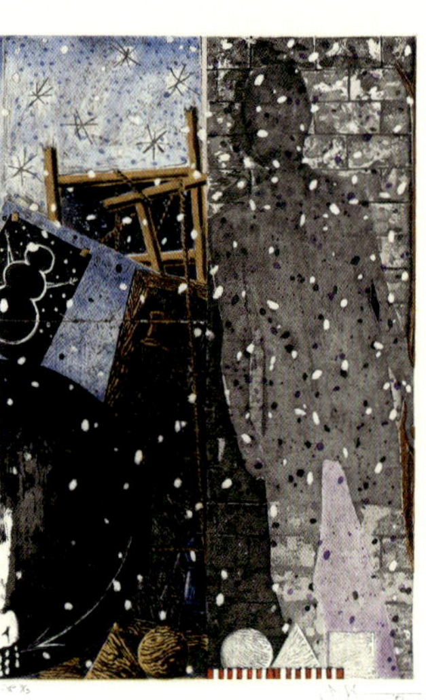

27 ***Art in America*, 2013**
29 ***Gray Alphabets*, 1968**

28 ***Light Bulb*, 1966**
30 ***Target with Four Faces*, 1979**

31 ***Winter*, from the Seasons, 1987**

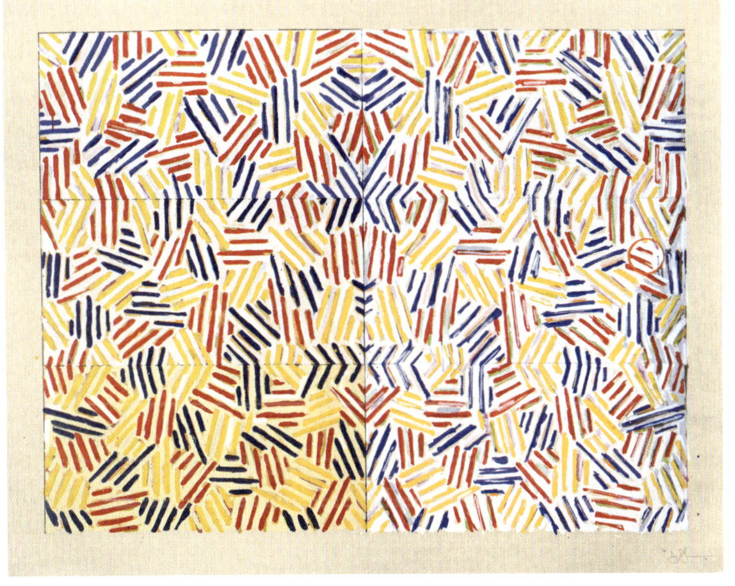

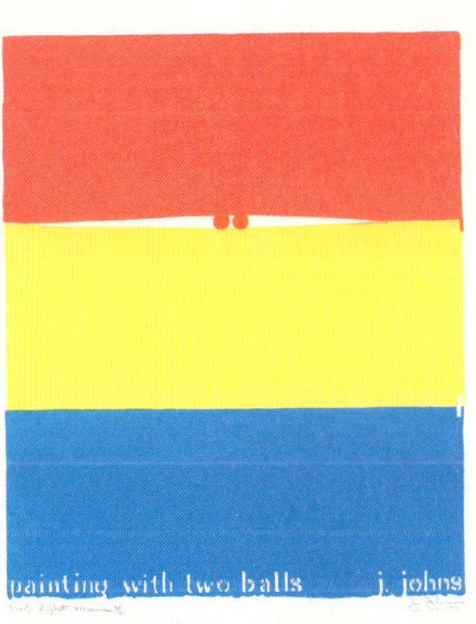

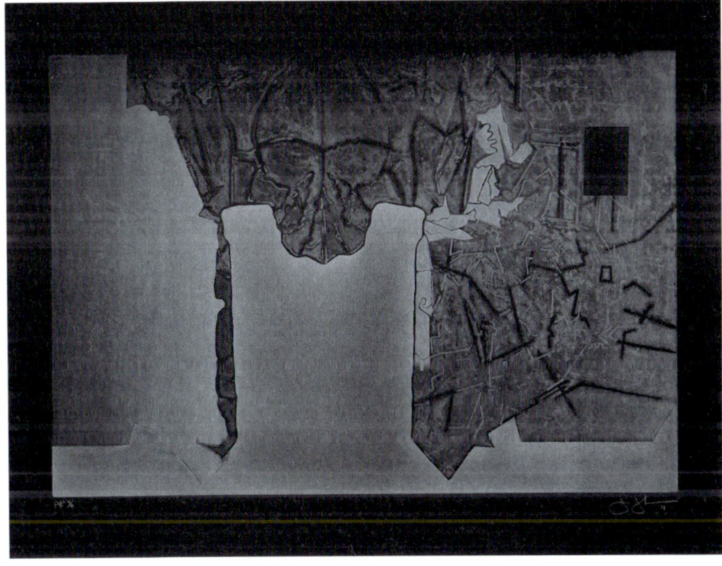

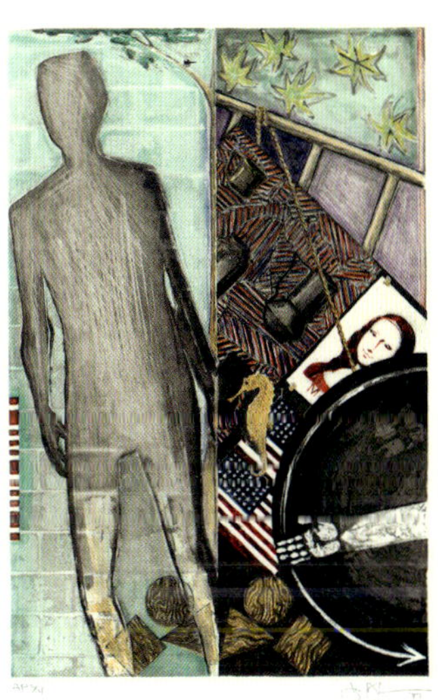

32 ***Corpse and Mirror***, 1976

33 ***Painting with Two Balls***, 1971

34 ***Regrets***, 2014

35 ***Summer***, from the Seasons, 1987

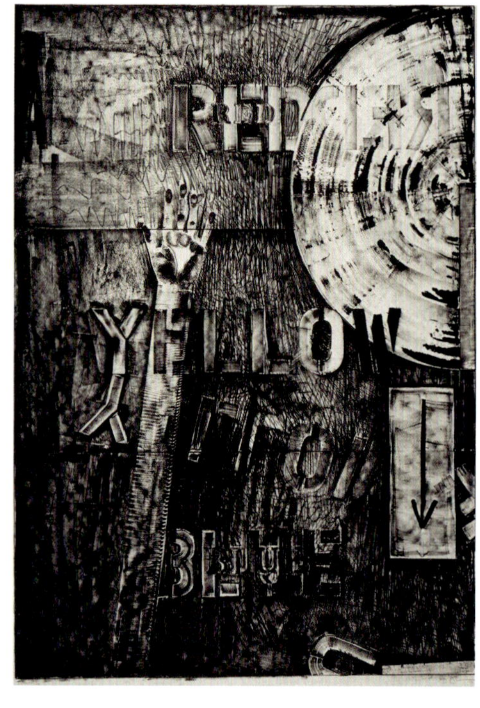

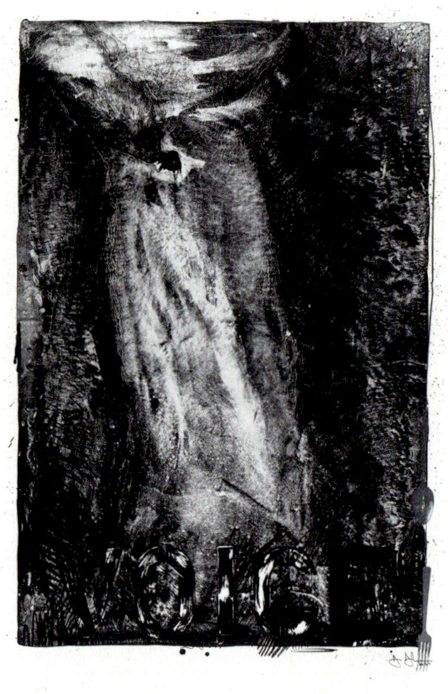

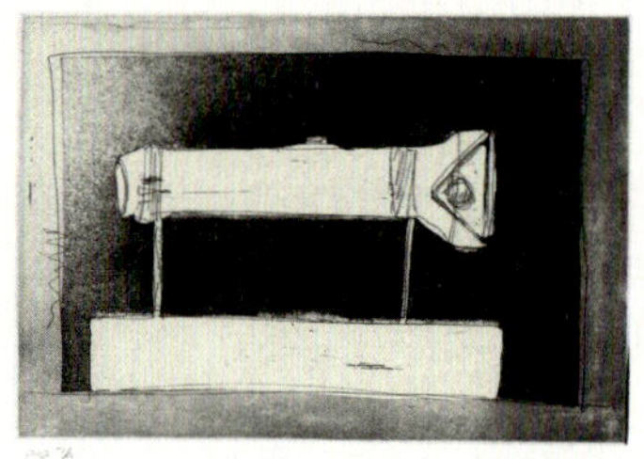

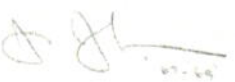

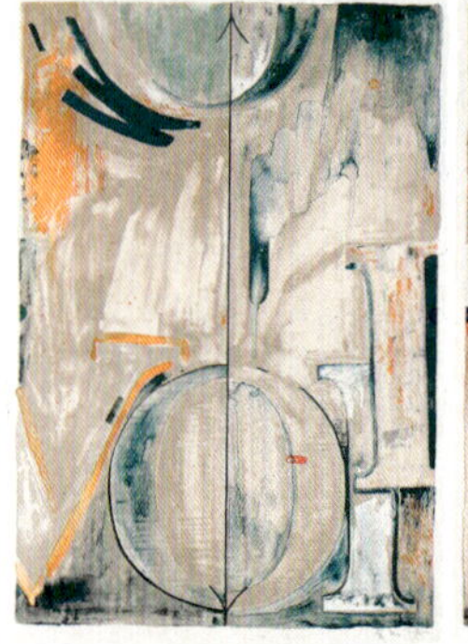

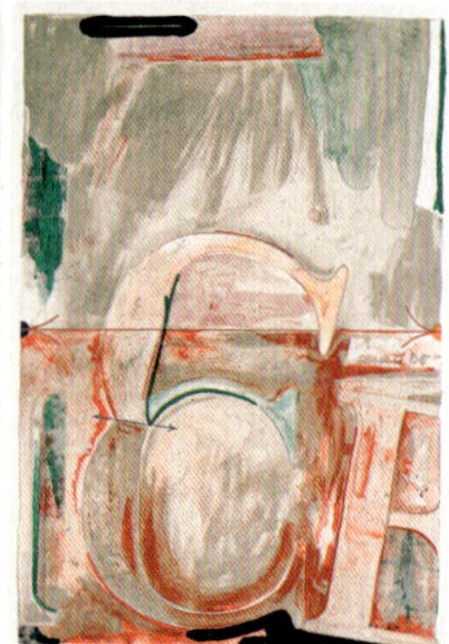

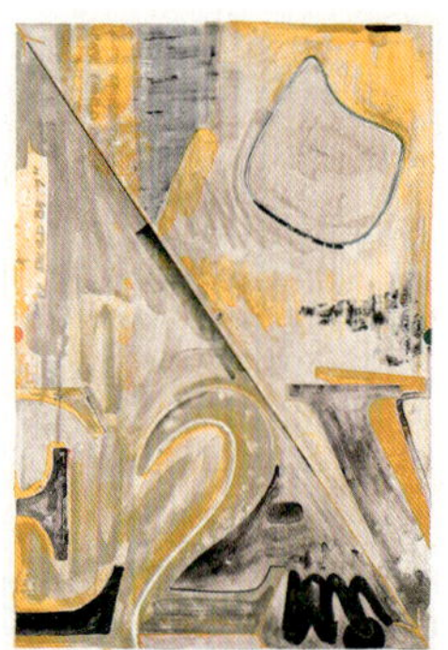

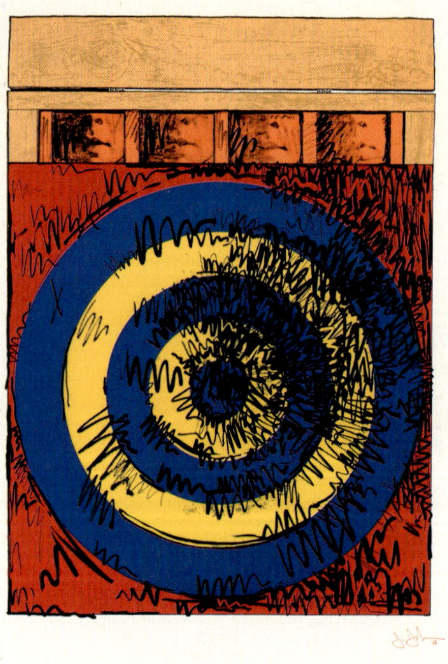

36 ***Land's End*, 1979**
39 ***Voice 2*, 1982**

37 ***Voice*, 1967**
40 ***Target with Four Faces*, 1968**

38 ***Flashlight I*, from 1st Etchings, 2nd State, 1969**

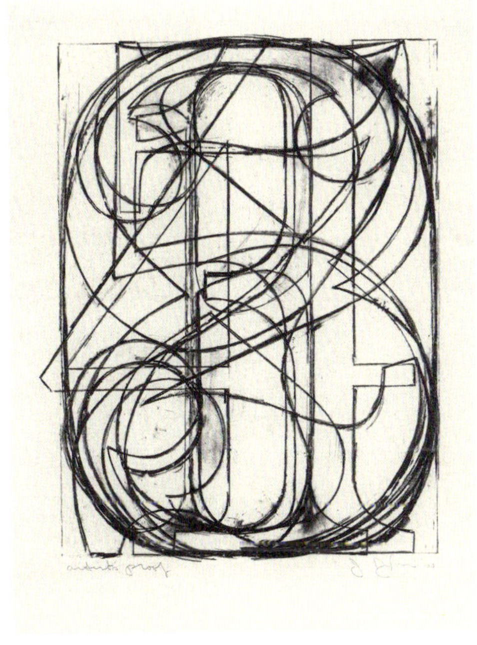

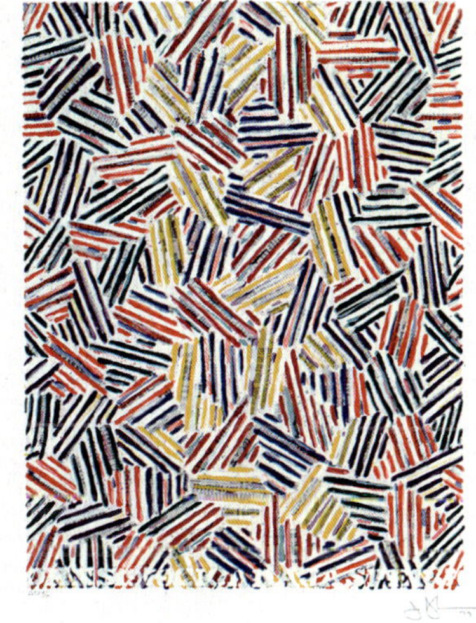

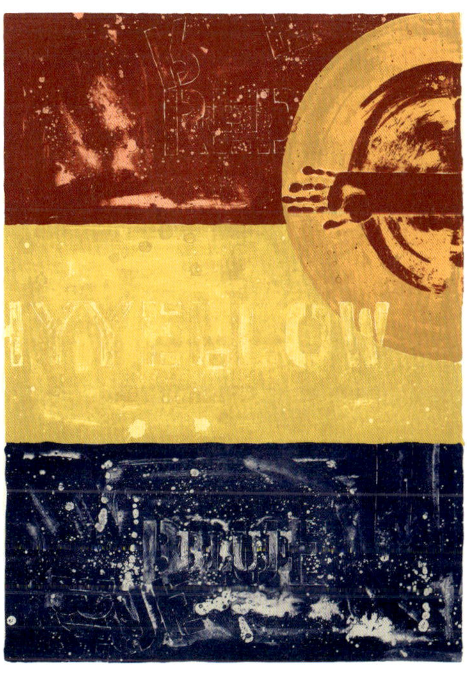

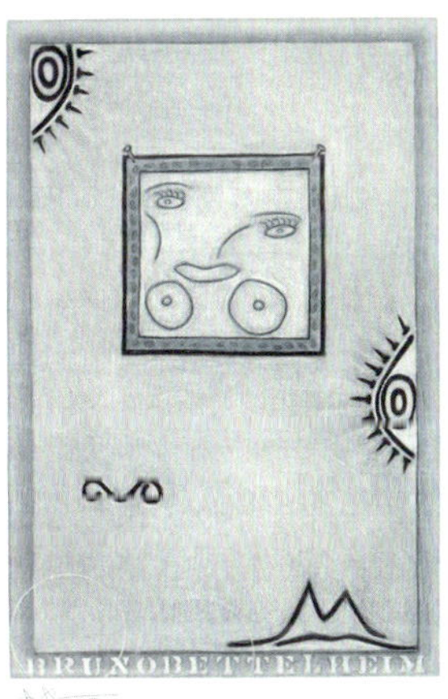

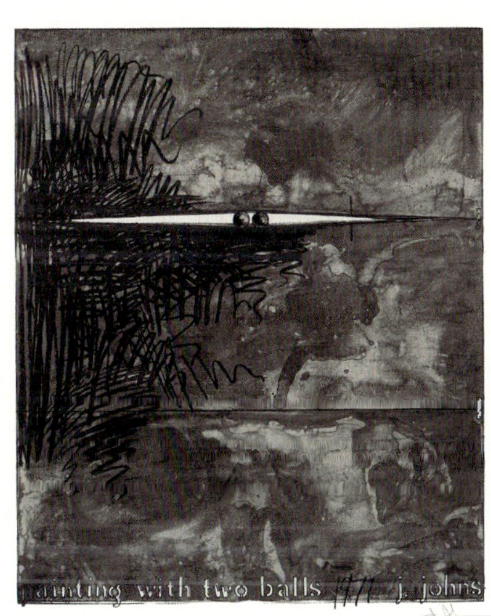

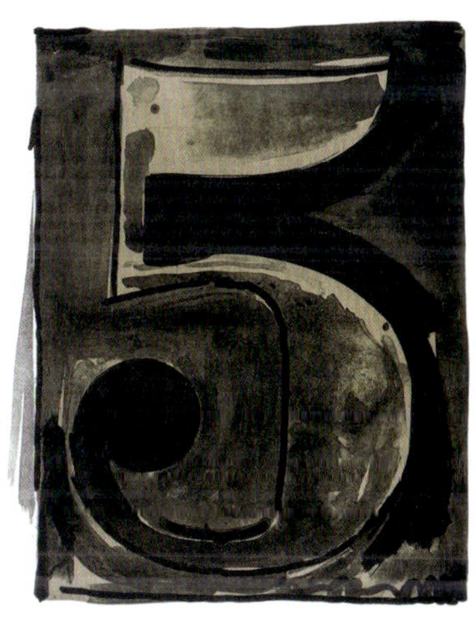

41 ***0 through 9*, 1960**
42 ***Cicada*, 1979**
43 ***Periscope I*, 1979**
44 ***Untitled*, 1995**
45 ***Painting with Two Balls (Exhibition Poster)*, 1971**
46 ***Figure 5*, from Black Numeral Series, 1968**

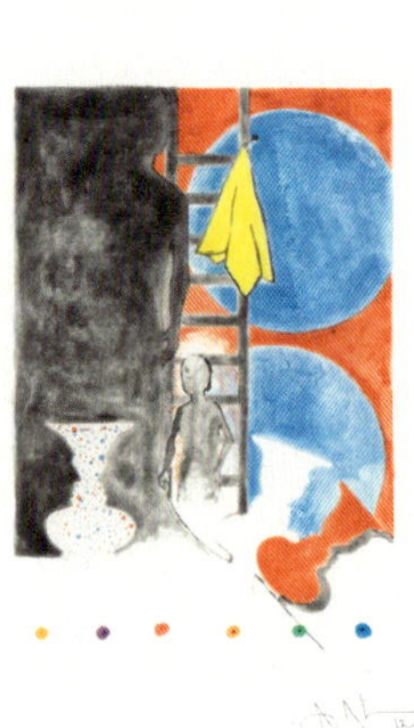

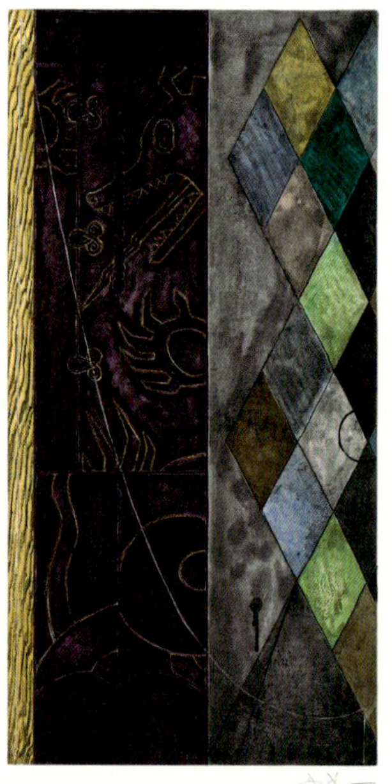

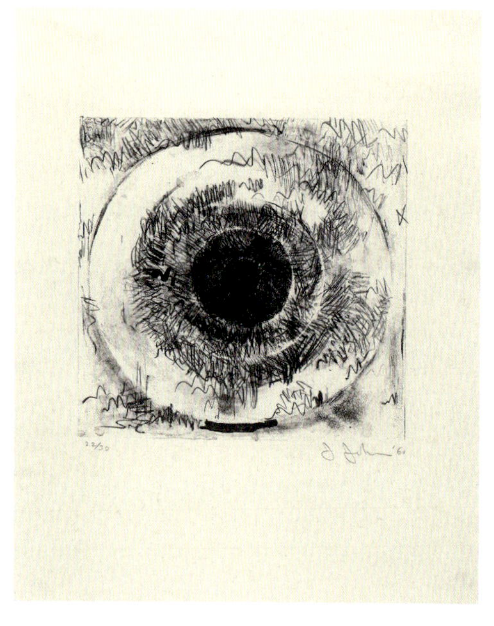

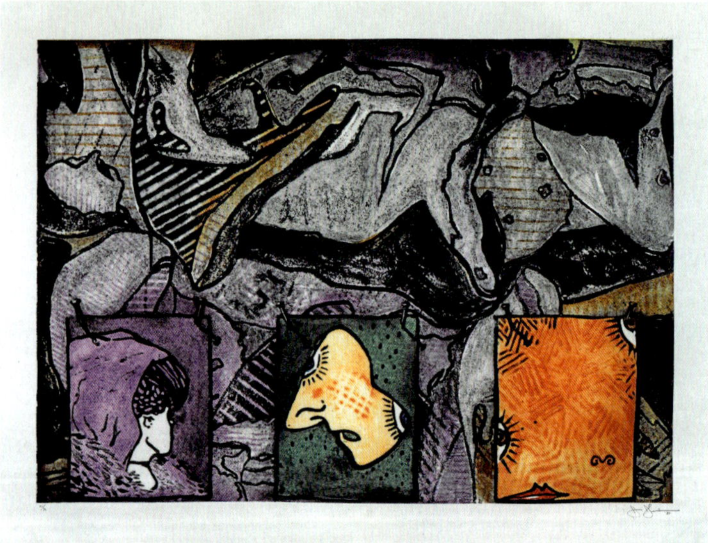

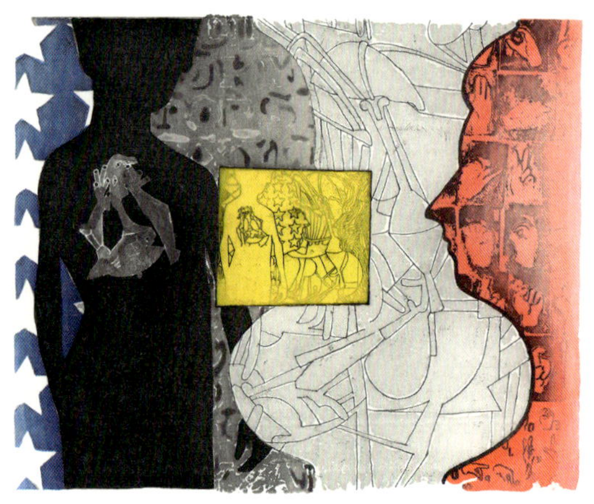

47 ***Untitled*, 2012**
50 ***Untitled*, 1988**

48 ***Untitled*, 1999**
51 ***Untitled*, 2010**

49 ***Target*, 1960**

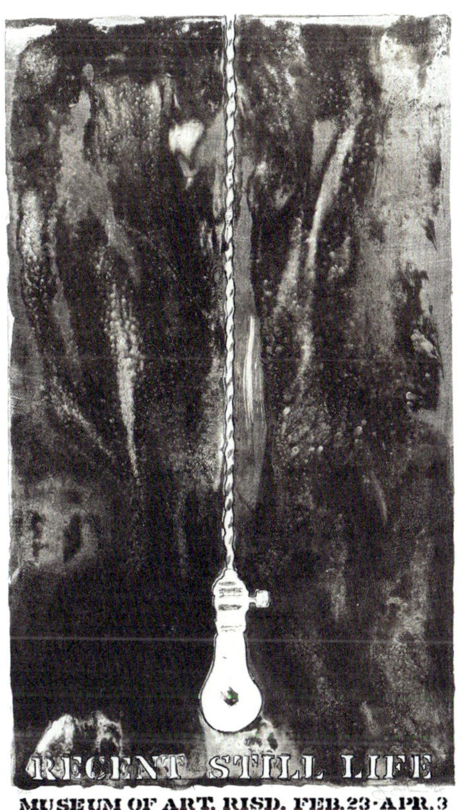

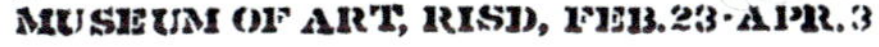

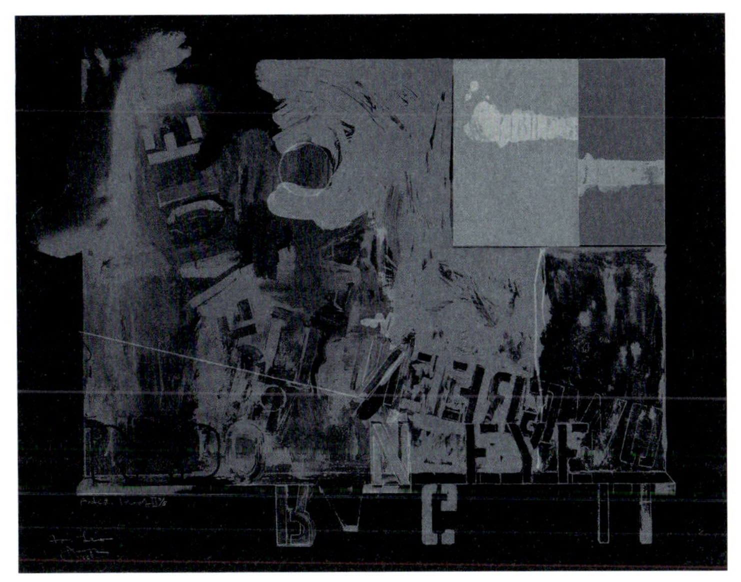

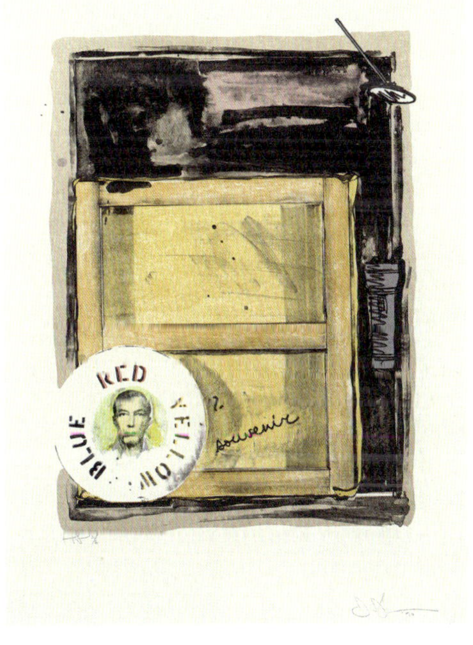

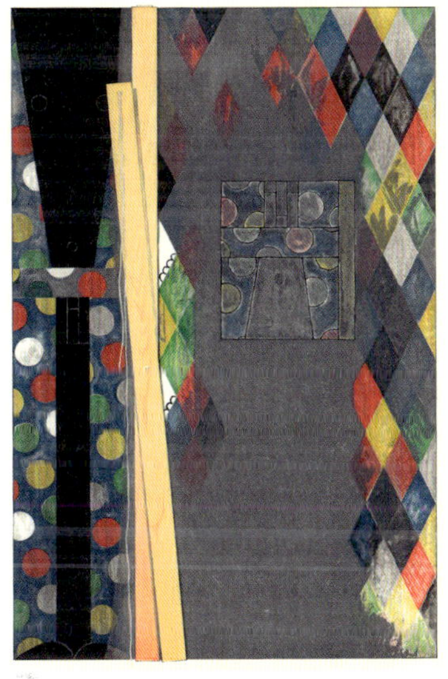

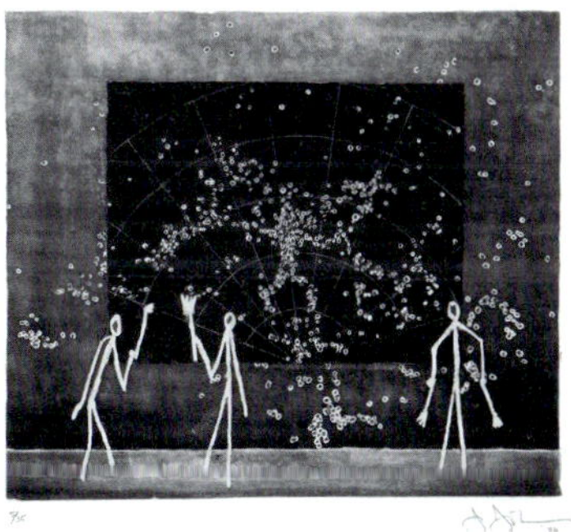

52 ***Recent Still Life*, 1966**

54 ***Souvenir*, 1970**

53 ***Passage II*, 1966**

55 ***Bushbaby*, 2004**

56 ***Untitled*, 2020**

Exhibition as Composition: Repetition and Difference

Sandra Skurvida

This exhibition—distributed across two cities and two museums with their distinct collections of works by Jasper Johns—has been conceived to produce difference, apart from the generality of a retrospective. It is not the first time many of these masterworks have been seen—they may be "known" to the mind's eye—yet each viewing over time produces a unique imprint of the original. Each viewing, paradoxically, repeats the irreplaceable, becoming something unique or singular in the present that has no equivalent in the past.

The walls of the Philadelphia Museum of Art, seen through *The Large Glass* by Marcel Duchamp (p. 198, fig. 3), are not a blank slate for this exhibition; on the contrary, in Johns's own words, they "attack it, are absorbed or reflected by it."[1] The new galleries of the Whitney Museum of American Art do not yet bear any imprints and may facilitate diffusion of memory according to Duchamp's dictum, "to reach the Impossibility of sufficient visual memory to transfer from one like object to another the memory imprint."[2] This Duchampian stopgap in the transfer of the memory from one aesthetic phenomenon to another is put to the test via arrangement of Johns's prints in the Philadelphia exhibition according to the chance operations method conceived by John Cage in the 1950s, when he and Johns were kindred spirits, and applied to writing music and poetry, as well as to exhibition making. Chance encounters activate the mind and engage the public in the production of meaning, rather than preserving an imprinted history of previous viewings.

Fig. 1 **Marcel Duchamp (American, b. France, 1887–1968). Facsimile note from *The Bride Stripped Bare by Her Bachelors, Even (The Green Box)*, published 1934 by Edition Rrose Sélavy, Paris**
Philadelphia Museum of Art; the Louise and Walter Arensberg Collection, 1950-134-986

Distrust in the validity of sensory perception pervaded the atmosphere of post–World War II art, affecting artists in various ways. Johns, among the doubters, had mentioned Duchamp's "*impossibility of transfer*" in his very first published statement, in 1959.[3] The following year, Duchamp's notes from *The Bride Stripped Bare by Her Bachelors, Even (The Green Box)* of 1934 (fig. 1; see also p. 155, pl. 14) were published in English for the first time, in the typographic version by Richard Hamilton.[4] In it, the note about difference in repetition was transcribed as follows:

> To lose the possibility of identifying/recognizing
> 2 similar objects—
> 2 colors, 2 laces
> 2 hats, 2 forms whatsoever
> to reach the Impossibility of
> sufficient visual memory
> to transfer
> from one
> like object to another
> the memory imprint
> —Same possibility
> with sounds; with brain facts

Johns signaled his keen interest in this statement in a short review of Hamilton's publication, concluding with a quote—a note to self, as it were: "'lose the possibility of identifying … 2 colors, 2 laces, 2 hats, 2 forms'; the vision of an alphabet 'only suitable for the description of this picture.'"[5] He returned to this formula in a sketchbook (fig. 2):

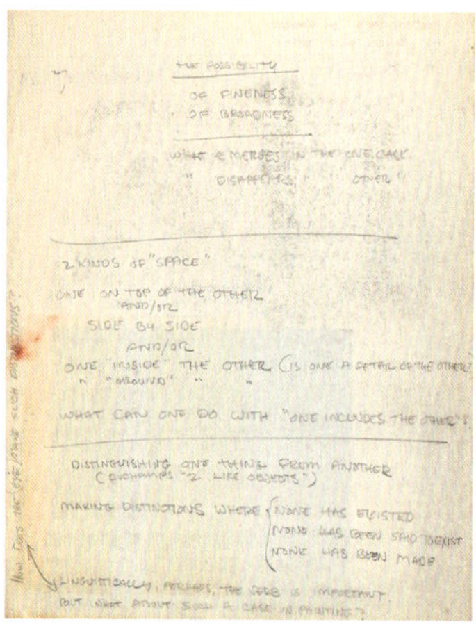

Fig. 2 **Sketchbook page, Book B, c. 1967**
Collection of the artist and Henry R. Kravis, 548.2008

> Distinguishing one thing from another
> (Duchamps "2 like objects")
>
> Making distinctions where
> { none has existed
> { none has been said to exist
> { none has been made
> ?
> How does the (eye) make such distinctions?
> ↓
> Linguistically, perhaps, the verb is important.
> But what about such a case in painting?[6]

Duchamp's note left an imprint in the minds of his successors. Years later, a seventy-five-year-old Cage responded to an interviewer's question—about whether he had any professional concerns then that he didn't have before—with a paraphrase of Duchamp's note via Johns: "to reach the impossibility of transferring from one like image to another the memory imprint. So that if you see Coca-Cola bottles, you're supposed to reach the impossibility of remembering the first Coca-Cola bottle when you look at the second one."[7] Although Cage's Coca-Cola references Andy Warhol, Johns's beer cans came first in the form of *Painted Bronze* (1960; p. 177, pl. 1; and p. 185, pl. 1). Each presumed repetition presents a similarity containing a difference—these permutations are in themselves an exposition of the note's continuing production of meaning. As Gertrude Stein put it, "The only thing that is different from one time to another is what is seen and what is seen depends upon how everybody is doing everything."[8]

Johns has taken the Duchampian "imprint" literally; he made his first prints in 1960, the same year he became familiar with *The Green Box*. The correspondences between Johns's prints and Duchamp's notion of "imprint" are implicated in the way Johns distributes the whole into parts and puts them back together again, a characteristic of the artist's process that is especially evident in his printmaking. Starting with numbers (*0 through 9* [1960; p. 75, pl. 1]) and continuing with letters (*Alphabet* [1969]), Johns conceived of structure as the only suitable description of the picture—the picture being equal to the sum of its parts, whereas the parts can become parts of another picture. The artist first traced the number stencils by hand in charcoal, all ten superimposed within one frame, and then printed the composite image, flattening the drawing within a lithograph the same way that Duchamp counterfeited his scripted notes in the printed form. The space is compressed in the merger. Duchamp's loose notes in *The Green Box*, on the other hand, retain their spatial autonomy—they can be perused at will, displayed, and put back into the box, without regard to a particular order. Duchamp's boxes model a kind of private exhibition, displayed by the viewer, and capable of producing a great variety of visual imprints.

Duchamp, Johns, and Cage used textuality as their source—textual structure can be parsed out into its elements, which are put together in various syntactic combinations bearing different meanings. *The Large Glass* has been deconstructed in *The Green Box*, resetting the semantic relationship of the whole to its parts—the parts appear in the aftermath of the making of the piece, in retrospection—as an index or glossary for the whole, which is difficult to grasp without the supplement. This reversible correlation of the source and imprint moved artwork, according to Johns, "into a field where language, thought and vision act upon one another."[9] Writing about Duchamp, Johns charted his own field of operative vision.

Conflation of artwork and display in Duchamp's boxes and Johns's prints determines both artists' construction of the pictorial space, in which superimposition of layers implies time as a visual imprint of simultaneity, evident in *0 through 9* and *Alphabet*. The enfolding and unfolding of space imply movement—it is not surprising that Johns collaborated with the Merce Cunningham Dance Company, which provided a stage for transmedial encounters among dancers, artists, and musicians. In his set design for the 1968 Cunningham ballet *Walkaround Time* (fig. 3), based on *The Large Glass*, Johns animated the dynamics of simultaneity (in time) and superimposition (in space). With Duchamp's permission, Johns isolated the seven elements of *The Large Glass* and transferred them onto transparent vinyl, which was stretched on sectional metal frames. These "imprints in space," distributed around the stage in various arrays during the dance, were brought back into the arrangement of *The Large Glass* at the end of the performance. The see-through, walk-through set suggested variability of pictorial space and its changing semantics.

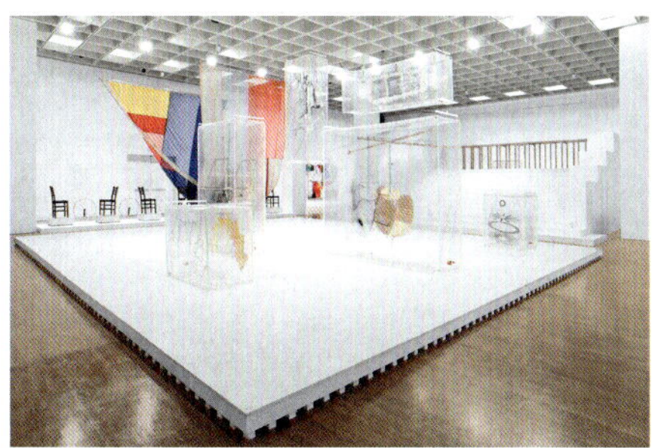

Fig. 3 **Johns's set elements for Merce Cunningham's *Walkaround Time* (1968) installed in the exhibition *Dancing around the Bride: Cage, Cunningham, Johns, Rauschenberg, and Duchamp*, Philadelphia Museum of Art, October 30, 2012–January 30, 2013**
Library and Archives, Philadelphia Museum of Art

Both Johns and Cage transitioned toward a new phase in their work at the end of the 1960s—the close of an era, which, for them, was personally signified by the death of the artist they revered. Cage created a visual art object in Duchamp's memory, *Not Wanting to Say Anything about Marcel* (1969; fig. 4). The title paraphrases Johns's response to an invitation from a magazine "to say something about Marcel," to which he replied, "I don't want to say anything about Marcel." For Cage, "not wanting" implied dissociation "from desires, taste and memory," opening up the space of engagement with "anything." *Not Wanting* comprises two lithographs and eight Plexigrams, each made up of eight transparent silkscreened panels inserted vertically into a wooden base. The piece is a container of fragmented, multilayered textual material, prefiguring the networked information environment of the twenty-first century. He sourced the material for this composition through chance operations using the 1955 edition of the *American Dictionary* and composed it into chance-determined arrangements within the panels. The choice of material echoes Duchamp's use of a random definition of "imprint" (*imprimer*) for the lyrics to his *Musical Erratum* (1913): "to make an imprint; mark with lines; a figure on a surface; impress a seal on wax" (*Faire une em-prein-te; mar-quer des traits; u-ne fi-gure sur une sur-face; im-pri-mer un sceau sur ci-re*).[10] In addition to artisanal work with leather, paints, and varnishes, *imprimer* implies leaving a mark and reproducing printed matter. This "random" word holds a key to Duchamp's future works and those of his successors—in particular Johns, whose work process often called for tracing figures on a surface of a pictorial plane—making an imprint of the present.

For Cage, imprinting meant producing a series of chance encounters leading toward indeterminacy, a process he programmed as a compositional apparatus—and, subsequently, as a computer application—to be used outside the author function. All the elements used in the making of *Not Wanting* were selected through a set of

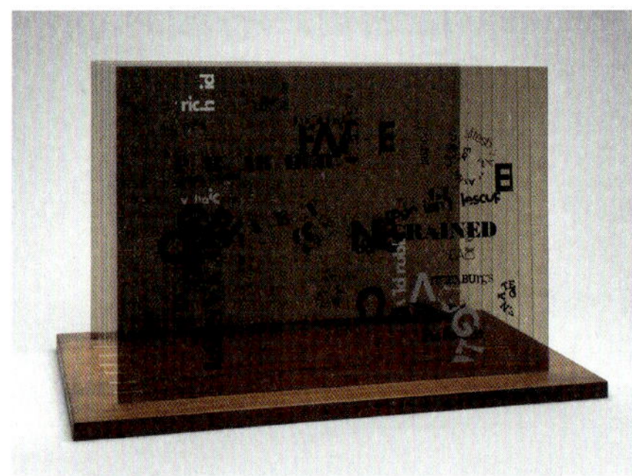

Fig. 4 **John Cage (American, 1912–1992) with Calvin Sumsion (American, 1942–2014). *Plexigram I*, from the portfolio *Not Wanting to Say Anything about Marcel*, published 1969 by Eye Editions, Cincinnati**
Plexigram (comprising eight silkscreened Plexiglas panels and one walnut base), each panel: 14 × 20 × 1/8 in. (35.6 × 50.8 × 0.3 cm). Philadelphia Museum of Art; purchased with the Lola Downin Peck Fund, 1970-38-1b

chance operations derived from the *I Ching* (*Book of Changes*).[11] Three coins were tossed three times to make every choice—which pages of the dictionary were used and which sections of those pages, determined according to a grid of sixty-four squares (the number of hexagrams in the *I Ching*, as well as squares on a chessboard). The next series of chance operations would determine the placement of the selected elements within the field of composition on each of the sixty-four panels, also mapped on a grid. The system was expanded to include charts of typefaces and colors to be used in the printing. This abbreviated outline makes it evident that while the process incorporated chance, it was anything but random. Rather, it was devised to circumvent habitual aesthetic choices, meandering, and improvisation. In an exhibition, the panels within each Plexigram may be arranged at random, leaving it to the installers to make an order within the predetermined framework.[12] Two versions of the fixed, chance-determined arrangements of the panels on the plane are represented in *Not Wanting* in a pair of lithographs. This multipart composition proposed fixity and change as defining factors of an exhibition, with Plexigrams modeling the stages of a changing display.

In *Not Wanting*, Cage tackled the potential of changing display in the context of a singular art object. His transmedial compositions of music, text, and visual art share the same structure of chance operations. Repetition of the same operation on a wide variety of material produces difference, but a difference without a predetermined concept—what Gilles Deleuze describes as "indifferent difference."[13] Cage's late compositions for museums projected variability—and, ultimately, indeterminacy—of meaning and its historical evolution as a counter to fixed, retrospective overview. The composer's curatorial activities at visual art institutions began in the mid-1980s; his last composition for museum, *Rolywholyover A Circus for Museum by John Cage*, is the most willingly forgotten instance of indeterminacy in the history of exhibition making (figs. 5-7).[14] The conceptual premise of this work was "to create a dynamic environment where people, art and all would co-exist in a compositional environment that exemplified a real situation where hierarchies were leveled off as much as possible, and where people enjoyed the opportunity to become more aware of the possibilities of self-government."[15] The procedure driving this composition was similar to the chance operations used in the making of *Not Wanting*, except that the compositional elements were artifacts and events rather than text fragments. This exhibition concept corresponded with the postmodern ahistoricity proposed by Jean-François Lyotard and displayed in his curation of the labyrinthine, linguistically structured exhibition *Les immatériaux* at the Centre Pompidou in Paris in 1985. The deconstructive drive in art practices of the preceding decade—such as by Johns and Cage—has been imprinted in the coeval theoretical considerations. This art-theoretical structural drive, envisioning a global situation as a changing multiplicity, opened up to a decentered, ahistorical worldview. Cage's museological project acts as a lens magnifying this moment of transition, and therefore deserves special attention today.

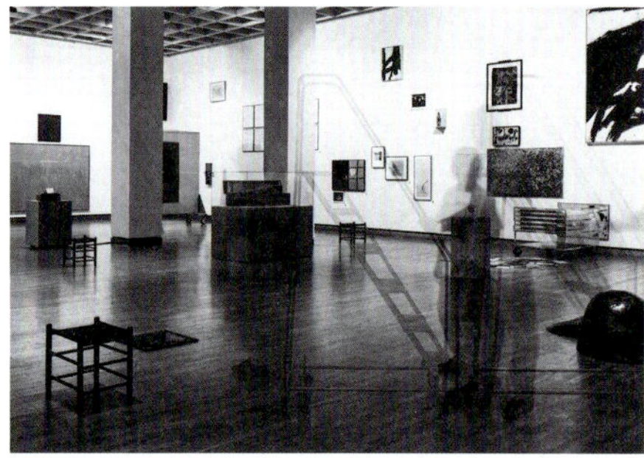

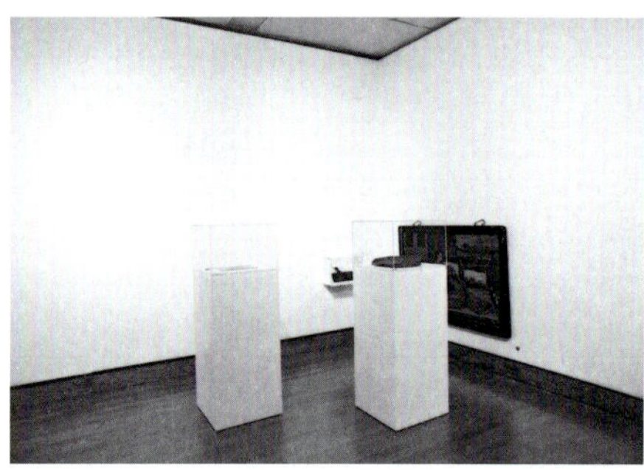

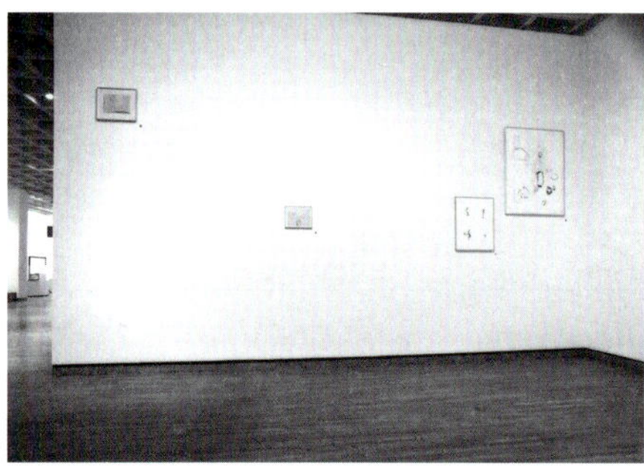

Figs. 5-7 **Installation views, *Rolywholyover A Circus for Museum by John Cage*, Philadelphia Museum of Art, June 4–July 30, 1995**
Library and Archives, Philadelphia Museum of Art

The original iteration of *Rolywholyover* comprised several distinct parts. Circus, an extensive collection of artworks from within Cage's circle, signified his artistic alliances and influences, representing a kaleidoscopic personal history of twentieth-century art. Museumcircle comprised objects selected by the curators from the widest possible range of museums in the area, to be installed within a decontextualized display of Circus.[16] Cage Gallery was dedicated to the composer's prints and watercolors, which he had been making since 1975, and serves as a prototype for the display of Johns's prints in the Philadelphia presentation of *Jasper Johns: Mind/Mirror*. Within *Rolywholyover*, all the art and nonart objects were installed according to Cage's method of chance operations. The walls and floors of the galleries were mapped according to a grid—similar to the making of *Not Wanting*, but in three-dimensional space—and positions of the objects were determined using chance operations, taking into account their sizes and display requirements (wall or floor), and stipulating no overlaps. The Circus display was dynamic, with daily changes to the installation, whose movements were choreographed for the specific space and time frame of the exhibition. The objects within Museumcircle and Cage Gallery remained static in their chance-determined positions. This composition for museum, comprising static and dynamic parts, was integrated through the principle of indeterminacy, as a changing network of connections did not settle on any particular display solution.

Such semantic volatility is also characteristic of Johns's formal solutions. Speaking of his Catenary series, he described his own paintings as "connections among all the various ideas we have of space, or connections of thought, or what? Connections to what you're calling emptiness, and what I'm calling fullness."[17] His self-referential paintings since the 1980s suggest a randomized display of the mind on which all the work done and seen has left an imprint. In two untitled paintings of 1984 (figs. 8, 9), Johns's series of prints Casts from Untitled (1973–74; p. 164, pls. 17–22), along with other artworks and objects in his possession, appear "taped" to a virtual board, signaling impermanence. This mental display changes from one painting to the other—as Cage quoted Johns in his essay on the artist's work and thought process: "*It moves. It moved. It was moved. It can, will, might move. It has been moved. It will be moved (can't have just it).*"[18]

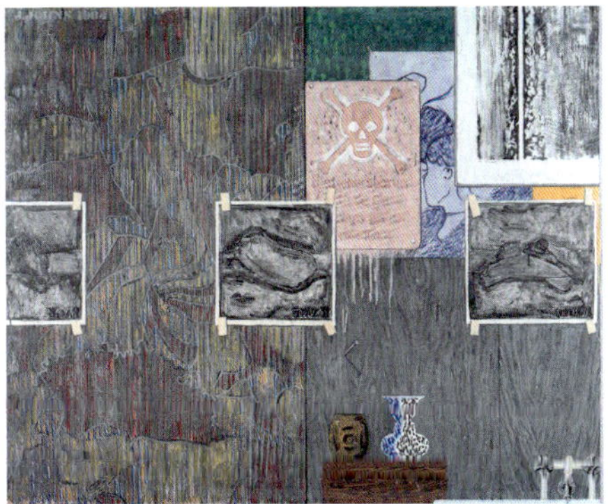

Fig. 8 ***Untitled*, 1984**
Encaustic on canvas, 63 ½ × 75 in. (161.3 × 190.5 cm). The Eli and Edythe L. Broad Collection

Johns and Cage share a structural, methodical process that limits the seemingly endless range of elements at one's disposal to a particular set to be used in multiple experimental takes. Each take reveals new aspects in the changing arrays—repetition breeds difference. Johns's superimposition of elements within his works resembles Cage's principle of simultaneity, realized in his compositions of music and for museums. In the Philadelphia exhibition, the proposed installation of Johns's prints arranged according to Cage's chance operations program suggests an active engagement among the contributors—the artist and composer continuing their exchange, activating the space of the exhibition, and engaging spectators in a process of viewing as production of meaning. Procedural chance applied to a curated selection of prints multiplies the semantic trajectories of the exhibition with every move. The changing installation makes all involved in its making—artists, curators, installers—responsible for mapping the mental trajectories within. This intersection of multiple significations is evident in Cage's compositions, including the mesostic form of his texts, in which a vertical phrase intersects lines of horizontal text:

intention Disappears
with Use. (johns.)
aspeCts
otHer
thAn
those we had in Mind
Produce attention.[19]

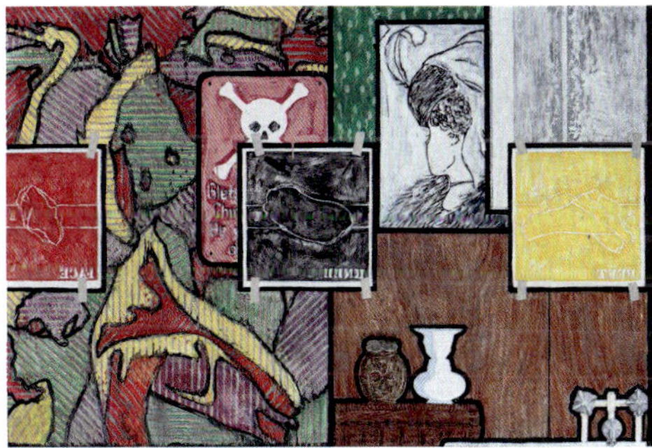

Fig. 9 ***Untitled*, 1984**
Encaustic on canvas, 50 × 75 in. (127 × 190.5 cm). Collection of the artist

Institutions are designed to manage randomness. A museum regulates the contents and conditions of display (lighting, temperature, sound, and movement of the audience), as well as the production of meaning within an exhibition—what relates to what, and how. The regimens of museum experience are intended to stop time in its tracks, despite the fact that an exhibition itself is "*a kind of object which as it changes or falls apart (dies as it were) or increases in its parts (grows as it were) offers no clue as to what its state or form or nature was at any previous time.*"[20] A conventional museum exhibition conveys predetermined knowledges that are supposed to remain stable, not change in front of one's eyes from one moment to the next. Subjecting a curatorial selection of Johns's prints to Cage's chance operations forfeits this finitude—the work of showing and viewing is never finished. "Exhibition" becomes a verb, a movement of meaning here and now, imprinting unstable traces in the memory of the observer. A chance display asks, "Why does the information that someone has done something affect the judgment of another? Why cannot someone who is looking at something do his own work of looking?"[21] A changing display asks museumgoers to see the art as if for the first time, without the imprint of knowledge, in order to produce a unique "memory imprint." This push and pull between habit and chance was conceived to pry open our access to conscious randomness—a certain freedom of the mind, which, commonly declared as part and parcel of art, is most difficult to attain in practice.

1 Jasper Johns, "Duchamp," *Scrap*, no. 2 (December 23, 1960): 4; reprinted in Carlos Basualdo and Erica F. Battle, eds., *Dancing around the Bride: Cage, Cunningham, Johns, Rauschenberg, and Duchamp*, exh. cat. (Philadelphia: Philadelphia Museum of Art, 2012), 87.
2 *The Writings of Marcel Duchamp*, ed. Michel Sanouillet and Elmer Peterson (New York: Da Capo, 1973), 31.
3 Jasper Johns, ["Statement"], in *Sixteen Americans*, ed. Dorothy C. Miller, exh. cat. (New York: Museum of Modern Art, 1959), 22; quoted in John Cage, "Jasper Johns: Stories and Ideas," in *Jasper Johns*, exh. cat. (New York: Jewish Museum, 1964); reprinted in *A Year from Monday: New Lectures and Writings by John Cage* (Middletown, CT: Wesleyan University Press, 1967), 79. Throughout this essay, italics, in original, signify quotations by Cage from Johns's notebooks and published statements. In the context of this essay on correspondences between Johns and Cage, Johns is quoted from writings by Cage.
4 Marcel Duchamp, *The Bride Stripped Bare by Her Bachelors, Even: A Typographic Version by Richard Hamilton of Marcel Duchamp's "Green Box,"* trans. George Heard Hamilton (New York: George Wittenborn, 1960), n.p.
5 Johns, "Duchamp," 4.
6 Jasper Johns, "Book B, c. 1967," in *Jasper Johns: Writings, Sketchbook Notes, Interviews*, ed. Kirk Varnedoe (New York: Museum of Modern Art, 1996), 61.
7 John Cage, "Art: Becoming John Cage," interview by Barbara Isenberg, *Los Angeles Times*, September 5, 1993, https://www.latimes.com/archives/la-xpm-1993-09-05-ca-31975-story.html (accessed May 28, 2020).
8 Gertrude Stein, *Composition as Explanation*, The Hogarth Essays, 2nd ser., no. 1 (London: Hogarth, 1926), 6.
9 Jasper Johns, "Marcel Duchamp (1887–1968)," *Artforum* 7, no. 3 (November 1968): 6.
10 For the translation, see Sanouillet and Peterson, *Writings of Duchamp*, 34.
11 John Cage, *To Describe the Process of Composition Used in "Not Wanting to Say Anything about Marcel"* (Cincinnati: Eye Editions, 1969), 1.
12 John Cage and Calvin Sumsion, "Colophon," in Cage, *To Describe the Process*, n.p.
13 Gilles Deleuze, *Difference and Repetition*, trans. Paul Patton (New York: Columbia University Press, 1994), 15.
14 The project was initiated in 1989 by Julie Lazar, then curator at the Los Angeles Museum of Contemporary Art, and premiered there in September 1993, a year after Cage's death. Over the next two years, it traveled to the Menil Collection, Houston; the Guggenheim Museum SoHo, New York; the Art Tower Mito Contemporary Art Center, Tokyo; and the Philadelphia Museum of Art. The three spaces that follow *Rolywholyover* in the title *Rolywholyover   A Circus for Museum by John Cage* reflect the syntactic spatiality of Cage's composition.
15 Julie Lazar, correspondence with the author, February 5, 2010.
16 For a detailed description of this project, see Sandra Skurvida, "John Cage, *Rolywholyover   A Circus*, 1993," in *The Artist as Curator*, ed. Elena Filipovic (Milan: Mousse, 2017), 229–45.
17 Jasper Johns, quoted in Amei Wallach, "A Master of Silence Who Speaks in Grays," *New York Times*, September 5, 1999. See also Scott Rothkopf, *Jasper Johns: Catenary*, exh. cat. (New York: Matthew Marks Gallery, 2005).
18 Jasper Johns, quoted in Cage, "Johns: Stories and Ideas," in *A Year from Monday*, 80.
19 John Cage, "36 Mesostics Re and Not Re Duchamp" (1968), in *M: Writings '67–72* (Middletown, CT: Wesleyan University Press, 1973), 28.
20 Johns, quoted in Cage, "Johns: Stories and Ideas," 77.
21 Cage, "Johns: Stories and Ideas," 75.

Archive

Few, if any, artists in recent history have had careers as intimately entwined with museums as Jasper Johns. He had a running start, appearing in his first museum exhibition at New York's Jewish Museum in 1957 at the age of twenty-six, and the twinned facts of his enduring acclaim and great longevity have contributed to a succession of annual exhibitions and acquisitions spanning sixty-five years. This story is as much about institutions as it is about people. Alfred H. Barr, the first director of the Museum of Modern Art, along with curator Dorothy Miller, inaugurated a still-unfolding tale at MoMA when they acquired Johns's work from his first solo exhibition at the Leo Castelli Gallery in 1958, and the baton has passed for decades to subsequent generations of curators and patrons, each of whom has added new works, exhibitions, and perspectives. Such relationships have crossed the globe, marked by moments of discovery, collaboration, competition, friendship, and even tragedy, as with the untimely deaths of two of Johns's ardent curatorial champions, Kirk Varnedoe of MoMA and Christian Geelhaar of the Kunstmuseum Basel, whom Johns memorialized with gifts of cherished paintings to their beloved institutions. Collections and exhibition histories accumulate through so many personal twists and turns, and it is archives that bear them crucial and lasting witness. Both the Whitney Museum of American Art and the Philadelphia Museum of Art count among those institutions with whom Johns has had the longest and closest associations, making possible and all the more meaningful the present retrospective.

Johns is one of the only artists alive to have visited all four of the Whitney's locations, from its original home on West Eighth Street and its brief midtown site to its building on Madison Avenue and its current one on Gansevoort Street. He first saw the work of Jackson Pollock and Isamu Noguchi at the initial venue in 1949, and he exhibited at the second in five consecutive installments of the Annual Exhibition of Contemporary American Painting from 1959 to 1963. Since then, he has participated in over sixty exhibitions and collection displays, including that for the 2015 opening of the Gansevoort Street location. Johns's first painting to enter the museum's holdings was *Studio* (1964; pp. 130–31, pl. 2), and today its collection comprises 218 of his works. In 1975, then-director Thomas Armstrong embarked on a major retrospective, which was installed two years later by Johns's friend David Whitney, a curator known for his sensitive eye. *Newsweek* dubbed Johns "Super Artist" on the occasion of the show (p. 310, pl. 6), which traveled internationally and was accompanied by a monograph by novelist Michael Crichton.[1]

Johns and the Whitney once again garnered headlines in 1980 when the museum acquired *Three Flags* (1958; p. 62, pl. 2) from the collection of Emily and Burton Tremaine for one million dollars, which the front page of the *New York Times* declared a record price for the work of a living artist (p. 312, pl. 13). Referencing his upbringing during the Depression, Johns remarked dryly of the figure, "It has a rather neat sound, but it has nothing to do with painting."[2] That same year, Johns designed a poster celebrating the Whitney's fiftieth anniversary (p. 312, pl. 12), juxtaposing images of American flags with fifty and forty-eight stars, the number of states in 1980 and at the time of the museum's founding. He reprised this honor with a broadside featuring *Two Maps* (1965; p. 61, pl. 1) from the Whitney's collection to mark the museum's seventy-fifth birthday in 2005 (p. 314, pl. 24). That two of Johns's best-known motifs are emblems of the United States has made his works de facto icons of a museum dedicated to the art of that nation, while the coincidence of the Whitney's founding and Johns's birth in 1930 has meant they share parallel histories. For nearly a century, Johns's rise has been inextricably linked to the Whitney's ambitions for both itself and the art it advocates.

Johns first came to the Philadelphia Museum of Art with Robert Rauschenberg in 1957 in search of Marcel Duchamp's work. The visit was partly motivated by critic Robert Rosenblum's use of the term "Neo-Dada" in a review of a Castelli Gallery group exhibition in which Johns participated.[3] In 1954, Louise and Walter Arensberg had donated their extraordinary collection to the Philadelphia museum, making Duchamp's art one of the cornerstones of its holdings. The relationship between the institution and the reluctant genius deepened when, in 1969, his secret project *Étant donnés* (1946–66) was posthumously unveiled in one of the museum's galleries. Reports of this mysterious work drew artists and scholars from all over the world, and that September, Johns, along with an entourage that included artists Richard Hamilton, Tomio Miki, Aiko Miyawaki, and Robert Morris, as well as writers Suzi Gablik and Roberta Bernstein, made a memorable pilgrimage to Philadelphia to view it (p. 318, pl. 5). There they were greeted by Anne d'Harnoncourt, a young curatorial assistant who had worked on the installation along with curator Walter Hopps and Paul Matisse, the artist's son. D'Harnoncourt would later become the museum's longtime director and a dear friend of Johns.

In 1970, the Philadelphia Museum of Art organized its first monographic exhibition of Johns's work, *Jasper Johns: Prints, 1960–1970*, and just a few years later, d'Harnoncourt asked the artist to lend a number of his sculptures to replace Duchamp's works that would be traveling as part of a 1973 retrospective. Many of these sculptures have remained on long-term view to this day, alongside other loans and important acquisitions, including *Catenary (I Call to the Grave)* (1998; p. 267, pl. 1), in a gallery permanently devoted to the artist's work (p. 322, pl. 23). In 1988, Johns represented the United States in the Venice Biennale under the Philadelphia Museum of Art's auspices with *Jasper Johns: Work Since 1974*. Johns was awarded the biennale's grand prize, the Golden Lion (p. 320, pl. 13), and the exhibition made a triumphant homecoming to Philadelphia later that year.

Over the years, the connection between the museum and the artist has continued to grow. In 2012–13, his work appeared alongside that of his most intimate collaborators and their enigmatic paterfamilias in *Dancing around the Bride: Cage, Cunningham, Johns, Rauschenberg, and Duchamp*, organized by Carlos Basualdo and Erica Battle. Animated by music, dance, and vital interconnections, the exhibition explored the lasting impact of Duchamp on the quartet of younger Americans, bringing Johns's Philadelphia journey full circle.

—Scott Rothkopf, with Carlos Basualdo, Sarah B. Vogelman, and Lauren Young

1 Mark Stevens with Cathleen McGuigan, "Super Artist: Jasper Johns, Today's Master," *Newsweek*, October 24, 1977, 66–68, 73, 77–79; Michael Crichton, *Jasper Johns* (New York: Harry N. Abrams in association with the Whitney Museum of American Art, 1977).

2 Jasper Johns, quoted in Grace Glueck, "Painting by Jasper Johns Sold for a Million, a Record," *New York Times*, September 27, 1980.

3 Robert Rosenblum, "Castelli Group," *Arts* 31, no. 8 (May 1957): 53.

Archive

Whitney Museum of American Art

1 Johns with *Flag on Orange Field* (1957; p. 66, pl. 6) during the installation of *Jasper Johns*, 1977. Frances Mulhall Achilles Library and Archives, Whitney Museum of American Art, New York; Photograph Collection, box 3, folder 16

2 Excerpt from the artist questionnaire for *Studio* (1964; pp. 130–31, pl. 2), the first work by Johns to enter the museum's collection, 1966. Cataloguing and Documentation Office, Whitney Museum of American Art, New York; object files, 66.1a–c

3 Letter from Johns supporting a campaign by artists invited to participate in the 1969 Annual Exhibition of Contemporary American Painting for a day of free admission at the Whitney, 1969. Frances Mulhall Achilles Library and Archives, Whitney Museum of American Art, New York; Records of the Office of the Director, series I, Lloyd Goodrich, box 6, folder 15, SC.69.3a–g

4 Johns at the opening of *Jasper Johns*, 1977. Frances Mulhall Achilles Library and Archives, Whitney Museum of American Art, New York; Photograph Collection, box 3, folder 15

5 Exhibition catalogue for *Jasper Johns*, 1977, by Michael Crichton, with a cover illustration designed by Johns. New York: Abrams and the Whitney Museum of American Art

6 *Newsweek*, October 24, 1977, with a profile of Johns on the occasion of *Jasper Johns*

7 *Savarin* (1977), lithograph (reproduced as a poster for *Jasper Johns*, 1977), 53 ½ × 31 ⅜ in. (135.9 × 79.7 cm), James V. Smith/ULAE, ed. no. A/B 4/14. Whitney Museum of American Art, New York; gift of the artist, 77.109

8 Correspondence between Whitney director Tom Armstrong and Johns, 1975. Frances Mulhall Achilles Library and Archives, Whitney Museum of American Art, New York; Exhibition Records, 1931–2004, box 81, folder 13

9 Correspondence between Armstrong and Johns, 1975. Frances Mulhall Achilles Library and Archives, Whitney Museum of American Art, New York; Exhibition Records, 1931–2004, box 81, folder 13

10 Exhibition model for *Jasper Johns*, 1977. Frances Mulhall Achilles Library and Archives, Whitney Museum of American Art, New York; Exhibition Records, 1931–2004, box 82, folder 6

11 Installation view, *Jasper Johns*, 1977

12 *Two Flags (Whitney Anniversary, 1980)*, 1980, lithograph (reproduced as a poster commemorating the museum's fiftieth anniversary), 50 × 33 ¾ in. (127 × 85.7 cm), Serge Lozingot and Martin Klein/Gemini, 4/11 AP. Whitney Museum of American Art, New York; fiftieth anniversary gift of the artist, 80.10

13 *New York Times*, September 27, 1980, with coverage of the Whitney's acquisition of *Three Flags* (1958; p. 62, pl. 2)

14 Notes for a toast given by Armstrong at the opening of *Jasper Johns: Savarin Monotypes*, 1982. Frances Mulhall Achilles Library and Archives, Whitney Museum of American Art, New York; Exhibition Records, 1931–2004, box 115, folder 26

15 Armstrong and Johns with *Three Flags* (1958; p. 62, pl. 2) after the museum acquired the work, 1980. Courtesy Jasper Johns

16 Study for *Three Flags*, 1958, charcoal on paper, 4 ¼ × 9 ½ in. (10.8 × 24.1 cm). Whitney Museum of American Art, New York; gift of the artist, 90.9

17 Installation view, *Jasper Johns: Savarin Monotypes*, 1982, with seven *Savarin* prints (all 1982; left to right, p. 210, pls. 6–8; p. 211, pl. 12; p. 209, pl. 5; p. 211, pls. 13, 14)

18 Flora Miller Biddle and Fiona Donovan, granddaughter and great-granddaughter of museum founder Gertrude Vanderbilt Whitney, with Johns at the opening of *The Drawings of Jasper Johns*, 1991

19 Gilbert Maurer, James Rosenquist, Leo Castelli, Robert Rauschenberg, Roy Lichtenstein, Johns, and Leonard A. Lauder at the opening of *Robert Rauschenberg: The Silkscreen Paintings, 1962–1964*, 1990

20 Installation view, 1983 Biennial Exhibition, with *Between the Clock and the Bed* (1981) and *In the Studio* (1982; p. 235, pl. 13); Phillip Maberry, *Paradise Found* (1983); Ellen Brooks, *Guarded Future* (1982); and Louise Bourgeois, *Shredder* (1983)

21 Exhibition catalogue for *The American Century: Art & Culture, 1950–2000*, 1999, by Lisa Phillips, with *Three Flags* (1958; p. 62, pl. 2) on the cover. New York: W. W. Norton and the Whitney Museum of American Art

22 Group portrait of artists featured in *The American Century: Art & Culture, 1950–2000*, 1999

23 Installation view, *Full House: Views of the Whitney's Collection at 75*, 2006, with David Salle, *Sextant in Dogtown* (1987); Sherrie Levine, *La Fortune (After Man Ray): 4* (1990) and *Large Gold Knot: 1* (1987); and *Racing Thoughts* (1983; p. 186, pl. 2)

24 Poster for the Whitney's seventy-fifth anniversary, 2005, with *Two Maps* (1965; p. 61, pl. 1)

25 Catalogue for *Artists for the Whitney of the Future: A Benefit Auction Sold to Benefit the Whitney Museum of American Art's New Building Project*, 2013, with *Untitled* (2012) on the cover

26 Letter from Whitney director Adam D. Weinberg to Johns, 2012

27 Installation view, *America Is Hard to See*, 2015, with Lari Pittman, *Untitled #16 (A Decorated Chronology of Insistence and Resignation)* (1993); *Racing Thoughts* (1983; p. 186, pl. 2); and Jean-Michel Basquiat, *Hollywood Africans* (1983)

28 Joel Shapiro and Johns at the opening of *America Is Hard to See*, 2015, with Keith Sonnier, *Ba-O-Ba, Number 3* (1969) and Thomas Downing, *Five* (1967)

Philadelphia Museum of Art

1 Johns examining Robert Rauschenberg's *Interview* (1955) at the opening of *Dancing around the Bride: Cage, Cunningham, Johns, Rauschenberg, and Duchamp*, 2012. Library and Archives, Philadelphia Museum of Art

2 Pamphlet for *Jasper Johns: Prints, 1960–1970*, 1970, with *Souvenir* (1970; p. 299, pl. 54) on the cover. Library and Archives, Philadelphia Museum of Art; Directors' Exhibition Records

3 Johns and curator Richard S. Field at the opening of *Jasper Johns: Prints, 1960–1970*, 1970. Library and Archives, Philadelphia Museum of Art; Marketing and Public Relations Department Records

4 Marcel Duchamp (American, b. France, 1887–1968), *Étant donnés: 1° la chute d'eau, 2° le gaz d'éclairage …* (*Given: 1. The Waterfall, 2. The Illuminating Gas …*), 1946–66, mixed-media assemblage: (exterior) wooden door, iron nails, bricks, and stucco; (interior) bricks, velvet, wood, parchment over an armature of lead, steel, brass, synthetic putties and adhesives, aluminum sheet, welded steel-wire screen, and wood; pegboard, hair, oil paint, plastic, steel binder clips, plastic clothespins, twigs, leaves, glass, plywood, brass piano hinge, nails, screws, cotton, collotype prints, acrylic varnish, chalk, graphite, paper, cardboard, tape, pen ink, electric light fixtures, gas lamp (Bec Auer type), foam rubber, cork, electric motor, cookie tin, and linoleum, 95 ½ × 70 × 49 in. (242.6 × 177.8 × 124.5 cm). Philadelphia Museum of Art; gift of the Cassandra Foundation, 1969-41-1

5 Mark Lancaster, Tomio Miki, Aiko Miyawaki, Lavinia Russell, Roberta Bernstein, Johns, Lois Long, Suzi Gablik, Robert Morris, John Russell, Rita Donagh, and Richard Hamilton on the museum's East Terrace soon after the installation of Duchamp's *Étant donnés*, 1969

6 Johns with collector Elizabeth Bliss Parkinson Cobb at the opening of *Marcel Duchamp*, 1973. Library and Archives, Philadelphia Museum of Art; Marcel Duchamp Exhibition Records

7 The American Pavilion at the 43rd Venice Biennale, which featured the exhibition *Jasper Johns: Work Since 1974*, organized by the Philadelphia Museum of Art, 1988. Library and Archives, Philadelphia Museum of Art; Special Exhibitions Department Records

8 *New York Times Magazine*, June 19, 1988, with a profile of Johns on the occasion of the Venice Biennale presentation of *Jasper Johns: Work Since 1974*. Library and Archives,

Philadelphia Museum of Art; Special Exhibitions Department Records

9 Exhibition catalogue for *Jasper Johns: Work Since 1974*, 1988, by Mark Rosenthal, with a detail of *Fall* (1986; p. 190, pl. 8) on the cover. Philadelphia: Philadelphia Museum of Art. Library and Archives, Philadelphia Museum of Art

10 Johns with *Untitled* (1983; p. 243, pl. 12) and the center sheet of *Voice 2* (1982) during the installation of *Jasper Johns: Work Since 1974* in Philadelphia, 1988. Library and Archives, Philadelphia Museum of Art; Marketing and Public Relations Department Records

11 Johns with *Spring* (1986; p. 190, pl. 7) at the Venice Biennale, 1988. Library and Archives, Philadelphia Museum of Art; Marketing and Public Relations Department Records

12 Installation view, *Jasper Johns: Work Since 1974* at the Venice Biennale, 1988, with *Foirades/Fizzles* (1976; pp. 166–67, pls. 26–33), *Racing Thoughts* (1984; p. 187, pl. 3), and *Cicada* (1979). Library and Archives, Philadelphia Museum of Art; Special Exhibitions Department Records

13 Curator Mark Rosenthal accepting the Golden Lion at the Venice Biennale for *Jasper Johns: Work Since 1974*, 1988. Library and Archives, Philadelphia Museum of Art; Marketing and Public Relations Department Records

14 *Philadelphia Inquirer*, June 27, 1988, with coverage of the Golden Lion award. Library and Archives, Philadelphia Museum of Art; Special Exhibitions Department Records

15 *Philadelphia Inquirer Magazine*, October 23, 1988, with a profile of Johns on the occasion of the Philadelphia presentation of *Jasper Johns: Work Since 1974*. Library and Archives, Philadelphia Museum of Art; Special Exhibitions Department Records

16 Museum president Robert Montgomery Scott, Katherine Sachs, museum director Anne d'Harnoncourt, Johns, and Mark Rosenthal at the Philadelphia opening of *Jasper Johns: Work Since 1974*, 1988. Library and Archives, Philadelphia Museum of Art; Marketing and Public Relations Department Records

17 Postcard from Johns to d'Harnoncourt, 1989. Library and Archives, Philadelphia Museum of Art; Anne d'Harnoncourt Records

18 Letter from Merce Cunningham to d'Harnoncourt, 1987. Library and Archives, Philadelphia Museum of Art; Marcel Duchamp Exhibition Records

19 Museum events calendar highlighting *Jasper Johns: Process and Printmaking*, 1999, with a detail of *Figure 5* (1969; p. 86, pl. 45) on the cover. Library and Archives, Philadelphia Museum of Art; Special Exhibitions Department Records

20 Installation view, Philadelphia presentation of *Jasper Johns: Work Since 1974*, 1988. Library and Archives, Philadelphia Museum of Art

21 Donors celebrating the acquisition of *Catenary (I Call to the Grave)* (1998; p. 267, pl. 1), 2001. Library and Archives, Philadelphia Museum of Art

22 *New York Times*, July 20, 2001, with coverage of the acquisition of *Catenary (I Call to the Grave)* (1998; p. 267, pl. 1). Library and Archives, Philadelphia Museum of Art; Marketing and Public Relations Department Records

23 Installation view of gallery 277 (Sachs Gallery), a space permanently dedicated to works by Johns, mostly on long-term loan from the artist, 2016. Library and Archives, Philadelphia Museum of Art

24 Johns with museum trustees and longtime collectors Keith and Katherine Sachs and curator Carlos Basualdo at Sachs Gallery dedication, 2014. Library and Archives, Philadelphia Museum of Art

25 Merce Cunningham Event performed during *Dancing around the Bride*, 2013, featuring former Merce Cunningham Dance Company members, from left: Marcie Munnerlyn, Emma Desjardins, Brandon Collwes, Krista Nelson, John Hinrichs, and Andrea Weber. Library and Archives, Philadelphia Museum of Art

26 Philippe Parreno and Johns at the opening of *Dancing around the Bride*, 2012. Library and Archives, Philadelphia Museum of Art

27 Johns and curator Joseph J. Rishel at the opening of *Dancing around the Bride*, 2012. Library and Archives, Philadelphia Museum of Art

28 Duchamp's *Apolinère Enameled* (1916–17) and Johns's *Painted Bronze* (1960; p. 206, pl. 2) during installation of *Dancing around the Bride*, 2012. Library and Archives, Philadelphia Museum of Art

Whitney Museum of American Art

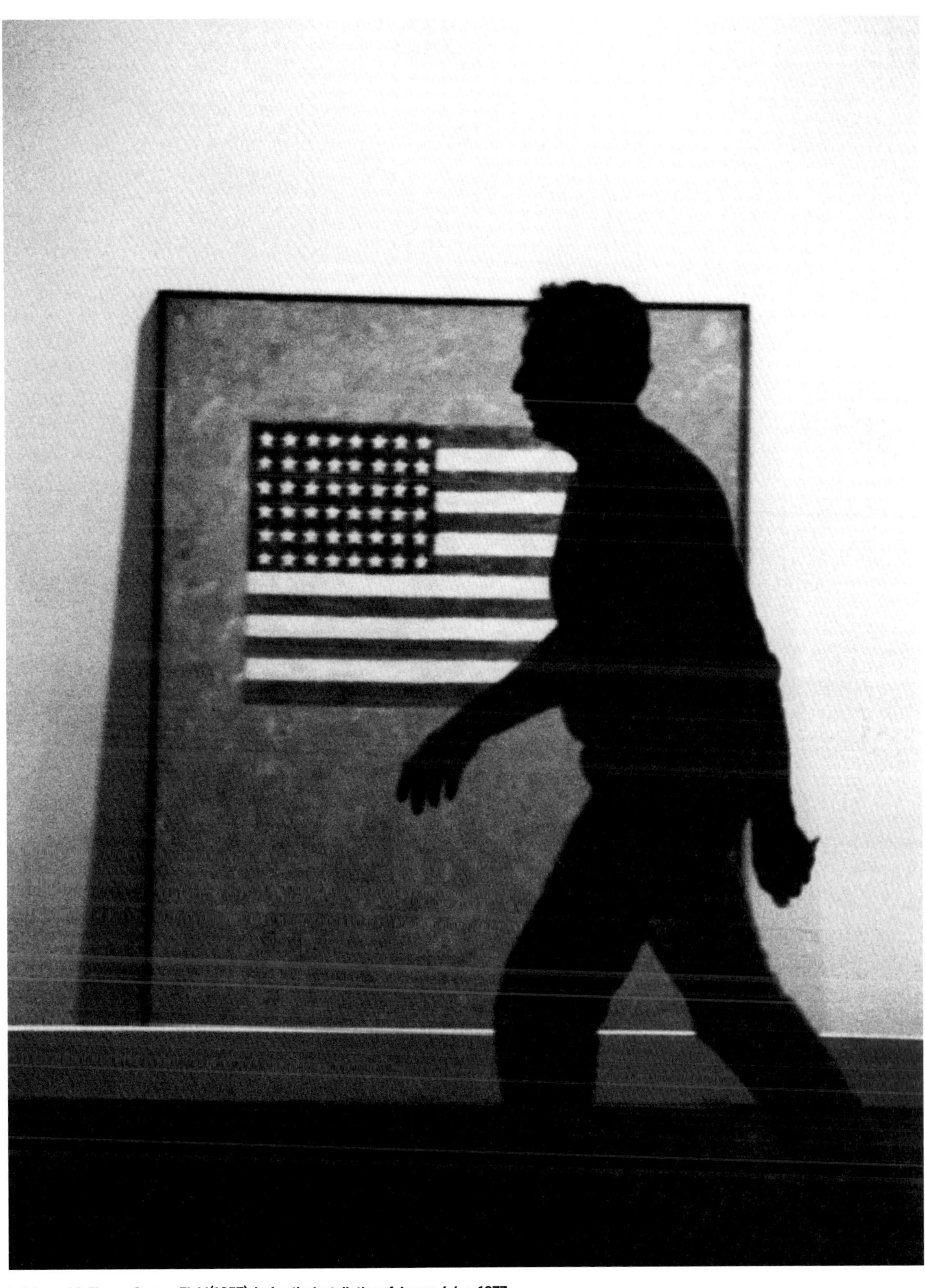

1 Johns with *Flag on Orange Field* (1957) during the installation of *Jasper Johns*, 1977

Where and when was this work exhibited before the Museum acquired it?

Leo Castelli Gallery, 1966

Will you kindly give us information about the subject of this work, the ideas expressed in it, the circumstances under which it was executed, any comments you would like to make on it, or any other information which would be of interest in the future:

THE DOOR FORM WAS MADE BY BRUSHING THE STUDIO DOOR WITH BLUE PAINT AND PRESSING THE CANVAS AGAINST IT.
A PALM LEAF WAS BRUSHED WITH RED AND PRESSED AGAINST THE CANVAS TO PRODUCE ONE FORM. THE LEAF CAME FROM A TREE IN MY YARD. THE OBJECTS WERE IN MY STUDOO AT THE TIME I MADE THE PAINTING.

Date April 26, 1966 Signed Kay Bearman for Jasper Johns
Castelli Gall.

2

I WISH TO JOIN WITH OTHER ARTISTS AND MEMBERS OF THE ART COMMUNITY REQUESTING CHANGES IN MUSEUM POLICY. I WOULD LIKE TO SEE THE WHITNEY MUSEUM IMMEDIATELY ESTABLISH A FREE DAY EACH WEEK. THIS WOULD GIVE MANY MORE PEOPLE ACCESS TO THE WORKS OF ART THE MUSEUM NOW HOUSES.

Jasper Johns

JASPER JOHNS

3

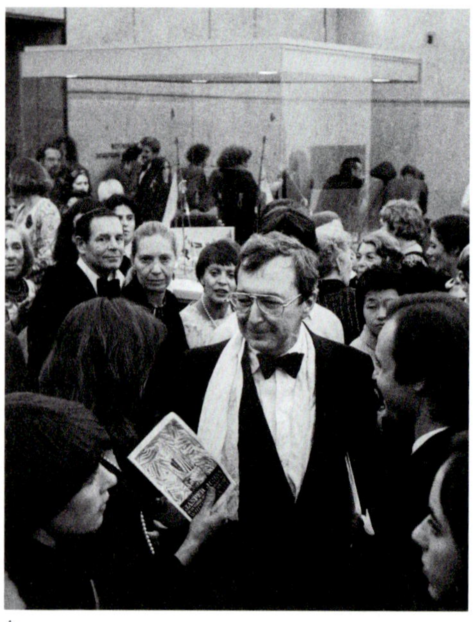

4

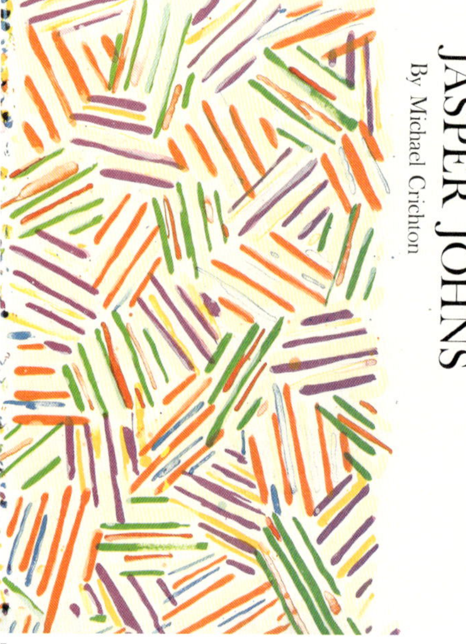

5

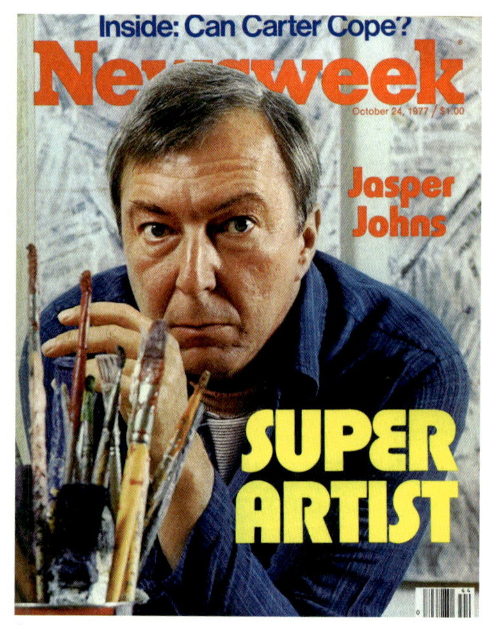

6

2 **Excerpt from the artist questionnaire for *Studio* (1964), the first work by Johns to enter the museum's collection, 1966**

3 **Letter from Johns supporting a campaign by artists invited to participate in the 1969 Annual Exhibition of Contemporary American Painting for a day of free admission at the Whitney, 1969**

4 **Johns at the opening of *Jasper Johns*, 1977**

5 **Exhibition catalogue for *Jasper Johns*, 1977, with a cover illustration designed by Johns**

6 ***Newsweek*, October 24, 1977, with a profile of Johns on the occasion of *Jasper Johns*, 1977**

JASPER JOHNS
18 OCTOBER 1977 · 22 JANUARY 1978
WHITNEY MUSEUM
OF AMERICAN ART

7

January 24, 1975

Mr. Jasper Johns
Terres Barses
Marigot
St. Martin
French West Indies

Dear Jasper:

It was a great pleasure to meet you. I am extremely pleased that you are enthusiastic about an exhibition of your work at the Whitney Museum of American Art in early spring of 1977. We are anxious to make this a complete presentation of your outstanding accomplishments in drawings, prints, paintings and sculpture.

The exhibition will be presented on the third and fourth floors of the Museum and will be scheduled for approximately three months. I shall begin to investigate the possibilities of traveling the exhibition to Paris, Amsterdam, Tokyo, and the west coast of the United States.

Leo Castelli has related your thoughts about the scholarship in connection with the exhibition. Together with your help I would like to put together the team which you have indicated you feel could do the best job. I will be in charge of the exhibition. David Whitney will be invited to make the selections of your work and be responsible for the installation. Marcia Tucker, curator of the Whitney, will write a catalogue essay. We plan to arrange for additional essays and will ask Leo Steinberg and perhaps Robert Rosenblum to contribute to the catalogue.

It is planned that the catalogue would be the soft cover version of a major hardcover book, and we will begin to look for a publisher to join us in this venture.

8

JASPER JOHNS
TERRES BASSES
MARIGOT
ST. MARTIN, F.W.I.

I Feb. '75

Dear Tom,

Thank you very much for your letter. I hope that your optimism toward the exhibition will continue and will encounter no obstacles.

Whatever "thoughts about scholarship" Leo related to you must have been his own. I don't remember having any when I was in NY and I've none now, unfortunately. Steinberg and Rosenblum would be excellent men to have write but I doubt that either wishes to write more about my work than he has already written. I have no information about Tucker's interest in or knowledge of my work but in NY I read two things that she had written and am delighted that she should do an essay.

I spoke with David Whitney before I left to ask if he were willing to work with the exhibition and if he had any ideas about texts. He said nothing would make him happier, to the first, and no, to the second. I'm pleased that you agree to his making the selections and hope that you have spoken with him. He worked for me for a couple of years and is very knowledgeable about the things I've made.

Pontus Hulten wanted a show of my drawings now being circulated in England by The Arts Council to go to Paris. Lenders' refusals to extend loans make the Paris show impossible and I have taken the liberty of telling Pontus to contact you if he should be interested in having the Whitney show go there.

I shall be in NY toward the end of March before going to Paris to continue trying to make some etchings with Aldo Crommelynk. I look forward to seeing you then.

With best wishes,

As ever,

9

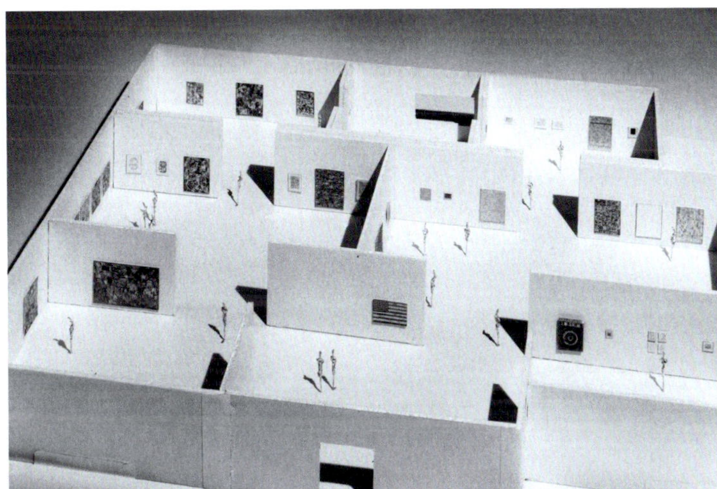

10

11

7 *Savarin* (1977), lithograph reproduced as a poster for *Jasper Johns*, 1977

8 Correspondence between Whitney director Tom Armstrong and Johns, 1975

9 Correspondence between Armstrong and Johns, 1975

10 Exhibition model for *Jasper Johns*, 1977

11 Installation view, *Jasper Johns*, 1977

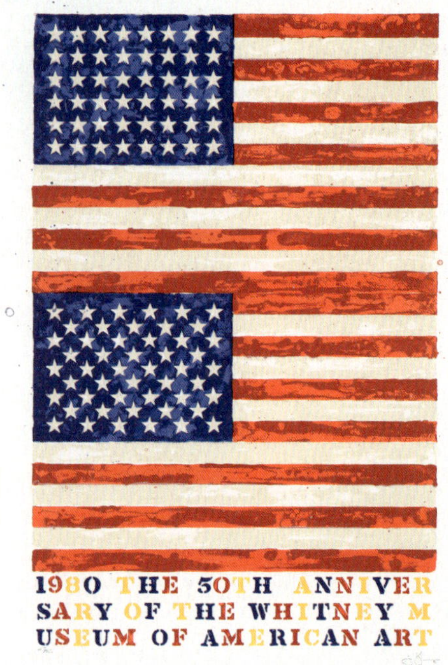

12

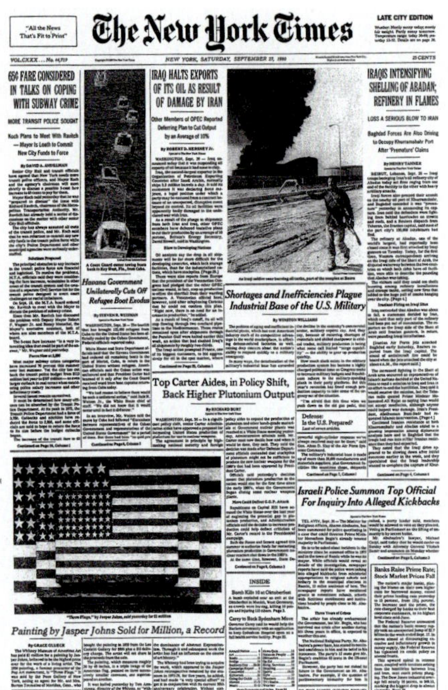

"All the News That's Fit to Print"

The New York Times

LATE CITY EDITION

NEW YORK, SATURDAY, SEPTEMBER 27, 1980

65¢ FARE CONSIDERED IN TALKS ON COPING WITH SUBWAY CRIME

IRAQ HALTS EXPORTS OF ITS OIL AS RESULT OF DAMAGE BY IRAN

IRAQIS INTENSIFYING SHELLING OF ABADAN; REFINERY IN FLAMES

Havana Government Unilaterally Cuts Off Refugee Boat Exodus

Shortages and Inefficiencies Plague Industrial Base of the U.S. Military

Top Carter Aides, in Policy Shift, Back Higher Plutonium Output

Israeli Police Summon Top Official For Inquiry Into Alleged Kickbacks

Painting by Jasper Johns Sold for Million, a Record

13

A TOAST TO JASPER JOHNS 17 NOVEMBER 82

Jasper--

The Whitney is committed to you, and we want to thank you for the great trust you have placed in us: the exhibition in 1977, with the original Savarin poster; the 50th Anniversary poster; and now this beautiful exhibition--and the many personal kindnesses which you've blessed us with, individually and collectively.

I'd like to be able to articulate how much your work means to me--and have the words of someone whose work I also love to speak for me and maybe for us all--

This is the true creator, the waver

Waving purpling wands, the thinker

Thinking gold thoughts in a golden mind,

Loftily jingled, radiant,

The joy of meaning in design

Wrenched out of chaos...the quiet lamp

For this creator is a lamp

Enlarging like a nocturnal ray

The space in which it stands, the shine

Of darkness, creating from nothingness....

"The Sail of Ulysses" Wallace Stevens

14

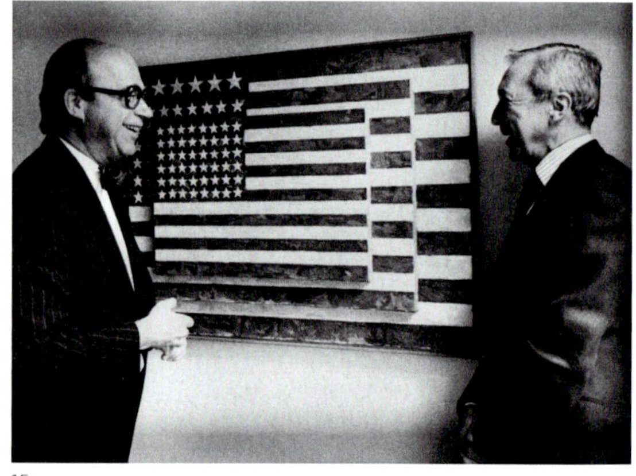

15

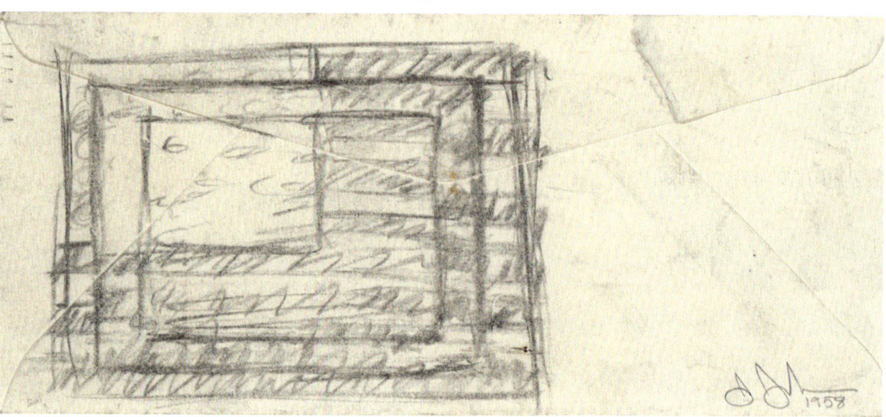

16

12 ***Two Flags (Whitney Anniversary, 1980)*** **(1980), lithograph reproduced as a poster commemorating the museum's fiftieth anniversary**

13 ***New York Times*****, September 27, 1980, with coverage of the Whitney's acquisition of** ***Three Flags*** **(1958)**

14 **Notes for a toast given by Armstrong at the opening of** ***Jasper Johns: Savarin Monotypes*****, 1982**

15 **Armstrong and Johns with** ***Three Flags*** **(1958) after the museum acquired the work, 1980**

16 **Study for** ***Three Flags*****, 1958**

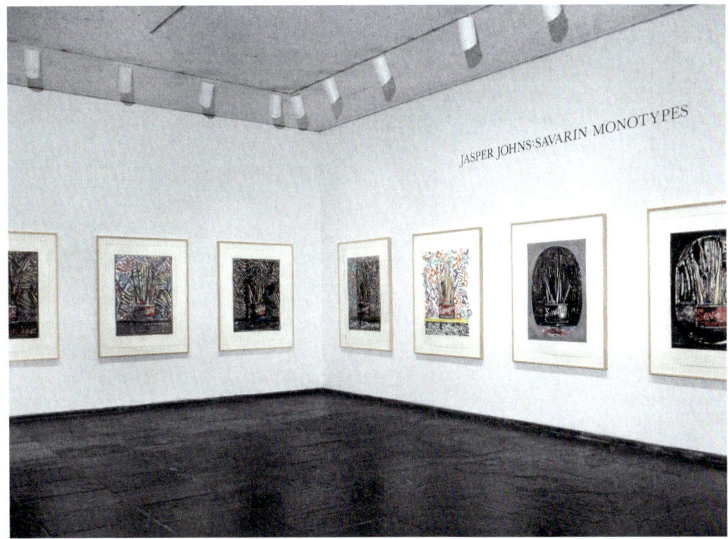

17

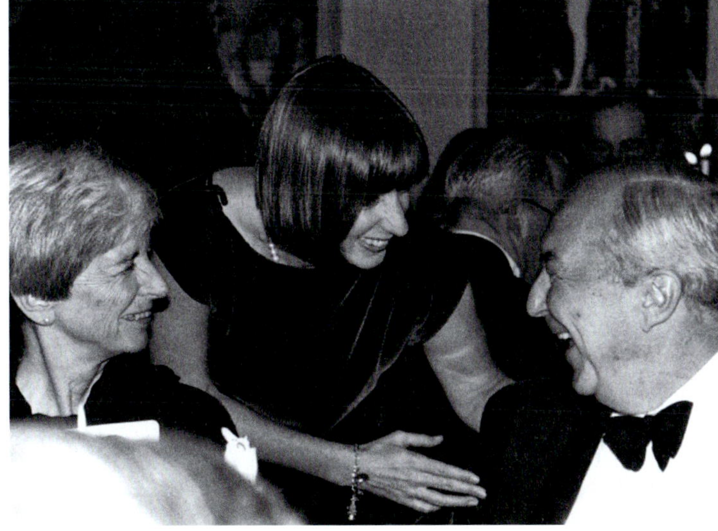

18

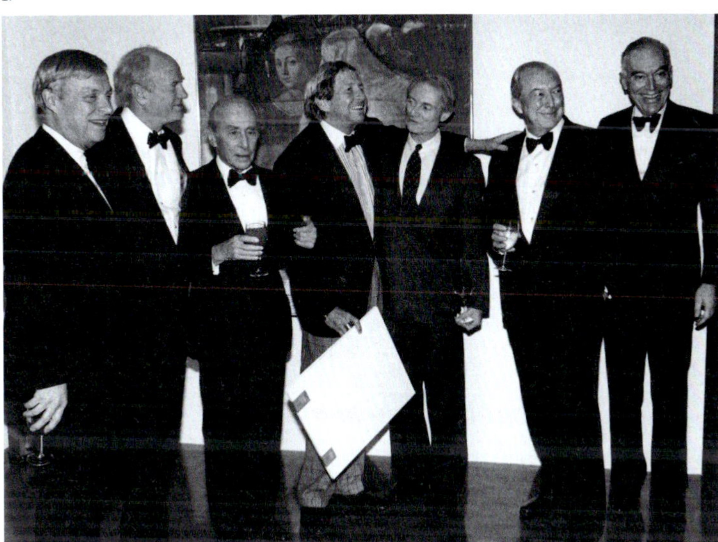

19

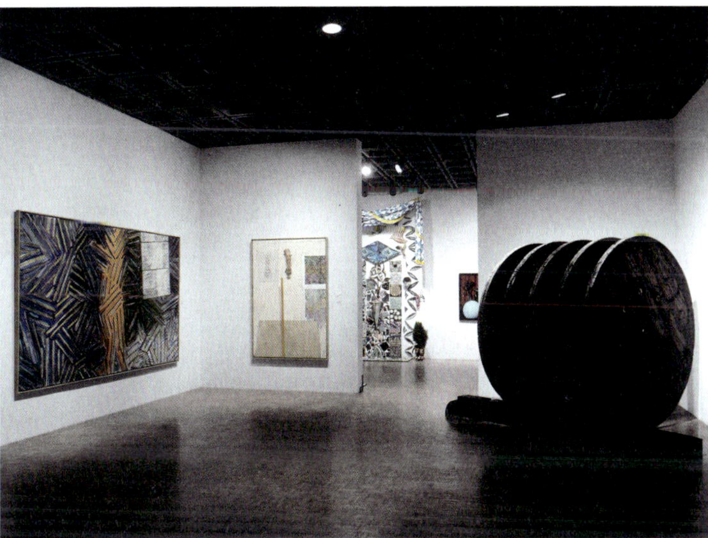

20

17 **Installation view, *Jasper Johns: Savarin Monotypes*, 1982, with seven *Savarin* prints (all 1982)**

18 **Flora Miller Biddle and Fiona Donovan, granddaughter and great-granddaughter of museum founder Gertrude Vanderbilt Whitney, with Johns at the opening of *The Drawings of Jasper Johns*, 1991**

19 **From left: Gilbert Maurer, James Rosenquist, Leo Castelli, Robert Rauschenberg, Roy Lichtenstein, Johns, and Leonard A. Lauder at the opening of *Robert Rauschenberg: The Silkscreen Paintings, 1962–1964*, 1990**

20 **Installation view, 1983 Biennial Exhibition, with *Between the Clock and the Bed* (1981) and *In the Studio* (1982); Phillip Maberry, *Paradise Found* (1983); Ellen Brooks, *Guarded Future* (1982); and Louise Bourgeois, *Shredder* (1983)**

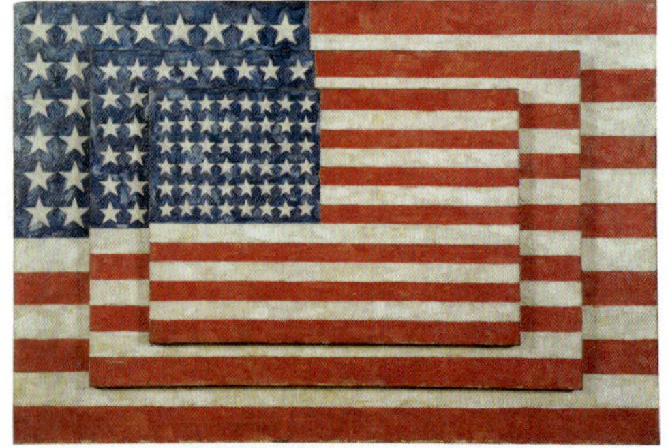

21

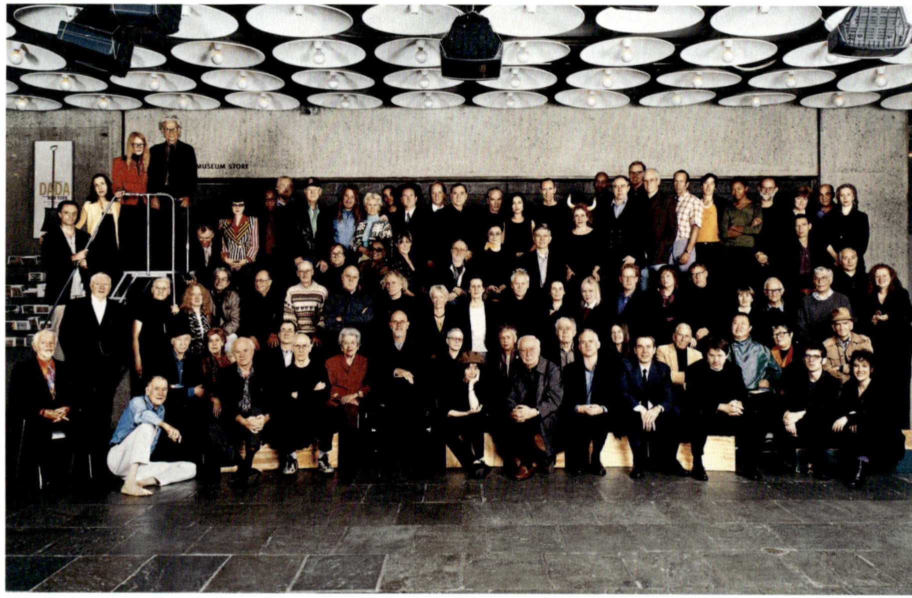

22

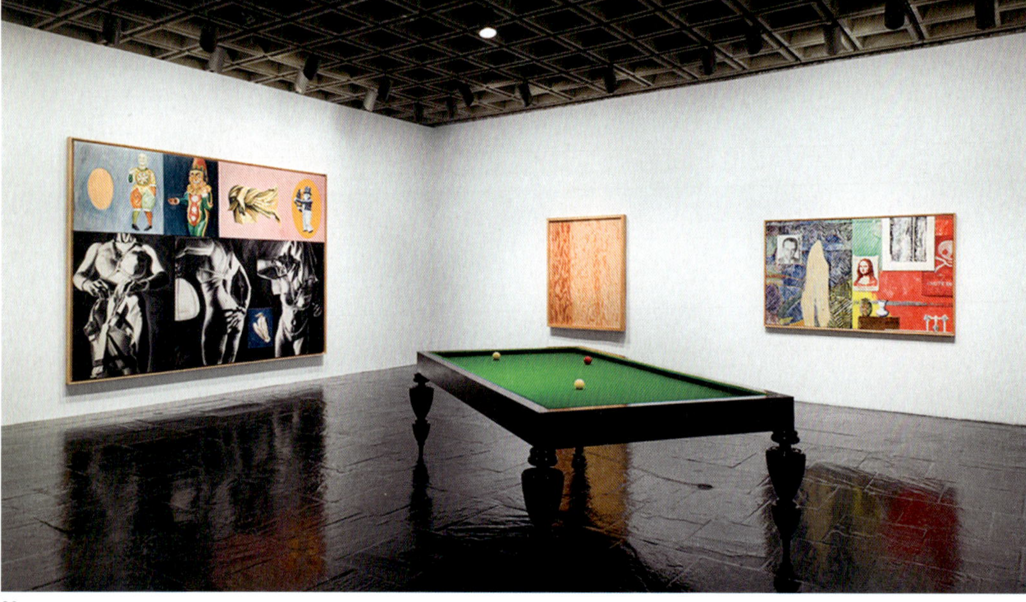

23

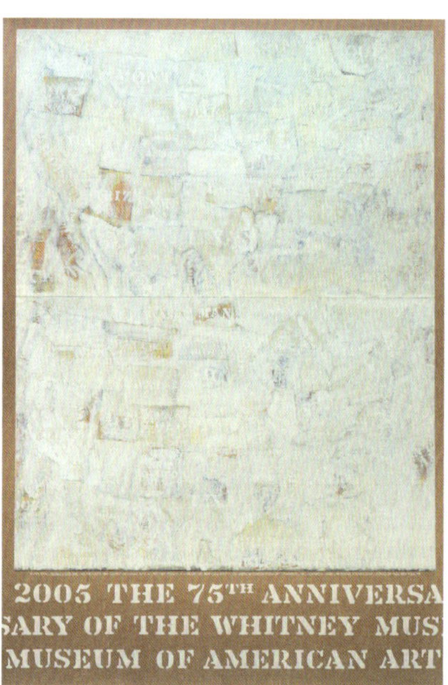

24

21 **Exhibition catalogue for *The American Century: Art & Culture, 1950–2000*, 1999, with *Three Flags* (1958) on the cover**

22 **Group portrait of artists featured in *The American Century: Art & Culture, 1950–2000*, 1999, with Johns seated front row, just right of center**

23 **Installation view, *Full House: Views of the Whitney's Collection at 75*, 2006, with David Salle, *Sextant in Dogtown* (1987); Sherrie Levine, *La Fortune (After Man Ray): 4* (1990) and *Large Gold Knot: 1* (1987); and *Racing Thoughts* (1983)**

24 **Poster for the Whitney's seventy-fifth anniversary, 2005, with *Two Maps* (1965)**

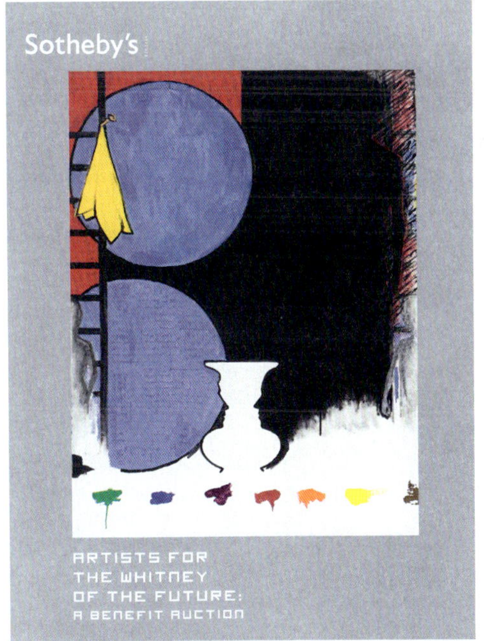

25

WHITNEY

14 July 2012

Adam D. Weinberg
Alice Pratt Brown Director

Dear Jasper–

I recently heard the wonderful news from Flora and Donna about your willingness to participate in the auction to benefit the new downtown Whitney. I am profoundly touched, grateful and honored by your generosity.

While I like to think that you and your art have benefitted by the support of the Museum, I can say, incontestably, that the Whitney and more importantly

26

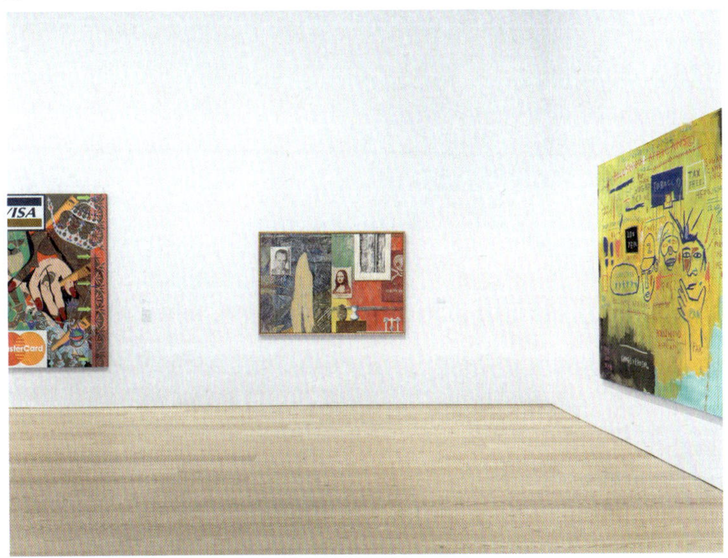

27

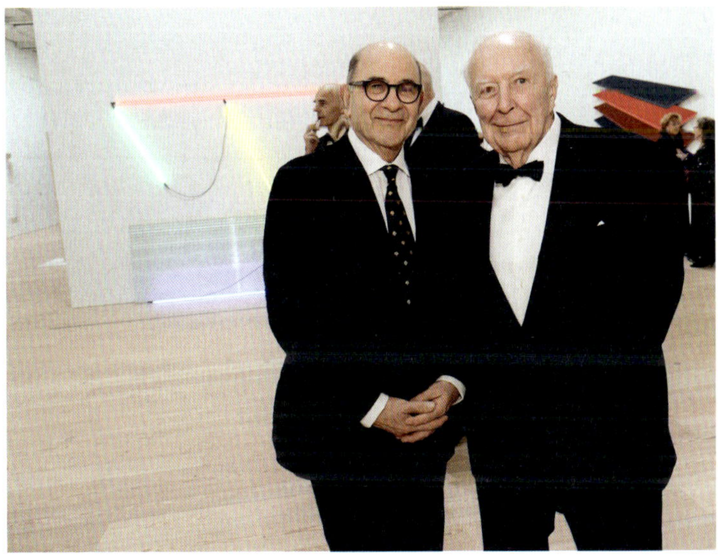

28

25 **Catalogue for *Artists for the Whitney of the Future: A Benefit Auction Sold to Benefit the Whitney Museum of American Art's New Building Project*, 2013, with *Untitled* (2012) on the cover**

26 **Letter from Whitney director Adam D. Weinberg to Johns, 2012**

27 **Installation view, *America Is Hard to See*, 2015, with Lari Pittman, *Untitled #16 (A Decorated Chronology of Insistence and Resignation)* (1993); *Racing Thoughts* (1983); and Jean-Michel Basquiat, *Hollywood Africans* (1983)**

28 **Joel Shapiro and Johns at the opening of *America Is Hard to See*, 2015, with Keith Sonnier, *Ba-O-Ba, Number 3* (1969) and Thomas Downing, *Five* (1967)**

Philadelphia Museum of Art

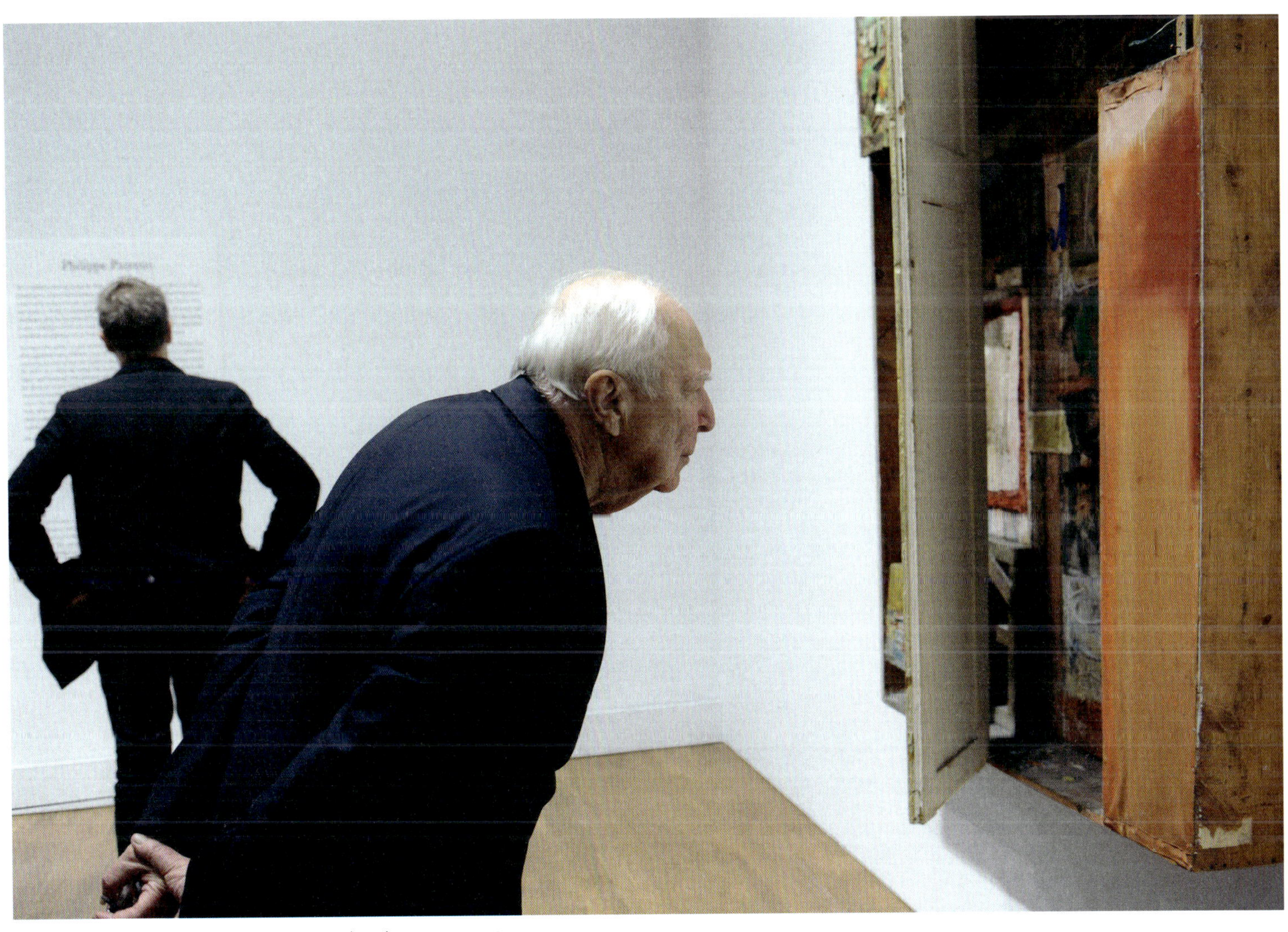

1 Johns examining Robert Rauschenberg's *Interview* (1955) at the opening of *Dancing around the Bride: Cage, Cunningham, Johns, Rauschenberg, and Duchamp*, 2012

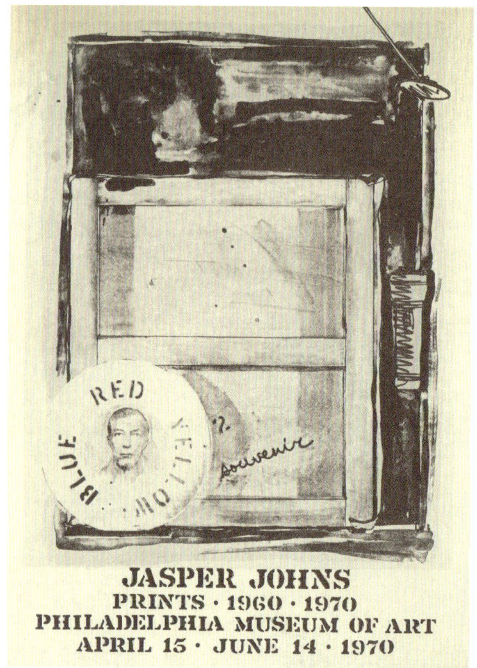

2

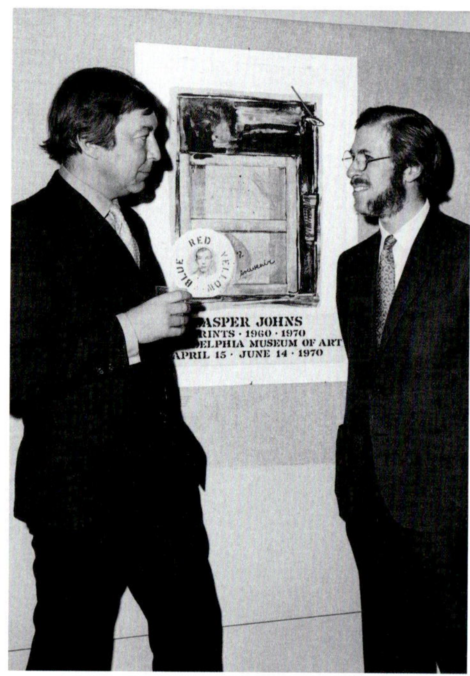

3

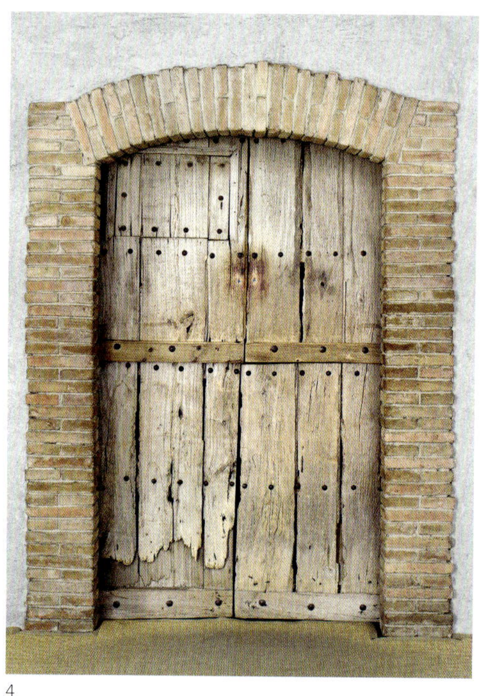

4

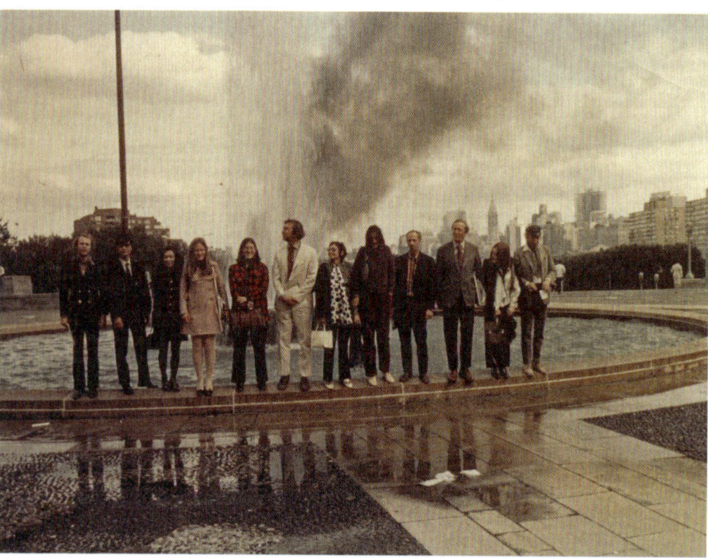

5

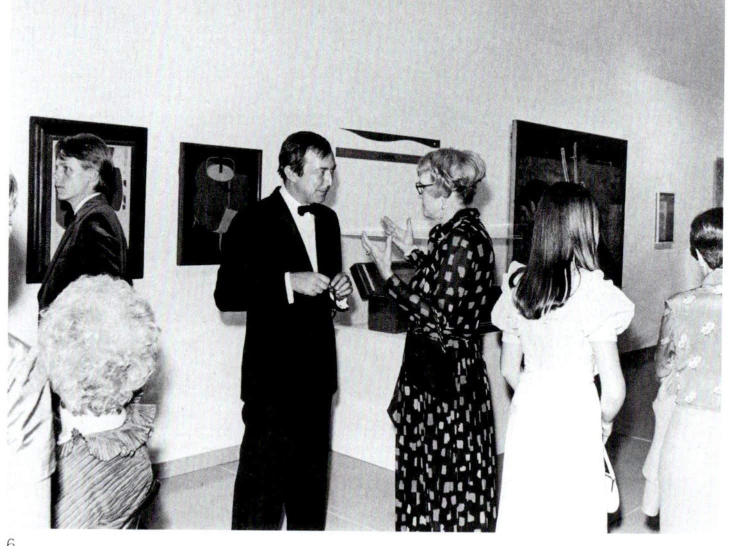

6

2 **Pamphlet for *Jasper Johns: Prints, 1960–1970*, 1970, with *Souvenir* (1970) on the cover**

3 **Johns and curator Richard S. Field at the opening of *Jasper Johns: Prints, 1960–1970*, 1970**

4 **Marcel Duchamp, *Étant donnés: 1° la chute d'eau, 2° le gaz d'éclairage …* (*Given: 1. The Waterfall, 2. The Illuminating Gas …*), 1946–66**

5 **From left: Mark Lancaster, Tomio Miki, Aiko Miyawaki, Lavinia Russell, Roberta Bernstein, Johns, Lois Long, Suzi Gablik, Robert Morris, John Russell, Rita Donagh, and Richard Hamilton on the museum's East Terrace soon after the installation of Duchamp's *Étant donnés*, 1969**

6 **Johns with collector Elizabeth Bliss Parkinson Cobb at the opening of *Marcel Duchamp*, 1973**

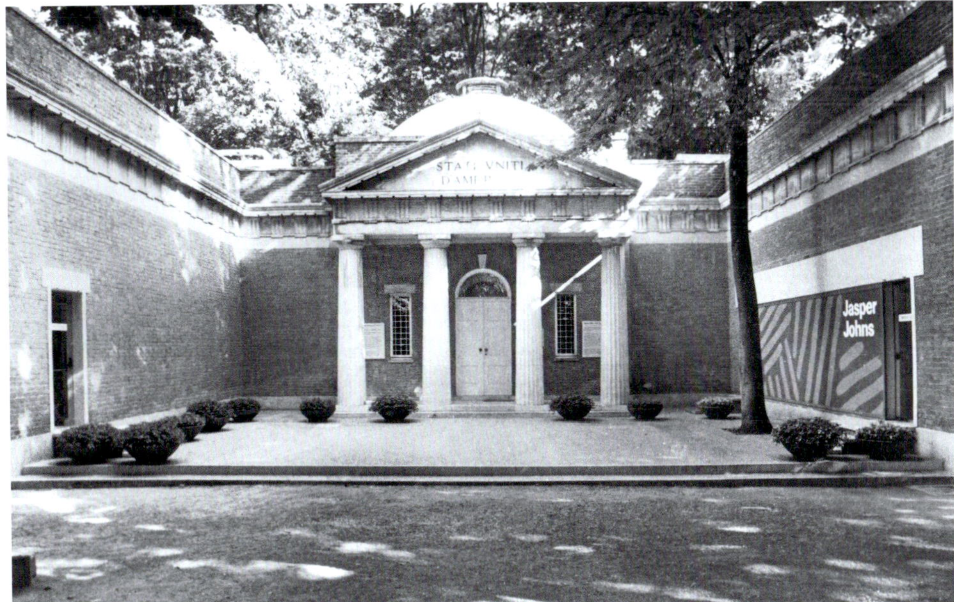

7

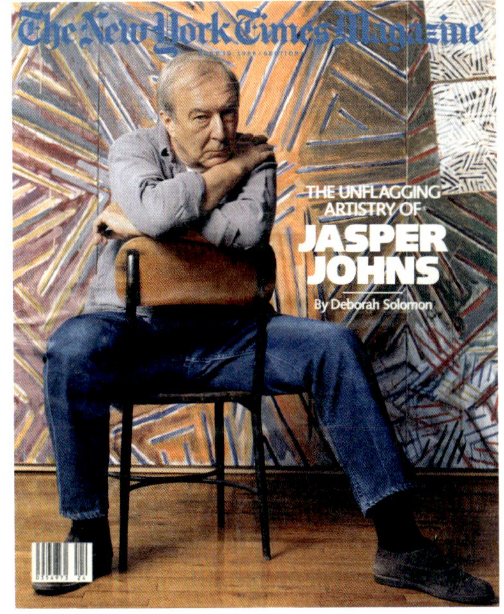

8

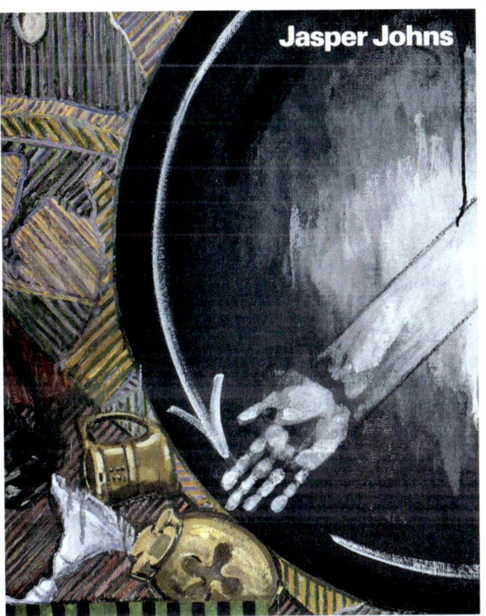

9

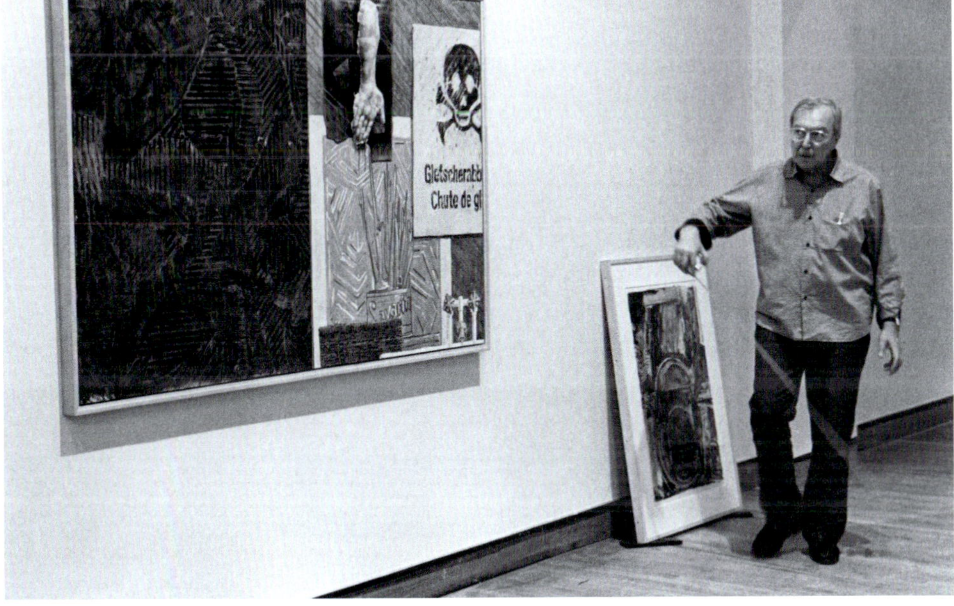

10

7 **The American Pavilion at the 43rd Venice Biennale, which featured the exhibition *Jasper Johns: Work Since 1974*, organized by the Philadelphia Museum of Art, 1988**

8 ***New York Times Magazine*, June 19, 1988, with a profile of Johns on the occasion of the Venice Biennale presentation of *Jasper Johns: Work Since 1974***

9 **Exhibition catalogue for *Jasper Johns: Work Since 1974*, 1988, with a detail of *Fall* (1986) on the cover**

10 **Johns with *Untitled* (1983) and the center sheet of *Voice 2* (1982) during the installation of *Jasper Johns: Work Since 1974* in Philadelphia, 1988**

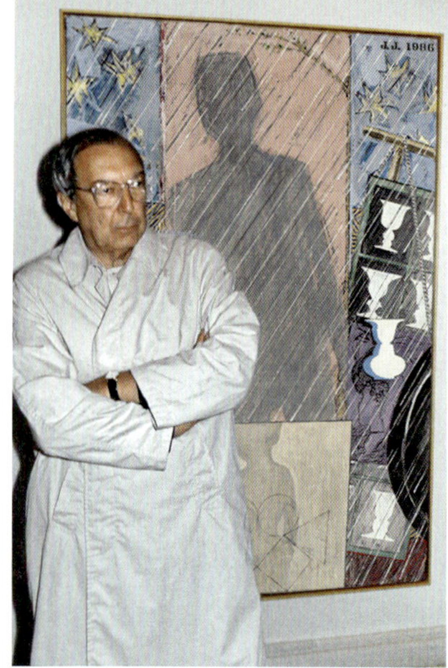

11

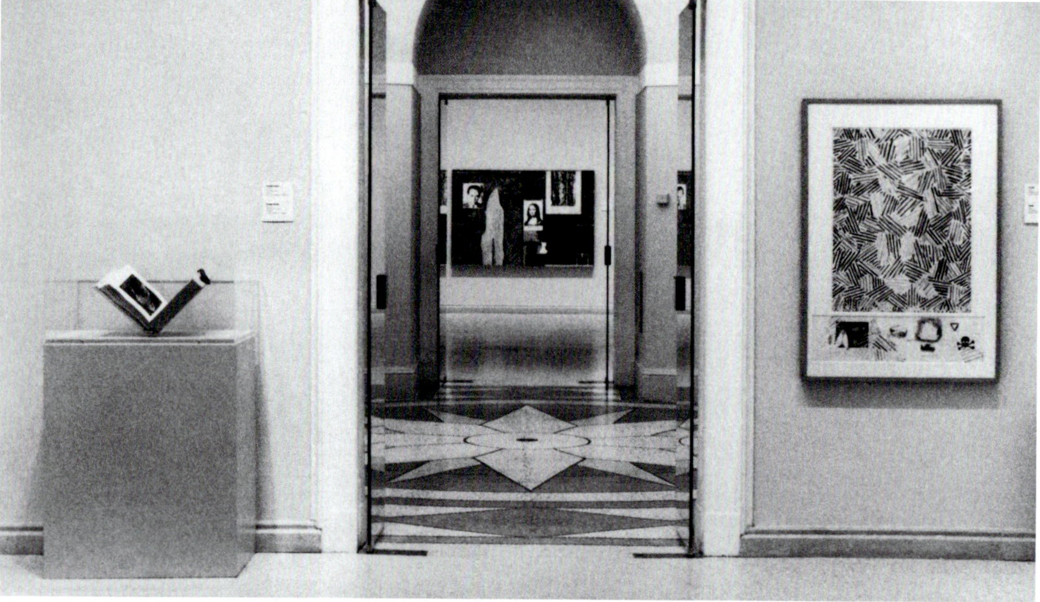

12

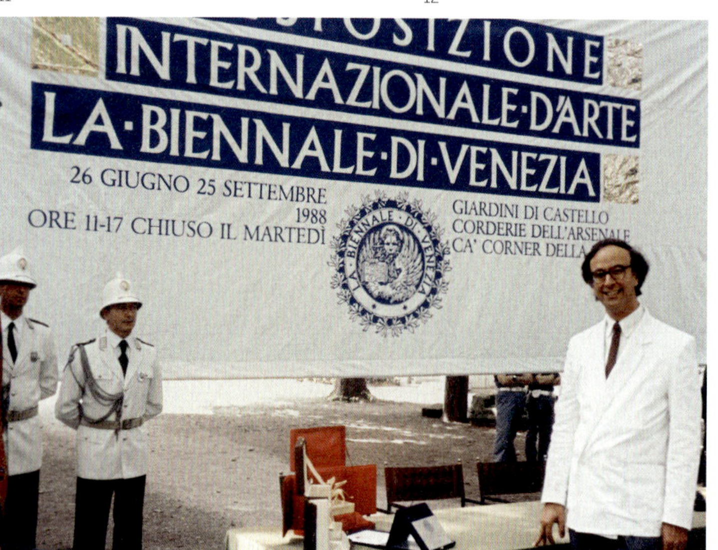

13

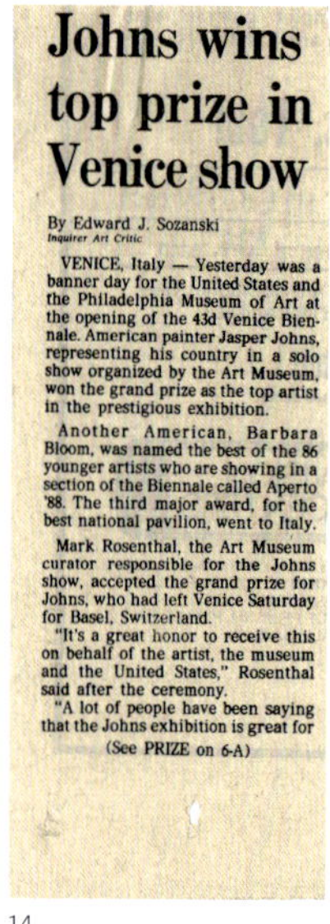

Johns wins top prize in Venice show

By Edward J. Sozanski
Inquirer Art Critic

VENICE, Italy — Yesterday was a banner day for the United States and the Philadelphia Museum of Art at the opening of the 43d Venice Biennale. American painter Jasper Johns, representing his country in a solo show organized by the Art Museum, won the grand prize as the top artist in the prestigious exhibition.

Another American, Barbara Bloom, was named the best of the 86 younger artists who are showing in a section of the Biennale called Aperto '88. The third major award, for the best national pavilion, went to Italy.

Mark Rosenthal, the Art Museum curator responsible for the Johns show, accepted the grand prize for Johns, who had left Venice Saturday for Basel, Switzerland.

"It's a great honor to receive this on behalf of the artist, the museum and the United States," Rosenthal said after the ceremony.

"A lot of people have been saying that the Johns exhibition is great for

(See PRIZE on 6-A)

14

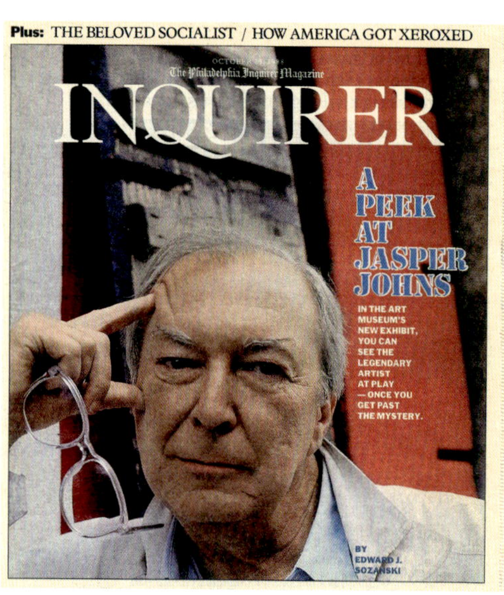

15

11 **Johns with *Spring* (1986) at the Venice Biennale, 1988**

12 **Installation view, *Jasper Johns: Work Since 1974* at the Venice Biennale, 1988, with *Foirades/Fizzles* (1976), *Racing Thoughts* (1984), and *Cicada* (1979)**

13 **Curator Mark Rosenthal accepting the Golden Lion at the Venice Biennale for *Jasper Johns: Work Since 1974*, 1988**

14 ***Philadelphia Inquirer*, June 27, 1988, with coverage of the Golden Lion award**

15 ***Philadelphia Inquirer Magazine*, October 23, 1988, with a profile of Johns on the occasion of the Philadelphia presentation of *Jasper Johns: Work Since 1974***

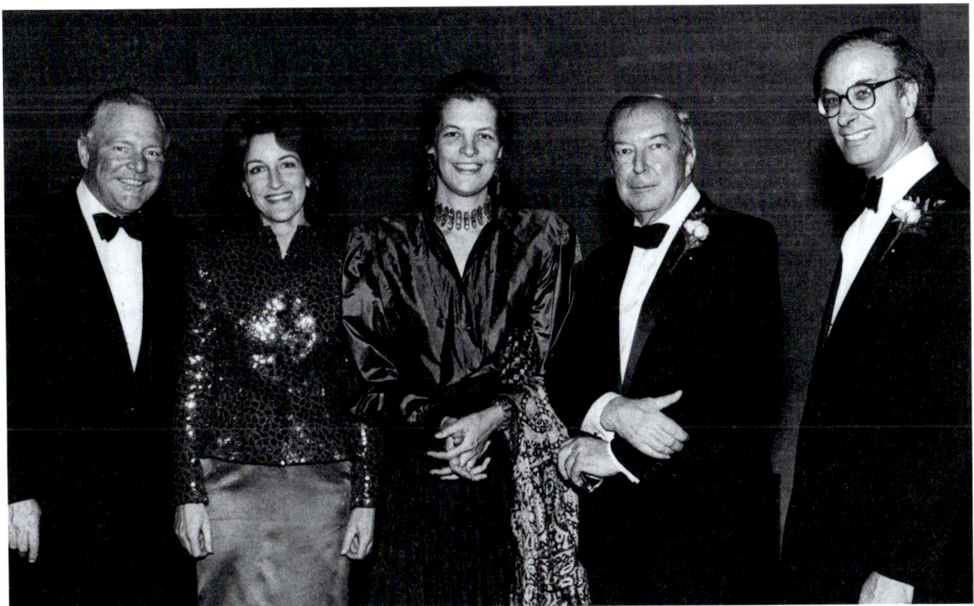

16

20 Dec. 89

Nr. 670
JASPER JOHNS (geb. 1930)
Flag above white with collage, 1955.
Leihgabe Kunstmuseum Basel

Dear Anne,
Best to you and Joe for the holidays. Thanks for the Cezanne sketchbooks. Am glad you saw the show in Basel. I thought it was wonderful too. Am off to St. M., hoping to see you in the New Year.
J

Verlag Öffentliche Kunstsammlung Basel
Vertrieb Reiter Kunstverlag AG, CH - 8123 Ebmatingen
Reproduktion verboten - G 89/1

DEC 20

17

AdH

NOV 12 1987

XC-DR
BA
JR

10/31/87

Dear Anne;
Just a note to thank you for having us with Marcel. After all our worries that the set, being unused for so long, wouldn't hold up, it did o.k. Looked good too.
The dancers were all delighted with their dinner with you, and I had a marvelous time at the reception after the Event. So many friends.
I'm off to Frankfurt this week for JC's Europeras. Love to Joe & you. Happy Halloween!
Merce

MERCE CUNNINGHAM

18

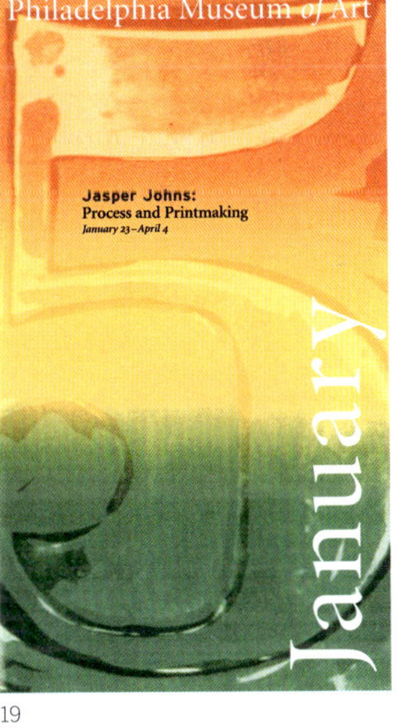

19

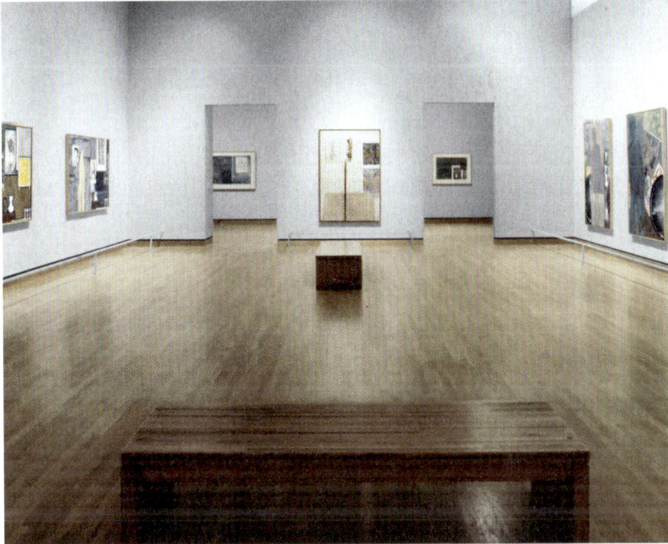

20

16 From left: museum president Robert Montgomery Scott, Katherine Sachs, museum director Anne d'Harnoncourt, Johns, and Mark Rosenthal at the Philadelphia opening of *Jasper Johns: Work Since 1974*, 1988

17 Postcard from Johns to d'Harnoncourt, 1989

18 Letter from Merce Cunningham to d'Harnoncourt, 1987

19 Museum events calendar highlighting *Jasper Johns: Process and Printmaking*, 1999, with a detail of *Figure 5* (1969) on the cover

20 Installation view, Philadelphia presentation of *Jasper Johns: Work Since 1974*, 1988

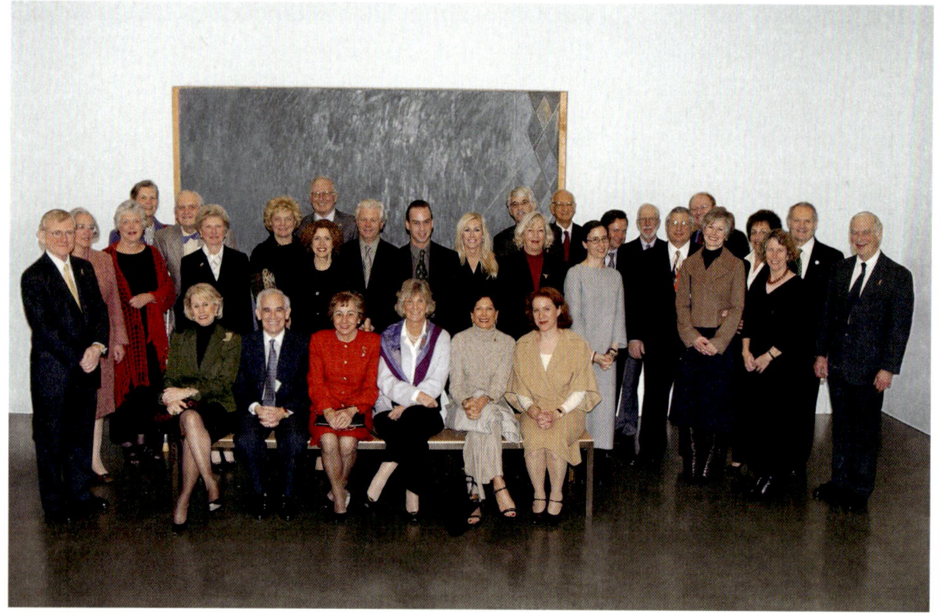

21

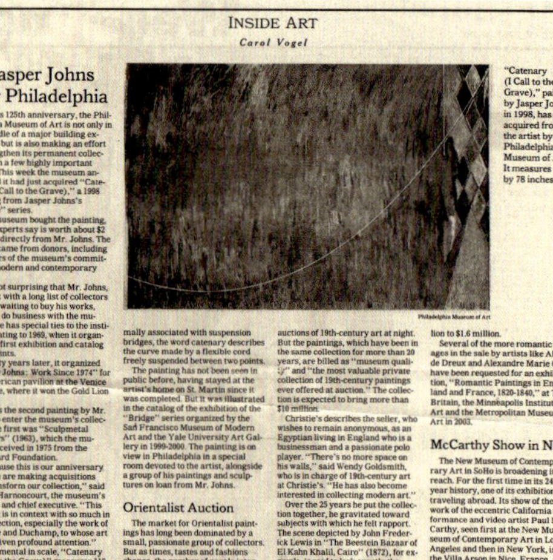

INSIDE ART

Carol Vogel

A Jasper Johns For Philadelphia

For its 125th anniversary, the Philadelphia Museum of Art is not only in the middle of a major building expansion but is also making an effort to strengthen its permanent collection with a few highly important works. This week the museum announced it had just acquired "Catenary (I Call to the Grave)," a 1998 painting from Jasper Johns's "Bridge" series.

The museum bought the painting, which experts say is worth about $2 million, directly from Mr. Johns. The money came from donors, including members of the museum's committee on modern and contemporary art.

It is not surprising that Mr. Johns, an artist with a long list of collectors eagerly waiting to buy his works, chose to do business with the museum. He has special ties to the institution dating to 1969, when it organized the first exhibition and catalog of his prints.

Twenty years later, it organized "Jasper Johns: Work Since 1974" for the American pavilion at the Venice Biennale, where it won the Gold Lion Award.

This is the second painting by Mr. Johns to enter the museum's collection. The first was "Sculpmetal Numbers" (1963), which the museum received in 1975 from the Woodward Foundation.

"Because this is our anniversary year, we are making acquisitions that transform our collection," said Anne d'Harnoncourt, the museum's director and chief executive. "This painting is in context with so much in our collection, especially the work of Cézanne and Duchamp, to whose art he has given profound attention."

Monumental in scale, "Catenary (I Call to the Grave)" measures 118 inches long by 78 inches high. It is in tones of gray encaustic, an ancient technique involving pigment suspended in melted wax, which Mr. Johns is frequently credited with reviving.

The material sets rapidly, allowing every brush stroke to remain distinct. A diamond-patterned harlequin motif appears on the right side of the canvas; a white string is suspended across the canvas from wooden slats that tilt outward along the left and right edges of the painting.

The title may seem strange. Normally associated with suspension bridges, the word catenary describes the curve made by a flexible cord freely suspended between two points.

The painting has not been seen in public before, having stayed at the artist's home on St. Martin since it was completed. But it was illustrated in the catalog of the exhibition of the "Bridge" series organized by the San Francisco Museum of Modern Art and the Yale University Art Gallery in 1999-2000. The painting is on view in Philadelphia in a special room devoted to the artist, alongside a group of his paintings and sculptures on loan from Mr. Johns.

"Catenary (I Call to the Grave)," painted by Jasper Johns in 1998, has been acquired from the artist by the Philadelphia Museum of Art. It measures 118 by 78 inches.

Philadelphia Museum of Art

Orientalist Auction

The market for Orientalist paintings has long been dominated by a small, passionate group of collectors. But as times, tastes and fashions change, the number of people interested in those 19th-century images, once described by the French painter Eugène Fromentin as "inflamed landscapes under a blue sky," has grown considerably. In contrast with Impressionist and modern art, there are still top-quality works available and they are relatively inexpensive.

Christie's is selling Orientalist paintings by such masters of this genre as Jean-Léon Gérôme, John Frederick Lewis, Gustave Bauernfeind and Ludwig Deutsch in a single-owner evening sale on Oct. 31. Sotheby's and Christie's rarely go to the trouble and expense of holding auctions of 19th-century art at night. But the paintings, which have been in the same collection for more than 20 years, are billed as "museum quality" and "the most valuable private collection of 19th-century paintings ever offered at auction." The collection is expected to bring more than $10 million.

Christie's describes the seller, who wishes to remain anonymous, as an Egyptian living in England who is a businessman and a passionate polo player. "There's no more space on his walls," said Wendy Goldsmith, who is in charge of 19th-century art at Christie's. "He has also become interested in collecting modern art."

Over the 25 years he put the collection together, he gravitated toward subjects with which he felt rapport. The scene depicted by John Frederick Lewis in "The Beestein Bazaar of El Kahn Khalil, Cairo" (1872), for example, is said to look exactly the same as it did when it was painted more than a century ago. Estimated at $2 million to $3 million, it captures Cairo's principal bazaar, from its architecture to the bustling crowd. The painting was once owned by Lord Leverhulme, the well-known British collector.

The sale also includes five paintings by Gérôme. Among the best is "The Pelt Merchant of Cairo" (1869), which depicts a merchant draped in a tiger's skin holding a helmet that is now in the permanent collection of the Walters Art Museum in Baltimore. It is estimated at $1.2 million to $1.6 million.

Several of the more romantic images in the sale by artists like Alfred de Dreux and Alexandre Marie Colin have been requested for an exhibition, "Romantic Paintings in England and France, 1820-1840," at Tate Britain, the Minneapolis Institute of Art and the Metropolitan Museum of Art in 2003.

McCarthy Show in Nice

The New Museum of Contemporary Art in SoHo is broadening its reach. For the first time in its 24-year history, one of its exhibitions is traveling abroad. Its show of the work of the eccentric California performance and video artist Paul McCarthy, seen first at the New Museum of Contemporary Art in Los Angeles and then in New York, is at the Villa Arson in Nice, France, through Sept. 23. The show will then be at Tate Liverpool from Oct. 18 to Jan. 13.

"Sure, it makes some money, but it's more about extending the life of an exhibition," said Lisa Phillips, the New Museum's director.

The New Museum has also changed its hours; it is now open one more day a week, on Tuesdays. The hours are now Tuesdays through Sundays from noon to 6 p.m. and Thursdays to 8 p.m. The museum will no longer be open until 8 p.m. on Saturdays and Sundays; but it has extended its Thursday hours.

22

23

24

21 **Donors celebrating the acquisition of *Catenary (I Call to the Grave)* (1998), 2001**

22 ***New York Times*, July 20, 2001, with coverage of the acquisition of *Catenary (I Call to the Grave)* (1998)**

23 **Installation view of gallery 277 (Sachs Gallery), a space permanently dedicated to works by Johns, mostly on long-term loan from the artist, 2016**

24 **Johns with museum trustees and longtime collectors Keith and Katherine Sachs, center, and curator Carlos Basualdo, right, at Sachs Gallery dedication, 2014**

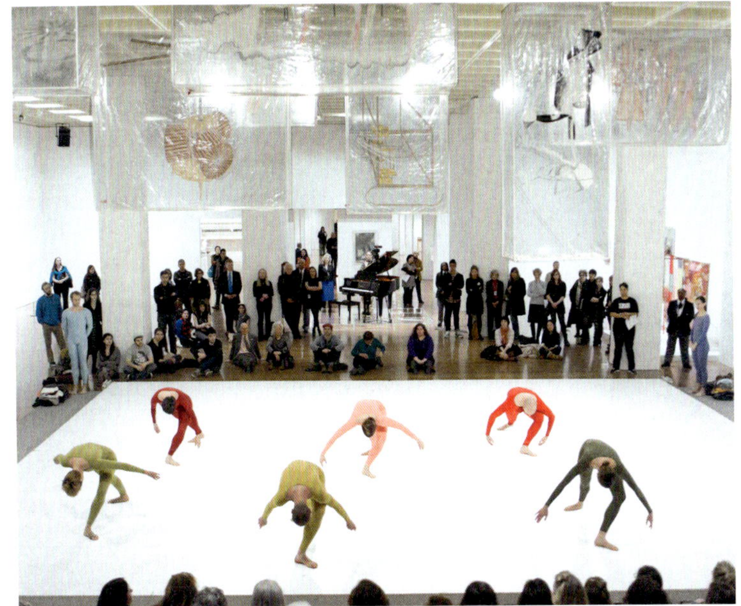

25

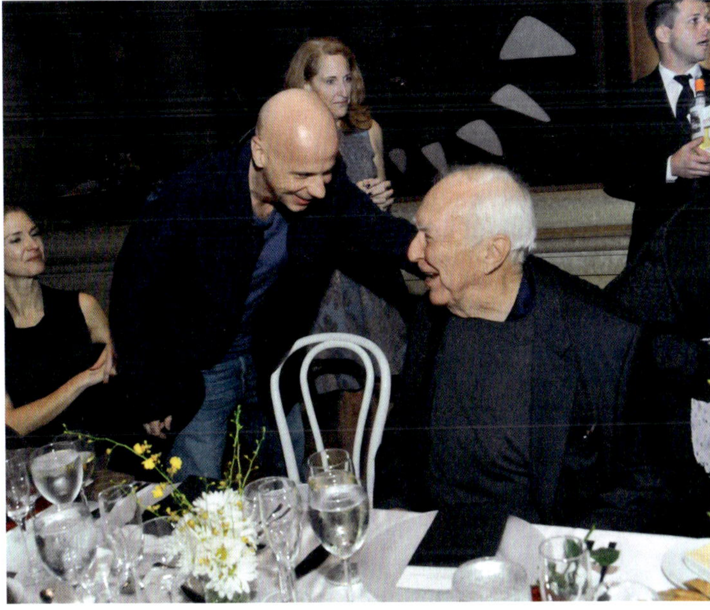

26

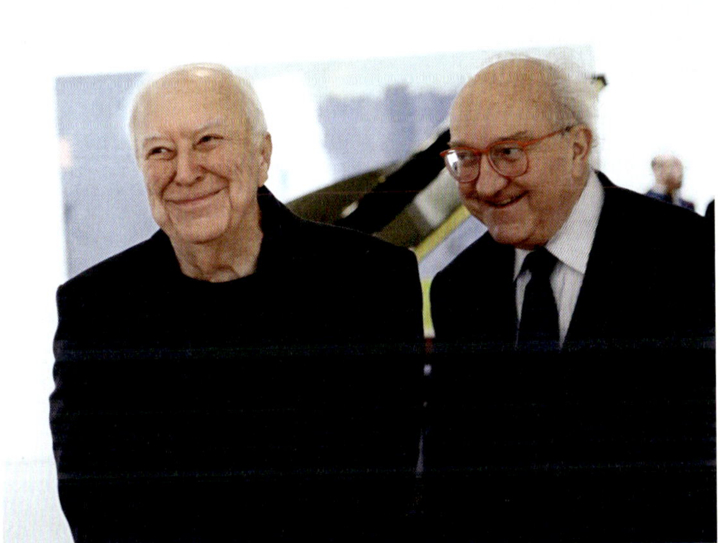

27

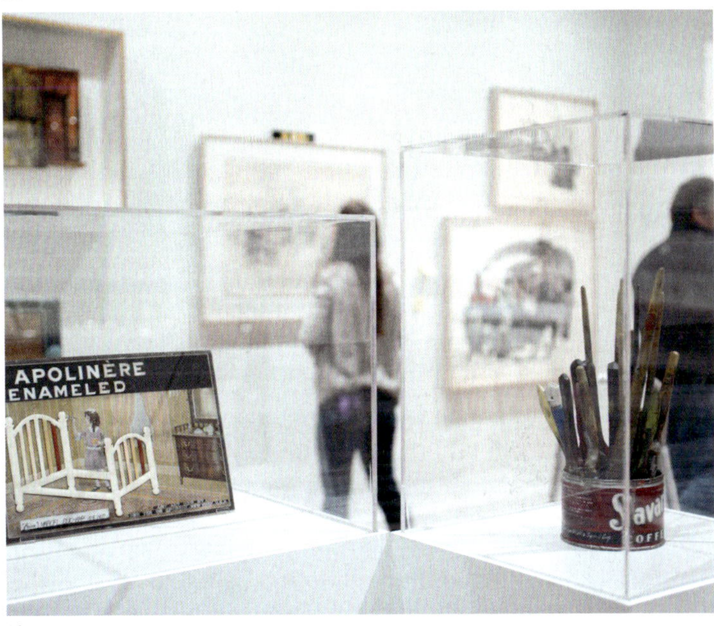

28

25 Merce Cunningham Event performed during *Dancing around the Bride*, 2013

26 Philippe Parreno and Johns at the opening of *Dancing around the Bride*, 2012

27 Johns and curator Joseph J. Rishel at the opening of *Dancing around the Bride*, 2012

28 Duchamp's *Apolinère Enameled* (1916–17) and Johns's *Painted Bronze* (1960), foreground left and right, during installation of *Dancing around the Bride*, 2012

Jasper Johns: Master of Chance

Carlos Basualdo

> Art is only the way in which the anonymous ones we call artists, by maintaining themselves constantly in relation with a practice, seek to constitute their life as a form of life: the life of the painter, of the carpenter, of the architect, of the contrabassist, in which, as in every form-of-life, what is in question is nothing less than their happiness.
> —Giorgio Agamben, "Archeology of the Work of Art" (2019)

To stop and look at a work by Jasper Johns is to fall into a trap. His paintings, sculptures, prints, and drawings usually present themselves to the viewer as a totality, self-contained, calling for close examination. Upon that, they reveal themselves as layered, scrupulously encrypted with the time and accidents of their own making, a deliberate collection of premeditated marks erased by other marks. Their seductiveness is revealed as opacity, and the opacity as sheer weight and density. Inevitably, the question of meaning comes to the surface, but the surface is ever receding from view. One looks instinctively for an answer in the examination of another work, and then another. Each of them clarifies something, but obscures something else. In the end, the paradox is that the actual perception of a work by Johns becomes a promise, indefinitely postponed. For all the glorious presence that they offer, they consign their viewer to a wandering absence. Looking at a work becomes thinking about it in relation to another. Our initial attraction, purely sensorial, becomes an insistent reflection in our minds. The work is both there, right in front of us, and elsewhere. We see ourselves in the act of chasing. Inactuality and actuality: when confronting the work, it speaks of the past (or the future); when thinking about the work, it talks about the (our own) present. The following paragraphs constitute a preliminary attempt to understand the paradoxical character of Johns's work, its emphatic existence between concrete things and imagined thoughts.

In an altogether insightful essay titled "Archeology of the Work of Art," the Italian philosopher Giorgio Agamben gives an account of the emergence of the "artistic machine" of modernity, the configuration of forces that delimit the notion of art in modern times.[1] Agamben defines modern art as a Borromean knot constituted by the interconnection among three elements: work (*ergon*), creative operation (*energeia*), and the artist. "It is not possible," Agamben writes, "even if it is always attempted, to either separate them or to make them coincide or, even less, to play one off against the other." This state of affairs finds its raison d'être in the divinization of the artists in the Renaissance, as Agamben describes it: "the disastrous transposition of the theological vocabulary of creation onto the activity of the artist." In ancient times, on the other hand, the sole repository of the creative operation was the work, which stood alone and separate from its maker, whose status was plainly that of an artisan. Contemporary art, Agamben argues, with its emphasis on authorship, process, and performance, completes the transference of *energeia* in detriment of the finished work, which seems to progressively assume a secondary role.

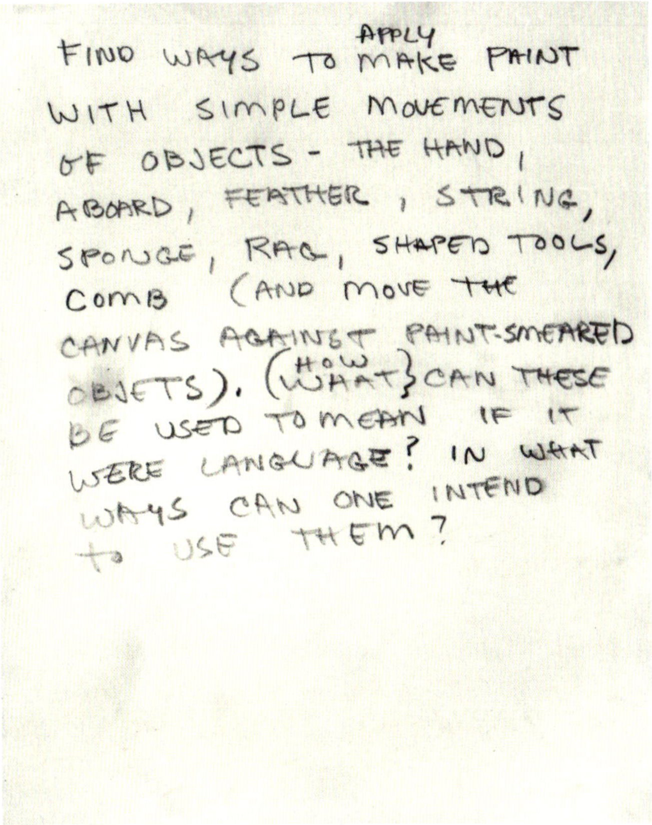

Fig. 1 **Sketchbook page, Book A, c. 1963. Courtesy of the artist**

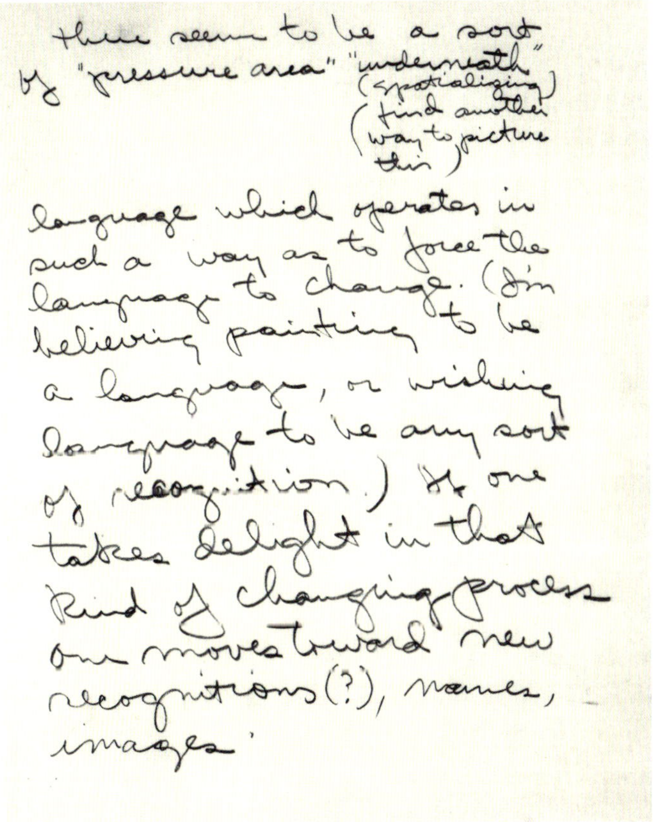

Fig. 2 **Sketchbook page, Book A, c. 1963–64. Courtesy of the artist**

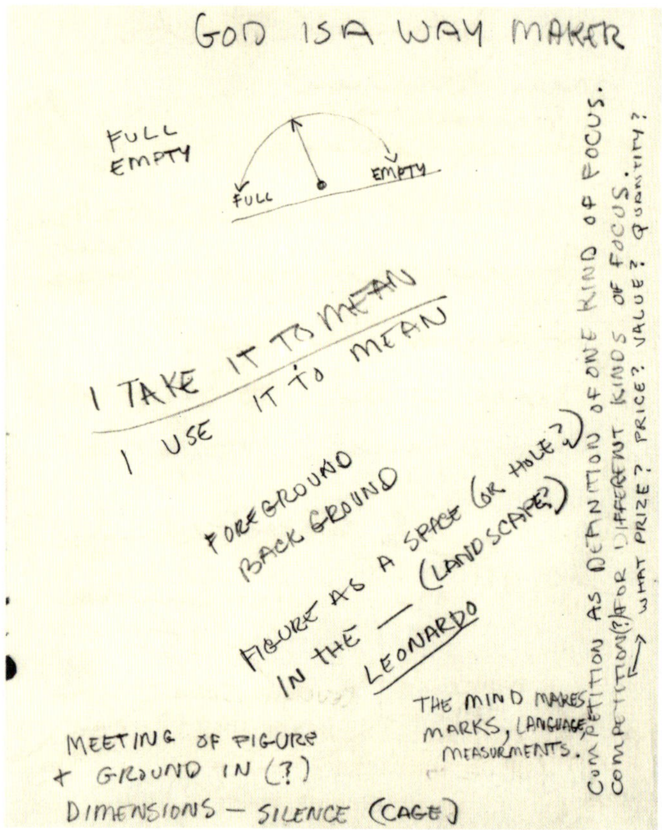

Fig. 3 **Sketchbook page, Book A, c. 1963–64. Courtesy of the artist**

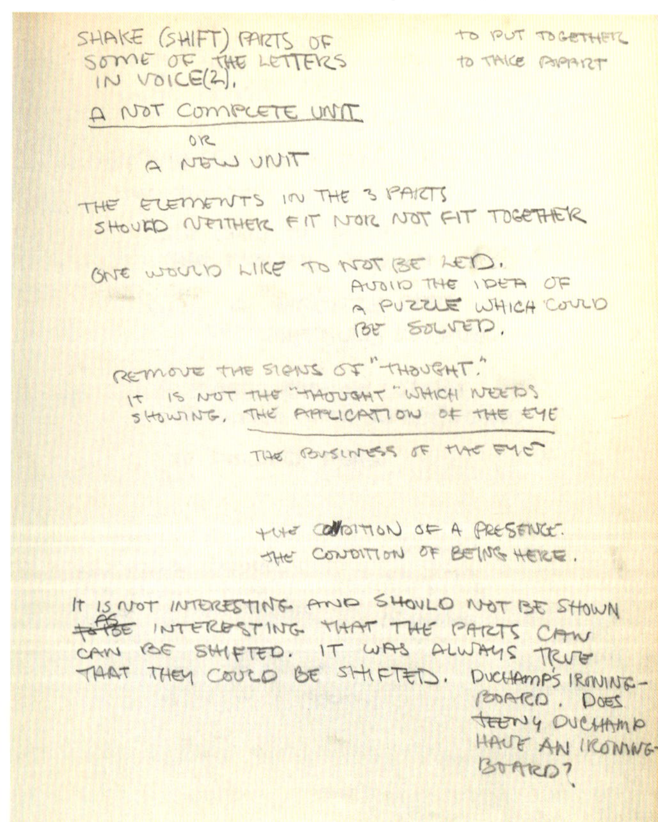

Fig. 4 **Sketchbook page, Book B, c. 1968. Courtesy of the artist**

Agamben identifies in Marcel Duchamp's readymades a direct attack on the work-artist-operation interconnection. In the readymade, according to Agamben, there is no work, as the object is industrially produced; no artist operation, as the object is not the result of an artistic process; and no artist, as the one who signs it is "a simple living being."[2] Here, Agamben is obviously referring to a specific readymade, *Fountain* from 1917, signed by the infamous R. Mutt. Two main objections to Agamben's argument about the readymades emerge at this point. The first is that it does not account for the position that the readymades occupy in the overall context of Duchamp's work, nor for the instability of their very definition, a quality that seems to have been constitutive of this class of objects for the artist. Second, Agamben seems to gloss over the fact that, in a text written by Louise Norton—and likely inspired by Duchamp himself—published in 1917 right after the scandal provoked by the presentation of *Fountain* in the first exhibition of the Society of Independent Artists in New York, the status of the object is clearly defined in relation to the agency of the author. "Whether Mr. Mutt with his own hands made the fountain or not has no importance. He CHOSE it. He took an ordinary article of life, placed it so that its useful significance disappeared under the new title and point of view—created a new thought for the object."[3] Far from an attack on the artistic machine of modernity, the readymade, or, to be specific, *Fountain*, reinforces its paradoxical nature by placing the creative energy squarely within the operational reach of the self-declared artist and, specifically, her capacity to choose, to decide on, its potential meanings. The main context for that operation is, in fact, not so much the institutional framework of an art exhibition or a museum, but the life itself of the artist. Several decades later, Duchamp would tell the Belgian filmmaker Jean Antoine that his greatest achievement was "using art, to create a *modus vivendi*; ... that is, ... trying to make my life into a work of art itself, instead of spending my life creating works of art in the form of paintings or sculptures."[4] In Duchamp's version of the machine of modernity, the emphasis is placed almost exclusively on the artist, who conducts her life as a continuous performance, so that the production of actual works becomes subordinated to the potential form that her life acquires. In fact, the creative energy becomes synonymous with the absence of work and the artist is consequently exalted, or reduced, to the role of a "breather," as Duchamp frequently put it, a living being. This is perhaps the actual knot confronting contemporary art, and it might be possible to characterize the contribution of many artists in the second half of the twentieth century by locating their work—and their life—in relation to these coordinates. Johns is no exception.

Two opposing, entangled forces are at play in the work of Jasper Johns. On the one hand, it is evident that he has deeply absorbed the legacy of Duchamp, while on the other, his work, in its seductive materiality, seemingly contradicts it. Johns has alchemically transformed the French-born artist's provocation about life made into art by developing a self-referential practice wherein the self is notoriously absent. Indefinitely suspending signification, Johns's work offers to the viewer an interminable landscape where signs are tirelessly recombined and no stable meaning is ever allowed to emerge. For Johns, life seems to be conceived solely as the life of the work, existing in order to be painstakingly mapped onto its progressive material digressions. Every object produced, whatever its medium, is for the artist an excuse for other works to be made, and the indefinite set of all his works is the ultimate context in which each of them finds its place. Paradoxically, in a world where no meaning is stable or definitive, each of Johns's works appears complete, even lapidary. The reason for this state of things is that Johns places creative energy both in the process leading to the work and in its completed manifestation, resulting in a dialectic between presence and absence, originality and repetition, and movement and stasis that has made his work as seemingly cryptic as it is stimulating and influential.

Little studied so far, Johns's sketchbooks serve as a guide to understanding the relevance of process in his work, as well as the intimate connection between language and images in his practice.[5] Johns's first notebook dates from the early 1960s and largely reflects the impact of Duchamp's notes for *The Green Box* (1934; p. 155, pl. 14) on his work.[6] The notebook was destroyed in a fire in Johns's studio in Edisto Beach, South Carolina, on November 14, 1966, but was partially recovered through photographs of its pages that the Japanese critic Yoshiaki Tōno had arranged to be taken during Johns's extended visit to Japan in 1964. Johns continues to keep notebooks to this day and to use them to register practical comments on the making of his work, unrealized proposals, and abstract reflections on the correspondence among words, actions, and materials. His notes make evident that materials, actions, and images as used in an artwork are all literally conceived as signifiers for Johns. For the artist, any activity related to the making of a work involves setting in motion a process of signification. "Find ways to apply/make paint with simple movements of objects—the hand, a board, feather, string, sponge, rag, shaped tools, comb (and move the canvas against paint-smeared objects). (How/What) can these be used to mean if it were language? In what ways can one intend to use them?" (fig. 1). In the context of Johns's practice, language in particular and signification in general thus serve as bridges between objects and actions, mediating between the emphasis on process and the studied quality of his "definitely unfinished" works. There seems to be no meaning outside language, which is a virtual synonym for consciousness in Johns's work. In another quote: "There could be another sort of coloration. Try to achieve that. Perhaps let every color stand for another color. Perhaps begin with a picture that already exists. Proceed to make a translation" (fig. 9). Even a cursory look at his sketchbooks reveals that Johns subjects to examination every aspect of his creative endeavor. This examination, which is as circuitous and implacable as the rest of his work, takes the form of a distancing. The more intimate the work becomes, the more remote: a reflection in the mirror of the mind.

Johns's relentless emphasis on process has inspired many generations of artists, including key figures such as Richard Serra and Bruce Nauman. Perhaps what they have found in this aspect of Johns's work is the possibility of conceiving of a form of artistic agency divorced from biography and the trappings of subjectivity, so that it is no longer a matter of "life as a work of art" but instead artistic process as a form of life. On the other side of the equation, Johns's endless fascination with the material products of that process (even if conceptually unfinished) results in the making of extremely seductive objects in the forms of paintings, drawings, sculptures, and prints—although, strictly speaking, few of Johns's works can be properly described without challenging conventional definitions. The iconicity of Johns's work can be ascribed to his equivocal successes as a maker. Equivocal in the sense that, as the great modernist that he is,

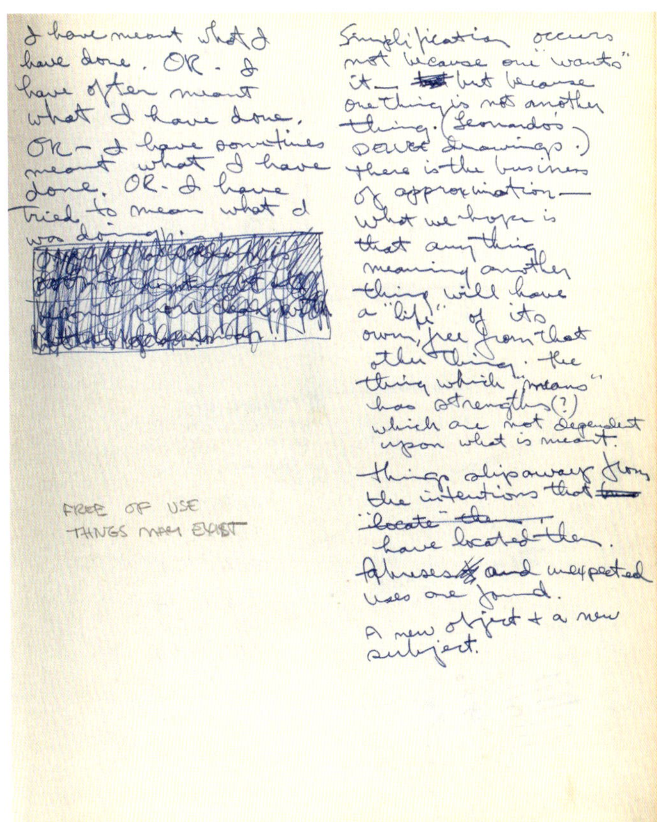
I have meant what I have done. OR - I have often meant what I have done. OR - I have sometimes meant what I have done. OR - I have tried to mean what I was doing.

FREE OF USE THINGS MAY EXIST

Simplification occurs not because one "wants" it — but because one thing is not another thing. (Leonardo's deluge [?] drawings.) there is the business of approximation — what we hope is that anything meaning another thing will have a "life" of its own, free from that other thing. The thing which "means" has strengths(?) which are not dependent upon what is meant.

things slip away from the intentions that have located them. Abuses and unexpected uses are found.

A new object + a new subject.

Fig. 5 **Sketchbook page, Book B, c. 1970. Courtesy of the artist**

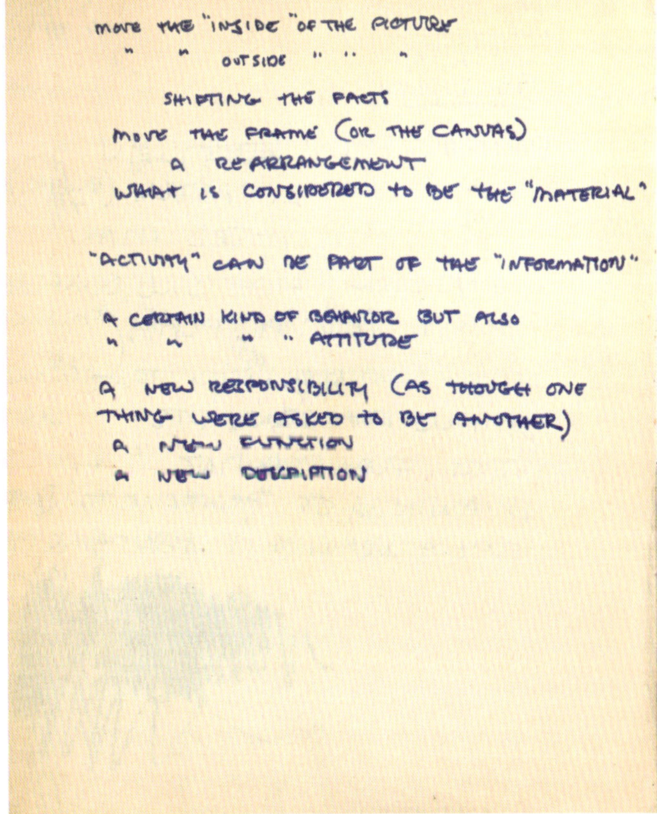
MOVE THE "INSIDE" OF THE PICTURE
" " OUTSIDE " " "
SHIFTING THE PARTS
MOVE THE FRAME (OR THE CANVAS)
A REARRANGEMENT
WHAT IS CONSIDERED TO BE THE "MATERIAL"

"ACTIVITY" CAN BE PART OF THE "INFORMATION"

A CERTAIN KIND OF BEHAVIOR BUT ALSO
" " " " ATTITUDE

A NEW RESPONSIBILITY (AS THOUGH ONE THING WERE ASKED TO BE ANOTHER)
A NEW FUNCTION
A NEW DESCRIPTION

Fig. 6 **Sketchbook page, Book C, c. 1970–71. Courtesy of the artist**

Fig. 7 **Sketchbook page, Book C, c. 1970–71. Courtesy of the artist**

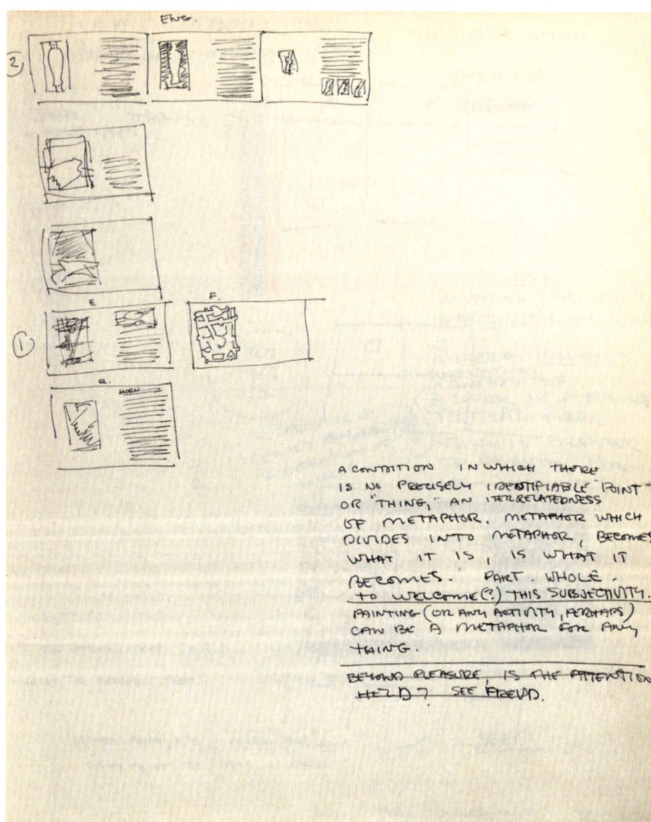

Fig. 8 **Sketchbook page, Book B, c. 1974–76. Courtesy of the artist**

he articulates his practice mainly as research and experimentation rather than as an exercise of mastery for itself. Mastery, for Johns, is simply accidental, a form of grace. In sum, Johns offers the viewer two opposing paths—the dissolution of subjectivity in the material evidence of the work or its alchemical transformation in process. He opts for neither, and leaves those who follow him alone with this impossible paradox. Ultimately, Johns's work defines a special place where language reigns supreme and yet no meaning is stable, where nothing is proper yet everything belongs.

Postscript (Summer 2020)

In truth, the "brokenness" that is such an intimate aspect of Johns's work, and that takes the form of a profound and incessant interrogation about the use and value of signs, can be said to operate simultaneously at the semantic, sociological, and psychological levels. Considering otherwise would amount to a forced reductionism, the assumption that meaning can be restricted and controlled, an illusion that the implacable logic of his work definitively shatters. As in an Indian myth from the *Puranas*, its meaning is ceaselessly displaced, traversing disparate levels of signification, endlessly dismantling any conventional frame of reference that might allow us to reduce it to a fixed system of interpretation. Once we consider the implications of this mode of operation, the semantic reach of the visual signs in Johns's work expands irrepressibly. The impossibility of connecting the features of a face as a marker of subjectivity, as in *Montez Singing* (1989; p. 235, pl. 10)—a work described as a semi-explicit reference to a painting by Pablo Picasso—may be seen as both a denunciation and a symptom of the fractures of a society constructed upon the most brutal exploitation of entire classes of people, under the banner of ethnic difference. Physiologically, the work speaks the language of autoimmune disease; it is art as a disease turned into language. Gloriously symptomatic, deeply aware, Johns uses everything at his disposal to elevate pain to manifestation, to literalize the geological fractures of his own subjective and national identity, to mourn the impossibility of a common language and the unrealized aspirations of modernity, and to find in the deep recesses of silence a redeeming glimpse of self-reflection.

1 Giorgio Agamben, "Archeology of the Work of Art," in *Creation and Anarchy: The Work of Art and the Religion of Capitalism*, trans. Adam Kotsko (Stanford, CA: Stanford University Press, 2019), 8–9.
2 Agamben, "Archeology," 12.
3 Louise Norton, "The Richard Mutt Case," *The Blind Man*, no. 2 (May 1917): 5.
4 Marcel Duchamp, interview by Jean Antoine (1966), *Art Newspaper*, March 1993.
5 The dating of specific pages in Johns's sketchbooks is highly challenging and, to some degree, hypothetical due to the fact that the artist does not date his notes or the individual pages. The dates attributed to the pages illustrated as figures 1, 2, 4, 6, and 7 in this essay are based on those in Kirk Varnedoe, ed., *Jasper Johns: Writings, Sketchbook Notes, Interviews* (New York: Museum of Modern Art, 1996). Those attributed to the pages illustrated as figures 3, 5, and 8–12 are the author's approximations, based on Varnedoe's dating and the relation of the content to known works by the artist.
6 The notes for *The Green Box* were published in 1960 in *The Bride Stripped Bare by Her Bachelors, Even: A Typographic Version by Richard Hamilton of Marcel Duchamp's "Green Box,"* trans. George Heard Hamilton (New York: George Wittenborn, 1960). Johns wrote a review of this book; see Johns, "The Green Box," *Scrap*, no. 1 (December 23, 1960): 4.

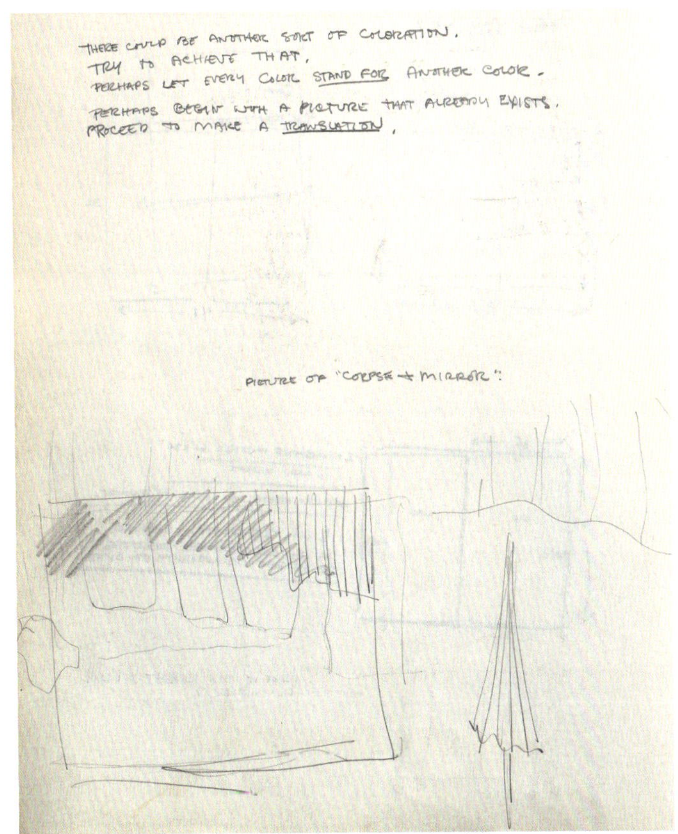

Fig. 9 **Sketchbook page, Book B, c. 1974–76. Courtesy of the artist**

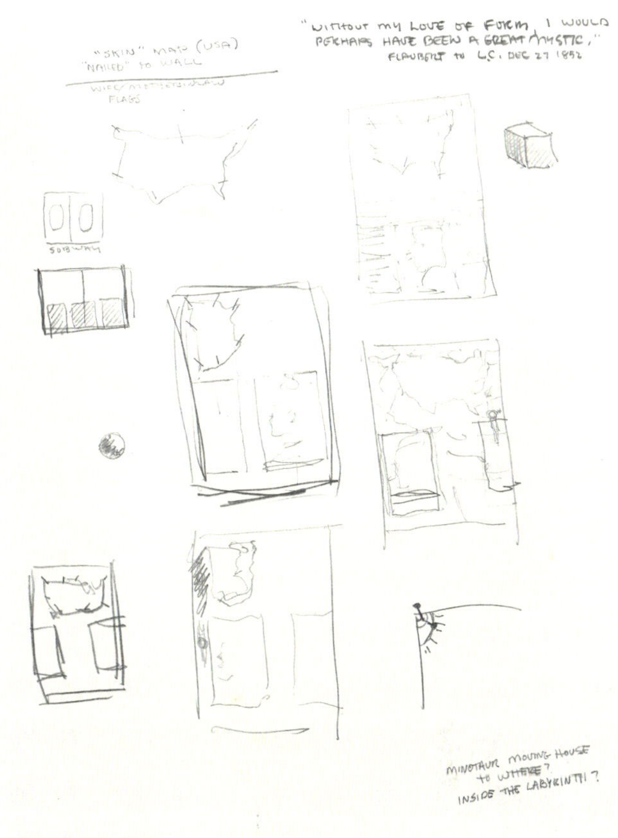

Fig. 10 **Sketchbook page, Book E, c. 1982–88. Courtesy of the artist**

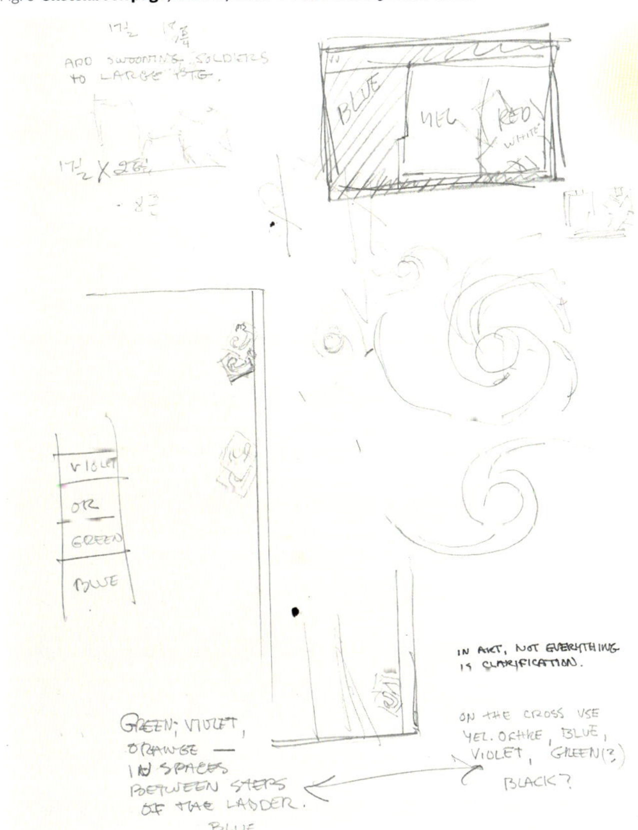

Fig. 11 **Sketchbook page, Book E, c. 1992–95. Courtesy of the artist**

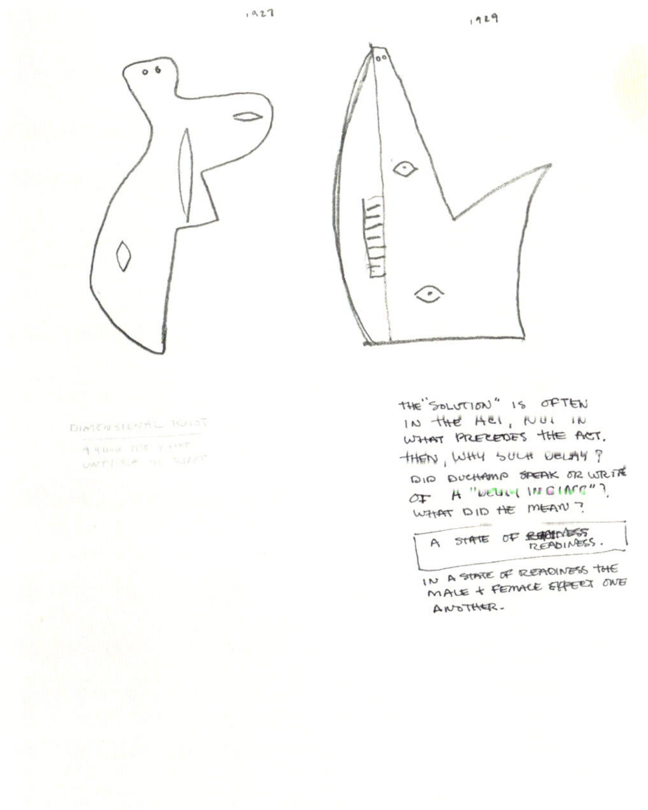

Fig. 12 **Sketchbook page, Book E, c. 1995–98. Courtesy of the artist**

Exhibited Works Not Illustrated

PHILADELPHIA MUSEUM OF ART

***Figure 5*, 1955**
Encaustic and collage on canvas
17 3/8 × 14 in. (44.1 × 35.6 cm)
Collection of the artist

***Figure 0*, 1959**
Encaustic and collage on canvas
20 1/8 × 15 1/8 in. (51.1 × 38.4 cm)
Ludwig Museum Koblenz, Germany

***Small Numbers in Color*, 1959**
Encaustic on wood
10 1/8 × 7 1/8 in. (25.7 × 18.1 cm)
Collection of the artist

***Light Bulb*, 1960**
Plaster (two parts)
4 1/8 × 5 7/8 × 4 in. (10.5 × 14.9 × 10.2 cm) overall
Collection of the artist

***Light Bulb*, 1960 (cast 1964)**
Bronze (two parts)
Ed. no. 2/4
4 × 5 7/8 × 3 7/8 in. (10.2 × 14.9 × 9.8 cm) overall
Collection of Barbara Bertozzi Castelli

***Ten Numbers*, 1960**
Charcoal and graphite pencil on paper (ten sheets)
13 1/2 × 11 in. (34.3 × 27.9 cm) average sheet size
The Cleveland Museum of Art; John L. Severance Fund, 2001.10

***Figure 3*, 1961**
Bronze
25 1/2 × 19 3/8 in. (64.8 × 49.2 cm)
Ed. no. 1/4
Collection of the artist

***Figure 3*, 1961**
Plaster and wire
26 1/2 × 20 in. (67.3 × 76.2 cm)
Collection of the artist

***4 the News*, 1962**
Encaustic and collage on canvas with objects (four panels)
65 × 50 1/8 in. (165.1 × 127.3 cm) overall
Kunstsammlung Nordrhein-Westfalen, Düsseldorf, Germany

***No*, 1964**
Graphite wash, graphite pencil, charcoal, and gouache on paper
20 3/8 × 17 1/2 in. (51.8 × 44.5 cm)
The Museum of Modern Art, New York; gift of Sarah-Ann and Werner H. Kramarsky, 114.2004

***White Target*, 1964–66**
Ink and graphite pencil over offset reproduction on paper
11 1/2 × 8 5/8 in. (29.2 × 21.9 cm)
Toyama Prefectural Museum of Art and Design, Japan

***The Critic Smiles*, 1965**
Ink on paper
11 × 8 1/2 in. (27.9 × 21.6 cm)
Private collection

***0*, 1966**
Graphite, graphite pencil, and pastel on paper
8 1/2 × 6 5/8 in. (21.6 × 16.8 cm)
Greenville County Museum of Art, South Carolina; museum purchase from the Arthur and Holly Magill Fund

***Map for Hisachika Takahashi's "From Memory Draw a Map of the United States,"* c. 1971**
Ink on paper
17 1/2 × 22 3/4 in. (44.5 × 57.8 cm)
Rocio and Boris Hirmas Collection

***Knee*, 1973–74**
Lithograph: one stone, two aluminum plates
30 3/4 × 22 3/4 in. (78.1 × 57.8 cm)
Serge Lozingot, Edward Henderson/Gemini
Ed. no. 3/47
Philadelphia Museum of Art; purchased with the SmithKline Beckman Corporation Fund, 1986-62-7

***Foirades/Fizzles*, 1976**
Bound book with thirty-three intaglios: thirty-eight copperplates, four aluminum plates; box with lithograph
13 × 10 in. (33 × 25.4 cm) overall (closed)
Atelier Crommelynck, Bill Law/Petersburg Press
Ed. no. 50/250
Philadelphia Museum of Art; promised gift of Keith L. and Katherine Sachs

***Foirades/Fizzles*, 1976**
Bound book with thirty-three intaglios: thirty-eight copperplates, four aluminum plates; box with lithograph
13 × 10 in. (33 × 25.4 cm) overall (closed)
Atelier Crommelynck, Bill Law/Petersburg Press
Ed. no. 72/250
Whitney Museum of American Art, New York; purchase, with funds from the Print Committee, 84.52

***Foirades/Fizzles*, 1976**
Bound book with thirty-three intaglios: thirty-eight copperplates, four aluminum plates; box with lithograph
13 × 10 in. (33 × 25.4 cm) overall (closed)
Atelier Crommelynck, Bill Law/Petersburg Press
Ed. no. 248/250
Collection of the artist

***Figure 4*, 1977**
Ink on plastic
13 1/4 × 11 1/2 in. (33.7 × 29.2 cm)
The Museum of Fine Arts, Houston; gift of Janie C. Lee in memory of Kevin Henke, 81.208

***Usuyuki*, 1979**
Screenprint
34 1/4 × 50 in. (87 × 127 cm)
Hiroshi Kawanishi/SPA
WP (newsprint)
National Gallery of Art, Washington, DC; Patrons' Permanent Fund and Special Friends of the National Gallery of Art, 2010.116.79

***Usuyuki*, 1979–81**
Screenprint
29 3/8 × 47 in. (74.6 × 119.4 cm)
Hiroshi Kawanishi/SPA
Proof
National Gallery of Art, Washington, DC; Patrons' Permanent Fund and Special Friends of the National Gallery of Art, 2010.116.78

***Untitled (Secondaries with Black)*, 1991**
Etching and aquatint
41 3/4 × 77 1/2 in. (106 × 196.9 cm)
John Lund, Hitoshi Kido, Craig Zammiello/ULAE
TP
The Museum of Fine Arts, Houston; museum purchase funded by Caroline Wiess Law in memory of Genevieve Favrot Peterkin, 94.726

***Untitled*, 1997**
Etching and aquatint
37 7/8 × 76 in. (96.2 × 193 cm)
Aldo Crommelynck/Atelier Crommelynck
TP
National Gallery of Art, Washington, DC; Patrons' Permanent Fund and Special Friends of the National Gallery of Art, 2010.116.525

***Untitled*, 1997**
Etching and aquatint
42 1/2 × 24 1/4 in. (108 × 61.6 cm)
Aldo Crommelynck/Atelier Crommelynck
TP
National Gallery of Art, Washington, DC; Patrons' Permanent Fund and Special Friends of the National Gallery of Art, 2010.116.492

***Untitled*, 1998**
Etching and aquatint
42 × 77 5/8 in. (106.7 × 197.2 cm)
Aldo Crommelynck/Atelier Crommelynck
TP
National Gallery of Art, Washington, DC; Patrons' Permanent Fund and Special Friends of the National Gallery of Art, 2010.116.516

***Untitled*, 1998**
Intaglio
14 7/8 × 11 in. (37.8 × 27.9 cm)
John Lund/Low Road Studio
TP
Private collection

***Untitled*, 1998**
Intaglio
15 × 11 in. (38.1 × 27.9 cm)
John Lund/Low Road Studio
TP
Private collection

***Untitled*, 1998**
Intaglio
15 × 11 in. (38.1 × 27.9 cm)
John Lund/Low Road Studio
TP
Private collection

***Untitled*, 1998**
Intaglio
15 × 11 in. (38.1 × 27.9 cm)
John Lund/Low Road Studio
TP
Private collection

***Untitled*, 1998**
Intaglio
15 × 11 in. (38.1 × 27.9 cm)
John Lund/Low Road Studio
TP
Private collection

***Untitled*, 1998**
Intaglio
15 × 11 in. (38.1 × 27.9 cm)
John Lund/Low Road Studio
TP
Private collection

***Untitled*, 1998**
Intaglio
15 × 11 in. (38.1 × 27.9 cm)
John Lund/Low Road Studio
TP
Private collection

***Untitled*, 1998**
Intaglio
15 × 11 in. (38.1 × 27.9 cm)
John Lund/Low Road Studio
TP
Private collection

***Untitled*, 1998**
Intaglio
15 × 11 in. (38.1 × 27.9 cm)
John Lund/Low Road Studio
TP
Private collection

***Untitled*, 1998**
Intaglio
15 × 11 in. (38.1 × 27.9 cm)
John Lund/Low Road Studio
TP
Private collection

***Untitled*, 1998**
Intaglio
15 × 11 in. (38.1 × 27.9 cm)
John Lund/Low Road Studio
TP
Private collection

***Untitled*, 1998**
Intaglio
15 × 11 in. (38.1 × 27.9 cm)
John Lund/Low Road Studio
TP
Private collection

***Untitled*, 1998**
Intaglio
20 ½ × 14 ½ in. (52.1 × 36.8 cm)
John Lund/Low Road Studio
TP
Private collection

***Untitled*, 1998**
Intaglio
20 ½ × 14 ½ in. (52.1 × 36.8 cm)
John Lund/Low Road Studio
TP
Private collection

***Untitled*, 1998**
Intaglio
22 ½ × 15 in. (57.2 × 38.1 cm)
John Lund/Low Road Studio
TP
Private collection

***Untitled*, 1998**
Intaglio
24 × 18 in. (61 × 45.7 cm)
John Lund/Low Road Studio
TP
Private collection

***Bushbaby*, 2005**
Ink on plastic
36 ¼ × 25 ¼ in. (92.1 × 64.1 cm)
Collection of the artist

***Figure 1*, 2011**
Graphite pencil on tan paper mounted on paper
14 ¾ × 11 ⅜ in. (37.5 × 28.9 cm) irregular
Collection of the artist

***Figure 3*, 2011**
Graphite pencil on tan paper mounted on paper
14 ¾ × 11 ⅜ in. (37.5 × 28.9 cm)
Collection of Judy Hart Angelo

***Untitled*, 2012**
Monotype
30 ¾ × 22 ½ in. (78.1 × 57.2 cm)
John Lund/Low Road Studio
Collection of the artist

***Untitled*, 2012**
Monotype
36 ¼ × 24 ⅜ in. (92.1 × 61.9 cm)
John Lund/Low Road Studio
Collection of the artist

***Untitled*, 2014**
Acrylic on canvas
20 ½ × 29 ½ in. (52.1 × 74.9 cm)
Private collection

***Untitled*, 2014**
Unique etching on paper mounted on paper support: six plates
43 ½ × 78 ¾ in. (110.5 × 200 cm)
Collection of the artist

Gutai Group
***Happy New Year*, 1967**
Twenty-nine works in various mediums
Various dimensions
Collection of Barbara Bertozzi Castelli

Arata Isozaki (Japanese, b. 1931)
***Marilyn Curves*, c. 1965**
Acrylic (three panels)
20 ⅛ × 7 ⅞ in. (51.1 × 20 cm) each
Collection of Jasper Johns

Katy Martin (American)
***Hanafuda/Jasper Johns*, 1978–81**
DVD (from Super 8 mm film), color
33 min.
Courtesy of the artist

Tomio Miki (Japanese, 1937–1978)
***Ear*, 1960**
Chromed plastic, injection mold
3 × 2 ⅛ × 2 ⅜ in. (7.6 × 5.4 × 6 cm)
Collection of Jasper Johns

Aiko Miyawaki (Japanese, 1929–2014)
***Work #35*, 1969**
Brass
3 ⅛ × 3 ⅛ × 3 ⅛ in. (7.9 × 7.9 × 7.9 cm)
Collection of Jasper Johns

Aiko Miyawaki
***Scroll*, 1976**
Oil on canvas
9 ¾ × 175 in. (24.8 × 444.8 cm)
Collection of Jasper Johns

Aiko Miyawaki
***Golden Egg*, c. 1982**
Bronze (two objects)
⅞ × 2 ½ × 1 ⅞ in. (2.2 × 6.4 × 4.8 cm) each
Collection of Jasper Johns

Ugo Mulas (Italian, 1928–1973)
***Jasper Johns, Numbers, Edisto Beach*, 1965**
Vintage gelatin silver print mounted on aluminum
19 ¾ × 26 ⅝ in. (50.2 × 67.6 cm)
Ugo Mulas Archive, Milan

Ugo Mulas
***Jasper Johns, Numbers, Edisto Beach*, 1965**
Vintage gelatin silver print mounted on aluminum
26 ⅝ × 19 ¾ in. (67.6 × 50.2 cm)
Ugo Mulas Archive, Milan

Yoshiaki Tōno (Japanese, 1930–2005) Photocopies of Keiji Sakai's Photographs of Johns's sketchbook pages, c. 1964
Acrylic box designed by Katsuhiro Yamaguchi (Japanese, 1928–2018)
Courtesy Jasper Johns

Shūzō Takiguchi (Japanese, 1903–1979) and Kazuo Okazaki (Japanese, b. 1930)
***Oculist Witnesses after Marcel Duchamp*, 1977**
Plexiglas and metal with fitted case
10 ¼ × 10 ½ × 10 ¼ in. (26 × 26.7 × 26 cm)
Ed. no. 3/100
Collection of Jasper Johns

WHITNEY MUSEUM OF AMERICAN ART

***Untitled*, 1954**
Oil and collage mounted on canvas
9 × 9 in. (22.9 × 22.9 cm)
The Menil Collection, Houston

***Flag Above White with Collage*, 1955**
Encaustic and collage on canvas
22 × 19 in. (55.9 × 48.3 cm)
Kunstmuseum Basel, Switzerland; gift of the artist in memory of Christian Geelhaar, 1994

***White Numbers*, 1959**
Encaustic and collage on canvas
53 × 40 ⅛ in. (134.6 × 101.9 cm)
Private collection

***Flashlight*, 1960**
Bronze and glass
Ed. no. 1/3
4 ⅞ × 7 ⅞ × 4 ⅜ in. (12.4 × 20 × 11.1 cm)
Collection of Thomas H. Lee and Ann Tenenbaum

***Light Bulb*, 1960 (cast and painted 1964)**
Bronze and oil paint (two parts)
Ed. no. 4/4
4 ⅛ × 5 ⅞ × 4 in. (10.5 × 14.9 × 10.2 cm) overall
Collection of the artist; on long-term loan to the Philadelphia Museum of Art, 1979

***Watchman*, 1966**
Graphite wash, metallic powder, graphite pencil, and pastel on paper
38 × 26 ½ in. (96.5 × 67.3 cm)
The Museum of Modern Art, New York; gift of the family of Victor W. Ganz in his memory, 323.1989

Study for *In Memory of My Feelings*, 1967
Ink and graphite pencil on plastic
12 ½ × 19 in. (31.8 × 48.3 cm)
Collection of the artist

Study for *In Memory of My Feelings*, 1967
Ink and graphite pencil on plastic
12 ½ × 19 in. (31.8 × 48.3 cm)
Collection of the artist

Study for *In Memory of My Feelings*, 1967
Ink and graphite pencil on plastic
13 ⅛ × 11 in. (33.3 × 27.9 cm)
Collection of the artist

Studies for *0-9*, 1968
Watercolor and graphite pencil on paper (ten sheets)
4 ⅝ × 4 in. (11.7 × 10.2 cm) each (approx.)
Collection of Jason Blum

***Tracing*, 1977**
Ink on plastic
11 × 13 in. (27.9 × 33 cm) sight
Collection of David and Lindsay Shapiro

***Cicada*, 1981**
Six silkscreens: nineteen screens
22 ¼ × 18 ¼ in. (56.5 × 46.4 cm) each
Kenjiro Nonaka, Hiroshi Kawanishi/JJ and SPA
Ed. no. 5/5
Whitney Museum of American Art, New York; promised gift of Emily Fisher Landau

***Cicada Sketches*, 1981**
Colored ink on plastic
14 × 15 ½ in. (35.6 × 39.4 cm)
Ryobi Foundation

***Untitled (Blue)*, 1981**
Watercolor and graphite pencil on paper
8 ½ × 6 in. (21.6 × 15.2 cm)
Collection of Maxine Groffsky and Winthrop Knowlton

***Land's End*, 1982**
Black ink and colored ink on plastic
36 ¼ × 28 ⅛ in. (92.1 × 71.4 cm)
Collection of the artist

***Untitled*, 1990**
Oil crayon, graphite pencil, and watercolor on paper mounted on paper
17 ⅞ × 13 ⅞ in. (45.4 × 35.2 cm)
Collection of the artist

***Nothing at All Richard Dadd*, 1992**
Graphite pencil on paper
41 ¼ × 27 ½ in. (104.8 × 69.9 cm)
The Museum of Modern Art, New York; gift of Kathy and Richard S. Fuld, Jr., 304.2002

***Untitled*, 1995**
Oil on canvas
66 × 44 in. (167.6 × 111.8 cm)
Irving Stenn Jr. Family Collection

***Untitled*, 1995**
Lithograph
41 ⅜ × 53 ¼ in. (105.1 × 135.3 cm)
Doug Bennett, Bill Goldston, Douglas Volle, Bruce Wankel, Lorena Salcedo-Watson/

ULAE
Ed. no. 24/49
Whitney Museum of American Art, New York; purchase with funds from the Print Committee, 96.71

***Untitled*, 1998**
Colored pencil on plastic
10 × 6 ½ in. (25.4 × 16.5 cm)
Collection of Meredith and Conley Rollins

***Untitled*, 1998**
Graphite pencil and colored pencil on plastic
8 × 5 ¼ in. (20.3 × 13.3 cm)
Collection of the artist

***Three Flags*, 2000**
Acrylic and graphite pencil on four sheets of plastic
11 × 7 ½ in. (27.9 × 19.1 cm)
Collection of the artist

***Untitled*, 2011**
Acrylic, crayon, graphite pencil, and colored pencil on fabric mounted on paper
27 ⅝ × 28 ½ in. (70.2 × 72.4 cm)
Collection of the artist

Ugo Mulas (Italian, 1928–1973)
***Jasper Johns*, 1964**
Vintage gelatin silver print
9 ⅞ × 14 ½ in. (25.1 × 36.8 cm)
Ugo Mulas Archive, Milan

Ugo Mulas
***Jasper Johns, Edisto Beach*, 1965**
Vintage gelatin silver print
6 ¼ × 8 ⅝ in. (15.9 × 21.9 cm)
Ugo Mulas Archive, Milan

Ugo Mulas
***Jasper Johns, Edisto Beach*, 1965**
Gelatin silver print
11 ¾ × 15 ¾ in. (29.9 × 40 cm)
Ugo Mulas Archive, Milan

Ugo Mulas
***Jasper Johns, Edisto Beach*, 1965**
Gelatin silver print
15 ¾ × 11 ¾ in. (40 × 29.9 cm)
Ugo Mulas Archive, Milan

Ugo Mulas
***Jasper Johns, Map, Edisto Beach*, 1965**
Vintage gelatin silver print mounted on aluminum
23 ½ × 19 ½ in. (59.7 × 49.5 cm)
Ugo Mulas Archive, Milan

Lenders to the Exhibition

Allen Family Collection
Judy Hart Angelo
Archives of American Art, Smithsonian Institution, Washington, DC
The Art Institute of Chicago
The Baltimore Museum of Art
David R. Baum and Tilly Macalister-Smith
Bayerische Staatsgemäldesammlungen, Pinakothek der Moderne, Munich
Jason Blum
Irma and Norman Braman
The Broad Art Foundation
The Eli and Edythe L. Broad Collection
Barbara Bertozzi Castelli
The Cleveland Museum of Art
Nancy and Steve Crown
Dallas Museum of Art
Des Moines Art Center, Iowa
Beth Rudin DeWoody
Glenn Dubin and Dr. Eva Dubin
Mr. and Mrs. Michael D. Eisner
Abigail R. Esman
Aaron I. Fleischman Collection
Forman Family Collection
Kathy and Richard S. Fuld, Jr.
Larry Gagosian
Gail and Tony Ganz
Kate Ganz
Glenstone, Potomac, Maryland
Greenville County Museum of Art, South Carolina
Esther Grether Family Collection
Anne Dias Griffin
Maxine Groffsky and Winthrop Knowlton
Agnes Gund
Marlene Hess and James D. Zirin
Samuel and Ronnie Heyman
Rocio and Boris Hirmas Collection
Hirshhorn Museum and Sculpture Garden, Smithsonian Institution, Washington, DC
Marguerite and Robert Hoffman
Marguerite Steed Hoffman
The Jewish Museum, New York
Jasper Johns
Kristen and Alex Klabin
Kolodny Family Collection
Kravis Collection
Laura Kuhn
Kunstmuseum Basel, Switzerland
Kunstsammlung Nordrhein-Westfalen, Düsseldorf, Germany
Emily Fisher Landau
Barbara and Richard S. Lane
Janie C. Lee
Thomas H. Lee and Ann Tenenbaum
Susan Lorence
Los Angeles County Museum of Art
Ludwig Museum Koblenz, Germany
Matthew Marks
Katy Martin
Susan and Larry Marx
The Menil Collection, Houston
The Metropolitan Museum of Art, New York
The Robert and Jane Meyerhoff Collection
The Middleton Family Collection
Minneapolis Institute of Art
MMK Museum für Moderne Kunst, Frankfurt am Main
Andrew Monk
Ugo Mulas Archive, Milan
Museum Ludwig, Cologne
Museum of Contemporary Art, Chicago
The Museum of Contemporary Art, Los Angeles
The Museum of Fine Arts, Houston
The Museum of Modern Art, New York
National Gallery of Art, Washington, DC
Nerman Family Collection
The Newhouse Collection
Marsha and Jeffrey Perelman
Philadelphia Museum of Art
Meredith and Conley Rollins
The Rose Art Museum, Brandeis University, Waltham, Massachusetts
Donna Perret Rosen and Benjamin M. Rosen
Ryobi Foundation
The Keith L. and Katherine Sachs Collection
San Francisco Museum of Modern Art
Louisa Stude Sarofim
Andrew and Denise Saul
Virginia Cowles Schroth
Seattle Art Museum
Monique H. and Gregg G. Seibert
Jeffrey Seller and Josh Lehrer
Sezon Museum of Modern Art, Nagano, Japan
David and Lindsay Shapiro
Jack Shear
Jon and Mary Shirley
Ayea and Mikey Sohn
The Sonnabend Collection
Irving Stenn, Jr., Family Collection
Margaret Leng Tan
Lisa and Steven Tananbaum
Toyama Prefectural Museum of Art and Design, Japan
Walker Art Center, Minneapolis
Mildred L. and Morris L. Weisberg
Whitney Museum of American Art, New York
Zygi and Audrey Wilf
Yale University Art Gallery, New Haven

Private collections

Contributors

Emmanuel Alloa is professor of aesthetics and philosophy of art at the University of Fribourg, Switzerland. He is the author of *Resistance of the Sensible World: An Introduction to Merleau-Ponty* (New York: Fordham University Press, 2017) and *Looking through Images: A Phenomenology of Visual Media* (New York: Columbia University Press, 2021), and he recently coedited *Dynamis of the Image: Moving Images in a Global World* (Berlin: De Gruyter, 2020).

Andrianna Campbell-LaFleur is an independent scholar based in Windsor, Connecticut. Her writing has appeared in *Artforum* and *frieze*, and she contributed essays to *Julie Mehretu* (New York: DelMonico Books–Prestel, 2019) and *Robert Rauschenberg* (New York: Museum of Modern Art, 2016). She curated *Vanishing Points* at the James Cohan Gallery, New York, in 2017; and with Daniel S. Palmer, she cocurated *DECENTER NY/DC: An Exhibition on the Centenary of the 1913 Armory Show* at the Luther W. Brady Art Gallery, George Washington University, Washington, DC, in 2013. With Robert Campbell-LaFleur, she is currently writing a photography book centered on regional Connecticut landmarks.

Carroll Dunham is an artist based in New York. *Into Words: The Selected Writings of Carroll Dunham* was published in 2017 by Badlands Unlimited, New York.

Flavio Fergonzi is professor of the history of contemporary art at the Scuola Normale Superiore, Pisa, Italy. He is the author of *Una nuova superficie: Jasper Johns e gli artisti italiani, 1958–1966* (Milan: Electa, 2019), *Marino Marini: Visual Passions* (Milan: Silvana, 2018), and *Filologia del 900: Modigliani, Sironi, Morandi, Martini* (Milan: Electa, 2013).

Ruth Fine is an independent scholar based in Philadelphia after a four-decade career with the National Gallery of Art, Washington, DC, where she curated several exhibitions of Jasper Johns's drawings and prints and selections from the Johns Proofs Archive. She is the editor of *Procession: The Art of Norman Lewis* (Berkeley: University of California Press, 2015), and curator of a forthcoming retrospective of photographs by Frank Stewart.

Michio Hayashi is professor of art history and visual culture at Sophia University, Tokyo. He is the author of *An Empty Space: Mel Bochner* (New York: Akira Ikeda Gallery, 2009) and the seven-volume *Painting Dies Twice, or Never* (Tokyo: Art Trace, 2003–9). He recently contributed to *Damien Hirst: Cherry Blossoms* (Paris: Fondation Cartier pour l'Art Contemporain, 2021).

Terrance Hayes is a writer and poet, and professor of English at New York University. His books include *American Sonnets for My Past and Future Assassin* (New York: Penguin Poets, 2018), *To Float in the Space Between: A Life and Work in Conversation with the Life and Work of Etheridge Knight* (Seattle: Wave Books, 2018), *How to Be Drawn* (New York: Penguin Books, 2015), and *Lighthead* (New York: Penguin Books, 2010).

Michael Ann Holly is the Starr Director Emerita of the Research and Academic Program, Clark Art Institute, Williamstown, Massachusetts. Her publications include *The Melancholy Art* (Princeton: Princeton University Press, 2013), *Past Looking: Historical Imagination and the Rhetoric of the Image* (Ithaca, NY: Cornell University Press, 1996), and *Panofsky and the Foundations of Art History* (Ithaca, NY: Cornell University Press, 1984).

Ralph Lemon is a visual artist, writer, and choreographer based in Brooklyn and the founder and artistic director of Cross Performance Inc. He is the author of *Come home Charley Patton* (2013), *Tree: belief/culture/balance* (2004), and *geography: art/race/exile* (2000)—comprising writings, choreographic scores, process notes, drawings, and photographs from the creation and performances of his project *The Geography Trilogy*—all published by Wesleyan University Press, Middletown, Connecticut.

Alexander Nemerov is the Carl and Marilynn Thoma Provostial Professor in the Arts and Humanities and the chair of the Department of Art and Art History at Stanford University. His most recent book is *Fierce Poise: Helen Frankenthaler and 1950s New York*, published by Penguin in 2021.

R. H. Quaytman is an American artist best known for her painting practice that is organized into chapters, like an ongoing book dating back to 2001. Her most recent exhibition, *The Sun Does Not Move, Chapter 35*, opened in 2019 at the Muzeum Sztuki in Łódź, Poland, and traveled to the Museu de Arte Contemporânea de Serralves in Porto, Portugal, in 2020. Her work is represented in the collections of the Museum of Contemporary Art, Los Angeles; the Museum of Modern Art, New York; the San Francisco Museum of Modern Art; the Solomon R. Guggenheim Museum, New York; the Stedelijk Museum, Amsterdam; the Tate, London; and the Whitney Museum of American Art, New York, among many others. She is currently working on an exhibition that will open in fall 2021 at Wiels in Brussels.

Jennifer L. Roberts is the Elizabeth Cary Agassiz Professor of the Humanities at Harvard University, Cambridge, Massachusetts. She is the author of *Transporting Visions: The Movement of Images in Early America* (Berkeley: University of California Press, 2014), *Jasper Johns / In Press: The Crosshatch Works and the Logic of Print* (Cambridge, MA: Harvard Art Museums, 2012), and *Mirror-Travels: Robert Smithson and History* (New Haven: Yale University Press, 2004), and coauthor of *Jasper Johns: Catalogue Raisonné of Monotypes* (New York: Matthew Marks Gallery; New Haven: Yale University Press, 2017).

Drew Sawyer is the Phillip Leonian and Edith Rosenbaum Leonian Curator of Photography at the Brooklyn Museum. He is the editor of *The Sun Placed in the Abyss* (Columbus, OH: Columbus Museum of Art, 2016), and he coedited *Art after Stonewall, 1969–1989* (New York: Rizzoli Electa, 2019).

Sandra Skurvida is a scholar and curator based in New York and Bremen, Germany. With a focus on the contemporary and its permutations, she has contributed essays on art-historical investigations of transmedia on John Cage, including "Technologies of Indeterminacy: John Cage Invents" in *Hybrid Practices: Art in Collaboration with Science and Technology in the Long 1960s* (Oakland: University of California Press, 2019) and "John Cage, *Rolywholyover A Circus*, 1993" in *The Artist as Curator: An Anthology* (Milan: Mousse, 2017). Her monograph on John Cage, *John Cage: Composing the Common*, is forthcoming.

Colm Tóibín is a writer of novels, short stories, and criticism; the Irene and Sidney B. Silverman Professor of the Humanities at Columbia University, New York; and chancellor of the University of Liverpool, England. His most recent book is *Mad, Bad, Dangerous to Know: The Fathers of Wilde, Yeats, and Joyce* (New York: Scribner, 2018), and his novels include *House of Names* (New York: Scribner, 2017), *Nora Webster* (New York: Scribner, 2014), *Brooklyn* (New York: Scribner, 2009), and *The Master* (New York: Scribner, 2004). *The Magician* is forthcoming in 2021 from Scribner.

Hannah Yohalem is the coexecutive director of Vital Spaces, Santa Fe, New Mexico. Her writing has appeared in *Dance Research: The Journal of the Society for Dance Research* and *Performa Magazine*.

Index

Page numbers in **bold** type indicate illustrations.

Photography Credits

Except as noted, photographs of paintings and sculptures by Jasper Johns are courtesy of the Wildenstein Plattner Institute, New York; photographs of drawings by Johns are courtesy of the Menil Collection, Houston; and photographs of prints by Johns are courtesy of Universal Limited Art Editions.

Artwork by Jasper Johns © 2021 Jasper Johns/VAGA at Artists Rights Society (ARS), New York, except as noted. Prints published by ULAE © 2021 Jasper Johns and ULAE/VAGA at Artists Rights Society (ARS), New York. Prints published by Gemini © 2021 Jasper Johns and Gemini/VAGA at Artists Rights Society (ARS), New York

The following credits apply to all images for which separate acknowledgment is due.

Ronald Amstutz, courtesy Matthew Marks Gallery, New York: p. 262, pls. 14, 18; p. 273, pl. 13

The Art Institute of Chicago: p. 242, pl. 6; photograph by Taku Saiki, Tokyo: p. 48, pl. 19; photographs by Jamie Stukenberg, Professional Graphics, Rockford, Illinois: p. 33, pl. 1; p. 34, pl. 2; p. 38, pl. 9; p. 39, pl. 13; p. 44, pl. 4; p. 45, pl. 5; p. 47, pls. 12-14, 16, 17; p. 65, pl. 5; p. 66, pl. 9; p. 69, pl. 20; p. 70, pl. 24; p. 81, pl. 16; p. 83, pl. 26; p. 85, pl. 39; p. 98, pl. 1; p. 99, pl. 2; p. 106, pl. 6; p. 118, pl. 2; p. 134, pl. 11; p. 161, pl. 4; p. 181, pl. 4; p. 182, pl. 6; p. 239, pl. 1; p. 243, pls. 9, 10; p. 267, pl. 1

© 2021 Artists Rights Society (ARS), New York/SIAE, Rome: p. 26, fig. 2

Image © The Estate of Francis Bacon/Bridgeman Images: p. 278, fig. 4

Image courtesy Mel Bochner: p. 247, fig. 3

Courtesy Castelli Gallery, New York: pp. 97, 101, 103, 107

Christie's, New York: p. 46, pl. 9

© 2021 Dedalus Foundation, Inc./Artists Rights Society (ARS), New York: p. 108, fig. 3

Thomas R. DuBrock: p. 244, pl. 16

© Association Marcel Duchamp/ADAGP, Paris/Artists Rights Society (ARS), New York, 2021: p. 155, pl. 14; p. 198, fig. 3; p. 300, fig. 1

Michael Fredericks, courtesy Matthew Marks Gallery, New York: p. 85, pl. 35; p. 192, pls. 16, 19

Courtesy Gemini G.E.L., Los Angeles, © 2021 Jasper Johns and Gemini/VAGA at Artists Rights Society (ARS), New York: pp. 86-87, pls. 40-49; p. 154, pls. 5-10; p. 164, pls. 17-22

President and Fellows of Harvard College, Cambridge, Massachusetts, photograph by Katya Kallsen: p. 43, pl. 3

Paul Hester: p. 48, pl. 23

Eleanore Hopper, courtesy Ronald Feldman Fine Arts, New York: p. 126, pl. 27

Kogo Inoue, Tokyo © The Wildenstein Plattner Institute, New York, 2021: pp. 120-21, pl. 4; p. 123, pl. 11

Courtesy Jasper Johns: p. 139, fig. 1; p. 152, pl. 3; p. 300, fig. 2; pp. 325-29, pls. 1-12; photographs by Akira Kanayama: p. 124, pl. 17; p. 125, pls. 19, 22

© 2021 Jasper Johns and Gemini/VAGA at Artists Rights Society (ARS), New York: p. 285, pl. 1; p. 287, pl. 3; p. 291, pl. 13; p. 294, pl. 29; p. 296, pl. 36; p. 297, pls. 43, 46

© 2021 Jasper Johns and Multiples, Inc./VAGA at Artists Rights Society (ARS), New York: p. 290, pl. 10

© 2021 Jasper Johns and Petersburg Press/VAGA at Artists Rights Society (ARS), New York: p. 294, pl. 30

© 2021 Jasper Johns and Simca Print Artists, Inc./VAGA at Artists Rights Society (ARS), New York: p. 73, pl. 35; p. 127, pl. 30; p. 295, pl. 32; p. 297, pl. 42

© 2021 Jasper Johns and ULAE/VAGA at Artists Rights Society (ARS), New York: p. 50, fig. 1; p. 67, pl. 13; p. 68, pls. 14, 15; p. 73, pl. 37; p. 190, pl. 10; p. 191, pl. 12; p. 192, pl. 17; p. 195, pl. 30; p. 221, figs. 2, 3; p. 288, pl. 4; p. 289, pl. 5; p. 290, pls. 6-8; p. 291, pls. 12, 14, 15; p. 292, pls. 18, 20, 21; p. 293, pls. 22-24, 26; p. 294, pls. 28, 31; p. 295, pls. 34, 35; p. 296, pls. 37-39; p. 297, pls. 41, 44; p. 298, pls. 48, 49; p. 299, pls. 52-55

Jasper Johns Studio, Sharon, Connecticut: pp. 216-17, pl. 3; p. 265, pls. 30-34; p. 299, pl. 56; © 2021 Estate of Madeline Gins. Reproduced with permission of the Estate of Madeline Gins: p. 125, pl. 20; imaging by John Hill: p. 139, fig. 1; p. 325, figs. 1-3; © Ari Imai: p. 125, pl. 23; © Kanayama Akira and Tanaka Atsuko Association: p. 124, pl. 15; © Estate of Tomio Miki: p. 125, pl. 21; © Ushio + Noriko Shinohara: p. 124, pl. 18; © Shūzō Takiguchi/M. Kawamura 2021: p. 124, pl. 16; photographs by Jerry L. Thompson: p. 84, pls. 30-33; p. 218, pls. 4-9; p. 219, pls. 10-15; p. 263, pls. 19-23; pp. 270-71, pl. 4; p. 275, pls. 22, 24; photograph by Dorothy Zeidman: p. 188, pl. 4

© 2021 Joseph Kosuth/Artists Rights Society (ARS), New York: p. 196, fig. 2

The LIFE Picture Collection via Getty Images: p. 277, fig. 3

Light Blue Studio, courtesy Craig F. Starr Gallery, New York: p. 69, pl. 21

Photograph courtesy Fondazione Piero Manzoni, Milan © 2021 Artists Rights Society (ARS), New York/SIAE, Rome: p. 25, fig. 1

Sergio Martucci: p. 67, pl. 12

Courtesy Matthew Marks Gallery, New York: p. 49, pl. 27; p. 195, pl. 33; p. 258, pl. 2; p. 261, pls. 10, 11; p. 264, pls. 24-29; p. 269, pl. 3; p. 273, pl. 11; p. 274, pls. 15-19

Rob McKeever, courtesy Gagosian Gallery, New York: p. 157, pl. 1; p. 242, pl. 7

The Metropolitan Museum of Art, New York, photographs by Jamie Stukenberg: p. 64, pl. 4; p. 72, pl. 34

Minneapolis Institute of Art, photograph by Charles Walbridge: p. 76, pl. 2

Courtesy Donald Moffett and Marianne Boesky Gallery, New York and Aspen. Artwork © Donald Moffett: p. 53, fig. 3

© Ugo Mulas heirs. All rights reserved: p. 132, pls. 3, 4, 6; p. 133, pls. 7-9; p. 134, pl. 14; p. 135, pl. 16

Museum für Moderne Kunst, Frankfurt: p. 46, pl. 7

The Museum of Modern Art, New York/Art Resource, New York, photograph by Peter Butler: p. 68, pl. 18; photograph by Robert Gerhard: p. 137, pls. 23-26; photograph by Jon Wronn: p. 244, pl. 15

Courtesy National Gallery of Art, Washington, DC: p. 127, pls. 29, 31; p. 160, pl. 3; p. 162, pls. 5-10; p. 163, pls. 12-16; p. 213, pl. 1; pp. 214-15, pl. 2; p. 222, figs. 4, 5

© Arnold Newman Properties/Getty Images: p. 109, fig. 5

Ohara Museum of Art, Kurashiki, Japan: p. 123, pl. 14

Photographs courtesy Fondazione Giulio e Anna Paolini, Turin © Giulio Paolini: p. 27, figs. 4, 5

Philadelphia Museum of Art Photography Studio: pp. 150-51, pl. 2; p. 166, pls. 26-29; p. 167, pls. 30-33; pp. 301-3, figs. 3-7

© 2021 Estate of Pablo Picasso/Artists Rights Society (ARS), New York; photograph by Adrien Didierjean, image © RMN-Grand Palais/Art Resource, New York: p. 248, fig. 4

Markus Redert Fotografie, Neuwied, Germany: p. 80, pl. 7

© Rheinisches Bildarchiv, Cologne: p. 66, pl. 6; pp. 158-59, pl. 2; p. 177, pl. 1

Courtesy Sezon Museum of Modern Art, Karuizawa, Nagano, Japan: p. 83, pl. 27

State Russian Museum, Saint Petersburg: p. 100, pl. 8

Glenn Steigelman: p. 122, pl. 5; p. 234, pl. 7; p. 237, pl. 22

© 2021 Frank Stella/Artists Rights Society (ARS), New York: p. 196, fig. 1

Jamie Stukenberg, Professional Graphics, Rockford, Illinois: p. 41, pl. 1; p. 46, pl. 8; p. 48, pls. 20-22; p. 49, pl. 25; p. 67, pl. 11; p. 70, pl. 23; p. 71, pl. 29; p. 73, pls. 36, 38; p. 82, pls. 22; p. 83, pl. 24; p. 85, pl. 37; p. 122, pls. 6, 7; p. 123, pl. 12; p. 126, pl. 28; p. 132, pl. 5; p. 134, pl. 13; p. 135, pl. 17; p. 155, pls. 11-13; p. 163, pl. 11; p. 165, pls. 23-25; p. 190, pl. 6; p. 191, pl. 11; p. 193, pl. 22; p. 234, pl. 6; p. 234, pl. 8; p. 236, pls. 14, 17, 18; p. 237, pls. 21, 23; p. 242, pls. 3-5; p. 243, pl. 8; p. 244, pl. 17; p. 245, pls. 19-22; p. 260, pls. 6, 7; p. 272, pls. 7-9; © The Wildenstein Plattner Institute, New York, 2021: p. 22, fig. 1; p. 35, pl. 3; pp. 36-37, pl. 4; p. 38, pls. 5-8, 10; p. 39, pls. 11, 12, 14; p. 42, pl. 2; p. 46, pls. 6, 10, 11; p. 47, pl. 15; p. 48, pl. 18; p. 49, pls. 24, 26; p. 61, pl. 1; p. 62, pl. 2; p. 63, pl. 3; p. 66, pls. 7, 8; p. 67, pl. 10; p. 68, pls. 16, 17; p. 70, pls. 25, 26; p. 71, pls. 27, 30; p. 72, pl. 31; p. 75, pl. 1; p. 77, pl. 3; p. 78, pl. 4; p. 79, pl. 5; p. 80, pls. 6, 8-11; p. 81, pls. 12-15; p. 82, pls. 18, 19, 21, 23; p. 83, pl. 29; p. 85, pl. 34; p. 100, pls. 3-7; pp. 104-5, pl. 1; p. 106, pls. 2-5; p. 117, pl. 1; p. 119, pl. 3; p. 126, pl. 25; pp. 130-31, pl. 2; p. 135, pl. 15; p. 136, pls. 19, 20, 22; p. 139, fig. 2; p. 149, pl. 1; p. 153, pl. 4; p. 168, fig. 1; p. 169, fig. 2; p. 170, fig. 3; p. 171, fig. 4; pp. 178-79, pl. 2; p. 180, pl. 3; p. 182, pls. 5, 7-9; p. 183, pls. 10-14; p. 185, pl. 1; p. 186, pl. 2; p. 187, pl. 3; p. 189, pl. 5; p. 190, pls. 7, 8; p. 191, pls. 13, 14; p. 193, pls. 20, 21; p. 206, pl. 2; pp. 232-33, pl. 4; p. 234, pl. 5; p. 235, pls. 9-11, 13; p. 236, pl. 16; p. 237, pl. 19; pp. 240-41, pl. 2; p. 243, pls. 11, 12; p. 244, pl. 14; p. 245, pl. 18; p. 248, fig. 5; p. 251, fig. 1; p. 257, pl. 1; p. 272, pl. 5; p. 273, pls. 10, 12; p. 275, pl. 23; p. 303, figs. 8, 9

Tate London © Tate, Liverpool, 2021: p. 82, pl. 20

Jerry L. Thompson: p. 69, pls. 19, 22; p. 72, pl. 33; p. 83, pls. 25, 28; p. 85, pl. 36; p. 135, pl. 18; p. 136, pl. 21; p. 190, pl. 9; p. 191, pl. 15; p. 192, pl. 18; p. 193, pl. 23; p. 194, pls. 25-29; p. 229, pl. 1; p. 230, pl. 2; p. 235, pl. 12; p. 237, pl. 20; p. 259, pl. 3; p. 261, pls. 9, 12; p. 262, pls. 15–17; p. 268, pl. 2; p. 273, pl. 14; p. 274, pl. 20; p. 275, pls. 21, 25; p. 278, fig. 5; © The Wildenstein Plattner Institute, New York, 2021: p. 71, pl. 28; p. 126, pl. 24

Courtesy Tokyo Opera City Art Gallery: p. 122, pl. 10

© Alan Turner. Photograph by Zindman/Fremont: p. 246, fig. 2

Photos courtesy Universal Limited Art Editions: p. 195, pl. 33; p. 260, pl. 8; p. 261, pl. 13

Photo: Joshua White, JWPictures.com: p. 81, pl. 17; p. 122, pls. 8, 9; p. 123, pl. 13; p. 195, pls. 31, 32; p. 231, pl. 3; p. 260, pl. 5

Whitney Museum of American Art, New York: p. 126, pl. 26; p. 205, pl. 1; p. 207, pl. 3; p. 208, pls. 4, 5; p. 209, pl. 5; p. 210, pls. 6–11; p. 211, pls. 12–17; p. 244, pl. 13; p. 298, pl. 47; © 2021 Jasper Johns and ULAE/VAGA at Artists Rights Society (ARS), New York: p. 129, pl. 1; photograph by Tim Nighswander/Imaging4Art: p. 295, pl. 33

Public domain image via Wikimedia Commons: p. 53, fig. 2

Photography © Dorothy Zeidman: p. 236, pl. 15; p. 246, fig. 1

Dorothy Zeidman, courtesy Matthew Marks Gallery, New York: p. 260, pl. 4; p. 272, pl. 6

Philadelphia Museum of Art Board of Trustees

Whitney Museum of American Art
Board of Trustees

This book was published on the occasion of the exhibition *Jasper Johns: Mind/Mirror*, organized by the Philadelphia Museum of Art and the Whitney Museum of American Art, New York. The organizing curators are Carlos Basualdo, Keith L. and Katherine Sachs Senior Curator of Contemporary Art, Philadelphia Museum of Art, and Scott Rothkopf, Senior Deputy Director and Nancy and Steve Crown Family Chief Curator, Whitney Museum of American Art, with Sarah B. Vogelman, exhibition assistant, in Philadelphia and Lauren Young, curatorial assistant, in New York.

Philadelphia Museum of Art
September 29, 2021–February 13, 2022

Whitney Museum of American Art, New York
September 29, 2021–February 13, 2022

In Philadelphia:

Bank of America is the National Sponsor

BANK OF AMERICA

Generous support is provided by Constance Hess Williams and Sankey Williams and Matthew Marks, and through the museum's endowment with the Daniel W. Dietrich II Fund for Excellence in Contemporary Art, the Annenberg Foundation Fund for Major Exhibitions, the Jill and Sheldon Bonovitz Fund for Exhibitions, the Robert Montgomery Scott Endowment for Exhibitions, and the Kathleen C. and John J. F. Sherrerd Fund for Exhibitions.

Major support is provided by the museum's Contemporary Art Committee, The Davenport Family Foundation, Ellsworth Kelly Foundation and Jack Shear, Agnes Gund, Leonard and Judy Lauder, Ms. Jennifer S. Rice and Mr. Michael C. Forman, The Sachs Charitable Foundation, Helen and Charles Schwab, and the Women's Committee of the Philadelphia Museum of Art—including special gifts from the estates of Patricia Sweet Clutz and Phyllys "Fifi" Fleming.

Significant support is provided by Constance R. Caplan, the Robert Lehman Foundation, Marsha and Jeffrey Perelman, and an anonymous donor.

Additional support is provided by Irma and Norman Braman, Clarissa Alcock Bronfman and Edgar Bronfman Jr., Isabel and Agustín Coppel, Aaron and Leslee Cowen, Roberta and Carl Dranoff, Jaimie and David Field, Kathy and Richard Fuld, Mrs. Ronnie F. Heyman, Linda and George Kelly, Sueyun and Gene Locks, Richard and Nancy Lubin, Susan and James Meyer, Leslie Miller and Richard Worley, Mitchell and Hilarie Morgan Family Foundation, The Pew Center for Arts & Heritage, Lyn M. Ross, Howard Sacks and Vesna Todorović Sacks, Katie and Tony Schaeffer, Karen Goodman Tarte, Robbi and Bruce Toll, and two anonymous donors.

Jasper Johns: Mind/Mirror benefited from a grant from the National Endowment for the Arts and is supported by an indemnity from the Federal Council on the Arts and the Humanities.

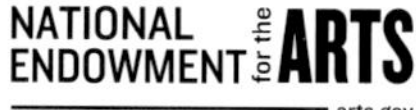

This accompanying publication was made possible by the Wyeth Foundation for American Art, The Davenport Family Foundation, Barbara Bertozzi Castelli, Jean-Christophe Castelli and Lisa Silver, and Craig F. Starr.

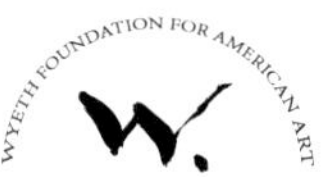

The exhibition celebration is generously sponsored by

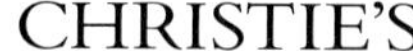

In New York:

Jasper Johns: Mind/Mirror is presented by

Leonard and Judy Lauder

Leadership support is provided by

Kenneth C. Griffin
Susan and John Hess

Bank of America is the National Sponsor

BANK OF AMERICA

The presentation is sponsored by

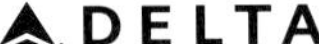

RALPH LAUREN

Generous support is provided by Judy Hart Angelo; Neil G. Bluhm; Matthew Marks; and Kevin and Rosemary McNeely, Manitou Fund.

Major support is provided by the Barbara Haskell American Fellows Legacy Fund; The Brown Foundation, Inc., of Houston; Nancy and Steve Crown; Anne and Joel Ehrenkranz; Ellsworth Kelly Foundation and Jack Shear; Agnes Gund; Kristen and Alexander Klabin; Helen and Charles Schwab; the Whitney's National Committee; and an anonymous donor.

Significant support is provided by Constance R. Caplan, Marguerite Steed Hoffman and Tom Lentz, the Jon and Mary Shirley Foundation, Sueyun and Gene Locks, Susan and Larry Marx, Marsha and Jeffrey Perelman, Donna Perret Rosen and Benjamin M. Rosen, and Stefan T. Edlis and H. Gael Neeson Foundation.

Additional support is provided by Aaron and Leslee Cowen, Kathy and Richard Fuld, Johanna and Leslie Garfield, Ashley Leeds and Christopher Harland, Mrs. Ronnie F. Heyman, Sheila and Bill Lambert, Barbara and Richard Lane, Margo Leavin, Janie C. Lee, Richard and Nancy Lubin, Martin Z. Margulies, the National Endowment for the Arts, Monique and Gregg Seibert, Norman Selby and Melissa Vail Selby, and Gloria Spivak.

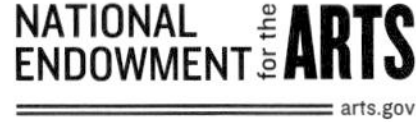

This exhibition is supported by an indemnity from the Federal Council on the Arts and the Humanities.

Support for the catalogue is provided by Barbara Bertozzi Castelli, Jean-Christophe Castelli and Lisa Silver, Craig F. Starr, and the Wyeth Foundation for American Art.

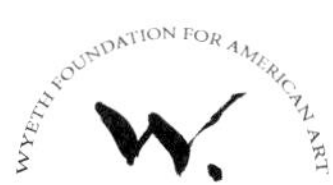

The opening dinner is sponsored by

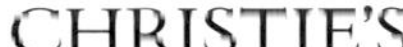

Colophon

Additional copyright notices and photography credits can be found on pages 342–43.

Whitney Museum of American Art
99 Gansevoort Street
New York, NY 10014
whitney.org

Philadelphia Museum of Art
2525 Pennsylvania Avenue
Philadelphia, PA 19130-9040
philamuseum.org

Distributed by
Yale University Press
302 Temple Street
P.O. Box 209040
New Haven, CT 06520-9040
yalebooks.com/art

Cataloging-in-publication data is on file with the Library of Congress.

Library of Congress Control Number
2021019315

ISBN 978-0-300-25425-9

Project manager: Beth Huseman
Editorial coordinator: Jacob Horn
Editors: Sarah Noreika and David Updike
Book and typeface design: A2/SW/HK, London
Production: Richard Bonk
Proofreader: Stephanie Salomon
Indexer: David Luljak
Printing and binding: Trifolio, Verona, Italy

Typeset in A2 Record Gothic
Printed on 135gsm Galerie Art Volume

Printed and bound in Verona, Italy

Second printing

Jacket, front, first row (all works listed from left): *Racing Thoughts*, 1983 (p. 186, pl. 2); *Target*, 1992 (p. 244, pl. 14); *Painted Bronze*, 1960 (cast and painted 1964; p. 185, pl. 1); *Untitled*, 1997 (pp. 232–33, pl. 4). Second row: *Painting with Ruler and "Gray,"* 1960 (p. 38, pl. 10); *Harlem Light*, 1967 (pp. 104–5, pl. 1); *Savarin*, 1982 (p. 208, pl. 4); *Untitled*, 2014 (p. 262, pl. 18). Third row: *Green Angel*, 1990 (p. 183, pl. 11); *Three Flags*, 1958 (p. 62, pl. 2); *Skin with O'Hara Poem*, 1965 (p. 134, pl. 12); *Figure 9*, from Color Numeral Series, 1969 (p. 87, pl. 49); *Thermometer*, 1959 (p. 100, pl. 6). Fourth row: *Painting with Two Balls*, 1971 (p. 295, pl. 33); *According to What*, 1964 (pp. 150–51, pl. 2); *Untitled*, 2018 (p. 274, pl. 18); *Target*, 1957 (p. 39, pl. 11); *Summer*, 1985 (p. 180, pl. 3). Fifth row: *Untitled*, 1983 (p. 243, pl. 12); *0 through 9*, 1965 (p. 83, pl. 27); from *5 Postcards*, 2011 (p. 263, pl. 19); *Usuyuki*, 1982 (pp. 120–21, pl. 4); *Untitled*, 1987 (p. 229, pl. 1). Front flap, first row: *Device*, 1961–62 (p. 193, pl. 20); *Perilous Night*, 1982 (p. 242, pl. 6); *Savarin*, 1982 (p. 210, pl. 6); *Map*, 1963 (p. 70, pl. 24). Second row: *Souvenir*, 1964 (p. 118, pl. 2); *Target with Four Faces*, 1968 (p. 296, pl. 40); *The Seasons*, 1989–90 (p. 230, pl. 2). Third row: *Untitled*, 2010 (p. 273, pl. 10); *Field Painting*, 1963–64 (p. 149, pl. 1); *White Flag*, 1955 (p. 64, pl. 4); *Figure 4*, 1959 (p. 81, pl. 13). Fourth row: *Studio II*, 1966 (p. 106, pl. 2); *Arrive/Depart*, 1963–64 (p. 153, pl. 4); study for *Regrets*, 2012 (p. 190, pl. 9). Fifth row: *Four Panels from Untitled 1972 [C Panel]*, 1973 (p. 162, pl. 6); *Flashlight*, 1960 (p. 183, pl. 13); *Untitled*, 2014 (pp. 216–17, pl. 3). Back, first row: *Studio*, 1964 (pp. 130–31, pl. 2); *From Henri Monnier*, 2000 (p. 272, pl. 6); *0–9*, 2008 (cast 2009; p. 84, pl. 30); *Flags I*, 1973 (p. 73, pl. 35). Second row: *Untitled*, 2010–11 (p. 274, pl. 20); *Map*, 1961 (p. 63, pl. 3); *Untitled*, 2018 (p. 264, pl. 24); *Untitled*, 1996 (pp. 214–15, pl. 2). Third row: *Figure 8*, 1959 (p. 81, pl. 15); *Flag on Orange Field*, 1957 (p. 67, pl. 11); *Untitled*, 1972 (pp. 158–59, pl. 2); *Untitled*, 2014 (p. 195, pl. 33). Fourth row: *Corpse and Mirror II*, 1974–75 (pp. 178–79, pl. 2); *Untitled (Leo Castelli)*, 1984 (p. 234, pl. 5); *Fragment—According to What: Leg and Chair*, 1971 (p. 152, pl. 3); *Two Maps II*, 1966 (p. 68, pl. 14); *Target with Four Faces*, 1955 (p. 42, pl. 2); *Savarin*, 1982 (p. 209, pl. 5). Fifth row: *False Start*, 1959 (p. 99, pl. 2); *Painted Bronze*, 1960 (p. 206, pl. 2); *Untitled (Halloween)*, 1998 (p. 136, pl. 22); *Skull*, 1971 (p. 190, pl. 6); *Mirror's Edge*, 1992 (p. 188, pl. 4); *Souvenir 2*, 1964 (p. 119, pl. 3). Back flap, first row: *Untitled*, 1998 (p. 136, pl. 19); *Untitled*, 1990 (p. 236, pl. 18); *Flag*, 1960–87 (p. 66, pl. 9); *Racing Thoughts*, 1984 (p. 187, pl. 3). Second row: *Two Flags*, 1985 (p. 244, pl. 13); *Usuyuki*, 1981 (p. 245, pl. 19); *Figure 7*, 1959 (p. 80, pl. 6); *Valentine*, 2010–11 (p. 195, pl. 32); *Device Circle*, 1959 (p. 100, pl. 7). Third row: *Winter*, 1986 (p. 181, pl. 4); *Painting with Two Balls*, 1960 (p. 38, pl. 8); *Flashlight*, 1960 (cast c. 1979; p. 183, pl. 14); *A Souvenir for Andrew Monk*, 1987 (p. 231, pl. 3); *Periscope (Hart Crane)*, 1963 (p. 182, pl. 6). Fourth row: *Usuyuki*, 1979–81 (p. 126, pl. 24); *Four Panels from Untitled 1972 [D Panel]*, 1973 (p. 163, pl. 16); *Targets*, 1966 (p. 46, pl. 7); *Fragment—According to What: Bent "Blue" (Second State)*, 1971 (p. 154, pl. 6). Fifth row: *Moratorium*, 1969 (p. 72, pl. 32); *Wall Piece*, 1968 (p. 106, pl. 3); *Watchman*, 1967 (p. 293, pl. 24); *Untitled*, 1990 (p. 237, pl. 23)

Cover, front and back: detail from *Untitled*, 2020 (p. 299, pl. 56)